P9-CRH-229

#71005-1.

ANGLO-SAXON PSYCHOLOGIES IN
THE VERNACULAR AND LATIN TRADITIONS

LESLIE LOCKETT

Anglo-Saxon Psychologies in the Vernacular and Latin Traditions

UNIVERSITY OF TORONTO PRESS
Toronto Buffalo London

© University of Toronto Press Incorporated 2011
Toronto Buffalo London
www.utppublishing.com
Printed in Canada

ISBN 978-1-4426-4217-1

Printed on acid-free, 100% post-consumer recycled paper with vegetable-based inks.

Library and Archives Canada Cataloguing in Publication

Lockett, Leslie, 1974–
Anglo-Saxon psychologies in the vernacular and Latin traditions / Leslie Lockett.

(Toronto Anglo Saxon series)
Includes bibliographical references and index.
ISBN 978-1-4426-4217-1

1. English literature – Old English, ca. 450–1100 – History and criticism.
2. Psychology in literature. 3. Mind and body in literature. I. Title.
II. Series: Toronto Anglo-Saxon series

PR179.P79L63 2011   829'.09353   C2010-907474-2

University of Toronto Press gratefully acknowledges the financial assistance
of the Centre for Medieval Studies, University of Toronto, in the publication of
this book.

Publication of this book has been aided by a grant from the Medieval Academy
of America.

University of Toronto Press acknowledges the financial assistance to its publishing program of the Canada Council for the Arts and the Ontario Arts Council.

 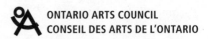

University of Toronto Press acknowledges the financial support of the Government
of Canada through the Canada Book Fund for its publishing activities.

Contents

Acknowledgments

Heartfelt gratitude is due to the faculty and librarians of the Medieval Institute at the University of Notre Dame, who nurtured my diffuse interests and taught me how to pursue them, especially Stephen Gersh, Calvin Bower, Jill Mann, Tom Noble, and Maura Nolan. For their stimulating insights and encouragement over the past several years I extend warm thanks to Tom Hall, Miranda Wilcox, Britt Mize, and Owen Phelan. Since coming to The Ohio State University I have been fortunate to enjoy the friendship and guidance of many talented colleagues, among whom I wish particularly to thank Marlene Longenecker, Lisa Kiser, Ethan Knapp, Richard Green, Karen Winstead, and David Herman. Helpful criticisms from these colleagues and from the anonymous readers for the Press have rooted out many errors and infelicities from this book; those that remain are entirely my own. Special gratitude is due to librarian Anne Fields and to the Interlibrary Loan staff at The Ohio State University, and to Valerie Lee, who as chair of the English Department showed me enormous patience and kindness when it was sorely needed.

For the resources, both time and funding, that have helped me bring this project to fruition, I am indebted to the University of Notre Dame, The Ohio State University, the University of Toronto Centre for Medieval Studies, and the Medieval Academy of America, which granted me a dissertation fellowship and a publication subvention. For permission to print the image on the book jacket I wish to thank Christine Ritchie, Librarian of University College, Oxford. And for their expertise and flexibility, I wish to thank editors Suzanne Rancourt and Barb Porter and copyeditor Miriam Skey of the University of Toronto Press.

There are three persons for whom I can scarcely begin to articulate the depth of my gratitude, affection, and admiration. Michael Lapidge and

Katherine O'Brien O'Keeffe co-directed my dissertation; they were and continue to be rigorous teachers, inspiring mentors, and generous friends. My husband Drew Jones has, through countless hours of conversation, helped me hone my arguments and fine-tune my writing. More importantly, he has given me a happy home in which to study and write.

   I dedicate this book to the memory of my father.

Note to Readers

Throughout this study, translations of Latin, Old English, and Old Saxon texts are my own except where specified otherwise. Where no edition is specified in the footnotes, quotations of Old English verse follow Krapp and Dobbie (eds), *Anglo-Saxon Poetic Records*, except for quotations of *Beowulf*, which follow Klaeber. Quotations of the Bible are taken from Weber et al. (eds), *Biblia Sacra iuxta vulgatam versionem*, and English translations of the Vulgate follow *The Holy Bible: Douay-Rheims Version*; in the discussion of the Hebrew biblical idiom in chapter 3, however, I have relied upon Metzger and Murphy (eds), *The New Oxford Annotated Bible*, to supply passages not quoted in my secondary sources.

In quoting from editions of ancient and medieval texts, I have silently regularized certain features of capitalization (especially when quoting the Vulgate) and punctuation (especially in the quotations of parallel definitions of the noun in chapter 5); I omit editorial diacritics from quotations in Old English and Latin and retain them in Old Saxon and Greek; and wherever possible I omit symbols marking editorial emendations. Wherever my alterations have implications for the reader's understanding of the text, I have made a clear note of them. In Latin texts I have regularized the spelling such that lowercase *u* and *i* replace *v* and *j* respectively, and the character *æ* has been substituted for hooked *e*; in Old English, I have replaced yogh with *g* and the ampersand with *ꝼ*.

Abbreviations

1 Cor, 2 Cor	First and Second Letters to the Corinthians
ACMRS	Arizona Center for Medieval and Renaissance Studies
Acts	Acts of the Apostles
Alms	*Almsgiving*, ed. ASPR 3
And	*Andreas*, ed. ASPR 2
ASE	*Anglo-Saxon England*
ASPR	Krapp and Dobbie (eds), The Anglo-Saxon Poetic Records, vols 1–6
Assmann	Assmann (ed.), *Angelsächsische Homilien und Heiligenleben*
Az	*Azarias*, ed. ASPR 3
BaP	Bibliothek der angelsächsischen Prosa
BAV	Biblioteca Apostolica Vaticana
BCLL	Lapidge and Sharpe, *A Bibliography of Celtic-Latin Literature 400–1200*
Beo	*Beowulf*, ed. Klaeber
BHL	*Bibliotheca hagiographica latina*
BL	British Library
BNF	Bibliothèque Nationale de France
BSB	Bayerische Staatsbibliothek
BT	Bosworth, *An Anglo-Saxon Dictionary*, ed. and rev. Toller
Carnicelli	Alfred the Great, *King Alfred's Version of St. Augustine's Soliloquies*, ed. Carnicelli
CCC	Corpus Christi College
CCCM	Corpus Christianorum, Continuatio Mediaeualis
CCSL	Corpus Christianorum, Series Latina

CH I	Ælfric, *Ælfric's Catholic Homilies: The First Series*, ed. Clemoes
CH II	Ælfric, *Ælfric's Catholic Homilies: The Second Series*, ed. Godden
CH Comm.	Godden, *Ælfric's Catholic Homilies: Introduction, Commentaries, and Glossary*
ChristB	*Christ II (Ascension)*, ed. ASPR 3
ChristC	*Christ III (The Judgment)*, ed. ASPR 3
Cons.	Boethius, *De consolatione philosophiae*
CPL	Dekkers and Gaar, *Clavis Patrum Latinorum*
CSASE	Cambridge Studies in Anglo-Saxon England
CSEL	Corpus Scriptorum Ecclesiasticorum Latinorum
Dan	*Daniel*, ed. ASPR 1
DEdg	*The Death of Edgar*, ed. ASPR 6
Deor	*Deor*, ed. ASPR 3
Diff.	Isidore, *Differentiae uerborum*
DK	Diels (ed.), *Die Fragmente der Vorsokratiker*
DOE	Healey et al., *The Dictionary of Old English: A to G Online*
DRA	Alcuin, *De ratione animae*
Eccl	Ecclesiastes
Ecclus	Ecclesiasticus (Sirach)
EETS	Early English Text Society
– o.s.	– original series
– s.s.	– supplementary series
El	*Elene*, ed. ASPR 2
ep., epp.	*epistola(e)*
Eph	Letter to the Ephesians
Etym.	Isidore, *Etymologiarum sive Originum libri XX*
Ex	*Exodus*, ed. ASPR 1
Fates	*The Fates of the Apostles*, ed. ASPR 2
Finn	*The Battle of Finnsburh*, ed. ASPR 6
fol., fols	folio(s)
Fort	*The Fortunes of Men*, ed. ASPR 3
frag., frags	fragment(s)
GenA	*Genesis A*, ed. ASPR 1
GenB	*Genesis B*, ed. ASPR 1
Gifts	*The Gifts of Men*, ed. ASPR 3
GL	Keil (ed.), *Grammatici Latini*
Gn	Genesis

Gneuss, *Handlist*	Gneuss, *Handlist of Anglo-Saxon Manuscripts*
Godden and Irvine	[?Alfred the Great], *The Old English Boethius*, ed. and trans. Godden and Irvine
GuthA	*Guthlac A*, ed. ASPR 3
GuthB	*Guthlac B*, ed. ASPR 3
Heb	Letter to the Hebrews
Hl	*Heliand*, ed. Behaghel
HomFr I	*Homiletic Fragment I*, ed. ASPR 2
HÜWA	Primmer (series ed.), *Die handschriftliche Überlieferung der Werke des heiligen Augustinus*
Instr	*Instructions for Christians*, ed. Rosier
Is	Isaiah
JDay I	*Judgment Day I*, ed. ASPR 3
JDayII	*Judgment Day II*, ed. ASPR 6
JEGP	*Journal of English and Germanic Philology*
Jer	Jeremiah
Jud	*Judith*, ed. ASPR 4
Jul	*Juliana*, ed. ASPR 3
Ker, *Catalogue*	Ker, *Catalogue of Manuscripts Containing Anglo-Saxon*
Klaeber	Klaeber, *Klaeber's Beowulf and the Fight at Finnsburg*, ed. Fulk et al.
KRS	Kirk, Raven, and Schofield, *The Presocratic Philosophers*
Lam	Lamentations
Lapidge, *ALL* 1	Lapidge, *Anglo-Latin Literature 600–899*
Lapidge, *ALL* 2	Lapidge, *Anglo-Latin Literature 900–1066*
Lapidge, *Library*	Lapidge, *The Anglo-Saxon Library*
Law, *GG*	Law, *Grammar and Grammarians in the Early Middle Ages*
Law, *ILG*	Law, *Insular Latin Grammarians*
Lk	The Gospel of Luke
LS	Ælfric, *Ælfric's Lives of Saints*, ed. Skeat
m.	metrum
Mald	*The Battle of Maldon*, ed. ASPR 6
Max I	*Maxims I*, ed. ASPR 3
ME	Middle English
MGH	Monumenta Germaniae Historica
– Epist.	– Epistolae
– PLAC	– Poetae latini aevi carolini

Miller	*The Old English Version of Bede's Ecclesiastical History of the English People*, ed. and trans. Miller
MnE	Modern English
MRune	*The Rune Poem*, ed. ASPR 6
MS, MSS	manuscript(s)
MSol	The metrical *Solomon and Saturn*, ed. ASPR 6
Mt	The Gospel of Matthew
Napier	Napier (ed.), *Wulfstan: Sammlung der ihm zugeschriebenen Homilien*
NQ	*Notes and Queries*
n.s.	new series; nuova serie
OE	Old English
OS	Old Saxon
par.	paragraph(s)
Phoen	*The Phoenix*, ed. ASPR 3
PIMS	Pontifical Institute of Mediaeval Studies
PL	Migne (ed.), Patrologia Latina
PPs	*Paris Psalter*, ed. ASPR 5
pr.	prosa
Prec	*Precepts*, ed. ASPR 3
Prv	Proverbs
Ps	Psalm(s)
RB	*Revue Bénédictine*
Rid	*Exeter Book Riddles*, ed. ASPR 3
Rim	*The Rhyming Poem*, ed. ASPR 3
Ruin	*The Ruin*, ed. ASPR 3
SC	Sources Chrétiennes
Sea	*The Seafarer*, ed. ASPR 3
Sent.	Isidore, *Sententiae*
SGen	*The Saxon Genesis*
Soul I	*Soul and Body I*, ed. ASPR 2
Soul II	*Soul and Body II*, ed. ASPR 3
Suppl.	Ælfric, *Homilies of Ælfric: A Supplemental Collection*, ed. Pope
Syn.	Isidore, *Synonyma de lamentatione animae peccatricis*
UL	[Cambridge,] University Library
Wan	*The Wanderer*, ed. ASPR 3
Wife	*The Wife's Lament*, ed. ASPR 3

ANGLO-SAXON PSYCHOLOGIES IN
THE VERNACULAR AND LATIN TRADITIONS

Introduction: Toward an Integrated History of Anglo-Saxon Psychologies

The book of Genesis recounts an incident in which the patriarch Noah, having become quite drunk on wine produced in his own vineyard, lies disrobed in his tent. Noah's middle son, Ham, enters the tent and commits the shameful act of looking at his naked father; Noah consequently curses Ham and the future progeny of Ham's son Canaan. The events leading up to the climactic moment of the curse are told with remarkable brevity in the Latin Vulgate: 'Coepitque Noe uir agricola exercere terram et plantauit uineam. Bibensque uinum inebriatus est et nudatus in tabernaculo suo.'[1] The Old English biblical epic *Genesis A* renders an account of the same episode, but it includes a brief digression, not present in the Vulgate, on the physiological and psychological effects of Noah's drunkenness:

> . He lyt ongeat
> þæt him on his inne   swa earme gelamp,
> þa him on hreðre   heafodswima
> on þæs halgan hofe   heortan clypte.
> Swiðe on slæpe   sefa nearwode
> þæt he ne mihte   on gemynd drepen
> hine handum self   mid hrægle wryon
> and sceome þeccan.[2]

---

1 Gn 9:20–1: 'And Noe, a husbandman, began to till the ground, and planted a vineyard, and drinking of the wine was made drunk, and was uncovered in his tent.'
2 *GenA* 1566b–73a: 'Within his tent, he scarcely perceived that which happened so wretchedly when the dizziness in his breast seized his heart, in the dwelling of the holy man. His mind constricted greatly in his sleep, so that he himself, stricken in his mind, was unable to cover himself in clothes with his hands and conceal his genitals.'

Under the influence of alcohol, Noah's coordination and judgment are impaired by dizziness, which in OE is called *heafodswima*, literally a 'floating' or 'swimming' of the head. This word vividly captures the subjective perception that dizziness is localized in the head, where it causes sensory impairment, disturbing both vision and balance. When this dizziness impairs Noah's cognition and rational judgment, however, it is unequivocally acting in his chest (*on hreðre*), where it squeezes or constricts the organ of the heart (*heortan clypte*). When the heart is squeezed, the mind too is constricted (*sefa nearwode*), with the result that Noah's capacity for reasoned judgment is diminished, and he fails to conceal his nakedness.

Readers who are well acquainted with OE literature may recognize in this passage from *Genesis A* an unusually vivid articulation of a pattern that recurs regularly throughout the OE corpus: the correlation of psychological distress with changes in the internal dimensions and temperature within the chest cavity. Verse and prose diction alike are peppered with common turns of phrase and compound words that reflect such a correlation. For instance, the poetic compound *bolgenmod*, meaning 'enraged,' may be translated literally as 'swollen-minded'; its counterpart in prose diction, *hatheort*, literally means 'hot-hearted' but is translated as both 'angry' and 'rash.' In the Exeter Book poem known as *Precepts*, a father admonishes his son, 'Yrre ne læt þe æfre gewealdan, / heah in hreþre, heoroworda grund / wylme bismitan.'[3] And in *Genesis B*, before Adam and Eve have succumbed to temptation, Satan broods with anger and jealousy, such that 'Weoll him on innan / hyge ymb his heortan.'[4] Each of these examples links the violent emotion of anger with heat and swelling in or around the heart, but the OE corpus provides many variations on this theme. Sometimes the heart is susceptible to milder negative emotions and intense positive emotions. The prose account of the Seven Sleepers relates that 'wurdon heora eagan afyllede mid tearum and angmode geomrodon ealle heora heortan,'[5] and one prose life of Guthlac describes the saint's love for God as 'on hys heortan hat and byrnende.'[6] Furthermore,

---

3 *Prec* 83–5a: 'Never allow anger, the sea of hostile words high in your breast, to have power over you or to pollute you with its boiling over.'

4 *GenB* 353b–4a: 'Inside him, his mind seethed around his heart.'

5 *Legend of the Seven Sleepers*, lines 222–3 (ed. Magennis, *The Anonymous Old English Legend of the Seven Sleepers*, 40): 'Their eyes were filled with tears, and with constricted minds they all mourned in their hearts.'

6 *Life of St Guthlac* 2.90–1 (ed. Gonser, *Das angelsächsische Prosa-Leben des heiligen Guthlac*, 111): 'hot and burning in his heart.'

the psychological distress that afflicts the heart may be cognitive rather than emotional, as in the case of drunken Noah (although the distinction between the cognitive and the emotional is a conceptual opposition that the Anglo-Saxons invoked very rarely).[7] In the absence of psychological distress, the 'default' state of the heart is roomy and unencumbered: in *Genesis B*, when Satan's messenger has succeeded in bringing about the downfall of Adam and Eve, he rejoices, saying, 'Forþon is min mod gehæled, / hyge ymb heortan gerume.'[8]

This brief selection of examples suggests a loose psycho-physiological pattern, in which psychological disturbances are associated with dynamic changes of pressure and temperature in the chest cavity. These physical changes resemble the behaviour of a fluid in a closed container, which expands and presses outward against the walls of the container when heated, threatening either to boil over or to burst the container if too much heat is applied. When the moment of intense emotion or distress passes, the contents of the chest cavity cool off and are no longer subject to excess pressure, just as if a heat source were removed from a container of boiling liquid. Several studies of this psycho-physiological pattern in OE have labelled it the 'container metaphor' of mental activity.[9] This pattern is not peculiar to OE; in fact, linguists, anthropologists, psychologists, and philosophers have described many ancient and modern cultural variants of this psycho-physiological pattern, which they often refer to as the 'hydraulic metaphor' or 'hydraulic model' of the mind.[10] Among these choices, I prefer 'hydraulic model' because it alludes to the physically dynamic dimension of the pattern – the correlation between increased heat and increased pressure – while leaving open the question of whether this concept of the mind is necessarily metaphorical. I will use the phrase 'hydraulic model' often in the following pages, as shorthand for a complicated bundle of

---

7 Low, 'Approaches to the Old English Vocabulary for "Mind,"' 15; Godden, 'Anglo-Saxons on the Mind,' 286–7 and 291.

8 *GenB* 758b–9a: 'My mind is therefore healed; my mind is spacious around my heart.'

9 Low, 'The Anglo-Saxon Mind'; Mize, 'The Representation of the Mind as an Enclosure in Old English Poetry'; Mize, 'Manipulations of the Mind-as-Container Motif'; Matto, 'A War of Containment'; Wehlau, *The Riddle of Creation*; Harbus, *The Life of the Mind in Old English Poetry*.

10 Among others, on the hydraulic model in the philosophy of emotions, see Solomon, 'Getting Angry'; in cognitive linguistics, Kövecses, *Metaphor and Emotion*, 142–63 (where the term 'container metaphor' is preferred); and in transcultural psychiatry, Hinton and Hinton, 'Panic Disorder, Somatization, and the New Cross-Cultural Psychiatry,' esp. 162–5.

concepts: it denotes both the central pattern of psycho-physiological associations and their less frequently represented entailments, and it additionally implies the localization of mental activity in the midsection of the body, usually in the chest, and sometimes in the abdomen, but not in the brain. Chapter 1 of this study contextualizes the mind-body partnership within the fourfold anthropology of body, mind, soul, and life-force that characterizes most OE literature, and chapter 2 describes in detail the varied depictions of the mind-body relationship and the hydraulic model that are found in both OE verse and OE prose.

The Status of the Hydraulic Model in Anglo-Saxon Thought

Until recently, modern readers have usually understood the hydraulic model of mental activity in OE to be a metaphor in the traditional sense: a non-essential and counterfactual figure of speech that equates two non-identical entities for the purpose of embellishment or evocation. For modern Western readers, the hydraulic model so plainly conflicts with even a layman's understanding of the physiology of emotion that we instinctively assume that the Anglo-Saxons shared our grasp of the disjunction between the hydraulic model and the way the mind 'really' works. Precisely this assumption implicitly underlies (among other studies) Joyce Potter's explication of images of seething in *Beowulf*. Potter claims that the words *wylm* 'swelling, seething' and *weallan* 'to swell, to seethe' acquired their central role in images of psychological distress by virtue of a metaphorical projection of macrocosmic, environmental seething, in the form of stormy seas and destructive fires, onto the microcosmic emotional landscape. 'It is, in fact, establishment of a correspondence between the elemental matter of water or fire and the throbs of the human heart, in waxing and waning, which makes the *wylm-weallan* word-complex not only generally poetic and imagistically creative, but precisely metaphoric,' Potter explains. 'Largely, the metaphor lives through the Old English manner of taking the abstract for the concrete and vice versa.'[11]

This argument is potentially illuminating but relies wholly on the assumption that the hydraulic model was purely metaphorical for the composer(s) and audiences of *Beowulf*. If it is reasonable to interpret literally the poem's images of microcosmic seething, much of Potter's reading is called into question: Was emotional seething necessarily 'abstract'

---

11   Potter, '*Wylm* and *weallan* in *Beowulf*: A Tidal Metaphor,' 192.

for the Anglo-Saxons? If emotional seething was truly abstract, why was it invariably mapped onto the chest and heart, and not onto the back, the brain, or the extremities? Most crucially for Potter's argument, could the direction of influence within the microcosmic-macrocosmic parallels actually have worked in the other direction? Eric Stanley, in a classic essay on OE poetic diction, is alert to this problem, and he cautions readers of OE to beware of unwarranted assumptions about the metaphoricity of any imagistic language that recurs throughout the poetic corpus. 'With some Old English figurative diction,' he points out, '… it is not possible to be sure if the figure was not as real to the Anglo-Saxons as the reality that gave rise to the figure.'[12] For instance, several OE poems employ phrases such as *forstes fetre*, 'with a fetter of frost' (*Max I* 75a) and *isgebinde*, 'with an ice-bond' (*Beo* 1133a) to characterize the ability of water to bind to itself when frozen. This 'fetters of frost' motif exemplifies 'the difficulty the modern reader has in evaluating the extent of Old English poetic diction,' says Stanley. 'He has no means of establishing if, what seems to him so imaginative an example of imagery, was not a scientific fact to the Anglo-Saxons; for how else is the solidifying of water to be explained?'[13]

Although Stanley briefly examines the images of *wylm* and *weallan* in his essay, he does not seriously consider whether the seething of the mind or the heart might have been 'a scientific fact to the Anglo-Saxons.' Nearly fifty years after Stanley's essay first appeared, Soon Ai Low pondered precisely this question in her PhD dissertation which, though unpublished, remains one of the most clear-sighted and valuable studies of the mind in OE literature to date. Employing George Lakoff and Mark Johnson's earlier writings on the role of metaphor in cognition, Low argues persuasively that the hydraulic model (or 'container metaphor') that dominates portrayals of the mind in OE literature is not a metaphor in the traditional sense of a superfluous literary ornament. Rather, it is a conceptual metaphor, which may be defined briefly as 'a systematic mapping of entities and relations from a sensorimotor source domain to a target domain that is abstract.'[14] Conceptual metaphors function not only in literary language but at the level of popular belief, where it is useful to conceptualize the

12 Stanley, 'Old English Poetic Diction and the Interpretation of *The Wanderer, The Seafarer,* and *The Penitent's Prayer,*' 235.
13 Ibid., 250–1.
14 M. Johnson, *The Meaning of the Body,* 165.

abstract life of the mind according to an analogy with the concrete, observable behaviour of heated fluid in a closed container.[15]

Although it is crucial to Low's overall argument that the hydraulic model be classified as a conceptual metaphor, she thoughtfully concludes her study by reflecting on how easily the prejudices of the typical modern reader may lead us to see metaphor where it does not exist. Following up her earlier discussion of 'melting minds and hearts' as manifestations of a conceptual metaphor THE MIND IS LIQUID, Low proposes that

> it may be a mistake to think of Old English melting minds as being metaphorical, because they may reflect actual belief about physiological processes. This is a real problem in using metaphor theory for the investigation of cross-cultural concepts, because we may wrongly perceive conceptual incongruities where none actually exist, or vice versa ... Our problem is one of insufficient data, not one of inadequate methodology. We simply do not know enough about the Anglo-Saxon worldview to make watertight judgements about what they would have perceived as metaphor, what physiology.[16]

I agree with Low that as long as we confine our investigation to the corpus of OE verse and prose narratives, we will have 'insufficient data' to determine whether the hydraulic model served as a literal representation of popular belief in a volatile, corporeal mind, or whether it was merely a conceptual tool that brought an abstract mind within the grasp of everyday cognition and linguistic expression. However, I do not accept that the question of metaphoricity brings us necessarily to a methodological impasse.

While it is true that the corpus of OE literature cannot per se demonstrate that the hydraulic model is *not* metaphorical, it is equally true, I would argue, that our usual motivations for reading the hydraulic model metaphorically are extraneous to the literature. In other words, we read the hydraulic model as metaphor because of the assumptions and predispositions we bring to our reading. One of these predispositions, which I will call the 'modernist bias,' arises from the strong mind-body dualism that dominates the thought of modern Western readers, often unconsciously, to the extent that we impose our concept of an oppositional mind-body relationship on the psychologies of other cultures. The 'medievalist bias,' on the other hand, is proof that a little learning can be a dangerous thing:

15 Low, 'The Anglo-Saxon Mind,' 55.
16 Ibid., 184–5.

scholarly readers, aware that the writings of Augustine of Hippo exerted a profound influence on the intellectual landscape of the medieval West, are prone to read 'Christian literature,' including literature merely copied by Christians, through the lens of Augustine's psychology, which emphasizes the oppositional relationship between the body and the incorporeal soul, while treating the transcendent soul and the rational mind as a single entity. I propose to move beyond Low's methodological impasse, first by overturning the modernist bias through a careful application of theories borrowed from cognitive linguistics and transcultural psychiatry, and second, by overturning the medievalist bias through a demonstration that non-Augustinian opinions on the soul, the mind, and incorporeality persisted throughout the Anglo-Saxon period, even among the literate and learned.

The Modernist Bias

Quite a few of the hydraulic-model idioms found in Modern English are recognizably descended from OE antecedents. For example, the passage from *Precepts* quoted above characterizes anger in a way that would sound familiar to any speaker of MnE: anger boils up inside and threatens to overwhelm a person's self-control. One might now speak – or, more likely, sing – about carrying a burning love in one's heart; a millennium ago, the *Chronicle*-poem *Death of Edgar* lamented that violence against Edgar's monastic establishments brought grief to everyone who 'on breostum wæg byrnende lufan / metodes on mode.'[17] We use the word 'cold' to describe someone who is aloof or emotionally indifferent; Beowulf, likewise, predicts that Ingeld's 'wiflufan / æfter cearwælmum colran weorðað.'[18] Because many hydraulic-model idioms have undergone little change in the transition from OE to MnE, and because the MnE idioms are obviously metaphorical, some readers have jumped to the conclusion that the OE idioms, too, were always used and understood metaphorically.[19] However,

---

17 *DEdg* 20–1a: 'carried in their breast a burning love of the Creator in their mind.'
18 *Beo* 2065b–6: 'love for his wife will become cooler in the wake of seething anxieties.'
19 The modernist bias implicitly underlies the tendency, in most discussions of the 'container metaphor' in OE, to dive into the question of *how* this model of the mind is metaphorical before considering *whether* it is metaphorical: see for example Kay, 'Metaphors We Lived By,' in which several families of MnE conceptual metaphors are said to descend from OE conceptual metaphors (esp. 282–3 on the 'container metaphor' of the mind).

this line of reasoning presupposes that the Anglo-Saxons shared our modern understanding of the physiology of emotion; that they believed that the mind and mental states were abstract; that they predicated concrete attributes (cardiocentric localization, spatial and thermal changes) of the mind only in order to make it easier to think and talk about something abstract and elusive. We presuppose such things because we project back onto the Anglo-Saxons our own relentlessly dualistic view of the mind-body relationship. It is very difficult for a dualist to take at face value that the mind is an organ in the chest cavity that is responsible for thinking, even though this is just what most OE literature tells us. The relatively young discipline of transcultural psychiatry and the interdisciplinary field of metaphor studies, both of which have generated significant corpora of scholarship on the hydraulic model in many languages and cultures, offer compelling reasons to set aside our modern, dualist bias and to examine afresh the nature of the mind-body relationship in Anglo-Saxon texts.

Transcultural Psychiatry as an Antidote to Dualist Prejudices

As the subdiscipline of transcultural psychiatry emerged in the first half of the twentieth century, one of its initial objectives was to improve the efficacy of Western psychiatric practitioners who served primarily non-Western populations of patients.[20] A serious hindrance to the success of these doctors has been the Western tendency to impose upon non-Western cultures a strong mind-body dualism. This tendency manifests itself as an overly rigid conceptual division between psychological and somatic disorders, which often leads to the suspicion that patients are malingering or deluded if they practice 'somatization,' that is, if they claim to suffer bodily distress even though they are diagnosed only with a disorder that Western medicine recognizes as psychological.[21] Calling for a reorientation of the Western practitioner's fundamental attitude toward other cultures' mind-body holisms, numerous scholars in the field of transcultural psychiatry have observed that mind-body dualists are actually a minority, in the contemporary global community as well as from a historical perspective. While Westerners regard mind-body holism and somatization as cultural idiosyncracies that demand special explanation, as if dualism were the most natural or normal understanding of the mind body relationship,

---

20 For a compact account of the emergence and evolution of the discipline, see Bains, 'Race, Culture and Psychiatry.'
21 Kirmayer et al., 'Somatization and Psychologization,' 258.

from a global perspective the phenomena that appear unusual and in need of special explanation are actually mind-body dualism and 'psychologization,' that is, the rigid conceptual separation between the mental and the bodily.[22]

It is precisely this tendency toward mind-body dualism that keeps the typical modern reader of OE from taking seriously the deeply holistic representations of mind and body that characterize so much OE literature. The purpose of introducing into this study theories borrowed from transcultural psychiatry is to minimize the reader's dualist biases and to increase the reader's receptivity to the nuances of Anglo-Saxon psychologies, which, although geographically 'Western,' predate the early modern Cartesian influence that underlies the secular dualism characteristic of modern Western cultures. With a heightened awareness of how our own post-Cartesian dualism distorts our observations of other cultures' notions of mind, we are in a position to take better advantage of the recent advances made in scholarship at the intersection of cognitive science and metaphor theory, especially the notion of embodied realism, which has enormous explanatory potential when applied to the problem of the hydraulic model.

Embodied Realism and the Origins of the Hydraulic Model

Lakoff and Johnson define embodied realism as 'the view that the locus of experience, meaning, and thought is the ongoing series of embodied organism-environment interactions that constitute our understanding of the world.'[23] For our purposes, embodied realism suggests that the co-activity of intense mental experiences and chest-centred sensations of heat and pressure have positively influenced, or at least strongly constrained, the formation of the hydraulic model of the mind, which many readers classify as a conceptual metaphor. A growing body of cross-cultural studies of conceptual metaphors is strengthening the case for embodied realism: when a particular conceptual metaphor transcends the boundaries of chronologically and geographically disparate cultures, the simplest explanation for this transcendence is that the metaphor has originated independently in disparate cultures, under the constraint of bodily experience. Nonetheless, debate continues over the validity of embodied

---

22 Kleinman and Kleinman, 'Somatization,' 435.
23 Johnson and Lakoff, 'Why Cognitive Linguistics Requires Embodied Realism,' 249.

realism and over the respective roles of embodiment and culture within this framework, especially as it applies to the hydraulic model of the mind. Because embodied realism plays an indispensable part in my efforts to circumvent the methodological impasse identified by Low, I have undertaken a substantial cross-cultural and diachronic study of the hydraulic model, with the goal of corroborating the hypothesis that the hydraulic model arose independently in many different cultures under the influence of the bodily sensations that accompany intense mental events. The results of this cross-cultural study appear in chapter 3. There, building upon the foundation of embodied realism, I propose a method by which we might assess whether a conceptual system whose formation was strongly constrained by embodied experience necessarily represents metaphorical thought, or whether it might be a literal expression of folk psychology. This approach proceeds in several stages:

1 In a given cultural or textual community, when a current concept (such as the hydraulic model of the mind) is strongly constrained by embodied experience, and there is no evidence that this embodied concept must compete with rival concepts that are not based in embodied experience, then there is no reason to call that concept a metaphor, *whether a modern observer would regard it as literally true or not.* The embodied concept has the status of folk belief, and where idioms rooted in that concept appear in texts, they are used literally.
2 Everyday idioms generated by the embodied concept will continually reinforce the culture's predisposition to accept the embodied perception as literally true.
3 When a concept (such as the hydraulic model) is continually reinforced by both embodied experience and everyday idioms, it will be very difficult for a rival concept, especially one that seems counterintuitive in light of embodied experience (such as the notion that the mind is in the brain rather than in the chest cavity) to supplant the embodied concept or to usurp its status as a literal truth. Only a rival concept that is backed by some authority that the cultural community regards more highly than common sense or personal experience will be able to supplant the embodied concept.
4 When a particular stratum of the culture adopts the rival conceptual model but continues to use the idioms generated by the obsolescent embodied concept, those idioms become metaphors.
5 The introduction of a rival concept at elite levels of learned discourse does not guarantee that the embodied concept has been supplanted at lower levels of learned discourse or among the population at large. It is

reasonable to expect that when a particular stratum of the culture has actually assimilated the rival concept (and thus has begun to use the embodied concept only metaphorically), the authoritative status and sustained presence of that rival concept will leave traces in that part of the textual record (if there is any) that is most closely linked with that stratum of the culture. The effect of such stratification is that within a single culture, an embodied concept may be understood literally by some textual communities while at the same time it is used metaphorically by others.

These five points provide an alternative to the uncritical perpetuation of the modernist bias. Rather than projecting backwards onto Anglo-Saxon literature an assessment of metaphoricity which relies on a post-Cartesian view of the mind-body relationship, we can identify discrete stages in the development of an embodied concept from folk belief to metaphor. The key to this approach is embodied realism, which undergirds this whole line of reasoning by acknowledging, first, the human tendency to allow bodily experience to guide our conceptualization of things that are difficult to understand, and second, the durability of conceptual models that are daily reinforced by subjective experience and the linguistic expressions of that experience.

Overturning the Medievalist Bias

The five points outlined above also suggest a responsible means of countering the medievalist bias. The hydraulic model itself indicates that the mind is corporeal, localized in or near the heart, and subject to spatial and thermal changes; in OE narrative, this notion of the corporeal mind goes hand-in-hand with the fourfold anthropology that distinguishes sharply between the mortal mind and the immortal soul. It is tempting to generalize that the surviving corpus of OE literature owes its manuscript transmission to men and women who were educated in the Christian tradition, which was particularly influenced by the thought of Augustine of Hippo, either directly or through encyclopedic and homiletic digests of his works. Since Augustine taught a dualist anthropology, in which the mind formed part of the incorporeal and immortal soul, those who espoused his teachings could not have employed or received the hydraulic model literally: this, in brief, is the basis of the medievalist bias.

A quarter-century ago, Malcolm Godden brought to the attention of Anglo-Saxonists the adoption and adaptation of Augustinian psychology by several highly educated Anglo-Saxons: chiefly Alcuin, Alfred, and

Ælfric.[24] Yet these authors' grasp of patristic philosophies of mind cannot be considered representative of that of ordinary Anglo-Saxons, or even of the men and women of various levels of learning who recorded most of the OE and Anglo-Latin references to the mind that have come down to us. No book-length study has yet examined Anglo-Saxon psychologies outside the OE corpus, so I have structured chapters 4 through 8 and the epilogue in such a way that they might fill this gap in the scholarship while also tracing the assimilation, by diverse textual communities of Anglo-Saxons, of concepts of mind, soul, and substance that rivalled the tradition of cardiocentric psychology. This history of Anglo-Saxon psychologies may then serve as a backdrop against which to assess whether the hydraulic model evolved from folk belief into metaphor during the Anglo-Saxon period, and if so, when and how this occurred.

Although chapters 4 through 8 are methodologically traditional, they reveal quite unexpected contours in the history of Anglo-Saxon thought. Chapter 4 musters all available forms of textual evidence in order to demonstrate that prior to the eleventh century the dominant psychological discourses consulted in Anglo-Saxon libraries were not those of Augustine and other representatives of the Platonist-Christian tradition: instead, the ideas about the soul and the mind that were most widely disseminated at all levels of literate culture were those contained in the *Dialogi* of Gregory the Great and the encyclopedic works of Isidore. The psychological content of these works, best described as eclectic, readily harmonizes with the Anglo-Saxons' cardiocentric psychology and anthropomorphic conception of the soul. Chapter 5 focuses on the texts that the Anglo-Saxons used in elementary instruction in Latin grammar and metrics. At this stage of education, students were not learning about the soul or the mind per se, but the grammarians' division of all nouns into those that signify corporeals and those that signify incorporeals had a markedly non-Platonist influence on their perception of substance and their understanding of incorporeality.

Chapters 6 through 8 examine the texts that form the backbone of Godden's classical tradition in Anglo-Saxon psychology, but at each stage the contextualization of these texts shows that the process of acquiring, assimilating, and disseminating Platonist-Christian doctrines on the soul and substance was ever an uphill battle. Alcuin's *De ratione animae*, which was written not in England but in Francia with the support of Carolingian

---

24 Godden, 'Anglo-Saxons on the Mind,' 271–85.

library resources, is staunchly Augustinian. However, a lesser-known Anglo-Saxon named Candidus Wizo, first Alcuin's pupil and later his colleague in Francia, rejected the fundamental Platonist doctrine of the soul's incorporeality and embraced instead the Stoicizing Christian position that ascribed incorporeality to God alone. As I argue in chapter 6, Candidus's Stoicizing Christian psychology was not altogether unusual for either an Anglo-Saxon or a Carolingian thinker of his day, although Alcuin would have his readers believe that Augustine's teachings on the soul were the only ones in circulation. Chapter 7 considers how two Alfredian translations, the *OE Boethius* and the *Soliloquies*, embrace the Platonic concept of the unitary soul but fall short of assimilating the complex Platonist-Christian implications of incorporeality: a testimony to the difficulty of internalizing doctrines so difficult and counterintuitive in the absence of a formal and systematic education. Finally, in chapter 8 I highlight Ælfric's Platonist-oriented opposition to the materialism – psychological and otherwise – that characterized the Anglo-Saxon popular mentality and that was reinforced in the homilies preached by Ælfric's contemporaries in the late tenth and eleventh centuries. In every case, the Augustinian or Platonist-Christian approach to the soul and to substance, which is usually assumed to be the default approach in any early medieval literate community, is demonstrably confronted with challenges from popular, Stoicizing, and eclectic alternatives.

It is not until chapter 8, where I consider Ælfric's dissemination of an anti-materializing agenda and a firmly Augustinian psychology in the form of vernacular homilies, that there is any sign of a serious challenge to cardiocentrism and the hydraulic model at middling and lower levels of literate culture and in the population at large. I consider the early eleventh century therefore to be the earliest possible point at which the Anglo-Saxons' cardiocentric psychology and hydraulic model of the mind met their first substantial challenge by a rival theory that was disseminated beyond the confines of the most elite literate milieux. According to the model I propose in chapter 3, therefore, the early eleventh century is the earliest possible point at which the metaphorization of the idioms associated with cardiocentrism and the hydraulic model could have begun on a broad, popular scale.

In the epilogue, I look ahead to the 'long eleventh century,' from around 990 to around 1110, and briefly consider additional challenges that confronted the hydraulic-model idiom in various textual communities as the eleventh century unfolded and the Norman Conquest brought radical changes to the content of Anglo-Saxon libraries. But my study properly ends with Ælfric because, having identified his homilies as the first challenge to the status of cardiocentrism and the hydraulic model as espoused by the general population, I conclude that the metaphorization of these concepts could not have begun in earnest until around the year 1000 at the very earliest, by which point nearly all surviving OE poetry had already been copied down. I would not encourage readers to assume uncritically that every manifestation of these concepts in OE literature is meant literally, any more than I would encourage them to perpetuate the assumption that such concepts are necessarily metaphorical. Instead I urge the reader to approach cardiocentrism and the hydraulic model as concepts that were, for most of the Anglo-Saxon period, likely used and received non-metaphorically, and to draw firm conclusions only *after* investigating whether a given text emanated from a circle that had already confronted and assimilated concepts of the mind that rivalled the embodied concepts of cardiocentrism and the hydraulic model.

1 Anglo-Saxon Anthropologies

Early Christian thinkers disagreed about the number of substances that make up the human being. Some favoured a tripartite anthropology that attributed to human nature a fleshly body, an animating soul (*anima* in Latin, *psuchê* in Greek), and an intellectual spirit (*spiritus* in Latin, *pneuma* in Greek). Others insisted that the spirit was merely a part of the soul, and consequently human nature comprised only two substances,[1] flesh and a 'unitary' soul, so called because it united in a single entity the powers to animate and govern the body, all mental activity, and the capacity to survive the death of the body and live on in the afterworld.[2] A handful of learned Anglo-Saxon discourses on psychology espouse a bipartite anthropology and understand the soul to be a unitary soul, and late in the Anglo-Saxon era, Ælfric of Eynsham employed the OE word *sawol* to signify the rational, incorporeal, and unitary soul that his Christian Latin authorities called *anima*. Yet in most OE literature – especially poetry, in which the diction is less constrained by the language of Latin source texts – the word *sawol* signified not a unitary soul but only that part of the human being that participated in the afterlife. The power to enliven the flesh belonged to another entity, the *feorh* (also called *ealdor* and *lif*), while the

---

1 Although a small number of Latin texts attest support for tripartition well into the early Middle Ages, by the fourth century the tripartite anthropology was favoured primarily in the East; in the West, from the time of Ambrose, Christian thinkers gradually became more rigidly opposed to tripartition. For an overview of these competing opinions on human nature through the Carolingian period, see Law, *Wisdom, Authority and Grammar in the Seventh Century*, 60–6 and 132–6.

2 I borrow the term 'unitary soul' from Bremmer, *The Early Greek Concept of the Soul*, whose anthropological terminology in turn relies on the types of soul established in the writings of the mid-twentieth-century ethnologists Ernst Arbman and Åke Hultkrantz.

functions that we might label psychological or mental belonged to yet another entity, the *mod* (which went by many names, including *hyge, sefa,* and *ferhð*). This fourfold anthropology of body, mind, life-force, and soul underlies most of the narrative and lyric representations of human beings in the OE corpus.[3] The central objectives of this chapter are to explore each element of this fourfold anthropology and to examine salient points of disagreement between the Anglo-Saxon fourfold anthropology and the bipartite anthropology favoured by many of the Latin Fathers.

A few aspects of the argument presented in this chapter will be familiar to readers who have encountered Malcolm Godden's distinction between 'the classical tradition' and 'the vernacular tradition' in Anglo-Saxon psychology, or Soon Ai Low's parallel observation that 'expert psychology' and 'common-sense psychology' coexisted in Anglo-Saxon thought.[4] It is a regrettable loss to literary critics and intellectual historians that Low did not publish her dissertation, where she most fully explores the notion of common-sense psychology in OE poetry. Godden's groundbreaking essay 'Anglo-Saxons on the Mind,' on the other hand, is now widely cited as the first and last word on Anglo-Saxon psychology, and yet readers usually oversimplify his paradigmatic distinction between 'classical' and 'vernacular,' emphasizing these broad categories at the expense of the subtlety with which Godden treats the idiosyncrasies of particular authors and works within each tradition. Given the less than ideal reception of both Godden's and Low's work, and given the circumscribed scope of Godden's essay (which he calls 'the product of some rather tentative researches'),[5] my opening chapter presents an opportunity to recapitulate, refine, and augment the claim that many OE narratives transmit an understanding of mind and soul that departs significantly from the psychological discourse of (among others) Augustine of Hippo and Ælfric of Eynsham. The division that I posit here between narrative and discursive treatments of psychological topics is not intended as a rigid generic binary but rather as a convenient shorthand that admittedly leaves room for gray

---

3 The present chapter is not meant to be a comprehensive study of the semantic boundaries of the terms for *mind* and *soul* in OE, which has already been executed by Phillips in his unpublished PhD dissertation, 'Heart, Mind, and Soul in Old English: A Semantic Study.' For further study of OE words for mind and soul, see also Low, 'The Anglo-Saxon Mind,' 1–47, and 'Approaches to the Old English Vocabulary for "Mind"'; Soland, *Altenglische Ausdrücke für 'Leib' und 'Seele,'* 52–5 and 106–10; and Anderson, *Folk-Taxonomies in Early English,* 327–51.
4 Godden, 'Anglo-Saxons on the Mind'; Low, 'The Anglo-Saxon Mind.'
5 Godden, 'Anglo-Saxons on the Mind,' 271.

areas. I call a text 'narrative' if it delivers information about an individual mind or soul in order to explain a particular psychological event that occurs in the course of a larger narrative; I apply the terms 'discourse' and 'discursive' to texts whose express purpose is to present generalizations about the nature of human minds and human souls.[6]

Physical Aspects of the Soul-Body Relationship

The OE word *sawol* signifies an entity that joins the body at the beginning of the life-span, leaves the body at death, and participates in the afterlife: this much is true throughout the corpus of OE literature, in narrative as well as in theological discourse. *Sawol* is more or less interchangeable with *gast* as a name for the human soul, although the word *gast* has an additional range of meanings not shared by *sawol*: *gast* can refer to God (especially the Holy Spirit), angels, saints, demons, the monster Grendel, fire, breath, and the mortal soul of non-human animals.[7] The life-span is coterminous with the residence of the *sawol* in the body: in the words of Cynewulf, a person's earthly life-span endures 'þenden god wille / þæt he her in worulde wunian mote, / somed siþian sawel in lice.'[8]

Several types of animation coincide with the soul's entrance into the body: the creation of Adam and Eve, the ensoulment of ordinary people before birth, the resuscitation of corpses, and the general resurrection of the dead in the end times.[9] When Jesus addresses the crowds at the Last Judgment in *Christ III*, he explains that at the creation of Adam he supplied mankind with both body and soul: 'Of lame ic þe leoþo gesette, geaf ic ðe lifgendne gæst.'[10] If Adam and Eve had not subsequently sinned, they

---

6 Low invokes roughly the same distinction between narrative texts, which employ common-sense psychology, and discursive texts, which employ philosophical psychology: see 'The Anglo-Saxon Mind,' 43; and 'Approaches to the Old English Vocabulary for "Mind,"' 20.

7 See the *DOE*, s.v. *gāst, gǣst*: the entry is exceptionally thorough and provides abundant textual evidence for these and other meanings of *gast*. MnE *spirit* aptly translates OE *gast* because both terms incorporate a wide range of supernatural and ethereal entities; however, where *gast* clearly refers to the human soul I have usually translated it into MnE as *soul*.

8 *ChristB* 817b–19: 'as long as God desires that he be allowed to dwell here in the world, that his soul be allowed to journey along in the body.' See also *Soul II* 39b–40.

9 Visionary experiences in which the *sawol* temporarily departs from the body are treated separately below.

10 *ChristC* 1381: 'From mud I prepared limbs for you; I gave you a living soul.'

would not have had to suffer death, but would have enjoyed the ongoing union of body and soul: 'ac æfter fyrste to þam færestan / heofonrices ge-fean hweorfan mostan, / leomu lic somud ond lifes gæst.'[11] Adam and Eve are a special case, having been created rather than born, but ordinary hu-mans must also have their souls and bodies joined before birth, an event that OE narratives treat somewhat obliquely. Enoch's bodily assumption into heaven is referred to as a journey 'on þam gearwum þe his gast onfeng / ær hine to monnum modor brohte.'[12] The individuals present at the Last Judgment are described, likewise, as 'sawla gehwylce þara þe sið oþþe ær / on lichoman leoþum onfengen.'[13] Several opinions about the manner and timing of the body's ensoulment have early Christian precedents: among Latin authors, some Neoplatonists claimed that pre-existent souls were im-planted into bodies, while Creationists held that God created a new soul for every conception, and Traducianists claimed that soul and body were both generated by the parents at conception.[14] The corpus of OE narratives at-tests no communal preference for any one of these positions. The foregoing passages from *Genesis A* and *Christ III* suggest the embodiment of pre-existing souls, as does the poem *Instructions for Christians*, whose speaker observes, 'Þu ful gearowe na wast wege þines gastes, / hu heo ðe on com oððe hwær heo æror was,'[15] though the larger framework of Neoplatonist-Christian psychology is not in evidence in any of these poems. Whether the *Soul and Body* poems imply the pre-existence of souls is more difficult to

---

11 *GuthB* 836–8: 'But after a time, they might have turned toward the most delightful joy of the heavenly kingdom, the limbs together with the body and the soul of life.'

12 *GenA* 1212–13: 'in the trappings [i.e., the body] that his soul received before his mother brought him forth among men.' The Vulgate account of Enoch's bodily assumption is somewhat oblique (Gn 5:24), but subsequent references (Ecclus 44:16; Ecclus 49:16; and Heb 11:5) make it clear that Enoch was understood to have been taken up in the flesh, without experiencing bodily death: an event memorably illustrated on p. 61 of Oxford, Bodleian Library, Junius 11 (which can be viewed in several facsimile editions, the most recent being Muir, *A Digital Facsimile of Oxford, Bodleian Library, MS. Junius 11*).

13 *ChristC* 1067–8: 'every soul who, at some point, received bodily limbs.'

14 Cross and Livingstone (eds), *Oxford Dictionary of the Christian Church*, s.v. 'Creationism' and 'Traducianism.'

15 *Instr* 221–2: 'You do not thoroughly comprehend the journey of your soul, how it en-tered into you or where it was before.' Rosier, 'Instructions for Christians,' prints *gearo þe* where I have adopted Robinson's emendation to *gearowe* ('Notes and Emendations to Old English Poetic Texts,' 120). The masculine noun *gast* does not agree with the feminine pronoun *heo* that refers back to it twice in line 222 (and once more in 223); perhaps a copyist substituted *gastes* for feminine *sawles* but did not change the pro-nouns accordingly.

ascertain. The damned soul of the *Soul and Body* poems claims that he was commissioned to animate a specific body that was already formed: 'ic wæs gæst on þe from gode sended,' the soul tells his former body; 'þe þurh engel ufan of roderum / sawle onsende þurh his sylfes hond, / meotud ælmihtig.'[16] The special intervention of God perhaps suggests that this poet had in mind a Creationist view of the body-soul union, but it is not stated outright that the soul was newly created for the occasion of ensoulment.[17]

In OE verse, both the resuscitation of corpses and the general resurrection of the dead at the Last Judgment parallel the ordinary ensoulment of the body before birth. A dead youth is brought back to life in *Elene*; one minute he is 'sawlleasne, / life belidenes lic,' but when the True Cross is raised above him, 'He sona aras / gaste gegearwod, geador bu samod / lic ond sawl.'[18] Elsewhere, when St Andrew resuscitates some recently drowned Mermedonian soldiers, the narrator of *Andreas* tells us that 'Þa þær ofostlice upp astodon / manige on meðle, mine gefrege, / eaforan unweaxne, ða wæs eall eador / leoðolic ond gastlic.'[19] In New Testament and Latin patristic portrayals, the general resurrection of the body in the end times is quite distinct from the resuscitation of corpses: in the final book of *De ciuitate Dei*, for instance, Augustine explains that the flesh will be resurrected in spiritualized form, without any corruption or deformity and in the form it possessed at the prime of life.[20] Such precise theological distinctions are not the stuff of OE poetry, however, and OE verse narratives typically portray resuscitation and resurrection in virtually identical terms. The narrator of *Judgment Day I*, looking ahead to the general resurrection, foretells that 'beoð þonne gegædrad gæst ond bansele, / gesomnad to þam siþe'; likewise, the narrator of *Christ III* declares that each dead

---

16 *Soul II* 43: 'I was a spirit sent into you by God'; *Soul II* 24–6a: 'by means of an angel coming down from heaven, the almighty Ruler infused you with a soul, by his own hand.'

17 The same ambiguity is present in a rare OE discursive statement on ensoulment in a treatise on prenatal development (*On the Human Foetus*, ed. Cockayne, *Leechdoms, Wortcunning and Starcraft*, 3.146), where it is said of the developing fetus, 'On þam þriddum monþe he biþ man butan sawle' (In the third month he is a human without a soul). Clearly the body exists unanimated for a length of time, but whether it is then animated by a pre-existent soul or a newly created one is left unsaid.

18 *El* 876b–7: 'soulless, the body of the one departed from life'; *El* 887b–9a: 'He arose at once, equipped with a soul, his body and soul both together.'

19 *And* 1625–8a: 'Then, as I have heard say, many an adolescent boy speedily stood up there, as a group, when the bodily and the spiritual were all united.'

20 See esp. *De ciuitate Dei* 22.21 (ed. Dombart and Kalb, CCSL 47–8, 841–2); the key scriptural text underlying Augustine's thought is 1 Cor 15:42–4.

man raised for the Last Judgment 'hafað ætgædre bu, / lic ond sawle.'[21] Later in *Christ III* there appears a hint of familiarity with patristic teachings on the resurrection of the body:

> Ðonne weoroda mæst   fore waldende,
> ece ond edgeong,   ondweard gæð
> neode ond nyde,   bi noman gehatne,
> berað breosta hord   fore bearn godes,
> feores frætwe.[22]

Despite the poetic appellations given to the soul and the body in these lines, their reunion at the resurrection is indistinguishable from the revival of a corpse, with one exception: the crowd is said to be *edgeong*, 'made newly young,' a word possibly inspired by the patristic theory that the general resurrection will restore the body of a thirty-year-old to those who have died in old age.[23]

Although some OE texts invoke the well-worn topos of the soul's imprisonment by the body, others treat the soul's enclosure in the flesh not as a moral affliction but simply as a fact of nature. The narrator of *Christ III*, for instance, exhorts his audience to be forthcoming when they confess their sins, because 'Ne mæg þurh þæt flæsc se scrift / geseon on þære sawle.'[24] More specifically, the soul resides in the midsection of the body, not in the head. When St Guthlac dies, the narrator of *Guthlac B* relates that 'Nu of hreþerlocan / to þam soþan gefean sawel fundað'; in *Genesis A*, God floods the earth in order to exterminate 'lica gehwilc þara þe lifes gast / fæðmum þeahte,' and Hagar melodramatically predicts that 'of heortan hunger oððe wulf / sawle and sorge somed abregde.'[25] Suggestions that

---

21 *JDay I* 102–3a: 'at that time the soul and the bone-house will be gathered, brought together for that journey'; *ChristC* 1035b–6a: 'will have both together, body and soul.' See also *JDay I* 40–3b, in which 'neither blood nor bone' will remain forever in the grave because men will bring both body and soul to the Last Judgment.

22 *ChristC* 1069–73a: 'Then the greatest of multitudes, everlasting and made newly young, goes forth into the presence of the Ruler, some willingly and others under compulsion; called by name, they will bear before the Son of God the treasure of their breast, the trappings of their life.'

23 As an analogue see, for instance, Augustine, *De ciuitate Dei* 22.15 (ed. Dombart and Kalb, CCSL 47–8, 834).

24 *ChristC* 1305b–6a: 'The confessor cannot see through the flesh into the soul.'

25 *GuthB* 1263b–4: 'Now, from out of the enclosure of the chest, the soul hastens toward true joy.' *GenA* 1281–2a: 'every creature that concealed the soul of life in its bosom';

the soul might reside in the head are, in contrast, extremely scarce in OE literature of any sort.[26]

The most rigorously Platonist of early Christian thinkers rejected all theories about the bodily seat of the soul, on the grounds that the soul's incorporeality entailed its non-spatial disposition; it could not be localized any more in one part of the body than in another because it was indivisible and therefore whole in every part of the body. The most learned Anglo-Saxons had some knowledge of Latin authors who advocated this particular understanding of the soul,[27] but outside the writings of Ælfric, the idea that the soul was truly incorporeal, indivisible, and non-localized has left little impression on OE literature. Of course Anglo-Saxon authors frequently depicted an oppositional relationship between soul and body, but this opposition did not depend on a notion of true incorporeality; the soul was distinguished from the flesh of the human body but not from bodily substance altogether. Within the OE contexts in which the body-soul opposition is most commonly invoked, such as moral exhortations and exempla, it is not very meaningful to emphasize the soul's lack of physical substance: it is much more effective to emphasize that the short-term gratification of the body is cheap in comparison with the eternal bliss of the soul. Accordingly, it is the soul's durability, not strict immateriality in the Platonist sense, that typically underpins the opposition of body and soul in OE narratives. Guthlac, confident that he will be receiving his reward in heaven, describes the imminent departure of his own soul: 'tydrað þis banfæt, / greothord gnornað, gæst hine fyseð / on ecne geard, utsiþes georn / on sellan gesetu.'[28] The 'eternal dwelling' of the soul contrasts sharply with the imminent decay of the body, underscored by the

---

GenA 2278–9: 'hunger or a wolf will pull the soul and sorrow together from my heart.' See also *Beo* 2819b–20, *Gen A* 1608b–10a, and *GenA* 2639b–41a (quoted below).

26 I am aware of only one OE statement that the *sawol* might occupy the head: it occurs in one of the prose *Solomon and Saturn* dialogues, and I discuss it further at the end of chapter 5 below. As I argue in a forthcoming article called 'Anglo-Saxon Knowledge of the Functions of the Brain,' based on the availability of the relevant Latin source texts and on references to the brain and the head in OE and Anglo-Latin literature, the idea that the transcendent *sawol* or the highly personalized *mod* was housed in the head did not gain currency in England prior to the eleventh century, although a few authors may have been acquainted with the idea that the brain participated in sensory processing.

27 On Anglo-Saxon adaptations of Platonizing Christian theories of the soul, see esp. chapters 6 and 8 below, on the works of Alcuin and Ælfric.

28 *GuthB* 1265b–8a: 'this bone-vessel grows weak, the earthen treasure [i.e., the body] mourns, the soul prepares itself, eager for its outward journey into the eternal dwelling, into better resting-places.'

compound *greothord*, which Bradley aptly translates as 'treasure-house of dust.'[29] The opposition between the soul's transcendence and the body's putrescence applies equally to damned and blessed individuals. Concerning the monstrous Holofernes, now slain, the *Judith*-narrator says, 'Læg se fula leap / gesne beæftan, gæst ellor hwearf / under neowelne næs';[30] similarly, in *The Phoenix*, the prophet Job anticipates his death, saying,

> Þeah min lic scyle
> on moldærne   molsnad weorþan
> wyrmum to willan,   swa þeah weoruda god
> æfter swylthwile   sawle alyseð
> ond in wuldor aweceð.[31]

The divergent fates of body and soul are not mere facts of nature: especially in Christian didactic contexts, they provide a rationale for pursuing the moral high ground in times of temptation or weakness. Guthlac, beset by devils who rack his body painfully in hopes that he will renounce his faith, explains to the devils that they have no power over him, because he values his transient body little, and the worst they can do to his soul is to send it on to heaven.

> Ne mæg min lichoma   wið þas lænan gesceaft
> deað gedælan,   ac he gedreosan sceal,
> swa þeos eorðe eall   þe ic her on stonde.
> Ðeah ge minne flæschoman   fyres wylme
> forgripen gromhydge   gifran lege,
> næfre ge mec of þissum wordum onwendað   þendan mec min gewit gelæsteð.
> Þeah þe ge hine sarum forsæcen,   ne motan ge mine sawle gretan,
> ac ge on betran gebringað.[32]

---

29 Bradley, *Anglo-Saxon Poetry*, 280.
30 *Jud* 111b–13a: 'Afterwards the foul corpse lay dead; the soul turned elsewhere underneath the deep earth.'
31 *Phoen* 563b–7a: 'Although my body must grow rotten in its earthen tomb, to the delight of worms, still the God of hosts will release my soul after the hour of death and raise it up in glory.' See also *And* 227b–9.
32 *GuthA* 371–8: 'Confronted by its own transient nature, my body cannot avoid death, but it must falter, as must this whole earth on which I stand. Even if you hostile creatures overwhelm my body in a surge of fire, with the greedy flame, you will never turn me away from these words, as long as my mind sustains me. Even if you afflict my body with pains, you may not reach my soul, but you will lead it to a better place.'

Juliana, likewise, tells her demonic tormentor that she privileges her soul's welfare over her body's, since her body will become food for worms:

Ic þære sawle ma
geornor gyme   ymb þæs gæstes forwyrd
þonne þæs lichoman,   se þe on legre sceal
weorðan in worulde   wyrme to hroþor,
bifolen in foldan.[33]

The moralized opposition between the transient body and the transcendent soul, stressing the negligibility of bodily gratification and denial in comparison with the eternal damnation or bliss of the soul, is as commonplace in OE verse as in early medieval Latin literature, but it must be stressed that OE articulations of this commonplace do not carry all the implications of the more philosophically complex opposition between the body and the incorporeal, unitary *anima*.

The Soul's Life in the Body

The passages adduced so far depict the soul actively turning toward the afterworld, with more or less enthusiasm, as it leaves the dying body. But what else does the soul do during its existence in the body? Is it capable of thought, of governing the actions of the body, of autonomous action? A thorough answer to this question requires that we approach it from several angles, examining how soul and body interact at death, how they interact during life, and the extent to which the soul and the mind share characteristic activities.

OE poetry is rich in circumlocutions pertaining to death, some of which imply that death is brought on by extrinsic forces alone, with neither soul nor body playing an active role in the process. In *Genesis A*, for instance, God says to the fallen Adam, 'þe is gedal witod / lices and sawle,' a turn of phrase that makes death sound as natural and as inevitable as the separation of leaves from the trees in autumn.[34] Even when violent circumstances inflict pain upon the body, the moment of death may simply 'divide' or 'loosen' the body from the soul: the demonic spirits who attack St Guthlac attempt

---

33 *Jul* 413b–17a: 'I care more – and more earnestly – about the ruin of the soul, of the spirit, than about the ruin of the body, which must become a delight for worms, in its grave on earth, buried in the ground.'
34 *GenA* 930b–1a: 'For you, separation of body and soul is a certainty.'

'þurh sarslege sawle gedælan / wið lichoman,' and the Mermedonians who attack St Matthew 'banhringas abrecan þohton, / lungre tolysan lic ond sawle.'[35] In these expressions, external forces are responsible for separating the soul from the body, and words such as *gedælan* and *tolysan* are emotionally neutral, suggesting neither resistance nor cooperation by soul or body.

Another class of circumlocutions characterizes the separation of soul and body as an undesired or unforeseen deprivation. In *Genesis A*, for example, King Abimelech is warned that 'Þe abregdan sceal / for þære dæde deað of breostum / sawle þine,' and in *Andreas*, the slain prison guards are called 'gaste berofene, / fægra flæschaman.'[36] Even more menacingly, the OE *Phoenix* personifies death as a bloodthirsty warrior who leaves bodies 'bereft' of their former partners:

> þonne deað nimeð,
> wiga wælgifre,   wæpnum geþryþed,
> ealdor anra gehwæs,   ond in eorþan fæðm
> snude sendeð   sawlum binumene
> læne lichoman,   þær hi longe beoð
> oð fyres cyme   foldan biþeahte.[37]

In these three passages, body and soul are still passive victims of death, but instead of the emotional neutrality of the earlier passages, words such as *abregdan* 'to rip out,' *berofene* 'bereft,' and *binumene* 'deprived' imply that the removal of the soul occurs under duress, as if soul or body were resisting their separation.[38] This idea is articulated more concretely in several poems that refer to soul and body as one another's 'kinsmen' or 'beloved.' The narrator of the *Soul and Body* poems opens by remarking how grievous it will be when death 'asundrað þa sibbe, þa þe ær somud wæron, / lic ond sawle!'[39] Similarly, Cynewulf, in his soliloquy at the end of

---

35 *GuthA* 227–8a: 'to divide his soul from his body by means of a painful blow'; *And* 150–1: 'sought to smash his joints, suddenly to unhinge body and soul.'

36 *GenA* 2639b–41a: 'Because of that deed, death must rip your soul out of your breast'; *And* 1084b–5a: 'bodies of the doomed, bereft of their souls.'

37 *Phoen* 485b–90: 'Then death, that bloodthirsty warrior, strengthened with weapons, takes the life of each individual and speedily sends the transitory bodies, deprived of souls, into the bosom of the earth, where they will remain for a long time, covered by soil, until the advent of the fire.' This passage is not known to depend upon any Latin source: see Griffith, 'The Sources of *The Phoenix.*'

38 See *DOE* s.v. *abregdan*, esp. A, A1; *be-reafian*; *be-niman*.

39 *Soul II* 4–5a: 'separates those kinsmen who were once together, body and soul.'

Juliana, depicts a close and loving friendship between body and soul, whom he calls 'wedded partners':

> Is me þearf micel
> þæt seo halge me   helpe gefremme,
> þonne me gedælað   deorast ealra,
> sibbe toslitað   sinhiwan tu,
> micle modlufan.   Min sceal of lice
> sawul on siðfæt,   nat ic sylfa hwider,
> eardes uncyðgu.⁴⁰

Cynewulf describes a body and a soul that cling to one another and resist the dissolution of their bond; it is Cynewulf's anxiety over this dissolution that moves him to petition St Juliana, since he does not know his soul's final destination. The clinging together of soul and body, whether naturally or wilfully, is not efficacious, since they cannot actually turn away death, yet the depiction of a familial or wedded love joining soul and body together during life implies that the soul is capable, at least, of inclining toward life and resisting death. The fullness of the individual's will and emotions, however, does not reside in the soul. In *Guthlac B*, as the saint anticipates his own death, 'Næs him sorgcearu / on þas lænan tid, þeah his lic ond gæst / hyra somwiste, sinhiwan tu, / deore gedælden.'⁴¹ While the bond of affection between soul and body implies their reluctance to be divorced from one another, Guthlac himself – who appears to be something other than his soul or his body – is not sorrowful or anxious. By the force of Guthlac's will or by the grace of God, his state of mind is not determined by the state of his soul. As the narrator confirms a few lines later, the source of Guthlac's calm and self-control, contrary to the inclinations of his *sawol*, is his *mod*: 'Ða wæs Guðlace ... mod swiþe heard.'⁴²

The *sawol* appears to possess more autonomy in the death-scenes of individuals who are looking forward to the rewards of the afterlife. In other passages from *Guthlac B* already cited above, the soul of the saint is

---

40 *Jul* 695b–701a: 'I have a great need that the saint provide assistance to me when the two wedded partners, dearest of all, depart from me, sever their friendship, their great, heartfelt affection. My soul must go on a journey from the body; I myself, ignorant of its resting place, do not know where.'

41 *GuthB* 966b–9a: 'He had no anxiety about this transitory time, even though his body and soul, the two wedded partners, would sever their beloved cohabitation.'

42 *GuthB* 976a–7: 'Then Guthlac's mind was very resolute.'

less inclined to cling to the body; it 'prepares itself eagerly' for the afterlife and 'hastens' out of the body toward heaven. Even a soul that is merely saved rather than saintly may actively embrace death; according to the opening lines of *Guthlac A*, when a blessed man dies, his soul does not try to prolong its friendship with the body: 'Ofgiefeþ hio þas eorþan wynne, / forlæteð þas lænan dreamas, ond hio wiþ þam lice gedæleð.' The angel who meets the blessed soul as it leaves the body speaks to the soul, saying, '"Nu þu most feran þider þu fundadest / longe ond gelome."'[43] The Christian individual who exerts control over the departure of his soul from his body is thereby marked as holy, following the example set by Christ and by the martyr Stephen at their deaths.[44] Non-Christians who exert control over their soul's departure from the body are likewise marked as heroes, and their souls appear to possess some degree of agency in this moment of heroism. When Beowulf knows his death to be imminent, 'he chose the funeral pyre' and 'his soul travelled out of his breast to seek the judgment of the just.' When mortally wounded, Byrhtnoth, both Christian and hero, beseeches God to allow his soul to journey out of the body and to reach heaven unscathed by demons.[45] Nonetheless, if these passages truly ascribe agency to the soul rather than simply serve to mark a character's heroic or Christian merit, the soul's agency is still relatively ineffectual, being limited to cooperation or resistance in the face of death.

The Capabilities and Behaviours of the Soul during Life

The corpus of OE poetry offers only two sustained considerations of the soul's activities during its life in the body: *Riddle* 43 in the Exeter Book[46]

---

43 *GuthA* 2b–3: 'The soul gives up the joy of this earth, abandons these transitory delights, and departs from the body'; *GuthA* 6–7a: '"Now you can journey to the place which you have been striving after long and diligently."'
44 Christ 'releases his spirit' as he dies on the cross (Lk 23:46), and Stephen, in imitation, utters the words 'Receive my spirit' as he is stoned to death (Acts 7:58). In the poem *Christ III*, at lines 1452b–3, Jesus addresses the crowds at the Last Judgment and recounts the scene of his death: 'ic anne forlet / of minum lichoman lifgendne gæst' (I relinquished my one living spirit from my body).
45 *Beo* 2817–20; *Mald* 173–80.
46 Below I quote Williamson's text of the 'Soul and Body' riddle (*The Old English Riddles of the Exeter Book*, 96) because his punctuation is preferable to that of ASPR 3 (see Williamson's remarks, 279–80). For the sake of consistency I follow the ASPR numbering of the Exeter Book riddles, according to which 'Soul and Body' is no. 43, although in principle I accept Lapidge's and Williamson's renumbering of the riddles to account for the fact that the text printed as the first three riddles in ASPR 3 is actually a single

and the poem called *Soul and Body*, which survives in two versions.[47] The solution to *Riddle* 43 in the Exeter Book is generally agreed to be 'soul and body.' The soul is an *indryhtne … giest* 'distinguished guest' who is *æþelum deorne* 'beloved for his nobility' (lines 1–2a), while the body is called an *esne*. It is worth scrutinizing the nuances of meaning attached to the word *esne*, which the speaker uses three times in just sixteen lines, in order to elucidate the precise status imputed to the body in this riddle. In the OE laws, *esne* is the specialized term for a servant of indeterminate status, superior to the slave (*ðeow* or *wealh*) but subordinate to the free labourer (*ceorl*).[48] In non-legal prose as well as poetry and glosses, *esne* may retain the same general meaning of 'servant,' often rendering Latin *seruus*,[49] but the compounds *esnemann* and *esnewyrhta*, which render Latin *mercenarius* 'hired man' and *operarius* 'day-labourer,' again underscore that the *esne* has more autonomy than a slave.[50] Although the word *esne* signals some degree of social inferiority, it may also connote youth, skills, strength, and masculinity. OE poets, translators, and glossators used *esne* to render the gender-specific Latin words *adulescens* and *iuuenis* 'young man' and *uir* 'husband' or 'man'; perhaps most significantly, the adverb *esnelice* does not mean 'obsequiously' or 'slavishly' but rather 'manfully' (Latin *uiriliter*).[51] In this sense Byrhtferth uses the word *esne* when he exhorts his male students to labour diligently to learn their computus: 'Swa gedafenað esnum þam orpedan, þonne he god weorc ongynð, þæt he þæt geornlice beswynce, þeah hine deofol mid his lymum wylle gedreccan.'[52] In *Riddle* 43, therefore, the repeated use of the term *esne* implies that the body is the soul's social subordinate, its hireling but not its slave; and that the body labours, not abjectly, but with skill and strength, and to its own advantage.

---

riddle (Lapidge, 'Stoic Cosmology and the Source of the First Old English Riddle,' 4–9; Williamson, *The Old English Riddles of the Exeter Book*, 127–33.)

47 *Soul and Body I*, preserved in the Vercelli Book, is atelous but includes the addresses of both the blessed soul and the damned soul; *Soul and Body II*, in the Exeter Book, includes only the damned soul's address. On the relationship between the texts, see Moffat, *The Old English* Soul and Body, 1–9.

48 Pelteret, *Slavery in Early Mediaeval England*, 84–5 and 271–4.

49 *DOE*, s.v. *esne* 1, 1.a, 1.b.

50 *DOE*, s.v. *esne-mann, esne-wyrhta*.

51 *DOE*, s.v. *esne* 2, 3; *esnelice*.

52 Byrhtferth, *Enchiridion*, 3.1.125–7 (ed. Baker and Lapidge, *Byrhtferth's Enchiridion*, 128): 'So it befits the bold young man, when he begins a good work, that he labour at it diligently, though the devil with his henchmen wishes to afflict him' (trans. ibid., 129).

The rest of the speaker's characterization of the body-soul relationship in *Riddle* 43, as it turns out, corroborates all these implications of the epithet *esne*. As a hired labourer, the body 'must go forth on that journey' with his master the soul, but the body has the choice to serve his master either honourably or wrongly.

> Gif him arlice
> esne þenað   se þe agan sceal
> on þam siðfate,   hy gesunde æt ham
> findað witode him   wiste ond blisse;
> cnosles unrim   care, gif se esne
> his hlaforde   hyreð yfle,
> frean on fore,   ne wile forht wesan
> broþor oþrum.[53]

The fate of both master and servant together is wholly contingent on whether the servant chooses to obey. If the servant is unruly and disrespectful, 'that will cause harm to both of them' (*him þæt bam sceðeð*) when they pass from this world (11b). According to the conditions of this relationship, the soul is a master in name only: it has no responsibility for making decisions and has no recourse when the body misbehaves in ways that threaten to injure them both. The epithets 'noble' and 'beloved' give the impression that the soul is naturally inclined toward good; moreover, while the body-as-servant can potentially destroy both of them by being disobedient, there is no consideration of the possibility that the soul could be a bad master. The choice between worthy and ignoble behaviour rests entirely with the body, and the soul is not so much the body's active master as the body's passive model of good behaviour. The faculties of moral deliberation and will are properties of the body alone.

Riddle 43 in the Exeter Book attempts, at least, to idealize the soul-body relationship as that of master and servant, even if closer examination uncovers that the servant is virtually autonomous. The *Soul and Body* poems,

---

53 *Rid* 43 [41], lines 4b–11a (ed. Williamson, *The Old English Riddles of the Exeter Book*, 96): 'If the servant, who must go forth on that journey, serves him honourably, they will certainly obtain for themselves sustenance and joy when they are safe at home, but they will obtain a countless number of sorrows for their family if the servant ill obeys his lord, his master along the way, and if one brother is unwilling to be fearful of the other.' Some editors interpret *agan* (line 5) as two words, *a gan*, which is metrically preferable but does not change the meaning appreciably: see ASPR 3.346.

however, do not even gesture toward the ideal of the beneficent soul as master of the body. Instead, they invert this relationship, especially where the damned soul addresses a domineering body to whom it was bound unwillingly. During their life together, the body afflicted the soul (17b), worked against it (59b), starved it of spiritual goods, and imprisoned it: 'þu me þy heardan hungre gebunde / ond gehæftnadest helle witum!' the soul says to its erstwhile body. 'Eardode ic þe on innan. No ic þe of meah-te, / flæsce bifongen.'[54] Though the soul is now damned, it was originally God's gift to the body and could potentially have 'stabilized' it, according to what the soul tells the body:

Þær þu þonne hogode   her on life,
þenden ic þe in worulde   wunian sceolde,
þæt þu wære þurh flæsc   ond þurh firenlustas
stronge gestyred   ond gestaþelad þurh mec,
ond ic wæs gæst on þe   from gode sended,
næfre þu me swa heardra   helle wita
ned gearwode   þurh þinra neoda lust.[55]

The responsibility for moral deliberation and awareness (suggested by the verb *hogode*) is borne by the body; the soul's capacity to 'stabilize' the body is ineffectual and falls far short of strict governance. Faced with this imbalance of power, the damned soul absolves itself of all responsibility, demanding of the body, 'Hwæt, wite þu me, werga!'[56] The narrator has already explained that the soul's fate in the afterlife depended on the deeds of the body in which it abided,[57] but the damned soul did not spend its earthly life berating or exhorting or cajoling the body in hopes of correcting its sinful behaviours. Instead, resigned to the fate that its sinful body was preparing for it, and knowing itself to be incapable of improving its own lot, the damned soul lay low and waited for death. Now the soul

---

54 *Soul II* 28–31a: 'You oppressed me with severe hunger and shackled me with the torments of hell! I dwelt within you; surrounded by flesh, I was not able to go out from you.'
55 *Soul II* 39–45: 'If you had realized at that time – here during life on earth, when I had to inhabit you – that you were powerfully swayed by the flesh and by wanton desires, and you were stabilized by me, and I was your soul, sent into you by God, then you never would have prepared for me the pain of such harsh punishments in hell, through your desire for pleasures.'
56 *Soul II* 22a: 'Indeed, do you blame *me*, you criminal!'
57 *Soul II* 5b–8.

reproaches its body, saying, 'Þæt me þuhte ful oft / þæt wære þritig þusend wintra / to þinum deaðdæge. Hwæt, ic uncres gedales bad / earfoðlice.'[58] Tormented by its life in the body, the soul still dreaded leaving that life, because damnation was sure to follow.

As *Soul and Body* portrays the soul-body relationship, the soul offers nothing more than a static example of benignity, which the body is free to reject. This characterization applies not only to the damned soul; when the blessed soul addresses its body, it reveals that it, likewise, has won a better fate not because it was more virtuous or more powerful than the damned soul, but because it happened to reside in a body that chose poverty and self-denial. The blessed soul praises its body for rejecting earthly comforts: 'Fæstest ðu on foldan ond gefyldest me / godes lichoman, gastes dryncess. / Wære ðu on wædle, sealdest me wilna geniht.'[59] Even the virtue of humility is credited to the body: as the blessed soul says to the body, 'Bygdest ðu þe for hæleðum ond ahofe me on ecne dream.'[60]

The soul's utter helplessness in the *Soul and Body* poems has surprised some modern readers, who expect a Christian text to depict a unitary soul, endowed with free will and reason, and fully capable of disciplining the body's appetites.[61] It is incorrect, however, to suppose that all Christian Latin discourse conformed to a single opinion concerning the extent of the soul's responsibility for sin: even within the corpus of Latin homiletic materials that depict the soul's address to the body, some texts portray a helpless soul victimized by inherently vicious flesh, and others ascribe to the soul a significant role in governing the actions of the body.[62] Allen Frantzen has proposed that the apparent inversion of the expected soul-body relationship in the OE *Soul and Body* poems is not heterodox but is due to the influence of penitential literature, with its emphasis on bodily

---

58 *Soul II* 32b–5a: 'Always it seemed to me that it would be thirty thousand years until the day you died. Alas, I waited in misery for our separation.'

59 *Soul I* 142–4: 'In this world you fasted, and you filled me with sustenance for the body and the drink of the soul. You existed in poverty, gave to me an abundance of delights.'

60 *Soul I* 151: 'You bowed down before the saints and lifted me up into eternal joy.'

61 Frantzen, 'The Body in *Soul and Body I*,' surveys the critical arguments that the poem is theologically heterodox because it dwells on the subjugation of the soul to the sinful body, and he usefully contrasts the content of *Soul and Body I* with Augustine's treatment of the moral relationship between soul and body in *De ciuitate Dei* (76–8).

62 Two contrasting opinions are represented by the Nonantola version of the 'Macarius' homily and the pseudo-Augustinian *Sermo ad fratres in eremo 49*, which Calder and Allen include among the analogues of the OE *Soul and Body* poems: see their translations in *Sources and Analogues of Old English Poetry*, 40–50.

mortification. If the soul-body hierarchy in the poem is out of step with patristic teachings, Frantzen concludes, it is 'only because the soul's responsibility is not expressed' in the poem, 'because the poet's subject is not theology, but penitential practice.'[63] While Frantzen's explanation is convincing, there is a simpler alternative, namely that the *sawol* of the OE *Soul and Body* poems is not identical to the unitary *anima* of many patristic Latin texts. Its responsibility for sinful behaviour is 'not expressed' because it has none, since the faculty of deliberation and will and agency reside in another component of the human being.

The portrait of the *sawol* that emerges from these texts is of an entity that is incapable of autonomous action or of efficacious thought while residing in the body. That is to say, the *sawol* may have the capacity to form opinions or to harbour desires and aversions, but it cannot use these 'thoughts' to influence the body, to mount an internal conflict with the mind, or to bring about the fulfilment of any of its desires, as long as it is enclosed in the flesh. As death approaches, the blessed or heroic individual's soul encounters its first opportunity to actively pursue a desire, that is, its desire to leave the body. To better understand the soul's exclusion from efficacious participation in the individual's everyday thoughts and actions during life, it is useful to compare the soul with the mind, and to ascertain what exactly the mind does for the individual.

The Distinction between Soul and Mind in the Vernacular Tradition

Four of the basic OE terms for the part of the human being responsible for thought are *mod, hyge, sefa,* and *ferhð,* all of which are typically translated as MnE 'mind.' *Mod* additionally means 'courage' or 'pride' in many contexts, while the latter three terms belong primarily to the poetic lexicon.[64]

---

63 Frantzen, 'The Body in *Soul and Body I,*' 81. Notably, in Frantzen's essay, which appeared three years before Godden's 'Anglo-Saxons on the Mind,' he admonishes scholars who would be 'prepared to argue that literate Anglo-Saxons dispensed two grades of truth and then to prove that *Soul and Body I* belongs with the inferior kind' (85). A two-tiered model of Anglo-Saxon thought on the soul-body relationship is precisely what Godden argues for and what the textual evidence corroborates, although Godden does not label the vernacular tradition 'inferior' to the classical tradition.

64 Godden, 'Anglo-Saxons on the Mind,' 287–9; Low, 'Approaches to the Old English Vocabulary for "Mind."' Low's response to Godden's definition of *mod* is articulated in 'Pride, Courage, and Anger: The Polysemousness of Old English *Mod,*' esp. 84–5. Phillips, 'Heart, Mind, and Soul in Old English,' devotes individual chapters to each of the words *mod, hyge, sefa,* and *ferhð*; see also Harbus's response to Phillips (*The Life of the*

Some intriguing studies have attempted to show that *mod, hyge, sefa,* and *ferhð* are distinct faculties,[65] but for the purpose of this study it is more useful to lump together these four simplices, along with related compounds and many terms that refer to more specific psychological faculties and events, to render a holistic account of 'the mind,' as we may for convenience's sake call that entity that executes all psychological tasks, including reason, will, deliberation, emotion, contemplation, governance of the body, and so on. Beyond a very small group of discursive texts that replicate the Platonic tripartition of the soul into the rational, the irascible, and the concupiscible,[66] the Anglo-Saxons did not conceive of reason and emotion as different classes of thought or localize them in different bodily seats.[67] In fact, the OE lexicon evidently includes no precise equivalents for MnE 'emotion' or 'emotional' as non-pejorative alternatives to 'reason' or 'rational.' The opposite of OE *gesceadwislic* 'rational' or 'reasonable' is *ungesceadwislic* 'irrational,' but this and related words denote the non-rational thought processes of beasts and the ravings of madmen rather than ordinary emotions.[68]

Though I have already demonstrated how a few specific classes of narrative suggest that the *sawol* was excluded from efficacious mental activity, it remains for us to examine how this division of labour holds up across the

---

Mind in Old English Poetry, 34–5); and McGowan, 'Year's Work in Old English Studies: Lexicon, Glosses,' 35–6.

65 Phillips takes for granted that *mod, hyge, sefa,* and *ferhð* each signified a distinct psychological faculty, and moreover, that authors throughout the Anglo-Saxon period used the word *sawol* to signify a unitary soul, just as Ælfric did ('Heart, Mind, and Soul in Old English,' esp. 7, 16–17). I find Low's criticisms of Phillips's methodology to be well-founded ('The Anglo-Saxon Mind,' 20, and 'Mental Cultivation in *Guthlac B*,' 626–8), but Harbus accepts, with reservations, Phillips's view of the relationship between *sawol* and *anima* (*The Life of the Mind in Old English Poetry*, 35–6). Richard North argues that there are significant semantic differences among *mod, hyge, sefa,* and *ferhð* and their Germanic cognates (*Pagan Words and Christian Meanings*, 63–98).

66 This group includes Alcuin's *De ratione animae*, the Alfredian OE *Boethius*, and Ælfric's Nativity Homily (*LS* 1), on which see chapters 6–8 below.

67 Godden, 'Anglo-Saxons on the Mind,' 289, 291; Godden, 'The Psyche and the Self: Some Issues in *Beowulf*,' 50; Low, 'Mental Cultivation in *Guthlac B*,' 628–9; Low, 'Approaches to the Old English Vocabulary for "Mind,"' 15; Harbus, *The Life of the Mind in Old English Poetry*, 37–8.

68 Certainly there are OE words that denote an abundance or excess of emotion, many of which are rooted in bodily sensations of heat and swelling in the chest (see Roberts, Kay, and Grundy, *A Thesaurus of Old English*, 1.430–2), yet none of these words seems to denote, without pejoration, a category of thought that is distinguished from *gescead* 'reason' on the basis of its content alone.

corpus of OE narrative and whether the mind was similarly excluded from activities proper to the soul. The second of these questions is the simpler of the two because the range of activities proper to the *sawol* is very narrow. As shown already, the *sawol* enters the body at animation, departs at death, and does very little in between; its primary purpose is to represent the individual in the afterworld. The mind, in contrast, does none of these things. As a rule, the entity called *mod, hyge,* and *sefa* is not said to leave the body at death or to participate in the afterlife,[69] and the few exceptions that have been proposed are unconvincing.[70] (*Ferhð* is a difficult case, which demands closer scrutiny below, in order to disambiguate *ferhð* from *feorh* as far as possible.)

That the *sawol* was excluded from efficacious mental activity is corroborated by a great deal of OE narrative evidence.[71] Notably, in *The Wanderer* and *The Seafarer,* the two poems most famous as meditations on the life of the mind, the word *gast* never appears, and the *sawol* appears only once and refers to a dead person present at the Last Judgment.[72] In other poems, where several synonyms referring to the mind are collocated in apposition or in parallel structure, the words *sawol* and *gast* are studiously avoided. A well-known example appears in Byrhtwold's battlefield exhortation in *The Battle of Maldon*: 'Hige sceal þe heardra, heorte þe cenre, / mod sceal þe mare, þe ure mægen lytlað.'[73] Less familiar are the

---

69 Godden, 'Anglo-Saxons on the Mind,' 289; Low, 'Mental Cultivation in *Guthlac B,*' 626; Moffat, *The Old English* Soul and Body, 18–19; Phillips, 'Heart, Mind, and Soul in Old English,' 19; Richard North, *Pagan Words and Christian Meanings,* 64–5.

70 Failure to recognize that *sawol* and *mod* are discrete entities introduces problems into several studies, including Hultin, 'The External Soul in *The Seafarer* and *The Wanderer*'; Salmon, '*The Wanderer* and *The Seafarer,* and the Old English Conception of the Soul'; Smithers, 'The Meaning of *The Seafarer* and *The Wanderer.*' Godden, 'Anglo-Saxons on the Mind,' 289 n. 47, suggests that *Guthlac A,* lines 25–9, might depict the *mod* rising to heaven in the afterlife, but the poem states that this ascent occurs 'þonne he his ænne her / gæst bigonge' (while he cultivates his one soul here), that is, during earthly life.

71 Even Phillips, who mistakes the *sawol* of OE narrative for the unitary soul of theological discourse, admits his surprise 'that *gast* and *sawol* occur in so few non-transcendent structures,' that is, that they rarely exhibit any behaviours at all except during and after the body's death: see 'Heart, Mind, and Soul in Old English,' 291.

72 The word *gæstlic* does occur in *The Wanderer,* but it seems to mean 'frightening' or 'profound,' as opposed to its usual use in discursive OE as a calque on Latin *spiritualis*: see Smithers, 'The Meaning of *The Seafarer* and *The Wanderer,*' 141–2. *Sawol* appears at *Sea* 100a (see below).

73 *Mald* 312–3: 'The mind must be firmer, the heart fiercer, and the mind [*or* courage] greater, as our strength shrinks.'

portrait of the estranged son in the metrical *Solomon and Saturn*, who 'hafað wilde mod, werige heortan, / sefan sorgfullne,'[74] and the sixth teaching delivered in *Precepts*, which includes all four simplex terms for the mind in just seven lines:

> Ongiet georne   hwæt sy god oþþe yfel,
> ond toscead simle   scearpe mode
> in sefan þinum   ond þe a þæt selle geceos.
> A þe bið gedæled;   gif þe deah hyge,
> wunað wisdom in,   ond þu wast geare
> ondgit yfles,   heald þe elne wið,
> feorma þu symle   in þinum ferðe god.[75]

Varied diction was clearly important to this poet, but even though the mental activities here described include moral deliberation and the cultivation of Christian virtues, *sawol* and *gast* are excluded, and mental activity is imputed exclusively to the mind.

Although the soul is, as a rule, uninvolved in psychological activity, two groups of exceptions merit closer scrutiny. First, the soul appears to be thinking or feeling emotions four times in *Guthlac A*, twice in the signed poems of Cynewulf, twice within a five-line segment of *Andreas*, and twice in *Daniel*.[76] Guthlac's *gast* is a repository of hope, and Juliana's *gast* is a repository of contempt.[77] Guthlac vows to submit to God in his

---

74 *MSol* 379–80a: 'possesses an untamed mind, a wretched heart, an anxious mind.' Cf. *MSol* 66–7, where *sawol* appears in a parallel construction with *sefa* and *mod* in a fashion that leaves their relationship to one another unclear. This passage is of particular interest because Anlezark has recently theorized that the metrical *Solomon and Saturn* was composed in Dunstan's milieu of mid-tenth-century Glastonbury (*The Old English Dialogues of Solomon and Saturn*, 49–57). If this is true, one might reasonably argue that *MSol* 66–7 represents a rare poetic reference to the unitary soul. For further discussion, see the epilogue below.

75 *Prec* 45–51: 'Understand fully what is good or evil, and continually distinguish between them with incisive thought, in your mind, and always choose for yourself the better. This will ever be granted to you: if your mind is strong, wisdom will dwell within it, and you will fully grasp the meaning of evil. Guard yourself always against it, and keep yourself always pure, upright in mind.'

76 In addition to the lines quoted below, see *GuthA* 544b, *GuthA* 258b, *El* 471a, and *And* 858b.

77 *GuthA* 170b–1a: 'He in gæste bær / heofoncundne hyht' (In his *gast* he bore heavenly hope); *Jul* 34–5a: 'freondrædenne ... heo from hogde, / geong on gæste' (in her *gast* the young woman hated married life).

gastgemyndum or 'thoughts of the *gast*,' and St Andrew's companions report to him their mystical vision in order that he might 'prudently consider it in the thoughts of the *gast*' (*ongitan gleawlice gastgehygdum*).[78] Most exceptional are the passages from *Daniel*; at one point *gast* and *mod* are even set in apposition as the narrator recounts how Nabuchadnosor recovered from his temporary insanity.

> Þa he eft onhwearf
> wodan gewittes,   þær þe he ær wide bær
> herewosan hige,   heortan getenge.
> Þa his gast ahwearf   in godes gemynd,
> mod to mannum,   siððan he metod onget ...
> [S]iðfæt sægde   sinum leodum,
> wide waðe   þe he mid wilddeorum ateah,
> oðþæt him frean godes   in gast becwom
> rædfæst sefa,   ða he to roderum beseah.[79]

One could argue that *gast* and *mod* are not quite synonyms, but that the *gast* turns to heavenly matters (*godes gemynd*) while the *mod* turns to earthly thoughts; still, the *gast* is undeniably engaged in memory in line 629 and (in a rather obscure construction) it feels the psychological influence of the *sefa* in lines 650b–1a.

It is not impossible that these passages are indeed attestations of the unitary soul fully engaged in mental activity, though this would be surprising in texts that otherwise adhere to the vernacular tradition. There is, however, another explanation. In all ten of these passages the psychologized entity is the *gast*, not the *sawol*, and in all ten passages, *gast* bears alliterative stress. Now, there is no OE word for 'mind' that begins with g, but there is one beginning in s, namely *sefa*. Most likely, the authors of these few poems (of which all but *Daniel* either are attributed to Cynewulf or share many similarities with his work) considered it suitable to call the mind *gast* because of its elusive or hidden (though by no means incorporeal) nature.

---

78 *GuthA* 600b–3b, *And* 859–61.
79 *Dan* 626b–30, 648–51: 'Then he again recovered from his crazed thought, near to his heart where he had long borne the mind of a warrior; then his *gast* returned to the memory of God, his mind turned back to his people, once he had recognized his Ruler ... He told his people about the adventure, the distant route he had roamed with wild animals, until prudent thoughts of the Lord God came upon him in his *gast*, when he looked to the heavens.'

They would not have called the mind *sawol* because, first, they had re-course to *sefa* when looking for a term for 'mind' that alliterated in *s*; and second, *sawol* does not share the semantic flexibility of *gast* and cannot be used to signify a variety of elusive or invisible entities. Because this group of exceptions seems to be motivated by metrical concerns and does not use *gast* in a way that is difficult to reconcile with some of its usual meanings, I conclude that these exceptions do not disrupt the usual division of labour between the transcendent soul and the thinking mind.

A second group of exceptional passages portrays the *sawol* temporarily leaving the body of a living person and experiencing visions of the after-world, during which the soul possesses greater agency, personality, and mental acuity than it typically possesses in its ordinary life in the body. Because the soul undergoes this experience while released from the body, one might say that these narratives are not exceptional at all, and that the soul's faculties are augmented by a temporary departure from the body just as they are by its permanent departure. All the same, these depictions of soul-travel merit comparison with narratives of mind-travel, because the contrast between them throws into relief the division of labour be-tween soul and mind.

Whether the Anglo-Saxons understood mind-travel to be a physical, spatial phenomenon or only a figural representation, temporary depar-tures of the mind (*mod, hyge, sefa, ferhð*) are associated with memories and imaginations of earthly people and places. It is the mind alone that temporarily abandons the speaker's breast in *The Seafarer* (*hyge*, 58a; *modsefa*, 59a) and *The Wanderer* (*mod*, 51; *ferhð*, 54; *sefa*, 57b), and in both poems, these departures from the body bring on visions of people and places in *this* world, not the next, as Peter Clemoes has amply dem-onstrated.[80] Given the amount of scholarly attention paid to the theme of *mens absentia cogitans* in these two poems, it is surprising that *mod* is always interpreted as either 'soul' or 'temper' in that much-discussed line in the Finnsburh episode of *Beowulf*: 'ne meahte wæfre mod / forhabban in hreþre.'[81] Summing up the opinions of earlier scholars, Chickering ex-plains that 'This free-standing phrase can mean "the soul left the body," i.e., Finn was killed, or "the anger (*mod*) of the Danes burst out in action." The poet has so placed the phrase that the undefined "spirit" (*mod*) seems

---

80   Clemoes, '*Mens absentia cogitans* in *The Seafarer* and *The Wanderer*.'
81   *Beo* 1150b–1a: 'the restless mind was unable to remain in the breast.'

an impersonal agent acting of its own accord.'[82] There is no precedent for the use of *mod* to signify the transcendent soul or the life-force, so I reject that reading altogether. To interpret *mod* as 'courage' or 'temper' is unobjectionable, but the context of the Finnsburh episode is better served if we interpret *mod* as the mind travelling out of the breast in the act of remembering. While the mutually hostile parties of Danes and Frisians are forced to winter together, they can hope to maintain peace only if they can banish memories of past violence between them. Despite their best efforts, 'the restless mind was unable to remain in the breast,' that is, the men could not restrain themselves from recalling old hostilities, as intimated by the immediately preceding lines:

Swylce ferhðfrecan   Fin eft begeat
sweordbealo sliðen   æt his selfes ham,
siþðan grimne gripe   Guðlaf ond Oslaf
æfter sæsiðe   sorge mændon,
ætwiton weana dæl.[83]

Because Guthlaf's and Oslaf's minds refuse to stay in the breast but instead travel in memory to the terrible scene of Hnæf's slaying by Finn's men, the remembrance of unavenged injuries sparks a renewal of the feud, and Finn's hall is bloodied again.[84]

In contrast, OE narratives in which the *sawol* or *gast* temporarily journeys out of the body are accounts of visionary experiences of the afterworld rather than of memory or imagination. In *Andreas*, for example,

---

82 Chickering, *Beowulf: A Dual-Language Edition*, 329. Klaeber's glossary supplies 'temper' as the meaning of this occurrence of *mod* (413, s.v. *mod*), and Godden translates *mod* as 'feelings' ('Anglo-Saxons on the Mind,' 288–9).

83 *Beo* 1146–50a: 'Likewise did a cruel death by the sword eventually come upon bold-minded Finn at his own home, after Guthlaf and Oslaf complained about the fierce attack and the grief that followed their sea-journey and blamed Finn for a large measure of their misery.' I take the 'fierce attack' to be the Frisians' slaying of Hnæf and the 'sea-journey' to be the Danes' initial voyage to Finn's stronghold, although other interpretations have been advanced, which are reviewed most clearly and accessibly by Chickering, *Beowulf: A Dual-Language Edition*, 327–9; see also Klaeber, 190–1.

84 Whether Guthlaf and Oslaf avenged Hnæf's death alone or with reinforcements does not affect my interpretation of the *mod wæfre* as the mind travelling in memory, because the remembrance of unavenged injuries could equally well have bolstered Guthlaf's and Oslaf's own courage or goaded their allies into assisting them in killing Finn: on the crucial role of memory in medieval Germanic accounts of feud, see Lockett, 'The Role of Grendel's Arm in Feud, Law, and the Narrative Strategy of *Beowulf*.'

the men aboard the ship reveal to St Andrew that they have experienced a remarkable vision of heaven: eagles 'seized our souls while we were sleeping' (*us ofslæpendum sawle abrugdon*) and lifted them up to heaven, where they witnessed a heavenly host offering praise and adoration to God.[85] A similar experience befell the Monk of Much Wenlock, who reported his vision first-hand to the Anglo-Saxon missionary Boniface (Wynfrith). According to the OE rendering of Boniface's account, the monk 'cwæð þæt him geeode þurh nedbade þæt his lichama wære seoc geworden, and he wæs semninga þy gaste benæmed.'[86] As the monk rises toward heaven, the whole earth grows smaller beneath him, and he watches demons and angels competing to win souls of the recently deceased. At the conclusion of this otherworldly vision, 'þa bibudon þa eadigan englas þæt his sawul ahwyrfde eft buton yldinge to his lichaman.'[87] A third instance occurs in the OE version of Bede's account of the vision of Fursey, who, while desperately ill, experiences two visions of souls in the afterlife. At first we are told only that Fursey is 'taken out of the body' (*alæded of lichoman*) and 'led back into the body' (*eft læded in lichoman*).[88] During one of these journeys, a damned soul tormented by flames touches Fursey's shoulder and face, burning him. When Fursey returns to the body, for the rest of his life the burn is visible on his body, as a 'tacen þære bærnnisse, þæt he on his sawle aræfnde.' It is amazing, the narrator concludes, that 'þætte seo sawl in deagolnisse þrowiende wæs, þæt se lichoma eawesclice foretacnode.'[89]

---

85   *And* 859–70. For the Latin text of the 'Bonnet Fragment' that underlies this episode in *Andreas*, see Brooks, *Andreas and the Fates of the Apostles*, 177–8.

86   *Wynfrith's Letter*, lines 7–8 (ed. Sisam, 'An Old English Translation of a Letter from Wynfrith to Eadburga,' 213): 'said that because of bodily pain it happened that his body became sick, and he was suddenly taken away in spirit.' Boniface first related this story in a Latin letter of the year 716/17; the OE translation of this letter survives in an eleventh-century manuscript, which Sisam maintains is not the translator's original (ibid., 207).

87   *Wynfrith's Letter*, lines 195–6 (ed. Sisam, 'An Old English Translation of a Letter from Wynfrith to Eadburga,' 222): 'Then the blessed angels ordered his soul to travel back into his body without delay.' Note that Boniface's Latin text does not indicate which part of the monk – soul, spirit, or otherwise – was returned to the body; the angels commanded 'ut sine mora ad proprium rediret corpus' (ibid., 223). It was the translator's decision, therefore, to specify that the monk's *sawol* travelled out of and into the body during this visionary experience.

88   *OE Bede* 3.19 (ed. Miller, 212, lines 4 and 11).

89   *OE Bede* 3.19 (ed. Miller, 216, lines 13–14): 'token of the burn that he suffered upon his soul'; ibid., lines 15–17: 'that which the soul was suffering in secrecy, the body manifested openly.' Bede's story of the vision of Dryhthelm (*OE Bede* 5.13; ed. Miller, 422–36) does

The narrative evidence thus supports a clear distinction between the *sawol*, which leaves the body temporarily to visit the afterworld, and the *mod*, which travels from the breast while engaged in memory or imagination. The soul and the mind are functionally and substantially discrete entities, and the *sawol* is fully actualized and psychologized only outside the body.[90]

The Intimacy of the Mind-Body Partnership

In *Soul and Body II*, the damned soul attributes to its erstwhile body various mental states, such as desire, forethought and the lack thereof, and the capacity to experience shame,[91] yet the soul also accuses the body of having been 'powerfully influenced by the flesh and by sinful desires.'[92] These lines of the soul's address do not make sense if its addressee is nothing more than the unconscious flesh. It is more accurate to conceive of the soul's addressee as a mind-body complex, or as a body composed of both unthinking flesh and thinking flesh, the latter being the organ of the mind. Either of these configurations challenges the modern reader's predisposition to think of mind and body as opposing forces. OE narrative does not typically portray internal conflict as a battle between mind and body, and the mantra 'mind over matter' has no part in OE descriptions of self-control under duress. Instead, mind and body typically share one will, and it is up to these two mortal elements of the human being to act in a manner that will harm or help the immortal soul. The *Soul and Body* poems are not alone in depicting a mind-body complex charged with the care of the soul. *Gifts of Men*, a little-studied poem in the Exeter Book, catalogues the various skills and temperaments allotted by God to men, among which is the ability to provide for the needs of the soul: 'Sum her geornlice gæstes þearfe / mode bewindeþ, ond him metudes est / ofer eorðwelan ealne

---

not specify whether it is the soul, mind, or life-force that leaves Dryhthelm's body; however, the fact that he experiences his vision after death implies that his *sawol* travels to the afterworld for a time before re-entering his corpse.

90 As Godden ('Anglo-Saxons on the Mind,' 277) points out, the OE *Boethius* suggests that it is the *gast* that departs from the body during dreams (B-text, ch. 34, lines 307–9; ed. Godden and Irvine, 1.328), but this is said in a discursive context, and the psychological vocabulary of the OE *Boethius* is applied in an inconsistent fashion (see chapter 7 below), so this passage does not pose a significant challenge to the narrative division of labour between the mind and soul in their respective journeys out of the body.

91 *Soul II* 19b–21 and 22b–3 (forethought), 31b–2 (desires), and 46 (potential shame).

92 *Soul II* 41–2a: 'þurh flæsc ond þurh firenlustas / stronge gestyred.'

geceoseð.'[93] As long as the soul is 'here' in the world, according to the speaker, it has little power to provide for itself, so it falls to the *mod* to choose either that which will lead to the soul's salvation or that which will gratify the mind and the body.[94]

If the soul's addressee in *Soul and Body* is a mind-body complex, does it follow that the mind decays in the grave along with the body? A heroic speech by Guthlac, delivered as he battles a troop of devils, intimates that the mind does in fact share in the body's mortality rather than the soul's transcendence. Guthlac acknowledges that the devils are likely to destroy both his 'fleshly covering' (*flæschoman*) and the intellect (*gewit*) sheltered within it, but even when they have deprived him of speech and thought, his *sawol* will never succumb to injury – in fact, the destruction of the mind-body complex frees the soul to travel to 'a better place.'[95] The speaker of *The Seafarer* makes a similar point as he observes that when life ends, the body will not be able to perform its customary tasks, which include sensory processing, motor control, and thought: 'Ne mæg him þonne se flæschoma, þonne him þæt feorg losað, / ne swete forswelgan ne sar gefelan, / ne hond onhreran ne mid hyge þencan.'[96] The Seafarer's choice of words suggests that 'thinking with the mind' is just another task executed by the body, and that the mind is just another organ of the body, the one that happens to be endowed with the faculty of thought, as other organs are endowed with the faculties of sensory perception or digestion or motion. The lines that immediately follow (97–102) depict the immortal *sawol* facing God's judgment in heaven, where it cannot benefit from the gold placed in the grave: a blunt reminder of the mortality and uselessness of all that the transcendent soul leaves behind.

Though in this chapter I have adduced only those OE depictions of the mind that underscore the distinctions between mind and soul, with respect to substance, function, and durability, there remains much to be said about the mind-body complex and the physiology of mental activity, to which all of chapter 2 is devoted. To conclude the present chapter's exploration of the fourfold anthropology of OE narrative, I investigate

---

93 *Gifts* 86–8: 'Some people here diligently embrace in the mind the needs of the soul and choose for themselves the favour of the Creator above all worldly riches.'

94 Godden makes a similar point concerning the homiletic soul-body dialogues in both prose and verse ('Anglo-Saxons on the Mind,' 289).

95 *GuthA* 374–8a, quoted in full above.

96 *Sea* 94–6: 'When the life-force abandons it, then the flesh-covering will not be able to devour sweets, nor to feel a wound, nor to move its hand, nor to think with the mind.'

the most elusive of the four components of the human being, namely the life-force, in order to distinguish it as clearly as possible from the soul and from the mind.

The Elusive *feorh*: The Transient Life-Force

Though OE narrative frequently focuses on the activities of the mind-body complex and on the life of the soul outside the body, the entity called *feorh* 'life-force' plays only a marginal role in narratives and in literary meditations on the human condition, probably because it has less personality, less agency, less power, and less durability than any other component of the human being. The *feorh* is also the most challenging part of the human being to characterize consistently across the OE corpus. The boundary between soul and life-force is blurred by the fact that they share a few important traits and behaviours, and moreover, some texts attest that the word *feorh* was occasionally confused or conflated with the word *ferhð*, which properly signifies the mind or some part thereof. Even though OE narratives preserve a few exceptions, the preponderance of evidence supports a single pattern of usage, in which the *feorh* is functionally and substantially discrete from both soul and mind.

The Transient Life-Force and the Transcendent Soul

The words *feorh, ealdor,* and *lif* all signify a component of the living human being that vivifies the body and dissipates upon departing from the body at death. Among these three, *ealdor* belongs primarily to the poetic lexicon, while *feorh* and *lif* occur in both verse and prose. All three terms also share a range of more abstract meanings, such as 'the condition of being alive' or 'the life-span.'[97] If the life-force and the soul appear to be interchangeable in certain texts, this is in part because the animation of the body requires the presence of both, and both depart at death, a similarity reflected in the formation of compound words. The element *-gedal* 'separation' is prefixed with *sawol-* and *gast-* as well as with *feorh-, ealdor-,* and *lif-*, to form compound nouns meaning 'death,' while adjectives meaning 'dead' are formed by prefixing the element *-leas* '-less' with *sawol-* and *gast-* as well as *ealdor-* and *lif-*. *Sawlberend* and *gastberend* 'bearing a

---

97 *DOE* s.v. *feorh* 1.c and 2; and s.v. *ealdor²* 1.a; BT s.v. *lif*. *Feorh* and *ealdor* thence have an even more abstract meaning in expressions such as *to ealdre,* 'always'; *on widan feore,* 'evermore'; and others: *DOE* s.v. *ealdor²* 2 and s.v. *feorh* 5.

soul,' as well as *feorhberend* and *feorheacen* 'bearing a life-force,' are attested as epithets meaning 'a living being.'

Furthermore, like the soul, the life-force is prominent in narratives of animation and death. At the creation of Adam and Eve, for instance, God instils in them both soul and life-force: 'Feorh in gedyde, / ece saula.'[98] The life-force must also enter ordinary living beings before they are born or hatched. The speaker of *Riddle* 10 ('Barnacle Goose') explains, 'Hæfde feorh cwico, þa ic of fæðmum cwom / brimes,'[99] and conversely, the speaker of *Riddle* 9 ('Cuckoo') alludes to his period of incubation in the egg as a time when he did not yet have either *feorh* or *ealdor*: 'Mec on þissum dagum deadne ofgeafun / fæder ond modor; ne wæs me feorh þa gen, / ealdor in innan.'[100] Also like the soul, the life-force is mentioned in a variety of OE circumlocutions pertaining to death. Of the Mermedonian youths killed in a flood, it is said that 'they lost their life-force because of the surge of the sea' (þurh flodes fær feorh aleton); Hrothgar memorably declares that Grendel's mere is so terrifying that a hart pursued by hounds 'would sooner give up his *feorh*, his *ealdor*, on the shore' (ær he feorh seleð, / aldor on ofre) than plunge into the water to save himself.[101] Cynewulf uses a similar turn of phrase in recounting the martyrdom of St James, who 'sceolde / fore Herode ealdre gedælan, / feorh wið flæsce.'[102]

Additionally, the life-force is spatially enclosed in the body, just as the soul is, and it may be released when the outer fortification of the flesh is breached. As Beowulf anticipates his defeat in battle against the dragon, the narrator reports that 'no þon lange wæs / feorh æþelinges flæsce bewunden,' and the *Genesis A*-narrator employs vivid language to explain that God sent the Flood to punish mankind: 'wuldorcyninges / yða wræcon arleasra feorh / of flæschoman.'[103] In one particularly grisly scene in *Andreas*, a devil goads the crowd to use their sharp swords to 'perforate'

98 *GenA* 184b–5a: '[God] placed inside them life, an eternal soul.'
99 *Rid* 10, 6–7a: 'I had a living life-force when I came forth from the bosom of the sea.' On the medieval legend that the barnacle goose hatched from a barnacle shell, having incubated under water, see Williamson, *The Old English Riddles of the Exeter Book*, 161–3.
100 *Rid* 9, 1–3a: 'Father and mother recently deposited me unliving [*scil.* as an egg, in a host bird's nest]; at that time there was not yet life-force in me, no life within.'
101 *And* 1629; *Beo* 1370b–1a.
102 *Fates* 35b–7a: 'had to part from his life-force, to separate his life-force from his flesh, because of Herod.'
103 *Beo* 2423b–4: 'The prince's life was not much longer entwined in the flesh'; *GenA* 1384b–6a: 'The waves of the glorious king banished the wicked men's life-force from the flesh-covering.'

St Andrew's flesh and thereby to compromise its ability to hold in the life-force: 'Lætað wæpnes spor / iren ecgheard, ealdorgeard sceoran, / fæges feorhhord,' the demon urges.[104] Occasionally the seat of the life-force, like that of the soul, is specifically localized in the region of the chest. The breast-armour that rests over Beowulf's shoulder, accordingly, provides special protection for his life-force: 'Him on eaxle læg / breostnet broden; þæt gebearh feore, / wið ord ond wið ecge, ingang forstod.'[105]

Beyond these similarities, the behaviour and character of the life-force diverges sharply from that of the soul. First, the life-force succumbs to bodily injuries that the soul transcends. The opening lines of *Riddle* 43 ('Soul and Body') briefly catalogue some bodily afflictions that cannot kill the soul (here playing the role of 'guest'):

> Ic wat indryhtne   æþelum deorne
> giest in geardum,   þam se grimma ne mæg
> hungor sceððan   ne se hata þurst,
> yldo ne adle.[106]

A strikingly similar list in *The Seafarer* enumerates harms that can destroy the life-force: 'adl oþþe yldo oþþe ecghete / fægum fromweardum feorh oðþringeþ.'[107] Reading these passages side-by-side underscores that the transient life-force is vulnerable to the same bodily injuries that cannot harm the immortal soul. The life-force is even included in the *Genesis A*-narrator's catalogue of transitory possessions that people ordinarily leave behind at death, 'þonne him god heora / æhta and ætwist eorðan gestreona / on genimeð and heora aldor somed.'[108] It is unthinkable that the *sawol* would be included in such a list, because it is the *sawol* that proceeds to the afterlife.

With respect to the lines quoted above from *The Seafarer*, one might point out that the life-force is said to be driven out of the body, not

---

104 *And* 1180b–2a: 'Allow the wake of the weapon, the hard-edged iron, to perforate the dwelling of the life-force, the life-enclosure of the doomed man.'
105 *Beo* 1547b–9: 'On his shoulder lay breast-armour of woven mail; it protected the life-force, stood firm against point and against entry of blade.'
106 *Rid* 43, 1–4a: 'I know a distinguished man, beloved for his nobility, a guest in the dwellings, whom terrible hunger cannot harm, nor hot thirst, old age, nor disease.'
107 *Sea* 70–1: 'Disease or old age or sword-hatred squeezes the life-force out of the departing doomed.'
108 *GenA* 1207b–9: 'when God snatches from them their belongings and their sustenance, the treasures of the earth, and their life at the same time.'

destroyed outright. It seems, however, that for the life-force, being driven out of the body is tantamount to destruction, because it has no independent existence outside of the body. Whereas the mind and the soul are capable of undertaking temporary journeys outside the bodies of the living, there can be no departure of the *feorh* that does not result in death. Additionally, unlike the soul, which is very often depicted travelling immediately to a place of reward or punishment when released from the dying body,[109] the journey of the life-force out of the dying body does not tend toward a new destination. It may be called *feorh uðgenge* 'departing life-force,'[110] but it does not arrive anywhere. Nor does it linger to share in the body's decay: when fire consumes the body of the Phoenix, 'lif bið on siðe, / fæges feorhhord, þonne flæsc ond ban / adleg æleð.'[111] The absence of the words *feorh* and *ealdor* from depictions of the general resurrection, where body and soul are reunited, suggests that the life-force did not continue to exist either in the grave or in the afterworld during the interval between the individual's death and the Last Judgment. It is tempting to explain the ephemerality of the life-force by positing that the words *feorh* and *ealdor* signify nothing more than the abstract state of being alive; on the other hand, if this were the case, we would expect *feorh* and *ealdor* to be collocated with words connoting eternity and immortality, analogous to expressions such as *ece lif* 'eternal life,' *lif butan ende* 'life without end,' and *sawles lif* 'the life of the soul.' To the best of my knowledge, *feorh* and *ealdor* in their more concrete sense of 'life-force' can never be *ece* or *butan ende*, nor are these words ever used to signify the life of the *sawol*

---

109 Among many examples, see *GuthB* 1265b–8a, *Jud* 111b–13a, *Phoen* 563b–7a, *Jul* 695b–701a, all discussed above, and *Instr* 221–3.

110 *Beo* 2123b.

111 *Phoen* 220b–2a: 'The life-force, the life-treasure of the one fated to die, will be on its way while the pyre burns flesh and bone.' See also *Phoen* 485b–90, discussed above, in which death takes away the *ealdor* and sends the body into the tomb and the soul into the afterworld. There is an exceptional instance at *Beo* 1210–11, where Hygelac's life-force is said to journey into the possession of others: 'Gehwearf þa in Francna fæþm feorh cyninges, / breostgewædu, ond se beah somod' (Then the life-force of the king, his corslet, and his necklace together travelled into the possession of the Franks). Given that the treasures travelling with Hygelac's *feorh* are all transient earthly goods, and given that later in the poem (2141a) Beowulf uses the phrase *feorh oðferede* 'I carried off her life-force' as a circumlocution meaning 'I killed her,' it is unlikely that the journey of Hygelac's *feorh* into his enemies' hands is meant to suggest its enduring existence outside the body. More likely it is merely a polite way to say that the Franks killed Hygelac and plundered the corpse. Cf. *DOE*, s.v. *feorh* 4.

in isolation from the body.[112] From the composite portrait of the life-force that emerges from numerous narratives, we may conclude that it is one of four discrete parts of the human being, a substance or energy that vivifies the flesh and ceases to exist when it departs from the dying body.

Despite the clear distinction between the soul's immortality and the life-force's ephemerality, words for soul and life-force occasionally appear in syntactic constructions – particularly parallel structures and apparent appositions – that encourage the reader to interpret both words as signifying the same entity. For instance, the speaker of Exeter Book *Riddle* 39 describes an inanimate but well-travelled entity (most likely Speech or Dream) by way of this paradox: 'Ne hafað hio sawle ne feorh, ac hio siþas sceal / geond þas wundorworuld wide dreogan.'[113] Here and throughout the OE poetic corpus it can be difficult to know whether soul and life-force are paired disjunctively, implying that they are two different things, or whether soul and life-force are two names applied to a single entity for the sake of varied diction. This sort of confusion occurs in a number of OE narratives pertaining to the animation and the death of bodies, because at these times soul and life-force come and go in tandem. As mentioned above, the *Genesis A*-narrator describes how God brought Adam and Eve to life: 'Feorh in gedyde, / ece saula. Heo wæron englum gelice, / þa wæs Eve, Adames bryd, / gaste gegearwod.'[114] Concerning the murderous cruelty of the Mermedonians, the narrator of *Andreas* remarks, 'Feorh ne bemurndan, / grædige guðrincas, hu þæs gastes sið / æfter swyltcwale geseted wurde.'[115] And when Grendel retreats to his mere, mortally wounded, we are told that 'Deaðfæge deog, siððan dreama leas / in fenfreoðo feorh alegde, / hæþene sawle.'[116] In each of these three passages, *feorh* is juxtaposed with *sawol* or *gast* such that one could reasonably argue on

112 Interestingly, the most abstract temporal meanings of *feorh* and *ealdor*, 'the span of life' or 'a long time,' appear in idioms such as *to ealdre* and *widan feore* 'for a long time,' and these idioms are often qualified by the adverb *ece* 'eternally' and the phrase *butan ende* to form expressions such as 'always and forever.'
113 *Rid* 39, 16–17: 'It has neither soul nor life, yet it shall make journeys far and wide over this wonderful universe.' On the long-contested solutions to this riddle, see Harbus, '*Exeter Book Riddle 39* Reconsidered.'
114 *GenA* 184b–7a: '[God] placed inside them life, an eternal soul. They were like the angels when Eve, wife of Adam, was endowed with a soul.'
115 *And* 154b–6: 'The eager warriors did not fret about their life, about how the journey of the soul would be directed after the agony of death.'
116 *Beo* 850–2a: 'Doomed to death, he hid until, deprived of joy, he lay down his life, his heathen soul, in the fen.'

syntactic grounds that they are in apposition to one another and share a single referent. Yet in each passage, where immortality or religious orientation is ascribed to the *sawol* or *gast*, the *feorh* has neither. God grants to Adam and Eve both *feorh* and *sawol*, but only the *sawol* is 'eternal,' and it is the *gast* that renders them immortal 'like the angels.' In *Andreas*, the Mermedonian warriors are prepared to give up both life and soul in battle, but the *gast* is said to undertake a 'journey' after death, and the *feorh* is not. Last, as Grendel dies, he gives up both *feorh* and *sawol*, but the adjective 'heathen' is applied to the *sawol*, underscoring that the soul, not the life-force, bears the identity of the individual into the afterworld.

The moral implications of the ephemerality of the life-force are further borne out by the cheapness of the life-force in comparison with the soul. In *Genesis A*, for instance, when God makes a new covenant with Noah after the Flood, he decrees that 'Ælc hine selfa ærest begrindeð / gastes dugeðum þæra þe mid gares orde / oðrum aldor oðþringeð.'[117] The implication is that the murderer suffers a greater loss than his victim does, or as A.N. Doane explains, 'punishment is not merely "blood for blood" but the soul of the murderer against the life of the slain (the murdered victim loses *aldor*, but the murderer loses *gastes duguðe*).'[118] Similarly, in *Andreas*, though the Mermedonians have already lost their lives (*feorh gesealdon*) in a flood, St Andrew continues to worry about the ongoing welfare of their souls, and he prays to God 'ðæt þa gastas, gode orfeorme, / in wita forwyrd, wuldre bescyrede, / in feonda geweald gefered ne wurdan.'[119] Though both life-force and soul have been taken from these young men, the threat of punishment in the afterlife extends only to their souls; the *feorh* is cheap in comparison.

The Blood and the Life-Force

In the course of his argument that the word *synsnædum* (*Beo* 743a) means 'sinful morsels,' Fred Robinson has examined the strong association of blood with both the soul and the life-force, an association attested in both OE verse and the pastoral discourses of Ælfric and Wulfstan. These two authors exhibit an 'almost obsessive concern with the Old Testament

---

117 *GenA* 1521–3a: 'Anyone who drives the life-force out of another person with the point of a spear first deprives himself of the nobility of his soul.'
118 Doane, *Genesis A: A New Edition*, 275.
119 *And* 1617–19: 'that their souls, destitute of good, deprived of glory, might not be borne into destruction caused by punishments, into the possession of devils.'

injunction against the drinking of blood,' which Robinson attributes to a 'widely held' belief 'that blood was identical with the soul.'[120] To illustrate that this belief was also manifest in OE verse, he points to God's command to Noah in *Genesis A*, in which *blode* is linked by apposition with *sawldreore*: 'Næfre ge mid blode beodgereordu / unarlice eowre þicgeað, / besmiten mid synne sawldreore.'[121] In the course of his argument he proposes translating *feorhlastas* (*Beo* 846b) as 'bloody track (lit[erally], track of the soul),' and he explains how the walls of Finn's hall could be 'hroden/ feonda feorum,' which he takes to mean 'reddened (or stained) with the souls of the foes.'[122] Though Robinson's conflation of soul and *feorh* may be imprecise, it does not at all diminish the persuasiveness of his interpretation of *synsnædum*. Less convincing, however, is Robinson's claim that the Anglo-Saxons believed that the soul was identical with the blood. Mary Clayton has demonstrated that this cannot be true of Ælfric, whose discursive works unequivocally teach that the human soul (*sawol*) is incorporeal.[123] There is also reason to doubt that Robinson's characterization of Anglo-Saxon belief can be sustained by the evidence of OE narrative.

Although OE authors specify the bodily seat of the life-force far less often than that of the soul or the mind, a few poems point to a loose association between the life-force and the blood. When Juliana is holding the devil in captivity, he confesses to her, 'Eac ic sume gedyde / þæt him banlocan blode spiowedan, / þæt hi færinga feorh aleton / þurh ædra wylm.'[124] Though these lines indicate that the devil's victims lost their life-force when their blood was spilled, it does not follow that the life-force is the blood or even that it resides in the blood: the loss of blood is one of many events that causes the life-force to abandon the body in OE verse.[125]

---

120 Robinson, 'Lexicography and Literary Criticism: A Caveat,' 102–3.

121 *GenA* 1518–20: 'At your table, never eat the meat with the blood, the soul-blood polluted with sin, contrary to what is fitting.'

122 Robinson, 'Lexicography and Literary Criticism,' 104.

123 In her note, 'Blood and the Soul in Ælfric,' Clayton takes issue with Robinson's essay specifically; for a broader discussion of Ælfric's understanding of the relationship between blood and soul, see Clayton, 'An Edition of Ælfric's *Letter to Brother Edward*,' 266–9 and 275–6; and on Ælfric's teachings on the soul's incorporeality, see chapter 8 below.

124 *Jul* 475b–8: 'I also caused some people to spew blood from their bone-locks, to let go their life immediately by the boiling over of their blood vessels.'

125 *Sea* 70–1, quoted above, mentions three deaths that drive the *feorh* out of the body, though only one of the three is a bloody death; see also *The Fortunes of Men* for a long catalogue of bloody deaths alongside bloodless ones such as starvation, burning, and old age.

And conversely, one may spill a great deal of blood without losing one's life-force; such is the unpleasant fate that God tells St Andrew is in store for him: 'Is þe guð weotod, / heardum heoruswengum scel þin hra dæled / wundum weorðan, wættre geliccost / faran flode blod. Hie þin feorh ne magon / deaðe gedælan, þeh ðu drype ðolie.'[126] To cite a similar example from a prose narrative, in an Ash Wednesday homily by Ælfric (LS 12), a man who flouts the Lenten fast vomits up blood as punishment for his sin, but he does not lose his *feorh*: 'eode him to kicenan . þa hwile ðe se bisceop mæssode and began to etenne . he feoll þa æt ðære forman snæde under-becc geswogen . and spaw blod . ac him gebyrede swa ðeah þæt feorh earfoðlice.'[127] The implication of these two passages is that blood loss may be associated with loss of *feorh*, but the *feorh* is not identical to the blood, unless it is possible for one to lose just a bit of *feorh*. Based on the characteristics of *feorh* elsewhere in OE narrative, this seems no more likely than becoming just a bit pregnant. Either a person has *feorh* and lives, or he lacks *feorh* and is dead. Perhaps the common thread that links together the passages cited by Robinson is not a belief that human blood is identical to the human soul or the life-force, but rather the metonymic use of *sawol* and *feorh*, both as simplices and in compounds, to signify mortality, much as in the compounds and circumlocutions pertaining to death that were discussed above. The *sawoldreor* that spills from Beowulf during his fight with the dragon is so called because enough blood is shed to bring about the soul's departure from the body.[128] As for *feorhlastas* and the phrase 'hroden / feonda feorum': to presume that *feorh* means 'blood' rather misses the point that in both situations, enough blood has been spilled that people have died. The poet uses the word *feorh* to signal the idea of mortality, not that of bodily fluids.

---

126 *And* 951b–5: 'For you a battle is destined; your body must be split apart by wounds and severe sword-strokes, and the blood must come out in a flood just like water. They cannot cut off your life by means of death, though you may suffer a blow.'

127 Ælfric, *LS* 12, lines 60–4 (ed. Skeat, *LS*, 1.264): 'he went to the kitchen while the bishop celebrated Mass, and he began to eat. Then at the first bite he fell down backwards and unconscious, and he vomited blood, but nevertheless, with difficulty he preserved his life.'

128 *Beo* 2693a; this 'mortal blood' is spilled when the dragon attacks Beowulf for the third and final time. I am less concerned with *sawoldreore* in *GenA* 1520b (on which see above) because in that context it refers to the souls of animals rather than humans; Clayton discusses the differences between human and animal *sawol* for the Anglo-Saxons and for Old Testament law in 'Blood and the Soul in Ælfric,' 366.

Exceptional Uses of *feorh* and the Likelihood of Diachronic Change

Though abundant evidence attests that the Anglo-Saxons distinguished the transient life-force from the transcendent soul, there are some notable exceptions to the patterns of usage established above for the word *feorh*. In the OE verse translation of Ps 87:3 the speaker laments, 'Forðon is sawl min sares and yfeles / fæste gefylled; is min feorh swylce / to helldore hylded geneahhe.'[129] The Latin text underlying these OE verses reads, 'quia repleta est malis anima mea et uita mea in inferno adpropiauit,'[130] so it is easy to rationalize the OE poet's use of *feorh*: *gefylled* is the most obvious translation for *repleta*, and among the three words typically used to translate *uita*, *feorh* is the only one that alliterates with *gefylled* (the others being *ealdor* and *lif*). This rationalization does not change the fact that, for whatever reason, the author of this verse rendering of the Psalms considered it not wholly incongruous to speak of the *feorh* being threatened by otherworldly torments. In conjunction with this anomaly, it bears mentioning that the glossator of the Lindisfarne Gospels and the glossator of Mark and Luke in the Rushworth Gospels habitually use the word *sawol* to gloss *anima*, while in contrast, the glossator of Matthew in the Rushworth Gospels demonstrates a sensitivity to the distinction between *feorh* and *sawol*, and he accordingly uses *feorh* to gloss *anima* where it means 'life-force' but uses *sawol* to gloss *anima* where it means 'transcendent soul.'[131] The scope of the present chapter does not extend either to diachronic analysis or to OE glosses on the Bible, but I propose that further study in both of those directions would show that under the influence of the relationship between *anima* and *uita* in the Vulgate, the originally clear distinction between *sawol* and *feorh* became blurry; or in other words, as the word *sawol* came to signify a unitary soul,

---

129 *PPs* 87:3, lines 1–3: 'Therefore my soul is heavily filled with sorrow and evil; my *feorh* likewise is bent down very near to the gate of hell.'
130 Ps 87:4 in the Roman Psalter version (ed. Weber, *Le Psautier romain*, 215): 'For my soul is filled with evils: and my life hath drawn nigh to hell.'
131 The Rushworth Gospels are preserved in Oxford, Bodleian Library, Auct. D. 2. 19; on the two glossators' contributions and the relationship of these glosses to those in the Lindisfarne Gospels, see Ker, *Catalogue*, no. 292. The Rushworth glosses are printed in Skeat, ed., *The Holy Gospels in Anglo-Saxon, Northumbrian, and Old Mercian Versions*, 25–245. Phillips is aware of the Rushworth glossators' different methods of glossing *anima*, but I do not entirely agree with his interpretation of the evidence ('Heart, Mind, and Soul in Old English,' 256–8); on the changing relationship between *feorh* and *sawol* see also La Farge, *'Leben' und 'Seele' in den altgermanischen Sprachen*.

by the later Anglo-Saxon period *feorh* came to signify one of several elements or faculties of the unitary *sawol*. If this could be demonstrated, it
would make sense of the seeming redundancy of the *sawol* and the *feorh*
entering and leaving the body in tandem at the beginning and the end of life:
they originally held distinct responsibilities, with the *feorh* enlivening the
flesh and the *sawol* abiding in the body until it went on to represent the individual in the afterlife.

The second anomaly in narrative uses of *feorh* results from the conflation
or confusion of similar words, *feorh* and *ferhð*. Confusion of this sort occurs
often enough that some consider the two words to be synonyms and close
etymological relatives.[132] A handful of poetic passages arguably (though by
no means certainly) impute psychological attributes or personality to the
feorh in contexts where we expect to find *ferhð* instead.[133] Conversely, on
several occasions in both prose and verse, the word *ferhð* appears in contexts
pertaining to death and the duration of life, where *feorh* is expected. For instance, in *The Fortunes of Men*, *feorð* appears unexpectedly in the depiction
of a fatal fall from a tall tree: 'Þonne he on wyrtruman / sigeð sworcenferð,
sawle bireafod, / fealleþ on foldan, feorð biþ on siþe.'[134] Neither poet nor
scribe habitually called the life-force *feorð*, since *feorh* appears nearby in the
phrase *feores orwena* 'despairing of his life' (line 40). The presence of *feorð*
in line 26b likely resulted from scribal error encouraged by the presence of
the compound *sworcenferð* in the previous line.[135]

But are all such confusions of *feorh* and *ferhð* due to copyist errors,
or were they considered near enough in meaning to be interchangeable?
Roberta Frank describes three occurrences of *ferhð* appearing in prose
passages where *feorh* is expected, all in eleventh-century copies of the *OE
Bede*. In an early tenth-century copy of the *OE Bede* (Oxford, Bodleian

---

132 Frank, 'Poetic Words in Late Old English Prose,' 100; Holthausen, *Altenglisches ety-
    mologisches Wörterbuch*, s.v. *feorh* and *fierhð* [*sic*]; Phillips, 'Heart, Mind, and Soul in
    Old English,' 64–81 and 250–6. Phillips wishes to conflate *feorh* and *ferhð* but distin-
    guishes the *feorh/ferhð* from the transcendent soul.
133 *Ex* 404a: *feores frofre* ('as a comfort to the ?*feorh*'); *El* 680b: *feores ingeþanc* ('intention
    of the ?*feorh*'); see also *Finn* 19a and *Mald* 317a. The expression *ful freolice feorh*
    ('very excellent *feorh*,' *GenA* 1618a) is likely not an error for *ful freolice ferhð* but
    rather a metonymic use of *feorh* to stand in for 'living being.'
134 *Fort* 24b–6: 'Then he drops to the base of the tree, his mind gone dark, deprived of his
    soul; he falls to the ground, his life-force is on its way.'
135 See also *ferhðbana*, which would mean 'mind-killer,' at *Ex* 399a, copied by the same
    scribe who twice used the more sensible form *feorhbana* 'deadly killer' at *GenA* 1020a
    and 2088a. In *Beowulf* the word *ferhðgeniðla* (2881a) appears to be a confused spelling
    of *feorhgeniðla* 'deadly enemy' (969a, 1540a, and 2933b).

Library, Tanner 10), one instance of the phrase *wide ferh in ecnesse* 'forever in eternity' shows the effects of Anglian smoothing, which has reduced the *eo* diphthong of *feorh* to a simple *e*. At the same locus, three eleventh-century copies have *færð* or *ferhð* where the Tanner Bede has *ferh*. Frank suggests two possible explanations: 'An eleventh-century scribe, not recognizing smoothed *ferh* as *feorh*, may have supplied a final -ð; it is also possible that poetic *ferhð* was chosen to close the scriptural quotation.'[136] In other words, she acknowledges that Anglian smoothing contributed to the copyists' confusion, but she also maintains that the substitution was made more felicitous by the near-synonymy of *feorh* and *ferhð*.[137] R.D. Fulk offers a firmer opinion about which of these two explanations underlies *feorh/ferhð* confusion in poems that have an Anglian recension in their histories; he argues that copyists' misinterpretation of the smoothed form *ferh* is wholly responsible for the confusion of two words that he regards as quite distinct in meaning. '[I]nstances of *wideferhð* … must be scribal alterations of *-ferh*: *wideferhð* is semantic nonsense, and *-ð* must have been added because *-ferh*, without breaking, looked odd … Indeed, it is difficult to imagine how *wideferhð* could have arisen except from an Anglian exemplar.'[138] To be sure, there remain a few instances of *feorh/ferhð* confusion that cannot be explained by Anglian smoothing, but by far the bulk of the textual evidence supports the conclusion that most poets and scribes did not use these words as interchangeable synonyms.[139]

In this chapter I have explained that the *mod* is distinct from the *sawol*, that the *sawol* is distinct from the *feorh*, and that the *feorh* is distinct from the *ferhð*, but I have not yet addressed what the *mod* or the *ferhð* is and what it does, or how it is linked to the body in a close-knit partnership. With the mind firmly distinguished from the other invisible parts of the human being, I can proceed in chapter 2 to elaborate on Anglo-Saxon understandings of the nature of the mind, with special attention to the way authors of OE verse and prose narratives describe the physiology of mental activity in terms of spatial and thermal changes within the chest cavity: changes in which the transcendent soul and the transient life-force do not participate.

---

136 Frank, 'Poetic Words in Late Old English Prose,' 100.
137 Ibid., 100: '*Ferhð* is substituted … for the synonymous, more common, and probably cognate *feorh*.'
138 Fulk, *A History of Old English Meter*, 299 n. 74 and 300; on Anglian smoothing, with particular attention to *ferhð* and *feorh*, see ibid., 298–301.
139 I have not assembled the relevant evidence at this juncture to facilitate the direct comparison of *feorh* with *ferhð*, but this conclusion is amply supported by the textual evidence for *feorh* discussed above, the characterizations of the *ferhð* given below in chapter 2, and many additional passages in the *DOE*, s.v. *feorh* and *ferhþ*.

2 The Hydraulic Model of the Mind in Old English Narrative

The word *breostsefa* occurs nine times in the OE corpus, in six different poems.[1] Like many OE compound-formations, *breostsefa* implies a relationship between its two elements, the breast and the mind, without specifying the nature of the relationship. Yet the meaning of the compound is not in doubt, because the OE corpus abounds in detailed depictions of the mind's activity within the chest cavity and of the spatial and thermal changes wrought in the chest cavity by changing psychological conditions. This chapter documents the nature and behaviour of the mind-in-the-breast as portrayed in the distinctive OE verse and prose idioms. I have deferred until chapter 3 the question of whether the Anglo-Saxons used the concept of the mind-in-the-breast literally or metaphorically.

Manifestations of the *breostsefa* in OE Verse

The sheer variety of the diction and syntax in OE verse depictions of the mind's residence in the breast is remarkable. Analysis of a large sample of passages depicting the behaviour of the *breostsefa* makes it clear that OE poets agreed about certain core features of the relationship between the mind (including mental states and contents) and the organs of the chest cavity, such as the cardiocentric containment of the mind, and the correlation of intense mental events with increased heat and pressure. At the same time, however, the peripheral details of the relationship between the mind and the breast were highly variable. Consequently, the behaviour of the

---

1 The word appears in *The Phoenix, Juliana, Vainglory, Christ I, Guthlac A* (twice), and *Elene* (three times); it is not attested in prose or glosses.

mind-in-the-breast may be more accurately described as a series of varia-tions on a theme rather than as a precisely replicated pattern.

The simplest representations of the mind-body relationship convey the localization of mental states in the heart or chest by means of prepos-itional phrases (commonly with *in, on, ymb*, and *æt*): 'wæs seo treowlufu / hat æt heortan'; 'Yrre ne læt þe æfre gewealdan, / heah in hreþre'; 'Sar eft gewod / ymb þæs beornes breost.'[2] The *Daniel*-poet favoured more unusual prepositional phrases when discussing Nabuchadnosor's tempor-ary insanity: at first 'his mod astah, / heah fram heortan,' but later 'he eft onhwearf / wodan gewittes, þær þe he ær wide bær / herewosan hige, heortan getenge.'[3] Although it is conventional in MnE to point out the cardiocentric location of emotion or contemplation in the breast only in order to call attention to its intensity, OE poems localize mundane mental activity in the breast too, such as ordinary thought, skill, expectation, in-tention. '[S]eo sceal in eagan, snyttro in breostum, / þær bið þæs monnes modgeþoncas,' reads one gnomic statement in *Maxims I*; in *Elene* it is reported of Judas that 'him gebyrde is / þæt he gencwidas gleawe hæbbe, / cræft in breostum.'[4] St Matthew praises God's omniscience, saying, 'Þu ana canst ealra gehygdo, / meotud mancynnes, mod in hreðre,' and Job anticipates his soul's ascent to heaven with the words, 'Me þæs wen næfre / forbirsteð in breostum.'[5] Conversely, a lost or diminished mental virtue is said to be removed from the breast, as when Moses tells the Israelites, 'Eow is lar godes abroden of breostum.'[6] Even when mental activity is represented as an action rather than a thing, this too occurs within the chest cavity: 'Gehyge on þinum breostum þæt þu inc bam twam meaht

---

2 *ChristB* 538b–9a: 'that faithful love was hot at the heart'; *Prec* 83–4a: 'Do not ever allow anger, high in your breast, to control you'; *And* 1246b–7a: 'Grief again travelled through-out the man's breast.'

3 *Dan* 596b–7a: 'his mind [*or* pride] rose up high from his heart'; *Dan* 626b–8: 'then he again reversed his insane state of mind, there where he earlier had openly displayed, close to his heart, the mind of a warrior.'

4 *Max I* 122–3: 'Seeing must reside in the eye and wisdom in the breast, where a man's mind-thoughts are'; *El* 593b–5a: 'it is an innate characteristic in him that he holds in his breast prudent answers and skill.' See also *El* 1142b–5a: 'Heo gefylled wæs / wisdomes gife, ond þa wic beheold / halig heofonlic gast, hreðer weardode, / æðelne innoð' (She was filled up with the gift of wisdom, and the heavenly Holy Spirit resided in that habi-tation and guarded her breast, her splendid heart).

5 *And* 68–9: 'You alone, ruler of mankind, know the intention of everyone, the mind in the breast'; *Phoen* 567b–8a: 'For me, the expectation of [salvation] will never break apart in my breast.'

6 *Ex* 268b–9a: 'The teaching of God has been torn from your breast.'

/ wite bewarigan,' suggests Satan's messenger to Eve in *Genesis B*.[7] Alternatively, thoughts and emotions may 'belong to' the heart and breast, in a sense that is both locative and agentive, in expressions which employ a subjective genitive (e.g., *heortan geþoht*) or a compound noun (e.g., *breostceare*):

> A scyle geong mon   wesan geomormod,
> heard heortan geþoht,   swylce habban sceal
> bliþe gebæro,   eac þon breostceare,
> sinsorgna gedreag.[8]

Some poets create a similar effect by foregrounding the mind's localization in the breast while the mind endures a specific psychological event, as in statements such as 'him wæs geomor sefa, / hat æt heortan' and 'Þa wæs modsefa myclum geblissod / haliges on hreðre.'[9] In another variation on the theme, one might carry (*wegan*) emotions in the heart or chest, as does Beowulf's grandfather Hrethel, who 'heortan sorge / weallinde wæg,' as well as every Englishman mourning the death of King Edgar, who 'on breostum wæg byrnende lufan / metodes on mode.'[10] Less often, psychological states are said to impinge directly upon the chest or the heart rather than upon a mind contained therein. When Abraham learns that he does not have to kill Isaac, the narrator of *Genesis A* comments that 'Hæfde Abrahame / metod moncynnes, mæge Lothes, / breost geblissad.'[11] On a more gloomy note, the wretched speaker of *The Rhyming Poem* laments, 'Nu min hreþer is hreoh, heofsiþum sceoh, / nydbysgum neah,' and the

---

7 *GenB* 562–3a: 'Think in your breast about how you two can both guard yourselves from punishment.'
8 *Wife* 42–5a: 'A young man must always be sorrowful in mind, the thought of his heart must be cruel. Likewise must he have a cheerful countenance as well as anxiety in his breast, a multitude of endless miseries.' On compounds beginning in *breost-*, *heort-*, and *hreðer-* that signify the mind, see Low, 'Approaches to the Old English Vocabulary for "Mind,"' 12; and Mize, 'The Representation of the Mind as an Enclosure in Old English Poetry'; neither of these essays discusses compounds that join *breost-*, *heort-*, and *hreðer-* to words for mental states, such as *heortgryre* 'heart-terror.'
9 *El* 627b–8a: 'his mournful mind was hot at his heart'; *And* 892–3a: 'Then the mind of the holy man was greatly delighted in his breast.'
10 *Beo* 2463b–4a: 'carried a seething sorrow in his heart'; *DEdg* 20–1a: 'carried in his breast a burning love of the Creator in his mind.'
11 *GenA* 2923b–5a: 'The creator of the human race had gladdened the breast of Abraham, kinsman of Lot.'

narrator of *Judgment Day II* warns that in the last days 'bið þæt earme breost / mid bitere care breged and swenced.'[12] This selection of syntactically diverse portrayals of the *breostsefa* does not exhaust all the configurations in which OE poetry juxtaposes mental activity and the organs of the chest cavity, but it brings to light the dominant idioms. Despite the consistent localization of mental activity in the chest cavity, the variability in these idioms reminds us that we are not dealing with a philosophically systematic theory of mind-body interaction but with a collection of individual, sometimes idiosyncratic, attempts to describe the invisible workings of the mind. The same will be true of the mind-body interactions discussed in the following pages: the literary representation of each consists of a recognizable core 'symptom' that is variously attributed, sometimes to the mind, sometimes to the heart or breast, and sometimes to mental states or contents.

Emotional Distress and Cardiocentric Heat

Foremost among the physical phenomena that accompany mental events is the production of heat in the chest cavity. Heat generates or is generated by distress (most often anger and grief) and sometimes by the experience of strong positive yearnings (intense love, longing for God, desire for wisdom or learning). Yet some intense mental states are never associated with cardiocentric heat, such as fear, relief, joy, and contentment. Because heat is characteristic of such a diverse range of mental states, both positive and negative, clarity demanded that a poet specify the contents or condition of the mind along with each reference to cardiocentric heat. Such depictions provided opportunities for OE poets to exercise their skills in repetition and variation. In *Judith*, for example, while the heroine anticipates slaying Holofernes, she laments, 'Þearle ys me nu ða / heorte onhæted ond hige geomor, / swyðe mid sorgum gedrefed.' She then turns her complaint toward God and prays, 'Gewrec nu, mihtig dryhten, / torhtmod tires brytta, þæt me ys þus torne on mode, / hate on hreðre minum.'[13] In this passage,

---

12 *Rim* 43–4a: 'Now my breast is troubled, fearful in its mournful journeys, close to troubles'; *JDay II* 213b–4: 'that miserable breast will be frightened and afflicted with sharp anxiety.'

13 *Jud* 86b–8a: 'Now my heart is severely heated and my mind miserable, greatly stirred up with sorrows'; *Jud* 92b–4a: 'Now, mighty Lord, brilliant-minded dispenser of glory, avenge that which is so cruel to me in my mind, so hot in my breast.'

it happens that heat is associated with the bodily seat of the mind, while the more abstract attributes are associated with the mind: Judith's heart is heated while her mind is mournful; her enemy's crime is hot in her breast, but cruel in her mind. It is tempting to construe passages like this as evidence for a clear-cut division of labour, as though the mind engaged in abstract thought or emotion while physiological symptoms affected the bodily seat of the mind. However, this tidy generalization does not hold up, because the mind and its contents can themselves generate heat or suffer from it. OE poets frequently characterize the mind as 'hot at the heart': 'Him wæs geomor sefa / hat æt heortan, hyge murnende.'[14] Mental states of hatred, love, and sadness can burn and be hot as well, as illustrated by these examples: 'brandhata nið / weoll on gewitte'; 'him drihtnes wæs / bam on breostum byrnende lufu'; 'Gnornsorge wæg / hate æt heortan, hyge geomurne, / meðne modsefan.'[15] One memorable passage in *Elene* attributes to Judas a 'fiery-hot love' and knowledge or understanding (*gewitt*) that has been kindled to the point of boiling:

> Him ða gleawhydig   Iudas oncwæð,
> hæleð hildedeor;   him wæs halig gast
> befolen fæste,   fyrhat lufu,
> weallende gewitt   þurh witgan snyttro.[16]

Bradley aptly translates *weallende* as 'ebullient,' a word that in MnE connotes both the mental intensity and the physical state of boiling that characterize Judas's state of mind.[17] Cynewulf's reference to the *weallende gewitt* brings us to the next stage of the behaviour of the *breostsefa*: in the mind-in-the-heart, as elsewhere in nature, intense heat causes swelling, seething, and boiling.

---

14 *ChristB* 499b–500: 'Their mind was miserable, hot at their heart; their mind was mourning.' See also *El* 627–8a (quoted above), *And* 1708b–9, and *GuthB* 1208–9.

15 *And* 768b–9a: 'a fiery hot hatred swelled in their mind'; *GenA* 190b–1: 'love of the Lord was burning in the breast of both [*scil.* Adam and Eve]'; *GuthB* 1335b–7a: 'he carried hot sorrow in his heart, a miserable mind, a dejected mind.' See also *GenB* 776b–7a, *DEdg* 20–1a (quoted above), and *ChristB* 537b–40a (discussed below).

16 *El* 934–7 (editorial punctuation altered): 'Then the wise-minded Judas, the brave hero, answered him; the Holy Spirit was speedily granted to him, fiery hot love and an ebullient understanding, through the cleverness of the wise man.'

17 Bradley, *Anglo-Saxon Poetry*, 188.

Cardiocentric Heat and the Boiling Mind

Most depictions of psychological seething and boiling rely on words from one of two families: that which includes *weallan* and *wylm*, or that which includes *belgan*. Weallan 'to swell, boil, seethe' and *wylm* 'that which wells up or boils' refer primarily to the surging or bubbling up of a liquid, often but not always caused by heat. These words and related compounds appear in many non-mental contexts, especially in depictions of sea-water.[18] In mental contexts, words belonging to the *weallan/wylm* group are associated with negative emotions and also with more positive states of intense love and the desire for God; therefore, words denoting specific states of mind must also be present in order to clarify the exact cause of swelling and seething.

The simplex *belgan* 'to swell up (in anger)' and its related compounds have a more restricted range of meanings: they are associated solely with anger but not with love, desire, or even other 'hot' negative emotions such as anxiety and grief. Among *belgan* and its OE relatives, some signify solely the internal swelling associated with rage,[19] while others signify external, visible swelling. The noun *belg*, for instance, had a variety of meanings, all related to swollen, bulging things such as pouches, wine-skins, bellows, and hills.[20] The verb *bealcettan* 'to belch, spew forth' and related words signify that something inside the body wells up and comes out of the body, or that the swelling of the body is externally visible.[21] There is only tenuous evidence that any individual word in the *belgan*-group was used to denote both psychological and visible swelling during the Anglo-Saxon period,[22] but other medieval Germanic languages did not restrict the use of individual words in this family to either the visible or the

---

18 See Potter, '*Wylm* and *weallan* in *Beowulf*: A Tidal Metaphor.'
19 *DOE*, s.v. *belgan, gebelgan, gebylgan, gebylged*, all of which refer only to swelling associated with negative emotion.
20 *DOE*, s.v. *belg, bylg*.
21 *DOE*, s.v. *bealcan, bealcettan, belced-sweora*.
22 *DOE* indicates that two meanings are attested for the rare word *bylgan*: 'to anger, offend, provoke' and 'to bellow at someone' (s.v. *bylgan*¹ and *bylgan*²). For the verb *abelgan*, which usually means 'to provoke someone to anger,' the *DOE* indicates one possible occurrence in which it means '? to swell, make (oneself *dat.*) larger' (s.v. *abelgan* 1). Additionally, the participle *bylged* 'swollen in anger' may be the first element in a compound *bylgedbreost*, reconstructed from MS *by led breost* in the first line of Exeter Book *Riddle* 81 ('Weather-cock'): see *DOE*, s.v. *bylgedbreost*; ASPR 3.372; and Williamson, *The Old English Riddles of the Exeter Book*, 362–3 (where this riddle is no. 77).

psychological domain, and certain cognates of *belgan* in those languages did indeed signify the swelling of rage as well as the external swelling of both living and inanimate entities.[23] Consequently, it is not entirely certain that speakers of OE were cognizant of the conceptual connection between the more psychologized words of the *belgan* family and the concept of cardiocentric swelling; nonetheless, the frequent juxtaposition of *belgan* and its relatives with images of cardiocentric heat suggests that the connection was probably recognized to some extent.[24]

Mental seething and swelling are variously predicated of the mind itself, of mental states, and of the mind's bodily seat. Most often, the entity that seethes is an intensely negative emotion or thought. When Guthlac confronts a pack of devils, the narrator reports, 'Ða wæs eft swa ær ealdfeonda nið, / wroht onwylled'; elsewhere, the Egyptians' renewed persecution of the Israelites prompts the *Exodus*-narrator to observe, 'Wæron heaðowylmas heortan getenge.'[25] The *Beowulf*-poet relies especially heavily on the *wylm* and *weallan* family; for instance, he juxtaposes the verb *weallan* with a compound in -*wylm* where Beowulf remarks that 'Ingelde / weallað wælniðas ond him wiflufan / æfter cearwælmum colran weorðað.'[26] The contents of the mind may seethe and boil even if they are not particularly impulsive or acute; sometimes an insidious thought works on the mind slowly, almost imperceptibly, over a space of time, as simmering water softens tough food. In such a manner do the seductive lies of Satan's

---

23 Carey, 'Fir Bolg,' and Henry, 'Furor Heroicus,' compare OE *bolgen* and Germanic cognates with Celtic cognates; see also Holthausen, *Altenglisches etymologisches Wörterbuch*, s.v. *belgan*. Related Germanic words include Old Frisian *belga*, Old High German *belgan* and Old Saxon *belgan*, all of which mean both 'to swell up' and 'to be angry,' and Old Norse *bólginn* 'swollen', *belgja* 'to cause to swell,' and *bylgja* 'a surge, a swelling.' Holthausen notes the connection linking the verb *belgan* with OE *bielg* and its Germanic cognates, which encompass a range of 'swollen' containers, such as a sack, bellows, and the belly.

24 It is possible that they were ignorant of the idea of spatial deformation that is etymologically inherent in *belgan*, just as MnE speakers are often unaware that *anxiety*, *anguish*, and *anger* share etymological roots in the semantic domain of spatial constriction and narrowness, but it is equally possible that the spatial connotations of *belgan* were as transparent to the average Anglo-Saxon as the spatial connotations of *depression* are to the present-day Western speaker of English.

25 *GuthA* 390–1a: 'Then the hatred and the enmity of the ancient enemies were made to boil up again, just as before'; *Ex* 148: 'Surges of aggression were touching their heart.' See also *Beo* 2463b–4a (quoted above), *Beo* 1992b–4a (discussed below), and *GuthA* 614b–15.

26 *Beo* 2064b–6: 'in Ingeld mortal hatred will boil up, and his love for his wife will become cooler in the wake of seething anxieties.'

messenger seethe in Eve's mind: 'Lædde hie swa mid ligenum and mid listum speon / idese on þæt unriht, oðþæt hire on innan ongan / weallan wyrmes geþeaht.'[27] In the *Metres of Boethius*, the personification of Wisdom likewise observes that greed simmering in the mind makes men reckless: 'Ac hit is sæmre nu, / þæt þeos gitsunc hafað gumena gehwelces / mod amerred, þæt he maran ne recð, / ac hit on witte weallende byrnð.'[28] Among the four simplex terms for 'mind,' poets most often selected *hyge* for depictions of mental seething, likely for the sake of alliteration. For example, when Satan is consumed with rage and jealousy, the *Genesis B*-narrator reports, 'Weoll him on innan / hyge ymb his heortan,' and St Andrew's Mermedonian converts are distraught at his departure from their land, to the extent that 'Þær manegum wæs / hat æt heortan hyge weallende.'[29] The *Genesis A*-narrator encapsulates the seething of the mind in a compound noun *hygewælm*, which aptly communicates the intensity of the hatred and rage that propel Cain to murder Abel: 'Hygewælm asteah / beorne on breostum, blatende nið, / yrre for æfstum.'[30]

Many of the foregoing passages remind us that the seething of the mind and of its contents occurs in the region of the heart; this localization is made even more plain when the heart and breast themselves boil and seethe. Witnessing the destruction wrought on his people by the enraged dragon, Beowulf worries that he has angered God, and because of this worry, 'breost innan weoll / þeostrum geþoncum, swa him geþywe ne wæs.'[31] Elsewhere, when Christ's followers watch him disappear into the skies at his Ascension, they are tormented by their passionate love for him: 'Þær wæs wopes hring; / torne bitolden wæs seo treowlufu / hat æt heortan, hreðer innan weoll, / beorn breostsefa.'[32]

---

27 *GenB* 588–90a: 'Thus with lies he counselled Eve and with pleasures he affirmed her in that misdeed, until the thought of the serpent began to seethe inside her.'

28 *OE Boethius*, C-text, metre 8, lines 42b–5 (ed. Godden and Irvine, 1.414): 'But it is worse now in that this greed has hindered the mind of every man so that he does not care for anything more, but seething in his mind it burns' (trans. ibid., 2.117).

29 *GenB* 353b–4a: 'Inside him, his mind seethed around his heart'; *And* 1708b–9: 'For many people, the mind was hot and seething around the heart.'

30 *GenB* 980b–2a: 'Mental boiling rose up within the man's breast: pale hatred, anger caused by envy.' The manuscript reads *hyge wæl mos teah*, with *wæl* at the end of a line, but editors emend to *hygewælm asteah*.

31 *Beo* 2331b–2: 'his breast seethed inside him with dark thoughts, as was not normal for him.' See also *Beo* 2113b–14.

32 *ChristB* 537b–40a (editorial punctuation altered): 'There was the sound of weeping; that faithful love, bitterly oppressed, was hot around the heart; the chest swelled inwardly; the mind-in-the-breast burned.'

Mental swelling, however, is not necessarily as ominous as the previous examples suggest: intensely positive mental states can swell up and even seethe in the breast. We have already seen that 'fiery-hot love' fuelled the 'boiling intellect' of Judas.³³ The narrator of *The Phoenix* characterizes faithful Christians as those who 'geheoldan halge lare / hate æt heortan, hige weallende / dæges ond nihtes dryhten lufiað,' suggesting that intellectual or spiritual enlightenment can set the mind to boiling.³⁴ Somewhat more cryptically, he also states that a 'boiling of the intellect' beneficially goads the Phoenix into reincarnating himself: it is necessary, the narrator explains, 'þæt he þa yldu ofestum mote / þurh gewittes wylm wendan to life.'³⁵ *Andreas* is especially rich in portrayals of beneficial mental swelling. When the apostles Andrew and Matthew are joyfully reunited, the narrator tells us that 'Hreðor innan wæs / wynnum awelled.'³⁶ Christ, appearing in disguise, praises Andrew's wisdom, which causes Christ's own mind to expand joyfully: 'min hige blissað, / wynnum wridað, þurh þine wordlæðe, / æðelum ecne.' Andrew responds by telling Christ that his own breast 'blooms inwardly' with the wisdom he has gained from their conversation: 'snyttrum bloweð, / beorhtre blisse, breost innanweard.'³⁷ The verbs *blowan* and *wridan* usually signify vegetable growth and do not, per se, connote that heat is the cause of mental swelling in these last two passages, but it is not unprecedented for these verbs to convey the image of swelling in conjunction with mental heat.³⁸

Implications of the Hydraulic Model of Mental Activity

Thus far, the behaviours of the mind-in-the-breast may be summed up as a series of thermal and spatial events:

1 Mental activity happens in an enclosed bodily space, usually localized in or around the *heorte*, or in the *breost* or *hreðer*.

---

33 *El* 934–7 (quoted above).
34 *Phoen* 476–8: 'keep holy doctrines hot at their heart and, while boiling in their mind, cherish the Lord day and night.'
35 *Phoen* 190–1: 'that he [*scil.* the Phoenix] be able to transform his old age into life right away, by means of a surge of the intellect.'
36 *And* 1018b–19a: 'their breast was swollen inwardly with joy.'
37 *And* 634b–6a: 'my mind exults, blossoms with joys because of your words, which are endowed with excellence'; *And* 646b–7: 'the breast blossoms inside with wisdom, with bright bliss.'
38 See, for instance, *Rim* 45b–8a (discussed below) and *And* 767.

2 Certain intense mental states coincide with the production of cardio-centric heat, but this heat is attributed variously to the mind, to the mind's contents or condition, and to the fleshly organs of the chest cavity.

3 Intense mental activity may also coincide with cardiocentric swelling, boiling, or seething, but this spatial deformation is attributed variously to the mind, to the mind's contents or condition, and to the fleshly organs of the chest cavity.

Despite variations within the pattern, the fundamental mechanism operating in the mind-body complex during an intense mental experience remains consistent. This mechanism is analogous to the physical behaviour of a container of fluid exposed to heat, and hence scholars across several disciplines refer to such portrayals of mental activity as the 'hydraulic model' of the mind.[39] An intense thought or emotion is analogous to a source of heat energy, so it provides heat when it arises in or near the container, which is in turn analogous to the mind or to the fleshly organs of the chest cavity. When a thought or emotion transfers its energy to the container and its contents, they too become hot, and they begin to seethe and expand.

This model makes sense of the observation that different poems attribute heat and seething variously to the emotions, to the mind, and to the mind's bodily seat, in a seemingly haphazard fashion: it is not haphazard after all, but within the scope of this model, all three of these entities have the capacity to participate in heat and seething. A heightened awareness of this ubiquitous model of the mind, furthermore, considerably enhan-

---

39 See chapter 3 for additional bibliography. In other disciplines, particularly in cognitive approaches to metaphor, scholars carefully differentiate hydraulic models of mind, which liken the mind only to a heated liquid, from models that liken the mind to a gas or a solid that likewise responds to psychological heat by expanding. Although some OE depictions of the mind-in-the-breast arguably liken mental activity to the heating of a solid or a gas rather than that of a liquid, the present study does not demand that we pay close attention to this distinction, because if (as I will argue) the OE hydraulic model is based on a folk understanding of the physiology of emotion, then liquid, solid, and gaseous contents of the chest cavity would all be expected to participate to some degree in narratives of intense mental events. Note, however, that the OE expressions that suggest that the solid, fleshly organs of the chest cavity swell in response to psychological heat ought to be distinguished from the very rare OE passages that portray the mind as a solid that melts rather than expands under the influence of heat: on the 'melting mind,' see Low, 'The Anglo-Saxon Mind,' 112–13.

ces the clarity of a number of difficult passages and words in OE verse. Familiarity with the hydraulic model provides a structural framework for interpreting verse portrayals of complex mental mechanisms; it counters the scholarly tendency to over-psychologize our readings and translations of depictions of the mind-body complex; and it sheds new light on subtle deployments of the hydraulic model that may go unnoticed by the modern observer.

Complex Mental Mechanisms

A passage discussed above, in which Christ's followers mourn his departure at his Ascension, exemplifies the sort of language that is elucidated by the hydraulic model. The mental event portrayed in these lines is fuelled by the disciples' faithful love, which is *hat æt heortan*, causing the mind-in-the-breast to burn (*beorn breostsefa*). Consequently, the whole container seethes or swells inwardly (*hreðer innan weoll*), increasing the internal pressure within the container, and the love in their breasts becomes oppressed (*bitolden*). The metrical *Solomon and Saturn* provides another constellation of symptoms of mind-body distress that are neatly illuminated by the hydraulic model. Saturn, a pagan prince, is heated up, not by anger or love, but by the anguish of frustration with his studies. He says to Solomon: 'Nænig manna wat, / hæleða under hefenum, hu min hige dreoseð, / bysig æfter bocum; hwilum me bryne stigeð, / hige heortan neah hædre wealleð.'[40] Saturn's mind 'gives out' under the stress of his studies; he characterizes his consequent mental distress as a 'flame' that arises within him. Fuelled by this flame, his mind seethes near his heart, in a fashion that increases the internal pressure within this mind-body container, as suggested by the adverb *hædre* 'oppressively.' (Both of these passages only hint adverbially at an increase in internal pressure, which is among the peripheral symptoms of mental distress that will receive further attention below.)

The OE idiom of emotional and verbal restraint is also shaped by the hydraulic model of mental activity. The speaker of the poem known as *Precepts* invokes the hydraulic model as he warns his son to restrain himself from outward displays of anger: 'Yrre ne læt þe æfre gewealdan, / heah in hreþre, heoroworda grund / wylme bismitan, ac him warnað þæt

---

40 *MSol* 59b–62: 'No man, no hero under heaven, knows how my mind fails, occupied with books: sometimes the flame rises up in me, my mind seethes oppressively near my heart.'

/ on geheortum hyge.'⁴¹ In these lines, anger is analogous to a flame: it can presumably be controlled when it is small, but when it grows too high, the flame of anger within the container of the chest cavity can dominate (*gewealdan*) the individual in whom it burns. Such strong heat energy is dangerous, because the 'sea of hostile words' contained within the chest may pollute the angry individual with its boiling over (*wylme bismitan*).

Because the modern reader is inclined to think of the mental and the physical as discrete and even opposing categories, translators and lexicographers often supply overly psychologized meanings for words that actually denote spatial or thermal changes, for the purpose of clarifying the psychological content of hydraulic-model imagery. On the occasion of Beowulf's homecoming, for instance, Hygelac admits to having harboured doubts and worries about the outcome of his nephew's journey: 'Ic ðæs modceare / sorhwylmum seað, siðe ne truwode / leofes mannes.'⁴² These lines are the reason why the Bosworth-Toller dictionary includes a cumbersome tertiary definition for *seoðan*: 'to prepare food for the mind, to make fear, hope, etc., subjects with which the mind may be occupied; cf. to feed a person with hopes.'⁴³ *Seoðan* is primarily a transitive verb meaning 'to boil' or 'to cook in a liquid,' and Ælfric's *Glossary* supplies the gloss *ic seoðe* for the Latin *coquo* 'I cook.'⁴⁴ The ordinary meaning of this verb is further clarified by its regular appearances in medical recipes, as in this remedy for a 'smear' to counteract foggy vision: 'finoles wyrttruman gecnuadne gemeng wið huniges seaw; seoð þonne æt leohtum fyre listelice oþ huniges þicnesse.'⁴⁵ The reader who understands how the hydraulic model operates has no need to concoct a special psychologized definition for *seoðan*, because it is wholly sensible for Hygelac to say, 'I boiled the anxiety of my mind in surges of sorrow.' Once we are familiar with the implications of the hydraulic mechanism governing Hygelac's emotions, it is not necessary to psychologize the translation of a word such as *seoðan* and, in so doing, to efface the meaning of the OE idiom.

---

41 *Prec* 83–6a: 'Do not ever allow anger, high in your chest, to control you, nor allow the sea of hostile words to pollute you with its boiling over, but a man ought to protect himself against that in his courageous mind.'

42 *Beo* 1992b–4a: 'Because of this [*scil.* Beowulf's journey] I boiled the anxiety of my mind in surges of sorrow; I did not have faith in the undertaking of the beloved man.'

43 BT, s.v. *seoþan*, III.3.

44 BT, s.v. *seoþan*, I; Ælfric, *Glossary* (ed. Zupitza, *Ælfrics Grammatik und Glossar*, 175).

45 *Leechbook II* 1.2.9 (ed. Cockayne, *Leechdoms, Wortcunning, and Starcraft*, 2.30; editorial punctuation altered): 'Again, mix pounded root of fennel with liquid honey; then simmer it attentively over a gentle flame until it is the thickness of honey.'

Anthropomorphism and the Hydraulic Model in The Ruin

Because the hydraulic model correlates heat and seething with a wide range of intense mental states, OE poets usually indicate which specific mental state fuels the spatial and thermal changes in a given narrative. How would it affect the audience's reception if a text portrayed cardiocentric heat and seething *without* naming a specific thought or emotion? I suspect that the Anglo-Saxon audience would have recognized the psychological implications of these cardiocentric symptoms and sought other contextual indices of a specific thought or emotion. The modern audience, on the other hand, is likely to overlook the psychological connotations of heat and seething imagery unless we are prepared to recognize the hydraulic model where it appears. Consider, for instance, the description of the decaying baths in *The Ruin*.

> Stanhofu stodan,   stream hate wearp
> widan wylme;   weal eall befeng
> beorhtan bosme,   þær þa baþu wæron,
> hat on hreþre. Þæt wæs hyðelic.
> Leton þonne geotan   [................]
> ofer harne stan   hate streamas.[46]

One needs no special knowledge of the hydraulic model to recognize that the ascription of the human body parts *bosm* and *hreðer* anthropomorphizes the ruined baths,[47] but if the audience is not sensitive to the hydraulic-model diction that pervades the poet's description of the water welling up from the hot springs, it is easy to overlook that this literary device operates on another level as well. The hot water issuing from the stream is described as a *wylm*, a surge, evoking the image implicit in the many compound nouns that signify the violent surge of emotions in the breast (e.g., *cearwylm, breostwylm, sorhwylm*). This surge of hot liquid originates in the *bosm* and the *hreðer* of the ruined building. In the 'bosom' of these

---

46 *Ruin* 38–43.
47 W.C. Johnson, for instance, has argued on wholly different grounds that *The Ruin*'s 'animation and sense of place rely on the archaic equivalence of body, dwelling, and city,' and that the poem is best understood as another manifestation of the anthropomorphizing tendencies of the Exeter Book *Riddles*, especially since *The Ruin* immediately precedes *Riddle* 61 and arguably belongs to the larger series of riddles in the Exeter Book: see 'The Ruin as Body-City Riddle,' esp. 398–9.

buildings, a *weal* (line 39b) is enveloping all the contents of this room or cavity. This word *weal* is usually taken to be the word *weall* with two *l*'s, meaning 'wall,' which makes sense enough as a feature of the ruined buildings. Yet two other nouns with identical spelling are also attested in Old English: the neuter noun *weall*, meaning 'a boiling liquid,' and the feminine noun *weall*, denoting an abstract quality of seething or fervour;[48] both nouns are related to the verb *weallan* and the noun *wylm*. In this light, *weal* in line 39b evokes an 'overflow' of hot water that bubbles out of the spring (although this does not rule out the possibility of a word play, such that *weal* means both the overflow of water and a stone wall). I propose translating this section of *The Ruin* as follows:

> And the stone courts were standing and the stream warmly spouted its ample surge, and the overflow enveloped all in its bright bosom where the baths were, hot at its heart: that was appropriate. Then they allowed to pour forth the hot streams over the grey stone.

For a reader who is aware of the psychological significance of heat and seething in the breast, this constellation of images – the seething liquid and the 'bosom' of the buildings – unmistakably evokes emotional distress. Some form of distress, whether anger or sorrow or longing, is certainly appropriate to the context of the poem, since the previous seventeen lines recall that the buildings were once glorious in appearance and full of joyous, wealthy inhabitants, long since destroyed by plague and decay. The hot surges that now course through the 'breast' of these ruins are the anthropomorphized stones' expression of loneliness and loss; the narrator even observes that 'it was appropriate' (*Þæt wæs hyðelic*) for the buildings' bosoms to seethe, as if already mourning their future desolation.

Peripheral Features of the Hydraulic Model

Three further phases of hydraulic-model mental activity follow logically upon the premise that the mind-in-the-breast behaves like a container of fluid heated by intense mental events. The first two are coolness and roominess, which represent the 'default' thermal and spatial states of the mind-in-the-breast when it is calm or in full command of its faculties,

---

48 See BT s.v. *weall, -es*, neuter; s.v. *weall, -e*, feminine; cf. also the first element of the compound *weallhat*, 'boiling hot' (BT s.v. *weall-hat*).

when the heat energy and swelling of psychological distress and desire are absent or dissipated. The third is constriction, which represents the most intense and potentially dangerous cardiocentric response to intense distress: as the mind-in-the-breast seethes and swells, it presses outward on the walls of its container, and for as long as it lacks sufficient space to function freely, its faculties are impaired.

Mental Cooling

Arriving on the Danish shore, Beowulf tells the coast-guard that he has come to exterminate the monster infesting Hrothgar's hall, 'gyf him edwenden æfre scolde / bealuwa bisigu, bot eft cuman – / ond þa cearwylmas colran wurðaþ.'[49] Later, Beowulf surmises that Ingeld's marriage to the peace-weaver Freawaru will be short-lived, because 'Ingelde / weallað wælniðas, ond him wiflufan / æfter cearwælmum colran weorðað.'[50] Though these two passages end with nearly identical words, they assign contrary values to the state of mental cooling. In the first instance, Beowulf obviously wants to help Hrothgar by cooling his 'boiling anxieties,' but for Ingeld, a negative heat energy drives out the peaceable and pleasurable heat of the passion he once felt for his wife. Thus mental cooling, like mental heat, can signify both positive and negative states of mind. In fact, mental cooling is invoked most often as a cause or symptom of martial, spiritual, or intellectual weakness. For the *Guthlac A*-narrator, the coolness of man's love for Christ is one sign that the world is in dramatic decline: 'Woruld is onhrered, / colaþ Cristes lufu, sindan costinga / geond middangeard monge arisene.'[51] The father-figure who dispenses advice in *Precepts* seems to be more resigned to the pervasiveness of spiritual tepidity than alarmed by it: 'Nis nu fela folca þætte fyrngewritu / healdan wille, ac him hyge brosnað, / ellen colað, idlað þeodscype.'[52] The gloomy speaker of *The Rhyming Poem* shares this attitude. Like the cooling of summer, the cooling of courage is so inevitable as to be proverbial: 'searohwit solaþ,

---

49 *Beo* 280–2: 'if a change should ever come to him later on, a remedy for the trouble of his injuries, and if his boiling anxieties should become cooler.'
50 *Beo* 2064b–6: 'in Ingeld mortal hatred will boil up, and his love for his wife will become cooler in the wake of seething anxieties.'
51 *GuthA* 37b–9: 'The world has been turned upside-down: love for Christ grows tepid; many trials have arisen throughout the world.' (Cf. Mt 24:12.)
52 *Prec* 67–9: 'At present there are not many people who are willing to uphold the ancient scriptures, but their minds decay within them, their courage cools, their learning becomes useless.'

sumurhat colað, / foldwela fealleð, feondscipe wealleð, / eorðmægen ealdaþ, ellen colað.'[53]

Fear and terror, more acute than the dissipation of courage, are also forms of mental coldness. Persons experiencing acute fear are often *acol* 'chilled' and *acolmod* 'cold-minded,' which differentiates them from sufferers of chronic anxiety and dread, who endure mental heat. In *Daniel*, Nabuchadnosor is chilled by his prescient dreams: 'Wearð he on þam egesan acol worden, / þa he ne wisse word ne angin / swefnes sines.'[54] When St Andrew sends a group of murderous Mermedonians into the sea to be drowned, it is said of their compatriots on shore, 'Þa wearð acolmod, / forhtferð manig folces on laste.'[55] Even a pack of demons can be cold with fear when an angel orders them to bring back Guthlac unharmed: 'Ða wearð feonda þreat / acol for ðam egsan.'[56] The words *acol* and *acolmod* are, like their 'hot' counterparts, insufficient to specify the nature of the emotion or thought that lowers the temperature of the mind-in-the-heart. In each of the foregoing passages, fear is specifically named as the source of this mental chill, preventing the reader from mistaking it for another kind of mental coldness, which users of MnE might call 'cold-bloodedness' or 'cold-heartedness.' This is the state of mind that Beowulf foresees for Ingeld, whose love for his wife will grow so cold that he no longer cares about preserving his ties with her family. The Mermedonians who want to eat St Matthew are called *caldheorte* 'cold-hearted' because their desire to kill is not fuelled by the heat of anger, courage, or vengeance; they are merely *wælgrædige* 'greedy for carnage' and disdainful of proscriptions against cannibalism. The *Andreas*-narrator underscores that their hearts are cold not because of fear but because they are not warmed by any normal, humane passions: 'Cirmdon caldheorte, (corðor oðrum getang), / reðe ræsboran. Rihtes ne gimdon, / meotudes mildse.'[57]

---

53 *Rim* 67–9: 'Brilliant whiteness becomes soiled; summer heat cools; earthly wealth fails; enmity boils up; earthly power becomes obsolete; courage cools.'

54 *Dan* 124–6a: 'He had become chilled by that terror, when he did not understand the meaning or the origin of his dream.'

55 *And* 1595b–6: 'Many of the people left behind became cold-minded, fearful-minded.'

56 *GuthA* 691b–2a: 'Then the troop of demons became chilled on account of their terror.' See also *And* 376b–7a, *And* 1265b–9a, and *GenA* 1953b–6a.

57 *And* 138–40a: 'Cold-hearted, cruel counsellors cried out, one troop versus another. They took no notice of what was right or of the merciful Lord.' See also *Az* 166–7, where the narrator calls Nabuchadnosor *acolmod* at a point in the narrative when it is impossible to discern whether this chill signifies cruelty to the youths in the oven or fear upon the realization that those youths are protected by an angel.

Mental Roominess

Picture a tea kettle full of boiling water, whistling as hot air presses out through the spout. Remove the kettle from the heat, and the whistling stops promptly because the air inside, beginning to cool, exerts less pressure on the walls of the kettle. In the same manner, when the heat energy of intense mental states dissipates, the swollen and pressured mind-in-the-breast becomes 'roomy,' regaining plenty of space to function comfortably within the chest cavity, and no longer suffering from an excess of pressure. The narrator of *Genesis B* provides a vivid pair of before-and-after illustrations showing the devils' emotional responses to Adam and Eve. Before the Fall, when Satan is enraged and jealous of the two humans, the narrator states, 'Weoll him on innan / hyge ymb his heortan.'[58] While Satan is chained in hell, another devil makes the journey to Eden to coax Eve to eat the fatal fruit. Exulting in his success and the humans' downfall, the deputy devil expresses his joy as an alleviation of constriction: 'Forþon is min mod gehæled, / hyge ymb heortan gerume, ealle synt uncre hearmas gewrecene / laðes þæt wit lange þoledon.'[59] The mind (*hyge*) that earlier seethed around his heart is no longer heated by anger, so its swelling retreats, leaving the heart unconstricted and 'roomy.' A similar reaction occurs in the breast of the heroine Judith almost instantaneously after Holofernes collapses in drunkenness. Entering his tent, Judith is miserable and uncertain, and her heart is 'heated'; she says, 'Þearle ys me nu ða / heorte onhæted ond hige geomor,' and she begs God to avenge 'þæt me ys þus torne on mode, / hate on hreðre minum.'[60] God immediately answers her prayers by freeing her mind from its constriction: 'Þa wearð hyre rume on mode, / haligre hyht geniwod.'[61] With her mind no longer constricted by the heat of distress, she is able to slay Holofernes without further hesitation.

One's mind need not first be impaired by the heat and constriction of distress in order to benefit from increased roominess. In *Genesis B*, Satan's messenger, trying to tempt Adam to eat from the forbidden tree, promises

---

58 *GenB* 353b–4a: 'his mind swelled inwardly around his heart.'
59 *GenB* 758b–60a: 'Therefore my mind is healed; my mind is spacious around my heart; avenged are all our sufferings from this misery that we have long endured.'
60 *Jud* 86b–7, 93b–4a (discussed above).
61 *Jud* 97b–8a: 'Then it became roomy in her mind; hope was renewed in the holy woman.' Compare Bradley's heavily psychologized translation, which effaces the role of mental roominess in the hydraulic model of the mind: 'So hope was abundantly renewed in the holy woman's heart' (*Anglo-Saxon Poetry*, 499).

him that the fruit will make him more beautiful and will make his breast spacious: 'nim þe þis ofæt on hand, / bit his and byrige. Þe weorð on þinum breostum rum, / wæstm þy wlitegra.'[62] Just what is meant by this roominess in the breast becomes clear as we learn how the fruit affects Eve: it sharpens her sensory perception and her apprehension of beauty (*GenB* 564–7, 600–9), augments her range of vision and hearing (666b–77), and strengthens her knowledge and powers of persuasion (568–9). Although Eve's breast was not constricted by suffering before she ate the fruit, all of these mental benefits of cardiocentric roominess cause her mind to feel 'light,' as she tells Adam: 'Wearð me on hige leohte / utan and innan, siðþan ic þæs ofætes onbat.'[63] Mental roominess appears to have been considered universally beneficial, whether it befell one who desperately needed relief from mental constriction or simply improved the mind from ordinary to extraordinary. Roominess, moreover, is a flexible enough symptom to encompass both emotional and intellectual improvements: in the preceding passages, Satan's messenger and Judith are made 'spacious' by happiness and fervour respectively, but the cardiocentric 'roominess' brought on by the forbidden fruit sharpens Eve's sensory and cognitive faculties, and likewise, in the final fitt of *Elene* (which I will discuss further below), Cynewulf represents his journey from ignorance to spiritual enlightenment as the acquisition of 'rumran geþeaht ... on modes þeaht.'[64]

Given the range of positive thoughts and emotions that can bring on mental roominess, it is worth paying close attention to the way we translate the adjective *rum* and the compound *rumheort*. The latter is usually treated as a calque on Latin *magnanimus* 'generous,' which meaning is then transferred to occurrences of *rum* in psychological contexts. In discussions of almsgiving and hospitality, a 'roomy heart' is doubtless a marker of generosity, as in the first two lines of the poem *Almsgiving*: 'Wel bið þam eorle þe him on innan hafað, / reþehygdig wer, rume heortan.'[65] The meaning of the phrase *rume heortan* is firmly resolved by the speaker's statement, a few lines later, that this same man 'mid ælmessan ealle toscufeð / synna

---

62 *GenB* 518b–20a: 'grasp for yourself this fruit in hand, bite it, and taste. In your breast it will become roomy, and your appearance will become more radiant.'

63 *GenB* 676b–7: 'It has become light [i.e., not heavy] in my mind, outwardly and inwardly, since I bit into that fruit.'

64 *El* 1240b–1b: 'a roomier faculty of thought ... in the thought of his mind.'

65 *Alms* 1–2: 'Well will it be with the nobleman, the right-minded man, who has within him a roomy heart.'

wunde.'[66] Likewise, according to *Maxims I*, the ideal woman ought to be 'rumheort … / mearum ond maþmum,'[67] in which context *rumheort* can only mean 'generous.' On the other hand, where *rum* appears in the passages discussed earlier in this section, context prohibits the interpretation of *rum* as 'generous,' because generosity does not strengthen Judith to kill Holofernes, nor is Satan's deputy more generous after the Fall, nor does Eve become more generous by eating the forbidden fruit. Fortunately, an understanding of the hydraulic model clarifies that a 'roomy heart' is the bodily symptom of an extraordinarily good emotional or intellectual state, rendering it unnecessary to concoct several psychologized definitions of *rum* to suit its meanings across a range of contexts.

In this light, it is useful to re-evaluate the usual assumptions about the meaning of Beowulf's first words to the Danish coast-guard, which include the phrase *rumne sefan*, often assumed to mean 'generous mind.' To declare the purpose of his visit, Beowulf announces, 'Ic þæs Hroðgar mæg / þurh rumne sefan ræd gelæran / hu he frod ond god feond oferswyðeþ';[68] then he immediately offers to cool Hrothgar's *cearwylmas* or 'boiling worries' by exterminating Grendel. Beowulf's 'roomy mind' will enable him to succeed where Hrothgar has failed: not in the realm of generosity, for Hrothgar is unquestionably generous as king and as host, but in clear-sightedness and fortitude in battle (recall the significance of Eve's and Judith's roomy minds), both qualities which are diminished in Hrothgar as long as his mind is constricted by *cearwylmas*.

The roomy heart is, in one important respect, different from all other hydraulic-model symptoms discussed so far. Unlike mental heat and seething and cooling, all of which can be associated with both positive and negative states of mind, roominess is always a beneficial, healthy quality for the mind-in-the-breast to possess. It is useful to keep this in mind as we examine the opposite phenomenon, namely the constriction of the mind-in-the-breast, because it will shed light on how to integrate the textual evidence for psychological constriction with the rest of the hydraulic model.

---

66 *Alms* 8–9a: 'will do away with all the wounds of sin by means of alms.'
67 *Max I* 86b–7a: 'roomy-hearted with respect to horses and treasures.'
68 *Beo* 277b–9: 'Thanks to my roomy mind I can teach Hrothgar a remedy for this matter: how he, wise and good, may overpower his enemy.'

Involuntary Constriction of the Mind

When a liquid is heated in a closed container, the pressure of the contents rises as the temperature rises; if the temperature rises enough, the internal pressure may become so intense that it threatens to rupture the walls of the container. In an analogous manner, when the distressed mind is hot and seething, the pressure within the chest cavity rises, pressing outward on the walls of the container while inwardly constricting all the contents of the chest cavity. As mentioned above, complex hydraulic-model images in *Christ II* and the metrical *Solomon and Saturn* mention constriction as a by-product of the heat and seething of the mind-in-the-breast: the blazing love in the breasts of Christ's disciples is 'grievously oppressed,' and when Saturn is overwhelmed by his studies, his mind 'wells up oppressively.'[69] Also mentioned earlier was the 'fiery-hot hatred' seething in the breast of the Mermedonians; this violent emotion reaches its peak when 'murderousness' constricts the mind and its contents: 'Þær orcnawe wearð / þurh teoncwide tweogende mod, / mæcga misgehygd morðre bewunden.'[70] In passages such as these, the constriction of the mind-in-the-breast is easily recognized to be the culmination of an intensely distressing episode that began with cardiocentric heat and seething. Yet throughout the poetic corpus there are many depictions of psychological 'narrowness' that do not fit so neatly into the hydraulic model. Sometimes the symptoms of heat and seething are absent; sometimes cardiocentric heat and seething are present but 'narrowness' is predicated of something other than the mind-in-the-heart; sometimes depictions of cardiocentric constriction are embellished with biblical images of captivity and enslavement to sin; sometimes 'narrowness' appears to be a wholly psychologized concept, without any reference to cardiocentric events. Taken together, this body of textual evidence points to the conclusion that psychological constriction is not solely the culmination of cardiocentric heat and seething: constriction is an unfavourable state associated with many forms of distress, and as such, the concept of psychological constriction is not wholly dependent on the hydraulic model of mental activity, even though hydraulic-model phenomena are one possible path to psychological constriction.

---

69 *ChristB* 538a and *MSol* 62 (see above).
70 *And* 770b–2: 'Through their blasphemy the men's doubting mind and their errors, hemmed in by murderousness, were there made manifest.'

The epilogue to *Elene*, in which Cynewulf describes his own conversion from ignorance to spiritual enlightenment, exemplifies the complications attending the concept of psychological constriction.

> Nysse ic gearwe
> be ðære ... riht[71]   ær me rumran geþeaht   1240
> þurh ða mæran miht   on modes þeaht
> wisdom onwreah.   Ic wæs weorcum fah,
> synnum asæled,   sorgum gewæled,
> bitrum gebunden,   bisgum geþrungen,
> ær me lare onlag   þurh leohtne had   1245
> gamelum to geoce,   gife unscynde
> mægencyning amæt   ond on gemynd begeat,
> torht ontynde,   tidum gerymde,
> bancofan onband,   breostlocan onwand,
> leoðucræft onleac.[72]   1250

Although sorrow (*sorgum*, line 1243) is elsewhere characterized as a 'hot' emotion, heat and seething are conspicuously absent from these lines, much as the *Genesis B*-poet makes no mention of mental cooling occurring in Eve's breast when she acquires mental roominess by eating the forbidden fruit. Instead, the biblical topos of enslavement to sin provides the dominant imagery in the epilogue to *Elene*, which echoes, for instance, Prv 5:22: 'iniquitates suae capiunt impium et funibus peccatorum suorum constringitur.'[73] The way Cynewulf maps his release from psychological constriction onto the midsection of the body is, nonetheless, reminiscent of the hydraulic model: God relieves him of two afflictions, sinfulness and ignorance, and in so doing he loosens the breast-chamber (*breostlocan*

---

71 In the manuscript this half-line reads *be ðære riht* with no gap, which is unmetrical, and there is no editorial consensus on an appropriate emendation: see ASPR 2.149.

72 *El* 1239b–50a: 'I did not fully grasp the truth of the [*word missing in MS*] before wisdom in its glorious power uncovered a more spacious faculty of thought in the thinking of my mind. I was stained by deeds, fettered by sins, tormented by sorrows, bound by grief, oppressed by hardships, before the mighty King laid upon me his teaching in a gentle manner, as a consolation to a hoary old man; before he bestowed and founded in my mind a blameless gift, revealed its brilliance and sometimes increased it, unbound the bone-chest, loosened the breast-enclosure, unlocked the power of the limbs [*or* power to compose song].'

73 'His own iniquities catch the wicked, and he is fast bound with the ropes of his own sins.' This parallel is suggested by Gradon, *Cynewulf's Elene*, 71.

onwand) where Cynewulf was constricted by his afflictions. The relief that his newfound wisdom brings to Cynewulf is characterized as a 'roomier faculty of thought' (*rumran geþeaht*). *Genesis A* provides further examples of the compatibility of cardiocentric constriction imagery with biblical imagery of enslavement and captivity: when the Lord admonishes Abraham, 'Ne læt þu þin ferhð wesan / sorgum asæled,' and when the narrator states that the Lord 'wiste ferhð guman / cearum on clommum,'[74] it is impossible to tell which of these strands of imagery was foremost in the poet's mind.

The concept of psychological constriction is further complicated by what we might call incomplete hydraulic-model scenarios. In *Deor*, no other hydraulic-model activity precedes the speaker's statement, 'Sæt secg monig sorgum gebunden, / wean on wenan';[75] in *The Wanderer*, a man long deprived of his lord's company is constricted by sorrow and sleep: 'sorg ond slæp somod ætgædre / earmne anhogan oft gebindað.'[76] Elsewhere, sorrow is characteristically associated with heat and seething, and although neither attribute is mentioned in these passages, the constriction denoted by the verb *gebindan* is clearly a marker of psychological distress. The same is true of the two lines of the *Rune Poem* that pertain to the rune *nyd*, whose name means 'distress.' The gist of these lines is that hardship builds character in the long run, even though it is unpleasantly tight within the breast: 'ᚾ [nyd] byþ nearu on breostan, weorþeþ hi ðeah oft niþa bearnum / to helpe and to hæle gehwæþre, gif hi his hlystaþ æror.'[77] Again, heat and seething are absent, even though the constriction is specifically said to impinge upon the breast. In other instances, mental heat and seething are localized in the breast while the attribute of narrowness is transferred elsewhere: for example, Beccel confesses to his mentor Guthlac that 'Oft mec geomor sefa gehþa gemanode, / hat æt heortan, hyge gnornende /

---

74 *GenA* 2196b–7a: 'Do not let your mind be fettered with sorrows'; *GenA* 2794b–5a: 'knew the mind of the man, chained by anxieties.'

75 *Deor* 24–5a: 'Many a man sat, constricted by sorrows, anticipating misery.' Low, 'The Anglo-Saxon Mind,' provides additional examples of mental constriction (97) but her discussion of mental expansion and contraction does not systematically integrate these phenomena with other hydraulic-model symptoms (ibid., 96–9).

76 *Wan* 39–40: 'sorrow and sleep all at once oppress the wretched loner.'

77 *MRune* 27–8: 'Distress is tight in the chest; nevertheless, afflictions often become both a help and a healing for people, if they attend to it early enough.' In the manuscript, the word *nyd* 'distress' is represented by a rune. On these lines and on the passage in *Elene* that collocates the rune *nyd* with images of constriction (discussed below), see Halsall, *The Old English* Rune Poem, 121–2.

nihtes nearwe,'[78] as though the night itself is figuratively constricting because of the cardiocentric distress that Beccel suffers. The Seafarer, likewise, is tormented by external and internal constriction during the lonely night-watch:

> þær mec oft bigeat
> nearo nihtwaco   æt nacan stefnan,
> þonne he be clifum cnossað.   Calde geþrungen
> wæron mine fet,   forste gebunden,
> caldum clommum,   þær þa ceare seofedun
> hat ymb heortan.[79]

With his feet bound on the outside by 'cold fetters' of frost and his chest cavity smothered by the heat of anxieties that 'sigh around the heart,' the Seafarer transfers the quality of narrowness to the noun *nihtwaco*, with the effect of making his sensation of constriction as vast and all-encompassing as a sleepless night on the ocean.

From the transferred epithet 'narrow night-watch' it is a small step to the most abstract uses of 'narrowness' as a near-synonym for 'distress,' much like Latin *angustia*, without any explicit reference to the mind-in-the-heart or the heat of distress. Beowulf, for instance, endures 'narrowness' while losing his battle against the dragon: 'nearo ðrowode / fyre befongen se ðe ær folce weold.'[80] In compounds, the element *nearu-* connotes distress, but it is not always readily apparent that such usages are connected to the notion of cardiocentric constriction: for example, in *Elene*, Cyriacus prays for God's help *on nearwe* 'in his distress' when he can't find the nails of the True Cross, which had been hidden *þurh nearusearwe* 'by means of grievous trickery.'[81] It is more difficult to make out what Cynewulf is saying about *nyd* and narrowness in his runic signature in *Elene*: 'ᚾ [Yr]

---

78 *GuthB* 1208–10a: 'Often my mournful mind admonished me with anxiety, narrowly in the night, my mournful mind hot near my heart.' See also *Fates* 104, where *nyd* and *nihtes nearowe* are again collocated.

79 *Sea* 6b–11a: 'There the narrow night-watch has often fallen to me, at the stern of the ship as it bumps against the rocks. My feet were squeezed by the cold, bound by frost, with cold fetters, while hot anxieties sighed around my heart.' The phrase *ceare seofedun* is unusual; literally, it means 'anxieties sighed,' but in light of the hydraulic model 'sighing' evokes the audible exhalation of air emanating from a simmering liquid.

80 *Beo* 2594b–5: 'he who once governed the people suffered constriction, besieged by fire.'

81 *El* 1102a and 1108a.

gnornode / † [nyd] gefera, nearusorge dreah, / enge rune.'[82] Yet whatever the syntactic relationship between *yr* and *nyd* may be, it is plain that the *yr* is tormented by sorrow and a secret that are 'constricting' or 'tight' and therefore threatening to mental well-being. In cases such as these, in which the poet makes no explicit connection between psychological constriction and the other symptoms of the hydraulic model, is it nonetheless appropriate to understand the mind-in-the-heart as the implicit locus of such constriction? Two of the most detailed depictions of the mechanism of mental constriction demonstrate that even in the absence of 'hot' categories of thought and emotion, spatial constriction within the chest cavity is in fact firmly associated with changes in the behaviour and spatial disposition of the mind-in-the-breast.

Involuntary Constriction and Drunkenness in Genesis A

The *Genesis A* account of Noah's drunkenness already made a brief appearance in the introduction because it includes the most physiologically precise account of psychological constriction in all of OE literature. The narrator recounts that after drinking too much wine, Noah retires to his tent and disrobes before passing out, an irrational behaviour that demands explanation:

> He lyt ongeat
> þæt him on his inne   swa earme gelamp,
> þa him on hreðre   heafodswima
> on þæs halgan hofe   heortan clypte.
> Swiðe on slæpe   sefa nearwode
> þæt he ne mihte   on gemynd drepen
> hine handum self   mid hrægle wryon
> and sceome þeccan.[83]

This is not just an elaborate metaphor: the words 'He lyt ongeat þæt' establish that, while Noah is unaware of the mind's physiological response

---

82 *El* 1259b–61a: 'The horn (Y), his comrade in duress (N), would mourn, and he would suffer oppressive grief, a confined secret' (trans. Bradley, *Anglo-Saxon Poetry*, 195–6).

83 *GenA* 1566b–73a: 'Within his tent, he scarcely perceived that which happened so wretchedly when the dizziness in his breast seized his heart, in the dwelling of the holy man. His mind constricted greatly in his sleep, so that he himself, stricken in his mind, was unable to cover himself in clothes with his hands and conceal his genitals.'

to drunkenness, the narrator is about to explain what is actually happening in Noah's mind-in-the-breast. The adverb *earme* 'miserably' underscores that Noah is in distress, and the phrase *on hreðre* indicates the internal bodily location of the distress. In his chest, dizziness or sensory confusion (*heafodswima*) grips Noah's heart. Consequently, his mind is constricted or squeezed (*sefa nearwode*), impairing his judgment, with the result that he does not cover his nakedness. Heat and seething are not mentioned, but this passage has something quite rare among portrayals of the mind-in-the-breast: a clear indication of the direction of cause and effect. The conjunction *þæt* in line 1571a indicates that the narrowing of the mind is a physiological precondition whose result is the impairment of Noah's modesty or his motor control or both.

Another infamous instance of startling irrationality in the Genesis narrative occurs after Lot and his two daughters are delivered from the destruction of Sodom. Living in isolation in a cave, the daughters believe that they will never find husbands with whom they might procreate, so they give Lot so much wine that they can have sex with him without his knowing what he is doing. Because such shocking behaviour by an otherwise respectable man demands explanation, the narrator again illustrates how alcohol was able to transform the dimensions of Lot's mind-in-the-heart:

> Hie dydon swa;   druncnum eode
> seo yldre to   ær on reste
> heora bega fæder.   Ne wiste blondenfeax
> hwonne him fæmnan to bryde   him bu wæron,
> on ferhðcofan   fæste genearwod
> mode and gemynde,   þæt he mægðe sið
> wine druncen   gewitan ne meahte.[84]

This episode includes fewer physiological details, but the crucial event is the same: alcohol constricts Lot in his mind and breast, with the result that he cannot prevent or even perceive the incestuous activity in which he ordinarily would refuse to partake.

Putting these passages together with those in the previous section, we can draw the following conclusions. Mental constriction is unequivocally

---

84 *GenA* 2600–6: 'Thus they did: the older daughter went first to both girls' father, into his bed while he was drunk; the white-haired man was not aware that the two women were as brides to him. In his mind-chamber, in his mind and his memory, he was tightly constricted to the extent that he, being drunk on wine, was unable to understand the undertaking of his kinswomen.'

dangerous, just as mental roominess is always beneficial. The episodes of Lot's and Noah's drunkenness show that mental heat and seething are not necessary precursors to constriction, but they also underscore that even when heat and seething are absent, the functioning of the mind-in-the-breast can be impaired by constriction from other sources. Conversely, since mental heat and seething are not unequivocally harmful phenomena, they need not lead to constriction. In this light, it is likely that even the most abstract references to psychological narrowness are implicitly connected to the idea that mental constriction injures the mind-in-the-breast, even when that connection is obscured by imagery that the present-day reader recognizes more readily, including the topos of enslavement to sin.

Voluntary Constriction of the Mind and Its Contents

The burning heart, the seething mind, and the burdened breast persist in MnE idioms of emotional distress, but the OE and MnE conventional representations of self-restraint diverge sharply. In MnE, we conventionally map the internal conflict between rational and irrational impulses onto the head and the heart, but the head is conspicuously absent from the OE portrayals of the mind; it is excluded from nearly all Anglo-Saxon representations of mental activity, be they literal or metaphorical, verse or prose, vernacular or Latin. The cultural and conceptual niche that in MnE is occupied by the conventional opposition of head and heart is filled, in OE literature, by the struggle of the individual to restrain the seething contents of his breast. Because seething leads to increased internal pressure, these contents naturally want to escape from their container in the form of words or tears. Eric Jager, among others, has already documented that OE poets commonly depicted the chest as the repository of thoughts and speech.[85] It remains to be explored how the OE poets involved the repository of the breast in narratives of internal psychological conflict. The individual's control over the contents of the breast depends on the physical suppression of emotional heat and seething, so that the pressure in the breast cannot force words and tears out of their container in imprudent or uncontrolled ways.[86]

---

85 Jager, 'The Word in the "Breost"'; and Jager, 'Speech and the Chest in Old English Poetry.'
86 Matto has addressed a portion of this question in his article entitled 'A War of Containment: The Heroic Image in *The Battle of Maldon*,' but his 'container metaphor' does not include the symptoms of cardiocentric heat and seething that are vital to the hydraulic model as a whole.

In OE verse, it is not inherently shameful to allow intense emotions to propel words and tears out of the breast. St Andrew weeps and prays passionately while his breast burns with distress, but the narrator does not suggest that his outburst is inappropriate for a man or for a Christian: 'Þa com hwopes hring / þurh þæs beornes breost, blat ut faran, / weoll waðuman stream, ond he worde cwæð: / "Geseoh nu, dryhten god, drohtað minne!"'[87] Nor does the *Beowulf*-narrator indicate that the hero is imprudent to allow a shout to burst out of his breast when he is swollen with rage at the dragon: 'Let ða of breostum, ða he gebolgen wæs, / Weder-Geata leod word ut faran, / stearcheort styrmde.'[88] When Beowulf is 'swollen' and his heart is 'rigid,' the words fly forcefully out of his breast as he allows them. Some two hundred lines later, when he is on the verge of death and no longer *gebolgen*, the contents of his breast are no longer pressurized, and they emerge so weakly that only 'the point of a word' can breach its container: 'wordes ord / breosthord þurhbræc.'[89] Additionally, if an utterance that ought to be kept in the breast is not propelled out by mental heat and pressure, then the suppression of that utterance is not terribly challenging. The speaker of *Instructions for Christians* advises the foolish man to keep his *unwisdom* sealed up in his breast:

> Betere bið þe dusige,   gif he on breostum can
> his unwisdom   inne belucan,
> þonne se snotere   ðe symle wile
> æt his heahþearfe   forhelan his wisdom.[90]

Since foolishness is not a 'hot' state of mind, the restraint of foolish words in the breast does not merit the rigorous cardiocentric struggle that keeps words of anger and grief from escaping.

Beowulf's and St Andrew's outbursts aside, it is a recurring theme in OE poetry that a man – and I do mean *man* in the gendered sense – ought to keep the contents of his breast locked up in situations in which speaking

---

87   *And* 1278b–81: 'Then the ghastly sound of weeping advanced through the man's breast, travelling outward; the gushing of a flood welled up, and he spoke aloud: "Now, Lord God, behold my condition!"'
88   *Beo* 2550–2a: 'Then, when he was swollen with rage, the prince of the Weder-Geats allowed a word to travel out from his breast; the rigid-hearted man roared.'
89   *Beo* 2791b–2a: 'the point of a word broke through the breast-container.'
90   *Instr* 71–4: 'The foolish man, if he knows how to lock his ignorance inside his breast, is better than the wise man who always wants to conceal his wisdom in his great need.'

and weeping would be shameful or detrimental to his relationships with other men and hence to his reputation.[91] *The Wanderer* provides the most thorough treatment of the social implications of cardiocentric restraint. The figure of the Wanderer idealizes the 'noble custom' of keeping the contents of the mind sealed up no matter what they may be. 'Ic to soþe wat,' he says with resignation, 'þæt biþ in eorle indryhten þeaw, / þæt he his ferðlocan fæste binde, / healde his hordcofan, hycge swa he wille.'[92] To do otherwise would threaten one's good reputation, so anyone who is 'eager for glory' restrains even his grief: 'Forðon domgeorne dreorigne oft / in hyra breostcofan bindað fæste.'[93] Accordingly, although he is miserable and far from home, the Wanderer declares, 'ic modsefan minne sceolde ... feterum sælan.'[94] Outward signs of aggression and boastfulness likewise demand that the prudent man regulate them by means of cardiocentric restraint:

> Wita sceal geþyldig,
> ne sceal no to hatheort   ne to hrædwyrde ...
> ne næfre gielpes to georn,   ær he geare cunne.
> Beorn sceal gebidan,   þonne he beot spriceð,
> oþþæt collenferð   cunne gearwe
> hwider hreþra gehygd   hweorfan wille.[95]

---

91 Discretion is a womanly virtue as well: the speaker of *Maxims I* reveres the woman who can keep a secret (83b–6a). However, most OE narratives of the individual's struggle to maintain silence by containing words in his breast happen to involve male speakers and characters.

92 *Wan* 11b–14: 'I know for a fact that it is a noble custom for a man to bind firmly his mind-enclosure, to hold onto his treasure-chest [i.e., his word-hoard], let him think what he will.'

93 *Wan* 17–18: 'Therefore the man who is eager for glory often locks up tight in his breast-chamber that which is grievous.'

94 *Wan* 19–21: 'I must confine my mind with fetters.'

95 *Wan* 65b–72: 'The wise man must be forbearing; he must not be too hot-hearted or too quick to speak ... and never too eager to boast before he is fully cognizant. When a man is going to speak a boast, he ought to bide his time until, bold-minded, he knows well which way the thought of his breast wants to turn.' Carey and Henry both maintain that the first element of the word *collenferð* literally means 'swollen,' as if from a hypothetical verb **cwellan*, 'to swell,' which would add to the hydraulic-model imagery in these lines: see Carey, 'Fir Bolg,' 80; and Henry, 'Furor Heroicus,' 237–8. Both of these studies also point out that the OE heroic epithet *eacen*, usually translated 'mighty,' literally means 'enlarged,' which is suggestive of the hero's swelling up with martial aggression.

The Wanderer recommends a state of emotional balance, in which a man's mind is firm or swollen (*collenferð*) enough to follow through on the boasts that he makes public, but his mind is not *so* hot (*no to hatheort*) that his thoughts gush out faster or more forcefully than he can control. The same balance ideally governs the publicizing of grief, since the narrator declares in the closing lines of the poem that 'ne sceal næfre his torn to rycene / beorn of his breostum acyþan, nemþe he ær þa bote cunne.'[96] Idle complaints are unbecoming in a man, but it is respectable for him to speak of ills that he intends to remedy promptly. Throughout *The Wanderer*, references to the breast, especially those compounds that underscore the capacity of the breast to contain and restrain the mind, suggest that the breast is instrumental in the regulation of one's own speech. Specifically, the best way to prevent a shameful display of grief or aggression is to avoid an excess of mental pressure in the chest cavity. Pressure is the most important condition to regulate: though mental heat *can* lead to extreme pressure and mental constriction, it is also possible for mental heat to be moderate or even beneficial, but no good ever comes of excessive pressure on the *breostsefa*.

Other poems add to our understanding of the physiological aspects of voluntary constriction. Recall that in the poem *Precepts*, a father advises his son, 'Yrre ne læt þe æfre gewealdan, / heah in hreþre, heoroworda grund / wylme bismitan.'[97] The source of the father's anxiety is not anger per se but self-control; not mental heat but excess mental pressure. When anger swells up too 'high in the breast,' it is no longer subject to the individual's control, but its heat causes an unstoppable torrent of hostile speech to boil over and exceed the walls of its pectoral container, shamefully polluting the speaker. The mechanism by which a man keeps such untoward displays of emotion sealed in the breast is given the special name of 'mind-tethers' by the *Beowulf*-narrator, as he explains how Hrothgar copes with his intense sadness at Beowulf's departure from Denmark:

> Wæs him se man to þon leof,
> þæt he þone breostwylm   forberan ne mehte
> ac him on hreþre   hygebendum fæst
> æfter deorum men   dyrne langað
> born wið blode.[98]

---

96 *Wan* 112b–13: 'a man must never publicize the miseries of his breast too readily, unless he already knows of a remedy.'
97 *Prec* 83–5a (see above).
98 *Beo* 1876b–80a: 'That man was so beloved that Hrothgar could not restrain the seething in his breast; rather, a hidden longing for that beloved man, secured in his breast by the

The meaning of this passage depends on the meanings of *breostwylm*, which some readers interpret as the flow of weeping or tears out of the breast. Although such a rendering of *breostwylm* can be harmonized with the hydraulic model, it is difficult to reconcile with the next lines of the poem, which state that the king *succeeds* in keeping his feelings 'secret' and 'fixed in his breast.' How can the king fail to restrain his weeping *but* keep his longing hidden in his breast? An awareness of how the hydraulic model operates makes it unnecessary to formulate any meaning for *breostwylm* other than the literal: 'boiling in the breast.' Beowulf is so beloved that when he departs, Hrothgar cannot prevent his breast from boiling, *but* his hidden longing remains firmly tethered in the breast. The heat of Hrothgar's emotion, while wilfully constrained inside the pectoral container, burns all the more fiercely and transmits its heat to the blood. The word *hygebendum* evokes a mechanism by which an individual might counteract the outward pressure of the seething mind-in-the-breast, as if the mind-tethers were muscles that could be flexed at will to keep words and tears from escaping from the breast, but at the risk of increasing the heat and pressure inside the chest cavity.

The Hydraulic Model in The Rhyming Poem, *lines 43–50*

An understanding of the role of hydraulic-model mechanisms in narratives of verbal self-restraint is particularly fruitful when applied to *The Rhyming Poem*, whose unusual lexicon and textual cruces have posed perennial challenges to readers. In lines 1–42 of *The Rhyming Poem*, the speaker reminisces about the wealth, power, friends, and allies who enriched his life for many years. The adverb *nu* 'now,' at the start of line 43, marks the moment of the reversal of his fortunes, and here the speaker begins to describe the grave distress that has afflicted him since his downfall. I give here the text of lines 43–50, primarily following the ASPR text but incorporating several changes about which I have commented below.

Nu min hreþer is hreoh,   heofsiþum sceoh,
nydbysgum neah;   gewiteð nihtes in fleah

---

tethers of his mind, burned into his blood.' BT, s.v. *wið*, II.c, suggests translating *born wið blode* as 'burnt against the blood, heated his blood?' The preposition *wið* governing the dative usually indicates a facing position or a position of contact or close proximity, which orientation I may have exaggerated by rendering *wið* as 'into,' but no other MnE preposition captures the idea that the heat of longing is transferred to the blood by prolonged contact in a pressurized environment.

se ær in dæge wæs dyre.   Scriþeð nu deop ond feor,   45
brondhord gebrowen,   breostum in forgrowen,
flyhtum toflowen.   Flah is geblowen
miclum in gemynde;   modes gecynde
greteð ungrynde   grorn oferpynde,
bealofus byrneð,   bittre toyrneð.   50

In lines 43–4a the speaker foregrounds cardiocentric distress: the breast is
'agitated,' 'timid,' and 'close to distress.'[99] The cause of this distress is the
sudden departure of the speaker's *dyre*, an elusive word which in this context is likely to mean 'beloved,' 'brave,' or 'precious.' If *dyre* means 'brave,'
then the person whom the speaker has lost may be one of the noble warriors formerly in his retinue, in which case his flight is emblematic of the
transience of hardiness and courage, as is often lamented in conjunction
with the *ubi sunt* motif in OE elegy. I favour the interpretation of *dyre* as
the 'beloved,' because the acuteness of the speaker's distress better befits a
personal loss than a meditation on transience in general, although I do not
mean to imply that the 'beloved' is necessarily a lover: the *Beowulf*-poet
twice calls *Beowulf* the 'beloved' (*leof, deor*) of Hrothgar in the passage
that depicts Hrothgar restraining his acute grief by means of 'mind-tethers'
(1876b–80a, quoted above).

In line 45b, where the manuscript reads *deop feor*, I have only added the
conjunction *ond* which very easily could have been neglected by the copyist, especially if his exemplar used the symbol ⁊ to represent the word.[100]
Most editors, including Krapp and Dobbie in ASPR 3, emend to *in feore*,
supposing that *feore* is the dative of *feorh*, and equating the latter with
'soul' or 'insides' or even 'self.'[101] The *feorh*, the transient life-force, is impersonal and ephemeral, lacking in psychological and bodily attributes: it
would be very surprising to find that an OE poet used the word *feorh* to
represent the bodily seat of the mind and the psychological victim of the
heat of the *brondhord*, or that he intended *in feore* to parallel *breostum* in
46b. Without emendation, the manuscript reading *feor* can be plausibly

---

99 I accept the usual emendation of MS *heow siþum* (43b) to *heofsiþum*, 'mournful undertakings,' although emending to *hreowsiþum* 'sorrowful undertakings,' as at least one
editor has proposed (see ASPR 3.313), would conform better to the poet's tendency to
use the same consonant cluster in all alliterating positions within a line.
100 This solution is favoured by Wentersdorf, 'The Old English "Rhyming Poem": A
Ruler's Lament,' 285.
101 See further ASPR 3.313–14; Macrae-Gibson, *The Old English Riming Poem*, 32–3;
Mize, 'The Representation of the Mind as an Enclosure,' 84 n. 78.

interpreted as the adverb 'far'; thus, the *brondhord* in 46a 'now creeps, deep and far,' an interpretation that is confirmed by further descriptions of its spatial extent in the lines that follow.

Several scholars have endeavoured to pin down the meaning of *brondhord*, but rarely have they taken into account the mechanics of the mind according to the hydraulic model.[102] The first element of the compound means 'fire,' while the second element, *-hord*, has as its primary meaning 'treasure' or 'treasure-chest.' In psychological contexts, often collocated with *heorte* or *breost*, the word *hord* refers to the things treasured up in the chest, namely the mind and the mind's thoughts and emotions.[103] In the present context, therefore, *brondhord* likely means 'burning thought,' which makes good sense in light of the hydraulic model.

I propose a new emendation at line 46a, replacing the manuscript reading *geblowen* (not emended in ASPR or elsewhere) with *gebrowen*. As the text stands in the manuscript, both 46a and 47b end in *geblowen*, and although the use of repetition rather than real rhyme occurs elsewhere in the poem, this instance of repetition could easily be attributed to scribal error resulting from homoeoteleuton. Emending to *gebrowen* improves both the sense and the alliteration of the line. *Gebrowen* is the past participle of *gebreowan*, 'to brew,' which contributes to the hydraulic-model narrative a vivid image of moderate heat and prolonged, gentle simmering.[104] Additionally, the replacement of *geblowen* with *gebrowen* produces double alliteration on the consonant cluster *br-*. Double alliteration is not metrically necessary, but the poet does appear to have aimed to use double alliteration as often as possible throughout *The Rhyming Poem*, and where the poet uses double alliteration, he is generally meticulous about alliterating on the same consonant cluster or on the same single consonant throughout

---

102 Schaar, '*Brondhord* in the Old English Rhyming Poem,' includes a summary of earlier opinions; see also J.E. Cross, 'Aspects of Microcosm and Macrocosm,' 11–15; Macrae-Gibson, *The Old English Riming Poem*, 48–9; Wentersdorf, 'The Old English *Rhyming Poem*: A Ruler's Lament,' 285–6. Britt Mize is undecided as to whether *brond-* in the compound *brondhord* signifies a sword or a flame, but in his explication of this passage he invokes the 'container metaphor' and is accordingly aware that these lines portray 'the eruption of something dangerous from mental containment': see 'The Representation of the Mind as an Enclosure,' 84–5.

103 See, e.g., *HomFr I* 5b–6: 'ond þæt facen swa þeah / hafað in his heortan, hord unclæne' (and yet he has deceit in his heart, an unclean treasure).

104 Cf. the *OE Orosius* 1.1 (ed. Bately, *The Old English Orosius*, 17): 'ne bið ðær nænig ealo gebrowen mid Estum' (there is no beer brewed among the Ests). See also the *DOE*, s.v. *gebreowan, gebrowen*; and BT, s.v. *twybrowen* 'twice-brewed.'

a given line. Though it is metrically permissible, he seldom mixes different clusters or mixes single and clustered consonants in alliterating positions within one line.[105]

The speaker next reveals that the *brondhord* is 'insidious' and it 'flourishes greatly in the memory' (lines 47b–8a). The affliction of the speaker's mind reaches its peak when his grief is *efenpynde*, according to the MS; neither this compound nor its second element is otherwise attested, and I have adopted the emendation, suggested by Sievers and followed by some later editors, of *efenpynde* to *oferpynde*, which is also unattested in OE but is plausible as a compound of the intensifying prefix *ofer-* and the participle of the hypothetical verb **pyndan* 'to impound.'[106] The compound would therefore mean 'exceedingly penned in,' which fits neatly into the extended hydraulic-model imagery running throughout this passage. Incorporating all of the changes suggested above, I translate lines 43–50 as follows:

> Now my breast is agitated, timid in its mournful undertakings, close to distress. He has departed in flight by night, who earlier in the day was beloved. Now there creeps a fire-thought, deep [and] wide, brewed and grown large inside the breast, dispersed by its travels. Insidious, it [*scil.* the fire-thought] flourishes greatly in the memory. Vast grief affects the condition of the mind when it is penned in too much: inclined toward evil, it burns; it moves around violently.

Considered together, lines 43–50 present a coherent and very detailed portrayal of the suffering of the mind-in-the-breast when an individual voluntarily constrains his grief in the breast over a long period. At the first mention of the *brondhord* or 'burning thought,' its motion in the breast is subtle and insidious: to describe it the speaker uses the verb *scriðan* 'to creep,' which is typically predicated of shadows and supernatural creatures.[107] In the present context the word is suggestive of the subtle agitation

---

105 There are few exceptions to this observation, such as line 40, where alliteration falls on *foldan, freoþode, folcum*. Double alliteration on consonant clusters occurs in twenty of the poem's 87 lines, whereas double alliteration on combinations of single and clustered consonants occurs in only five other lines (one of which is 43, which demands emendation; see above). On double alliteration and related ornaments in other poems, see Orchard, 'Artful Alliteration in Anglo-Saxon Song and Story.'

106 On Sievers's emendation see ASPR 3.314; Krapp and Dobbie retain MS *efenpynde* in their edition.

107 In *Beowulf*, for instance, ordinary humans cannot *scriðan*, but demons, shadows, the dragon, and Grendel (the shadow-traveller, *sceadugenga*) can *scriðan*. See also T.D. Hill, '"Hwyrftum scriþaðˮ: *Beowulf*, line 163.'

of a fluid that has not reached the boiling point. But this low burning gradually grows more agitated. After it 'creeps,' the burning thought is 'brewed' (*gebrowen*), that is, cooked at a moderate intensity; then it seethes and swells, becoming 'expanded' (*forgrowen*), and finally it is 'dispersed by its flights' (*flyhtum toflowen*), or in other words, the burning is spread throughout the chest cavity, in the same way that Hrothgar's secret longing 'burned into the blood.' When this thought is disseminated throughout the chest, the mind can scarcely avoid dwelling upon it; the speaker tells us that the burning thought 'flourishes in the memory.' Because the speaker's 'vast grief' is bottled up inside without hope of escape (*oferpynde*), it becomes more intense. The growing magnitude of the speaker's distress is represented in psychological terms, in that his grief 'affects the condition of the mind' (*modes gecynde greteð*) and becomes 'inclined toward evil' (*bealofus*), but it is also communicated in physiological terms, by the increasing motility of the burning emotion in the chest, which began by 'creeping' and now reaches its peak when it 'runs to and fro violently' (*bittre toyrneð*), like water at a rapid boil. It is no coincidence that the constricted contents of the speaker's breast become 'inclined toward evil,' and thus dangerous to himself and others, only at the point when boiling and agitation culminate in constriction (if that is indeed what *oferpynde* signifies): among all the stages of the hydraulic model, only constriction is unequivocally injurious.

The Hydraulic Model of Mental Activity in OE Prose

Narrative and discursive treatments of mental activity in OE prose have received much less scholarly attention than their verse counterparts. This imbalance gives the misleading impression that the hydraulic model is merely a poetic trope, invoked to elevate the diction of verse portrayals of the mind, and consequently that it functions as a literary ornament rather than as a practical conception of how the mind works. Yet the mental mechanisms characteristic of OE verse also pervade the prose corpus, including OE works by authors whose discourses on the soul and on the mind are rightly assigned to the classical tradition in Anglo-Saxon psychology. The core features of the prose hydraulic model are identical to those attested in the verse corpus: the mind-in-the-breast is susceptible to heat, seething, and swelling during intense thought and emotion of both positive and negative varieties, and the dissipation of mental energy renders the mind cool. At the same time, the lexicon of the prose hydraulic-model idiom is quite distinct from that found in OE poetry, and certain hydraulic-model symptoms receive proportionally more attention, or bear a weightier social stigma, in prose narratives than in poems. Ideally, a thorough study of the hydraulic model in OE prose would attend carefully to the diction of the Latin sources underlying most of the relevant OE texts, and it would systematically examine a sufficiently broad sample of texts to sustain observations about translation practices and OE psychological vocabulary across the prose corpus. The objectives of the following pages are much more modest: they are simply to demonstrate that the hydraulic model did indeed flourish in OE prose (not to mention in the Christian Latin sources of OE prose) and thereby to discourage the assumption that the hydraulic model was an ornament peculiar to the poetic register rather than a practical, explanatory model of mental activity.

The *Thesaurus of Old English* offers a striking first impression of the centrality of hydraulic-model idioms in prose portrayals of the mind.[108] The *Thesaurus* groups OE words according to semantic field, noting which words are *hapax legomena* and which appear solely in verse or in glosses. In the field of 'Ardour, fervour, strong feeling' (§08.01.01.01) the editors include forty-six OE words: twenty-eight of these connote heat or fire or swelling, and among these, only two appear solely in verse. The heading 'Want of interest or concern, indifference' (§08.01.01.02.01) includes thirteen words, among which seven pertain to cool or tepid temperature; none of these seven is restricted to verse. 'Anger' (§08.01.03.05.02) includes eighty-eight words and phrases, among which twenty-six connote heat or seething or swelling; only four of these twenty-six are restricted to the poetic corpus. Under the heading 'Misery, trouble, affliction' (§08.01.03.07.02), six words contain the element *hefig*; nine contain either *ang* or *nearu*; two more connote swelling or binding; and only one of these seventeen words is a poetic term. The lexical building-blocks of the hydraulic model are obviously present in OE prose; it remains to consider how they are employed in prose narratives.

Prose Treatments of the Mind-in-the-Breast

Freed from metrical constraints, authors of OE prose found innumerable ways to characterize the behaviour and attributes of the mind-in-the-heart. As in the poetic corpus, the mind-in-the-heart is responsible for

---

108 Roberts, Kay, and Grundy, *A Thesaurus of Old English*; the semantic fields discussed here appear at 1.430–52.

both rational thought and emotion: the breast or heart can contain every mental activity or attribute, from thought and worry,[109] to anger, love, and goodwill,[110] and from 'spiritual love,' wisdom, and virtue,[111] to learning[112] and the understanding of scripture[113] and the 'gift of God.'[114]

Perhaps contrary to the modern reader's expectations, *mod* and *heorte* when mentioned in tandem do *not* represent a complementary pair such as the intangible and the bodily, or the rational and the passionate. Most collocations of *heorte* with *mod* and its synonyms, in fact, give the impression that they are functionally identical, especially by juxtaposing heart and mind in parallel constructions and doublets. One Maundy Thursday homily, for instance, twice uses the doublet *heorte and modgeðanc innan*

109 *The Legend of the Seven Sleepers*, lines 402–3 (ed. Magennis, *Seven Sleepers*, 46): 'þæt ilce geþanc and seo sylfe carfulnyss þe heom amang þam nihtslæpe wæs on heora heortan' (that same thought and the same worry, which was upon them during the night's sleep, was upon their hearts). For the *breost* as the locus of profound thought, which is contrasted with the superficial act of sensory perception, see *Durham Proverbs* 17 (ed. Arngart, 'The Durham Proverbs,' 292): 'Blind byþ bam eagum se þe breostum ne starat' (He who does not look with the breast is blind in both eyes).

110 Ælfric, *LS* 16, lines 341–2 (ed. Skeat, *LS* 1.360): 'yrre hæfð wununge on ðæs dysegan bosme' (anger has its dwelling place in the bosom of the fool). (Cf. Eccl 7:10.) Ælfric, *LS* 29, line 273 (ed. Skeat, *LS* 2.186): St Denis is praised for 'seo lufu . and welwillendnys þe wunað on þinum breoste' (the love and goodwill that dwell in your breast).

111 *Life of St Guthlac*, ch. 2 (ed. Gonser, *Prosa-Leben*, 109): 'wæs he … mid gastlicre lufan his heorte innan gefylled' (his heart was filled inwardly with spiritual love); ch. 20 (ibid., 170): 'a wæs swetnys on his mode and snyttro on his breostum' (there was always sweetness in his mind and wisdom in his breast); ch. 20 (ibid., 170): 'him næfre elles on hys muðe næs buton Cristes lof, ne on his heortan butan arfæstnys' (there was never in his mouth anything except praise of Christ, nor in his heart anything except virtue).

112 Ælfric, *CH II* 9, lines 26–8 (ed. Godden, *CH II*, 73): 'He hlod ða mid þurstigum breoste ða flowendan lare. ðe he eft æfter fyrste mid hunigswettre þrotan þæslice bealcette' (With his thirsting breast he absorbed the teaching that flowed forth, which, after the first interval, he poured out again with his honey-sweet throat).

113 Alfred, *Pastoral Care*, ch. 17 (ed. Sweet, *King Alfred's West-Saxon Version of Gregory's Pastoral Care*, 125): 'gif ðara haligra gewrita ondgit bið on ðam breostum ðæs godan recceres … eac sceal bion on ðæm breostum ðæs monnan swetnes' (if the understanding of the Holy Scriptures exists in the breast of the good teacher, likewise there must also be sweetness in that man's breast).

114 *Life of St Guthlac*, ch. 2 (ed. Gonser, *Prosa-Leben*, 112): 'þa wæron þa wæstmberendan breost þæs eadigan weres mid godes gife gefyllede and mid þam lareowdome þæs hean magistres godes' (Then the fruitful breast of the blessed man was filled with the gift of God and with the teaching of God, the celestial schoolmaster).

to refer to the conscience or the moral-deliberative faculty.[115] The homilist of Blickling 2 portrays both mind and heart engaged in prayer when he writes, 'Cleopian we nu in eglum mode ʒ inneweardre heortan'; when lust and wickedness enter the heart, the homilist continues, people become 'on heora mode mid mislicum geþohtum onstyrede, þæt seo stemn þære heortan bið swiþe gedrefed on þæm gebede.'[116] Ælfric attributes to both mind and heart the capacity to 'see' God through faith,[117] and elsewhere he uses the words *mod, heorte,* and *ingehygd* within a single sentence to signify interiority and sincere intention: 'Ac ne cwæð þu na mid wordum þæt þu wylle mildsiæn, and ælcige swaðeah wiðinnæn ðinre heortan; for þan ðe God isihð þin ingehyd swytellice, þeah ðe men nyten hwæt ðu on mode bihydest.'[118] Loosely translating a remark made by Gregory the Great on Mt 7:3, Alfred writes, 'Sio gedrefednes ðære ungeðylde on ðæm mode ðæt is se smala cið, ac se yfela willa on ðære heortan ðæt is se greata beam.'[119] A brief note, dating to the late twelfth century or later, instructs singers to chant their psalms 'swa mycel swa ðu meaht mid inreweardan heortan. na mid efestlican wordan. ac mid geþencendan mode.'[120] Dozens of similar examples pervade the OE prose corpus, on the basis of which Low has

---

115 Assmann homily 13, lines 54–5 (ed. Assmann, 153): 'se feond … his heortan and his modgeðanc innan to ðan lærde and scynde' (the devil persuaded and corrupted his heart and the inner thought of his mind'); lines 167–9 (ibid., 158–9): 'he æghwilcne ænne man sceawað, æghwæðer ge ða dæda utan, ge eac ða heortan and þone modgeðanc innan' (he [*scil.* Jesus] will examine each man individually, both his outward deeds and even the heart and the inner thought of the mind).

116 Blickling homily 2 (ed. Morris, *Blickling Homilies,* 19): 'Now we cry out in our troubled mind and in our inner heart … [they are] stirred up in their mind by wandering thoughts, so that the voice of the heart is sorely disturbed in prayer.'

117 Ælfric, Irvine homily 3, lines 127–9 (ed. Irvine, *Old English Homilies from MS. Bodley 343,* 65): 'Þeo unleaffulnesse is þare heortæ blindnysse, and þe soða geleafa onliht þone mon, þe mæg mid his mode his Scyppend iseon' (Unbelief is blindness of the heart, and the true faith enlightens the man who is able to see his Creator with his mind). See also Ælfric, *Suppl.* 17, lines 121–6 (ed. Pope, *Suppl.* 2.572).

118 Irvine homily 2, lines 181–4 (ed. Irvine, *Old English Homilies from MS. Bodley 343,* 44): 'But do not say with words that you wish to be merciful, and still delay within your heart; because God sees your inward thought clearly, although men do not know what you keep hidden in your mind.'

119 Alfred, *Pastoral Care,* ch. 33 (ed. Sweet, *Pastoral Care,* 225): 'The distraction of impatience in the mind, that is the small mote, but ill will in the heart, that is the massive beam.'

120 'Directions to Recite the Penitential Psalms' in Cambridge, UL, Ii. 1. 33 (ed. Ker, *Catalogue,* 24): 'as much as you are able, with the inward heart – not with hasty words but with thoughtful mind.'

observed that the relationship between mind and heart is one of 'prag-matic synonymy': they are not absolutely identical but can serve equally well in most contexts to signify the entity responsible for thought.[121]

In a sizable minority of instances in which terms for the mind or men-tal activity are collocated with the word *heorte* (and to a lesser extent, the word *breost*), the relationship between them is instead that of the part to the whole: the heart signifies the deepest part of the mind, in a sense that is both spatial and psychological. The heart is the most secluded and protect-ed part of the mind-in-the-breast, a bodily container within a container; its contents are accordingly less likely to be manifested externally, less likely to be known truly by other people, less likely to be muddled by conflicting influences. When the heart is differentiated at all from the mind, therefore, it is usually in order to emphasize that its contents are the most silent, the most permanent, the most inscrutable, or the most sincere of all the contents of the mind. Because the heart can restrain thoughts from being released as speech, 'in the heart' serves as a periphrasis for 'silently.' For example, the translator of the *Seven Sleepers* legend rendered the Latin words 'cogitabat in semetipso dicens' with the OE 'he þohte on his heortan and cwæð to him sylfum,'[122] and similarly, where the Latin *Letter of Alexander to Aristotle* reads 'Sursum, inquit, omnes intuemini et de quibus quisque rebus consul-turus est occulto cogitet silentio, nemo palam pronuntiet,' the OE transla-tor has written, 'lociað nu ealle up ⁊ be swa hwylcum þingum swa ge willon frinan, þence on his heortan deagollice, ⁊ nænig mon his geþoht openum wordum ut ne cyðe.'[123] Depictions of the heart and breast as a protective container for memories foreshadow the MnE idiom of 'learning by heart.' It is said, for instance, of St Nicholas that when he attended church as a

---

121 Low, 'Approaches to Old English Vocabulary for *Mind*,' 17. Low asserts that *mod* and *heorte* are interchangeable names for the 'inner principle,' and she thus includes *sawol* in a relationship of pragmatic synonymy with *mod* and *heorte*, but as I will argue in subsequent chapters, *sawol* and *mod* are pragmatically synonymous in very few OE works outside the writings of Ælfric; even Alfred sometimes maintains a conceptual boundary between them.

122 Latin *Legend of the Seven Sleepers*, line 233 (ed. Magennis, *Seven Sleepers*, 84): 'He was pondering and speaking inwardly to himself.' OE *Legend of the Seven Sleepers*, lines 470–1 (ibid., 48): 'He thought in his heart and spoke to himself.'

123 Latin *Letter of Alexander to Aristotle*, ch. 36 (ed. Orchard, *Pride and Prodigies*, 220): 'Everybody direct your contemplation upward, and let each individual who is going to ask a question ponder these things in hidden silence: nobody should speak out loud.' OE *Letter of Alexander to Aristotle* ch. 36 (ibid., 248): 'Everybody look upward, and think secretly in your heart about whatever you wish to find out, and let no one speak his thought aloud in audible words.'

child, 'swa hwæt swa he þærinne geherde rædan of halgan gewritum, eall he
hit on his heorte behydde ꝼ fæste belaf on his gemynde.'[124] An OE prognos-
tic text offers this advice concerning dreams: 'On syx nihta. þæt þe þonne
þince þæt þu geseo. þæt beo fæst on þinum breostum. wite þæt þin geþanc
ne leose.'[125] Being the most protected part of the mind, the heart also holds
those contents of the mind that are the least susceptible to corruption and
the least accessible to human comprehension. Writing to Wulfstan, Ælfric
alludes to the heart's capacity to protect the mind from corruption: 'we
habban sceolan ures modes clænnysse on ure heortan.'[126] Elsewhere, while
preaching, he alludes to the heart's inscrutability, saying, 'Ne ðam heofen-
lican deman nis nan neod æniges mannes gewitnysse. se ðe þurhsihð ælces
mannes heortan. and gewisslicor wat þæs mannes mod þonne he sylf.'[127]

Mental Heat in the Prose Idiom

In most respects, the nature and behaviour of mental heat in OE prose dif-
fers little from that of OE verse: it is a prominent symptom of acutely aggressive states of mind (anger, cruelty, and illicit desires including lust), of
prolonged intense suffering (sorrow and anxiety), and of energetic en-
thusiasms of a more positive nature (keenness for learning, love for God
and other people). Anger and cruelty, for example, are as likely to burn per
se as they are to set people on fire: the prose translation of Ps 2:13 reads,
'for þæm þonne his yrre byð onæled, þonne beoð eadige þa þe nu on hine
getrywað,'[128] but in Wærferth's translation of the Dialogues, Zalla the
Goth 'abarn ꝼ aweoll mid þy bryne þære unmætestan wælhreownesse,' and
some irritable Lombards become 'swyðlice mid yrre onælde.'[129] Ælfric,

---

124 Life of St Nicholas, lines 55–6 (ed. Treharne, The Old English Life of St Nicholas, 84):
    'Whatever he there heard being read out from Holy Scripture, he stored it all in his
    heart, and it remained firmly in his memory.'
125 Dream lunary, lines 6–7 (ed. Chardonnens, Anglo-Saxon Prognostics, 900–1100, 451):
    'On the sixth night, whatever you think you see at that time, let it be firmly fixed in
    your breast; take care that you do not lose hold of that thought.'
126 Ælfric, First Old English Letter for Wulfstan (Brief II), ch. 31 (ed. Fehr, Die Hirtenbriefe
    Ælfrics, 84): 'In our heart we must hold fast to the purity of our mind.'
127 Ælfric, CH II 39, lines 153–5 (ed. Godden, CH II, 332): 'The heavenly judge has no
    need of the testimony of any man; his sight penetrates the heart of every man, and he
    knows the mind of a man more certainly than the man himself does.'
128 Alfred, Prose Psalter, Ps 2:13 (ed. O'Neill, King Alfred's Old English Prose Translation
    of the First Fifty Psalms, 101): 'Therefore when his anger is kindled, then will they be
    fortunate who now trust in him.'
129 Wærferth, Dialogues 2.31 (ed. Hecht, Bischof Wærferths von Worcester Übersetzung
    der Dialoge Gregors des Grossen, 162): 'burned and seethed with the burning of the

because he conceived of the mind as part of the unitary soul, occasionally suggests that the *sawol* too behaves according to the hydraulic model; in his adaptation of the pseudo-Basilian *Admonitio ad filium spiritalem*, he urges his fellow monks, 'Adræf fram ðinre sawle ælce yfelnysse. and seo hatung ne ontende ðine heortan nates hwon.' Should a monk nonetheless fall prey to anger, Ælfric continues, 'ne læt ðu ðæt yrre licgean on ðinre heortan ofer sunnan setlunge. ac foh to sibbe æror. and adræf ða hatheortnysse fram ðinre sawle hraðe.'[130] It is noteworthy that Ælfric considered it appropriate to employ cardiocentric and hydraulic-model imagery in his narrative and hortatory writings even though he staunchly defended the incorporeality of the unitary soul in his psychological discourses; it bears repeating, however, that the potential conflict between these two concepts of mind would have been observed by very few other OE authors, since most Anglo-Saxons firmly distinguished mind from soul, as demonstrated in chapter 1.

Cardiocentric heat accompanies illicit desires of all kinds. The young widow Galla refuses to remarry because she rejects 'þam hatiendan luste þyses middaneardes,'[131] and Fursey's angelic guide in the afterworld explains that 'Swa swa se lichama bið ontend ðurh unalyfede lustas. swa eac byrnð seo sawul ðurh neadwis wite.'[132] In Wærferth's OE *Dialogues*, the devil sets Benedict aflame with sexual desire by implanting in his mind the vision of a woman: 'mid swa mycclum fyre onælde þam Godes þeowan þæt mod in þæs wifes ansyne, þæt he uneaðe hine sylfne geheold in his agenum breoste for ðam lege þæs wifes lufan.'[133] After Benedict has quenched the fires of

---

most immense ferocity'; *Dialogues* 3.37 (ibid., 250): 'strongly inflamed with anger.' Where Hecht prints two versions of the text in parallel columns, I quote version C, which follows the text of Cambridge, CCC, 322. On the relationship among the versions of the *Dialogues*, see Godden, 'Wærferth and King Alfred: The Fate of the Old English *Dialogues*.'

130 Ælfric, *Admonitio ad filium spiritualem*, ch. 5 (ed. Norman, *The Anglo-Saxon Version of the Hexameron of St. Basil*, 44–6): 'Drive every wickedness from your soul, and do not let enmity [*or* heat] kindle your heart in any way ... do not let that anger linger in your heart past the setting of the sun, but rather resume your friendship and drive the hot-heartedness from your soul immediately.' Perhaps Ælfric has here introduced a hydraulic-model pun on *hatung*, which with a short *a* means 'heat' and with a long *a* means 'enmity,' both of which are fitting in context.

131 Wærferth, *Dialogues* 4.14 (ed. Hecht, *Wærferths Übersetzung*, 279): 'the burning desire for this world.'

132 Ælfric, *CH II* 20, lines 107–8 (ed. Godden, *CH II*, 193): 'Just as the body is inflamed through unlawful desires, so also does the soul burn by means of a fitting punishment.'

133 Wærferth, *Dialogues* 2.2 (ed. Hecht, *Wærferths Übersetzung*, 101): 'Because of the woman's appearance, the mind of God's servant burned with such a great fire that he could scarcely restrain himself in his breast on account of the fire of his love for the woman.'

lust by rolling around in a patch of thorns and nettles, the episode concludes with Gregory's explanation that 'in geogoðhade þæs lichaman costung wealleþ, ⁊ þonne fram þam fiftigoðan geare colað seo hæte þæs lichaman.'[134] The mechanism by which lust arises and is extinguished parallels one aspect of the verse hydraulic-model idiom discussed above: as mental heat increases within the closed container of the breast, it becomes ever more difficult not to allow the contents of the mind to boil up and to escape in the form of shamefully manifest words or actions. In Benedict's case, Gregory later reports that at its peak, sexual desire nearly compelled Benedict to abandon monasticism altogether. But this is a problem that plagues the young: when advanced age diminishes the heat of lust inherent in the body, temptation 'cools' and is less likely to 'seethe' or 'well up,' Gregory teaches.

Although mental heat is most commonly associated with acutely passionate episodes, it can equally accompany chronic forms of suffering. The narrator of the *OE Bede*, for instance, often speaks of the heat of sorrow and anxiety. When Adamnan has had a premonition that the monastery at Coldingham will be destroyed by fire, anticipation of this tragedy sinks him into grief: 'þa geswearc se Godes mon semninga ⁊ ongan hatlice ⁊ biterlice wepan, ⁊ þa unrotnesse his heortan mid his andwlitan tacnunge ypte ⁊ cyðde.'[135] Passionately positive mental states, such as single-minded love for God, also generate heat in the mind-in-the-breast. On his deathbed, St Martin holds 'seo Godes lufu toðæs hat ⁊ toðæs beorht on his heortan,'[136] and Pope Vitalius, writing to Oswiu of Northumbria after his conversion to Christianity, acknowledges the king's newfound 'aarfæstnesse willan ⁊ his hate Godes lufan.'[137] Burning love of another person can be virtuous too, if it grows out of a clearly Christian motivation: Pope Gregory is said to have become 'swiþe mid þære blæsan soþere lufe ontend' for the Anglo-Saxons when he discovered that they were in need of Christianization.[138]

---

134   Wærferth, *Dialogues* 2.2 (ed. Hecht, *Wærferths Übersetzung*, 102): 'In youth the temptation of the body boils up, and then from age fifty the heat of the body cools.'

135   *OE Bede* 4.26 (ed. Miller, 352): 'Then suddenly the man of God darkened and began to weep hotly and bitterly, and the sadness in his heart came forth and made itself manifest in visible form on his face.'

136   Blickling homily 18 (ed. Morris, *Blickling Homilies*, 225): 'love for God so hot and so bright in his heart.' See also *Life of St Guthlac*, ch. 2, lines 72–3 and 90–1 (ed. Gonser, *Prosa-Leben*, 110–11).

137   *OE Bede* 3.21 (ed. Miller, 248): 'desire for virtue and his heated love of God.'

138   Æthelwold of Winchester, 'An Account of King Edgar's Establishment of Monasteries' (ed. Whitelock et al., *Councils and Synods* I/1.144): 'strongly inflamed with the blaze of true love.'

Hatheortnes in the Prose Hydraulic Model

The noun *hatheortnes* and the adjective *hatheort*, which rarely occur in verse,[139] signify something more than the sum of their parts, because they are not wholly interchangeable with other representations of cardiocentric heat. That is, to be *hatheort* is not the same as being *hat æt heortan*, a condition that accompanies both destructive and virtuous passions in the verse corpus. *Hatheortnes* sometimes appears to be nothing more than an intense manifestation of or inclination toward anger; in the OE *Life of Machutus*, for instance, Redwala is characterized as 'mid hatheortnesse onæled. ⁊ mid gedrefdum gaste. ⁊ yrsiendum mode,'[140] and in a close translation of Gregory's *Pastoral Care*, Alfred says of the ideal teacher that 'he swa stiere ðæm ungeðyldegum irsunga, swa he ðone hnescan ðafettere on recceleste ne gebrenge; ⁊ ðeah swa tilige hi to onælenne, swa hi ða hatheortan ne forbærnen.'[141] However, *hatheortnes* need not be associated with anger at all; in translations and glosses it commonly renders *iracundia*, *furor*, and *zelus*, and the glossator of the Eadwine Psalter translates Latin *zelus* with the doublet *hatheortnesse uel wodnesse*.[142] Drunkenness may stimulate *hatheortnes*, according to an OE gloss on the *Liber scintillarum* that reads 'druncennyss soðlice gedrefednysse cenð geþances hatheortnysse heortan lig galnysse.'[143] *Hatheortnes* in turn aggravates other vices, not limited to anger: in Blickling 5 the homilist discusses the loss of sexual appetite in persons approaching old age: 'eal se lichoma geunlustaþ þa

---

139 The noun *hatheortnes* occurs once in the *Metres of Boethius* (25.47), which takes over a great deal of prose diction from the prose *OE Boethius*; the corresponding passage in the prose is discussed below. The adjective *hatheort* appears once in *The Wanderer*, line 66, in a list of temperamental traits that the wise man possesses only in moderation, such as readiness to boast, desire for wealth, hesitation to do battle, boldness. On this passage and other examples of moderation as a heroic ideal, see Gwara, '*Forht* and *fægen* in *The Wanderer* and Related Literary Contexts of Anglo-Saxon Warrior Wisdom.'

140 *Life of Machutus* (ed. Yerkes, *The Old English Life of Machutus*, 65, lines 17–18): 'set on fire with hot-heartedness and with an agitated spirit and impassioned mind.'

141 Alfred, *Pastoral Care*, ch. 60 (ed. Sweet, *Pastoral Care*, 453): 'he should rein in the irascibility of the impatient man in such a way that he does not lead the mild and pliable man into negligence, and yet he should strive to inflame them in such a way that the hot-hearted do not burn destructively.'

142 Ps 68:10 in the Eadwine Psalter (ed. Harsley, *Eadwine's Canterbury Psalter*, 116): 'hot-heartedness or insanity.'

143 *OE Liber scintillarum*, ch. 28 (ed. Rhodes, *Defensor's* Liber scintillarum, 106): 'Drunkenness truly spawns agitation of the thought, hot-heartedness of the heart, the flame of desire.' Defensor's source for the Latin text is Isidore of Seville, *Sententiae* 2.43.1.

geogoðlustas to fremmenne þa þe he ær hatheortlice lufode, ⁊ him swete
wæron to aræfnenne ... Hwær bið la þonne se idla lust, ⁊ seo swetnes þæs
hæmedþinges þe he ær hatheortlice lufode?'¹⁴⁴ Clearly this man's hot-
heartedness is associated with immoderate desire, not with anger.

Immoderation, in fact, is the essence of *hatheortnes*; it adds a dimension of danger and sinfulness to any other passion to which it is attached.
Accordingly, though prose diction allows for Christian love to be *hat on
heortan*,¹⁴⁵ *hatheortnes* does not fuel Christian love. Acts that may be done
in moderation or in love are at risk of being undermined or perverted by
hatheortnes: the narrator of the *OE Bede* observes that 'þeah ðe þæt wiite
hwene heardor ⁊ strongor don sy, þonne is hit of lufan to donne, nales of
welme ne of hatheortnesse.'¹⁴⁶ The homilist of Vercelli 4 even names 'the
hot-hearted' among the classes of sinners who are destined for hell: 'Þær
sculon bion þa þe ic ær nemde, ⁊ þa niðigan ⁊ þa æfstigan ⁊ þa yðbylgean ⁊
þa hatheortan ⁊ þa gramhydigan ⁊ þa struderas ⁊ þa þeofas ⁊ þa manswaran
⁊ þa leogeras ⁊ þa gytseras.'¹⁴⁷ Within the framework of the hydraulic model, therefore, *hatheortnes* seems to be a particularly heightened cardiocentric heat energy that fuels ordinary irrationalities to the point where they
are beyond an individual's control; unlike other forms of cardiocentric
heat, *hatheortnes* always carries a threatening connotation. Note also that
the Vercelli 4 homilist also mentions, right before the *hatheortan*, a group
of sinners called the *yðbylgean*, the irritable or 'easily swollen.' This is one
of three occasions in this homily when the vice of *hatheortnes* is paired
with the related vice of *gebelge*, which is irritability or 'swollenness.'¹⁴⁸

---

144 Blickling homily 5 (ed. Morris, *Blickling Homilies*, 59): 'His whole body loathed to act
     upon the youthful lusts that he once had loved hot-heartedly and that had been sweet
     for him to contemplate ... Where then is the vain lust, and the sweetness of sexual
     intercourse, which he once loved hot-heartedly?'
145 *Life of St Guthlac*, ch. 2 (ed. Gonser, *Prosa-Leben*, 111): 'he wæs geþyldig and ead-
     mod; and a seo godcunde lufu on hys heortan hat and byrnende' (He was patient and
     obedient, and always that divine love was hot and burning in his heart). See also
     Blickling homily 18 (ed. Morris, *Blickling Homilies*, 225), quoted above.
146 *OE Bede* 1.16 (ed. Miller, 68): 'Even though that punishment may be carried out
     somewhat more stringently and forcefully, it is to be given in love, not at all in seeth-
     ing and hot-heartedness.'
147 Vercelli homily 4, lines 48–51 (ed. Scragg, *The Vercelli Homilies and Related Texts*, 92):
     'Those whom I named earlier will be in hell, as well as the malicious and the envious
     and those who are easily swollen with rage and the hot-hearted and the cruel and rob-
     bers and criminals and perjurers and liars and misers.'
148 Vercelli homily 4, lines 138–9 and 310–11 (ed. Scragg, *Vercelli Homilies*, 96 and 102–3);
     see also the *OE Vision of St Paul*, lines 61–7 (ed. Healey, *The Old English Vision of
     St Paul*, 67).

The foregoing passage from the *OE Bede*, too, pairs *hatheortnes* with *wylm*, another word suggesting the mental seething that follows naturally upon the heating of the mind in *hatheortnes*. Although the condition of *hatheortnes* is not identical to the state of being *hat æt heortan*, the concept of *hatheortnes* is no less a part of the hydraulic model than the less dangerous forms of cardiocentric heat.

From Cardiocentric Heat to Seething and Swelling

As in verse, words from the *weallan/wylm* family are prominent in OE prose depictions of the mental seething and boiling up that result from intense cardiocentric heat. Seething may accompany vicious states of mind such as anger and the vindictiveness that is born of frustration: for instance, when St Alban refuses the judge's order to sacrifice to idols, the judge becomes 'mid miclum wylme ⁊ yrre onstyred';[149] and one glossator of Prv 19:3 writes that when a man is tripped up by his own foolishness, then 'ongean god he weald on mode.'[150] Alfred praises the man who 'forbygð ðone wielm ⁊ ðone onræs his hatheortnesse,' and Wærferth characterizes the cruel Goth named Zalla as 'mid weallendum geþohte ⁊ mid unwittignysse þæs þweoran modes.'[151] Unlike *hatheortnes*, however, the mental seething signified by *weallan* and *wylm* is not uniformly vicious. In the OE *Pastoral Care*, Alfred observes that 'Oft eac ða grambæran wenað ðæt hiera undeaw sie sumes ryhtwislices andan wielm,' and soon thereafter he advises, 'Ne bið se no gefylled ðæs Halgan Gæsðæs se ðe on ðære smyltnesse his monðwærnesse forlæt ðone wielm ryhtwislices andan, oðða eft on ðæm wielme ðæs andan forlæt ðone cræft ðære monnðwærnesse.'[152] According to Alfred's words, the seething of an impassioned state of mind such as *anda* 'violent emotion'[153] may be justified and even 'righteous' – and not only from the seething person's point of

---

149 *OE Bede* 1.7 (ed. Miller, 36): 'stirred up by great seething and anger.'

150 *OE Liber scintillarum*, ch. 24 (ed. Rhodes, *Defensor's* Liber scintillarum, 95): 'against God he seethes in his mind.'

151 Alfred, *Pastoral Care*, ch. 40 (ed. Sweet, *Pastoral Care*, 297): 'turns away from the seething and the onrush of his hot-heartedness.' Wærferth, *Dialogues* 2.31 (ed. Hecht, *Wærferths Übersetzung*, 163): 'with seething thoughts and with irrationality in his depraved mind.'

152 Alfred, *Pastoral Care*, ch. 40 (ed. Sweet, *Pastoral Care*, 289 and 291): 'Often even the irascible man believes that his vice is the boiling over of some justifiable anger … He is not filled with the Holy Spirit who, in the tranquillity of his meekness, ignores the welling up of righteous anger, or again in the welling up of anger neglects the power of meekness.'

153 See *DOE*, s.v. *anda*, for uses that signify both virtuous and vicious types of intense emotion.

view. Mental seething can also be fuelled by passionate displays of virtue, including Christian love and the love of learning. According to the OE *Rule of Benedict*, there are good and evil manifestations of *anda*, and as soon as monks turn away from the evil one, 'þysene oþerne mid hatan wylme soðre lufe geornlice began.'[154] Likewise, in the story of the monk Antonius, his desire for Christian wisdom causes him to seethe inwardly: 'þa þa he swiðe geornlice ˥ mid mycclum wylme his lustes smeade þa halgan spræca godcundra boca, ne sohte he na in þam swa swyþe snyttru ˥ wisdomes word, swa he sohte dædbote ˥ inbryrdnesse wop, to ðon þæt þurh þa onwæcenesse his mod aburne.'[155]

In contrast to the *weallan/wylm* family of words, which can signify the energetic seething of both positive and negative mental states, the verb *belgan* and its relatives signify only the mental swelling associated with anger and aggression: as the Blickling 3 homilist explains, 'gif us hwa abylgþ, þonne beo we sona yrre, ˥ willaþ þæt gewrecan gif we magon.'[156] Swelling is variously predicated of the individual and the mind: Ælfric writes, for instance, 'Þa gebealh hine se cynincg and to his bedde eode. wende hine to wage wodlice gebolgen,'[157] but in the *OE Orosius*, when a river sweeps away one of Cyrus's best men, then the narrator reports that 'Ða gebeotode Cirus ðæt he his þegn on hire swa gewrecan wolde, þa he swa grom wearð on his mode ˥ wiþ þa ea gebolgen.'[158] The exclusively vicious character of the swelling denoted by the *belgan* family of words is underscored by the homiletic passages discussed above, in which those who are

---

154 Æthelwold of Winchester, OE *Rule of Benedict*, ch. 72 (ed. Schröer, *Die angelsächsischen Prosabearbeitungen der Benediktinerregel*, 131): 'They eagerly undertake this other [*scil.* the good zeal] with the hot welling up of true love.' See also Ælfric, *CH II* 9, lines 176–8 (ed. Godden, *CH II*, 77); and Napier homily 55 (ed. Napier, 286, lines 9–12).

155 Wærferth, *Dialogues* 4.49 (ed. Hecht, *Wærferths Übersetzung*, 337): 'when he, very eagerly and with a great boiling of desire, studied the holy speech of divine books, he did not so much seek there great insight and words of wisdom as he sought reparation for sins and weeping from contrition, to the extent that through that attentiveness his mind was set on fire.'

156 Blickling homily 3 (ed. Morris, *Blickling Homilies*, 33): 'If anything makes us swollen, then we are instantly angry, and we wish to be avenged on it, if we are able.'

157 Ælfric, *LS* 18, lines 178–9 (ed. Skeat, *LS* 1.394): 'Then the king swelled up and went to bed; he turned to face the wall, insanely swollen.' See also Wærferth, *Dialogues* 1.2 (ed. Hecht, *Wærferths Übersetzung*, 20, lines 22–6).

158 OE *Orosius* 2.4 (ed. Bately, *OE Orosius*, 43): 'When Cyrus boasted that he would thus take vengeance on that river on behalf of his thegn, then he became exceedingly cruel in his mind and swollen with rage against the river.' See also Ælfric, *CH I* 29, line 58 (ed. Clemoes, *CH I*, 420).

yðbylge 'easily swollen' are listed alongside the *hatheorte* and other classes of sinners in hell. Accordingly, the homilist of Vercelli 10 exhorts his audience, 'ne to yðbylge ne syn we, ne to langsum yrre næbben we.'[159]

Constriction of Mind

In prose as in verse, the distressed mind-in-the-breast may be subject to constriction, characterized either according to spatial disposition, as narrowness, or according to sensation, as pressure or heaviness. The Anglo-Saxons used the words *ang* and *nearu*, both meaning 'narrow,' along with some of their related compounds, to signify both psychological constriction and external, visible spatial narrowness. Perhaps unlike the words of the *belgan* family, therefore, *ang* and *nearu* and their relatives unquestionably retained some sense of spatial narrowness when used in psychological contexts. Although constriction always signifies distress rather than positive mental energies, the forms of distress that can produce constriction are more diverse than the limited forms of aggression associated with *belgan*. For instance, the *Letter from Alexander to Aristotle* employs words in the *nearu*-family to signify grave anxiety and grief. When the hostile terrain makes it impossible for Alexander to provide water to his men or his beasts, he explains to Aristotle, 'Þa wæs ic swiðe on minum mode generwed for ðæm dumbum nytenum, for þon ic wiste þæt men yþelicor meahton þone þurst arefnan þonne þa nietenu.'[160] Subsequently, he alarms his companions by refusing food after he hears prophesied his own betrayal and death; in Alexander's words, 'þa bædon mec mine geferan þæt ic on swa micelre modes unreto ⁊ nearonisse mec selfne mid fæstenne ne swencte.'[161] Similarly, according to Alfred's *Pastoral Care*, when Moses asks his kinsman Hobab to be the Israelites' guide through the desert, he makes this request for Hobab's own benefit, not because Moses himself was constricted by anxieties about their journey through dangerous and unknown territory: 'Ne

---

159 Vercelli homily 10, lines 51–2 (ed. Scragg, *Vercelli Homilies*, 198): 'let us not be too easily swollen, nor let us hold onto our anger too long.'

160 OE *Letter of Alexander to Aristotle*, ch. 13 (ed. Orchard, *Pride and Prodigies*, 232): 'Then I was sorely constricted in my mind on behalf of the dumb beasts, because I knew that men could more easily endure that thirst than could the beasts.'

161 OE *Letter of Alexander to Aristotle*, ch. 38 (ed. Orchard, *Pride and Prodigies*, 250): 'But my companions begged me not to torment myself with fasting in such great sadness and narrowness of mind.' See also Alfred, *Pastoral Care*, ch. 34 (ed. Sweet, *Pastoral Care*, 231), where the envious man is characterized as one who 'bið genierwed on his mode' (is constricted in his mind) when he witnesses someone else's good fortune.

spræc he hit no forðyðe his mod auht genierwed wære mid ðære uncyððe
ðæs siðfætes, forðæm hit wæs geweorðad mid ðæm andgiete godcundes
wisdomes, ⁊ wæs him self witga.'¹⁶²

The adjective *ang* and its relatives are equally flexible in signifying cardiocentric constriction arising from multiple and non-specific forms of distress.
According to Ælfric, a blind man who longs to be healed by St Swithun
prays to the saint 'mid innewerdre heortan, and mid angsumnysse,'¹⁶³ and
during the siege of Jerusalem, the inhabitants' starvation is so severe that
'Sume hi cuwon heora gescy. sume heora hætera. sume streow for þære
micclan angsumnysse þæs hatan hungres.'¹⁶⁴ In the anonymous OE *Life of
St Neot*, the saint comforts King Alfred, saying, 'Ac þonne þe ealre ang-
sumest byð on þine mode, geðænc þu min, ⁊ ic þe gescilde on Drihtenes
name.'¹⁶⁵ A text on dream-interpretation prognosticates that 'Gif him þince
þæt he on blacan horse ride þæt biþ his modes angnes.'¹⁶⁶ Constriction can
even be predicated of the heart itself, as in several glosses on Ps 60:3 which
read, 'to þe cleopode þaþa angud wearþ heorte min.'¹⁶⁷

The phenomenon of cardiocentric constriction, when characterized from
the perspective of sensory perceptions within the breast, exerts pressure
upon the organs of the chest cavity: consequently, mental constriction is also
called *hefignes* 'heaviness' in many prose texts. In the OE *Dialogues*, Gregory laments that he himself is 'geswænced mid hefigum sare minre heortan,'

162 Alfred, *Pastoral Care*, ch. 41 (ed. Sweet, *Pastoral Care*, 304): 'He spoke these words not
   because his mind was at all constricted by lack of knowledge of the journey – for it was
   endowed with the understanding of divine wisdom, and he himself was a prophet.'
163 Ælfric, *Life of St Swithun* (*LS* 21), line 208 (ed. Skeat, *LS*, 1.454): 'with his inner heart,
   and with anguish [*literally* narrowness].'
164 Ælfric, *CH I* 28, lines 47–9 (ed. Clemoes, *CH I*, 411): 'Some people gnawed on their
   shoes, and some on their garments, some on straw because of the enormous constriction of that hot hunger.'
165 *Life of St Neot* (ed. Warner, *Early English Homilies from the Twelfth Century MS.
   Vesp. D. XIV*, 131–2): 'But when it is the most constricted of all in your mind, think
   of me, and I will protect you in the name of the Lord.' See also the OE *Legend of the
   Seven Sleepers*, lines 222–3 (ed. Magennis, *Seven Sleepers*, 40): 'angmode geomrodon
   ealle heora heortan' (with constricted minds they all mourned in their hearts); and
   Æthelwold, OE *Rule of Benedict*, ch. 64 (ed. Schröer, *Die angelsächsischen Prosabearbeitungen der Benediktinerregel*, 120), which recommends that the ideal candidate for
   abbot be free from constriction of mind: 'Ne beo he drefende ne angmod' (He should
   be neither prone to agitation nor constricted in mind).
166 Dreambook, line 72 (ed. Chardonnens, *Anglo-Saxon Prognostics, 900–1100*, 299): 'If it
   seems to the dreamer that he rides on a pale horse, that signifies constriction of his mind.'
167 Gloss on Ps 60:3 in the Arundel Psalter (ed. Oess, *Der altenglische Arundel-Psalter*,
   106): 'To you I cried out when my heart was constricted.' The Latin text reads 'ad te
   clamaui dum anxiaretur cor meum.'

and the cruel Lombards are 'inælede mid hefigum yrre' when they martyr their Christian prisoners.[168] In the *Pastoral Care*, Alfred explains that a persistent and incorrigible sin is one 'ðætte hira modes innað yfele ⁊ hefiglice mid gefylled wæs.'[169] Like mental narrowness, mental heaviness can never result from virtuous forms of cardiocentric heat and seething; Wisdom implies as much when he asks Boethius the rhetorical question, 'Hu ne witon we þæt nan nearanes ne nan earfoðu ne nan unrotnes ne nan sar ne nan hefignes nis nan gesælð?'[170] Since mental heaviness is necessarily undesirable and detrimental, Ælfric forecasts that this condition will be altogether absent from heaven: 'Ælc man mæg ðær geseon oðres mannes geðoht, ne him næfre ne hingrað, ne hefigmod ne bið, ne him ðurst ne derað.'[171] As the verse *Genesis A* and *Genesis B* employed images of expansion and contraction to signify intellectual enlightenment and impairment *without* cardiocentric heat and seething, so does Alfred's prose maintain that heaviness alone, without other symptoms, can severely impair the mind's rational and verbal faculties: 'Oft ðonne ðæt hefige mod glit niðor ⁊ niðor stæpmælum on unnyttum wordum, oð hit mid ealle afielð, ⁊ to nauhte wirð.'[172] Yet unlike the mental constriction of the OE verse idiom, the mental heaviness of the OE prose idiom is not irrevocably associated with a sinful or dangerous loss of self-control, as an episode from the *Dialogues* demonstrates. When labourers rebuilding a church run out of bread during a famine, a miracle eventually replenishes their food supply; before the miracle is wrought, however, the holy man Sanctulus is 'heavily constricted inside' but nonetheless able to control his outward demeanour and offer encouragement: 'he frefrode hi mid luflicum wordum ⁊ heom geheht utan mid his muðe, þæt he him sylf næfde; ac he wæs swiðe hefiglice genyrwed innon, forþon þe he ne mihte begytan þone mete, þe he þam wyrhtum gehet.'[173] Finally, an episode in the

---

168 Wærferth, *Dialogues*, preface (ed. Hecht, *Wærferths Übersetzung*, 3): 'oppressed by a heavy sorrow on my heart'; *Dialogues* 3.28 (ibid., 233): 'set on fire with oppressive anger.'

169 Alfred, *Pastoral Care*, ch. 54 (ed. Sweet, *Pastoral Care*, 419): 'with which the bowels of the mind were sorely and oppressively full.'

170 Alfred, *OE Boethius*, B-text, ch. 24, lines 113–14 (ed. Godden and Irvine, 1.292): 'How can we be unaware that neither constriction nor hardship nor unhappiness nor injury nor heaviness is a blessing?'

171 Ælfric, *Suppl.* 11, lines 558–60 (ed. Pope, *Suppl.*, 1.446): 'Every man there can see the thoughts of another, and he never hungers nor is heavy-minded, nor does thirst torment him.'

172 Alfred, *Pastoral Care*, ch. 38 (ed. Sweet, *Pastoral Care*, 279): 'Then the heavy mind often slips gradually lower and lower in useless words, until it falls down entirely and comes to nothing.'

173 Wærferth, *Dialogues*, 3.37 (ed. Hecht, *Wærferths Übersetzung*, 251): 'he comforted them with loving words and outwardly promised them with his mouth that which he

prose *Life of Guthlac* accentuates the cardiocentrism of psychological constriction: when the saint's sister Pega finds out that Guthlac has died, 'heo
þa sona on eorðan feoll and mid mycelre hefignysse gefylled wearð, þæt heo
word gecweþan ne mihte. Mid þan heo þa eft hig gehyrte, heo þa of þam
breostum inneweardum lange sworetunge teah.'[174] The heaviness that Pega's
grief brings upon her breast is at first so intense that it impairs her faculty
of speech, but as soon as she recovers her consciousness – the words *heo hig
gehyrte* literally mean 'she heartened herself' – a sigh or a sob is expelled
from within her oppressed breast, and after that she is able to speak again.

Complex Hydraulic-Model Narratives Generated by OE Translators

The prose passages examined thus far exemplify individual symptoms of
mental activity, but as in verse, the hydraulic model in prose is a coherent
(though not rigidly consistent) system of describing mental activity, in
which one symptom follows upon another as the laws of nature dictate. To
illustrate this coherence, I have selected prose passages that not only adduce multiple hydraulic-model symptoms but also exceed, in quantity and
quality, the hydraulic-model imagery present in their Latin source texts.
Consider how the narrator of the *OE Bede* accounts for the changing
mental states of Eadwine, the future king of Northumbria, when he has
just been warned that his protector King Rædwald intends to betray him:

> he Eadwini ... sæt swiðe unrot on stane beforan þære healle, ꝼ ongon mid
> monegum hætum his geþohta swenced beon: ꝼ ne wiste, hwider he eode oðþe
> hwæt him selest to donne wære. Þa he þa longe mid[175] swigendum nearo-
> nissum his modes ꝼ mid þy blindan fyre soden wæs, þa geseah he semninga on
> midre niht sumne mon.[176]

---

did not possess; but on the inside he was very heavily constricted, because he was unable to obtain the food that he had promised to the builders.'
174 *Life of St Guthlac*, ch. 20 (ed. Gonser, *Prosa-Leben*, 167): 'then she immediately fell to the
ground and was filled up with a great heaviness, to the extent that she could not speak a
word. When she was revived, she drew out from within her breast a prolonged sob.'
175 At the words *Þa he þa longe mid* I follow the reading of Cambridge, Corpus Christi
College, MS 41, which Miller records in a separate volume (3.121), because the reading
preserved in Miller's base text (Oxford, Bodleian Library, Tanner 10) is syntactically
problematic.
176 *OE Bede* 2.9 (ed. Miller, 128): 'Very unhappy, Eadwine sat on a stone in front of the
hall, and he began to be oppressed by the manifold heat of his thoughts, and he did not

Though the corresponding passage of Bede's Latin text already adduces elements of the hydraulic model, the translator's modifications enrich these elements significantly. Bede reports that Eadwine 'is troubled by the manifold heat of the thoughts' (multis … cogitationum aestibus affici), but where Bede says Eadwine is 'troubled,' the OE translator says he is weighed down or oppressed, using the participle *geswenced* that is so commonly collocated with the words *hefig* and *hefignes*. Bede's Latin also mentions Eadwine's 'constrictions of mind and inward fire' (mentis angoribus et caeco … igni), but where Bede says that Eadwine was 'seized' or 'devoured' (*carperetur*) by these forces, the OE translator writes that Eadwine was 'cooked' or 'stewed,' using the word *soden*, which is the past participle of the verb *seoðan* discussed above.[177]

The translator of the *OE Bede* has elaborated upon the hydraulic-model imagery he found already present in his Latin source, but in translating the *OE Boethius*, Alfred went further and inserted an elaborate hydraulic-model narrative where Boethius's Latin *De consolatione philosophiae* has none. In the Latin, Philosophia concisely explains that those who are superficially the most powerful and wealthy suffer from other insidious psychological afflictions:

hinc enim libido uersat auidis corda uenenis,
hinc flagellat ira mentem fluctus turbida tollens,
maeror aut captus fatigat aut spes lubrica torquet.[178]

Despite the mixing of metaphors, this cluster of images lends urgency to what might otherwise be a fairly dry, moralizing observation: immoderate desire leads to further psychological disorder. The OE prose rendering of this passage is much longer than the original and also more cohesive with respect to its imagery:

---

know where he should go or what would be best for him to do. Then when he had for a long time been stewed in the silent constrictions of his mind and by the inward fire, then suddenly in the middle of the night he spied a certain man.'

177 For the full text of the Latin passage, see Bede, *Historia ecclesiastica* 2.12 (ed. Colgrave and Mynors, *Bede's Ecclesiastical History*, 178); the editors point out that the words *caeco carperetur igni* echo Vergil, *Aeneid* 4.2.

178 Boethius, *Cons.* 4 m. 2, lines 6–8 (ed. Bieler, CCSL 94, 70): 'For here desire overthrows the heart with avaricious poisons; here roiling anger brings on surges that batter the mind, which is worn down by repressed sorrow or tormented by slippery hope.'

> Forþam of þam unmette and þam ungemetlican gegerelan, of þam swetmettum and of misclicum dryncum þæs liþes onwæcnað sio wode þrag þære wrænnesse and gedrefð hiora mod swiðe swiðlice. Þonne weaxað eac þa ofermetta and ungeþwærnes, and þonne hi weorðað gebolgen þonne wyrð þæt mod beswungen mid þam welme þære hatheortnesse oððæt hi weorþað geræpte mid þære unrotnesse and swa gehæfte.[179]

Alfred has omitted the metaphors pertaining to poison and slipperiness that appear in the Latin, and he has consolidated the remaining images into a coherent mechanism, in which the mind, directly affected by what is put into and onto the body, warms and expands under the influence of psychological distress, culminating in the 'constrained' (*geræpte*) and 'bound' (*gehæfte*) condition of the distressed individuals.

Mental Cooling

When strong desires and emotions dissipate, so does their heat energy. Mental cooling, therefore, is a favourable condition if it results from the dissipation of illicit desires. According to the teaching that the *OE Bede* attributes to Pope Gregory, 'nemne ær þæt fyr þære unrehtan willunge from þam mode acolie, ne sceal he hine wyrðne telgan broðra ⁊ Godes þeowa gesomnunge, seðe hine gesiið hefigadne beon þurh yfelnesse unrehtes willan.'[180] Note also that as long as these desires are still hot, the wicked man suffers not only heat but also constriction, as he is 'weighed down' by his desires.

---

179 Alfred, *OE Boethius*, B-text, ch. 37, lines 15–21 (ed. Godden and Irvine, 1.346): 'Therefore because of extravagance and immoderate dress, because of sweetmeats and wines of all kinds, there arises an insane moment of wantonness that agitates their mind very powerfully. Then excess and impatience increase too, and when they [*scil.* excess and impatience] grow swollen, then the mind is battered by the boiling up of hot-heartedness, until these men become constrained by their distress and are thus imprisoned.'

180 *OE Bede* 1.16 (ed. Miller, 80): 'Unless that fire of wicked desire first cools in the mind, he who realizes that he is oppressed by the wickedness of improper desire must not consider himself worthy of his brothers and the gathering of God's servants.' See also Wærferth, *Dialogues*, 2.2 (ed. Hecht, *Wærferths Übersetzung*, 102), quoted above, in which Gregory teaches Peter that 'fram þam fiftigoðan geare colað seo hæte þæs lichaman'; and the OE *Liber scintillarum*, ch. 21 (ed. Rhodes, *Defensor's* Liber scintillarum, 87), according to which sexual desire 'butan clænum hlafe ⁊ wine acolað' (cools off without refined bread and wine). The ultimate source of Defensor's Latin text here is Terence, *Eunuchus* 732, as quoted in Jerome's *ep.* 54.

However, mental cooling in OE prose more frequently marks the dissipation of the heat that fuels passionately virtuous behaviours, and therefore mental tepidity was strenuously to be avoided. There survives a hymn, glossed in OE, in which the supplicants pray that 'sloth of the heart not abide' (ne slæwþ onwunige heortena) and that sins not 'cool the burning of the spirit' (acolige bryne gastes).[181] A number of OE texts communicate an abiding anxiety over psychological tepidity because it threatened an individual's ability to persevere in monastic obedience, in learning to read, in Christian charity, and even in the faith itself. According to an OE version of the *Rule of Benedict*, monks who desire to live as hermits are suspect figures, because without the support of the community they are especially prone to mental tepidity: 'hi mid ungesceade on þam frumwylme heora gecyrrednesse hy sylfe fulfremede taliaþ, ac hy swiþe recene awlaciaþ and swindende acoliaþ, þonne hy þa ealdan unðeawas and leahtras ascunian nellaþ … ne heora ealdra gebodum hyrsumian nellaþ, forþi ansetles wununge geceosaþ.'[182] Their conversion to the monastic order is called *frumwylm*, literally the 'original boiling up'; when this boiling fervour subsides and the monks grow spiritually cold, their tepid minds cannot sustain their virtuous intentions. Ælfric likewise worried about his fellow-monks' vulnerability to mental cooling in the arena of intellectual development. '[S]e ðe naðor nele ne leornjan ne tæcan, gif he mæg, þonne acolað his andgyt fram ðære halgan lare, and he gewit swa lytlum and lytlum fram gode,' says Ælfric in the introduction to his *Grammar*; 'is nu for ði godes þeowum and mynstermannum georne to warnigenne, þæt seo halige lar on urum dagum ne acolige oððe ateorige, swaswa hit wæs gedon on Angelcynne nu for anum feawum gearum.'[183] In the *Pastoral Care*, Alfred voices an anxiety that the hearts of spiritual

---

181 OE gloss on the hymn *Tu trinitatis unitas*, 4.1–4 (ed. Milfull, *The Hymns of the Anglo-Saxon Church*, 165).

182 'Be muneca cynne,' an addition to Æthelwold's OE *Rule of Benedict* (ed. Schröer, *Die angelsächsischen Prosabearbeitungen der Benediktinerregel*, 135): 'unreasonably, in the first welling up of their conversion, they think themselves perfect, but they very quickly cool down and, languishing, they grow cold, because they do not want to put away the old vices and sins … and they do not want to be obedient to the commands of their elders; therefore they choose a hermit's dwelling.'

183 Ælfric, *Grammar*, Preface (ed. Zupitza, *Ælfrics Grammatik und Glossar*, 3): 'If a man who is able wishes neither to learn nor to teach, then his understanding will cool in the absence of holy teaching, and in the absence of God he thus knows progressively less … Now the servants and monks of God must urgently take care that that holy teaching not cool off or dissipate in our day, as happened in England just a few years ago.'

leaders, if laden with worldly responsibilities, will grow cool in their love for God: 'forðæm oft ða heortan ðara reccera, sua sua we ær cuædon, ðonne hie mid ðissum hwilendlicum ðingum hie selfe abisegiað, ꝼ ðæm unwærlice ðiowiað, hi ðonne lætað acolian ða innecundan lufan.'[184] Even the heat of faith is susceptible to cooling: according to an anonymous homily on St Paulinus, when King Eadwine of Northumbria is killed, 'se cristendom mid Norðhembrum acolade swiðor þanne hi beþorfton.'[185] The homilist of Napier 50 likewise bemoans the fact that since the age of the early Christian martyrs, 'wearð se soða geleafa swiðe acolad þurh deoflice gedwolmen.'[186]

Mental Roominess

Although in the prose idiom a spacious mind and a roomy heart are signs of good spiritual health and increased mental perception, I have found no clear evidence that this roominess explicitly represents a relief from hydraulic-model symptoms of heat and constriction. In the prose corpus, *rummod* and *rumheort* and related compounds almost invariably denote generosity and liberality, except where they are used to translate the phrase *dilatato corde* 'with expanded heart' and similar expressions that are characteristic of Old Testament diction. For instance, several OE glosses on Ps 118:32 render the words 'dilatasti cor meum' as 'tobræddest heortan min,'[187] and where the Latin *Rule of Benedict* reads 'dilatato corde inenarrabili dilectionis dulcedine curritur uia mandatorum Dei,' the OE translator writes, 'he is us þeah to gefarenne mid rumheortum mode and mid godum and glædum geþance and mid gefyllednesse Godes geboda.'[188]

---

184 Alfred, *Pastoral Care*, ch. 18 (ed. Sweet, *Pastoral Care*, 139): 'as we said before, the hearts of rectors often allow their inner love to cool off when they occupy themselves with temporal things and devote themselves thereto without due caution.'

185 Homily on St Paulinus, lines 9–10 (ed. Sisam, 'MSS. Bodley 340 and 342: Ælfric's *Catholic Homilies*,' 151): 'Christianity among the Northumbrians cooled more markedly than was desirable for them.'

186 Napier homily 50 (ed. Napier, 270, lines 1–2): 'the true faith grew very chilled because of devilish heretics.'

187 Gloss on Ps 118:32 in the Arundel Psalter (ed. Oess, *Der altenglische Arundel-Psalter*, 195): 'Thou didst enlarge my heart.'

188 Æthelwold, OE *Rule of Benedict*, Prologue (ed. Schröer, *Die angelsächsischen Prosabearbeitungen der Benediktinerregel*, 5): 'we must nevertheless journey with roomy-hearted mind, with good and happy thoughts, in the fulfilment of God's commands.'

The most notable instance of mental expansion in OE prose occurs in the second book of Wærferth's translation of Gregory's *Dialogues*, when St Benedict experiences a miraculous vision. In this account, the occurrence and the content of the vision are explained as the result of the expansion of Benedict's mind. First he sees the whole world gathered into a single ray of light, and then he watches as the soul of Germanus of Capua is taken up to heaven in the form of a fiery ball. Gregory's interlocutor Peter asks how Benedict could possibly have seen the entire world at once, and Gregory patiently explains how spatial transformations in the soul and mind make it possible:

þeah þe heo [*scil.* seo sawl] lytles hwæt geseo of þam leohte þæs scyppendes, hire þynceð sceort eall þæt þær gesceapen byþ, forþon þe in þam leohte þære incundan gesihþe þæs modes sceat byð toleoðod ⁊ swa swiðe byð tobræded ⁊ aþened in Gode sylfum, þæt hit byþ ufor eallum middanearde, ⁊ seo sawl sylf þæs geseondan byð eac ofer hi selfe. ⁊ þonne heo byþ genumen in þæt Godes leoht ofer hi sylfe, heo byþ gebræded in ðam inran dælum, ⁊ þonne heo besyhð under hi sylfe, heo ongyteð hi upp ahafene, ⁊ hu lytel ⁊ sceort wæs, þæt þe heo ne mihte ymbfon ⁊ oncnawan, hulic þæt wæs, þa þa heo on lichaman wæs gehæfd ⁊ gehyned ... soðlice þæt þær gecweden wæs, þæt eall þes middangeard wære gegaderod beforan his eagum, nis hit na þy gecweden, þæt heofon ⁊ eorðe wære tosomne getogen, ac þæs geseondan mod wæs tobræded.[189]

The modern reader naturally understands this passage as a symbolic or metaphorical account, in which the expansion of perception is narrated as a spatial expansion. I do not wish to broach the question of metaphor at present, but I would point out that neither Gregory nor Wærferth uses words suggestive of analogies (e.g., *quasi, uelut, gelice, swa swa*). Instead, they both call Benedict's vision 'such a great miracle' (*tanti miraculi, swa*

---

189 Wærferth, *Dialogues* 2.35 (ed. Hecht, *Wærferths Übersetzung*, 173–4): 'Even if the soul sees any tiny bit of the light of its Creator, all creation will then seem small to it, because in the light of its inner sight the bosom of the mind is loosed, and it is so greatly broadened and stretched out in God himself, that it will be above the whole earth, and the very soul of the person having the vision will be above itself. And when it is taken into the light of God above itself, it will be broadened in its inner part, and when it gazes down below itself, it perceives that it has been raised up, and how tiny and small it had been, that it had been unable to grasp and understand its own condition when it was confined and oppressed in the body ... Truly was it said then that all this earth was gathered before his eyes; it is not thereby meant that heaven and earth were drawn together but that the mind of the person having the vision was broadened.'

myccles wundres), which would scarcely be warranted if they understood Benedict's mental expansion to be a metaphor rather than a real phenomenon.[190] In sum, the limited evidence for mental spaciousness in the prose corpus suggests that while there is good reason to think that this idiom does signify a spatial transformation of the mind-in-the-breast, it need not (and perhaps does not) occur as a form of relief from hydraulic-model symptoms of distress. Instead, as in the verse corpus, the roomy heart is a sign of extraordinary spiritual or mental well-being.

Conclusions

Much of the prose evidence for the hydraulic model depends directly upon hydraulic-model diction in its Latin sources. This circumstance makes it difficult to evaluate the relationship between the prose hydraulic model and Anglo-Saxon concepts of the physiology of mental activity, because on the basis of the prose corpus alone, one could arguably attribute the ubiquity of the hydraulic model to the influence of Latin sources that are rich in hydraulic-model imagery, especially Gregory, Isidore, Bede, and the anonymous Latin homilies and hagiographies. A juxtaposition of the verse and prose treatments of the hydraulic model, however, points to the conclusion that the Anglo-Saxon notion of the *breostsefa* and its hydraulic-model behaviours arose independently of Latin influence. The basic symptoms of heat, seething, constriction, and cooling are the same for the verse corpus as for the prose. At the same time, there are striking and systematic differences in the psychological, social, and spiritual values that prose and verse texts respectively attach to each symptom. In the verse corpus, beneficial mental cooling is well represented, and mental spaciousness frequently signifies positive mental attributes other than generosity; in constrast, in the prose corpus mental cooling is almost exclusively a sign of psychological failings, and in the rare instances in which mental spaciousness represents some quality other than generosity, there is no sign that it results from the relief of cardiocentric distress. The concept of *hatheortnes* is, moreover, virtually absent from the poetic corpus, though it is ubiquitous in the prose corpus; the verse corpus has no corresponding category of cardiocentric heat that is uniformly detrimental. And the theme of voluntary constriction of the contents of the chest cavity as a means of repressing shameful outward manifestations of negative

---

190 On Gregory's version of this material, see chapter 4 below.

emotion is much more developed in poetry than in prose, where the idea of keeping things locked in the breast is more likely to be associated with secrets, memorization, and silence (as a socially neutral alternative to vocalization, rather than as a sign of masculine virtue).

Is the Anglo-Saxon hydraulic model of mental activity a literary construct based on borrowings from the Latin and biblical idioms? The divergence between the verse and prose manifestations of the hydraulic model suggests that this cannot be so: it is inconceivable that the specialized language and the social values attached to symptoms of the hydraulic model in poetry diverged so markedly from those of prose in the short period of time between the introduction of Christian Latin literature to the Anglo-Saxons and the appearance of the first OE verse texts. It is far more likely that prior to their Christianization the Anglo-Saxons already employed the hydraulic model and attached culturally specific values to individual symptoms, and that OE and Latin hydraulic-model diction subsequently converged in OE prose translations of Latin texts. This is an important point to establish before we proceed to analyse the relationship between Anglo-Saxon writing and thought about the mind, because it allows us to be more confident that the hydraulic model in both verse and prose is not merely a superficial imitation of Latin diction.

How to mount a methodologically sound analysis of the relationship between Anglo-Saxon *narrative* writing and conceptualizations of the mind remains a challenge, however. Though ultimately I reject the generalization that the hydraulic model functioned as a conceptual metaphor throughout Anglo-Saxon literature, conceptual metaphor theory is a useful starting point because it offers a framework within which to analyse the relationship between linguistic expression and conceptualization. Specifically, within the now vast literature on conceptual metaphor, the notion of embodied realism illuminates how cognitive processes of constructing abstract conceptual models are strongly constrained by the sensory experience of inhabiting the human body. Not all scholars are in agreement that embodied realism is able to account for the hydraulic model of mental activity, however, so the following chapter begins with a defence of embodied realism and of its applicability to the study of Anglo-Saxon psychology.

3 The Hydraulic Model, Embodiment, and Emergent Metaphoricity

Though the previous chapter detailed the content of the Anglo-Saxons' cardiocentric psychology and the hydraulic model of the mind, as well as the prominence of these concepts in OE narrative, I have not yet addressed the more elusive question of their role in Anglo-Saxon thought. Was the hydraulic model a figurative representation of the mind, with which Anglo-Saxon authors ornamented their diction and elevated it into a more poetic register? Was the hydraulic model a conceptual metaphor that the Anglo-Saxons consciously invoked in narrative, as a stand-in for a more abstract model of mind that was incompatible with the narrative register? Or did the hydraulic model serve as a literal articulation of many Anglo-Saxons' understanding of the substance and behaviour of the mind-in-the-breast – in other words, was the hydraulic model used and understood literally?

Some scholars have thoughtfully arrived at the conclusion that these questions are insoluble, while others have uncritically assumed that conceptual metaphor theory satisfactorily accounts for the hydraulic model throughout the OE corpus.[1] I find neither of these positions wholly satisfactory; an enormous gap in the literary history and the intellectual history of the Anglo-Saxons will persist as long as we cannot understand the relationship between what the Anglo-Saxons wrote about the mind and how they thought about the mind. It is admittedly challenging to formulate a methodologically sound approach to this problem. The method I propose is founded upon the debunking of the two misapprehensions that I identified in the introduction: the modernist bias and the medievalist

---

1 Low, 'The Anglo-Saxon Mind,' and Stanley, 'Old English Poetic Diction,' reason that the question cannot be answered; see my introduction for further bibliography.

bias. Most of the present chapter is concerned with the modernist bias, that is, the present-day reader's inclination to interpret body and mind as wholly distinct and even opposed to one another, without taking into account whether a given text emanates from a culture in which mind-body dualism is as pervasive as it is in popular present-day Western thought. Ultimately, I maintain that only a small fraction of Anglo-Saxon authors used the hydraulic model as a conceptual metaphor; for the rest, cardio-centric psychology and the hydraulic model were literal representations of their conceptualization of the mind and its behaviours. The route by which I arrive at this conclusion nonetheless begins with conceptual metaphor theory because of its profound capacity to explain how cultures construct complex conceptual systems to account for things that are not readily accessible to observation, such as thought and emotion.[2]

Conceptual Metaphor and Embodied Experience

Literary critics have, for many centuries, understood metaphor to be the transfer of a name from that which it properly signifies to that which it does not signify, thereby endowing the latter with salient characteristics of the former, typically for the purpose of linguistic ornamentation. Underlying any metaphor is a statement of the type 'X is not-X,' which means (according to objectivist philosophers and literary critics) that metaphors are essentially falsehoods that represent objective realities less accurately than literal language can. Dissatisfied with the traditional view of metaphor as falsehood, George Lakoff and Mark Johnson argued in their seminal study *Metaphors We Live By*, which appeared in 1980, that some metaphors are not mere linguistic ornaments: they are indispensable cognitive tools that organize our conceptualization of abstract entities and

---

2 Though other contemporary and medieval theories of metaphor might profitably be applied to the OE hydraulic model, I employ conceptual metaphor theory because it is most conducive to an analysis of the relationship between folk theory and learned discourse, based on the durability of folk theories that originate in embodied experiences. Lakoff and Johnson's treatment of metaphor diverges from other metaphor theories with respect to several important issues; notably, whereas some theorists assert that an utterance is metaphorical only if it is consciously meant to be a metaphor, conceptual metaphor theory holds that metaphors are often spoken and acted upon unconsciously, and that it is the cognitive process underlying utterances and actions, rather than the speaker's or agent's intent, that determines metaphoricity.

moreover influence our behaviours with respect to those abstract entities.[3] In a conceptual metaphor such as ARGUMENT IS WAR, more concrete elements of the source domain WAR are mapped onto the target domain ARGUMENT and influence our conceptualization of abstract entities within that domain. The conceptual metaphor ARGUMENT IS WAR influences verbal utterances about argument, such as 'Your claims are *indefensible*' and 'If you use that *strategy*, he'll *wipe you out*,' but it also shapes the practice of argument itself: when we argue, we *attack* an *opponent*, we *gain and lose ground*, we mount a *counterattack* or *defend* our own position. 'It is in this sense that we live by the ARGUMENT IS WAR metaphor in this culture; it structures the actions we perform in arguing,' Lakoff and Johnson conclude.[4]

Notably, Lakoff and Johnson specify that the conceptual metaphor ARGUMENT IS WAR is peculiar to 'this culture.' Under the influence of another culture's markedly different conceptual metaphor, an abstraction such as argument can take on a markedly different form. 'Imagine a culture where an argument is viewed as a dance, with the participants as performers, and the goal being to perform in a balanced and aesthetic way,' Lakoff and Johnson propose; '*we* would probably not view them as arguing at all. It would be strange even to call what they were doing "arguing."'[5] Since the inception of conceptual metaphor theory, a number of studies have investigated the cross-cultural continuity and comprehensibility of metaphors and concluded that conceptual metaphors are least comprehensible across cultural boundaries 'when, for cultural reasons, the speaker and listener attach different connotations to the source domains.'[6] These studies typically target geographical, linguistic, and socio-economic barriers, but the same principle certainly applies to chronological barriers such as that which separates us from the Anglo-Saxons. One objective of the present chapter is to bring the present-day reader to a clearer understanding of

---

3 Lakoff and Johnson, *Metaphors We Live By*, 4–5. Their use of small capitals to mark phrases as conceptual metaphors has now become conventional in metaphor studies.
4 Ibid., 4.
5 Ibid., 4–5.
6 Littlemore, 'The Effect of Cultural Background on Metaphor Interpretation,' 274; see also Deignan, 'Metaphorical Expressions and Culture.' Deignan illustrates this point with the British expression 'that's not your cup of tea,' meaning 'that's not something you particularly like,' which would make little sense within a culture that did not particularly prize tea as a beverage and as a social ritual. The nearest Spanish equivalent of this expression is 'no ser santo de tu devoción,' literally 'not to be the saint of your devotion,' which is rooted in 'Catholic images not readily accessible to the non-Catholic majority of British English speakers, of praying through particular saints' (261).

ostensible metaphors in the OE psychological idiom, such as THE MIND IS CONTAINED IN THE BREAST or ANGER IS CARDIOCENTRIC HEAT, by way of a better understanding of the connotations that the Anglo-Saxons attached to the source domains CONTENTS OF THE BREAST and CARDIOCENTRIC HEAT. Conversely, metaphors are most comprehensible across cultural boundaries when their source domains are equally salient and carry similar connotations on both sides of that boundary. Among the most stable source domains is the experience of living in the human body, whose interactions with its environment are conditioned by its upright posture, its being held down by gravity, its involuntary physiological responses to distress and injury and illness. These non-culture-bound aspects of living in the human body influence the generation of conceptual metaphors 'on the basis of "conflations" in our experience – cases where source and target domains are coactive in our experience,' explain Johnson and Lakoff. 'For example, verticality and quantity are coactive whenever we pour juice into a glass or pile up objects. This is the experiential grounding for [the conceptual metaphor] MORE IS UP.'[7] Similarly, the fact that 'physical size typically correlates with physical strength, and the victor in a fight is typically on top' provides the experiential grounding for the conceptual metaphor HAVING CONTROL OR FORCE IS UP; BEING SUBJECT TO CONTROL OR FORCE IS DOWN, which is verbalized in idioms such as 'I am on top of the situation' and 'He is under my spell.'[8]

In the case of the OE hydraulic model, it is reasonable to posit that the coactivity of intense mental activity with chest-centred sensations of heat and pressure provided the experiential grounding for concepts such as THE MIND IS CONTAINED IN THE BREAST and ANGER IS CARDIOCENTRIC HEAT, but such a hypothesis may oversimplify the relationship between human physiology and the cognitive processes that generate conceptual metaphors. From the time of their earliest publications, Lakoff and Johnson have acknowledged that even the most fundamental orientational metaphors such as MORE IS UP are not wholly dictated by bodily experience; different cultures are prone to varying interpretations and verbalizations of the coactivities that link abstractions to bodily experiences.[9] Nonetheless, conceptual metaphor theory has faced challenges from several quarters,[10]

---

7 Johnson and Lakoff, 'Why Cognitive Linguistics Requires Embodied Realism,' 245–6.
8 Lakoff and Johnson, *Metaphors We Live By*, 15.
9 See, for instance, Lakoff and Johnson, *Metaphors We Live By*, 14 and 18–19.
10 See esp. Lakoff and Johnson, *Philosophy in the Flesh: The Embodied Mind and its Challenge to Western Thought*, 74–117; and Johnson and Lakoff, 'Why

particularly from cultural anthropologists who maintain that Lakoff and Johnson ascribe too influential a role to the cross-cultural consistency of bodily experiences and not enough of a role to cultural variation.[11] In response to this criticism, Lakoff and Johnson have articulated a corollary of conceptual metaphor theory that they call 'embodied realism,' according to which a combination of inborn, bodily-experiential, and cultural-experiential factors *constrain*, but do not absolutely determine, the selection and elaboration of suitable conceptual metaphors.[12]

Working within Lakoff and Johnson's paradigm of embodied realism, Zoltán Kövecses has generated numerous cross-cultural studies of conceptual metaphors involved in descriptions and expressions of anger. He proposes an exceedingly circumspect account of embodied realism with specific reference to metaphors for anger:

> The universality of actual physiological experiences might be seen as leading to the similarities (though not equivalence) in conceptualized physiology (i.e. the conceptual metonymies), which might be the basis of the similarity (though again not equivalence) in the metaphorical conceptualization of anger and its counterparts ... [I]t is not suggested that embodiment actually produces the [ANGER IS HOT FLUID IN A] PRESSURIZED CONTAINER metaphor, but that it makes a large number of other possible metaphorical conceptualizations

Cognitive Linguistics Requires Embodied Realism,' which both summarizes and rebuts the philosophical contention that conceptual metaphor theory represents a form of 'extreme empiricism' (246-8).

11 See esp. N. Quinn, 'The Cultural Basis of Metaphor.' In response to Lakoff and Johnson's *Metaphors We Live By*, Quinn writes, 'While I certainly agree that metaphors play some role in the way we comprehend and draw inferences about abstract concepts, I take issue with the claim that they or the schemas on which they are said to be founded actually constitute the concepts.' Metaphors do not independently produce concepts; instead, 'particular metaphors are selected by speakers, and are favored by these speakers, just because they provide satisfying mappings onto already existing cultural understandings' (64-5).

12 See esp. Johnson and Lakoff, 'Why Cognitive Linguistics Requires Embodied Realism': '[A]lthough aspects of our shared embodiment coupled with the commonalities of our shared environments will give rise to ... many shared conceptual metaphors, there is room within these general constraints for extensive cultural variation in the ways the meaning [is] extended and elaborated. For example, it is hard to imagine any creature with a body similar to ours, located within a gravitational field like the one we inhabit, that would not have some form of verticality [metaphor] ... However, there is great variability in the ways a notion of vertical orientation can be interpreted and the valuation that can be placed upon it' (251).

either incompatible or unnatural. It would be odd to conceptualize anger as, say, softly falling snow, an image completely incompatible with what our body is like and what our physiology does in anger. It is in this sense that the particular embodiment of anger is seen as limiting the choice of available metaphors for anger.[13]

Kövecses' insightful characterization of the role of embodied experience in the conceptualization of anger brings to light some of the reasons why conceptual metaphor theory has been such a fruitful tool for studying expressions and descriptions of psychological distress, in modern languages as well as in OE. Embodied realism provides a rationale for the coherence of a particular culture's metaphorical conceptualization of anger, since the source domain will be the fairly predictable bodily sensations and autonomic nervous responses to anger. Embodied realism also accounts for the cross-cultural consistency that has been observed in many comparative studies of anger metaphors, since most of the autonomic nervous responses to anger are not culture-bound, although culturally variable factors will influence the way those bodily responses are subjectively perceived and verbalized.

This is not to say that the theory of embodied realism is now universally accepted. In fact, one vocal opponent of Kövecses' work bases her arguments specifically on evidence drawn from the corpus of OE literature. Caroline Gevaert reasons that if the conceptual metaphors ANGER IS HEAT and THE MIND IS A PRESSURIZED CONTAINER are truly rooted in embodied experience, then they should be diachronically constant. As Gevaert interprets the textual evidence, vast differences separate the hydraulic-model metaphors of OE from those of ME and MnE. She arrives at the conclusion that if supposedly embodied metaphors exhibit any diachronic instability at all, then the whole theory of embodied realism is vitiated.[14] Unfortunately, Gevaert's argument is troubled by her misunderstanding of Lakoff's and Kövecses' claims[15] and by substantial

---

13 Kövecses, 'Metaphor and the Folk Understanding of Anger,' 66–7.
14 Gevaert, 'Anger in Old and Middle English: A "Hot" Topic?' and Gevaert, 'The ANGER IS HEAT Question: Detecting Cultural Influence on the Conceptualization of Anger through Diachronic Corpus Analysis.'
15 Gevaert writes, 'Lakoff's two central, mutually related claims [are that] the conceptualisation of anger is embodied and universal ... If the ANGER IS HEAT-conceptualisation does not prove to be universal, it may not be embodied and a cultural component may be involved' ('Anger in Old and Middle English,' 89). But as we have seen, Lakoff and Johnson have acknowledged the role of cultural variability in metaphor formation from

flaws in her methodology.[16] Several patently inaccurate assertions attest to her deep misunderstanding of the textual evidence: she claims that the OE translation of Boniface's letter to Eadburga is the only pre-850 text to use the word *hatheortnes*; that OE 'texts before 850 are purely Germanic ones'; that 'a person cannot be said to be *hot with sadness*'; and that 'The diachronic data show the ANGER IS FIRE metaphor to be of Latinate origin and to be confined to religious texts for a long time.'[17]

I would not mount such a detailed criticism of Gevaert's work if it were not for the influence her studies have had on Kövecses' own ongoing thought about embodied realism. In a paper that appeared in 2006, Kövecses modifies his claims about the diachronic stability in order to account for what he calls Gevaert's 'extremely important finding,' chiefly her claim 'that heat related words account for only 1.58 per cent of all the words describing anger before 850.'[18] Ultimately Kövecses adds flexibility to his articulation of embodied realism by making refinements that can better account for the interplay between embodied responses to anger and

---

their very first articulation of experientialism. Elsewhere Gevaert maintains that 'Kövecses made an objectively measurable increase in body temperature in angry people the very foundation of the embodiment theory' ('The ANGER IS HEAT Question,' 3), which misrepresents the significance that Kövecses places on measured autonomic responses to anger (cf. Kövecses, 'Anger: Its Language, Conceptualization, and Physiology in the Light of Cross-Cultural Evidence').

16 Gevaert bases her analysis solely on a corpus search for individual words signifying anger ('The ANGER IS HEAT Question,' 4–5), a method that in no way accounts for the rich OE lexicon of emotional distress that one encounters when actually reading OE texts. Moreover, unaware of the rich bibliography of relevant studies outside her own field, Gevaert states in studies published in 2002 and 2005 that 'only few people have shown an interest in the conceptualizations [of anger as heat] in older stages of the English language': see her 'The ANGER IS HEAT Question,' 4 and 11 n. 1; and 'The Evolution of the Lexical and Conceptual Field of ANGER,' 295 n. 5.

17 Gevaert, 'The ANGER IS HEAT Question,' 5–6 and 10; the same problems are replicated in Gevaert, 'The Evolution of the Lexical and Conceptual Field of ANGER.' Gevaert follows the Helsinki Corpus's assignment of OE texts to chronological groups: pre-850, 850–950, and 950–1050. According to its own website, the Helsinki Corpus uses multiple and inconsistent criteria in their chronological groupings: 'Periodization has been of primary importance (with regard to the date of the original text and the date of the manuscript),' according to Kytö, 'Manual to the Diachronic Part of the Helsinki Corpus of English Texts.' To clarify: the Latin letter of Boniface is dated to ca. 716, but the OE translation appears only in a mid-eleventh-century copy, which is not the translator's original (Ker, *Catalogue* no. 182, item 3; Sisam, 'An Old English Translation of a Letter from Wynfrith to Eadburga,' 205–11).

18 Kövecses, 'Embodiment, Experiential Focus, and Diachronic Change in Metaphor,' 1.

the culturally conditioned perceptions and expressions of those responses. But on the way to these valuable conclusions he rebroadcasts a number of Gevaert's errors.

Nonetheless, setting aside her flawed handling of the OE data, Gevaert's broader objection to embodied realism is worth further consideration, because it is representative of scholars' lingering doubts, both intellectual and visceral, about the role of embodied experience in the cognitive process of generating conceptual metaphors. Mistakenly believing that the OE data correlates anger with cardiocentric heat only under the influence of Christian Latin, Gevaert hypothesizes that the ANGER IS FIRE metaphor 'is certainly not motivated by metonyms referring to body heat ... The motivation for the ANGER IS FIRE metaphors is therefore most probably not body heat, but external fire.' This conceptual metaphor, she maintains, maps onto a volatile emotion the characteristic temperature and volatile nature of ordinary fire observed in nature or in domestic settings.[19] There is nothing inherently objectionable in this hypothesis, but it simply does not account for the cross-cultural and diachronic consistency (*not* iron-clad universality) of anger's bodily localization in the abdomino-thoracic cavity, nor does it account for the correlation of anger with cardiocentric pressure.

In fact, the more evidence is accumulated in support of the cross-cultural and diachronic recurrence of cardiocentrism and the hydraulic model, the more difficult it is to explain the evidence without recourse to some version of embodied realism. In the pages that follow, I have compiled numerous analogues of the OE hydraulic model, from cultures that vary geographically and diachronically from one another, with particular attention to the pervasiveness of the core hydraulic-model symptoms that were identified above in chapter 2: cardiocentrism, heat, seething, outward pressure and inward constriction in the abdomino-thoracic cavity.[20] The purpose of this compilation is to strengthen the case that the theory of embodied realism provides the soundest explanation for the origin of the hydraulic model in OE. It will then remain to be considered what embodied realism can tell us about a given culture's metaphorical or literal usage of a particular conceptualization and its linguistic expressions.

---

19 Gevaert, 'The ANGER IS HEAT Question,' 10.
20 Although some scholars use the term 'analogue' to signify the relationship between two texts that demonstrably derived shared material from a common source, I am using the term 'analogue' to signify texts that are genealogically unconnected but share notable features of content, style, structure, etc.: see Lapidge, 'The Comparative Approach,' 27.

Materialist Psychologies among the Presocratic Greeks

The surviving writings of the poets, philosophers, and physicians of the Greek-speaking areas of the Mediterranean during the Presocratic era (ca. 700 BC to the late fifth century BC) preserve a multiplicity of theories about the substance of the mind and of the soul, but one thing common to these psychologies was the absence of any concept of absolute immateriality of the sort later explored in Plato's dialogues.[21] With respect to the mind-body distinction in particular, Shirley Darcus Sullivan has asserted that in several genres of Greek literature predating Plato, 'the distinctions between material and immaterial, corporeal and incorporeal are not made to the degree that we make them. There is some perception of difference, but we encounter a continuum of physical and psychological rather than a sharp division between the two.'[22] At one end of this continuum is the *nous* 'mind,' which may be spatially localized but otherwise has no bodily attributes. Occupying the middle of the spectrum are *thumos* and *phrên*, both of which are organs of thought, emotion, and will: *thumos* is localized in the chest cavity and is loosely associated with blood and with the air in the lungs; *phrên* also loosely signifies some constellation of organs in the chest cavity,[23] in a manner analogous to OE *hreðer*. At the more physical end of the continuum are *kradiê*, *êtor*, and *kêr*, all of which mean

---

21 In the Homeric literature there is no suggestion that the human soul (*psuchê*) and the gods were anything other than material beings; subsequently, certain fifth-century poets and philosophers began to formulate material distinctions between soul and body, or between *noêta* 'things that can be thought about' and *aisthêta* 'things that can be perceived with the senses,' but they still understood the non-fleshly to be composed of more subtle materials such as *aithêr* and fire, and they understood even the invisible to have spatial extent. Renehan, 'On the Greek Origins of the Concepts Incorporeality and Immateriality,' argues that scholars who credit the Presocratics with the concept of an incorporeal or immaterial soul are using those terms too loosely (108–19); see also Popper, 'Comments on the Prehistoric Discovery of the Self,' who confirms that the majority of Presocratic thinkers were psychological materialists whose distinction between mind and body was based not on their respective substances but on the peculiar moral character of the mind.
22 Sullivan, *Psychological and Ethical Ideas: What Early Greeks Say*, 17.
23 Sullivan discusses the bodily localization and psychological characteristics of *nous*, *thumos*, and *phrên* in Homeric literature, in early lyric and elegiac poetry, and in the Presocratic philosophers (ibid., 18–70). On the anthropological category of the 'ego souls,' including *nous*, *thumos*, and *phrên*, and their independence from the *psuchê*, which is a 'free soul' that has agency only when outside the body, see Bremmer, *The Early Greek Concept of the Soul*, 53–63.

'heart,' signifying at once the fleshly organ and the bodily seat of emotion.[24] The localization of psychological faculties in the midsection of the body is not metaphorical in this literature. The first extant arguments favouring the brain as the locus of the specific mental faculties were advanced around the beginning of the fifth century BC by the physician Alcmaeon of Croton, who proposed, possibly on the basis of dissections, that 'the brain provides the senses of hearing and sight and smell, and from these memory and opinion come to be.'[25] Some decades later, cephalocentric psychology would slowly begin to gain traction, as theories favouring the localization of psychological activity in the brain were circulated under the name of Hippocrates (469–399 BC).[26] But during the era of Homer and Hesiod, cardiocentrism was not metaphorical, because there coexisted no cephalocentric or non-materialist alternative.

Cardiocentrism and the Hydraulic Model in Homer and Hesiod

The association of psychological states and events with the midsection of the body is particularly prominent in the language of Hesiod, who assigns all types of thought and emotion to the breast and its internal organs. In the *Theogony* he characterizes Eros as the god 'who overcomes the reason and purpose in the breasts [*en stêthessi*] of all gods and all men.'[27] Subsequently, as Zeus is drumming up support for a battle against the Titans, he opens his speech with the words, 'let me say what the spirit in my breast [*thumos eni stêthessi*] bids me,' and the giant Kottos replies with flattery: 'We know that you have exceeding intelligence [*prapides*, literally "diaphragm"] and exceeding insight [*noêma*].' As Zeus begins to fight the Titans, 'his lungs [*phrenes*] were filled with fury.'[28] In Hesiod's *Works and Days,* in the account of the gods' creation of Pandora, Hermes places 'in

---

24 Sullivan, *Psychological and Ethical Ideas*, 17 and 70–3.
25 Plato, *Phaedo*, 96b, cited in translation by Hankinson, 'Greek Medical Models of Mind,' 197. As Hankinson explains, in this part of Plato's dialogue, Socrates catalogues several Presocratic teachings on the nature of the mind; scholars have argued, and Hankinson accepts, that this view is attributable to Alcmaeon.
26 Hankinson, 'Greek Medical Models of Mind,' 207; see ibid., 203–8, for hydraulic-model mechanisms in the treatises of the Hippocratic corpus.
27 *Theogony*, lines 120–2. Quotations of Hesiod's verse follow West's translation of *Theogony; Works and Days*, and West's editions of the *Theogony* and of *Works and Days.*
28 *Theogony*, lines 644–5, 655–6, and 688.

her breast [stêthessi] ... lies and wily pretences and a knavish nature.'²⁹ Zeus scolds Prometheus, saying, 'You are pleased at having outwitted me [emas phrenas êperopeusas, literally "you have deceived my breast"].'³⁰ And the call of the crane, announcing the arrival of the rainy season, 'stings the heart [kradiên] of the man with no ox,' that is, it grieves the man who has no beasts to help him plough.³¹ Homeric verse likewise invokes a strongly cardiocentric psychology. In the opening exposition of the Iliad, for example, Apollo is 'angered in his heart' [chôomenos kêr].³² Shortly thereafter, Achilles' anger is accompanied by cardiocentric turmoil: 'within his shaggy breast [stêthessin] the heart [êtor] was divided two ways,' because he is uncertain whether he ought to slay Agamemnon 'or else to check the spleen [cholon] within and keep down his anger [thumon].' His deliberation continues until Athena arrives: Achilles 'was stirring up these matters throughout his breast and spirit [kata phrena kai kata thumon].'³³

In the foregoing lines concerning Achilles' deliberation, the act of self-restraint is expressed in the language of the hydraulic model: to keep his violent impulses hidden, Achilles needs to keep hot fluid and breath, cholos and thumos, tamped down in his midsection. This representation of voluntary cardiocentric constriction is complemented by passages elsewhere in the Iliad that portray other hydraulic-model symptoms. In Book 9, for instance, Meleagros succumbs to 'such anger [cholos, literally "bile"] as also causes the mind [noon] to swell in the chest [en stêthessi],'³⁴ exemplifying the mechanism by which a hot fluid in the chest cavity transfers its heat energy to the mind and causes seething or swelling. As an alternative to the swelling and constriction of the mind itself, the force of a strong emotion can grip the mind-in-the-breast from the outside and smother it: Helen thus offers her sympathy to her brother Hector, 'since for you especially,' she says, 'suffering wraps around your heart [ponos phrenas amphibebêken].'³⁵

---

29 Works and Days, lines 77–9.
30 Works and Days, line 55.
31 Works and Days, line 451.
32 Iliad 1.44–5 (trans. Lattimore, The Iliad of Homer). For the Greek text of the Iliad I have consulted Monro and Allen, Homeri opera, vol. 1.
33 Iliad 1.188–93; the first two translations follow Lattimore, The Iliad of Homer, and for the third clause I have substituted my own literal translation for Lattimore's much more elegant rendering, which reads 'he weighed in mind and spirit these two courses.'
34 Iliad 9.553–4 (translation mine).
35 Iliad 6.355 (translation mine).

Cardiocentrism and the Hydraulic Model in the Poem of Empedocles

The surviving writings of the major Presocratic philosophers attribute to the soul or intellect a material substance and a cardiocentric location.[36] Among the Presocratics, Empedocles of Acragas, who penned his philosophical works in Greek hexameters around in the mid-fifth century BC,[37] is the most vocal proponent of a cardiocentric psychology, and he explicitly envisions the physiology of thought as a system of pressurized channels, some filled with fluid and susceptible to heat – in other words, a hydraulic system. Empedocles localizes a number of mental faculties, including memory and rational judgment, in organs of the midsection of the body: the diaphragm (*prapidês*), the lungs and praecordia (*phrên*), and the innards or liver (*splanchna*). '[I]t is very hard indeed / for men, and resented, the flow of persuasion into their thought organ [*phrena*],' Empedocles observes; 'Blessed is he who obtained wealth in his divine thinking organs [*prapidôn*].'[38] Elsewhere he exhorts his audience, 'Hear my words; for learning will expand [*auxei*] your thought organs [*phrenas*],'[39] and he urges his listener to cultivate knowledge 'by dividing up the discourse [*logoio*] in your heart [*splanchnoisi*].'[40] For Empedocles, even divinity itself is not an immaterial entity but a mind-in-the-breast of unimaginable scale, 'a sacred and ineffable thought organ [*phrên hierê kai athesphatos*] / darting through the entire cosmos with swift thoughts.'[41]

---

36 See Kirk, Raven and Schofield, *The Presocratic Philosophers* (hereafter KRS) for Presocratic opinions on the substance and bodily seat of the soul and the intellect: esp. 203–8 on Heraclitus, 284–5 and 305–13 on Empedocles, 362–6 on Anaxagoras, and 441–52 on Diogenes of Apollonia.

37 The surviving fragments of Empedocles' works have traditionally been understood to belong to two distinct poems, *On Nature* and *Purifications* (see KRS, 282–3 and 320–1), but Brad Inwood now argues that the fragments represent a single poem, and he has accordingly reordered them: see *The Poem of Empedocles*, 8–19 (hereafter referred to as Inwood). In the following pages all quotations of Empedocles in English and in Greek follow Inwood, but I have also provided the numbers of the fragments according to the standard edition of Empedocles in Diels and Kranz, *Die Fragmente der Vorsokratiker* (hereafter DK). Square brackets around English words are Inwood's, but Greek words in square brackets have been added by me for clarity's sake.

38 Empedocles, frags. 2.2–3 and 4.1 (trans. Inwood; = DK 114.2–3 and 132.1).

39 Empedocles, frag. 25.14 (trans. Inwood; = DK 17.14).

40 Empedocles, frag. 3.3 (trans. Inwood; = DK 4.3).

41 Empedocles, frag. 110.4–5 (trans. Inwood; = DK 134.4–5). See also Inwood's commentary at p. 68; it should be noted that Empedocles makes this statement in the course of

Though the mind-organs in Empedocles' poem are cardiocentric containers, expanding as they accumulate sensory knowledge, they also seem to behave as limbs, extending outward to gather more sensory data. 'There was among them a man of exceptional knowledge, / who indeed obtained the greatest wealth in his thinking organs [*prapidôn*],' Empedocles reports, '... for whenever he reached out with all his thinking organs [*prapidessin*] / he easily saw each of all the things which are / in ten or twenty human lifetimes.'[42] To cultivate deeper wisdom, one must then store and meditate upon the data gleaned by sensory perception: 'For if, thrusting them[43] deep down in your crowded thinking organs [*prapidessin*], / you gaze on them in kindly fashion, with pure meditations, / absolutely all these things will be with you throughout your life.'[44]

The mechanism by which knowledge reaches the thinking organs is a physical one, dependent primarily on the sense organs. When Empedocles wants to describe the Divinity's ineffability, he writes, 'It is not achievable that we should approach [it/him] with our eyes / or grasp [it/him] with our hands, by which the greatest road / of persuasion extends to men's thought organ [*phrena*].'[45] These important lines indicate that, while Empedocles concedes that the deity cannot be apprehended by the senses, the primary means of acquiring knowledge of things other than the deity is the 'greatest road of persuasion' that bridges the sense organs and the thought organ. Effluences (*aporrhoiai*), which are emitted by every perceptible thing, enter the body when they come in contact with the sense organ that contains pores of the right shape and size; from there they travel through channels toward the blood housed in the chest cavity.[46] Perception of these

---

arguing against anthropomorphic conceptions of the deity, so he is not saying that the divine *phrên* is one bodily part of a vast anthropomorphic god.

42 Empedocles, frag. 6 (trans. Inwood; = DK 129).

43 The antecedent of 'them' is uncertain because this is the first line of the fragment. In the divergent arrangements of both Inwood and DK, the fragment preceding this one deals with the mechanism of sense perception. In Inwood's frag. 14 Empedocles discusses the reliability of the senses and mentions the 'passage for understanding' (*poros ... noêsai*) that allows external stimuli to be perceived, and in DK 109, Empedocles articulates the theory according to which each element is perceived by a like element in the intellect. In either arrangement, the antecedent of 'them' is either sensory perceptions or the thoughts that follow upon them.

44 Empedocles, frag. 16.1–3 (trans. Inwood; = DK 110.1–3).

45 Empedocles, frag. 109 (trans. Inwood; = DK 133).

46 On the sources that contribute to our understanding of this aspect of Empedocles' psychology, see Hankinson, 'Greek Medical Models of Mind,' 198–9; Inwood, 195–203; and KRS, 309–11.

effluences is executed by the blood around the heart. Empedocles says of the heart that it is 'nourished in seas of blood which leaps back and forth, / and there especially it is called understanding by men; / for men's understanding is blood around the heart [*haima gar anthrôpois perikardion esti noêma*].'[47] Surviving fragments of Empedocles' own poem do not account for the mechanism by which blood is capable of perception or understanding, but according to Theophrastus (370–287 BC), Empedocles taught that 'Thinking is of like by like, ignorance of unlike by unlike, thought being either identical with or closely akin to perception … So it is especially with the blood that they think; for in the blood above all other parts the elements are blended.'[48]

Additionally, Empedocles' description of respiration, in which *aithêr* is carried to the blood through channels that begin in the nostrils, is placed by both Diels and Inwood among the fragments dealing with sense perception, on the grounds that it portrays not only respiration but also the transmission of how olfactory *aporrhoiai* travel along the 'road of persuasion' from the nose to the thinking organ.

And all [animals] inhale and exhale thus: all have channels
empty of blood in the flesh, deep inside the body,
and at their mouths the extreme surface of the nostrils is pierced right through
with close-packed furrows, so that
they cover over the blood but a clear passage is cut in channels for aither.
Next, when the smooth blood rushes back from there,
seething air rushes down in a raging billow;
and when it [blood] leaps up, it exhales again –
as when a little girl plays with a clepsydra of gleaming bronze.[49]

If olfactory effluences travel through these channels along with the *aithêr*, as later testimonia suggest was Empedocles' opinion,[50] then the blood that meets the *aithêr* brought to the chest cavity would also perceive the effluences brought with it.

---

47 Empedocles, frag. 96 (trans. Inwood; = DK 105).
48 Theophrastus, *De sensu* 9 (trans. KRS, 311).
49 Empedocles, frag. 106.1–9 (trans. Inwood; = DK 100.1–9)
50 See Inwood, 202–3, for Aristotle's discussion of whether Empedocles' bloodless channels are filled with air, and 48–9, on the likely context of frag. 106 within Empedocles' poem.

Finally, because perception and knowledge depend upon the flow of *aporrhoiai* through open channels to the blood around the heart, Empedocles associates cognitive impairment with the constriction of the 'road of persuasion.' Wishing for his addressee Pausanias to maximize his mental capacity by attending to all the sensory data available to him, Empedocles advises him, 'Do not in any way curb the reliability of the other limbs by which there is a passage for understanding [*hoposêi poros esti noêsai*], / but understand each thing in the way that it is clear.'[51] Conversely, to be literally 'narrow-minded' is a pitiable condition combining ignorance and self-deception. Speaking of the narrow-minded, Empedocles writes,

> For narrow devices are spread throughout their limbs,
> but many wretched things strike in, and they blunt their meditations.
> And having seen [only] a small portion of life in their experience
> they soar and fly off like smoke, swift to their dooms,
> each one convinced of only that very thing which he has chanced to meet,
> as they are driven in all directions. But each boasts of having seen the whole.[52]

These pitiful men, with their clogged channels of sense-perception, stand in stark contrast to the knowledgeable man whom Empedocles admires so much for his ever-expanding *prapides*, as we saw above.

Cardiocentrism and the Hydraulic Model in Plato's *Timaeus*

Plato's account of human nature in the *Timaeus*, and especially his distribution of the soul among three bodily seats, is exceedingly difficult to reconcile with his other psychological works, in which he maintains that the soul – at least the rational, immortal part of the soul – is incorporeal. Whether the creation narrative in the *Timaeus* would have been received as doctrine or as myth in Plato's day is less germane to the present discussion than the observation that the tripartition of the soul in the *Timaeus* attempts to explain human psychological phenomena by accounting for the somatic accompaniments of psychological activity.

As the interlocutor Timaeus relates, the gods receive a portion of the substance of the immortal soul from the creator god. They proceed to fashion a mortal soul and a body as a vessel for both types of soul, but

---

51 Empedocles, frag. 14.7–8 (trans. Inwood; = DK 3.7–8).
52 Empedocles, frag. 8.1–6 (trans. Inwood; = DK 2.1–6).

they place the immortal soul in the head so that it might have only a narrow point of contact, via the neck, with the mortal soul. 'That part of the inferior soul which is endowed with courage and passion [*thumou*] and loves contention' is placed in the thorax, and that which is responsible for bodily appetites is set in the abdomen. Between them the diaphragm (*phrenas*) is laid as a barrier, to minimize the influence of the appetites on the passions.[53] The heart, enclosed in the breast with the passionate part of the soul, plays an important psychological role: by means of the blood it communicates distresses and appetites to other parts of the body so that they may respond appropriately:

> The heart, the knot of the veins and the fountain of the blood which races through all the limbs, was set in the place of guard, that, when the might of passion was roused by reason making proclamation of any wrong assailing them from without or being perpetrated by the desires within, quickly the whole power of feeling in the body, perceiving these commands and threats, might obey and follow through every turn and alley, and thus allow the principle of the best to have the command in all of them.[54]

Though it is necessary that the heart work harder during passionate episodes, the gods did not want it to become excessively hot and swollen. Therefore, explains Timaeus, they configured the other organs of the chest cavity in an arrangement that would best mitigate cardiocentric heat and swelling:

> But the gods, foreknowing that the palpitation of the heart in the expectation of danger and excitement of passion must cause it to swell and become inflamed, formed and implanted as a supporter to the heart the lung, which was, in the first place, soft and bloodless, and also had within hollows like the pores of a sponge, in order that by receiving the breath and the drink, it might give coolness and the power of respiration and alleviate the heat. Wherefore they cut the air channels leading to the lung, and placed the lung about the heart as a soft spring, that, when passion was rife within, the heart, beating against a yielding body, might be cooled and suffer less, and might thus become more ready to join with passion in the service of reason.[55]

53 Plato, *Timaeus* 70a (trans. Jowett, 1193). For the Greek text I have consulted Rivaud's edition (Plato, *Oeuvres Complètes*, vol. 10, *Timée – Critias*), 195–7.
54 Plato, *Timaeus* 70b (trans. Jowett, 1193).
55 Plato, *Timaeus* 70 c–d (trans. Jowett, 1193–4).

According to this account, the gods are less concerned with the heart's role in animation and nutrition of the body than with its ability to be dominated by the rational soul. While the heart is overheated, it swells outward and is in turn pressed upon by its surroundings. Apparently, as long as this state of arousal persists, the heart continues to send passionate and appetitive signals to the rest of the body. Because the lung is soft, as the heart swells against it the lung yields, minimizing the degree to which constriction impinges upon the function of the heart; because the lung brings in fresh air, it contributes to the cooling of the heart. Only when the heart is cool and free from constriction is it 'ready' to subject itself to the rational soul once more.

Hydraulic-Model Mechanisms in the Aristotelian *Problemata*

The cardiocentric heat and seething described in the *Timaeus* reappear in a Greek text known as the *Problemata*, questionably attributed to Aristotle (384–22 BC), consisting of a series of questions and answers about the mechanics of the human body, many of which treat the physiology of emotion.[56] The most salient difference between the hydraulic-model idiom of the *Timaeus* and that of the *Problemata* is that in the latter, the spatial change brought about by the heat is violent agitation, the boiling of the blood, rather than the more static swelling of the heart seen in the *Timaeus*. Yet the detrimental effect on cognition and deliberation is similar: 'when the soul is moved and travelling,' states the respondent in the *Problemata*, 'it is not possible either to feel or to think.' The respondent goes on to explain that internal physiological heat, arising from a variety of causes, is one source of violent motion of the soul and hence of cognitive impairment: 'This is why children, the intoxicated, and madmen cannot think; for owing to the quantity of heat within them the movement is very great and violent, but when this ceases they become more sensible; for as the

---

56 Opinions on the date of the work range from the third century BC to the fifth century AD, but Pierre Louis, the most recent editor of the *Problemata*, favours Aristotelian authorship for at least parts of the text (see his *Problèmes*, 1.xxiii–xxv), and the editors of a new collection of studies on the *Problemata* accept that 'The text as we have it today is a combination of materials from different sources and different periods, in which genuine Aristotelian texts have been mixed with later texts, e.g. by Theophrast' (De Leemans and Goyens, introduction, in their *Aristotle's* Problemata *in Different Times and Tongues*, ix–x). Because the present discussion treats the *Problemata* as an analogue rather than as a source of other hydraulic-model texts, the problems of authorship and date are not pressing.

mind is untroubled they can control it more.'[57] Again, in response to a question about why nervous people have sweaty feet, it is proposed that nervousness 'is an increase of heat, such as takes place in anger[.] For anger is a boiling of heat about the heart.'[58]

Are the 'very violent movement' (*kinêsis sphodrotatê*) of the soul and the 'boiling of heat about the heart' (*zesis tou thermou tou peri tên kardian*) metaphors or literal physiological facts for the respondent in the *Problemata*? Most texts offer no direct evidence to answer such a question, but in the case of the *Problemata*, the respondent claims outright that hydraulic-model idioms are not mere metaphors.

> Why is it that in a state of anger, when the heat collects within, men become heated and bold, but in a state of fear they are in the opposite condition? Or is not the same part affected? In the case of the angry it is the heart which is affected, which is the reason why they are courageous, flushed and full of breath, as the direction of the heat is upwards, but in the case of the frightened the blood and the heat escape downwards, whence comes the loosening of the bowels. The beating of the heart is also different (in the two cases), since with the frightened it is rapid and strongly punctuated as would naturally occur from a failure of heat, whereas in the case of the angry it functions as one would expect if more heat was collecting there; so the phrases 'to boil up [*anazein*],' 'to raise up one's anger [*to orinesthai ton thumon*],' 'to be stirred up [*tarattesthai*]' and similar expressions are not wrongly but quite naturally used of the temper.[59]

The author clearly asserts that, according to his knowledge of the internal physiology of emotion, expressions that attribute heat and swelling to the heart are spoken not wrongly (*kakôs*) but in accordance with nature (*oikeiôs*), that is, literally. I understand the adverb *oikeiôs* to mean 'literally'

---

57 Aristotle, *Problemata*, 30.14 (trans. Hett, *Aristotle's Problems*, 2.179; ed. Louis, *Problèmes*, 3.41).

58 Aristotle, *Problemata*, 2.26 (trans. Hett, *Aristotle's Problems*, 1.61; ed. Louis, *Problèmes*, 1.45). Cf. Aristotle, *De anima* 403a (trans. Lawson-Tancred, *De anima (On the Soul)*, 129): 'the natural philosopher and the dialectician would give a different definition of each of the affections, for instance in answer to the question "What is anger?" For the dialectician will say that it is a desire for revenge or something like that, while the natural philosopher will say that it is a boiling of the blood and hot stuff about the heart.'

59 Aristotle, *Problemata*, 27.3 (trans. Hett, *Aristotle's Problems*, 2.117–19; ed. Louis, *Problèmes*, 2.226–7). I have slightly modified Hett's translation by rendering very literally the three expressions in the last sentence.

on the basis of a similar usage in Aristotle's *Ars rhetorica*: the author contrasts metaphor (*metaphora*) with 'the natural,' which he calls *to oikeion*.[60] If *to oikeion* is that which is not *metaphora*, then in the context of *Problem* 27 it is reasonable to understand *oikeiôs* to mean 'not metaphorically' or 'as it happens in nature.'

Throughout the *Problemata*, in fact, the respondent explains all sorts of physiological phenomena that occur inside the body, where they cannot be observed by others, as microcosmic re-enactments of phenomena that are observable in nature. The construction of such explanations rests on whatever external symptoms may accompany the internal phenomenon, plus the individual's subjective perception, as sensed by his internal organs, of what is occurring inside him. Mechanisms to account for these forms of evidence are then proposed in accordance with the reasonable theory that human organs are made up of the same elements that make up everything else in nature and therefore will behave according to the same laws. For instance, after the respondent states that 'anger is due to fire, for it is by retaining a quantity of fire that [people] grow hot within,' he goes on to explain that this explanation is best supported by the observation that children turn red when they are angry, as they would turn red under the influence of any other form of heat. '[C]hildren first of all draw deep breaths and then grow red; for the amount of heat within being great and causing liquefaction makes them grow red, since if anyone were to pour abundant cold water over them they would cease to be angry, for their heat would be quenched.'[61] The application of this method of reasoning is not applied to hydraulic-model phenomena alone. When it is asked, 'Why is it that when men drink, they sweat less if they eat as well?' in reply it is proposed, 'Is it because the food absorbs the moisture, as if a sponge were put upon it, and it is possible to check the flow to a great extent, just as in streams by stopping the channels, by introducing food?'[62] The governing principle here is that the microcosm inside the human body is, in quite a literal fashion, subject to the same rules of nature that govern the macrocosm.

---

60 Aristotle, *Ars rhetorica* 1404b (ed. Roemer, *Aristotelis Ars rhetorica*, 178): 'to de kurion kai to oikeion kai metaphora mona chrêsima pros tên tôn psilôn logôn lexin' (The ordinary sense, the natural or literal sense, and metaphor are only serviceable for the style of bare language [i.e., prose]).
61 Aristotle, *Problemata*, 8.20 (trans. Hett, *Aristotle's Problems*, 1.191; ed. Louis, *Problèmes*, 1.139).
62 Aristotle, *Problemata*, 2.25 (trans. Hett, *Aristotle's Problems*, 1.61; ed. Louis, *Problèmes*, 1.44).

Stoic Psychology and Chrysippus's Defence of
Common-Sense Cardiocentrism

For the Stoics of ancient Greece and Rome, everything that had spatial
extent or the capacity to act upon or be acted upon by another entity was
a body.[63] Accordingly, they understood God and the human soul (*psuchê*)
to be corporeal, made of the subtle gaseous material known as *pneuma*. By
remaining in constant motion inward and outward, *pneuma* takes on a
specific *tonos* or tension and thereby lends both coherence and individual
character to the inert matter which it pervades; no two bodies contain
pneuma with identical *tonos*, and it is *tonos* that differentiates the capacities or behaviours of one type of *pneuma* from those of another. The particular sort of *pneuma* that makes up the human soul takes on eight
different tensions within the body and hence possesses eight distinct faculties, including the five senses, sexual reproduction, and speech. The eighth
part of the soul is the *hêgemonikon*, which governs the other faculties; it
is wholly rational and responsible for all mental and moral activity.[64]
Disruptions to the motion and the *tonos* of the soul also hamper its ability
to reason and hence cause irrational or emotional thought and behaviour.
'Physically speaking,' explains A.A. Long, 'emotions are extreme expansions or contractions of the mind's *pneuma*.'[65] Terms such as '*eparsis*
(swelling), *sustolê* (contraction), *tapeinôsis* (lowering), *diachusis* (melting),
ptoia (fluttering)' were used by the Stoics to describe the spatial deformation of the *pneuma* during the experience of strong emotions.[66] Moreover,
although the concept of mental heat is not as prominent in Stoic psychology as in that of the *Timaeus* or of the *Problemata*, the Stoics understood
anger, a sure source of disruptive expansions and contractions of the *pneuma*, to be a condition of seething around the heart.[67]

---

63 On the relationship between being and substance in classical Stoic thought, see
    Brunschwig, 'Stoic Metaphysics.' Selected topics in Stoic ontology and psychology are
    discussed in greater depth in chapters 4–6 below.
64 On the substance of the *pneuma*, types of *pneuma*, and the functions of the *hêgemoni-
    kon*, see Annas, *Hellenistic Philosophy of Mind*, 37–43 and 61–70; Long, 'Soul and Body
    in Stoicism,' 35–8 and 47–8; Long, 'Stoic Psychology,' 561–72; and Von Staden, 'Body,
    Soul, and Nerves: Epicurus, Herophilus, Erasistratus, the Stoics, and Galen,' 96–105. A
    more expansive treatment of pneumatic psychology is provided by Verbeke,
    L'Évolution de la doctrine du pneuma du Stoïcisme à Saint Augustin.
65 Long, 'Stoic Psychology,' 583.
66 Sedley, 'Chrysippus on Psychophysical Causality,' 329.
67 Lloyd, 'Emotion and Decision in Stoic Psychology,' 240.

Stoic opinion favoured the localization of the *hêgemonikon* in the heart. According to the Stoic philosopher Chrysippus of Soloi (ca. 280–205 BC), 'The heart is the location of the part where all these [parts of the *psychê*] meet, which is the governing part of the *psychê*. That is our doctrine.'[68] As Chrysippus was aware, however, Alcmaeon and the Hippocratics, among others, favoured the brain as the seat of the intellect, based on medical experimentation. Herophilus (ca. 330–250 BC) had even performed experiments that led him 'to specify more precisely than any precursor the location of the soul's central "ruling part": it is in "the ventricle of the brain which is its base."'[69] In his treatise *On the Soul*, now lost but known through fragments quoted by the Greek physician Galen (129–ca. 210 AD), Chrysippus acknowledges competing opinions but vigorously defends cardiocentric psychology, and he even maintains that the common-sense origin of cardiocentrism was a more powerful marker of authority than the empirical data that supported cephalocentrism:[70]

> [W]hile there is agreement about the other parts, people disagree about the governing part of the *psuchê* and have different theories about its location. Some say it is in the region of the chest, others in the head ... the place [of the *psuchê*] seems to elude us since we have neither a clear perception of it, as we had with the others [*scil.* the other parts of the *psuchê*], nor indications from which its location might be deduced. Otherwise there would not have been so much disagreement among physicians and philosophers.[71]

The problem that Chrysippus broaches is the same one that was raised earlier, with respect to the Aristotelian *Problemata*: since nobody can watch what happens inside the body during intense mental states, our conceptualization of the physiology of emotion rests, at least in part, upon the subjective sensations that accompany emotion, most of which are felt in

---

68 Chrysippus, *On the Soul*, preserved in Galen's *On the Doctrines of Hippocrates and Plato* (hereafter *PHP*) 3.1; quoted in translation by Long, 'Stoic Psychology,' 567. See further Sedley, 'Chrysippus on Psychophysical Causality,' esp. 326–31; and Annas, *Hellenistic Philosophy of Mind*, 20–6 and 68–70, on the influence exerted by contemporary medicine on the Stoics' pneumatic psychology and their cardiocentrism.
69 Von Staden, 'Body, Soul, and Nerves,' 87.
70 The preservation and refutation of Chrysippus's *On the Soul* in Galen, *PHP*, is thoroughly treated by Tieleman, *Galen and Chrysippus on the Soul: Argument and Refutation in the* De placitis *Books II–III*.
71 Chrysippus, *On the Soul* (=Galen, *PHP*, 3.1); quoted in translation by Long, 'Stoic Psychology,' 567.

the region of the heart. Chrysippus observes, 'I think that people in general are led to this belief' – that is, the belief that the *hêgemonikon* is located in the heart – 'because they are conscious, as it were, of their mental feelings taking place in the area of the chest and especially in the location of the heart – the sort of feelings especially associated with grief and fear and anger and passion.'[72] In another fragment of *On the Soul* preserved by Galen, Chrysippus indicates that hydraulic-model symptoms formed part of this common-sense psychology:

> The many have ... an inner perception of the passions of the mind happening to them in the region of the chest and especially the place assigned to the heart, as is especially the case in occurrences of grief and fear, in wrath and anger most of all; for impressions arise in us as if it [i.e. anger] were vaporized from the heart and were pushing out against certain parts and were blowing into the face and hands. [73]

These subjective perceptions of 'people in general,' which (as Chrysippus notes) are corroborated by the hydraulic-model idioms that pervade Homeric poetry, constitute what Chrysippus calls the *koinê phora*, the 'common opinion.'[74] Here and elsewhere, Chrysippus invokes the *koinê phora* not as a 'pre-scientific' and inferior alternative to the recent findings of the Greek physicians but as a legitimate source of support for Stoic theories. Chrysippus's refusal to privilege the physicians' empirical findings over those that corroborate everyday experience marks an interesting moment in the historical relationship between common-sense and expert psychologies.

The Physiology of Emotional Distress in the Hebrew Bible

Several recent studies approach idioms of mental activity in the Hebrew Bible from different angles yet arrive at similar conclusions: in the Hebrew Bible, thought and emotion are never localized in the brain, but rather in

---

72 Chrysippus, *On the Soul* (=Galen, *PHP* 2.7); quoted in translation by Long, 'Stoic Psychology,' 570.
73 Chrysippus, *On the Soul* (=Galen, *PHP*, 3.2.5; quoted in translation by Tieleman, *Galen and Chrysippus on the Soul*, 237).
74 Tieleman, *Galen and Chrysippus on the Soul*, 237–44. See also Annas, *Hellenistic Philosophy of Mind*, 68–70.

the chest cavity as well as in the abdomen;[75] additionally, distress is strongly correlated with heat and constriction. David B. Mumford, an academic psychologist whose study of the topic was motivated by his interest in cross-cultural similarities among bodily localizations of distress, finds that in the Hebrew Bible, intense negative emotion is most often identified as, or accompanied by, discomfort in the heart (*leb, lebab*),[76] bowels (*meim*), and belly or womb (*beten*), but not in the chest (*chazeh*); less often this discomfort impinges upon the bones and kidneys. Distress is not localized in the head except where the text makes reference to the eyes, which are said to generate tears or to grow dim.[77] Mark S. Smith additionally observes that the Hebrew idiom attributes a broad range of mental states and contents to the heart but involves the liver and innards only in severe distress.[78] Emotions are localized in the heart in passages such as Ps 13:2 ('How long must I bear pain in my soul, and have sorrow in my heart all day long?'); Ps 13:5 ('my heart shall rejoice in your salvation'); Is 61:1 ('he has sent me to bring good news to the oppressed, to bind up the brokenhearted'); and Jer 23:9 ('My heart is crushed within me, all my bones shake').[79] Rational and contemplative thought are also localized in the heart: see for instance Ps 33:11 ('The counsel of the Lord stands for ever, the thoughts of his heart to all generations'); and Ps 10:6 ('They think in their heart, "We shall not be moved"'). Many other examples could be adduced.[80]

The sensations that afflict the organs of the chest and abdomen are chiefly heat, violent upward motion, and constriction. According to Mumford, the word *chemah* 'anger, fury,' which occurs 110 times in the Hebrew Bible, is etymologically a very close relative of *chom* 'heat.' Heat in the heart is manifested in expressions such as Ps 39:3, 'My heart became hot within me.' The spatial change correlated with distress is typically an upward and agitated motion, as in Job 37:1: 'At this [*scil.* the wrath of

---

75 Smith, 'The Heart and Innards in Israelite Emotional Expression: Notes from Anthropology and Psychobiology,' 432 and n. 27; Robert North, 'Brain and Nerve in the Biblical Outlook,' 577 and 594–5.

76 Robert North is doubtful that the words *leb* and *lebab* necessarily signify the organ that pumps blood; in non-psychological contexts they may denote internal organs of the chest cavity more generally ('Brain and Nerve in the Biblical Outlook,' 592–4).

77 Mumford, 'Emotional Distress in the Hebrew Bible: Somatic or Psychological?' 93 and 95.

78 Smith, 'The Heart and Innards in Israelite Emotional Expressions,' 429–34.

79 Ibid., 429.

80 See esp. Mumford, 'Emotional Distress in the Hebrew Bible,' 94–5.

God] also my heart trembles, and leaps out of its place.'[81] Mumford observes that a number of words signifying distress have their etymological roots in the field of spatial constriction and binding. The words *tsarar, tsarah, tsar, tsir*, meaning 'trouble' or 'distress,' occur well over 100 times, and these are close relatives of *tsur* 'bound up,' 'hemmed in.' The word *chebel*, which occurs ten times in the Hebrew Bible, means 'agony' as well as 'rope' or 'bond,' and as Mumford observes, 'it implies a physical sensation of constriction or tightness,' as in Ps 18:4: 'The cords [*chebel*] of death encompassed me.'[82]

The Hebrew Bible also employs images of voluntary cardiocentric constriction to depict the action of restraining words within the breast. This voluntary constriction may occur with or without being impeded by cardiocentric heat. When distress makes it difficult to hold words within, the heart is hot, as in Ps 39:2–3: 'I was silent and still; I held my peace to no avail; my distress grew worse, my heart became hot within me. While I mused, the fire burned; then I spoke with my tongue.' But it is not necessary that heat be present for an individual to feel as though words are trying to force their way out of the chest cavity. In Job 32:18–20, Elihu says, 'For I am full of words; the spirit within me constrains me. My heart is indeed like wine that has no vent; like new wineskins, it is ready to burst. I must speak, so that I may find relief; I must open my lips and answer.'

Both Mumford and Smith interpret their findings as evidence that hydraulic-model idioms in the Hebrew Bible originated in the subjective perception of somatic accompaniments of strong emotions. 'The reason why the heart occupies such an important place in the biblical language of emotion is not hard to fathom,' writes Mumford. 'Emotional excitement, fear, and distress are all accompanied by cardiac sensations. In terms of somatic sensation, the heart is a much more plausible centre for the emotions than the brain.'[83] Smith likewise concludes that 'the location of emotional responses in various parts of the body in the Psalter was perhaps related to Israelite perceptions of physiological responses to emotions. In

---

81 The Hebrew Bible less often portrays the distressed heart sinking and growing soft, as in Ps 22:14: 'I am poured out like water, and all my bones are out of joint; my heart is like wax; it is melted within my breast': on the softening of the innards resulting in tears, see below. The Psalter appears to have directly inspired all but one of the instances of 'melting mind' in Old English: see Low, 'The Anglo-Saxon Mind,' 112–13 and 183–4.

82 Mumford, 'Emotional Distress in the Hebrew Bible,' 94–5.

83 Ibid., 96.

other words, Israelites associated emotions with the internal organs where the emotions were perceived to be felt physically.'[84]

As we have seen, some OE narratives integrate tears and weeping into narratives of hydraulic-model activity. According to a detailed study by Terence Collins, the biblical Hebrew idiom, too, depicts crying as an extension of internal hydraulic-model activity that reaches all the way up to the eyes. Ps 31:10 reads, 'My eye is wasted with grief; my throat and stomach also.' As Collins interprets this verse, it signals, first, that grief physically wears down those parts of the body that it affects; and second, 'the order in which the body parts are listed (eyes – throat – stomach) gives the picture of a continuous process involving the eyes and stomach as extremities with the throat holding a crucial position as the link between the two.'[85] Collins adduces a further example in Lam 2:11: 'My eyes are wasted through tears, my intestines are in turmoil, my liver is poured out on the ground, because of the destruction of the daughter of my people.' Says Collins, 'we are not dealing here with a metaphorical use of "wasting, longing." Rather the use of the word is to be accounted for in literal terms of physical wasting. The tears are said to make the eyes fail by depriving them of their vital substance which runs out in the form of water.'[86] On the basis of numerous Old Testament passages such as these, Collins offers a composite description of the physiological mechanism by which psychological distress generates tears:

> Distressing, external circumstances produce a physiological reaction in a man, which starts in his intestines and proceeds to affect his whole body, especially the heart. This physiological disturbance is actually a change in the physical composition of the inner organs, a general softening up, which initiates an outflow of the body's vital force. This outflow proceeds through the throat and eyes, and issues in the form of tears which are nothing less than the oozing out of the body's vital substance.[87]

This marks a subtle departure from the mechanism seen in OE narrative and elsewhere, by which tears and words are propelled out of the chest cavity by the outward force of increased pressure within the chest cavity. As Collins interprets the evidence, the internal organs grow soft rather

---

84 Smith, 'The Heart and Innards in Israelite Emotional Expressions,' 431.
85 Collins, 'The Physiology of Tears in the Old Testament: Part I,' 23.
86 Ibid., 20–1.
87 Ibid., 18.

than rigid before tears are generated. At the same time, core symptoms such as abdomino-thoracic heat and the seething up of liquid from the chest cavity remain consistent, even when the organs of the chest cavity grow flaccid rather than hard under the influence of psychological heat.

For the sake of compiling a more diverse body of evidence in support of the application of embodied realism to the hydraulic model, I turn now from ancient texts to a few medieval literatures that also rely on hydraulic-model symptoms in their psychological narratives and discourses. I have not treated classical and Christian Latin psychological idioms separately in this chapter, partly because of their closer relationships to ancient Greek and Hebrew idioms respectively, and also because the presence of hydraulic-model idioms in ancient and medieval Latin writing is implicit in the large number of OE prose translations that draw such idioms from Latin sources. The literary idioms of Old Saxon and Old Irish have of course been influenced to some extent by the idioms of the Hebrew Bible as well, but it is not likely that the psychological concepts present in these literatures entirely postdate the Christianization of the Saxons and the Irish, so the idioms of both literatures lend cultural and diachronic diversity to the evidence compiled here.

Cardiocentrism and the Hydraulic Model in Old Saxon Biblical Poetry

Heavily influenced by the idiom of the Vulgate Bible, but also genetically rooted in the Germanic tradition of versification that gave rise to OE poetry, the psychological idiom of Old Saxon (OS) narrative provides an interesting comparandum for the OE hydraulic model. The OS texts *Heliand* and *Genesis* are verse paraphrases of biblical narratives, and taken together they constitute a sizable majority of the surviving OS corpus. The fourfold constitution of the human being attested in these texts is very similar to that of OE narrative: the mind (OS *hugi, môd, sebo, môdsebo,* etc.) is an integral part of the transient, fleshly body, and this mind-body complex is regularly distinguished from the two entities that depart from it at death, namely the immortal soul (*seola, gêst*) and the ephemeral life-force (*ferah*).[88] As for the location of the *hugi,* it is telling that in *Heliand*

---

88 The boundary between immortal soul and transient life-force is more porous in these OS poems (e.g., *Heliand,* ed. Behaghel, 3350b–3a) than in OE narrative, probably due to the influence of Latin *anima* on OS *seola*: see Green, *Language and History in the Early Germanic World,* 284–5, and La Farge, *'Leben' und 'Seele' in den altgermanischen Sprachen.* Other studies that have explored the relationship among soul, mind, and body

and *Genesis*, none of the compounds beginning in *hôbid-* 'head' signify the mind or mental activity, whereas all of those beginning in *hert-* and *briost-* signify thoughts or emotions.[89] Such evidence strongly suggests not only that the authors of these poems conceived of the heart as the seat of the mind but also that they employed this cardiocentric psychology to the exclusion of any cephalocentric alternative.[90]

Localizations of all types of mental activity in the chest cavity are ubiquitous in the *Heliand*. Simeon, for instance, warns Mary that her infant son will later bring pain to her heart: '"Thu scalt noh," quað he, "cara thiggean, / harm an thînumu herton, than ina heliðo barn / uuâpnun uuîtnod."'[91] When the Jews gather for a holiday feast, the narrator reports, 'Quâmun managa / Iudeon an thene gastseli; uuarð im thar gladmôd hugi, / blîði an iro breostun.'[92] Among the forms of rational thought that reside in the breast are understanding and memory: when Mary first grasps the surprising fact that she has conceived a son by God, the *Heliand*-narrator says, 'siu ira breostun forstôd / iac an ire seƀon selƀo,'[93] and after finding Jesus, still a boy, speaking with the elders in the temple, 'Maria al biheld, / gibarg an ira breostun, sô huuat sô siu gihôrda ira barn sprecan / uuisaro

---

in OS include Augustyn, *The Semiotics of Fate, Death, and the Soul in Germanic Culture*, esp. 106–22 and 132–45 on soul and life-force, and 122–32 on the mind; Flowers, 'Toward an Archaic Germanic Psychology'; and Eggers, 'Altgermanische Seelenvorstellungen im Lichte des Heliand,' in which the terms *herta* and *briost* are purposefully excluded from consideration because the author presumes that cardiocentric psychology is purely metaphorical (270).

89 This assessment is based on the entries in Sehrt, *Vollständiges Wörterbuch zum Heliand und zur altsächsischen Genesis*.

90 This point is worth emphasizing because even OS specialists are prone to lapse into the MnE speaker's habit of using the notion of the heart to stand in for irrational thought and the head to stand in for rational thought: see, for instance, Murphy's cephalocentric interpretations of psychological narratives in the *Heliand*, lines 173b–4a and 3687b–90 (*The Heliand: The Saxon Gospel*, 10 and 120 n. 173).

91 *Heliand* 499b–501a: '"You must yet," he said, "take on sorrow, grief in your heart, when the sons of men kill him with weapons."' Cf. Lk 2:35, where Mary's soul (*animam*), not her heart, is afflicted. See also *Heliand* 5686b–9a. All quotations of and references to the *Heliand* (hereafter *Hl*) and the OS *Genesis* (hereafter *SGen*) follow Behaghel (ed.), *Heliand und Genesis*; translations are mine, made in consultation with Cathey (ed.), *Hêliand: Text and Commentary*, and Murphy (trans.), *The Heliand: The Saxon Gospel*.

92 *Hl* 2736b–8a: 'There came to the guest-hall many Jews; there, their minds grew delighted, happy in the breast.'

93 *Hl* 292b–3a: 'she understood in her breast and in her own mind as well.' See also *Hl* 2371b–2a.

uuordo.'[94] Even the driest and least emotional attributes of the mind, such as *bôkcraft* 'literacy,' reside in the breast: Herod summons all the most learned and eloquent men in Jerusalem, who 'an iro brioston bôkcraftes mêst / uuissun te uuârun.'[95] During his treatment of the Sermon on the Mount, the *Heliand*-narrator lingers over the subject of the mind; following the Gospel account, but contrary to the pattern observed in OE narrative, he maintains the container of the breast cannot keep secrets locked up indefinitely by sheer force of will:

> That mênid thoh breosthugi,
> managoro môdseƀon   manno cunnies,
> huuô alloro erlo gehuilic   ôgit selƀo,
> meldod mid is mûðu,   huilican he môd haƀad,
> hugi umbi is herte: thes ni mag he farhelan eouuiht,
> ac cumad fan them uƀilan man   inuuidrâdos,
> bittara balusprâca,   sulic sô hi an is breostun haƀad
> geheftid umbi is herte: simbla is hugi cûðid,
> is uuilleon mid is uuordun,   endi farad is uuerc aftar thiu.[96]

As in OE, the notion of containment in the heart here carries connotations of sincerity: one's real thoughts and feelings are sheltered there, though one might try to disguise them with contrary words and actions. Unlike the OE idiom, however, which makes the act of voluntary constriction of the breast's contents a prominent marker of idealized masculinity, the *Heliand*-narrator suggests that efforts to constrain one's truest thoughts are ultimately fruitless, and eventually one's words and deeds always fall into line with the contents of the breast.

---

94 *Hl* 830b–2a: 'Mary kept it all, hoarded in her breast whatever knowing words she heard her son say.' In this instance (among others) the diction is directly influenced by the cardiocentric diction of the biblical source text (Lk 2:51).

95 *Hl* 614b–15a: 'indeed knew the greatest book-learning in their breast.' See also *Hl* 4711b–12a.

96 *Hl* 1750b–8: 'Nevertheless, the mind-in-the-breast, the mind-thoughts of many of the human race, makes it clear how every man reveals himself, how he utters with his mouth what sort of mind he has, what sort of mind surrounds his heart. This he cannot conceal at all, but from a wicked person comes wicked counsel, vicious utterances, such as he holds in his breast, fettered around his heart. Always his mind will be made known, his intentions by means of his words, and his deeds will proceed accordingly.' Cf. Lk 6:45.

Among the various expressions that localize the mind in the breast, the prepositional phrases *umbi herta* 'around the heart' and *uuið herta* 'against the heart' most vividly draw attention to the spatial aspect of hydraulic-model activity. The phrase *umbi herta* is nearly always collocated with one of two adjectives, *sêr*, meaning 'sore,' or *hriuuig*, 'painful' or even 'pounding,'[97] as in the narrator's words concerning the distress of the disciples after the Last Supper: 'Thô uuarð môd gumon / suîðo gisuorken endi sêr hugi, / hriuuig umbi iro herte.'[98] Where the phrase *umbi herta* appears with *sêr* and *hriuuig* it suggests a particular spatial disposition of the contents of the chest cavity, in which the mind is wrapped around the heart such that, in moments of distress, the mind presses or strikes inward upon the heart and causes it pain. In some cases this combination of pain and pressure is described as a sensation of heaviness within the breast: concerning the rich man whom Jesus commands to give away all his belongings in order to attain the kingdom of heaven, the narrator says, 'Thô uurðun Kristes uuord kindiungumu manne / suîðo an sorgun, uuas imu sêr hugi, / môd umbi herte ... / uuas imu unôðo innan breostun, / an is sebon suâro.'[99] An equally oppressive spatial relationship between mind and heart is signified by the phrase *uuið herta* 'against the heart,' especially where it is collocated with forms of the verb *uuallan* 'to well up, to seethe,' which is cognate with OE *weallan*. Just before Christ predicts the downfall of Jerusalem, the narrator reports, 'Thô uuel imu an innen / hugi uuið is herte: thô ni mahte that hêlage barn / uuôpu auuîsien, sprak thô uuordo filu / hriuuiglîco.'[100]

---

97 Sehrt, *Vollständiges Wörterbuch zum Heliand*, supplies only psychologized meanings for *hriuuig*, such as *betrübt* 'distressed,' *bekummert* 'anxious,' and *traurig* 'sad,' but according to Orel, *hriuuig* is related to the OS verb *hreuwan* 'to cause pain,' physical as well as emotional, and the etymological roots of *hriuuig* and *hreuwan* lie in the domain of physical striking or pounding (*A Handbook of Germanic Etymology*, 186–7, s.v. **xrewwanan*, **xrewwaz*).

98 *Hl* 4670b–2a: 'Then the men's mind and thought grew very dark, throbbing around the heart.' See also *Hl* 803–4a; *Hl* 3177b–9a; *Hl* 4588b–9a; *SGen* 95b–6. Recall also that the before-and-after narrative of the state of the devils' hearts in the OE *Genesis B*, which is closely derived from (mostly missing portions of) the OS *Genesis*, includes the contracting and loosening of the mind around the heart (*ymb heortan*) as their mood changes (*GenB* 353b–4a and 758b–9a; see chapter 2 above).

99 *Hl* 3290–5a: 'Then the words of Christ truly became a source of sorrow for the young man; painful was his mind, the thought surrounding the heart ... in his breast he was heavy, in his mind he was weighed down.'

100 *Hl* 3687b–90a: 'When inside him his mind welled up against his heart, then the holy Son could not hold back from weeping: he then spoke many painful words.' See also *Hl* 606–8a.

The *Heliand*-poet had frequent recourse to the verb *uuallan* as well as the verb *belgan*, cognate with OE *belgan* 'to swell (with rage),' to characterize the effects of anger and other intense negative emotions within the chest cavity. For instance, Christ warns his followers not to offer sacrifices when motivated by malice: 'gi ne mugun mid gibolgono hugi / iuuuas gôdes uuiht te godes hûsun / uualdande fargeban.'[101] Though the *Heliand*-poet employed no cognates of OE *rummod* 'roomy-minded, generous,' Christ's warning may imply that while the mind is swollen by malice it cannot be 'roomy' enough to make a sincerely generous offering. In other instances, the narrator's diction underscores that mental swelling is a source of pain within the chest cavity: 'Thô uuarð im thes an sorgun hugi, / môd mornondi,' he says of Herod; '… he sô hriuuig sat, / balg ina an is briostun.'[102] Three verb forms signifying cardiocentric swelling are concentrated in a few lines of the dramatic scene in which Peter is provoked to cut off the ear of the high priest's slave.

> Thô gibolgan uuarð
> snel suerdthegan,   Sîmon Petrus,
> uuell imu innan hugi,   that he ni mahte ênig uuord sprekan:
> sô harm uuarð imu an is hertan,   that man is hêrron thar
> bindan uuelde.   Thô he gibolgan geng,
> suîðo thrîstmôd thegan   for is thiodan standen,
> hard for is hêrron: ni uuas imu is hugi tuîfli,
> blôð an is breostun.[103]

In this state of swelling and seething, Peter is incapable of uttering a word; this effect is quite the opposite of what we would expect in an OE narrative, where excessive cardiocentric swelling leads to mental volatility and vulnerability to unmanly outbursts. Perhaps this is because Peter's mental

---

101 *Hl* 1464b–6a: 'with a swollen mind you cannot give any of your goods to the Ruler at the house of God.'

102 *Hl* 720b–4a: 'His mind then fell into anxiety, his mind became mournful … thus he sat, in pain, and he swelled up in his breast.' See also *Hl* 1437b–9a, *SGen* 32b–3a, *SGen* 233b–8.

103 *Hl* 4865b–72a: 'Then Simon Peter, the bold sword-thegn, grew swollen; his mind seethed within him, so that he was unable to utter any word. Thus there came to be grief in his heart, because someone intended to tie up his lord there. Swollen, he then departed, the very bold-minded thegn, to stand before his king, resolute before his lord: his mind was not wavering, not timorous in his breast.'

swelling makes him *hard*, an adjective that can bear a positive connotation such as 'bold' or 'stoical,' or a negative one, such as 'hardened' or 'stubborn.' Yet there are instances in the *Heliand* in which cardiocentric turmoil and pressure send hot tears pouring out through the eyes, much like water boiling over and spilling out of its container.[104] Lazarus's sisters Martha and Mary both beseech Jesus to raise their brother from the dead, but it is Mary who stirs Jesus' compassion sufficiently to bring him to tears: 'griat gornundi, antat themu godes barne / hugi uuarð gihrôrid: hête trahni / uuôpu auuellun.'[105] These lines are suggestive of a full-fledged hydraulic-model mechanism in which the 'hot tears' are brought forth and sobs made to 'well up' by the emotional turbulence that Mary kindles in Jesus' breast, but admittedly not all the stages of this mechanism are plainly represented. A fuller picture of the physiology of tears is provided in the account of Peter's emotional reaction to the realization that he has just denied Christ for a third time.

> Thes thram imu an innan môd
> bittro an is breostun,   endi geng imu thô gibolgan thanen
> the man fan theru menigi   an môdkaru,
> suîðo an sorgun,   endi is selƀes uuord,
> uuamscefti uueop,   antat imu uuallan quâmun
> thurh thea hertcara   hête trahni,
> blôdage fan is breostun.[106]

Christ's prophecy, or Peter's memory of it, swells up (*thram*) in Peter's mind and breast;[107] Peter himself is also said to be swollen (*gibolgan*) as he

---

104 The mechanism is strikingly similar to that which Collins describes in the idiom of distress of the Hebrew Bible (see above), but in the passages that I quote here, which paraphrase New Testament material, the *Heliand*-poet is invoking a hydraulic-model mechanism for the production of tears without prompting from his biblical source.

105 *Hl* 4071–3a: 'Lamenting, she complained until the mind of God's son was moved: hot tears welled up with his weeping.'

106 *Hl* 5000b–6a: 'This swelled up in his mind, bitterly in his breast, and thus swollen he went from that place, the man went from the multitude, in a state of mind-worry and deeply in sorrow, and he bewailed his own words, his sinfulness, until there came hot and bloody tears welling up from his breast because of his heart-worry.'

107 Sehrt, *Vollständiges Wörterbuch zum Heliand*, glosses *thrimman*, which occurs only once in OS, as *anschwellen* 'swell up,' but Orel suggests the meaning 'to jump, to spring,' and indicates that *thrimman* is cognate with Latin *tremo* 'shake, quake' (*A Handbook of Germanic Etymology*, 425–6, s.v. **þremmanan*).

goes away to weep in solitude. In this context *gibolgen* seems much more likely to mean 'swollen' than 'enraged,' since Peter's state of mind is more sorrowful and anxious than angry, as indicated by the words *môdkaru, sorgun,* and *hertcara.* Because of this cardiocentric distress (*thurh thea hertcara*) whose most prominent symptom is swelling, his tears grow hot and come up boiling (*uuallan quâmun*) from his breast. The tears, in fact, are not only hot but bloody, emphasizing the severity of the pain and injury that his heart endures during this crisis.

While there is much that the OS hydraulic-model idiom shares with that of OE narrative, several salient differences stand out. With respect to the physiological mechanisms suggested by hydraulic-model idioms, frequent mention is made of cardiocentric swelling and seething and even the production of hot tears, but only very rarely is psychological heat mentioned on its own as a symptom of distress. Vigorous faith in God was likely conceptualized as a form of cardiocentric heat; this is the implication, at any rate, of the narrator's observation that the faith that a man 'considers in his heart' (*an is hertan gehugda*) is all too easily extinguished or 'cooled' by greed: 'than he imu farfâhid an fehogiri, / aleskid thene gilôbon.'[108] But throughout the *Heliand* and the OS *Genesis,* cardiocentric heat is much less prominent than cardiocentric firmness and softness, both of which can be virtuous or vicious depending on the context, much like cardiocentric heating and cooling in OE.

Cardiocentrism and the Heat of Passion in Medieval Irish Texts

'[T]hroughout the history of the Irish language,' writes Liam Mac Mathúna, 'the designation of the concept of "the heart" has been remarkably stable and uniform, being conveyed by *cride* and its orthographical and phonological successors.'[109] What Mac Mathúna calls the 'concept' of the heart encompasses the cluster of mental faculties and physical responses associated with the organ of the heart in other cardiocentric psychologies examined thus far, and this cardiocentrism appears in a number of different literary registers and discourses in early Irish.

---

108 *Hl* 2503–4a: 'when he entangles himself in greed, he chills his faith.'
109 Mac Mathúna, 'Lexical and Literary Aspects of "Heart" in Irish,' 1. In my ahistorical discussion of analogues I have avoided the vexed problem of dating the composition of premodern Irish texts that appear to be early medieval but survive only in later medieval or early modern manuscripts.

In legendary narratives, the heart was often the seat of the qualities that made a hero a hero. For instance, in the *Story of Mac Datho's Pig*, when Conall and Cet exchange honorific greetings upon meeting, Cet uses a long series of cardiocentric and hydraulic-model epithets to convey his esteem for Conall's hardiness: 'Fochen Conall, cride licce, londbruth loga, luchair ega, guss flann ferge fo chích curad crēchtaig cathbūadaig.'[110] That this heroic *cride* is a fleshly organ, and not just a metonymic representation of the mind or of courage, is brought home by one account of the hero Cú Chulainn's death. Mortally wounded, he looks into his chest cavity and observes the organ of the heart itself, and is surprised to find that, unlike the hearts of legendary heroes, his own is made of nothing but flesh and blood.

> ꝗ do chuirsion a ucht ꝗ urbhruinne risan choirthe ꝗ thug lámh ara chroidhe ꝗ do ghabh aga choimdechadh. 'Truagh sin,' ar Cú Chulainn, 'do-bheirim fom bhréithir ꝗ toingim fona déibh aordha, nárbh féidir nach croidhe cloiche nó cnámha nó iarainn do bhí ionnam, nach dénainn leth a ndernus do ghaisgedh nó do ghníomhartaibh.'[111]

But heroic poetry is not the only genre to psychologize the heart. An early medieval Irish text known as the *Cauldron of Poesy* ponders the origin and localization of the intellectual and artistic gifts that make a man a poet. The speech generated by the gift of poetry emanates from the chest cavity: 'dliucht sóer sóeras broinn / bélrae mbil brúchtas úad.'[112] The Irish cardiocentric

110 *Scéla mucce Meic Dathó*, 15.9–11 (ed. Thurneysen, *Scéla mucce Meic Dathó*, 14): 'Welcome Conall, heart of stone, angry heat of the hero, glittering of ice, red strength of anger beneath the breast of a champion who is covered in wounds and victorious in battle' (translation mine).

111 *Aided Con Culainn* (qtd by Mac Mathúna, 'Lexical and Literary Aspects,' 4): 'And [Cú Chulainn] placed his chest and his breast against the pillar and put his hand on his heart and proceeded to look at it. "That is a pity," said Cú Chulainn, "I give my word and I swear by the gods of the air, that I did not know until today that it was not a heart of stone or bone or iron that was within me, and if I had known that it was a heart of blood or flesh that was in me, I would not have done half of the valour or the deeds that I did"' (trans. ibid.).

112 *The Cauldron of Poesy*, lines 3–4 (ed. Breatnach, 'The Caldron of Poesy,' 62): 'a noble privilege which ennobles the breast is the fine speech which pours forth from it' (trans. ibid., 63). There is some disagreement over the location of the mental faculty involved in composing poetry: 'Where is the source of poetic art in a person; in the body or in the soul?' the *Cauldron*-speaker asks. 'Some say in the soul since the body does nothing without the soul. Others say in the body since it is inherent in one in accordance

idiom converges with that of the Bible in the mid-eighth-century Würzburg Glosses on the Pauline epistles, in which *cride* signifies the locus of belief, as in the gloss '.i. conrop inonn cretem bes hifar cridiu et anasberaid hó bélib';[113] *cride* is also the abode of God within a person and is therefore susceptible to being preyed upon by the devil, as indicated by the gloss '.i. athuidecht icride tar ési dæ.'[114] As in the OE idiom, the heart can be expanded by spiritual or intellectual enlightenment: another of the Würzburg Glosses reads '.i. badlethan formenme et forcride ocairitin indforcitil sa.'[115] The same cardiocentric localization of the mind – or psychologization of the heart – is also represented in medical discourse, again underscoring that this *cride* is a fleshly organ. The later medieval medical treatise *Regimen na sláinte* discusses psychological injuries as a source of damage to the organ of the heart: 'oir is fiadnuise neich eigin eagnaid co fuilid da namuid urchoideacha ag an craidi, .i. in midochus ⁊ in dobron ... ⁊ is mor an urchoid do-nid an da chinel so don chraidi.'[116]

Old Irish texts employ a hydraulic-model idiom as well, in which heat and swelling are the most prominent symptoms, and they are chiefly associated with anger, the battle-rage of heroes, and other aggressively passionate mental states. Several scholars have drawn attention to the etymological relationships that underscore the correlation of heat with intense mental states. 'The noun *grís* means "heat, fire, embers" and, figuratively, "ardour, valour, passion,"' observes Proinsias Mac Cana; other words denoting heat and redness, he continues, have given rise to causative verbs that denote the act of incitement or of provocation.[117] Likewise, Kim McCone points

---

with physical relationship, i.e. from one's father or grandfather' (lines 19–22; ibid., 64–5).

113 Würzburg Glosses 7d10, glossing 1 Cor 1:10 (qtd by Mac Mathúna, 'Lexical and Literary Aspects,' 9): 'i.e. so that the belief which is in your heart, and what ye utter with (your) lips may be the same' (trans. ibid.).

114 Würzburg Glosses 22b5, glossing Eph 4:27 (qtd by Mac Mathúna, 'Lexical and Literary Aspects,' 9): 'i.e. his [the devil's] coming into the heart in place of God' (trans. ibid.).

115 Würzburg Glosses 16a15, glossing 2 Cor 6:13 (qtd by Mac Mathúna, 'Lexical and Literary Aspects,' 9): 'i.e. let your mind and your heart be enlarged in receiving this teaching' (trans. ibid.).

116 *Regimen na sláinte*, lines 1642–7 (qtd by Mac Mathúna, 'Lexical and Literary Aspects,' 3–4): 'for it is the testimony of some wise person that the heart has two injurious enemies, that is despair and grief; and great is the damage which these two types do to the heart' (trans. ibid.). The date of this medical treatise has been estimated to fall within the first quarter of the fifteenth century.

117 Mac Cana, '*Laíded, gressacht* "Formalized Incitement,"' 84–5.

out that 'at the level of vocabulary *fichid* "fights" and *fichid* "boils" are homonyms, while *grís* "heat" and *bruth* "boiling heat" also mean "ardour, valour," *daig* "flame" can signify "hero" and so on.'[118] And again, according to Sayers, 'When Cú Chulainn fails to dispatch his opponents quickly, the verb employed to describe the satirical incitation given by Bricriu or Lóeg is *gressaid*, the same term as used to work a bellows. *Brostaid* "urges, incites" was used as well of stirring up a fire. The verb *grísaid* was also used for both incitation and causing to glow. Similarly, *bruth* "ardour, anger, fury" was used of a charge of metal put in a smelter and of the resulting molten mass.'[119]

Some of the symptoms that typically follow upon heat in other hydraulic-model idioms are present in medieval Irish literature as well, and in narrative they are not limited to anger and battle rage but also accompany profound grief. A poem attributed to Gormlaith, a tenth-century woman of the ruling class, supplies an instance of cardiocentric swelling: 'Fa Chloinn Uisnigh dob fearr clú / do bhí Deirdre mur tú anois, / a croidhe ina clíaph gur att.'[120] The bursting of the heart could be fatal; in *Aided Muirchertaig meic Erca* it is said of the widow Duaibhsech that after she witnessed the priests carrying her late husband's body, then 'ro mebaid cró-maidm dia craide 'na cliab ⁊ fuair bas fo chētōir ann sin do chumaid a fir.'[121] And in the *Táin Bó Cúailnge*, when a certain smith is devastated by the death of his hound, the narrator reports, 'Ba béim cride fri cliab leis.'[122]

This sharp and sometimes fatal cardiocentric pain that accompanies profound grief is often expressed in an idiom peculiar to Irish literature, in which the verb *cnómaidid* 'breaks like a nut' is collocated with *cride* 'heart.'[123] This expression appeared in the foregoing description of the widow Duaibsech's grief; likewise, Findabair's heart fatally 'breaks like a

118 McCone, *Pagan Past and Christian Present in Early Irish Literature*, 171.
119 Sayers, 'The Smith and the Hero: Culann and Cú Chulainn,' 243.
120 Gormlaith, *Poem* 8.4.1–3 (ed. Bergin, *Irish Bardic Poetry,* 210): 'Concerning Uisnech's famous children Deirdre was as I am now, until her heart burst [literally 'swelled'] within her bosom' (trans. ibid., 312). On attribution and dating, see ibid., 202–3.
121 *Aided Muirchertaig meic Erca* 46 (qtd by Mac Mathúna, 'Lexical and Literary Aspects,' 15): 'a great bursting forth of blood broke her heart in her breast and she died immediately from grief for her husband' (trans. ibid.).
122 *Táin Bó Cúalnge*, Recension II, line 894 (ed. O'Rahilly, *Táin Bó Cúalnge from the Book of Leinster*, 107): 'He felt it like a blow of the heart against the breast' (trans. ibid., 243). On this and subsequent passages drawn from Recension II of the *Táin*, see Mac Mathúna, 'Lexical and Literary Aspects,' 11–14.
123 Mac Mathúna, 'Lexical and Literary Aspects,' 11.

nut' when she learns that a struggle for her hand in marriage has resulted in the death of hundreds of excellent warriors: 'ro maid cnómaidm dá cride 'na clíab ar ⁊ féile ⁊ náre.'[124] Mac Mathúna reports several additional instances of this idiom, including that which appears in the closing lines of the *Táin Bó Cúailnge*, where the Brown Bull of Cooley dies after slaughtering countless people: 'Tuc a druim risin tilaig assa aithle ⁊ ro maid cnómaidm dá chride 'na chlíab.'[125]

In a later version of the Brown Bull of Cooley episode, the beast's heartbreak is manifested outside the body, for after his heart breaks like a nut, the narrator reports, 'do cuir a croidi 'na duibhlia dubhfhola tara bhel amach.'[126] It is not unusual in medieval Irish narratives to find that intense negative emotions cannot be concealed within the chest cavity but, against the sufferer's will, make themselves manifest on the outside of the body. Not all cases are as dramatic as that of the Brown Bull of Cooley; in response to humiliation, bubbles and blisters are said to be raised upon the cheeks as a severe effect of facial flushing.[127] At the other end of the spectrum are the grotesquely demonstrative transformations of Cú Chulainn by heat and swelling that accompany battle-rage. As a boy, when attacked by his young playmates, he 'became distorted,' opening his mouth so wide that his innards were visible; his hair appeared to be on fire, and a light shone above his head.[128] Later, as a seventeen-year-old, once he takes up arms to prove his valour, he cannot be vanquished until

---

124 *Táin Bó Cúalnge*, Recension II, line 3888 (ed. O'Rahilly, *Táin Bó Cúalnge from the Book of Leinster*, 107): 'her heart cracked like a nut in her breast through shame and modesty' (trans. ibid., 243).

125 *Táin Bó Cúalnge*, Recension II, lines 4916–17 (ed. O'Rahilly, *Táin Bó Cúalnge from the Book of Leinster*, 136): 'After that he turned his back to the hill and his heart broke like a nut in his breast' (trans. ibid., 272).

126 *Táin Bó Cúailnge*, Stowe version, lines 5094–8 (qtd by Mac Mathúna, 'Lexical and Literary Aspects,' 14): 'he threw up his heart in a black gushing of black blood out of his mouth' (trans. ibid.).

127 McCone, *Pagan Past and Christian Present*, explains, 'Like bubbles (*bolga*) rising to the surface of a heated cauldron's contents, blisters (*ferba, bolga*) are raised upon a cheek burned by the shame of satire or the like, as happened when the poet Néde lampooned Caier to force him out of the kingship ... Indeed, Cormac's Glossary defines *ferb* "blister" as "a bubble that comes upon a person's face after satire or after false judgement"' (173).

128 *Táin Bó Cúailnge*, Recension I, lines 428–34 (ed. and trans. O'Rahilly, *Táin Bó Cúailnge, Recension I*, 14 and 137). This passage is very frequently discussed in the secondary literature; see esp. McCone, *Pagan Past and Christian Present*, 171–2; and Enright, 'Fires of Knowledge.'

(having been distracted by three women who bare their breasts to him) Cú Chulainn is captured by the warriors of Emain, who extinguish the heat of his battle-rage with nothing more than cold water. These warriors, the narrator reports,

> seized him and cast him into a tub of cold water. That tub burst about him. The second tub into which he was plunged boiled hands high therefrom. The third tub into which he went after that he warmed so that its heat and its cold were properly adjusted for him. Then he came out and the queen, Mugain, put on him a blue mantle with a silver brooch therein.[129]

When Cú Chulainn again experiences the 'warp-spasm' as an adult, its outward manifestations are even more dramatic. His joints are violently distorted, and the muscles of his calves and his head grow to enormous proportions. Again he opens his mouth wide enough to reveal his innards, and 'his lungs and his liver fluttered in his mouth and his throat ... every stream of fiery flakes which came into his mouth from his throat was as wide as a ram's skin. The loud beating of his heart against his ribs was heard like the baying of a bloodhound.' This display culminates with 'the straight stream of blood which rose up from the very top of his head.'[130]

External Manifestations of the Hydraulic Model in Irish and Old Norse

There is no question that medieval Irish narratives associate aggressive and negative passions with cardiocentric distress, heat, swelling, and outward pressure, but does it all add up to a hydraulic model of the mind? The constellation of symptoms accompanying energetic mental states makes the Irish idiom a loose analogue of the OE hydraulic model, but there are important mechanical differences and social ramifications. The internal heat and swelling brought about by aggressive passions in Irish narrative are so frequently manifested on the outside of the body that any notion of voluntary cardiocentric constriction would be difficult to reconcile with the Irish idiom of distress. In other words, because there are outlets for psychological heat and swelling – the spewing of blood, the blisters that are raised on the face, the external swelling of the body – this idiom lacks

---

129 *Táin Bó Cúailnge*, Recension I, lines 814–19 (ed. and trans. O'Rahilly, *Táin Bó Cúailnge, Recension I*, 25 and 148).
130 *Táin Bó Cúailnge*, Recension I, lines 2245–78 (ed. and trans. O'Rahilly, *Táin Bó Cúailnge, Recension I*, 68–9 and 187).

the motif, prominent in OE narrative, in which the individual struggles to keep all perceptible signs of cardiocentric distress locked down in his chest cavity. One might say that the pectoral container is not 'sealed' in Irish narrative as it is in OE, and this difference affects both the mechanics and the ethics of the physiology of emotion.

The tendency to emphasize the external manifestations rather than the internal effects of psychological heat and swelling is a feature that the medieval Irish idiom shares with that of Old Norse literature, very possibly as a result of centuries' worth of cultural exchange beginning in the early Middle Ages. In the present chapter I have not included a section on Old Norse reflexes of the hydraulic model, but all of its core features are well represented in the literature: cardiocentric localization, heat, boiling, pressure and heaviness of the breast. External manifestations of these symptoms may be mild, as in the case of facial flushing, or extreme, as in this episode in *Njal's Saga*: 'Þórhalli Ásgrímssyni brá svá við, er honum var sagt, at Njáll, fóstri hans, var dauðr ok hann hafði inni brunnit, at hann þrútnaði allr ok blóðbogi stóð ór hvárritveggju hlustinni, ok varð eigi stǫðvat, ok fell hann í óvit, ok þá stǫðvaðisk.'[131] A certain amount of shame is nonetheless attached to such an unbridled outward display of grief: after Thorhall recovers from the aforementioned incident, the narrator states, 'stóð hann upp ok kvað sér lítilmannliga verða.'[132] Additionally, as in the foregoing account of the death of Cú Chulainn, in which he examines his own heart looking for physical markers of heroism, the fleshly organ of the heart plays a prominent role in Old Norse psychological narratives. In the *Skaldskaparmál* of the *Prose Edda*, the ingestion of the heart's blood of a dragon gives Sigurth the power to understand the language of birds, for example.[133] The poem *Atlakviða*, which forms part of the *Poetic Edda*, includes an episode in which the hearts cut from the breasts of two living men reveal, by their quivering and their stillness respectively, that one belonged

---

131 *Brennu-Njáls Saga*, ch. 132 (ed. Sveinsson, Íslenzk Fornrit 12, 344; trans. Magnusson and Pálsson, *Njal's Saga*, 277): 'Thorhall Asgrimsson was so shocked when he heard that his foster-father, Njal, had been burned to death, that his whole body swelled up; a stream of blood spouted from his ears and could not be staunched, until he fell down unconscious and the flow ceased of its own accord.'

132 *Brennu-Njáls Saga*, ch. 132 (ed. Sveinsson, Íslenzk Fornrit 12, 344; trans. Magnusson and Pálsson, *Njal's Saga*, 277): 'he got up and said that he had not behaved like a man.'

133 Snorri Sturluson, *Skaldskaparmál*, ch. 112–13 (trans. Byock, in Snorri, *The Prose Edda: Norse Mythology*, 97–8).

to a coward and one belonged to a hero.[134] In this tale, the physiological difference between cowardice and coolness, which in other literatures is typically known only to the narrator and the person experiencing the corresponding cardiocentric sensations, is revealed to a larger audience by an act of brutality that brings Hialli's and Hǫgni's hearts out of their breasts and before the eyes of others. The cardiocentric psychology of Old Norse narrative is, in fact, one of the most intriguing psychological idioms in all of medieval literature and is worthy of a much more detailed investigation, but it would not be possible in the scope of the present chapter to do justice to its complexity.[135] Additionally, since the purpose of the present compilation of hydraulic-model analogues is to support the theory of embodied realism, Old Norse can add little meaningful evidence to a body of data that already includes three literatures with which it shares significant cultural links: Old English, medieval Irish, and Old Saxon.

Ancient and Medieval Analogues as Evidence Corroborating Embodied Realism

The similarities between just the Homeric and biblical Hebrew psychological idioms are sufficiently striking to have led Mumford to speculate about the independent origins of each idiom in the bodily experience of emotional distress. 'Both Hebrew and Greek notions of the heart might have had common roots in the language and culture of the Phoenicians, from whom both languages derived their alphabets,' Mumford proposes. 'But a simpler explanation is at hand: emotional excitement, fear and distress are all accompanied by cardiac sensations ... The focus on the heart as the emotional center may have arisen independently in all these cultures.'[136] This reasoning, which is plausible when supported by data from only two unrelated cultures, becomes more compelling in light of the other ancient and medieval analogues adduced above.[137]

---

134 *Atlakviða* 23.3–10 and 25.3–10 (ed. and trans. Dronke, *The Poetic Edda, Volume I: Heroic Poems*, 8).
135 Some idea of the complex and profound differences that separate Old Norse concepts of the soul and mind from other Western Germanic psychologies may be gathered from Turville-Petre, *Myth and Religion of the North*, 221–30 and 269–74; Strömbäck, 'The Concept of the Soul in Nordic Tradition'; Flowers, 'Toward an Archaic Germanic Psychology.'
136 Mumford, 'Somatic Symptoms and Psychological Distress in the *Iliad* of Homer,' 147.
137 It bears mention that Simon Nicholson has undertaken a study of Anglo-Saxon concepts of emotion that proceeds along methodological lines very similar to those used

Up to this point I have treated the various permutations on the hydraulic model as analogues, so that I might prescind from examining their textual relationships with Anglo-Saxon psychologies. Without delving into this fraught problem in any detail, I would like to conclude this discussion of ancient and medieval analogues with a few general observations. The fact that the Anglo-Saxons shared some aspects of cardiocentrism and the hydraulic model with their continental Saxon contemporaries surely owes *something* to the concepts of the mind that were current among their common ancestors prior to the migrations of the Angles and the Saxons. Consequently, when we have already considered the OE hydraulic model in such detail, OS analogues offer only tenuous support for the embodied origins of the hydraulic model, because they arguably evolved from the same pool of northern Germanic concepts about mind and body. The biblical Hebrew and medieval Irish analogues are more useful in this regard. Obviously the Anglo-Saxons absorbed Old Testament diction into their own literature and had ongoing cultural contacts with the Celtic populations of the British Isles, but if any part of their cardiocentric psychology developed before the migration period – which seems likely, given that it is deeply ingrained in the diction of the least Christianized works of OE literature – then it necessarily originated independently of biblical and Irish influences. As for the ancient Greek analogues, their philosophical elaboration of hydraulic-model mechanisms occurred independently of any influence from Hebrew scriptures, and in turn, in the unlikely event that continental Germanic populations or the Anglo-Saxons or the Irish had direct knowledge of Greek literature or philosophy in the early Middle Ages, it is inconceivable that such knowledge was profound enough

---

in Mumford's studies of the *Iliad* and the Old Testament; Nicholson's objective was to evaluate whether Julian Leff was correct to posit that the Anglo-Saxons (like other cultures he deemed 'primitive') were indeed 'incapable of distinguishing between somatic and psychic aspects of moods' (Nicholson, 'The Expression of Emotional Distress in Old English Prose and Verse,' 327). I have not cited this study in any part of the foregoing discussion because even while arguing against Leff, Nicholson uncritically perpetuates Leff's assumption that the psychological and the somatic are necessarily as discrete in other cultures as they are in twentieth-century Anglo-American discourse. Consequently, Nicholson does not even entertain the possibility that the mind-in-the-heart might be non-metaphorical: he writes, for instance, 'Some words appear to carry connotations of bodily disturbance but in fact refer exclusively to states of mind. For example, *hatheortnes* is found in [the OE] *Boethius* and means anger or rage. *Breostcearu* is literally translatable as breast-care and means anxiety or grief' (ibid., 330). (On Leff's controversial studies of non-Western emotional idioms, see below.)

to have a formative influence over their dominant psychological idioms.[138] The Old Irish, ancient Greek, and biblical Hebrew analogues, placed alongside the hydraulic-model idioms of medieval Germanic literatures, therefore support the proposition that cardiocentrism and the hydraulic model originated independently in multiple cultures, a phenomenon most simply explained by the theory of embodied realism, which maintains that certain aspects of the subjective experience of living in the human body are cross-culturally consistent, and that they constrain and possibly even shape the formation of conceptual models along similar lines in disparate cultures.

With the exception of the hydraulic model of the Hebrew Bible, all of the analogues considered thus far belong to Indo-European cultures and languages. If embodied realism is truly the soundest explanation for the cross-cultural persistence of the hydraulic model, we should expect to find the hydraulic-model idiom manifested in even more disparate cultures and languages. Therefore I turn now from premodern literatures to a wholly different class of evidence: the data that cognitive linguists, anthropologists, psychologists, and psychiatrists have gathered in their investigations of idioms of mental activity in present-day cultures and languages worldwide.

Present-Day Analogues of the Hydraulic Model

The available evidence for present-day manifestations of the hydraulic model is drawn not from surveys of large corpora of literary or philosophical texts but from the brief glimpses of hydraulic-model phenomena that are afforded by linguistic, anthropological, and psychiatric investigations of idioms of distress. Expressions of anger are disproportionately prominent because cognitive linguists have employed cross-cultural studies of anger as the basis for developing theories of metaphor formation, including embodied realism. Moreover, for some cultures and languages I have access to a sizable and diverse body of evidence, while for others I have encountered only one or two idioms pertinent to the hydraulic model. Therefore, rather than examining individual cultures' hydraulic-model idioms one at a time, it is more expedient to sum up the cross-cultural evidence for each individual hydraulic-model symptom.

---

138 Lapidge leaves open the question of whether Theodore and Hadrian might have brought knowledge of Greek literature to a significant number of students at the Canterbury school ('The Comparative Approach,' 31), while Enright, 'Fires of Knowledge,' is more optimistic that the medieval Irish did in fact have knowledge of Greek epic.

Before I proceed to the data, I wish to foreground one very important disclaimer. Any comparison of ancient and medieval thought with
present-day non-Western analogues is likely to raise the spectre of the
old-fashioned anthropological primitivism that characterized the thought
of nineteenth- and early-twentieth century figures such as Durkheim
and Mauss. My rationale for setting OE psychological idioms alongside present-day analogues is altogether different from that of the earlier
anthropological tradition. What OE psychology has in common with
a significant number of psychological idioms used in present-day non-
industrialized cultures is *not* that they are 'primitive,' but rather that they
are free from the influence of Descartes, whose mind-body dualism exerts
so strong an influence on modern North American and European popular
concepts of the mind. Plenty of industrialized cultures still employ non-
Cartesian concepts of mind or rely upon hydraulic-model idioms rooted
in pre-Cartesian concepts of mind. Moreover, in cultures whose popular
psychologies are influenced by recent trends in neuroscience, laypersons
have superficial knowledge of the growing body of evidence that favours
psychological materialism and mind-body holism: consequently, the more
we learn about how our biochemistry constrains our behaviours and our
thoughts, the more naive and indeed 'primitive' our popular Cartesian
mind-body dualism will appear. And so I ask the reader to pay careful
attention to what I argue in the following pages: I do not claim that mind-
body holism is a peculiar feature of 'primitive' cultures, but rather (in
agreement with Kirmayer, Fabrega, and other specialists in cross-cultural
psychology) I claim that present-day mind-body dualism is a peculiar
feature of the relatively few cultures that have embraced Descartes, and
that among cultures outside the very small Cartesian minority, mind-body
holism is prevalent and is often articulated in the form of cardiocentrism
and a hydraulic model of the mind.

Cardiocentrism

Present-day cultures that employ idioms rooted in cardiocentric psychology do not all share a single understanding of the relationship between the
mind and the organ of the heart. For typical speakers of American English,
the localization of mental activity in the heart is metaphorical: individuals
who conceive of the brain as the seat of the mind nonetheless localize
mental activity in the heart to signal that such activity is more profound,
more personal, or more emotional than the dry, rational, ineffable activities of the brain. In contrast, the common-sense psychology current in

Jamaica actually localizes the mind in the chest cavity, near but not identical to the heart. In her study of Jamaican concepts of mind, cultural anthropologist E.J. Sobo writes,

> Once they have occupied the heart, emotions can occupy the *mind*, which is also situated in the chest and which is experienced as the voice that tells one what to do. Unlike the heart, the mind is not often pictured as a tangible or corporeal organ. People rarely drew it in the internal body drawings that they made for me. But they often said that it was there as they explained the anatomical illustrations that they made.[139]

Most of Sobo's Jamaican informants distinguish between the organ of the heart and the invisible mind that resides near the heart, but such a distinction is not made in all cardiocentric psychologies. The popular Jamaican understanding of the mind-body relationship is different from that which characterizes the cardiocentric psychology of the Punjabis, a major ethnic group originating in Pakistan and India. According to Inga Britt-Krause, Punjabi immigrants to Britain employ an idiom of distress that includes a condition called 'sinking heart,' which is thought to arise from the heat generated in the heart during the experience of intense distress, especially anger. One Punjabi interviewee quoted in Britt-Krause's study remarked, 'You can get [sinking heart] from all kinds of feelings. When you feel very angry and your body becomes hot, your heart is making a lot of heat and then your heart can sink or you can have a heart attack.'[140] Britt-Krause explains, '"The heart is sinking" is an English translation of *dil ghirda hai*. This refers to an illness or a state which may be physical or emotional or both. *Ghirna* means to fall, sink, drop, stumble or to be killed in battle.' As a corrective to the presupposition that 'sinking heart' is a metaphorical expression of a purely psychological condition, she proceeds to clarify that '"my heart is sinking" is not analogous to "I am worried." Punjabis label their illness [sinking heart] when feelings of anxiety are combined with physical sensations in the heart or chest.'[141] In other words, one and the same organ is the locus of the emotional distress and the somatic symptoms. Geographically near to the Punjabis but culturally distinct, the Newar ethnic group of the Kathmandu Valley in Nepal also subscribes to a strongly cardiocentric psychology. In his study of the emotional and moral dimensions of Newar psychology, anthropologist Steven

---

139 Sobo, 'The Jamaican Body's Role in Emotional Experience,' 322.
140 Britt-Krause, 'Sinking Heart: A Punjabi Communication of Distress,' 569.
141 Ibid., 566–7.

M. Parish writes that Newars 'take it for granted' that emotions, memory, moral deliberation, and other forms of thought 'are located in the chest, since for Newars the mind is in the heart, not the head.'[142] There is a sensory component to this cardiocentric model as well: 'Pain, sadness, fear, and grief are spoken of in terms of a heart in distress: a heart may sink, tremble, throb, flutter, or burn like fire ... The Newar heart can open and blossom like a flower in joy. It may fly away in fear or confusion, or burst in envy.' And one who lacks the conviction to follow through on what his conscience tells him to do is said by the Newars to lack 'heart blood.'[143]

The degree to which a cardiocentric or hydraulic-model idiom is used literally or metaphorically is intimately related to the concept of the mind-body relationship that operates alongside cardiocentrism and the hydraulic model within a specific culture. In the foregoing examples, the Jamaican model treats this relationship differently from the Punjabi model, and the available evidence pertaining to the Newar idiom does not make clear precisely what sort of mind-body relationship operates alongside their hydraulic-model idioms. In the following discussion of present-day analogues, it is not necessary to resolve the question of whether or to what degree cardiocentrism and the hydraulic model are used metaphorically in any given culture; still, it is important to avoid the presumption that all manifestations of cardiocentrism and the hydraulic model are as thoroughly metaphorical as they are in modern American usage, or conversely, that literal cardiocentrism necessarily implies that mind and heart are identical.

Cardiocentric Heat and Emotional Distress

Because comparative studies of idioms for emotional distress have provided the substrate for numerous studies in cognitive linguistics, there is abundant, cross-cultural documentation of the correlation of emotional distress, both chronic and acute, with internal heat, which is often localized in the chest cavity. In Japanese, anger is the emotion most closely linked with cardiocentric heat, hence the expression 'to experience anger to the degree that the chest becomes hot' (mune ga atsuku naru hodo no ikari o oboeru).[144] In their study of Zulu expressions of anger, Taylor and

---

142 Parish, 'The Sacred Mind: Newar Cultural Representations of Mental Life,' 315–16.
143 Ibid., 317–18.
144 Matsuki, 'Metaphors of Anger in Japanese,' 139. As in several other cultures' psychological idioms, this heat is likely to spread to the face and cause flushing; Matsuki cites the expression 'to get angry with a red/scarlet face' (kao a makka ni shite okoru).

Mbense report, 'When questioned about the physiological effects of anger, Zulu speakers invariably cite increased body temperature, and insist that an angry person is quite literally "hot."' The correlation of increasing body temperature with anger underlies Zulu idioms such as 'When he heard, he warmed up' (U-nele we-zwa wa-fudumala), and 'The police are eating flames' (Amaphoyisa a-dla amalangabi), meaning that the police are enraged.[145] In the West African language Wolof, the expression 'he heated my heart' (Tàngal na sama xol) means 'he made me angry.'[146] Idioms of anger in Mbula, an Austronesian language, localize the heat of anger somewhat lower in the midsection of the body, in the liver rather than in the heart: 'liver hot' (kete- (i)bayou) means 'very angry.'[147] Anger is not the only form of distress associated with increased body temperature, particularly in the chest cavity: for Iranian speakers of Arabic, the expression 'my heart is broiled as a kebab' or 'my heart is scorched' (urayim kebab olur) communicates the sort of distress that follows a traumatic event,[148] and the Polish phrase '[to] fever oneself' (gorączkować się) is a periphrasis for 'to be nervous.'[149] Additionally, in Chinese the phrase 'one's heart is like burning' (xin ji ru fen) describes a state of great anxiety.[150] As I will discuss further below, the Chinese idiom considers qi rather than heat to be the fuel that powers intense psychological states, but it is noteworthy that the experience of anxiety is nonetheless likened to burning.

Sobo's study of Jamaican popular psychology suggests a way in which the correlation of anger with body heat fits into a larger conceptual system and even a code of behaviour. Because anger 'comes with or generates heat,' Sobo explains, her informants maintain that 'drinking a glass of cold water literally cools it down.' Another way to cool the heat of anger is to allow it to escape the body in the form of words. '[P]eople ease anger's heat when they express or "throw hot words." One man confided that after people's hearts cool, they often fail to carry out the threats they hurl when the heat of anger loosens their tongues. That tongues loosen so should be of no surprise: heat applied to a frozen joint releases it.' The words that

145 Taylor and Mbense, 'Red Dogs and Rotten Mealies: How Zulus Talk About Anger,' 203–5.
146 Kövecses, 'Metaphor and the Folk Understanding of Anger,' 64.
147 Wierzbicka, Emotions Across Languages and Cultures, 301.
148 Good, 'The Heart of What's the Matter: The Semantics of Illness in Iran,' 37.
149 Mikołajczuk, 'The Metonymic and Metaphorical Conceptualisation of Anger in Polish,' 159.
150 Wierzbicka, Emotions across Languages and Cultures, 301.

escape the body need not be 'hot words' in order to have a cooling effect on the heart: Sobo reports that 'an evangelist who encountered a tense crowd when taking a bus near election time did her best to quench that group's potential for violence by getting them to "cool down" with spiritual songs.'[151] Whereas Sobo's study primarily sheds light on the effects of heat during episodes of acute distress, psychological heat may have similar effects on those who suffer from chronic anger or grief. Present-day Koreans apply the name *hwabyung*, which means both 'anger-illness' and 'fire-illness,' to an illness that plagues individuals who suppress external manifestations of intense emotions. As one recent study explains,

> Koreans link *Hwabyung* to lasting anger, disappointments, sadness, miseries, hostility, grudges, and unfulfilled dreams and expectations. When these emotions are not expressed openly and if they reach a threshold beyond which they cannot be kept under control, they are manifested physically in the form of *Hwabyung* ... An excess of the fire element in a person's constitution manifests itself behaviorally in expressions of anger. Conversely, pent-up anger disturbs the fire element to such a degree that serious illness may appear.[152]

I will have more to say about the somatic manifestations of *hwabyung* below, but even this brief introduction to the etiology of *hwabyung* foreshadows that other hydraulic-model symptoms will arise from the excess of emotional 'fire' if it is not released from the body in outward displays of distress.

Cardiocentric Boiling, Swelling, and Bursting

As discussed earlier, the overheated heart is occasionally said to 'melt,' as in the Hebrew Psalms, or to 'sink,' as in the Punjabi concept of 'sinking heart.' Much more commonly, however, the cardiocentric distress associated with negative emotions is expressed as the violent boiling, upward motion, or outward swelling of the contents of the abdomino-thoracic cavity. Boiling and seething are perhaps the most widely invoked symptoms of cardiocentric heat. In the Polynesian language known as Toraja, for instance, the expression 'my chest/breast is bubbling/boiling' (re'de

---

151 Sobo, 'The Jamaican Body's Role in Emotional Experience,' 324.
152 Pang, '*Hwabyung*,' 496–7.

ara'ku) means 'I am very angry,'[153] and in Hungarian, one might say 'Anger was boiling inside him' (Forrt benne a düh) or 'He is seething with anger' (Fortyog a dühtôl).[154] Zulu idioms for emotional distress include 'He boiled with anger' (Wa-ye-bila ulaka) and 'I felt my blood boil' (Nge-zwa ku-bila igazi);[155] similar expressions occur in Tunisian Arabic, such as 'He made my blood burn' (Haraq-l-i damm-i) and 'He lifted blood up to my head' (Talla3-l-i id-damm l-raaS-i), which is a periphrasis for 'I was flushed with anger.'[156] In Polish the fluid that boils during anger is not blood but gall: to say that someone is angry, one can use the expression 'gall boils itself in someone' (żółć się w kimś gotuje).[157] And although anger can impinge upon the chest cavity in the Japanese idiom, the initial phase of the boiling of anger, called *ikari*, is localized beneath the chest cavity, in the stomach: hence the expressions 'Anger boils the bottom of the belly' (Ikari ga hara no soko o guragura, saseru) and 'The intestines are boiling' (Harawata ga niekurikaeru).[158]

Because the chest cavity encloses solids and gases as well as liquids, it is not surprising that its contents, when heated, are sometimes said to swell like a heated solid or to burst like a balloon rather than to boil. Sobo offers a detailed description of this stage of the hydraulic model in Jamaican popular psychology. Even for some emotions that do not generate cardiocentric heat, the onset of intense emotion is first sensed in the organ of the heart; these emotions 'can be felt as the chest tightens, or when it feels as if it is filling up, or as other kinds of motion are registered therein.' Sobo goes on to explain that

> too much of an emotion can fill and 'enlarge' the heart or otherwise 'strain' it. A person overcome with sorrow and longing can die of a 'broken heart.' Grief can 'swell' the heart, causing it to burst if it does not gain 'expression' through tears, which carry out waste related to or caused by the grief but not the actual grief itself, which is, after all, a feeling like pain and so non-substantial.[159]

---

153 Wellenkamp, 'Everyday Conceptions of Distress,' 278 n. 10.
154 Kövecses, 'Metaphor and the Folk Understanding of Anger,' 56.
155 Taylor and Mbense, 'Red Dogs and Rotten Mealies,' 204.
156 Maalej, 'Figurative Language in Anger Expressions in Tunisian Arabic,' 57–8.
157 Mikołajczuk, 'The Metonymic and Metaphorical Conceptualisation of *Anger* in Polish,' 159.
158 Matsuki, 'Metaphors of Anger in Japanese,' 140; she adds that *guragura* is an onomatopoeic word that evokes the sound of boiling (150 n. 4).
159 Sobo, 'The Jamaican Body's Role in Emotional Experience,' 322.

The Jamaican psychological idiom is not alone in positing a stage at which the heart is overwhelmed to the point of bursting: in Tunisian Arabic we find the analogous expression 'My heart is going to explode' (qalb-i maši y-taršaq).[160] Alternatively, a similar sequence of events can play out over a slightly different area in the body's midsection. As mentioned already, in the Japanese idiom, the seething of anger begins in the stomach (*hara*), but as the stomach boils it is said to 'stand up' in the body's midsection: one may use the phrase 'the stomach stands up' (hara ga tatsu) to mean that one is angry. Matsuki reports that the standing up of the stomach can be the precursor to an outburst: 'I threw a book because *hara* rose up so much' (Anmari hara ga tatta node hon o nagatsuketa).[161] The moment when self-control capitulates to the seething of the stomach is captured in the remarkably vivid expression 'His patience-bag burst' (Kannin-bukuro-no o-ga kireta).[162]

Thoracic Constriction and Choking

In the Japanese idiom, if anger persists but the 'patience-bag' does not burst, the stomach continues to boil and to 'stand up' in the body's midsection, perhaps growing so tall that it interferes with the body parts above it. First it reaches the chest, as in the expression 'to feel strangled by *mune* [chest] because of the rise of *hara* [stomach]' (Haradatashisa ni mune o shimetsukerareru). Eventually anger may also reach the head: one can say of anger that it 'finally has come to the head' (toutou atama ni kita).[163] This is one of several possible ways to describe the excessive upward and outward pressure generated in the body's midsection by psychological seething and swelling. Several other languages describe the constriction stage of the hydraulic model in terms of strangulation and choking: among the Zulu idioms reported by Taylor and Mbense are statements such as 'He was so angry he choked' (Wa-thukuthela wa-cinana), 'He was so angry something stuck in his throat' (Wa-thukuthela wa-bind-wa), and 'When I told him, he inflated' (Nga-m-tshela qede wa-futh-eka), meaning that he reacted angrily.[164] According to Douglas Hollan, Toraja idioms of emotion are particularly tied to the condition of the breath (*penaa*), and the constriction of the

---

160 Maalej, 'Figurative Language in Anger Expressions in Tunisian Arabic,' 60.
161 Matsuki, 'Metaphors of Anger in Japanese,' 144–5.
162 Kövecses, 'Metaphor and the Folk Understanding of Anger,' 59.
163 Matsuki, 'Metaphors of Anger in Japanese,' 145–6.
164 Taylor and Mbense, 'Red Dogs and Rotten Mealies,' 200–1.

breath is correlated with several kinds of emotional distress and cognitive impairment. '[S]omeone with a "choked breath" (*pusa' penaanna*) feels dizzy, confused, bewildered, and so on,' explains Hollan. When one is afflicted by 'emotions like anger, frustration, intense grief, drunkenness, or possession ... one's breath becomes hot (*malassu penaanna*) and choked. Under such circumstances, one becomes confused, dizzy, and no longer conscious or aware of one's actions.'[165] Similarly, the Korean syndrome called *hwabyung* can culminate in serious physical pain perceived by the sufferer to be an enormous lump in the abdomen that presses on the lungs, impeding respiration, and on the intestines, impeding digestion. Pang writes that

> patients who had *Hwabyung* had experienced suppressed anger of long duration and frequently complained of gastric discomfort due to a sensation of epigastric mass and of a morbid fear of impending death ... According to traditional Korean medical principles, *Hwabyung* results when inner conflicts develop into a blood-muscle lump called *Hwa* in the epigastric region. The lump is related to pain and other physical symptoms by the sufferer ... although no evidence of it is found in biomedical physical examinations. Sufferers may also complain of epigastric mass, indigestion and other gastrointestinal symptoms, respiratory symptoms, and feelings of hotness.[166]

Alternatively, cardiocentric constriction may impinge upon the heart itself rather than the flow of breath; in these cases, the constriction is characterized as a sensation that the heart is being squeezed. In her study of the relationship between emotions and bodily sensations, Anna Wierzbicka adduces the Russian expression 'N's heart squeezed' (u N serdce šalos') as a communication of strong and unbridled feeling, and she mentions a similar Polish description of pangs of grief: 'My heart was being squeezed as I was leaving the places where I had been born and where I had grown up' (Serce ściskało mi się, gdym opuszczał okolicę, w której urodziłem się i wzrosłem).[167] A young female subject described in Byron J. Good's study of Iranian cardiocentric psychology complained of 'the sensation of her heart being squeezed (*darux*) and depressed ... She blamed this on the fact that she was 27, already had 5 children, was stifled by narrow living quarters, and lived with her mother-in-law as the head of the household.'[168]

165 Hollan, 'Emotion Work,' 46.
166 Pang, '*Hwabyung*,' 495 and 497.
167 Wierzbicka, *Emotions across Languages and Cultures*, 233 and 299.
168 Good, 'The Heart of What's the Matter,' 34.

Finally, the most idiosyncratic articulation of cardiocentric constriction must be that of the Zulus, who employ the quasi-onomatopoeic word *xhifi* to represent the 'squashing' of the heart by the initial violent attack of anger. 'The ideophone *xhifi* denotes "squashing" or "crunching something soft,"' explain Taylor and Mbense. Squashing in the heart 'specifically denotes the sudden onset of anger,' as in the expression 'My heart went *xhifi* when I saw him' (Inhliziyo i-th-é xhifi ngi-m-bona), meaning 'I suddenly felt hot-tempered when I saw him.'[169]

Cooling and Spaciousness as Symptoms of Default or Favourable Mental States

Linguists, anthropologists, and transcultural psychiatrists have been interested primarily in idioms of distress, so there is very little available evidence of hydraulic-model idioms pertaining to positive and neutral mental states. Not surprisingly, where such evidence is available, it tends to correlate positive and neutral mental states with cardiocentric coolness, spaciousness, and lightness. For instance, in the Zulu idiom, which characterizes distress as constriction of the heart, the joyful heart is capable of expanding without constriction, as in the expression 'My heart overflowed with joy' (Inhliziyo yami ya-phuphuma injabulo).[170] The Austronesian language Mbula, which uses the phrase 'liver hot' to signify anger, uses the corresponding phrase 'liver cool' (kete-iluumu) to mean 'at peace.'[171] We have seen that the Toraja language correlates emotional distress with constriction of the breath; accordingly, as Hollan explains, 'Someone with a "large breath" (*kapua penaanna*) feels healthy, energetic, and proud … Under normal, healthy circumstances, one is cool (*masakke*) and one's breath unchoked, so that one feels alert, conscious (*mengkilala*), and aware of the implications of one's actions.'[172] And in Japanese, which emphasizes the internal pressure that builds up in the midsection of an individual who restrains his anger, the dissipation of anger is characterized as relief from

---

169 Taylor and Mbense, 'Red Dogs and Rotten Mealies,' 197–8. The authors further explain that *xhifi* is one of several hundred ideophones in the Zulu language; an ideophone names an entity according to a perceptible quality such as sound or movement or manner, and it is often onomatopoeic. 'The nearest thing in English to ideophones are forms like *whoosh* (indicating a rushing sound) and *boingk* (indicating a clanging sound)' (223–4 n. 4).
170 Taylor and Mbense, 'Red Dogs and Rotten Mealies,' 195.
171 Wierzbicka, *Emotions Across Languages and Cultures*, 301.
172 Hollan, 'Emotion Work,' 46; see also Wellenkamp, 'Everyday Conceptions of Distress,' 278 n. 10.

pressure and a consequent sensation of lightness: 'I feel light after having expressed my anger' (Okottara kimochi ga karuku natta).[173]

Analogues Lacking a Core Feature of the Hydraulic Mechanism

Finally, the data gleaned from present-day cultures indicates that some conceptualizations of the physiology of distress correspond to the hydraulic model, with respect to bodily localization and the quality of the sensations accompanying intense mental events, even when not all core symptoms of the hydraulic model are present. Traditional Chinese medicine teaches that the energy that fuels the emotional experience and its physiological symptoms is not heat but *qi*, so the distressed heart does not burn but, under the influence of *qi*, merely *feels* like burning. '*Qi* is energy that is conceptualized as a fluid that flows through the body. It is also a fluid that can rise and then produce an excess,' explains Kövecses. It resides variously in the heart, breast, spleen, or liver. In the context of the hydraulic model of emotions, *qi* acts very much like heat energy because it causes the container of the organ in which it resides to expand.[174]

Consequently, many Chinese idioms of emotional distress closely resemble those in other languages, but references to heat energy are rare. Ots observes that the phrase 'the liver likes to expand' (gan xi tiao da) is equivalent to the statement 'anger likes to expand.' If anger is not allowed to expand, 'it may also cause belching, vomiting, globus hystericus, and the retrosternal globe ... Interpretations are very graphic in this case: anger wants to rise and get outside, but it is concealed in the chest or the throat or leaves the mouth in a deformed way.'[175] The characterization of anger and its driving energy as an outward force is exemplified in idiomatic expressions such as 'one's *qi* wells up like a mountain' (qi yong ru shan) and 'the pent-up anger-*qi* in one's breast finally explodes' (yuji zai xiong de nuqi zhongyu baofa le).[176] A patient suffering from a chronic personality problem describes an episode of anger in similar terms: 'I felt such rage, I wanted to hit her. I still feel the rage surge through me when I think back to that event. It rises upward in my stomach and chest.'[177]

---

173 Matsuki, 'Metaphors of Anger in Japanese,' 142.
174 Kövecses, 'Metaphor and the Folk Understanding of Anger,' 60–1.
175 Ots, 'The Angry Liver, the Anxious Heart, and the Melancholy Spleen,' 40–1.
176 Kövecses, 'Metaphor and the Folk Understanding of Anger,' 60–1.
177 Kleinman and Kleinman, 'Somatization: The Interconnections in Chinese Society among Culture, Depressive Experiences, and the Meanings of Pain,' 459.

When the rise of anger is checked and not allowed to escape, one is said to experience thoracic depression (*xiong men*) or a feeling of pressure in the chest, called *men qi*:

> *Xiong* means 'chest,' *men* means 'tightly closed,' 'sealed,' and 'de-pressed' in the sense of the physical experience of a weight on the chest ... In the theory and practice of [traditional Chinese medicine] thoracic depression corresponds with the liver, e.g., blocked anger. This correspondence is expressed in the metaphor of *men qi*, translated as 'sulky.' It refers to the blocked *qi* of the liver and describes the urge of the *qi* to emerge while sealed within the chest and causing pressure on the chest.[178]

Clearly the idiom of emotional distress in Chinese traditional medicine is constrained by physiological accompaniments of emotion similar to those in other cultures, even though the concept of *qi* replaces the more widespread notion of heat energy.

Another system for conceiving of emotional distress has been named the 'pneumaulic' model by modern researchers, because it shares most of the salient traits of the hydraulic model, but the substance enclosed in the containers within the body is air or wind rather than liquid. Hinton and Hinton, who have studied idioms of anxiety and panic among the Khmer in Cambodia, explain that as their subjects conceive of it, anxiety 'frequently has a clear physiological correlate: a pressurized rise of multiple winds, ascending from blocked knee and elbow vessels, hitting upward from the belly, attacking the lungs and heart, distending the neck vessels, swirling cranial contents, causing dizziness and blurry vision, and shooting from the ears.' At the stage when this ascending wind reaches the thoracic cavity it 'impedes breathing [and] compresses the heart.'[179]

The Khmer concept of the physiology of anxiety naturally invites comparison with the hydraulic model, but Hinton and Hinton argue that Western research has failed to recognize the significance of a container-based conceptual system that has wind rather than liquid flowing through it.[180] I accept Hinton and Hinton's concern that Western psychological

---

178 Ots, 'The Angry Liver,' 43. Ots goes on to compare Chinese descriptions of thoracic depression with the idioms in which German, Turkish, and Afghan patients describe similar sensations of pressure in the chest resulting from emotional distress.
179 Hinton and Hinton, 'Panic Disorder, Somatization, and the New Cross-Cultural Psychiatry,' 164.
180 Ibid.

and medical practitioners might serve their patients more effectively by setting aside their familiarity with liquid-based folk physiologies of distress and paying close attention to the practical ramifications of a wind-based physiology. For our present purposes, however, even while being sensitive to the differences between the hydraulic and the pneumaulic, or between mental heat and *qi*, we can nonetheless map symptoms of the Chinese and Khmer physiologies of distress onto the same areas of the body that are affected by hydraulic-model activity in a remarkable range of unrelated cultures. Cultural variation among the hydraulic-model analogues unquestionably impinges upon the perceived anatomy of the abdomino-thoracic cavity, the direction of cause-and-effect mechanisms, and the social consequences of manifesting short- and long-term mental anguish, but culture has a much less noticeable effect on the core somatic accompaniments of distress.

Autonomic Responses and Subjective Perceptions

The biochemistry underlying the hydraulic model has lately captured the interest of the popular media. The *New York Times*, for instance, has recently reported on 'broken-heart syndrome' and 'the second brain.' The technical name for broken-heart syndrome is stress cardiomyopathy. In response to a deeply traumatic event, the sufferer of stress cardiomyopathy experiences intense pain in the heart and pressure in the chest that impedes breathing. These symptoms are often mistaken for signs of heart attack, but diagnostic tests indicate no blockage of the coronary arteries. Instead, 'emotional trauma causes the brain to release high doses of stress hormones. This hormonal blast paralyzes the muscle cells of the heart, preventing them from working to pump the blood.'[181] It is possible for a patient to recover from stress cardiomyopathy, but it is potentially fatal: some patients actually die of a broken heart. Lower down in the body's midsection, upper- and lower-abdominal discomfort experienced in response to stress and trauma is linked to the activity of the 'second brain,' a nervous system located in the gut, whose regulation of digestive enzyme secretion and peristalsis fluctuates in response to many of the same neurotransmitters whose presence in the brain regulates moods and emotions.[182]

---

181 Sanders, 'Heart Ache,' 28.
182 Brown, 'The *Other* Brain Also Deals with Many Woes,' includes an interview with physician Michael D. Gershon, who has published a general-audience book on the enteric nervous system, entitled *The Second Brain*. The demand for media coverage of these

Predating popular interest in the subject are several decades' worth of scientific research into the involuntary physiological mechanisms that underlie hydraulic-model symptoms. Several classic experiments are still cited regularly in current studies, including Averill's 1969 experiment in which he showed films to different groups of test subjects in order to induce grief and mirth (i.e., laughter, which is distinguished from happiness). He found that induced grief caused a measurable increase in blood pressure without an increase in heart rate, while the subjects who viewed the humorous film experienced a measurable increase in respiratory activity, partly related to the fact that they laughed during the film.[183] In a study published in 1983, Ekman et al. asked test subjects to 'relive' past emotional experiences; those who reported feeling anger, fear, and sadness as they relived past experiences had an elevated heart rate, while those who felt happiness, disgust, and surprise did not. Among the three emotions that caused heart rate to increase, only anger also produced an elevation in skin temperature.[184] Fundamentally similar results emerge from a 1997 meta-analysis of twenty-two studies of the autonomic responses to emotion completed over the previous twenty-four years: Cacioppo et al. report that 'discrete emotions such as happy, sad, fear, anger, and disgust cannot be fully differentiated by visceral activity alone, but followup meta-analyses did suggest that the negative emotions in this literature are associated with stronger ANS [autonomic nervous system] responses than are the positive emotions.'[185] Elevated blood pressure, increased cardiac output, and elevated heart rate were the most prominent responses to negative emotions in general; diastolic blood pressure was elevated by anger more than by sadness, and by sadness more than by happiness.[186]

In several respects, the data from these studies correspond to the crosscultural patterns in the hydraulic-model idioms adduced above. The

---

illnesses likely has much to do with the fact that intense heart pain and gastrointestinal distress that have no obvious physiological origin are sources of frustration for the doctor and of stigmatization for the patient, who may be told that his suffering is 'all in his head,' so to speak: on the phenomenon of somatization and its connotations, see below.

183 Averill, 'Autonomic Response Patterns during Sadness and Mirth,' 410–11.
184 Ekman, Levenson, and Friesen, 'Autonomic Nervous System Activity Distinguishes among Emotions,' 1209. Ekman et al. also report that when they re-analyzed their data without consideration for the validation criteria used in their original analysis, 'only the negative versus positive emotional distinctions remained; all distinctions among negative emotions were lost' (ibid., 1209).
185 Cacioppo et al., 'The Psychophysiology of Emotion,' 184.
186 Ibid., 181–3.

measured autonomic responses chiefly affect the operation of the heart and the lungs, and to a lesser extent, the digestive tract, so it is not surprising that the subjective perception of these responses centres on the chest cavity and, to a lesser extent, the abdomen. The finding of Ekman et al. that the strongest differences in autonomic responses separate negative from positive emotions, rather than one negative emotion from another, is congruent with the fact that many iterations of the hydraulic model correlate heat and constriction with generalized distress and coolness and expansiveness with the general absence of distress. Where there were signs of differentiation among the negative emotions, anger was distinguished from the others by a measurable increase in skin temperature and a sharper elevation of blood pressure.

Though Ekman et al. report that *measured* autonomic responses differ little among anger, fear, and sadness, respondents in a 1996 study by Hupka et al. consistently claimed that their subjective *perceptions* of those autonomic responses varied noticeably among the negative emotions. This study had a cross-cultural dimension as well, since its participants were 514 university students from Germany, Mexico, Poland, Russia, and the United States. Each participant 'rated 31 body components and products of physiological functions as to the extent to which they are the source of the feelings that accompany anger, envy, fear, and jealousy. In agreement with the social constructionist perspective, we expected cross-cultural differences in the ratings,' Hupka et al. explain.[187] But instead they found that perceptions of some physiological accompaniments of emotion – particularly those that are related to the hydraulic model – transcend cultural boundaries. 'We found that anger is reported to be felt across the five nations (listing the sites from rank 1 to 4) in the face, breath, head, and heart ... [T]he heart is reported to be involved in all four emotions, whereas the other sites are more selectively attributed to the emotions.'[188] Contrary to their expectations, Hupka et al. conclude that 'some of our corporeal loci ... corroborate previous findings that such reports of differentiated autonomic activity are shared across cultures.'[189]

The cross-cultural consistency documented by the controlled study of Hupka et al. pertains to everyday emotions, but clinical studies suggest that some of the bodily sensations associated with chronic and pathological

---

187 Hupka et al., 'Anger, Envy, Fear, and Jealousy as Felt in the Body: A Five-Nation Study,' 246.
188 Ibid., 255.
189 Ibid., 258.

psychological distress also transcend cultural boundaries. For example, Mumford et al. administered the Bradford Somatic Inventory (BSI), a bilingual (Urdu and English) questionnaire, to Pakistani and indigenous British patients presenting symptoms of anxiety and depression at medical clinics in their native countries. The BSI lists forty-six somatic symptoms commonly reported among depressed and anxious patients and asks the subjects to indicate whether they are experiencing those symptoms as part of their current state of depression or anxiety. Both ethnic groups reported experiencing discomfort in the chest and abdomen as well as fatigue and discomfort localized in the head; less common, but still shared between the two groups, were sensations of heat and of a globus blocking the throat and impeding breathing.[190] '[M]ost of the clusters of somatic symptoms show obvious similarities across the cultural divide,' Mumford et al. find. 'This would seem to suggest that the core somatic experiences, which these dimensions of functional somatic symptoms represent, are universal human experiences, largely independent of culture. These results certainly offer no support for the extreme position of cultural relativity espoused by some anthropologists.'[191] This is not to say that the British and Pakistani results were identical; within the core clusters of symptoms, there were cross-cultural differences of perception and expression. 'The process by which these unpleasant sensations reach consciousness, are interpreted, and are then acted upon is subject to cultural influence. Any explanatory model must incorporate both elements, culture and somatic awareness,' Mumford et al. conclude.[192]

In sum, the theory of embodied realism, not in its starkest version but tempered by an awareness of cultural variation, is the single best way to account for all the evidence pertaining to the cross-cultural consistency of the hydraulic model, including clinical studies of perceived somatic accompaniments of distress across cultural boundaries; controlled tests of the autonomic responses to induced emotional states; modern hydraulic-model idioms gathered from every corner of the globe; and the diachronic persistence of the hydraulic model in unrelated cultures dating back nearly three millennia. This evidence firmly sustains the conclusion that the Anglo-Saxons' cardiocentric psychology and hydraulic model are ultimately rooted in the coactivity of intense mental activity with sensations of heat, seething, and constriction in the abdomino-thoracic cavity; these roots likely reach

---

190 Mumford et al., 'The Bradford Somatic Inventory,' 382.
191 Ibid., 383–4.
192 Ibid., 384.

far back into the Germanic prehistory of OE. This is a rather circumspect claim, and it lacks a historical dimension, but it provides a firm foundation for two arguments that I would like to advance in tandem in the following pages. First, the coactivity of emotions with bodily sensations can constrain *non*-metaphorical conceptualization. Second, the theory of embodied realism provides the key to determining when and how cardiocentrism and the hydraulic model changed from literal expressions of folk psychology to conceptual metaphors in the history of the English language.

Embodied Realism and Metaphoricity

The theory of embodied realism, perhaps because it arose as a corollary of Lakoff and Johnson's theory of conceptual metaphor, is usually invoked only in discussions of metaphor formation. Serious consideration of the role of embodied realism in the generation of non-metaphorical concepts is, at present, discouraged by the cognitive-science turn in metaphor studies, which emphasizes the process of conceptual blending that dominates the human brain's methods of organizing abstract ideas.[193] In a monograph designed to introduce scholars in the humanities to applications of cognitive science, Patrick Colm Hogan states that 'a cognitive approach does not give us the answer' to the question of what distinguishes the literal from the metaphorical, and in fact, 'cognitive principles indicate that this is a misguided question.'[194] Elsewhere Fludernik et al. assert that 'the cognitive paradigm has not only replaced antiliteral and literary conceptions of metaphor; it has actually inverted the evaluation of these binary oppositions. In this view linguistic expression arises from strategic adaptations of body schemata that we project onto our environment.'[195] From this ahistorical, process-oriented perspective, the content- and context-based distinctions among literal, metonymic, and metaphorical language are utterly obsolete.

However, literary and intellectual historians cannot dispense with these content- and context-based categories if we have any interest in understanding the relationship between thought and language; these categories constitute the framework within which we evaluate whether a historical population of authors and audiences would have regarded a particular concept as 'truth-bearing' or as 'figurative,' irrespective of the scientific

193 On conceptual blending, see especially Fauconnier and Turner's influential monograph, *The Way We Think: Conceptual Blending and the Mind's Hidden Complexities*.
194 Hogan, *Cognitive Science, Literature, and the Arts: A Guide for Humanists*, 91.
195 Fludernik et al., 'Metaphor and Beyond: An Introduction,' 385.

accuracy that a modern observer would attach to such a concept. I am not advocating that the present-day reader return to the objectivist understanding of the metaphor as a false and logically deficient utterance; rather, I am urging present-day historians not to lose sight of the fact that most of the authors and audiences whom we study *were* objectivists, who distinguished between the literal and the metaphorical and – in technical discourse if not in narrative – privileged the literal as more truthful and more accurate than the metaphorical. I understand why cognitive theorists maintain that their work is most immediately germane to the process rather than the content of conceptualization, but I maintain that the model of cross-domain mapping and the theory of embodied realism are in fact compatible with, and exceedingly useful in, the historian's study of literal and metaphorical conceptual systems.

A Theory of Embodied Conceptualization and Emergent Metaphoricity

To begin, it is useful to clarify what separates the literal from the metaphorical, within the framework of cross-domain mapping rather than from an objectivist perspective. Consider a spectrum of possible relationships between the source and target domains of a conceptual system, as perceived by its historical user. At one end of the spectrum, where source and target domains are perceived as wholly discrete, we have metaphor, be it conceptual or ornamental, which implies a statement of the type 'X is not-X.'[196] At the other end of the spectrum, we have literal language, in which source and target domains are perceived to be not wholly discrete. In such a case, the mapping of the characteristics of the source onto the target domain is simply a literal truth; from the perspective of the historical user there might appear to be only a single domain, and no cross-domain mapping at all. Within this framework, I envision a process by which embodied realities can constrain or generate literal concepts, which may or may not eventually become metaphors, depending on whether the historical population changes its understanding of the relationship between source and target domains. I will first enumerate each stage of this process as a generalized theory and then illustrate the process with a specific example.

---

196 Metonymies may occupy intermediate positions on this spectrum, when source and target domains are not wholly discrete – say, in a concept of the type 'X^a is a salient part of X' – but the quality of the relationship between domains is as important in metonymy as is the perceived degree to which the domains are discrete, so the model of a metaphorical-to-literal spectrum can only partially accommodate metonymy.

Stage 1. When the coactivity of an embodied experience with a relatively abstract state or event constrains or shapes the formation of a conceptual system, salient characteristics of the embodied experience are mapped onto the abstract state or event, often in a way that concretizes and explains that which is most elusive about that state or event. If the historical user of that concept recognized a difference between the source domain of embodied experience and the target domain of the abstract state or event, then the cross-domain mapping has generated a metaphorical concept. But if the user of that concept acknowledged no substantial distinction between the source domain and the target domain, the cognitive process by which he formed that concept is not really cross-domain mapping, and the resulting concept is not metaphorical. For that historical user, the embodied reality is constitutive of reality.

Accordingly, if a present-day reader wishes to discern whether an embodied concept was metaphorical or non-metaphorical at a given point in history, the reader's own understanding of the relationship between source and target domains is irrelevant, even if it is objectively more accurate by present-day standards. The only responsible way to assess the metaphoricity of a concept in its historical context is to examine other texts or material evidence generated by the historical user's culture or textual community, in search of signs that the user did or did not acknowledge a substantial difference between the embodied source domain and the abstract target domain. If such an investigation turns up no evidence of a perceived division between source and target domain, then that culture or textual community likely did not consider the concept to be metaphorical, and it likely used idioms associated with that concept as literal expressions of their best understanding of the abstract state or event.

Stage 2. A non-metaphorical concept that originated in embodied experience may begin to migrate from the literal end of the spectrum toward the metaphorical, if some cultural influence triggers a new recognition that the abstract contents of the target domain are not accurately described by the experientially constrained features of the source domain. What was functionally a single conceptual domain is split into discrete source and target domains, and as their relationship changes, the conceptual system generated by cross-domain mapping may come to be perceived as metonymic or metaphorical within the historical culture or textual community affected by the triggering event.

What kind of cultural influence could trigger such a shift? The most likely candidates are learned discourses that challenge the common-sense or intuitive tendency to identify an embodied reality as an objective reality. But not just any learned discourse can effect this sort of shift across an entire culture. Often a conceptual system rooted in embodied experience generates everyday idioms, and in such a case, the repeated verbal references to that embodied conceptual system strengthen the tendency to interpret the embodied reality as common-sensical, natural, and accurate. Consequently, a conceptual system that is daily corroborated by both embodied experience and everyday idioms will be exceedingly difficult to uproot. In order for a rival conceptual system to trigger the division of the single embodied conceptual domain into discrete source and target domains, and thereby to supplant the embodied concept and usurp its status as a literal truth, that rival concept must be either inherently persuasive enough, or extrinsically authoritative enough by the standards of the historical culture in question, to trump intuition and common sense. The type of discourse that will sit atop the hierarchy of authoritative discourses will vary from one culture to another, and even among textual communities within a single culture: some ascribe the most authoritative status to empirical scientific data; for others, religious dogma outweighs science. And sometimes common sense and embodied realities outweigh both science and religion: as we saw above, the great Stoic philosopher Chrysippus defended cardiocentric psychology against the critiques of cephalocentric physicians and philosophers on the grounds that 'common opinion' understood the mind to be concentrated in that place where its activities were most perceptible to the senses, that is, in the chest cavity.

If the source of the counterintuitive rival concept is an institution that relies on written transmission of its authoritative or learned doctrines, then the process by which the rival concept challenges and eventually supplants the embodied concept will have left traces in the textual record. It may be the case that the rival concept supplants the embodied concept only within particular textual communities within the larger culture; it is not unusual for a counterintuitive conceptual system to be assimilated within a learned subculture while a common-sense theory continues to thrive among the population at large. Such a circumstance may result from limited dissemination of the counterintuitive concept or from the subculture's privileging of discourses that are not recognized by the general population to be more authoritative or persuasive than common-sense theories. For this reason, it may be easier for the historian to pinpoint the moment at which a counterintuitive rival concept *first* arises in learned discourse than to identify when that rival concept has wholly supplanted an embodied concept in the general population. During the period when counterintuitive rival concepts have been assimilated by particular textual

170 Anglo-Saxon Psychologies

communities, the historian should expect to find evidence of stratification in the usage of the embodied concept; it may well retain non-metaphorical status in narrative and some modes of discourse even while the counter-intuitive rival has supplanted the embodied concept in other modes of discourse. Accordingly, evidence for the assimilation of a counterintuitive rival concept within a specific textual community is insufficient to prove its assimilation in the culture at large.

Stage 3. Once the historical culture in question no longer considers the content of the target domain to be accurately or literally characterized by the salient features of the source domain of embodied experience, any concepts and idioms generated by cross-domain mapping that remain in use in that culture are rightly considered to be metonymies or metaphors.

Geocentrism and the Tenacity of Embodied Realities

As an illustration of the foregoing theoretical model of diachronic meta-phorization, consider the words 'sunrise' and 'sunset.' These words originate in the idea that THE SUN IS A HEAVENLY BODY THAT ORBITS THE EARTH, which represents the most intuitive explanation of the way the human body experiences the changing relative positions of the sun and the earth. People observed the sun moving upward relative to the horizon in the morning and downward relative to the horizon in the evening, and without any alternative theories available that might challenge their common-sense conclusion, they used the concepts of sunrise and sunset quite literally; the target domain THE SUN was thought to be accurately characterized by the features of the source domain A HEAVENLY BODY THAT ORBITS THE EARTH. An important historical insight is lost if we apply the label of metaphor to the concepts 'sunrise' and 'sunset' where they are used by cultures without any knowledge of non-geocentric models of the cosmos. Ælfric of Eynsham, for instance, uses the phrase *sunnan upgang* 'sunrise' in his scientific treatise *De temporibus anni*, written during the period 992 x 1002.[197] He clearly regards 'sunrise' as a literal and accurate description of the relative movements of sun and earth, for he also writes, 'Soðlice seo sunne gæð be Godes dihte betwux heofenan ˥ eorðan · on dæg bufon eorðan · ˥ on niht under ðysse eorðan ealswa feorr adune on nihtlicere tide under þære eorðan · swa heo on dæg bufon upastihð.'[198] Ælfric's use of the

197 Kleist, 'Ælfric's Corpus: A Conspectus,' 127.
198 Ælfric, *De temporibus anni* 1.18 (ed. Henel, *Ælfric's De temporibus anni*, 8): 'Truly the sun travels at the command of God between heaven and earth, and in the day it goes

phrase *sunnan upgang* exemplifies Stage 1 of the model outlined above, and it is easy to determine that Ælfric's usage is non-metaphorical because we know with certainty that he did not subscribe to a counterintuitive, heliocentric model of the cosmos.

What about Stage 2? Heliocentric models of the solar system had been proposed by natural philosophers in the West as early as the sixth century BC, but the use of the words 'sunrise' and 'sunset,' or of their ancient antecedents, such as Latin *solis ortus* and *occasus* or OE *sunnan upgang* and *setlung*, reinforce the user's inclination to conceive of the sun as a satellite that rises on one side of the earth and sets on the other side. Nothing in ordinary experience encourages one to replace the concept of a stationary earth with the concept of an earth that is rotating rapidly on its axis and orbiting the sun. Moreover, the geocentric model was staunchly defended as a matter of Christian dogma, to the extent that after Galileo's telescopic observations provided persuasive scientific evidence that the earth orbited the sun, the Catholic Church nevertheless condemned Galileo for promulgating heliocentric theories in the 1630s.

Presently in the United States, the assimilation of heliocentrism is incomplete and stratified. My own use of the terms sunrise and sunset represents a conceptual metaphor, exemplifying Stage 3 of the foregoing model: the embodied perception of the sun's rising and setting plays a role in my conceptualization of the passage of time, even though at the literal level, my embodied experience is trumped by my understanding of natural science.[199] On the other hand, even though most textual communities in the United States, from elementary school classrooms to mainstream religious communities, currently favour heliocentrism, nonetheless it was reported in 2005 that 'one adult American in five thinks the Sun revolves around the earth, an idea science had abandoned by the 17th century.'[200] This surprising

---

above the earth and at night it goes beneath this earth: it descends just as far down beneath the earth at night-time as it rises above the earth during the day.'

199 The notion that sunrise and sunset represent orientational metaphors is at odds with other theories of metaphor which regard the intention to communicate metaphorically as a prerequisite for metaphoricity. Lakoff's discussion of the conceptual metaphor SEXUALITY IS A PHYSICAL FORCE helpfully illustrates how the cognitive processes that lead us to utter metaphors and act on metaphorical concepts are in operation even when we are unconscious of them: see *Women, Fire, and Dangerous Things*, 409–15.

200 Dean, 'Scientific Savvy? In U.S., Not Much.' Dean's source for this statistic is Dr Jon D. Miller, a prominent researcher at the Northwestern University Medical School, who has for several decades conducted polls of Americans' knowledge of science on behalf of political, scientific, and non-profit organizations.

fact illustrates just how long it can take for a rival, counterintuitive concept to supplant a concept rooted in embodied perception and everyday idioms, even if that rival has science and mainstream religion on its side.

The concept of sunrise and sunset works well to illustrate my proposed model of diachronic metaphorization because most readers of this book agree, first, that modern science has satisfactorily demonstrated that the earth goes around the sun and, second, that many premodern textual communities acknowledged no distinction between the target domain THE SUN and the embodied source domain A HEAVENLY BODY THAT ORBITS THE EARTH.[201] Applying the same model of diachronic metaphorization to cardiocentric psychology and the hydraulic model, however, presupposes that at some point in history the users of these conceptual systems acknowledged no distinction between their embodied reality and objective reality, between the domains of ANGER and HEAT, or between the domains of EMOTION and CONTENTS OF THE CHEST CAVITY. Readers of this book are likely to resist the premise that the mental and the bodily could function as a single domain at any point in the prehistory of the English language, much less during the Anglo-Saxon period. The main reason for this resistance, however, has less to do with our understanding of Germanic and Anglo-Saxon concepts of mind and body than with our own present-day Western predisposition to think of mind and body as separate, and indeed oppositional, conceptual domains. As a corrective to this modernist bias, I turn next to a different perspective on cross-cultural conceptions of mind and body, drawn from the field of transcultural psychiatry, a discipline which has for some decades been engaged in training Westerners to shed their dualist presuppositions about the nature of the mind-body relationship.

Transcultural Psychiatry: An Antidote to Dualist Assumptions about Mind and Body

The subdiscipline of transcultural psychiatry was developed in the first half of the twentieth century, in part to increase the efficacy of Western psychiatric practitioners who served primarily non-Western populations

---

201 For another concrete example of diachronic metaphorization, though without consideration of the implications of embodied realism, see Geeraerts and Grondelaers, 'Looking Back at Anger: Cultural Traditions and Metaphorical Patterns,' who trace the history of humoral theory from its practical, non-metaphorical use in classical medical discourse to its early modern demise among scientific communities and its survival in present-day metaphorical expressions in European languages.

of patients, whether in non-Western countries or in communities of immigrants to Europe and North America.[202] (Much of the data adduced in my earlier discussion of the cross-cultural recurrence of the hydraulic model is, in fact, gleaned from studies in transcultural psychiatry.) Early efforts in this field treated non-Western psychological disorders as cultural variants of disorders acknowledged in Western psychiatry, such as depression and schizophrenia. Yet the results garnered by such studies were often vitiated by what Kleinman calls a category fallacy. 'Having dispensed with indigenous illness categories because they are culture-specific,' Kleinman explains, 'studies of this kind go on to superimpose their own cultural categories on some sample of deviant behavior in other cultures, as if their own illness categories were culture-free.'[203]

The reification of Western illness categories is but one of many category fallacies that the field of transcultural psychiatry calls attention to, and aims to correct, in both academic and clinical contexts. Among these, the most germane to our present discussion is the tendency to impose uncritically upon non-Western cultures the rigid Western separation, even opposition, between mind and body, based on moral inclinations as well as physical substance and ontological hierarchy. In the field of psychiatry, this tendency manifests itself in a rigid distinction between psychological and somatic disorders. Such a distinction cannot accommodate the fact that non-Western patients frequently present bodily complaints when their disorder is one that Western psychiatrists would view as essentially mental. This infelicitous imposition of Western dualism upon non-Western modes of experiencing and communicating illness has led to some particularly short-sighted arguments: for example, that primitive non-Western cultures lack the vocabulary necessary to express abstract emotional states.[204]

A more recent example is the frequently repeated supposition that non-Westerners are especially prone to somatization, that is, the articulation of mental distress in terms of bodily symptoms: this claim has been reviewed and criticized repeatedly in studies that compare the experience and conceptualization of specific mental disturbances in multiple cultures.[205] The

---

202 Bains, 'Race, Culture and Psychiatry: A History of Transcultural Psychiatry.'
203 Kleinman, 'Depression, Somatization, and the "New Cross-Cultural Psychiatry,"' 4.
204 Leff, 'Culture and the Differentiation of Emotional States'; he retracted this opinion in later writings.
205 See, for example, Kleinman and Kleinman, 'Somatization: The Interconnections in Chinese Society among Culture, Depressive Experiences, and the Meanings of Pain';

Western insistence on separating psychological and somatic disorders 'largely reflects the persistent mind-body dualism of Western medicine: psychiatric disorders are perceived as mental disorders, notwithstanding their prominent somatic symptoms,' according to Kirmayer et al. 'The label of somatization then serves to fit the recalcitrant patient and problem into the overall system of medicine (even if it offers little in the way of clarity).'[206] The implications for treatment are significant, because 'notwithstanding the current biological turn in psychiatry,' Westerners have a hard time shedding the suspicion that those who somatize their mental distress are either deluded or deceitful, either hysterical or malingering.[207] In order to provide successful treatment to patients with a holistic understanding of mental and physical disorders, Western practitioners are encouraged to set aside their own ingrained mind-body dualism and to understand the nature and causes of other cultures' mind-body holism.

Just as the discipline of transcultural psychiatry endeavours to improve psychiatric care by reorienting practitioners' perspectives on other cultures' concepts of mind, so can its tenets improve the present-day reader's grasp of historically distant cultures' concepts of mind. Transcultural psychiatry demonstrates that mind-body dualists are actually a minority within the contemporary global community: 'In other parts of the world, and in the experience of patients from many ethnocultural groups, the sharp distinction between psychological and somatic symptoms is far from obvious.'[208] Horacio Fabrega extends the same argument to encompass the diachronic global community of cultures whose psychologies we can study in written records: specifically, in ancient Greek medical theories, in the Indian medical tradition known as Ayurveda, and in Chinese traditional medicine (the latter two of which are still highly influential today). In Ayurveda, 'every facet of illness and disease can involve phenomena that cross the mind-body duality of the West.'[209] For example, Ayurvedic medicine attributes both insanity (*unmada*) and epilepsy (*apasmara*) to the same physiological mechanism: excess humours migrate to the heart, where the mind resides, and the mind malfunctions because these humours block the

---

Alexander et al., 'Mental Disorders in Patients with Noncardiac Chest Pain'; Kirmayer et al., 'Somatization and Psychologization.'
206 Kirmayer et al., 'Somatization and Psychologization,' 258 and 236.
207 Ibid., 258.
208 Ibid., 236.
209 Fabrega, 'Somatization in Cultural and Historical Perspective,' 186.

ducts and channels that connect the heart with the sense organs.[210] Though Westerners conceive of insanity as a mental disturbance and epilepsy as a bodily illness, Ayurveda assigns them the same etiology, because within Ayurveda the holistic domain of the person has not been fragmented into discrete mental and physical domains. Mind-body holism is also the reason why Ayurvedic medicine does not invoke the category of complaint that Westerners call somatization, in the sense of inappropriate reports or perceptions of somatic symptoms by those who suffer from mental disorders. According to Fabrega, the 'ontological distinction between mental and physical disease' that is a prerequisite to the category of somatization 'did not gain dominance in India. The theory of Ayurvedic medicine is powerfully unitary and functional in nature and does not distinguish ontologically among types or nature of medical disease.'[211]

Fabrega reiterates this historical argument with reference to traditional Chinese medicine, in which the organ of the heart is 'responsible for the expressions of a person's individuality, including consciousness, concentration, reasoning, and organized social action.'[212] We have already seen that Chinese idioms of acute psychological distress follow the pattern of the hydraulic model but rely on qi rather than mental heat as the source of energy that fuels mental mechanisms. Cardiocentric psychology 'underscores the holism implicit in Chinese medicine,' says Fabrega, and this holism explains why 'in classical Chinese medicine the idea of somatization as exaggerated, excessive, displaced, or peculiarly manufactured bodily symptoms simply does not exist.'[213] Kirmayer et al. echo Fabrega's argument, asserting that the lack of distinction between mental and physical illness 'does not mean that Chinese medicine ... dissolved the mind-body dualism of Western medicine: they never created it in the first place. The holism of Chinese medicine does not develop psychology as a separate realm of discourse.'[214]

The mind-body holism of the Ayurvedic and Chinese medical traditions is therefore not the result of some cultural influence on an originally dualist system; on the contrary, dualism never formed a part of these medicines, because neither philosophy, nor theology, nor natural science, nor

---

210 Obeyesekere, 'The Theory and Practice of Psychological Medicine in the Ayurvedic Tradition,' 160.
211 Fabrega, 'Somatization in Cultural and Historical Perspective,' 185.
212 Ibid., 188.
213 Ibid., 188–9.
214 Kirmayer et al., 'Somatization and Psychologization,' 258–9.

any other potentially authoritative rival system of thought has disrupted these cultures' phenomenologically based concept of mental and physical health as a single domain. If modern Westerners think that patients steeped in the Ayurvedic and Chinese medical traditions are prone to somatizing their mental distress, this perspective is the product of our own preconception that mental and physical distress are ontologically discrete. Kirmayer usefully turns the Western perspective on its head when he writes that *if* it is true that non-Westerners are more prone to somatization, 'it can only be because Westerners (who themselves comprise extremely diverse and divergent cultural groups) share some distinctive values or practices that contribute to the obverse of somatization, which has been termed *psychologization*.'[215] I find Kirmayer's articulation of the problem helpful because it urges the Western observer of other cultures' mind-body concepts to regard psychologization as stranger and more counterintuitive than somatization: not as the default or most natural conceptualization of mind and body, but as a corollary of 'distinctive values or practices.'[216] This perspective corroborates my earlier proposition that where phenomenologically based mind-body holism exists, it will continue to be used literally until some rival concept triggers the fragmentation of the embodied domain of 'the whole person' into the physical and the mental.[217] 'From the cross-cultural perspective, it is not somatization in China

---

215   Kirmayer, 'Cultural Variations in the Clinical Presentation of Depression and Anxiety,' 23.

216   I expect that some readers will find the theory underpinning my argument inherently objectionable, precisely because mind-body dualism is a linchpin of many present-day American and western European social policies and ideals, and conversely, because mind-body holism may be regarded as antithetical to certain aspects of Western scholarship in the humanities: on this conflict, see esp. M. Johnson, *The Meaning of the Body*, 2–15.

217   A new book by journalist Ethan Watters reports that such fragmentation of popular conceptions of the holistic mind-body complex is currently under way in several non-Western cultures. *Crazy Like Us: The Globalization of the American Psyche* (2010) documents how energetic global campaigns by Western pharmaceutical companies are marketing peculiarly Western illness paradigms (including anorexia, post-traumatic stress disorder, depression, and schizophrenia) to cultures that previously did not recognize the existence of these illnesses or employ the West's post-Cartesian approach to healing. As Watters shows, the encroachment of Western pharmaceuticals into Japan, Hong Kong, Tanzania, and Sri Lanka is triggering fundamental changes in these cultures' conceptualizations of illness and the mind-body relationship – changes that take root first among medical professionals and then spread to those patients who have the resources to purchase 'cures' as defined by Western paradigms. Watters's account provides ample, present-day illustrations of the stages of metaphorization of an embodied

and the West but psychologization in the West that appears unusual and requires explanation,' write Kleinman and Kleinman.[218] In the same vein, I maintain that from the cross-cultural perspective, it is not the concept of the mind-in-the-heart in Anglo-Saxon England but the disembodied and counterintuitive mind-in-the-soul, whether in Anglo-Saxon England or in the present day, that requires special explanation.

An Open-Minded Approach to the Possibility of Anglo-Saxon Mind-Body Holism

As Western mind-body dualism predisposes psychiatrists to impose unconsciously the concept of somatization on foreign experiences of illness, so does it predispose modern Western readers to impose upon other cultures a metaphorical interpretation of the corporeal mind and all the stages of the hydraulic model. Though the tenets of transcultural psychiatry do not prove that the OE hydraulic model originated as a non-metaphorical concept, they do demonstrate the intellectual advantage of casting aside present-day prejudices before evaluating concepts of mind and body held by cultures less influenced by Cartesian dualism than our own, be they pre-Cartesian or non-Western. With dualist prejudices set aside, the literary historian and the intellectual historian can evaluate Anglo-Saxon psychological idioms by historically appropriate standards, after scouring the textual record for signs of the presence, dissemination, and assimilation of any teachings that posed a serious challenge to any aspect of cardiocentric psychology and the hydraulic model of mental activity.

Though transcultural psychiatry can combat the modernist bias, there remains the medievalist bias, which plagues present-day readers who assume that the concept of the incorporeal, unitary soul was a basic tenet of church dogma and was therefore well known and fully assimilated wherever Christianity took hold in Anglo-Saxon England. All of the subsequent chapters in this book are dedicated to demolishing this assumption. Certainly from the arrival of Augustine of Canterbury onwards, we can find evidence that the most learned Christians in England were aware of at least some aspects of the Platonizing-Christian concept of the unitary, incorporeal soul. But as discussed earlier, the availability of a rival theory

---

reality as outlined above, especially Stage 2, in which embodied realities are supplanted by rival theories at different rates for different strata within a single culture.
218 Kleinman and Kleinman, 'Somatization: The Interconnections in Chinese Society among Culture, Depressive Experiences, and the Meanings of Pain,' 435.

in the very small textual community of England's educated elite is by no means sufficient to show that this rival theory took hold in the general population, or even at the level of those with middling educations. In each of the chapters that follow, I search within a specific textual community for teachings that directly challenged the cardiocentric localization of the mind and the hydraulic model of mental activity: for instance, the teaching that the mind was part of the soul, combined with the teaching that the soul was entirely without material substance, was incompatible with the idea that the mind was concentrated in any one part of the body or subject to thermal and spatial changes. Chapter 4 evaluates the evidence of the raw materials – the manuscripts of classical and patristic psychologies – that were available in Anglo-Saxon England to sustain the transmission of these rival theories. Then chapters 5 through 8 evaluate the nature of the rival theories that were available at different educational strata: at the top, figures such as Alcuin and Ælfric; one step below them, King Alfred; then those who acquired some Latin literacy through the formal study of grammars, riddles, and the rest of the literary curriculum; then the anonymous vernacular homilists, and finally the ordinary non-literate population. This approach makes it possible to gauge when, and to what extent, learned discourse on the mind and soul posed an authoritative and sustained challenge to cardiocentrism and the hydraulic model within each cultural community, which in turn makes it possible to narrow the window of time during which cardiocentrism and the hydraulic model began to shift from literal expressions of folk psychology to conceptual metaphors.

4 The Psychological Inheritance of the Anglo-Saxons

The historical backdrop against which we can measure the metaphoricity of the vernacular model of psychology – including both cardiocentrism and the hydraulic model – consists primarily of datable texts containing psychological discourse in the classical tradition. Godden has defined the classical tradition in Anglo-Saxon psychology as that strain of thought which is most directly indebted to the Platonist-Christian tradition, and I agree that this is an apt description of what sets the works of Alcuin, Alfred, and Ælfric apart from most OE narrative treatments of the mind and soul.[1] For the purposes of the present study, however, it is useful to conceive of the classical tradition more broadly: to define it as coterminous with those texts known to and written by the Anglo-Saxons that are most directly indebted to early Christian Latin theological and philosophical traditions. This expansion of the category of the classical tradition makes room for other strains of thought that clearly do not originate in the Anglo-Saxons' vernacular tradition, though they are, in crucial ways, distinct from the precise Platonist-Christian philosophies of mind generated by Augustine or Boethius.

I underscore the diversity of Christian psychological discourses in order to combat the medievalist bias, which leads modern scholars to dismiss, without further consideration, the notion that any moderately learned Anglo-Saxon could have taken seriously the cardiocentric psychology and the hydraulic model that characterize the vernacular tradition. Two basic misapprehensions underlie the medievalist bias: first, that before the Christianization of the Anglo-Saxons had even begun, psychological discourse

---

1 Godden, 'Anglo-Saxons on the Mind,' 271–85.

among Western Christian intellectuals was monolithically dominated by Augustinian opinions; and second, that direct and indirect knowledge of Augustine's psychological discourses was readily available in most Anglo-Saxon centres of learning. '[I]t would be much safer to assume that the English knew any given work of Augustine than that they did not,' wrote J.D.A. Ogilvy in 1936,[2] and this was the fundamental assumption underlying the dominant approach to OE poetry throughout the middle decades of the twentieth century. In the past two decades the study of patristic influence on OE verse has been carried out with greater circumspection,[3] but in other areas of Anglo-Saxon studies the medievalist bias still thrives. 'For the Anglo-Saxons, Augustine was the leading Latin writer,' according to a study published in 1993; 'Anglo-Saxon knowledge and use of Augustine were both broad and deep.'[4] Literate Anglo-Saxons are said to have espoused an 'Augustinian worldview,'[5] and Anglo-Saxon thinkers are supposed to have embraced an 'Augustinian synthesis' to the extent that they could not or would not recognize internal contradictions among their patristic source texts.[6] It is taken for granted that 'Augustine's works enjoyed a wide circulation in Anglo-Saxon England,' and therefore as we await the publication of the entry on Augustine in *Sources of Anglo-Saxon Literary Culture* (as one scholar remarked in 2007) the work of Ogilvy 'is still useful for showing how popular Augustine was in Anglo-Saxon England.'[7]

---

2 Ogilvy, *Books Known to Anglo-Latin Writers from Aldhelm to Alcuin, 670–804*; quoted (not in agreement, however) by Szarmach, 'The Meaning of Alfred's *Preface* to the *Pastoral Care*,' 70.

3 A healthy scepticism toward the pan-allegorical approach is well articulated by Joyce Hill, 'Confronting *Germania Latina*: Changing Responses to Old English Biblical Verse.'

4 J.F. Kelly, 'The Knowledge and Use of Augustine among the Anglo-Saxons,' 214 and 216.

5 Jolly, *Popular Religion in Late Saxon England*, treats the seemingly non-Christian elements of Anglo-Saxon texts and rituals with remarkable sensitivity, usefully problematizing binaries such as pagan-Christian and orthodox-unorthodox, but she repeatedly uses the phrase 'Augustinian worldview' to name the intellectual common thread uniting learned and ecclesiastical thought and ritual: see esp. 72–3.

6 N. Thompson, 'Anglo-Saxon Orthodoxy,' maintains that in the early medieval West, 'Most Christians assumed that there was a unified and harmonious body of doctrine set out in scripture, attested by the Fathers, and shared by the whole church without disagreement. This perception of unity, based on what Jaroslav Pelikan has called the Augustinian synthesis, impeded the recognition of contradictions or inconsistencies in the tradition' (46–7). Thompson further argues that this false sense of unity impeded Ælfric's comprehension of Paschasius and Ratramnus; cf. chapter 8 below.

7 Alcamesi, 'The *Sibylline Acrostic* in Anglo-Saxon Manuscripts,' 149; she is referring not to the first edition of Ogilvy's work quoted above but to the more circumspect 1967 revision.

These claims would be defensible if we had any reason to think that the typical Anglo-Saxon poet or homilist or hagiographer had access to a patristic library of the calibre of Bede's or Ælfric's, but every available form of evidence points in quite the opposite direction. This chapter takes initial steps toward overturning the medievalist bias, beginning with a survey of the diversity of late antique and early medieval psychological discourse, and concluding with an examination of the textual evidence for the dissemination of philosophical and theological opinions on the soul and on incorporeality in Anglo-Saxon England.

No system of categorization can satisfactorily capture the complexities of early medieval opinions on the mind, the soul, and the nature of their respective substances, but in the chapters that follow it will be useful to have established some shorthand by which to distinguish several strains of thought within the classical tradition. First is the Platonist-Christian psychology represented by Augustine and Boethius as well as lesser lights such as Claudianus Mamertus.[8] Then there is that marginalized category of Latin Fathers whose psychology – specifically their opinions on the substance of the soul and its relationship to the substance of the divine – was influenced less by Platonism than by Stoicism: among their more prominent representatives are John Cassian and Gennadius of Marseilles. I distinguish a third category as well, encompassing texts and authors whose psychology is best described as eclectic, in which a broadly Platonist orientation coexists with opinions about the soul or the mind that are not tied to any systematic philosophical or theological tradition. The *Dialogi* of Gregory the Great exemplify the category of eclectic psychology: of course Gregory maintains the incorporeality of the soul when he is compelled to do so in a discursive mode, but at the same time, Gregory's narratives, which far outweigh the discursive interludes in the *Dialogi*, encourage a cardiocentric conception of the mind and a spatial, even anthropomorphized understanding of the soul. One might say that they send a mixed message to their audience, even though there is no reason to doubt that Gregory himself had a firm grasp of Platonist-Christian psychology.

---

8 If it fell within the purview of this study to devote more attention to the differences among early Christian philosophical psychologies, it would be necessary to distinguish among Neoplatonist, Middle Platonist, and Platonist opinions, but attention to this detail is not useful here, since the Anglo-Saxons themselves did not recognize such distinctions. In the chapters that follow I use the term 'Platonist' as a catch-all category encompassing Platonist and Neoplatonist thinkers who asserted the incorporeality of the soul along with all its epistemological and ontological corollaries.

These categories – the Platonist, the Stoicizing, and the eclectic – will be used to distinguish various strains of Insular psychology in subsequent chapters, but the purpose of the present chapter is to evaluate what sort of psychological teachings the Anglo-Saxons inherited from their forebears. In the following pages I have provided an overview of the psychological opinions constituting each category along with a few prominent textual examples of each. Then at the end of the chapter I weigh the textual evidence for the availability and influence of Platonist, Stoicizing, and eclectic psychologies at different periods of Anglo-Saxon history.

Platonist-Christian Opinions on the Soul and on Substance

In subsequent chapters, where I invoke the category of Platonist-Christian psychology, or where I distinguish a 'strict' or 'Platonizing' concept of incorporeality from a non-philosophical definition of incorporeality, I use these terms to signify a specific and circumscribed set of ideas that allowed the more rigorous thinkers to invoke the idea of the incorporeal soul in the service of dialectical proofs of theological tenets. The following list of these premises is not at all intended to represent the diversity and complexity of Platonist-Christian psychological discourse: on the contrary, these few premises represent the barest skeleton of points of consensus among early medieval authors and texts that share a Platonist-Christian psychological orientation.

1 **The human soul (*anima*) is rational.** The concept of a unitary soul, which encompasses at least the rational faculties if not other mental faculties as well, separates the Platonist-Christian tradition from the Anglo-Saxons' vernacular tradition, in which soul and mind are separate entities.
2 **The human soul is incorporeal, as are angels and God.** The incorporeality of the rational spirits (i.e., human souls and angels) separates the Platonist-Christian tradition from that of Stoicizing Christian thinkers, who ascribed true incorporeality to God alone.
3 **That which is incorporeal lacks material substance.** The Platonist-Christian application of the term 'incorporeal' to entities that lack all material substance is distinct from non-Platonist uses of the term, in which the incorporeal is synonymous with the non-fleshly, or the invisible, or that which is composed of a very subtle material.
4 **That which is incorporeal by Platonist-Christian standards is immortal.** Although the soul's immortality is typically defended by

Christian authors regardless of their philosophical orientation or lack thereof, the Platonist-Christian tradition treats immortality as a natural corollary of incorporeality and builds upon this connection in dialectic.

5 **That which is incorporeal by Platonist-Christian standards is capable of perceiving incorporeal truths and can be perceived only by other incorporeals.** This epistemological corollary of the rational soul's incorporeality is not the same as the non-philosophical observation that something not present to the senses can be conjured up in memory or imagination. The faculty of *intellectus* by which the rational soul perceives incorporeals can perceive things that are wholly and permanently inaccessible to the senses. (In practice, not all incorporeals are equally accessible to the *intellectus* as long as the soul resides in the body.)

6 **Incorporeal truths, including the Ideas or Forms, are immortal, and they exist independently of the material world of particular things.** Of course this Realist position characteristically separates Platonist thought from the Aristotelian opinion that Universals are dependent on the existence of particular things, but more germane to the present study is that the very existence of wholly immaterial realities was foreign to the popular mentality of the Anglo-Saxons and their Frankish contemporaries, as discussed in chapter 8 below.

Other doctrines rooted in the Platonist tradition will surface in later chapters, but they need not be considered part of the common ground of consensus among Platonist-Christian authors and texts. A minority of early medieval discourses, for instance, maintains the existence of a world-soul that animates the cosmos; a minority also supports the theory of anamnesis or recollection, according to which all souls, before being implanted in bodies, existed on the plane of the incorporeal Forms and thence absorbed truths that remain latent but scarcely accessible within the rational soul during its tenure in the flesh. Additionally, not all Christian thinkers of a Platonist persuasion rigorously attached to the concept of the soul's incorporeality the same corollaries concerning its non-locality, non-spatial distribution, and indivisibility.[9]

---

9 On the conceptual relationship among incorporeality, place, and space in the fifth-century and ninth-century debates over the nature of the soul, see esp. Cristiani, 'L'Espace de l'âme.'

The six points listed above are not just the hallmarks of a Platonizing orientation in psychological discourse; they are also indispensable elements of psychology as it was put to use in dialectic in early medieval Christian milieux. John Marenbon has described early medieval philosophy, beginning with Alcuin's circle in the late eighth century, as a partnership between Aristotelian dialectic and Christian theology characterized by a Platonist understanding of substance. I will not attempt here to reproduce Marenbon's elegant explanation of the intellectual sleight-of-hand that allowed late antique adaptations of Aristotle's *Categories* to be put to use in the service of a largely Platonist (i.e., largely Realist) ontology.[10] Instead I would like to illustrate the nature of this particular marriage of Platonism with the *Categories* by considering the *Soliloquia*, one of Augustine of Hippo's early philosophical dialogues, which served as a favoured model for Carolingian authors as they developed their idiosyncratic mode of discourse on the soul. Close attention to the *Soliloquia* in their own right brings to light Augustine's reliance on the strict Platonist definition of incorporeality and its epistemological implications for the soul. Additionally, scrutiny of the *Soliloquia* at this juncture provides much-needed background information in anticipation of subsequent discussions of the psychological discourse of Anglo-Saxon scholars among the Carolingians (chapter 6) and of the OE adaptation of the *Soliloquia* (chapter 7).

Platonist-Christian Psychology in the Service of Dialectic

Augustine's *Soliloquia* depicts a conversation in which 'Augustine' articulates his fear and ignorance of certain matters, and in reply, Ratio (Reason) offers consolation and instruction. Augustine (i.e., the author) titled his dialogue *Soliloquia* to evoke the idea that Ratio resides within 'Augustine' himself (i.e., the interlocutor in the dialogue), even though 'Augustine' is initially uncertain who or where his interlocutor is.[11] Pervading and shaping the dialogue is 'Augustine's' fear that, even if the soul is immortal (which he does not take for granted), its afterlife might be devoid of individual mental activity, without which his existence will be dreary and futile, or perhaps his mind will regress to a childlike state.[12] During the course of

---

10 Marenbon, *From the Circle of Alcuin to the School of Auxerre*, 4–8, 12–15, and 22–9.
11 Augustine explains the name in *Retractationes* 1.4.1; cf. *Soliloquia* 1.1.1 (both discussed below in chapter 7).
12 *Soliloquia* 1.12.20 (ed. Hörmann, CSEL 89, 32.2–12) and 2.20.36 (ibid., 97.15–98.5); on these passages, see below.

Book 2, Ratio persuades 'Augustine' that his soul is immortal, but because the *Soliloquia* was never completed, Ratio does not address her interlocutor's worry about the quality of mental life in the afterlife. The anxieties expressed by the interlocutor 'Augustine' are rooted in the historical Augustine's own biography. As told in the *Confessiones*, Augustine's encounter with Cicero's *Hortensius* at age nineteen inspired him to reorder his priorities; in the *Soliloquia*, 'Augustine' tells Ratio that he renounced worldly pleasures and began to thirst for wisdom after reading Cicero fourteen years earlier.[13] The historical Augustine continued to esteem Cicero's writings and to wrestle with him as a worthy philosophical adversary throughout his life,[14] although he was deeply troubled by the closing passage of Cicero's *Hortensius*, which Augustine quotes at length in his *De Trinitate*. 'If this capacity of ours to perceive and to be wise is perishable and fleeting,' Cicero proposes, then he hopes wanly for 'a cheerful sunset to our days when we have completed our tasks.' But on the other hand, 'if we have eternal and divine souls [*animos*] ... we must suppose that the more these souls keep always to their course, that is to reason and to eager inquiry, and the less they mix themselves up in the tangled vices and errors of men, the easier will be their ascent and return to heaven.'[15] Augustine was disappointed in Cicero for doubting the immortality of the soul, and he attributed Cicero's error to the influence of the sceptics in the New Academy,[16] who promoted, as a philosophical ideal, the ceaseless search for truth. In composing the *Soliloquia*, Augustine strove to repudiate the scepticism that Cicero expresses in the closing lines of the *Hortensius*, concerning the immortality of the soul and its ongoing search for wisdom.[17]

---

13 *Confessiones* 3.4.7 (ed. Verheijen, CCSL 27, 30.5–10); *Soliloquia* 1.10.17 (ed. Hörmann, CSEL 89, 26.12–18).

14 The classic study of Augustine's engagement with Cicero is Testard, *Saint Augustin et Cicéron*; on the role of the *Hortensius* in Augustine's conversion, see 1.170–6; and on his renunciation of material luxuries and honours, see 1.132–6.

15 Augustine, *De Trinitate* 14.19.26 (trans. E. Hill, *The Trinity*, 391); for Latin text, see Mountain (ed.), CCSL 50A, 458.34–43.

16 *De Trinitate* 14.19.26 (ed. Mountain, CCSL 50A, 458.55–7).

17 On Augustine and scepticism, see O'Daly, *Augustine's Philosophy of Mind*, 162–71; and Watson's introduction to Augustine, *Soliloquies and Immortality of the Soul*, 5–6, 15–16; on the *Hortensius* and its relationship to the *Soliloquia*, see Testard's *index locorum* in *Saint Augustin et Cicéron*, 1.375 (*Soliloquia*); 1.373 (*De Trinitate* 14.19.26) and 1.377–8 (*Hortensius* frag. 97).

At the outset of the *Soliloquia* it quickly becomes clear that Ratio and 'Augustine' use the word *anima* to signify a unitary soul that incorporates a range of mental faculties. 'Augustine' points out that the *anima* possesses free will;[18] Ratio underscores that the soul utilizes reason and is capable of understanding.[19] Non-sensory perception (*intellectus*) is attributed variously to the *anima*, the *animus*, and the *mens*. Within the *Soliloquia* Augustine does not spell out the relationship among these terms, but in other works he specifies that the mind 'belongs to' and 'is pre-eminent in' the soul.[20] 'Augustine' immediately accepts that the *animus* belongs to·the *anima*, so Ratio does not belabour the point before using it as the foundation of her later argument: that the *anima* must be immortal because it perceives immortal realities. Other than 'Augustine's' doubt about its immortality, the only aspect of the *anima* that causes any confusion is its dual meaning, since *anima* can also signify the non-rational and mortal soul of beasts. Therefore when 'Augustine' claims to love the *anima*, Ratio asks teasingly, 'Therefore do you also love fleas and bugs?' 'Augustine' is compelled to specify that he loves only the *anima rationalis*, the rational soul that sets humans apart from beasts, irrespective of the good and evil traits of the human being in which it resides.[21]

Having established these basic characteristics of the rational *anima*, Ratio pauses to advertise the moral and spiritual benefits of believing in the immortality of the soul, with the implicit message that scepticism about the immortality of the rational *anima* undermines the moral compass. Faith, hope, and love must all be cultivated during life in order that the soul's looking for God might result in the soul's seeing God, although when the soul leaves the body and attains a clear vision of God, faith and hope will no longer be necessary, and only love will remain.[22] As the dialogue proceeds,

---

18 *Soliloquia* 1.1.4 (ed. Hörmann, CSEL 89, 8.13): 'arbitrium animae liberum est.' All translations of the *Soliloquia* are my own, but I have consulted Watson's translation of Augustine, *Soliloquies and Immortality of the Soul*.
19 *Soliloquia* 1.6.13 (ed. Hörmann, CSEL 89, 21.10): 'Aspectus animae ratio est' (Reason is the soul's sense of sight); 1.6.12 (ibid., 21.6–7): 'Sine tribus istis [*scil.* fide, spe, caritate] igitur anima nulla sanatur, ut possit deum suum uidere, id est intellegere' (Therefore without those three [*scil.* faith, hope, love] no soul is cleansed so that it can see – that is, understand – its God).
20 O'Daly, *Augustine's Philosophy of Mind*, 7–8; see, for instance, *De Trinitate* 15.7.11 (ed. Mountain, CCSL 50A, 474.7–475.13; trans. E. Hill, *The Trinity*, 403): 'Non igitur anima sed quod excellit in anima mens uocatur' (So it is not the soul but what is pre-eminent in the soul that is called mind).
21 *Soliloquia* 1.2.7 (ed. Hörmann, CSEL 89, 12.9–20).
22 *Soliloquia* 1.6.13–7.14 (ed. Hörmann, CSEL 89, 21.10–23.5).

Ratio elicits from 'Augustine' his philosophical orientation as an adherent of Cicero and a halfhearted sceptic: he embodies the bleak outlook and sense of purposelessness that Augustine had come to associate with scepticism by the time he penned his early dialogues. Despite his renunciation of most bodily desires and worldly pleasures, 'Augustine' is reluctant to sacrifice his friendships, bodily health, and life, not because he desires these things per se, but because the loss of them would hinder his pursuit of wisdom.[23] As mentioned above, 'Augustine' is acutely fearful that death will snuff out his mental faculties, even if it does not completely destroy the soul.[24] Ratio's objective is to assuage her interlocutor's fear by proving through dialectic that the *anima* is immortal. Because 'Augustine' already accepts that the *anima* is a unitary soul, incorporeal, and possessed of reason, within this Platonist-Christian framework it may be taken for granted that if the soul lives on past the death of the flesh that hinders its perception of incorporeal truths, its ability to perceive those truths will be restored.

The conversation that takes place in Book 1 of the *Soliloquia* is stretched out over the course of two different days. The first day's discussion ends inconclusively, in the middle of a consideration of impediments to human apprehension of truths. Early on the second day, Ratio's teaching turns from a general consideration of epistemological barriers to a pointed criticism of 'Augustine's' own blindness and – contrary to his claims that he had renounced so much of the material world – his ongoing entanglement in worldly desires. 'Augustine' grows despondent and begs Ratio to move ahead more quickly with her demonstration of the soul's immortality. Obliging his request, Ratio speeds through a breezy demonstration that proceeds according to these points:

1 Truth (*ueritas*) is not the same as a true thing (*uerum*).
2 Truth does not pass away when true things pass away.
3 Bodies necessarily pass away.
4 Truth is not a body.
5 Whatever exists must exist somewhere (*alicubi esse*).
6 Only a body can exist in a place (*esse in loco*); therefore, if truth is not a body, then it must exist 'somewhere' that is not a place.
7 Truth does not exist in mortal bodies.
8 'Truth exists, and it does not exist nowhere' (Est autem ueritas et non est nusquam).

---

23 *Soliloquia* 1.9.16 and 1.12.20–1 (ed. Hörmann, CSEL 89, 24.19–25.14 and 31.3–33.19).
24 *Soliloquia* 1.12.20 (discussed below).

9 If truth is to have a 'somewhere' in which to exist, then there must exist immortal, incorporeal things in which truth exists.

10 Nothing is true unless truth exists in it.

11 'It follows that true things do not exist unless they are immortal' (Conficitur non esse uera nisi quae sunt inmortalia).[25]

This argument unfolds with breathtaking speed because 'Augustine' assents readily to every assertion that Ratio makes. Her reasoning relies implicitly and unquestioningly on Platonic ontology and epistemology. The Forms, being incorporeal and therefore immortal and immutable, are the only things that exist fully, and they are constitutive of reality; the incorporeal part of a human being, which is interchangeably named anima, animus, and mens, is the only part of 'Augustine' that can apprehend the incorporeal Forms. None of this needed to be explained to Augustine's target audience. The sceptics whom Augustine wished to refute were not necessarily opposed to the reality of Forms but only to the notion that a human being, either in the body or after death, might attain certain knowledge of those incorporeal realities.[26]

As Book 2 begins, Ratio and 'Augustine' re-establish that what he most desires to know is whether he is immortal, and that he desires immortality not for the sake of life itself, but for the sake of prolonging his pursuit of knowledge.[27] As befits a dialogue that promotes a Platonist epistemology in the face of scepticism, the interlocutors are more ardently interested in intellectus than in the soul's other capacities, but since they understand the anima to be a unitary soul, intellectus is inseparable from the soul's life and existence. Accordingly, Ratio rearticulates 'Augustine's' inquiry: 'esse uis, uiuere et intellegere; sed esse ut uiuas, uiuere ut intellegas. Ergo esse te scis, uiuere te scis, intellegere te scis. Sed utrum ista semper futura sint an nihil horum futurum sit an maneat aliquid semper et aliquid intercidat an minui et augeri haec possint, cum omnia mansura sint, nosse uis.'[28]

25 Soliloquia 1.14.26–15.29 (ed. Hörmann, CSEL 89, 39.3–43.13); on this passage, see Watson's comments in Augustine, Soliloquies and Immortality of the Soul, 180–1; and O'Daly, Augustine's Philosophy of Mind, 186.

26 On Augustine's reception of the theory of Forms and its implications for epistemology, see O'Daly, Augustine's Philosophy of Mind, 189–99.

27 Soliloquia 2.1.1 (ed. Hörmann, CSEL 89, 46.9–26).

28 Soliloquia 2.1.1 (ed. Hörmann, CSEL 89, 47.7–13): 'R. You want to exist, to live, and to understand, but you want to exist in order to live, and to live in order to understand. Therefore you know that you exist, you know that you live, and you know that you understand, but you desire to know whether these [scil. the states of existing, living, and

When Ratio subsequently resumes her logical demonstration of the soul's immortality, she introduces the distinction between an accident and an inseparable property, a distinction originating in Aristotle's *Categories*. An accident exists in a thing in such a way that 'etiam seiungi atque alibi esse possit, ut hoc lignum in hoc loco, ut sol in oriente,' but an inseparable property exists in another thing in such a way that 'ab eo nequeat separari, ut in hoc ligno forma et species quam uidemus, ut in sole lux, ut in igne calor, ut in animo disciplina.'[29] Upon this distinction Ratio builds the following argument for the immortality of the *animus*:

> Omne, quod in subiecto est, si semper manet, ipsum etiam subiectum maneat semper necesse est. Et omnis in subiecto est animo disciplina. Necesse est igitur semper animus maneat, si semper manet disciplina. Est autem disciplina ueritas et semper, ut in initio libri huius ratio persuasit, ueritas manet. Semper igitur animus manet nec umquam animus mortuus dicitur.[30]

'Augustine' accepts the Aristotelian notion of accidents and inseparable properties in general, but he has doubts about whether a discipline is actually an inseparable property of the mind. As he points out, it is problematic to maintain that a learned discipline, such as disputation, is inseparably present in the minds of the unlearned.[31] Ratio declines to address his objection right away, and she intimates that she will come back to it in Book 3 of the dialogue (though Augustine never completed this third book).[32]

---

understanding] will exist forever; or whether none of them will continue to exist; or whether one might endure always while another perishes; or whether, if all of them are going to endure, they can be diminished or increased.'

29 *Soliloquia* 2.12.22 (ed. Hörmann, CSEL 89, 75.5–9): An accident 'can also be detached or exist elsewhere, like this wood in this place, like the sun in the east.' An inseparable property 'cannot be separated from its subject, like form and species in this wood which we see, like light in the sun, like heat in fire, like a discipline in the mind.'

30 *Soliloquia* 2.13.24 (ed. Hörmann, CSEL 89, 79.1–7): 'If everything which is in a subject endures always, it must be that the subject itself also endures always. And every discipline is in a subject, namely the mind. So it must be that the mind endures always, if the discipline remains always. Now, a discipline is truth, and truth endures always, as reason demonstrated at the beginning of the first book. Therefore the mind endures always, and the mind is never called "dead."'

31 *Soliloquia* 2.12.22–13.23 (ed. Hörmann, CSEL 89, 75.11–76.7) and 2.14.25 (ibid., 79.16–80.2).

32 *Soliloquia* 2.19.33 (ed. Hörmann, CSEL 89, 93.7–12). Augustine's notes preparatory to Book 3 have come down to us as *De immortalitate animae*, which he did not intend for publication in their present state: see Augustine, *Retractationes*, 1.5.1 (ed. Mutzenbecher,

Instead of addressing her interlocutor's objection right away, Ratio steers the conversation back toward the theory of Forms. It was earlier agreed that there can exist such a thing as a true body.[33] However, it must be admitted that (1) because bodies are necessarily subject to passing away, they cannot contain the same kind of truth that is found in the disciplines; and (2) just as triangles in nature are never the perfect triangles studied in geometry, so are all bodies in nature merely imitations of their Forms.[34] The part of this argument that 'Augustine' finds most difficult to grasp is that if a body actually achieved its ideal Form, it would not be a body anymore but an *animus*:

> R. ... ego puto corpus aliqua forma et specie contineri, quam si non haberet, corpus non esset, si ueram haberet, animus esset. An aliter putandum est?
> A. Adsentior in parte, de cetero dubito. Nam, nisi teneatur aliqua figura, corpus non esse concedo. Quomodo autem, si eam ueram haberet, animus esset, non satis intellego.[35]

Ratio's response does little to bolster or elucidate her extreme Realist assertions; she simply restates that the relationship between body and *animus* is analogous to that between natural shapes and shapes in geometry. 'Augustine' professes to be convinced, but one suspects that it was simply not worth the effort to explain here how the *animus* could be the body's Form, since this is not a necessary premise of Ratio's argument for the soul's immortality.[36] Book 2 then draws to an abrupt close. As mentioned earlier, in the final chapter 'Augustine' confesses his fear that his mind might revert to a childlike state, with diminished self-awareness, and in response, Ratio only reassures 'Augustine' that God will assist them in his

---

CCSL 57, 15–16); and Watson's comments in Augustine, *Soliloquies and Immortality of the Soul*, 198–9.

33 *Soliloquia* 1.15.28–9 (ed. Hörmann, CSEL 89, 41.11–44.2).
34 *Soliloquia* 2.17.31–19.33 (ed. Hörmann, CSEL 89, 87.17–93.6).
35 *Soliloquia* 2.18.32 (ed. Hörmann, CSEL 89, 91.1–8): 'R. I reckon that a body consists of some form and species; if it did not have form, it would not be a body, but if it had true form, it would be a mind. A. I agree in part, but I hesitate over the rest. For I grant that it would not be a body unless it were contained by some shape, but I don't fully understand how it would be a mind if it possessed true form.'
36 Augustine provides a more satisfactory explanation of how the *animus* is the body's Form in *De immortalitate animae*: see esp. 15.24 (ed. Hörmann, CSEL 89, 125.13–127.3) and Watson's comments in Augustine, *Soliloquies and Immortality of the Soul*, 211).

search for truth.[37] By the standards of dialectic, she has yet to craft a watertight demonstration that the unitary soul is immortal, and since Augustine never completed Book 3, Ratio never assuages her interlocutor's fear of a mentally diminished existence in the afterlife.

Imitators of Augustine's Method of Argumentation

Setting aside these unresolved logical flaws, however, the method of discourse exemplified in the *Soliloquia*, combining a heavily Realist approach to the Forms with the dialectical apparatus of Aristotle's *Categories*, was emulated by late antique defenders of Platonist psychology, such as Claudianus Mamertus, whose *De statu animae*, composed in 469 or 470, is a lengthy and acerbic refutation of the brief Stoicizing discussion of the soul put forth by Faustus of Riez (fl. ca. 455–80).[38] The relationship between strict incorporeality and epistemology is indispensable to Claudianus's logic: 'Intellectum uero localem non esse uel intellegendo cognoscimus, quia si intellectus localis est, locale erit et quod intellegitur. Nihil enim locale est, quod non et ipsum locus est. At si intellectus localis et in hoc deus, quia hoc intellegitur deus, ergo localis est deus.'[39] Since it is preposterous to suppose that God is localized, some part of the human being must be incorporeal in order to perceive God. Claudianus makes the most of opportunities to call his opponent's ideas preposterous: 'Persuadere mihi non possum,' he writes, 'quod philosophi huius [*scil.* Platonis] anima corporea fuerit, ac si forsan praecipiti lapsu stultitiae ulla anima corpus esse iudicanda est, illas equidem corporeas iudicauerim, quae corpus esse se credunt.'[40] That Claudianus could work sneers and satire into his treatise

---

37 *Soliloquia* 2.20.36 (ed. Hörmann, CSEL 89, 98.1–9).
38 On the dispute over the nature of the soul in fifth-century Gaul, see esp. Mathisen, *Ecclesiastical Factionalism and Religious Controversy in Fifth-Century Gaul*, 235–44; Fortin, *La querelle de l'âme*, esp. 15–110; and Madoz, 'Un caso de materialismo,' 206–10.
39 Claudianus Mamertus, *De statu animae* 1.14 (ed. Engelbrecht, CSEL 11, 58): 'We recognize by means of intellection that the intellect is not spatial, because if intellect is spatial, that which is apprehended by intellect will also be spatial. Nothing then is spatial which is not also itself a space. But if the intellect is spatial and God is in it, because God is apprehended by it, therefore God is spatial.'
40 Claudianus Mamertus, *De statu animae* 2.7 (ed. Engelbrecht, CSEL 11, 122–3): 'I cannot persuade myself that the soul of this philosopher [Plato] was corporeal, but if it must be judged, perhaps through some precipitous crisis of stupidity, that any soul is a body, I would reckon that it is the souls who believe themselves to be a body that are corporeal.'

on the incorporeal soul is suggestive of how comfortable he and his fifth-century audience were with this mode of discourse; the Carolingians would later learn from Augustine, Claudianus Mamertus, and others to cultivate a similar method of argumentation, but most of the Carolingians' philosophical texts cannot, sadly, match Claudianus's wit and sarcasm. To further explore the ideology of the opponent whose work Claudianus so vigorously denounces, I turn next to the Stoicizing strain of early Christian psychology.

The Corporeal Soul of Stoicizing Christian Thought

According to classical Stoic thought, true existence (*ousia*) can be ascribed only to bodies. A body is defined according to its substance, as that which 'has threefold extension together with resistance,' and according to its capacity, as that which demonstrably acts upon or is acted upon by another body.[41] According to its capacity, therefore, the human soul is a body: the Greek philosopher Cleanthes (ca. 330–ca. 230 BC) observes that the soul acts on the body, for 'when it feels shame and fear, the body turns red and pale respectively,' and it is acted upon by the body, because it feels pain when the body is sick or wounded.[42] Souls as well as God, the active principle of the universe, are made of an intelligent, rational, bodily substance called *pneuma*.[43] The only incorporeals in the classical Stoic universe are those things that can neither act upon or be acted upon by a body: these are place, time, the extra-cosmic void, and the *lekton* 'that which can be said.' To these, the Stoics attributed not true existence but only subsistence (*hupostasis*).[44]

In the classical Stoic ontological hierarchy, therefore, incorporeals occupy the lowest position, since they are denied true existence, while corporeals are on top. From the perspective of a Platonist, this ontological hierarchy is strangely inverted, since the upper levels of the Christian Platonist's ontological hierarchy are occupied by incorporeals such as God,

---

41 Brunschwig, 'Stoic Metaphysics,' 210–11; see also Long and Sedley, *The Hellenistic Philosophers*, 1.272–4.

42 Long and Sedley, *The Hellenistic Philosophers*, 1.272, §45A; see also Brunschwig, 'Stoic Metaphysics,' 211; and Annas, *Hellenistic Philosophy of Mind*, 41–2.

43 Brunschwig, 'Stoic Metaphysics,' 210–11; on the *pneuma*, see esp. Long, 'Stoic Psychology'; and Sedley, 'Chrysippus on Psychophysical Causality,' 325–31.

44 Brunschwig, 'Stoic Metaphysics,' 213; for further discussion of the *lekton*, see chapter 5 below.

(usually) angels, and human souls, while mutability and corruption prevent corporeals from being fully existent or fully real. As we look back at the history of early Christian psychologies, the dominance of Augustine and other Platonist thinkers obscures the presence of a significant minority who espoused and developed a more Stoicizing understanding of the substance of the soul.[45] I would even go so far as to say that our understanding of early Christian psychology is so tied to Platonist and Platonizing thought that it is hard to see how the Stoic and the Christian ontologies could have been considered at all compatible with one another. The survey of early Stoicizing Christian opinions on the nature of the soul that I set out here is perhaps more thorough than one might expect in a study of Anglo-Saxon psychologies, but it provides the necessary background material for chapters 5 and 6, in which I argue that Stoicizing opinions on the soul persisted among a significant minority of educated Christians in the West, for a considerably longer period than most modern scholars acknowledge.[46]

Some representatives of the Stoicizing minority are, undeniably, strange figures on the early Christian intellectual landscape.[47] For instance, in his treatise *De anima*, Tertullian (ca. 160–ca. 225 AD) rejects numerous tenets of Platonist psychology, preferring instead to localize the psychic *pneuma* in the blood around the heart and to promote the psychological materialism of the classical Stoics Zeno, Cleanthes, and Chrysippus, whom he cites by name.[48] Combining his pneumatic psychology with an exceedingly

---

45 Spanneut, *Le Stoïcisme des Pères de l'Église*, covers the influence of Stoicism on Christian thought, both Eastern and Western, from St Paul through Tertullian; on Stoicizing Christians from Tertullian to around the year 600, see Spanneut, *Permanence du Stoïcisme*, 130–78; Verbeke, *The Presence of Stoicism in Medieval Thought*, 21–35 (on psychological materialism); and Colish, *The Stoic Tradition from Antiquity to the Early Middle Ages*, vol. 2.
46 Both Spanneut and Verbeke make very brief mention of the strain of psychological materialism that persisted in Carolingian circles in the ninth century (Spanneut, *Permanence du Stoïcisme*, 180–1; and Verbeke, *Presence of Stoicism*, 35–8).
47 On psychological materialism in Christian thought predating Tertullian, see Spanneut, *Le Stoïcisme des Pères de l'Église*, 133–50; and Madoz, 'Un caso de materialismo,' 204–5. Paulsen, 'Early Christian Belief in a Corporeal Deity: Origen and Augustine as Reluctant Witnesses,' expands the discussion of early Christian materialism to include non-Stoicizing thinkers.
48 In *De anima* 5 Tertullian names his authorities, Stoic and otherwise, on the meaning of corporeality; in *De anima* 15 he discusses the localization of the soul. See also Colish, *The Stoic Tradition*, 2.19–25; and Verbeke, *The Presence of Stoicism in Medieval Thought*, 23–5.

literal reading of Genesis, Tertullian proposes that the substance of the soul is materially anthropomorphic:

> Recogita enim, cum deus flasset in faciem homini flatum uitae, et factus esset homo in animam uiuam, totus utique, per faciem statim flatum illum in interiora transmissum et per uniuersa corporis spatia diffusum simulque diuina aspiratione densatum omni intus linea expressum esse, quam densatus impleuerat, et uelut in forma gelasse. Inde igitur et corpulentia animae ex densatione solidata est et effigies ex impressione formata.[49]

It must be admitted that Tertullian's extreme anthropomorphism did not have a lasting or profound influence on later Stoicizing thought, though it is useful to see how Tertullian was able to merge his Stoic-oriented materialism with the Judeo-Christian tradition.[50]

Setting aside the issue of anthropomorphism, Tertullian's understanding of the spiritual substance of God and of the soul exerted a marked influence on the philosophy of mind articulated by Lactantius (ca. 240–ca. 320).[51] He follows Tertullian's lead regarding the corporeality of human souls and of angels,[52] but his opinion on the substance of God is not so clear, and in it scholars have identified strands of both Stoic and Platonist thought intertwined. It appears that Lactantius wanted to retain as much of the Stoic opinion as possible, including the concept of divine *pneuma*, while also rejecting two objectionable corollaries of the idea that the divine *pneuma* permeates the universe. The concept of divine *pneuma* could be taken to imply pantheism or animism: Lactantius rejects this implication outright in his *Institutiones diuinae*.[53] The second implication of the divine

---

49 Tertullian, *De anima* 9.7–8 (ed. Waszink, CCSL 2, 793): 'Recall that when God breathed the breath of life into the face of man, and man was made into a living soul, truly whole, that breath was immediately carried through the face into the interior and diffused throughout all the spaces of the body; and at the same time, having been condensed by the divine breath, it was pressed into every line of the body, which it filled up when it was condensed, and it solidified as if in a mould. From this, therefore, the corporeality of the soul was solidified by condensation and its likeness was formed by its moulding.'

50 See further Spanneut, *Le Stoïcisme des Pères de l'Église*, 150–66 and 210–22 on Tertullian's psychology, and 269–94 and 391–7 on his views of substance, God, angels, and demons.

51 Verbeke, *The Presence of Stoicism in Medieval Thought*, 25–6.

52 Lactantius, *De opificio Dei* 16.12 (ed. Perrin, SC 213, 196) and 17–18 (ibid., 198–206); see also Colish, *The Stoic Tradition*, 2.43.

53 Lactantius, *Institutiones diuinae* 2.9.16; see Colish, *The Stoic Tradition*, 2.40.

pneuma generated more lasting controversy. Because the divine *pneuma* is omnipresent and indistinct from the *pneuma* of human souls, one might infer that human souls are part of the divine essence. Such an inference would eventually be deemed heretical, for if the human soul were a part of the divine essence, it would be incapable of sin.

Now, there are aspects of Neoplatonist thought that had the potential to generate the same objectionable conclusion, so this is not a uniquely Stoicizing heresy, but the potentially heretical implications of the divine *pneuma* had a remarkable effect on the development of Stoicizing Christian ontology. To conceptualize an impenetrable boundary between the divine substance and the rest of the universe was entirely contrary to the tenets of classical Stoicism, but it was necessary, if Stoicizing Christians wished to avoid the pitfalls of heresy, to articulate an ontological and substantial distinction between God and his creatures. The solution adopted by a number of thinkers was to retain the view that being was a property of bodies alone, while asserting that God surpassed the realm of ordinary being by virtue of his incorporeality. This assertion marks a significant departure from the classical Stoic ontological hierarchy, in which incorporeals had *less* than ordinary being. And although the placement of an incorporeal at the top of the ontological hierarchy gives it a superficial resemblance to that of the Platonist tradition, the Stoicizing Christian thinkers continued to maintain that all God's creatures, including angels and human souls, were bodies.

Anxiety over the heretical implications of the divine *pneuma* shaped the psychological opinions of important late antique theologians including Hilary of Poitiers (ca. 300–ca. 368) and John Cassian (ca. 360–435). In his commentary on Matthew, for instance, Hilary asserts,

> Nihil est quod non in substantia sua et creatione corporeum sit et omnium siue in caelo siue in terra siue uisibilium siue inuisibilium elementa formata sunt. Nam et animarum species siue obtinentium corpora siue corporibus exsulantium corpoream tamen naturae suae substantiam sortiuntur, quia omne quod creatum est in aliquo sit necesse est.[54]

---

54 Hilary of Poitiers, *Comm. in Matthaeum* 5.8 (ed. Doignon, SC 254, 158): 'There exists nothing that is not corporeal in its substance and creation; and all things whether in heaven or earth, whether visible or invisible, are made of material elements. Even the species of souls, whether they possess bodies or issue from bodies, receive a corporeal substance in any case, according to their own natures, which is necessary for everything that is created.' See Colish, *The Stoic Tradition*, 2.123–5.

And Cassian, in the seventh of the *Collationes*, writes that God is the only truly incorporeal being; all creatures must be corporeal, even if only very thinly.

> Licet enim pronuntiemus nonnullas esse spiritales naturas, ut sunt angeli, archangeli ceteraeque uirtutes, ipsa quoque anima nostra uel certe aër iste subtilis, tamen incorporeae nullatenus aestimandae sunt. Habent enim secundum se corpus quo subsistunt, licet multo tenuius quam nostra sunt corpora, secundum apostoli sententiam ita dicentis: *et corpora caelestia, et corpora terrestria* [1 Cor 15:40], et iterum: *seminatur corpus animale, surgit corpus spiritale* [1 Cor 15:44]. Quibus manifeste colligitur nihil esse incorporeum nisi deum solum, et idcirco ipsi tantummodo posse penetrabiles omnes spiritales atque intellectuales esse substantias, eo quod solus et totus et ubique et in omnibus sit, ita ut et cogitationes hominum et internos motus atque adyta mentis uniuersa inspiciat atque perlustret.[55]

Marcia Colish explains, 'Cassian is grappling here with a genuine metaphysical problem that was to plague many medieval thinkers regardless of their philosophical allegiance ... [A]pparently unaware of any other philosophical way to distinguish created spiritual beings from God, Cassian falls back on the corporality of angels and human souls as a way of reinforcing the Christian doctrine of God's otherness.'[56]

I have already alluded to the dispute between Faustus of Riez and Claudianus Mamertus concerning the substance of the soul. The benign intention behind Faustus's letter was to reject an altogether different heresy, that of Arianism, according to which Christ is not of one substance with God the Father. In his discussion of the filiation of the Son, Faustus draws directly from Cassian the opinion that God alone is incorporeal,

---

55 Cassian, *Collationes* 7.13 (ed. Petschenig, CSEL 13, 192–3): 'For although we declare that some natures are spiritual, as are the angels, the archangels and the other powers, our soul itself and of course the subtle air, yet these are by no means to be considered incorporeal. They have a body appropriate to themselves by which they subsist, although it is far more refined than our own bodies. In the words of the Apostle: "There are heavenly bodies and earthly bodies." And again: "It is sown an animal body, and it rises a spiritual body." From this it is clear that nothing is incorporeal but God alone, and therefore only to him can every spiritual and intellectual substance be penetrable because he alone is whole and everywhere and in all things, such that he may examine and survey the thoughts and internal dispositions of human beings and all the inmost recesses of the mind' (trans. Ramsey, *The Conferences*, 256–7).
56 Colish, *The Stoic Tradition*, 2.122.

'for he alone is unbounded and diffused everywhere.'[57] And if God alone is incorporeal, then human souls and angels must be corporeal, an assertion which Faustus justifies by adducing patristic precedents. Some of the most learned Fathers, he argues, claim that everything that has been created appears to be a material substance and to be corporeal ('quicquid creatum est materiam uideri ... et corporeum esse'); additionally, the nature of souls and angels is necessarily corporeal because that nature is 'circumscribed with respect to its origin and its space' (initio circumscribatur et spatio).[58] Faustus was not alone in adopting a corporealist view of the soul; among the Christian literati of Gaul in the later fifth century, in fact, the corporealist faction appears to have outnumbered Claudianus Mamertus's allies who supported Augustine's Neoplatonizing psychology.[59]

A near-contemporary of Faustus, the late fifth-century priest Gennadius of Marseilles, is now known primarily as the continuator of Jerome's *De uiris illustribus*, but it was in another work, his *De ecclesiasticis dogmatibus*, that Gennadius vigorously asserted his Stoicizing opinion on the substances of God and of the soul. *De ecclesiasticis dogmatibus* articulates a series of orthodox positions on fundamental Church teachings and contrasts each with its heterodox alternatives.[60] Gennadius is strongly critical of earlier thinkers, of both Stoicizing and Platonist inclinations, including Tertullian, who failed to distinguish clearly between the substance of God and that of his creation.[61] In the same vein, he opposes any suggestion that the substance of creatures might be incorporeal like that of the deity:

---

57 Faustus, *Ep.* 3 (ed. Engelbrecht, CSEL 21, 174). On Faustus's reliance on Cassian, and the central purpose of *Ep.* 3, see Colish, *The Stoic Tradition*, 2.128–9; cf. Brittain, 'No Place for a Platonist Soul in Fifth-Century Gaul,' 245–7.

58 Faustus, *Ep.* 3 (ed. Engelbrecht, CSEL 21, 173). Because of Claudianus Mamertus's response, *Ep.* 3 is Faustus's most widely disseminated statement on the corporeality of the soul, but he reiterates his corporealist position in several other works: see Mathisen, *Ecclesiastical Factionalism and Religious Controversy in Fifth-Century Gaul*, 239.

59 Mathisen, *Ecclesiastical Factionalism and Religious Controversy in Fifth-Century Gaul*, 235–44, contextualizes Faustus's and Claudianus's quarrel within the ecclesiastical and literary networks of fifth-century Gaul; on the theological implications of the controversy, see also Verbeke, *The Presence of Stoicism in Medieval Thought*, 33–5; Fortin, *La querelle de l'âme*, esp. 15–110; and Madoz, 'Un caso de materialismo,' 206–10.

60 The standard edition of Gennadius's work appears in Turner's article entitled 'The *Liber ecclesiasticorum dogmatum*,' which (with Turner's 'Supplenda') includes an excellent study of early medieval citations and manuscripts of *De eccl. dogm.* as well as a history of false attributions of the text to other authors; see ibid., 78–9 for Turner's disambiguation of the three versions of *De eccl. dogm.* that are printed in the PL.

61 Gennadius, *De eccl. dogm.*, par. 4 (ed. Turner, 'The *Liber ecclesiasticorum dogmatum*,' 90).

nothing in nature is incorporeal or invisible or uncircumscribed except God; angels and human souls 'subsist bodily, though not in the flesh.'[62] As Colish explains, Gennadius put forth these assertions in order to combat the Origenist heresy, which maintained in error that angels and prelapsarian humans were purely spiritual beings, and that humans received their bodies only as a result of the Fall.[63] Gennadius's reasoning, however, is not based solely on ontological considerations: as a matter of natural philosophy, God is everywhere and the soul is circumscribed. The soul's localized nature makes it necessarily more corporeal than God.

In the final paragraph (54) of *De ecclesiasticis dogmatibus* Gennadius again raises the problem of the soul's substance, in a tone revealing his indignation that his own orthodoxy has been called into question by one of his contemporaries. 'Propter nouellos legislatores,' Gennadius writes, 'qui ideo animam tantum ad imaginem Dei creatam dicunt ut quia Deus incorporeus recte creditur etiam anima incorporea esse credatur, libere confitemur imaginem in aeternitate similitudinem in moribus inueniri.'[64] At issue is the extent to which the soul must replicate the characteristics of God, given that it is God's image and likeness. These *nouelli legislatores* insist that the soul is in the image of God to such a degree that it must share God's incorporeality; Gennadius counters that such a conclusion is not necessary, since the soul's immortality and its behaviour already reflect God's image and likeness respectively. Based on the likely dating of *De ecclesiasticis dogmatibus* between 470 and 490, Morin and Madoz have both suggested that this paragraph is a response to Claudianus Mamertus's lengthy and rhetorically overblown polemic against Stoicizing Christian psychology, the *De statu animae*, which was composed around 468.[65]

---

62 Gennadius, *De eccl. dogm.*, par. 11–12 (ed. Turner, 'The *Liber ecclesiasticorum dogmatum*,' 91–2); for the Latin text, see my chapter 6 below.

63 Gennadius mentions the Origenist heresy by name in ch. 14. On the controversies underlying *De eccl. dogm.*, par. 10–20, in which Gennadius treats errors pertaining to the Creation, see Colish, *The Stoic Tradition*, 2.130–1.

64 Gennadius, *De eccl. dogm.*, par. 54 (ed. Turner, 'The *Liber ecclesiasticorum dogmatum*,' 99): 'The recent *legislatores* proclaim that the soul alone is created in the image of God, to such an extent that we must believe that the soul is incorporeal, since God is rightly believed to be incorporeal. Because of those *legislatores*, we assert without reservation that the image of God is found in the soul's eternity, and the likeness of God is found in its behaviour.'

65 Madoz, 'Un caso de materialismo,' 207–9; Morin, 'Le *Liber dogmatum* de Gennade de Marseille et problèmes qui s'y rattachent,' 447. Par. 54 is present in the first recension of *De eccl. dogm.*, which circulated anonymously, and which Turner dates after 450 and Morin dates between 470 and 491; but par. 54 is absent from the second recension,

Although Morin does not adduce specific parallels between Gennadius's paragraph 54 and *De statu animae*, his suggestion is well-founded, since Claudianus Mamertus belabours the very point that Gennadius condemns:

> Sed sicut rei corporeae nulla imago esse potest nisi corpus, ita nequaquam imago incorporei inuenitur in corpore ... Si imago dei est humana anima, incorporei uidelicet imago est, si incorporei imago est, incorporea utique ipsa est. At si incorporea non est, incorporei prorsus imago non est. Sed incorporei imago est, incorporea igitur est: nam quia creata est, non est deus, quia imago dei est, non est corpus.[66]

I am less convinced, however, by Morin's hypothesis that the omission of paragraph 54 from the second redaction of *De ecclesiasticis dogmatibus* was due to the fact that Stoicizing materialism had become irrelevant by the late fifth century.[67] On the contrary, a significant contribution of Turner's study is his demonstration that *De ecclesiasticis dogmatibus* continued to be copied, and to be cited as orthodox and authoritative, for several centuries thereafter, although it was not always attributed to Gennadius:[68] I will have more to say about this in chapter 6 below.

Eclecticism in Patristic Psychological Discourse and Narrative

Under the rubric of eclectic psychological discourses I have placed a few texts that send mixed messages to the reader. They gesture toward the Platonist-Christian tradition by portraying a unitary soul and maintaining that it is incorporeal, but they undercut the full Platonist significance of

---

which circulated under Gennadius's name and must have been completed no later than ca. 500, when it was quoted in the *Statuta ecclesiae antiqua*.

66 Claudianus Mamertus, *De statu animae* 1.5 (ed. Engelbrecht, CSEL 11, 40–1): 'But just as the image of a corporeal thing can be nothing other than a body, so is the image of the incorporeal never found in a body ... If the human soul is the image of God, then clearly it is the image of an incorporeal, and if it is the image of an incorporeal, then the soul itself is certainly incorporeal. Now, if the soul is not incorporeal, it is definitely not the image of an incorporeal. But if the soul is the image of an incorporeal, it is therefore incorporeal: for since the soul was created, it is not a god, and since it is the image of God, it is not a body.'

67 Morin, 'Le *Liber dogmatum* de Gennade,' 447: 'alors que l'incorporéité de l'âme était généralement admise, on ait cru devoir retrancher ce chapitre avec celui qui le précède, comme n'ayant plus de raison d'être, rien que de naturel à cela.'

68 Turner, 'The *Liber Ecclesiasticorum Dogmatum*,' esp. 80–8, and 'Supplenda,' 109–13.

incorporeality by portraying the mind localized in the heart or by treating the soul as a spatial and material being, perhaps as an incorporeal in the loose sense of an entity that is distinct from the flesh rather than an entity that lacks material substance altogether. The distinction between Platonist-Christian and eclectic texts is neither scientific nor foolproof, but I put eclectic texts in their own category nonetheless, because it is necessary to acknowledge that not all Platonizing treatments of psychological topics were rigidly Platonist enough to teach an audience about the significance of the soul's incorporeality or the utility of such a concept in dialectic. Prominent examples of eclectic psychology are the *Dialogi* attributed to Pope Gregory the Great (590–604)[69] and several of the works of Isidore of Seville (ob. 636) that were best known to the Anglo-Saxons, including the *Etymologiae*, *Differentiae*, *Sententiae*, and *Synonyma*.

Gregory's *Dialogi*: Why Strict Incorporeality Is Incompatible with Narrative

The *Dialogi* depict a conversation in which the autobiographical persona 'Gregory' narrates, at the request of his deacon Peter, many miracles wrought by holy men and women in their own time and in the previous centuries; in the last of the four books, the conversation is driven by Peter's inquiries about the existence and immortality of the soul. Gregory states unequivocally on several occasions that the human soul is incorporeal. Yet any reader of the *Dialogi* who did not already espouse a thoroughly Platonist-Christian concept of the soul could not elicit from the *Dialogi* nearly the same understanding of the soul's incorporeality that is present, both implicitly and explicitly, in Augustine's *Soliloquia* or in other philosophically rigorous Platonist treatments of the soul. The narrative segments of the *Dialogi*, which far outweigh their brief passages of non-narrative discourse, give every impression of a soul that is spatially distributed and able to travel spatially outside the body; it is invisible under normal conditions, but in miraculous visions the soul is frequently revealed to be an anthropomorphic shade of the individual.

Among the accounts of Benedict's life and miracles in Book 2 of the *Dialogi*, for instance, is an episode in which Benedict, during his lifetime,

---

69 Paul Meyvaert, who regards the *Dialogi* as an authentic work of Gregory, surveys the long-standing controversy over the text's authorship in his essay 'The Authentic *Dialogues* of Gregory the Great.' The authorship debate does not impinge upon the present study, since the Anglo-Saxons believed the *Dialogi* to be an authentic work of Gregory.

sends out his soul thirty miles from Monte Cassino to appear in the dreams of an abbot and a prior, in order to deliver instructions as to where to lay the foundation for a new monastery. When Peter asks how it is possible that the soul could travel so far so fast, and how it could make itself under- stood in dreams, Gregory does nôt (as Alcuin and Ælfric would later do) deny the spatial reality of soul-travel; instead, he reminds Peter that 'it is totally obvious that the spirit is of a more mobile nature than the body,' and he cites a biblical precedent in which the soul of Habakkuk travelled from Judea to Chaldea to bring dinner to the prophet Daniel.[70] Gregory also recounts how Benedict, while praying in his bedroom at Monte Cassino, witnessed the soul of Germanus, bishop of Capua, ascending into heaven, and moreover, as Benedict himself later reported, the entire cosmos was presented before his eyes as if caught up in a single sunbeam.[71] Again, Peter asks how any man could possibly see the whole universe at once, and again, Gregory does not deny the spatial reality of the miraculous event but explains it with reference to the changing dimensions and location of the soul: 'animae uidenti creatorem angusta est omnis creatura. Quamlibet etenim parum de luce creatoris aspexerit, breue ei fit omne quod creatum est, quia ipsa luce uisionis intimae mentis laxatur sinus, tantumque expan- ditur in Deo, ut superior existat mundo.'[72] In other texts, Gregory regu- larly speaks of the ascent and descent of the mind in a metaphorical sense, but in those instances there is no suggestion that the mind's ascent alters the individual's visual perspective on the environment; in contrast, in these paragraphs of the *Dialogi*, Gregory conspicuously avoids any suggestion that Benedict's mystical experience was just a metaphorical one.

Occasionally, the corporealizing of the soul in Gregory's narratives is tempered by brief discursive reminders that there exists an imperceptible reality that exceeds that which is manifest to the senses, even in miracles. In Book 3, for instance, Gregory observes that invisible realities may be closer to the truth than what is visible, and that Peter should not admire the most easily perceptible miracles, such as the resuscitation of the dead,

---

70 Gregory, *Dialogi* 2.22.4 (ed. de Vogüé, SC 260, 204): 'Liquet profecto quia mobilioris naturae est spiritus quam corpus.'

71 Gregory, *Dialogi* 2.35.3 (ed. de Vogüé, SC 260, 238): 'sicut post ipse narrauit, omnis etiam mundus, uelut sub uno solis radio collectus, ante oculos eius adductus est.'

72 Gregory, *Dialogi* 2.35.6 (ed. de Vogüé, SC 260, 240): 'The whole of creation appears meagre to the soul that is looking upon its Creator. Even if it sees just a tiny part of the light of the Creator, everything that has been created will be made small from its per- spective, because the receptacle of the mind is made expansive by the very light of that inner vision, and in God it is enlarged so greatly that it stands above the universe.'

to such an extent that he neglects the miracles wrought upon the invisible soul, which are superior to bodily miracles.[73] To value the invisible above the visible, and the faculties of the mind above the bodily senses, is undoubtedly a Platonist-Christian gesture. But at the end of Book 3, Peter asks for proofs, either by reason or by exempla, of the immortality of the soul, which (says Peter) many people *within* the Church do not wholly accept.[74] Peter's inquiry is virtually identical to that of the interlocutor 'Augustine' in the *Soliloquia*, yet the explanations that Gregory provides in Book 4 make plain that a vast gulf separates the psychology of the *Dialogi* from that of Augustine's *Soliloquia* and other texts that ascribe to the soul the sort of incorporeality that satisfies the exigencies of dialectic. Augustine's *Soliloquia* caters to an audience who accepts that the soul is incorporeal by Platonist standards, who accepts the epistemological corollaries of incorporeality, and who values rational proofs. Gregory's *Dialogi*, in contrast, caters to those who resist believing in things that are inaccessible to the senses. And rather than instil in his audience an appreciation of the reality of incorporeals in their natural, imperceptible state, Gregory satisfies the materialist mentality of his audience by adducing visible and tangible evidence of the presence of incorporeals and bolstering his evidence with biblical exempla.

A few examples from Book 4 illustrate the character of Gregory's rhetoric. At the outset of this book Gregory observes that we humans, being carnal ourselves, are reluctant to accept the existence of the invisible (*inuisibilia*) because we cannot have first-hand knowledge (*experimentum*) of them. We are like a child born to an imprisoned mother and raised within her prison cell, who is reluctant to believe that such things as sun and stars, birds and horses really existed, solely on the basis of his mother's stories. Gregory's analogy is strikingly reminiscent of the famous allegory of the Cave in Plato's *Republic*, which illustrates the inferiority of sensible quasi-realities to those incorporeal realities that are apprehended only by the incorporeal soul. However, the ending of Gregory's analogy is decidedly non-philosophical: we must have faith in the testimony of our forebears, who through the Holy Spirit had first-hand knowledge (*experimentum*) of things that are invisible to us.[75] Shortly thereafter, Peter admits that he would like some concrete evidence of the soul's immortality. Gregory's first response to Peter's question is syllogistic, giving it the

73 Gregory, *Dialogi* 3.17.7 (ed. de Vogüé, SC 260, 340) and 3.37.9 (ibid., 416).
74 Gregory, *Dialogi* 3.38.5 (ed. de Vogüé, SC 260, 432).
75 Gregory, *Dialogi* 4.1.2–5 (ed. de Vogüé, SC 265, 18–22).

air of a dialectical demonstration: God fills and surrounds everything; he is uncircumscribed and invisible. Servants must bear some resemblance to those whom they serve; therefore God's servants must also be invisible. These invisible servants must be angels and the souls of the just. We can tell by the movement of the body that the soul is alive within the body; likewise, since the soul serves God after leaving the body, it must be invisible and immortal.[76] The structure and tone of Gregory's discourse are imitative of dialectic, but his reasoning is very loose; it is not a philosophical given but only a convenient supposition that servants resemble their masters, or that God must have invisible servants.

When Peter reiterates his request for proof of the soul's immortality, this time Gregory obliges him, not with dialectic but with accounts of visible and tangible manifestations. Miracles wrought at the tombs of saints demonstrate that those saints' souls must still be alive and thriving.[77] The souls of saints and apostles are sometimes visible to one who is dying or to those who are with the dying person.[78] And through faith and prayer, some people have been able to see souls, normally invisible, leaving their bodies at death, accompanied by bright lights and fragrant odours, by angelic songs or demon psychopomps.[79] The accumulation of narrative evidence, selected to satisfy the desire for concrete proofs of the soul's immortality, far overshadows Gregory's infrequent efforts to turn Peter's attention from visible manifestations toward invisible realities. Moreover, Gregory's diction never suggests that the epistemological mechanism underlying all these events is the incorporeal soul's intellection of incorporeal realities; rather, that which is naturally imperceptible is made miraculously perceptible to the senses. For the purpose of most of these narratives, the concept of the incorporeal is made virtually synonymous with the invisible.

At a few points in Book 4 Gregory does gesture toward a more complex notion of incorporeality by invoking its epistemological and spatial corollaries. When Peter asks how it happens that individuals on their deathbeds sometimes receive accurate premonitions of future events, Gregory's answer is threefold. Sometimes a miraculous revelation discloses future events; in other instances, souls that are in the process of shedding the flesh are 'divinely inspired' such that they 'cast the incorporeal eye of the

76 Gregory, *Dialogi* 4.5.4 (ed. de Vogüé, SC 265, 34–6).
77 Gregory, *Dialogi* 4.6.1 (ed. de Vogüé, SC 265, 38–40).
78 Gregory, *Dialogi* 4.12–18 (ed. de Vogüé, SC 265, 48–72).
79 Gregory, *Dialogi* 4.7–11 (ed. de Vogüé, SC 265, 40–8).

mind' upon the secrets of heaven.[80] Sometimes even impious and vicious souls can experience premonitions of future events, not with divine assistance but under their own power: 'uis animae aliquando subtilitate sua ea quae sunt uentura cognoscit.'[81] A greedy lawyer is able to foretell where he will be buried: how could this be possible, Gregory asks, except that 'the power and subtle nature of his soul foresaw it' (uis animae ac subtilitas praeuidebat)?[82] Though Gregory far more often has recourse to miraculous explanations, in at least this one instance he brings to the fore the idea that the soul's incorporeality *naturally* facilitates intellection of the incorporeal, even in the absence of divine assistance.

Gregory again confronts the complexities of strict incorporeality when he grapples with the conundrum of the incorporeal soul in the corporeal afterworld. When Reparatus, upon travelling to hell in a vision, witnesses vast funeral pyres burning, Gregory is quick to explain that hell is not actually full of burning wood; the vision of funeral pyres was granted so that Reparatus, and in turn others who heard of the vision, might be more terrified by the thought of roasting on a real wood fire.[83] Similarly, when Gregory recounts another vision of the afterworld in which a house built from gold bricks is seen in the midst of a flowery meadow, Peter scoffs, finding it 'ridiculous' that precious metals should be needed to dress up the joys of heaven. Gregory is quick to agree that such a detail cannot be taken seriously: 'Ex rerum, Petre, imaginibus pensamus merita causarum,' he explains, before elaborating an allegorical reading of the concrete attributes of the afterworld that were observed in this miraculous vision.[84] Yet Gregory is unwilling to make the same argument about hellfire. Peter is understandably baffled by the idea of a corporeal fire that can torment an incorporeal soul; within the Platonist-Christian tradition, even the likes of Augustine and Alcuin had difficulty accounting for the interactions between the wholly incorporeal soul and any corporeal entity.[85] In reply to Peter's question, Gregory offers several answers. If the incorporeal soul can be disposed in the fleshly body, why can it not be so disposed in a

---

80 Gregory, *Dialogi* 4.27.1 (ed. de Vogüé, SC 265, 86).
81 Gregory, *Dialogi* 4.27.2 (ed. de Vogüé, SC 265, 86): 'By virtue of its own subtle nature, the power of the soul sometimes comes to know what is going to happen.'
82 Gregory, *Dialogi* 4.27.3 (ed. de Vogüé, SC 265, 88).
83 Gregory, *Dialogi* 4.32.5 (ed. de Vogüé, SC 265, 108).
84 Gregory, *Dialogi* 4.37.15–38.5 (ed. de Vogüé, SC 265, 134–8): 'We use images of things, Peter, to evaluate the moral significance of underlying realities.'
85 On Augustine's approach to the problem in *De Genesi ad litteram*, which was borrowed by Alcuin, see chapter 6 below.

corporeal fire? And if the fallen angels, who are incorporeal, suffer in a corporeal fire, why can the soul not also be tormented by fire even before it is reunited with its body? Most interestingly, Gregory proposes that the corporeal fire does not actually burn the incorporeal soul, but it appears to the soul as though it were being burned, and this illusion causes it to suffer: 'Teneri autem per ignem spiritum dicimus, ut in tormento ignis sit uidendo atque sentiendo. Ignem namque eo ipso patitur quo uidet, et quia concremari se aspicit crematur.'[86] While Gregory strains to render a responsible account of the mechanism by which an incorporeal soul can experience a corporeal hell, he undermines the rhetorical efficacy of talking about hellfire in the first place, which is, as he elsewhere admits, to terrify listeners who are inclined to believe that the corporeal is more real than the incorporeal.

Overall, in the *Dialogi*, Gregory does not aim to correct this sort of materialist mentality as much as to accommodate it, and to teach his audience about the immortality of the soul in spite of it: he occasionally ascribes to the soul the sort of strict incorporeality that carries epistemological and spatial connotations, but these brief discursive moments are far outweighed by narratives of anthropomorphic souls and of the incorporeal made manifest to the senses. Would Gregory's *Dialogi* have posed a serious challenge to the cardiocentrism and the hydraulic model that constituted the folk psychology of many members of its Anglo-Saxon audience? I strongly doubt that any reader who did not come to the *Dialogi* already in possession of an understanding of the Platonist-Christian concept of incorporeality could have learned much about it from the *Dialogi*. The occasional psychologization of the soul in this text may have challenged the vernacular tradition's division of labour between the soul and the mind, but in the absence of a strict notion of the soul's incorporeality, the unity of soul and mind need not conflict with cardiocentrism and the hydraulic model.

Isidore's Juxtaposition of the Incorporeal Soul with Cardiocentrism

In Isidore's encyclopedic works, psychological eclecticism manifests itself not simply in an inconsistent approach to the meaning of incorporeality and the relationship between substance and epistemology, as in Gregory's *Dialogi*, but also in Isidore's ambivalence about the relationship between

---

86 Gregory, *Dialogi* 4.30.2 (ed. de Vogüé, SC 265, 100): 'We say that the spirit is held by the fire in such a way that it is tormented by seeing and feeling the fire: for it suffers from the fire because it sees the fire, and it is burned because it sees itself being burned.'

mind and soul, as well as frequent and apparently literal references to the heart as the seat of various emotional and rational faculties. Within the *Etymologiae*, and between the *Etymologiae* and others of Isidore's well-known writings such as the *Differentiae* (*De differentiis uerborum*), the *Sententiae*, and the *Synonyma*, there are myriad internal contradictions concerning these subjects. This inconsistency is not surprising given that the first three of these are encyclopedic texts; their compilation was driven more by the impulse to collect than by any need for systematic conceptual harmony within each text. The point of calling attention to these inconsistencies, therefore, is not to denigrate Isidore's thought but to explore whether Isidore's works posed a significant challenge to the cardiocentric psychology and hydraulic model of the mind that many Anglo-Saxon readers espoused.

Beginning with the fundamentals, Isidore teaches that the soul is unitary and incorporeal. Alcuin's and Ælfric's well-known descriptions of the unitary soul have as their ultimate source *Differentiae* 2.27, where Isidore explains that the one soul is called by different names because of its manifold faculties: 'Quae dum contemplatur, spiritus est; dum sentit, sensus est; dum sapit, animus est; dum intellegit, mens est; dum discernit, ratio est; dum consentit, uoluntas est; dum recordatur, memoria est; dum membra uegetat, anima est.'[87] Similar information appears in other texts of the *differentiae uerborum* genre, where it is not meant to be a statement about the *ratio animae* so much as a disambiguation of similar words.[88] Disambiguation is the central purpose of Isidore's *Differentiae uerborum* overall, but in this instance he notably adds a brief clarification of the soul's unitary nature: 'non tamen ita diuiduntur in substantia sicut in nomine, quia eadem omnia una est anima.'[89] He also renders a slightly more expansive account of the activities proper to each faculty that belongs to the unitary soul:

87   Isidore, *Diff.* 2.27 (ed. Andrés Sanz, CCSL 111A, 61): 'When it contemplates, it is *spiritus*; when it feels, it is *sensus*; when it knows, it is *animus*; when it apprehends with the intellect, it is *mens*; when it discerns, it is *ratio*; when it consents, it is *uoluntas*; when it remembers, it is *memoria*; and when it vivifies the limbs, it is *anima*.' On Alcuin's and Ælfric's adapatations of this material, see chapters 6 and 8 below.
88   E.g., the *Appendix Probi* (*GL* 4.202.5–6), associated with the fourth-century grammarian Probus (Kaster, *Guardians of Language*, 350); and a *Differentiae sermonum* preserved in Bern, Burgerbibliothek, Cod. 178 (s. ix), fols 111r–16r (*GL* 8.283.6–8).
89   Isidore, *Diff.* 2.27 (ed. Andrés Sanz, CCSL 111A, 61): 'Yet they are not divided in substance as they are in name, because all of those same faculties are one soul.'

Sicut enim spiritus pars animae est, pro quo imagines rerum corporalium in-
primuntur, sic animus pars eiusdem animae est, quo sentitur et sapitur; sicut
et mens eiusdem portio est, per quam omnis ratio intellegentiaque percipitur;
sicut uoluntas, qua intellecta consentiuntur; sicut memoria, qua meditata
rememorantur.[90]

This unitary soul is incorporeal; it is wholly devoid of material substance.
The word *anima* is etymologically related to Greek *anemos* 'wind,' Isidore
claims, because the Greeks thought that air inhaled through the mouth
animated the body, but this is proven false by the observation that the
developing fetus is ensouled in the womb long before it breathes air. 'Non
est igitur aer anima, quod putauerunt quidam qui non potuerunt incor-
poream eius cogitare naturam,' Isidore concludes, implying that only a
mental deficiency could lead someone to espouse psychological materialism.[91] In the *Differentiae* he reiterates that the soul is an incorporeal substance (*substantia incorporea*), containing within it neither earth, water,
air, nor fire.[92]

To what degree does Isidore's concept of incorporeality conform to that
of the more philosophical representatives of the Platonist-Christian tradition? He clearly attaches ontological and epistemological significance to
the concept of incorporeality, most of all in his discussions of the nature of
God. God lacks material substance; therefore he is wholly unchanging (*in-
commutabilis*), indivisible, of simple substance (*simplex*), and immortal.[93]
He is non-spatial (*inlocalis*) and he occupies the universe non-spatially,
such that he is whole everywhere;[94] he is invisible, yet his substance (*es-
sentia Dei*) is accessible to the angelic and the human intellect.[95] Isidore
also communicates that the sacraments embrace a corporeal reality as well
as an incorporeal reality. Concerning baptism, he explains that 'sicut aqua

---

90 Isidore, *Diff.* 2.27 (ed. Andrés Sanz, CCSL 111A, 60–1): 'Just as the spirit is the part of
the soul upon which images of corporeal things are impressed, so is the *animus* the part
of the same soul by which things are perceived and known; in this way too the *mens* is a
subdivision of the same soul, by which all reason and understanding is absorbed; likewise the will is the part by which things understood are approved; likewise memory is
the part by which things that have been pondered are called to mind again.'
91 Isidore, *Etym.* 11.1.7 (ed. Lindsay, *Etym.*): 'Therefore the soul is not air, as some people
have thought who were incapable of conceptualizing its incorporeal nature.'
92 Isidore, *Diff.* 2.25 (ed. Andrés Sanz, CCSL 111A, 57); see also *Diff.* 2.28 (ibid., 64–5).
93 Isidore, *Sent.* 1.1.1–6 (ed. Cazier, CCSL 111, 7–8); see also *Etym.* 7.1.18–28.
94 Isidore, *Sent.* 2.5 (ed. Cazier, CCSL 111, 11) and 1.2.1 (ibid., 8–9).
95 Isidore, *Sent.* 3.1–2 (ed. Cazier, CCSL 111, 12).

purgatur exterius corpus, ita latenter eius mysterio per Spiritum sanctum purificatur et animus ... Quae dum carnaliter fit, spiritaliter proficit; quomodo et in ipsa baptismi gratia uisibilis actus, quod in aqua mergimur, sed spiritalis effectus, quod delictis mundamur.'⁹⁶ The incorporeal aspect of the sacrament is no less a reality than its visible aspect; it simply occurs in the realm of incorporeal entities such as the soul and the Holy Spirit.

Thus far Isidore appears faithful to the teachings of his Platonizing Christian forebears: where his allegiance lay is evident in his heavy reliance on Augustine and on several works of Gregory (but not the *Dialogi*) for the material that he compiles in the *Sententiae*. But it is easy to find within these same three of Isidore's works a number of passages that disrupt the illusion of philosophical consistency. In his overview of elementary grammar, Isidore reproduces the simplistic definition of incorporeality that many late antique and early medieval grammarians used, namely, 'corporalia dicta, quia uel uidentur uel tanguntur, ut *caelum, terra*. Incorporalia, quia carent corpus; unde nec uideri nec tangi possunt, ut *ueritas, iustitia*.'⁹⁷ As discussed in chapter 5 below, this sense-based definition not only leaves a lot of grey areas unaccounted for between the corporeal and the incorporeal but also falls far short of the complex concept of incorporeality that can be put to use in dialectic. Isidore further muddies the relationship between substance and sensory perception when, in an effort to disambiguate *corpus* 'body' from *caro* 'flesh,' he states that *caro* refers to blood and bone, but *corpus* 'is usually tangible and visible, and though flesh can be called a body, sometimes also something airy (*aereum*), which is not subject to touch or to sight, is also called a body.'⁹⁸

Nor does Isidore consistently and unequivocally adhere to the idea that the soul is incorporeal in the Platonist-Christian sense. Occasionally his equivocation takes the form of an implicitly Stoicizing approach to the relationship between substance and ontological hierarchy. There is nothing untoward, from a Platonist perspective, in Isidore's assertion that God

---

96 Isidore, *Etym*. 6.19.48 and 6.19.52 (ed. Lindsay, *Etym*.): 'Just as the body is cleansed outwardly with water, so is the mind also purified in a hidden manner by the sacrament of baptism through the Holy Spirit ... When this is executed in the flesh it is beneficial for the spirit; in this way too there is a visible act in the very gift of baptism, namely that we are submerged in water, but also a spiritual result, namely that we are washed of our offences.'

97 Isidore, *Etym*. 1.7.3–4 (ed. Lindsay, *Etym*.): 'Corporeals are so called because they are seen and touched, such as *sky, earth*; incorporeals are so called because they lack a body, wherefore they can be neither seen nor touched, such as *truth, justice*.'

98 Isidore, *Diff*. 2.26 (ed. Andrés Sanz, CCSL 111A, 58–9).

alone is unchangeable, while angels and human souls are not unchangeable
(*inmutabiles non sunt*). But in the same passage he goes on to say, 'Quod
materiam habet unde existat, mutabile est, quia de informi ad formam
transit. Quod uero non habet materiam, inmutabile est, sicut Deus utique
est.'[99] The implication is that the mutability of angels and souls is a corollary of their materiality. In fact, Isidore elsewhere characterizes angels as
creatures that are composed of a spiritual substance (*spiritali substantia*)
and made changeable according to their nature (*natura mutabiles conditi*),
which take up bodies made of celestial air (*corpora ex caelesti aere sumunt*)
when they are sent as messengers to earth. Demons, being fallen angels,
are also 'ethereal in body' (*corpore aerei*).[100] Regarding the human soul, in
the *Etymologiae* Isidore includes a variant version of the aforementioned
'names of the soul' passage that appears in the *Differentiae*, but the version
in the *Etymologiae* states that the soul is called 'spirit' when it respires,
that is, when it breathes (*dum spirat, spiritus est*).[101] Though elsewhere he
insists that the soul, in its capacity as animating principle, cannot be identical to air, in the *Differentiae* he maintains that the body is in fact animated
by inhaled air: his sources claim that 'in pulmonibus uero aerem contin-
eri, qui a corde per uenas quas arterias uocant diffunditur, ut paulatim
inspirandi respirandique tractu totum animet corpus.'[102] And having elsewhere denied that the soul contains anything fiery in it, in the *Etymologiae*
Isidore explains that what makes snake venom lethal is its cold nature,
from which the soul's fiery nature naturally flees: 'Omne autem uenenum
frigidum est, et ideo anima, quae ignea est, fugit uenenum frigidum.'[103]
    Isidore's impulse to be more thorough than consistent also leads him
to introduce material that conflicts with the principle of the indivisible
unitary soul. He reports, though he does not endorse, Lactantius's teaching that the *anima* is that which animates the body and the *animus* is that
which senses and knows. This is why, according to Lactantius, the *animus*

---

99 Isidore, *Sent.* 1.1.2–3 (ed. Cazier, CCSL 111, 7): 'That which has material substance
   out of which it exists is changeable, because it goes from the unformed to the formed.
   That which has no material substance is immutable, as indeed God is.'
100 Isidore, *Diff.* 2.14 (ed. Andrés Sanz, CCSL 111A, 28–9).
101 Isidore, *Etym.* 11.1.13 (ed. Lindsay, *Etym.*).
102 Isidore, *Diff.* 2.17 (ed. Andrés Sanz, CCSL 111A, 44): 'In the lungs there is contained
   air, which is dispersed by the heart through the channels which are called arteries, so
   that gradually the air animates the entire body by the propulsion of breathing in and
   out.'
103 Isidore, *Etym.* 12.4.42 (ed. Lindsay, *Etym.*): 'All poison is cold, and therefore the soul,
   which is fiery, flees the cold poison.'

can cease to function in an individual who is still alive and animated by the *anima*.[104] Isidore's own ubiquitous cardiocentrism is also difficult to rec‑ oncile with the idea of the incorporeal, unitary soul, for if the mind is truly incorporeal, it is substantially indivisible and cannot be localized in a single part of the body. Cardiocentrism is a prominent feature of Isidore's narra‑ tive psychological idiom, which is on display much more in his *Synonyma de lamentatione animae peccatricis* than in his aforementioned encyclo‑ pedic works, where didactic discourse dominates. The *Synonyma* is meant to serve both penitential and rhetorical ends, and as such the speaker of the *Synonyma* is wretchedly mournful as he ponders his own sins, and highly repetitive as he models different idioms with which to express his misery and remorse: 'Anima mea in angustiis est, spiritus meus aestuat, cor meum fluctuat, angustia animi possidet me. Angustia animi affligit me, circumdatus sum omnibus malis ... oppressus angustiis.'[105] The images of cardiocentric heat, seething, agitation, and constriction in a liquid en‑ vironment, which are here associated with grief, give way to the bloodless heat and agitation produced by dread: 'in tanta formidine contabui miser, pallui miser, exsanguis effectus sum, emarcuit cor meum, pauore aestuo, formidinis metu tabesco, timor et tremor animam meam quassauerunt.'[106] With his bodily fluids all dried up by his fear of confessing his own sins, the speaker is unable to muster any tears of compunction; sin and fear combine to make it impossible for him to repent in mind or in body: 'non sufficit memoria referre tantorum criminum gesta. Peccata quoque mea mihi sensum doloris tulerunt, hebetudine cordis coagulatae sunt lacrymae, obriguit animus, nullo moerore compungitur.'[107] The speaker begs his own tears to return, to moisten his face so that he might weep as befits a sinner, and so that his soul might awaken from its stupor. Bloodless in fear and unable to cry, the speaker lacks the crucial liquid elements that must be present in order for his emotional physiology to function.

104 Isidore, *Diff.* 2.27 (ed. Andrés Sanz, CCSL 111A, 59–60); see also *Etym.* 11.1.11–12.
105 Isidore, *Syn.* 1.5 (PL 83.827–9): 'My soul is in straits, my spirit seethes, my heart is agitated, constriction of the mind besieges me. Constriction of the mind afflicts me, I am surrounded by all evils ... [I am] weighed down by constriction.'
106 Isidore, *Syn.* 1.14 (PL 83.831): 'in such great terror I have wasted away wretchedly, I have become a pale wretch, I have become bloodless, my heart has wasted away, I boil with fright, I waste away in fear of something dreadful, fear and trembling have shaken my soul.'
107 Isidore, *Syn.* 1.57 (PL 83.840): 'Memory does not suffice to report the commission of such great sins. My sins bring on a feeling of pain in me; my tears are coagulated be‑ cause of the dullness of my heart, my mind has stiffened, I am not pricked by sorrow.'

Isidore's vivid cardiocentrism is by no means restricted to the penitential and narrative registers: though one may be tempted to regard the cardiocentrism of the *Synonyma* as a literary flourish, it is not possible so to disregard the medical cardiocentrism present in his encyclopedic works. In the *Etymologiae*, under the heading 'On acute illnesses,' Isidore mentions a disorder called *cardiaca*, which takes its name from the heart (Greek *kardian*), because it brings on 'suffering of the heart with dreadful fear' (cordis passio cum formidabili metu).[108] He proposes a spurious etymological link between anger (*ira*) and fire: 'Iracundus dictus quia accenso sanguine in furorem conpellitur; *ur* enim flamma dicitur, et ira inflammat.'[109] He takes the cardiocentric connotations of *misericordia* 'mercy' quite seriously. '*Misericordia* is so called because it makes miserable (*miserum*) the heart (*cor*) of one who grieves over the distress of another,' Isidore writes; he must admit one exception to this etymological reasoning, however, because God possesses mercy even though he has no heart.[110] Isidore localizes the *anima*, in its capacity as animating principle, in the chest cavity: 'uiscera uitalia, id est circumfusa cordis loca, quasi *uiscora*, eo quod ibi uita, id est anima, continetur.'[111] The soul's rational and emotional activity is also localized in the heart; as Isidore explains, the word *cor* is associated with the word *cura*, care or anxiety, because 'in the heart all care and source of knowledge abides.'[112] The *praecordia*, moreover, are the spaces around the heart in which sensory perceptions are received; they are called *praecordia* 'because therein is the origin of the heart and of understanding.'[113] The heart is not the only organ which plays an

---

108 Isidore, *Etym.* 4.6.4 (ed. Lindsay, *Etym.*).

109 Isidore, *Etym.* 10.129 (ed. Lindsay, *Etym.*): 'A man is said to be prone to anger when he is driven into a rage because his blood has been kindled; indeed fire is called *ur*, and ire inflames a man.' Lindsay suggests that Isidore must have encountered this word *ur* as a corruption of *pûr*, the Greek word for fire, but I am persuaded by the suggestion that Isidore had in mind the Latin verb *uro* 'to burn': see the remarks of Barney et al. on p. 221 of their translation of the *Etym*.

110 Isidore, *Etym.* 10.164 (ed. Lindsay, *Etym.*); here I have borrowed the translation of Barney et al., *The* Etymologies *of Isidore of Seville*, 223.

111 Isidore, *Etym.* 11.1.116 (ed. Lindsay, *Etym.*): 'The *uiscera* are also called "vital organs" (*uitalia*), namely the places surrounding the heart (*cor*), as if the word were *uiscora*, because in that place life (*uita*), that is, the soul, is contained' (trans. Barney et al., *The* Etymologies *of Isidore of Seville*, 238).

112 Isidore, *Etym.* 11.1.118 (ed. Lindsay, *Etym.*): 'in eo enim omnis sollicitudo et scientiae causa manet.'

113 Isidore, *Etym.* 11.1.119 (ed. Lindsay, *Etym.*): 'eo quod ibi sit principium cordis et cogitationis.'

important role in thought and temperament according to humoral theory: the heart is the organ employed in knowledge, the spleen in laughter, the gall bladder in anger, and the liver in love.[114] And because of the heart's important role as the seat of the soul, it is the first organ formed in the developing human fetus: 'Primum autem aiunt cor hominis fingi, quod in eo sit et uita omnis et sapientia.'[115]

Further complicating the relationship among soul, mind, and body, Isidore transmits a few cephalocentric doctrines as well. He grants to the brain a role in sensory processing and remarks that sight is the most useful and the most adept of the bodily senses, which in turn he associates with the fact that the sense of sight is the nearest to the brain, 'from which all things flow' (unde omnia manant).[116] He also quotes, by way of Augustine, the Greek medical tradition's localization of mental faculties in three lobes of the brain: sensory processing in the front, motor control in the rear, and memory in the middle.[117] And although he asserts confidently, at one point in the *Differentiae*, that the mind is concentrated in the citadel of the head ('in capitis arce mens collocata est'), a few chapters later he also summarizes the Platonic tripartition of the soul as well as the ancient philosophical debate over whether the soul resides in the head, in the chest cavity, or throughout the limbs.[118] Overall, in the three encyclopedic works considered here, cardiocentric psychological doctrines considerably outweigh cephalocentric ones, but the heart-versus-head debate is only one aspect of the internal conflicts among these texts, since neither localization is wholly congruent with the strict incorporeality of the unitary soul that Isidore favours – some of the time.

Again, the point of discussing the eclectic nature (to put it mildly) of Isidore's psychology is not to hold up his doctrines to a standard of consistency that is ill suited to medieval encyclopedic works, but rather to show that an Anglo-Saxon reader could easily come away from the study of Isidore with no compelling reason to abandon his own concept of the mind-in-the-heart, nor to consider the soul to be incorporeal in the sense of immaterial rather than in the sense of non-fleshly. Having briefly described and illustrated the Platonist, Stoicizing, and eclectic strains of psychological discourse, I turn now to the textual evidence for the Anglo-Saxons' knowledge and use

---

114 Isidore, *Etym.* 11.1.127 (ed. Lindsay, *Etym.*).
115 Isidore, *Etym.* 11.1.143 (ed. Lindsay, *Etym.*).
116 Isidore, *Etym.* 11.1.20–1 (ed. Lindsay, *Etym.*).
117 Isidore, *Diff.* 2.17 (ed. Andrés Sanz, CCSL 111A, 35–6).
118 Isidore, *Diff.* 2.17 (ed. Andrés Sanz, CCSL 111a, 35) and 2.28 (ibid., 65–6).

of each, and thence to an assessment of whether Augustine was indeed the dominant influence upon psychology in literate milieux, as is commonly supposed by present-day readers.

Anglo-Saxon Reception of Platonist, Stoicizing, and Eclectic Psychologies

A quick glance at the author-index of Gneuss's *Handlist* or Lapidge's *Anglo-Saxon Library* gives the impression that a wide array of Latin patristic texts, especially those of Augustine, was available to the Anglo-Saxons. Closer scrutiny reveals, however, that a large proportion of these texts are very sparsely attested: some, only by post-Conquest manuscripts and booklists; others, by quotations in the works of Aldhelm or Bede alone. Teresa Webber and Rodney Thomson caution that prior to the twelfth century very few English and continental libraries were as large and diverse as Bede's library at eighth-century Wearmouth-Jarrow; Thomson memorably characterizes these rare libraries as 'a small archipelago in a sea of non-Latin-speaking semi-pagans.'[119] Anglo-Saxon centres of learning typically poured more resources into the acquisition of liturgical books, homiliaries and hagiographies, and school-texts for literary study than into biblical commentaries or the weightiest works of Ambrose, Augustine, and Jerome.[120] Thomas N. Hall writes, 'Remarkably, fewer than two dozen manuscripts survive written in pre-Conquest Anglo-Caroline minuscule containing a single work by Augustine, Ambrose, Jerome, or Gregory.'[121] This figure is not wholly attributable to slender rates of survival, since a substantial proportion of patristic works copied by English hands of the late tenth and eleventh centuries show signs of having been copied from continental exemplars, suggesting that exemplars were imported because they were unavailable in England.[122]

Though scholars who study the manuscript evidence have demonstrated decisively that only a slim selection of patristic material was available to the Anglo-Saxons between Bede's day and the Conquest, there persists,

---

119 Webber, 'The Patristic Content of English Book Collections in the Eleventh Century,' 192; Thomson, 'The Norman Conquest and English Libraries,' 31; Hall, 'Biblical and Patristic Learning,' 334.
120 Thomson, 'The Norman Conquest and English Libraries,' 29.
121 Hall, 'Biblical and Patristic Learning,' 334.
122 Rella, 'Continental Manuscripts Acquired for English Centers in the Tenth and Early Eleventh Centuries.'

among scholars who focus more on texts than on manuscripts, a habit of assuming that Augustine's opinion on a given topic, or a watered-down version thereof, was the 'default' opinion for any early medieval individual who had enough education to copy a manuscript or write a vernacular poem. This is a highly illogical assumption in the case of Augustine's Platonist teachings on the unitary soul, on substance and the reality of Forms, and on the epistemological corollaries of incorporeality, because all of these teachings contradict everyday experience. It is virtually impossible, therefore, for an individual to acquire even a serviceable understanding of these areas of Augustinian thought without engaging in sustained study of Augustine's theological discourses, or without at least receiving solid instruction in the basics of Platonist-Christian discourse. One could not absorb or intuit the fullness of Augustine's thought on these topics by doing the things that ordinary literate persons did, such as studying grammar and reciting psalms and preaching Latin homilies (even those of Augustine) and listening to the recitation of saints' lives. As a corrective to the habitual overestimation of Augustine's influence upon all strata of Anglo-Saxon culture, I have compiled here the evidence for Anglo-Saxon knowledge of a variety of Latin discourses dealing wholly or in part with the nature and substance of the soul and of the mind. I have divided them according to their Platonist, Stoicizing, or eclectic character, as in the foregoing discussion of individual texts.

Direct Knowledge of Platonist Teachings on the Nature of the Soul

There is little to say about the classical forebears of the Platonist-Christian tradition, because the Anglo-Saxons simply did not have direct knowledge of the landmark texts that explicitly treat substance and the unitary soul. Greek was not studied outside the circle of Theodore and Hadrian in late seventh-century Canterbury, so it is not surprising that we have no evidence of first-hand Anglo-Saxon knowledge of the major Greek philosophical treatments of the nature of the soul and mind, such as Plato's *Phaedo*, *Phaedrus*, and *Republic*, Aristotle's *De anima*, and Plotinus's *Enneads*.[123] Latin translations of Plato's *Timaeus* had been produced by both Cicero (now lost) and Calcidius (whose translation and commentary

---

123 On the direct and indirect transmission of Plato in particular, see Klibansky, *The Continuity of the Platonic Tradition during the Middle Ages*; Gersh, 'The Medieval Legacy from Ancient Platonism'; and Marenbon, 'Platonism – A Doxographic Approach: The Early Middle Ages.'

cover only the first half of the *Timaeus*, not including the section that treats the tripartition of the soul).[124] Cicero's translation was unknown in England, but Calcidius's work may have been available in Benedictine circles in the late tenth century.[125] A modest selection of works by the Greek Fathers was known in translation, but none of these is specifically concerned with psychology, and there is nothing to suggest Anglo-Saxon knowledge of Gregory of Nyssa's *De opificio hominis* (though this had been translated into Latin by Dionysius Exiguus and again by John Scottus Eriugena) or of Nemesius of Emesa's *De natura hominis* (which was first translated into Latin in the eleventh century).[126]

As for the foremost Latin discourses on the *ratio animae* (that is, on the nature of the soul from the perspective of natural philosophy, rather than a purely moral or eschatological perspective) that are staunchly Platonist in orientation, I have compiled here the available evidence for direct knowledge of these works in England.[127] Though the list may appear long and diverse, note that the vast majority of these works were known only in the most elite educational milieux, and mostly before 740 and after 980.

---

124 The tripartition of the soul in *Timaeus* 69d–70c is discussed in chapter 3 above. On the extent and arrangement of Calcidius's translation and commentary, see Dutton, 'Medieval Approaches to Calcidius,' 191–2; Dutton urges readers to keep an open mind to the possibility that Calcidius did generate a translation and commentary for *Timaeus* 53c–92c that was very soon lost.

125 Lapidge indicates that Calcidius's translation is quoted by Lantfred and by Abbo, both continental scholars who visited England for several years in the mid- to late tenth century (*Library*, 295); it is not known whether they had Calcidius with them when they were in England or if they left copies of his *Timaeus* translation behind when they returned to Francia. On indirect knowledge of Plato among the Anglo-Saxons, see Szarmach, 'The *Timaeus* in Old English.'

126 Siegmund, *Die Überlieferung der griechischen christlichen Literatur*, catalogues Latin translations of Greek works available in the West prior to the twelfth century; several Greek Fathers were available in translation in Anglo-Saxon England, but the available works do not include any major discourses on psychology: see Lapidge, *Library*, 292, 302, 307, 317, 322–3, and 335. On Latin translations of Galenic works that began to arrive in England the late eleventh century, see ibid., 303; Banham, 'A Millennium in Medicine?'; and my epilogue below.

127 One could adduce a longer list of works whose treatment of the soul is implicitly Platonist in spirit, but which do not explain the complexities of Platonist psychology; my list includes only those works from which a medieval reader might have gleaned an understanding of the soul that was sufficiently Platonist and sufficiently sophisticated to be put to use in dialectic, as exemplified by Augustine's *Soliloquia* and Claudianus Mamertus's *De statu animae* above.

Quotations in Anglo-Saxon homilies, hagiographies, and poetry are remarkably scarce.

Ambrose, *Hexameron* [CPL 123] was known to Aldhelm (ob. 709/710), Bede (ob. 735), Ælfric (fl. ca. 990–ca. 1010), Byrhtferth (ca. 970–ca. 1020), and the author of the OE poem *The Phoenix*.[128] It is possible, but far from certain, that borrowings from the *Hexameron* appear in the OE *Boethius*.[129] Clemoes suggests that the *Hexameron* may have provided the inspiration, perhaps through an intermediate source, for flight-of-the-mind passages in *The Wanderer* and *The Seafarer*, but he finds no firm evidence that direct knowledge of the *Hexameron* underlies either poem.[130] Of the four extant Anglo-Saxon MSS of the *Hexameron*, one dates to the turn of the eleventh century and another has eleventh-century English provenance; the others are post-Conquest, as are the two booklists that include this text.[131]

Augustine, *De anima et eius origine* [CPL 345] is quoted once by Bede, and then there is no further record of Anglo-Saxon knowledge antedating three MSS of the late eleventh and early twelfth centuries.[132]

Augustine, *De ciuitate Dei* [CPL 313] exemplifies the pattern of discontinuous attestation exhibited by many patristic texts over the course of the Anglo-Saxon period. This work was quoted or echoed several times by Aldhelm and the late seventh- or early eighth-century author of the *Liber monstrorum*, and many times by Bede; additionally, an excerpt (18.23, on the Sibylline prophecies) appears in a manuscript of the second half of the eighth century.[133] The next clear evidence of Anglo-Saxon use of *De ciuitate Dei* appears only in the late tenth and early eleventh centuries, with quotations and echoes in the works of Lantfred, Ælfric, and Byrhtferth. It is mentioned in one post-Conquest booklist, and there survive three MSS, two of which are certainly post-Conquest.[134] The evidence does not support J.F. Kelly's claim that *De ciuitate Dei* 'was very widely known'

---

128 Lapidge, *Library*, 280; see also Bankert, Wegmann, and Wright, *Ambrose in Anglo-Saxon England*, 18–22.
129 Discenza, 'The Sources of [the OE Translation of] Boethius, *The Consolation of Philosophy*.'
130 Clemoes, '*Mens absentia cogitans*'; and Bankert, Wegmann, and Wright, *Ambrose in Anglo-Saxon England*, 22.
131 Lapidge, *Library*, 279–80.
132 Ibid., 283.
133 Ibid., 284; see also Alcamesi, 'The *Sibylline Acrostic* in Anglo-Saxon Manuscripts.'
134 Lapidge, *Library*, 284. The doubtful MS is a fragment written on the continent in the ninth century, for which Gneuss tentatively suggests a tenth- or eleventh-century

or Ogilvy's claim that 'It is continually cited and quoted without citation' throughout the Anglo-Saxon period.[135]

Augustine, *Confessiones* [CPL 251] was used by Bede, Alcuin (active in England during the 770s and early 780s),[136] and Byrhtferth; two extant MSS are both post-Conquest.[137]

Augustine, *De Genesi ad litteram* [CPL 266] was known to Bede, Ælfric and Byrhtferth, and it survives in three post-Conquest MSS.[138]

Augustine, *De immortalitate animae* [CPL 256] appears not to have been known at all in Anglo-Saxon England.

Augustine, *De musica* [CPL 258], which includes a substantial discourse on the soul in Book 6, is attested by one quotation in a work of Aldhelm.[139]

Augustine, *Quaestiones in Heptateuchum* [CPL 270], which includes a consideration of the relationship between the soul and the blood according to the Levitican dietary laws, is attested by quotations in Theodore and Hadrian's *Biblical Commentaries* and in Bede, and then is not attested again except for a quotation by Lantfred.[140]

Augustine, *De quantitate animae* [CPL 257] is an *antecedent* source for a single line of Ælfric's Nativity homily.[141] It is preserved in a Salisbury MS of the late eleventh century, and it is also attested in one eighth-century booklist from Würzburg, within the region of Anglo-Saxon missionary activity.[142]

Augustine, *Soliloquia* [CPL 252], is quoted once by Aldhelm and once by Alcuin; its presence in England around the turn of the tenth century is firmly attested by the Alfredian OE adaptation of the work and by a MS

English provenance: see his 'Addenda and Corrigenda to the *Handlist of Anglo-Saxon Manuscripts*,' no. 760.3.
135 J.F. Kelly, 'The Knowledge and Use of Augustine among the Anglo-Saxons,' 215; Ogilvy, *Books Known to the English*, 82.
136 Most of Alcuin's works were penned on the continent; following Lapidge (*Library*, 228–9) I count only *De laude Dei* and the poem on the York library as secure evidence for the books available in later eighth-century York.
137 Lapidge, *Library*, 282.
138 Ibid., 285.
139 Ibid., 286.
140 Ibid., 290.
141 Godden, 'Anglo-Saxons on the Mind,' 282. The line in question appears to be synthesized from *De quantitate animae* and Cassiodorus's *De anima*, and as such is rather tenuous evidence for the direct knowledge of either of these works.
142 Lapidge, *Library*, 287.

dated 's. x¹,' possibly originating in southern England or in Mercia. One additional extant manuscript is of post-Conquest English provenance.[143]

Augustine, *De Trinitate* [CPL 329] was known to Acca of Hexham (ob. 740), Bede, Alcuin, Ælfric, and Byrhtferth. Surviving Anglo-Saxon MSS are limited to an eighth-century fragment, an early-eleventh-century fragment, and a post-Conquest MS; two further MSS and two booklists suggest that it was known in the milieu of the Anglo-Saxon missionaries in Germany.[144]

Augustine, *De uera religione* [CPL 264] is attested by two post-Conquest MSS and one post-Conquest booklist.[145]

Augustine, *De uidendo Deo* (*Epistola* 147) [CPL 262] is attested by quotations and echoes in the works of Acca of Hexham and Bede, and it is one of the sources of supplemental material used in Book 3 of the Alfredian *Soliloquies*. Manuscript evidence is limited to one continental copy with eleventh-century English provenance, and this text is mentioned in one post-Conquest booklist.[146]

Boethius, *De consolatione philosophiae* [CPL 878] is securely attested in England from the late ninth or early tenth century, and it is possible that Alcuin had a copy at York in the late eighth century.[147] The OE translation of the *Consolatio*, and the use of the *Consolatio* as a supplemental source for the OE *Soliloquies*, are roughly contemporary with the arrival (ca. 900) of an early ninth-century continental MS;[148] one English copy and three

---

143 Ibid., 291; on the OE *Soliloquies* and its transmission history, see below.
144 Lapidge, *Library*, 287; Ogilvy, *Books Known to the English*, 94.
145 Lapidge, *Library*, 288.
146 Ibid., 289; Ogilvy, *Books Known to the English*, 87.
147 The name *Boetius* appears in Alcuin's poem on the York library (line 1547), amid a group of authors of elementary texts on grammar, metrics, dialectic, and rhetoric. On this basis Lapidge suggests that Alcuin was more likely to have had Boethius's works on logic than the *Consolatio*; on the same grounds, Lapidge suggests that the presence of the name *Lactantius* (line 1552) amid other authors of Latin hexameters favours the conclusion that Alcuin knew the *Carmen de aue phoenice* rather than Lactantius's theological works such as *De opificio Dei* (*Library*, 230–1). I would not use this logic to rule out the presence of the *Consolatio* or *De opificio Dei* at York, as it is unlikely that Alcuin would have named an author multiple times if the library held works by that author belonging to several genres.
148 On Vatican City, BAV, Vat. lat. 3363, the ninth-century continental copy of the *Consolatio* bearing glosses in a late-ninth-century Welsh hand and signs of use in tenth-century Glastonbury, see Godden, 'Alfred, Asser, and Boethius.'

quotations in royal charters belong to the first half of the tenth century.[149] The text was especially well known from the mid-tenth century onward: it was used by Lantfred, Abbo of Fleury, Byrhtferth, and Goscelin (fl. s. xi²), and there survive thirteen MSS copied or imported between s. x² and s. xi med., two post-Conquest MSS, and two mentions in post-Conquest booklists.[150]

Cassiodorus, *De anima* [CPL 897] is an *antecedent* source for a single line of Ælfric's Nativity homily and a possible source for the first piece in his first series of *Catholic Homilies*;[151] other evidence is limited to one manuscript of eleventh-century English provenance and mention in one post-Conquest booklist.[152]

Cicero, *Disputationes Tusculanae* and *De re publica* are not known to have been present in Anglo-Saxon England.

Claudianus Mamertus, *De statu animae* [CPL 983] may have been introduced into England by Abbo of Fleury.[153] Indirect knowledge of *De statu animae* is more likely, by way of Abbo's *Explanationes in calculo Victorii* and Remigian commentaries on Boethius's *De consolatione philosophiae*, both of which replicate some of Claudianus's arguments for the incorporeality of the soul.[154]

149 Lapidge, *Library*, 293; *Fontes Anglo-Saxonici*; for charters S429 (Athelstan, 935), S438 (Athelstan, 937), and S470 (Edmund, 940), see S.E. Kelly, *The Electronic Sawyer*.
150 Lapidge, *Library*, 293–4; *Fontes Anglo-Saxonici*. On the dissemination of the OE *Boethius* and Latin commentaries on the *Consolatio*, see below.
151 Godden, 'Anglo-Saxons on the Mind,' 282; DeGregorio, 'Cassiodorus,' 7–8.
152 Lapidge, *Library*, 296; DeGregorio, 'Cassiodorus,' 7–8. Colish calls attention to Cassiodorus's self-contradictory blending of Neoplatonic and Stoic characteristics in his description of the soul, especially in his assertion that it is material but not corporeal (*The Stoic Tradition* 2.249–51), but I am not persuaded that the medieval reader of *De anima* would have recognized its affinities with the Stoicizing tradition so much as with the psychology of Augustine and Claudianus Mamertus. The *spiritalis substantia* of the soul is, according to Cassiodorus, circumscribed but non-spatially distributed, and he calls it *incorporea*, repeatedly denying that it is *corporalis* or possesses *corporalitas*. See *De anima*, ch. 3–4 (ed. Halporn, CCSL 96, 537–40), and note that the *apparatus fontium* includes far more citations of Augustine and Claudianus Mamertus than of Lactantius.
153 Lapidge suggests that Abbo possibly brought this work to Ramsey in the late 980s, since he had recently relied upon it in composing his *Explanationes in calculo Victorii* at Fleury in the early 980s, and the recently founded house of Ramsey presumably could not yet have acquired a library sufficient to support the composition of Abbo's *Quaestiones grammaticales* and *Passio S. Eadmundi* without being supplemented by books that Abbo brought from the continent (*Library*, 242–4).
154 Most of the MSS of Boethius's *Consolatio* noted above also contain a commentary; the commentary in Cambridge, UL, Kk. 3. 21 names 'Claudianus' as one of three authorities

Macrobius, *Comm. in Somnium Scipionis* was first used by Abbo and Byrhtferth, and all five extant Anglo-Saxon MSS (four of which contain only excerpts or fragments) date to the end of the tenth century or later.[155]

Among the Platonist psychological discourses on this list, the only one for which we can posit widespread Anglo-Saxon knowledge and use is Boethius's *De consolatione philosophiae*, though study of this text in England began only in the late ninth century.[156] Several of the works on this list are attested for the periods before roughly 740 and after roughly 980, but not for the intervening 250 years, and several others are attested only for the period after roughly 980, or only after the Conquest. If these discourses were available to the authors of OE poems and saints' lives during the period between Bede and Ælfric, they had almost no discernible influence, with the exception of Ambrose's *Hexameron* and the Latin works translated by Alfred's circle.

Indirect Knowledge of Patristic Christian-Platonist Teachings on the Nature of the Soul

Tied to the emergence of Boethius's *Consolatio* as an object of study, starting around the turn of the tenth century there became available in England several texts that mediated the transmission of Platonist-Christian psychology to Anglo-Saxon readers. These include Alcuin's *De ratione animae*, Latin commentaries on the *Consolatio*, and the Alfredian translations of the *Consolatio* and of Augustine's *Soliloquia*. Among these texts, Alcuin's *DRA* offers the most lucid introduction to the Augustinian unitary soul and the significance of its incorporeality. Its dissemination, however, was sparse; the two surviving Anglo-Saxon manuscripts both date to the later eleventh century,[157] and though quotations from *DRA* appear in the OE *Boethius* and Ælfric's Nativity Homily (*LS* 1; Belfour 9), it remains

---

for the tripartition of the soul (49v, line 54). On Abbo's use of *De statu animae*, see Peden's comments in her edition of Abbo's *Commentary on the Calculus of Victorius of Aquitaine*, xxxiii; the parts of the *Comm.* that depend most heavily upon Claudianus Mamertus are chapters 1.6–7, 1.12–16, 2.1, and 3.43–5.

155 Lapidge, *Library*, 320.
156 Moreover, as Malcolm Godden observes, some portion of the early medieval readership of the *Consolatio* studied its poetic form rather than its philosophical content: see 'The Alfredian Project and Its Aftermath,' 108–9.
157 Gneuss, *Handlist*, 467 and 749.5.

debatable whether Alfred and Ælfric knew the work directly.[158] *DRA* has been proposed as the source for the flight-of-the-mind passages in *The Seafarer* and in the second *Lorsch Riddle*; however, since the relevant passage in *DRA* is a nearly verbatim quotation of Lactantius's *De opificio Dei*, I regard the latter as a much more likely inspiration for these two poems' depictions of the mind-in-the-heart, a concept that conflicts sharply with Alcuin's stance on the incorporeal, unitary soul.[159]

The Latin commentaries on Boethius's *Consolatio*, especially those that lavish attention on the ninth *metrum* of Book 3, transmit information on the *ratio animae* drawn from the works of Augustine, Claudianus Mamertus, and Alcuin, among others.[160] Though some sort of commentary must have been available to support the Alfredian study and translation of the *Consolatio*, the manuscript evidence suggests that knowledge of the commentaries was quite restricted until the later tenth century: Gneuss lists eleven copies of the 'Remigian' commentaries, the earliest of which are dated 's. x².'[161]

As for the Alfredian translations themselves, as I argue in chapter 7, the *Soliloquies* succeeds in teaching the reader about the unitary nature of the soul but does not replicate Augustine's use of the Platonist understanding of incorporeality. Use of the OE *Soliloquies* is not attested in any other works except the OE *Boethius* (presumably by the same author), and the *Soliloquies* survives whole in a single copy of the twelfth century.[162] The OE *Boethius* attracted a somewhat broader tenth- and eleventh-century readership. Though only three manuscript witnesses have survived (one of which was lost in the nineteenth century), its dissemination is further

---

158 The content of Alcuin's *DRA* is treated at length in chapter 6 below. On the putative use of *DRA* by Alfred, see Szarmach, 'Alfred, Alcuin, and the Soul'; and by Ælfric, see Godden, 'Anglo-Saxons on the Mind,' 296–8; and Leinbaugh, 'Ælfric's *Lives of Saints* I and the Boulogne Sermon,' 193–7.

159 See n. 174 below as well as my discussion of the second *Lorsch Riddle* in chapter 5.

160 Selections of what the commentaries have to say about the soul at *Cons.* 3 m. 9 may be found in Szarmach, 'Alfred, Alcuin, and the Soul'; and Wittig, 'The "Remigian" Glosses on Boethius's *Consolatio Philosophiae* in Context,' 174–83.

161 Gneuss, *Handlist*, 178 (*ad indicem*, under 'Remigius of Auxerre'); on the use and manuscript tradition of the commentaries, see also Bolton, 'The Study of the Consolation of Philosophy in Anglo-Saxon England'; and Wittig, 'The "Remigian" Glosses on Boethius's *Consolatio Philosophiae* in Context,' 184–96.

162 Interestingly, the only other attestation of the OE *Soliloquies* is an excerpt of the opening prayer, preserved in an eleventh-century miscellany: see Szarmach, 'Alfred's *Soliloquies* in London, BL, Cotton Tiberius A. iii.'

attested by mentions in two medieval booklists,[163] a reference in Æthelweard's *Chronicle* (written around 980), quotations in several works of Ælfric, and echoes in the OE *Distichs of Cato*, composed in the later tenth or earlier eleventh century.[164]

The impact of these mediating texts on the overall availability of Platonist psychology in Anglo-Saxon England was circumscribed. Like many of the aforementioned patristic discourses, they were sparsely disseminated before the later tenth century. Alcuin's *DRA* and the Latin commentaries were most likely read as supplements to the study of the *Consolatio* itself, which was undertaken only by students who reached an advanced stage of the literary curriculum. The *OE Boethius* and the *Soliloquies*, which were the first texts to broadcast the concept of the unitary soul in OE, were theoretically accessible to a less scholarly audience, but they do not transmit the Platonist-Christian doctrine of the soul's strict incorporeality, with all of its epistemological corollaries.

Knowledge of Stoicizing Christian Psychology in Anglo-Saxon England

If Platonist psychological discourses were little known outside eighth-century Northumbria and the Benedictine milieu of the mid-tenth century onward, the central textual representatives of classical Stoic and Stoicizing Christian psychological discourse were even scarcer. There is no sign of direct knowledge of the ontological or psychological doctrines of classical Stoicism in Greek or Latin.[165] Evidence for the presence of Stoicizing Christian discourses on the *ratio animae* may be summed up briefly, because there is very little.

Cassian, *Collationes* [CPL 512] was used by Aldhelm, Bede, Asser (fl. 890s), Lantfred, and Ælfric,[166] and Cassian is cited by name as an authority on the tripartition of the soul in Remigian commentaries on Boethius's

---

163 See Godden and Irvine, 1.9–24, 1.34–41, and 1.543–4 on the manuscripts, and 1.42–3 on the booklists.

164 Ibid., 207–12 and 545–7.

165 On the Greek and Latin representatives of classical Stoicism, see Colish, *The Stoic Tradition from Antiquity to the Early Middle Ages*, vol. 1; see also Verbeke, *The Presence of Stoicism in Medieval Thought*, 1–19, on the facets of classical Stoic doctrine that exercised the greatest influence over the Latin authors of the Middle Ages (though, for the most part, not directly over the Anglo-Saxons).

166 Lapidge, *Library*, 295.

Consolatio.[167] The *Collationes* survive in one eighth-century MS from the region of Anglo-Saxon missionary activity; three further Anglo-Saxon MSS and one mention in a booklist all postdate the Conquest.[168]

Faustus of Riez, *Epistola* 3 (*Quaeris a me*) [CPL 963] is not attested on its own at any point during the Anglo-Saxon period, but a significant portion of the letter typically circulated anonymously as a preface to Claudianus Mamertus's *De statu animae*,[169] so it was likely introduced into England by Abbo of Fleury along with Claudianus's treatise.

Gennadius of Marseilles, *De ecclesiasticis dogmatibus* [CPL 958] survives in four Anglo-Saxon MSS, including one from the early eighth century, one from the late tenth, and two from after the Conquest, and it is mentioned in one post-Conquest booklist.[170] As I discuss in chapter 6 below, this text often circulated as part of collections of canons, and not always under Gennadius's name; it is probable that some of the many collections of canons in extant Anglo-Saxon MSS contain *De ecclesiasticis dogmatibus*, whole or in part.[171]

Hilary of Poitiers, *Comm. in Matthaeum* [CPL 430] is not known to have been used by the Anglo-Saxons; Hilary is the second writer listed in Alcuin's poem on the York library, but it is unclear which of his works was held there.[172]

Lactantius, *Institutiones diuinae* [CPL 85] is not known to have been transmitted to Anglo-Saxon England.

Lactantius, *De opificio Dei* [CPL 87] was used by Aldhelm and Lantfred.[173] Alcuin includes the name *Lactantius* in his poem on the York library, though it is unclear what work(s) might be meant. Passages in *The Seafarer* and the second *Lorsch Riddle* concerning the flight of the mind,

167 See, for instance, CUL Kk. 3. 21, 49v, line 54. Cassian treats the tripartition of the soul in *Collatio* 24.14; see chapter 6 below on Alcuin's adaptation of this material.
168 Lapidge, *Library*, 295.
169 See Engelbrecht's remarks at CSEL 11, viiii–x and 1; and CSEL 21, xlviii.
170 Lapidge, *Library*, 303–4.
171 For MSS of canons, see Gneuss, *Handlist*, 159 (*ad indicem*). It is also possible that Alcuin knew of this text while still in England; his poem on the York library lists Fulgentius (line 1544; see Lapidge, *Library*, 230), and if this is a reference to Fulgentius of Ruspe's *De fide ad Petrum*, the likelihood is good that *De ecclesiasticis dogmatibus* appeared in the same MS, although not necessarily under Gennadius's name, as these two texts very frequently travelled together (see, for instance, *HÜWA* II/1, 70–2 and 89–90, for ten MSS now in English libraries containing both texts; and *HÜWA* V/1, 93–5 and 117–19 for ten MSS now in German libraries containing both texts).
172 Lapidge, *Library*, 229.
173 Ibid., 319.

which some have supposed to depend on Alcuin's *De ratione animae*, were likely drawn from *De opificio Dei* instead,[174] especially given that Alcuin's Platonizing Christian psychology clashes with the vernacular psychology of *The Seafarer* and the staunchly materialistic understanding of the mind-in-the-heart portrayed in the second *Lorsch Riddle*.

Tertullian, *De anima* [CPL 17] is not known to have been transmitted to Anglo-Saxon England.

Clearly the dissemination of Stoicizing Christian opinions on the soul was quite restricted in Anglo-Saxon England, with Lactantius's *De opificio Dei* being the only work to exert any clear influence on literary output. Unlike some of the Platonist-Christian texts mentioned earlier, the Stoicizing Christian works that were available to the earliest Anglo-Saxon authors were not typically revived in the late tenth or eleventh centuries. As chapter 6 will demonstrate, Anglo-Saxon authors in Carolingian circles during the later eighth and earlier ninth centuries came into more frequent contact with the materialist psychology of Gennadius and possibly Faustus. Still, with the exception of *De opificio Dei*, nearly all of the known quotations or reminiscences of these Stoicizing texts by Anglo-Saxon authors, whether at home or abroad, occur in highly learned contexts, not in OE poetry or homilies or hagiographical prose.

The Dominance of Eclectic Psychological Discourse in Anglo-Saxon England

What were the lesser lights of Anglo-Saxon literary history learning about the nature of the soul? At all levels of education, and at all periods of Anglo-Saxon history, they were reading Gregory's *Dialogi* and the encyclopedic works of Isidore of Seville. Compare the scant transmission histories of the aforementioned Platonist-Christian and Stoicizing texts with the broad dissemination of these works whose psychological orientation I have classified as eclectic.

Gregory the Great, *Dialogi* [CPL 1713]. Of the nine extant MSS of the *Dialogi* used or produced in Anglo-Saxon England, only one postdates the Conquest, while three date to the early eleventh century, two to the tenth

---

174 The argument that the authors of these poems had direct knowledge of Alcuin's *DRA* is advanced by Clemoes, '*Mens absentia cogitans* in *The Seafarer* and *The Wanderer*'; and Lendinara, 'Gli *Aenigmata Laureshamensia*'; cf. Diekstra, '*The Seafarer* 58–66a: The Flight of the Exiled Soul to Its Fatherland,' who points out that the relevant section of *DRA* is a nearly verbatim quotation of Lactantius' *De opificio Dei* (434).

century, and three to the eighth century; Lapidge identifies another three copies of the *Dialogi* that were produced or used in the region of the eighth-century Anglo-Saxon missionaries in Germany. The *Dialogi* are mentioned in at least three Anglo-Saxon booklists and three booklists from the missionary milieu as well.[175] Knowledge of Gregory's *Dialogi* is further attested by quotations and echoes in the teachings of Theodore and Hadrian, the *Vita sancti Gregorii* by an anonymous monk of Whitby, Aldhelm, Bede, the *Old English Martyrology*, Felix (author of the *Vita sancti Guthlaci*), Willibald (author of the *Vita Bonifatii*), Wærferth, Alfred, Asser, Vercelli homily 14, the anonymous *Vision of Leofric*, Ælfric, Byrhtferth, Goscelin, and the authors of several Latin charters.[176] Alcuin mentions 'Gregorius summus' in his description of the library at York, but he does not specify which works of Gregory were held there.[177] Finally, although Wærferth's OE translation of the *Dialogi* is generally considered to have been lightly esteemed among Anglo-Saxon readers, its four surviving copies provide further evidence of Anglo-Saxon interest in the stories told by Gregory, and those four copies, incidentally, outnumber surviving copies of Alfred's *Boethius* and *Soliloquies* translations put together.[178] All told, the chronological and geographical range of attestations of Gregory's *Dialogi* makes it undoubtedly one of the best-known and most influential books in Anglo-Saxon history.

Isidore, *Etymologiae* [CPL 1186]. Nineteen extant Anglo-Saxon MSS contain part or all of the *Etymologiae*, among which at least eleven were in England before the eleventh century; one mention of the *Etymologiae* appears in a post-Conquest booklist.[179] This text was popular within the ambit of the Anglo-Saxon missionaries, as attested by six MSS of the *Etymologiae* used or produced in that milieu.[180] Additionally, there survives a continental witness to an epitome of the *Etymologiae* that Lapidge believes to have been compiled and glossed in OE by the very early eighth century.[181] Quotations and allusions indicate that the *Etymologiae*

---

175 Lapidge, *Library*, 304.
176 This list is compiled on the basis of *Fontes Anglo-Saxonici* and Lapidge, *Library*, 305. The charters in question are S55 (dated 757 but spurious: see S.E. Kelly, *The Electronic Sawyer*), S519 (King Eadred, dated 946), and S724 (King Edgar, dated 964).
177 Lapidge, *Library*, 229.
178 On the English reception of both the Latin and the OE versions, see esp. D.F. Johnson, 'Who Read Gregory's *Dialogues* in Old English?'; and Dekker, 'King Alfred's Translation of Gregory's *Dialogi*: Tales for the Unlearned?'
179 Lapidge, *Library*, 311. On the transmission of the *Etymologiae* in Anglo-Saxon England, see Lazzari, 'Isidore's *Etymologiae* in Anglo-Saxon Glossaries.'
180 Lapidge, *Library*, 311.
181 Lapidge, 'An Isidorian Epitome from Early Anglo-Saxon England.'

was known to Theodore and Hadrian, Aldhelm, the author of the *Liber Monstrorum*, Tatwine, Eusebius (Hwætberht), Bede, Boniface, Willibald, Alfred, Lantfred, Wulfstan of Winchester, Abbo, Ælfric, Byrhtferth, and possibly the translator of the *OE Orosius* and the authors of the OE poems *The Order of the World* and *The Phoenix*.[182] This is one of very few texts about which we can safely say that the vast majority of Anglo-Latin authors and the most prolific OE authors had direct knowledge of it.

Isidore, *Synonyma de lamentatione animae peccatricis* [CPL 1203]. There survive seven MSS of the *Synonyma* used or produced in Anglo-Saxon England, only one of which postdates the Conquest; two of these copies were produced in the eighth century and four in the tenth century.[183] Another five extant MSS of the *Synonyma* were used or produced in the area of the Anglo-Saxons' missionary activity in eighth-century Germany, and the *Synonyma* is mentioned in one tenth-century English booklist and one from the missionary milieu.[184] This work is among the sources used by Aldhelm, Alcuin (while still in England), and Ælfric Bata, the eleventh-century author of several schoolroom colloquies.[185] The *Synonyma* served as a direct source for Irvine homily 9 and for Vercelli homilies 10 and 22, and its indirect influence is attested by the frequent use of the *ubi sunt* motif in OE prose and verse.[186]

Isidore, *Sententiae* [CPL 1199]. Four pre-Conquest Anglo-Saxon MSS survive,[187] and the *Sententiae* appears on three booklists: an English one of the late eleventh or early twelfth century, and two lists from the region of

---

182 This list combines data found in Lapidge, *Library*, 311; *Fontes Anglo-Saxonici*; Di Sciacca, 'Isidorian Scholarship at the School of Theodore and Hadrian: The Case of the *Synonyma*,' 83–4; Law, 'The Study of Latin Grammar in Eighth-Century Southumbria,' 66; and the *apparatus fontium* in Glorie's edition of the *enigmata* of Eusebius and Aldhelm (CCSL 133).

183 Lapidge, *Library*, 312–13; it is not known when Salisbury, Cathedral Library, MS 173 arrived in England.

184 Ibid.

185 Ibid., 313; and Di Sciacca, *Finding the Right Words: Isidore's* Synonyma *in Anglo-Saxon England*, 149–74 (esp. 164–74 on Ælfric Bata). Di Sciacca elsewhere concludes tentatively that the evidence does *not* support the theory that Theodore and Hadrian had the *Synonyma* at their Canterbury school: see 'Isidorian Scholarship at the School of Theodore and Hadrian,' 91–103.

186 See Cross, '*Ubi sunt* Passages in Old English: Sources and Relationships'; Szarmach, 'A Return to Cotton Tiberius A. III, art. 24, and Isidore's *Synonyma*'; and Di Sciacca, *Finding the Right Words: Isidore's* Synonyma *in Anglo-Saxon England*, 109–48.

187 Lapidge, *Library*, 312. Two of these are eighth-century fragments, one a mid-tenth-century import, and one an early eleventh-century product of Canterbury.

Anglo-Saxon missionary activity in eighth-century Germany.[188] Quotations or echoes of the *Sententiae* appear in Bede's *Comm. in Genesin*, the anonymous Latin *uita* of St Birinus of Winchester, the *Vitae sanctorum Willibaldi et Wynnebaldi* penned by the Englishwoman Hygeburg who went as a missionary to Germany in the mid-eighth century, and one homily of Wulfstan II of York (ob. 1023).[189] A number of direct quotations also appear in a Latin charter, purporting to be of King Eadred and dated 949, which was probably composed by Dunstan.[190]

Isidore, *De differentiis uerborum* [CPL 1187]. This work survives, whole or in excerpts, in three eighth-century MSS and two post-Conquest MSS. It is mentioned in one post-Conquest English booklist and possibly in a tenth-century booklist, and it was possibly known to Theodore and Hadrian.[191]

In sum, several forms of textual evidence combine to demonstrate that it was not Augustine whose opinions on the soul were most widely read in England before the year 1000, nor was there abundant access to Platonist-Christian psychologies outside the most impressive centres of learning prior to the year 1000. Instead, Gregory's *Dialogi* and the works of Isidore of Seville were consulted from the seventh century to the eleventh, and they left their mark on many types of literature, including OE and Latin poetry, hagiography, homilies, grammars, riddles, scriptural exegesis, glossaries, colloquies, and charters. The textual inheritance shared by run-of-the-mill Anglo-Saxon authors was not the strict Platonizing-Christian psychology of Augustine and his ilk but the eclectic psychology of Gregory and Isidore, which, though loosely Platonizing, easily accommodated cardiocentrism, the hydraulic model, and non-philosophical approaches to the soul's incorporeality. Building upon this survey of the textual resources at the disposal of the Anglo-Saxons, the next four chapters investigate the psychological opinions generated by the Anglo-Saxons themselves. Alcuin and Ælfric, as we will see, were as staunchly Augustinian in their psychology as the 'medievalist bias' leads readers to presuppose, but these two authors were certainly in the minority.

---

188 Ibid., 312.
189 This list is based on Lapidge, *Library*, 312; *Fontes Anglo-Saxonici*; and Ogilvy, *Books Known to the English*, 170.
190 Charter S546: see Lapidge, 'Æthelwold as Scholar and Teacher,' 185–6; and S.E. Kelly, *The Electronic Sawyer*.
191 Lapidge, *Library*, 309 and 135–6; Di Sciacca, 'Isidorian Scholarship at the School of Theodore and Hadrian,' 84.

5 First Lessons in the Meaning of Corporeality: Insular Latin Grammars and Riddles

According to the manuscript evidence surveyed in the previous chapter, the majority of Anglo-Saxons who acquired Latin literacy prior to the late tenth century probably never picked up a manuscript copy of any of Augustine's discourses on incorporeality, epistemology, or the unitary soul. What, then, were the formative influences on the typical literate Anglo-Saxon's understanding of substance and the soul? Before he or she could study Gregory's *Dialogi* or consult Isidore's *Etymologiae*, virtually every Anglo-Saxon who underwent formal training in Latin learned some version of the following definition of a noun: 'Nomen quid est? Pars orationis cum casu, corpus aut rem proprie communiterue significans.'[1] I quote this definition from the *Ars minor*, the briefer of two grammar textbooks by the Roman grammarian Donatus (fl. ca. 350–60 AD), but students would have found the same information in Donatus's *Ars maior* as well as in numerous commentaries and an assortment of late antique technical grammars based on the work of Donatus. Many of these grammars digress upon the difference between *corpus* and *res*, or between the corporeal and the incorporeal things that nouns could signify. As the relationship between *corpus* and *res* became complicated by Christian teachings on God and the soul, new grammars generated during the early Middle Ages evolved ever lengthier digressions about the corporeal and incorporeal substances signified by nouns, and these digressions often treat corporeality and incorporeality as relative categories, more in the manner of the Stoicizing Christian tradition than that of the Platonists.

---

1 Donatus, *Ars minor* 2 (ed. Holtz, *Donat et la tradition*, 585): 'What is a noun? A part of speech with case, signifying a body or a thing, specifically or generally.'

The early medieval grammarians' preoccupation with *corpus* and *res*, moreover, found a concrete application in another genre of texts used in the elementary classroom: the Latin verse riddles, which students typically studied as they learned the rudiments of quantitative metre. The Anglo-Latin verse riddles in particular attest to students' and teachers' fascination with the relationship between the corporeal and the incorporeal. It is no coincidence, I think, that the Anglo-Latin riddles as well as the prose riddle-dialogues are among the only early medieval Latin texts to treat cardiocentric psychology in a semi-discursive register: as long as the early medieval classroom was not dominated by the Platonizing ontology and epistemology characteristic of Augustinian and Carolingian theological discourse, there was no reason to abandon the concept of the corporeal *breostsefa* in favour of the unitary, incorporeal *anima*.

These elementary schooltexts – the late antique technical grammars and commentaries, the early medieval exegetical grammars, the verse riddles, and the riddle dialogues – constitute the shared intellectual heritage of the majority of literate Anglo-Saxons through at least the mid-tenth century. Their presence in pre-1000 manuscripts far exceeds that of patristic discourses on the soul or on substance, and in contrast to the more advanced literary and theological texts which only the especially promising students might aspire to study, nearly everyone who acquired literacy encountered the grammars, often at a very young age. As such, in order to gauge what learned Anglo-Saxons thought about corporeality, the mind, and the soul, the grammars and riddles can tell us much more than can the exceptionally thorough patristic libraries consulted by theologians such as Bede and Ælfric.

Why Is the Noun Defined as *corpus aut rem significans*?

As already mentioned, even the pared-down *Ars minor* of Donatus foregrounds, in its very first lines, the idea that everything that can be signified by a noun is either a *corpus* or a *res*. If a student happened to be using Donatus's *Ars maior* instead, he would also learn that *Roma* and *Tiberis* are examples of proper nouns, while *urbs* 'city' and *flumen* 'river' are examples of appellative (i.e., common) nouns.[2] The latter are in turn divided into several types: 'Appellatiuorum nominum species multae sunt. Alia enim sunt corporalia, ut *homo, terra, mare*; alia incorporalia, ut *pietas*,

---

2 Donatus, *Ars maior*, 2.2 (ed. Holtz, *Donat et la tradition*, 614).

iustitia, dignitas.'[3] Every noun is thus either a corporeal or an incorporeal, but these are only the first two of many classes of common noun. Most of the other classes are formal rather than semantic: a noun is either a simplex or composed of multiple morphemes, either of Greek or Latin or mixed origin, and so forth. But in nearly all the technical grammars, *corporalia* and *incorporalia* are at the head of the list. If the *nomina incorporalia* were more or less the equivalent of what modern English grammar books call 'abstract nouns,' as Donatus's examples *pietas, iustitia, dignitas* suggest, then there would be some limited utility, for the elementary student, in being able to recognize that, for instance, third-declension nouns in *-tio, -tionis*; *-itas, -itatis*; or *-itudo, -itudinis* are 'incorporeal' and that their gender is feminine. Some of the grammars in the Donatus tradition do make use of the notion of *incorporalia* in explaining morphological trends such as these.[4] More often, however, the grammarians' digressions on the meaning of *corporalia* and *incorporalia* reveal that they were less interested in the morphology of *nomina incorporalia* than in what it meant for the external referents of those nouns to be incorporeal. And while it is understandable that teachers and students alike were more interested in the concept of incorporeality than in noun morphology, it does raise the question of how something with so little grammatical application made its way into a prominent position in elementary grammars to begin with.

The Greek terms *sôma* 'body' and *pragma* 'deed, occurrence, state of affairs' entered grammatical discourse within the framework of Stoic dialectic.[5] Because the Stoics attributed true existence only to bodies, they maintained that the purpose of nouns (and other nominal parts of speech)

---

3   Donatus, *Ars maior*, 2.3 (ed. Holtz, *Donat et la tradition*, 615): 'There are many types of common noun. Some are corporeal, such as *man, earth, sea*; others are incorporeal, such as *dutifulness, justice, worthiness.*'

4   E.g., Phocas, *De nomine et uerbo* 7.2 (ed. Casaceli, *De nomine et verbo*, 33): 'Rem autem incorporalem significantia pleraque a uerbis transferuntur et sunt generis feminini, ut *haec oratio, ratio, actio, statio, hortatio, religio*: et haec similiter nomina per casus omnes *o* producunt praeter nominatiuum et uocatiuum numeri singularis' (Very many nouns that signify an incorporeal thing are derived from verbs and belong to the feminine gender, such as *this speech* [< oro, -are], *reason* [< reor, -eri], *action* [< ago, -ere], *position* [< sto, -are], *encouragement* [< hortor, -ari], *reverence* [< religo, -are]: and likewise these nouns have a long *o* in all the cases except nominative and vocative singular).

5   What we know of Stoic grammatical theory has been assembled from writings in adjacent fields; the Stoics are not known to have produced any technical grammars: see Blank and Atherton, 'The Stoic Contribution to Traditional Grammar,' 310–14; and Luhtala, *Grammar and Philosophy in Late Antiquity*, 18–24. Our chief sources for Stoic grammatical theory are Book 7 of the doxography of Diogenes Laertius (fl. early third

was to name bodies. Verbs, in contrast, did not name bodies; verbs were used to predicate some state of affairs about bodies. The *pragma* 'state of affairs,' also called the *lekton* 'that which could be said,' was understood to be incorporeal; consequently, the *lekton* was one of the four things to which the Stoics ascribed only *hupostasis* 'subsistence' rather than true existence.[6]

How, then, did the Stoics' association of *sômata* with nouns and *pragmata* with verbs become transformed into the widespread assertion that nouns named both *sômata* and *pragmata*? According to Anneli Luhtala, the transformation occurred during late antiquity, when the Stoic understanding of corporeality met challenges from both Platonist Realism and the Aristotelian *Categories*. The grammarian Apollonius Dyscolus (fl. second century AD), whose teachings were heavily influenced by Stoic language theory, still perpetuated the Stoic doctrine that nouns signify bodies: this much is clear from his surviving treatise on syntax.[7] Apollonius's treatise on the noun, however, was lost. As it has been indirectly transmitted in grammatical scholia and in Priscian's *Institutiones grammaticae*, Apollonius's definition of the noun states that it signifies both *sômata* and *pragmata*.[8] Luhtala reasons that Apollonius's work on syntax more accurately reflects his real outlook on corporeality, and that scholiasts predating Priscian redacted Apollonius's definition of the noun in accordance with, first, the Platonist belief in corporeal and incorporeal realities, and second, the Aristotelian association of nouns with substances and verbs with accidents.[9] The structure of Apollonius's redacted definition of the noun became widespread among the earliest surviving Greek technical grammars, including the definitive *Tekhnê grammatikê* formerly attributed to Dionysius Thrax: 'Onoma esti meros logou ptôtikon, sôma ê pragma sêmainon, sôma men hoion *lithos*, pragma de hoion *paideia*, koinôs te kai idiôs legomenon, koinôs men hoion *anthrôpos*, *hippos*, idiôs

---

century AD) and the polemical *Aduersus mathematicos* of the sceptical philosopher Sextus Empiricus (fl. second century AD).

6 Long and Sedley have assembled the relevant excerpts from primary sources, with commentary, in *The Hellenistic Philosophers* 1.195–202; see also Long, 'Language and Thought in Stoicism'; Lloyd, 'Grammar and Metaphysics in the Stoa'; Frede, 'The Stoic Notion of a *lekton*.' On the Stoic incorporeals (place, time, the extra-cosmic void, and the *lekton*), see Brunschwig, 'Stoic Metaphysics,' 212–19.

7 Luhtala, *Grammar and Philosophy in Late Antiquity*, 85–6.

8 Ibid., 84; on Priscian's definition of the noun, see below.

9 Luhtala, *Grammar and Philosophy in Late Antiquity*, 86–90.

de hoion *Sôkratês*.'[10] The nouns chosen to illustrate the difference between *sôma* and *pragma* leave no doubt that these words no longer carry the specialized meanings that they had within the context of Stoic dialectic; they have been simplified to mean the referents of concrete and abstract nouns respectively.[11]

Definitions of this type were clearly the progenitors of Donatus's definition of the noun, which in turn became the prevalent definition of the noun in Latin technical grammars for several centuries. Donatus teaches that 'the noun is a part of speech with case, signifying a body [*corpus*] or a thing [*rem*] specifically or generally; specifically, as in *Roma* and *Tiberis*, and generally, as in *city* and *river*.'[12] One implication of this development is that, as instruction in Latin grammar grew ever more distant from classical Stoic dialectic, the grammarians who continued to define nouns as *corpus aut rem significans*, and likewise to divide common nouns into *corporalia* and *incorporalia*, were preserving a vestige of Stoic metaphysics that had very little bearing on morphology and none whatsoever on syntax. I suspect that it was their grammatical irrelevance that made these loci susceptible to frequent revisions by late antique and early medieval grammarians: they could digress speculatively on the meaning of corporeality at these loci without any risk of vitiating those parts of the definition of the noun that were actually relevant to the study of morphology and syntax.

---

10 Dionysius Thrax, *Tekhnê grammatikê*, 12 (ed. Uhlig, *Dionysii Thracis Ars grammatica*, 24): 'A noun is a part of speech with case, signifying a body or an abstraction (a body, such as *stone*, or an abstraction, such as *education*), which is meant generally or specifically (generally, such as *person, horse*, or specifically, such as *Socrates*).' Ch. 1–5 of this *Tekhnê* are still thought to be the authentic work of Dionysius (fl. ca. 100 BC); many scholars now believe that ch. 6–22, which deal with the parts of speech, are an addition of the fourth century AD. For arguments on both sides of the authorship question, see Law and Sluiter, *Dionysius Thrax and the Technê Grammatikê*.

11 The same can be said of many definitions of the noun preserved in the early Greek technical grammars printed by Wouters, *The Grammatical Papyri from Graeco-Roman Egypt*: see esp. 47–8 for Papyrus Yale 1.25, a fragmentary technical grammar from Egypt, probably of the first century AD. According to this text, a proper noun is 'lexis ousian idian sômatos ê pragmatos sêmainousa' (a word signifying the peculiar being of a body or thing): see ibid., 49.6–8; some words have been reconstructed. On the changing connotations of *pragma*, see Hadot, 'Sur divers sens du mot *pragma* dans la tradition philosophique grecque,' esp. 313–18; and on the adaptation of *pragma* into Latin grammars as *res*, see Grondeux, '*Corpus dicitur quidquid videtur et tangitur*: Origines et enjeux d'une définition,' 37–45; and Grondeux, '*Res* Meaning a Thing Thought: The Influence of the *Ars Donati*.'

12 Donatus, *Ars maior* 2.2 (ed. Holtz, *Donat et la tradition*, 614).

Corporeal and Incorporeal Nouns and Their Referents in the Donatus Tradition

Already in the mid-fourth century, Donatus's near-contemporary Charisius supplemented his discussion of *nomina appellatiua* with a simple rule for discerning the difference between the corporeal and incorporeal objects that were named by nouns.[13] Charisius explains: 'Appellatiua autem quae gene-raliter communiterque dicuntur quaeque in duas species diuiduntur, quarum altera significat res corporales, quae uideri tangique possunt, ut est *homo, terra, mare*, altera incorporales, ut est *pietas, iustitia, dignitas*, quae intellectu tantum modo percipiuntur, uerum neque uideri nec tangi possunt.'[14] Some grammarians proposed other ways to classify common nouns according to the nature of their referents; in his fourth-century *Instituta artium*, for example, Probus writes, 'Appellatiua autem sunt nomina animalium et inani-malium; sunt item et illa, quae ex aliqua re hominibus accidunt.'[15] Yet this means of classifying common nouns would never become as popular among Latin grammarians as the classifications according to corporeality and incorporeality.

Numerous Latin grammars distinguish between the *res corporales* and *res incorporales* signified by nouns on the basis of sight and touch, just as Charisius does: these include fourth- and early fifth-century texts such as Dositheus's *Ars grammatica*, the *Anonymus Bobiensis*, and Diomedes'

---

13 My research on the significance of *incorporalia* in late antique and early medieval Latin grammars was completed before the appearance of Grondeux's detailed study of the same topic, '*Corpus dicitur quidquid videtur et tangitur*: Origines et enjeux d'une définition,' which likewise traces philosophical and theological influences on the development of the grammatical concepts *corpus* and *res*, but with proportionally far less attention to the Insular grammars and more to the Carolingian and later medieval grammars. See esp. 37–52 for Grondeux's treatment of the Greek and late antique Latin grammars and scholia, which is considerably more detailed than the scope of the present chapter permits.

14 Charisius, *Ars grammatica* 1.6 (ed. Barwick, *Charisii Artis grammaticae libri V*, 193–4): 'There are common nouns, which are meant in a general or common way, and which are divided into two types, one of which signifies corporeal things, which can be seen and touched, such as *human, earth, sea*, and the other of which signifies incorporeal things, such as *dutifulness, justice, worthiness*, which are perceived by means of the intellect alone but can be neither seen nor touched.'

15 Probus, *Instituta artium* (*GL* 4.51): 'Common nouns are the names of animate beings and inanimate beings; there are also those which signify the non-essential qualities of people according to something extraneous.' The *accidentia* of the third group are what we would call adjectives, though these were typically treated under the rubric *De nomine*.

Ars grammatica.[16] Grammars of a second group, whose average date is slightly later than the first, maintain the sensory criteria for distinguishing between corporeals and incorporeals, but they are careless about distinguishing between nouns and their external referents. For instance, in his commentary on Donatus's *Ars minor*, Servius (fl. late fourth or early fifth century) provides the following explanation of the basic definition of the noun: 'Quod autem dixit corpus aut rem significare, hoc ipsius proprium est. Corporale autem nomen uel incorporale grammatici ita definierunt, ut corporale sit quidquid uidetur et tangitur, ut *lapis*; incorporale quod nec uidetur nec tangitur, ut *pietas*.'[17] The sixth-century grammarian Pompeius, whose *Commentum artis Donati* was evidently committed to writing by an amanuensis listening to Pompeius deliver a lecture, is memorably careless in this regard. To illustrate the properties of nouns, Pompeius says, 'Da quoduis nomen. Hector totum hoc habet: hic Hector casus est; Hector uidetur et tangitur, corporale est; Hector unius nomen est, ergo proprium est ... Puta marmor, uidetur et tangitur, corporale est; illud marmor est et illud marmor est, appellatiuum est; hoc marmor nominatiuus est.'[18] In these instances, at least the basis for assessing the corporeality of an external referent remains constant, and the relationship between *corporalia* and *incorporalia* as grammatical categories – that is, as groups of common nouns rather than groups of external referents – is straightforward. *Nomina corporalia* and *nomina incorporalia* are two sides of a single coin

---

16 Dositheus, *Ars grammatica* (*GL* 7.389–90); *Anonymus Bobiensis* (ed. de Nonno, *La Grammatica dell'*Anonymus Bobiensis, 2.12–18); Diomedes, *Ars grammatica* (*GL* 1.322). The dates I provide for these and other late antique grammarians follow Kaster, *Guardians of Language*, who includes a prosopography of third- through sixth-century grammarians at 237–79, followed by a prosopography of figures whose identities and careers are more obscure, at 380–440.

17 Servius, *Comm. in Donati artem minorem* (*GL* 4.406): 'He [*scil.* Donatus] said that a noun signified a body or a thing; this is its peculiar property. The grammarians define a corporeal noun or an incorporeal noun in this way: a corporeal noun is whatever is seen and touched, such as *stone*; an incorporeal noun is that which is not seen nor touched, such as *dutifulness*.' See also the similar statements in Servius's *Comm. in Donati artem maiorem* (*GL* 4.429) and in the *Ars grammatica* by Julian of Toledo (fl. 680s–90s) (ed. Maestre Yenes, *Ars Iuliani Toletani Episcopi*, 12).

18 Pompeius, *Commentum artis Donati* (*GL* 5.137): 'Give me any noun you like. Hector has all these properties: this Hector is an inflected form; Hector is seen and touched, it is corporeal; Hector is the name of one person, so it is proper ... How about marble? It is seen and touched, it is corporeal; that is marble and that is marble, it is a common noun; this marble is nominative.' On the likelihood that Pompeius's grammar was recorded during schoolroom lectures, see Kaster, *Guardians of Language*, 156–8.

and cannot overlap, because regardless of whether the corporeality of an external referent is in doubt, a noun either refers to a corporeal thing or it does not; a noun cannot be 'sort of' corporeal. Pompeius (among others) underscores this point: 'nequaquam inuenitur nomen, ut non sit aut corporale aut incorporale.'[19]

Some of the Latin grammars, however, betray the possibility that the meanings of *corporalia* and *incorporalia* are, in reality, not as simple as the grammarians would make them out to be. Servius, in the passage quoted above, stipulates that 'whatever is seen and touched' is the definition of a corporeal only insofar 'as the grammarians define it.' A Donatus commentary attributed to Sergius offers this explanation of the lemma *corpus aut rem*: 'Corporalia et incorporalia dicunt grammatici. Videris, quid dicant philosophi uel oratores. Interim grammatici corporale dicunt quod uidetur et tangitur, incorporale quid nec uidetur nec tangitur.'[20] The *Primae expositiones*, attributed to a different 'Sergius,' includes a similar disclaimer: 'Incorporale autem est, quod nec uidetur nec tangitur, ut puta *pietas, iustitia, dignitas*. Sed philosophi aliter disputant.'[21] And Pompeius, ever the most emphatic of the grammarians, declares to his students, 'Corporalia dicuntur nomina quae uidentur et tanguntur, incorporalia quae neque uideri neque tangi possunt, secundum grammaticos. Quid autem dicant philosophi de istis rebus, quid ad nos? Corporalis dicitur res apud grammaticos quae uideri potest et tangi, incorporalis quae nec uideri nec tangi potest.'[22]

The cause of this disagreement between the grammarians and the masters of other disciplines was surely that the grammatical definition of corporeality was too simplistic to serve philosophical discourse, especially dialectic. Although the late antique grammarians tended to cling to the

---

19 Pompeius, *Commentum artis Donati* (*GL* 5.137): 'never is there found a noun that is not either corporeal or incorporeal.'

20 Sergius, *Explanationes in artem Donati* (*GL* 4.490): 'The grammarians call them *corporalia* and *incorporalia*. You will see what the philosophers and the rhetors say. Nevertheless, the grammarians call *corporale* that which is seen and touched, and *incorporale* that which is neither seen nor touched.'

21 'Sergius,' *Primae explanationes Sergii de prioribus Donati grammatici* (*GL* 8.143): 'An incorporeal is that which is neither seen nor touched, such as *dutifulness, justice*, and *worthiness*. But the philosophers argue otherwise.'

22 Pompeius, *Commentum artis Donati* (*GL* 5.137): 'Nouns that are seen and touched are called corporeals, and those that can neither be seen nor touched are called incorporeals, according to grammarians. As for what the philosophers say concerning these matters – what is that to us? According to grammarians, a thing is called corporeal if it can be seen and touched, and incorporeal if it can neither be seen nor touched.'

same simplistic method of distinguishing corporeals and incorporeals when they talked about common nouns, at other loci in their grammars they occasionally acknowledge competing philosophical treatments of corporeality. One of the definitions of *uox* 'sound' that grammarians invoked, from at least the mid-fourth century, reads, 'Vox est aer ictus, sensibilis auditu, quantum in ipso est.'[23] Yet Diomedes, a slightly younger contemporary of Donatus, suggests that the simplicity of the foregoing definition might belie a point of contention among philosophers: 'Vox est, ut Stoicis uidetur, spiritus tenuis auditu sensibilis.'[24] In his massive *Institutiones grammaticae*, Priscian (fl. late fifth–early sixth century) paused to explore the implications of the corporeality of sound: 'Nam si aer corpus est, et uox, quae ex aere icto constat, corpus esse ostenditur, quippe cum et tangit aurem et tripertito diuiditur, quod est suum corporis, hoc est in altitudinem, latitudinem, longitudinem, unde ex omni quoque parte potest audiri.'[25] Pompeius evidently thought that the nature of sound was too sophisticated a topic to put before his grammar students, because in the introductory sentences of his *Ars* he says tersely, 'De uoce tractare quid est, hoc philosophorum est.'[26] Audax, in contrast, thought it better to share the underlying philosophical arguments with his readers:

Vox quid est? Aer ictus auditu sensibilis ... Vox corporalis est, an incorporalis? Secundum Stoicos corporalis, qui eam sic definiunt, ut nos in principio respondimus. Plato autem non esse uocem corpus putat: 'non enim percussus,' inquit, 'aer, sed plaga ipsa atque percussio, id est uox.' Democritus uero ac deinde Epicurus ex indiuisis corporibus uocem constare dicunt, corpus autem esse aut efficiens aut patiens.[27]

---

23 Donatus, *Ars maior* 1.1 (ed. Holtz, *Donat et la tradition*, 603): 'Insofar as it exists on its own, sound is air that has been struck, perceptible to the faculty of hearing.'
24 Diomedes, *Ars grammatica* (*GL* 1.420): 'Sound, as the Stoics understand it, is a subtle type of *pneuma* perceptible to the faculty of hearing.'
25 Priscian, *Institutiones grammaticae* 1.2.4 (*GL* 2.6): 'Now if air is a body, then sound also, which consists of air that has been struck, is demonstrably a body. Indeed when it touches the ear and is divided into three parts (that is, into height, width, and length), which is the property of a body, thence it can be heard from each and every direction.'
26 Pompeius, *Commentum artis Donati* (*GL* 5.96; editorial punctuation altered): 'It is the philosophers' job to explain what sound is.'
27 Audax, *De Scauri et Palladii libris excerpta* (*GL* 7.323): 'What is sound? Air that has been struck, perceptible to the faculty of hearing ... Is sound corporeal or incorporeal? It is corporeal according to the Stoics, who define sound just as we did in answering the initial question. Plato, however, thought that sound was not a body: "It is not air that has been struck," he said, "but the stroke itself and the act of striking: that is what

None of this is particularly germane to grammar or to the study of the Latin language more broadly construed, but some of the grammarians nonetheless indulged themselves in digressions on the topic of corporeality, in ways that reveal a non-scholarly curiosity about things (as opposed to the names of things) whose substance was difficult to evaluate. As in the foregoing discussions of *uox*, sometimes such difficulties were prompted by differences among philosophical concepts of corporeality: the fourth- or fifth-century *Fragmentum Bobiense de nomine*, for example, explains that 'Epicurei definiunt quidquid uisu aut tactu subiacet, hoc corpus esse,' with the interesting implication that 'unde et umbras corpora esse dicunt.'[28] But in many cases, and especially concerning the division of common nouns into *corporalia* and *incorporalia*, digressions and alterations seem to have been prompted by a combination of Christian and Platonic influences and ordinary empirical observations.

All of the grammars considered thus far have limited their examples of *incorporalia* to things that modern grammars would call abstract nouns, but the influences of Platonism and Christianity demanded that other sorts of beings be added to the list. Diomedes' *Ars grammatica*, which dates to the later fourth or early fifth century, may be the earliest surviving grammar to broach the problem of the divine substance. His discussion of common nouns is nearly identical to that of Charisius and the *Anonymus Bobiensis*, but he adds *deus* and several other things to his list of *res incorporales*: 'altera incorporales, quae intellectu tantum modo percipiuntur, uerum neque uideri nec tangi possunt, ut est *deus, pietas, iustitia, dignitas, sapientia, doctrina, facundia.'*[29] If the external referent of the common noun *deus* is incorporeal, this raises another problem, for all of the grammars discussed so far have divided only the common nouns into *corporalia* and *incorporalia*, but presumably names of deities would be proper nouns that signify incorporeals. The fifth-century grammarian Consentius does not suggest any sensory criteria for discerning corporeality, but he addresses

---

sound is." But Democritus and then Epicurus say that sound consists of indivisible bodies and that a body is that which acts or is acted upon.' The date of Audax's career falls somewhere between the mid-fourth century and the later seventh but cannot currently be determined with precision: see Kaster, *Guardians of Language*, 386.

28 *Fragmentum Bobiense de nomine*, par. 158 (ed. Mariotti, 'Il *fragmentum Bobiense de nomine*,' 68): 'The Epicureans claim that whatever is subject to sight *or* touch is a body: for this reason they also say that shadows are bodies.'

29 Diomedes, *Ars grammatica* (*GL* 1.322): 'Other nouns signify incorporeal things, which are perceived by the intellect alone but can be neither seen nor touched, such as *god, dutifulness, justice, worthiness, wisdom, teaching*, and *eloquence*.'

238 Anglo-Saxon Psychologies

the problem of nouns that are both *propria* and *incorporalia*: 'Corporalia uel communiter uel proprie significantur: communiter, ut *homo, mons, mare*; proprie, ut *Cicero, Caucasus, Hadriaticum*. Incorporalia sunt, ut *pietas, iustitia, eloquentia*; et haec exceptis deorum nominibus fere semper communiter significantur.'[30] As we shall see, early medieval lists of *incorporalia* were to become even more expansive, including such beings as *anima* and *angelus*, as grammatical discourse became more Christianized.

Alongside the philosophically motivated adaptations that late antique grammarians implemented, there are also signs that teachers and students occasionally found the grammatical definition of corporeality to be insufficient even to account for common-sense observations about the natural world. The grammarian Cledonius, a *senator* of probably the mid-fifth century, wrote an *Ars grammatica* that survives in a single manuscript of around the year 600.[31] Like the author of the aforementioned *Fragmentum Bobiense de nomine*, he was sensitive to the significance of the conjunctions used in sensory definitions of corporeality: 'Corporalia sunt quae et tanguntur et uidentur, ut *homo, terra, mare*; incorporalia sunt quae non tanguntur et uidentur, ut *caelum, sol, aer*; alia quae nec tanguntur nec uidentur, ut *pietas, iustitia, dignitas*.'[32] Cledonius conceivably created this intermediate category of *incorporalia* not to address philosophical concerns – he mentions no conflicting philosophical schools of thought – but in response to the curiosity of his students, who must have delighted in finding exceptional things in the natural world that would confound the paradigm that they learned in the classroom. It remains, however, difficult to explain why Cledonius classified heaven, sun, and air as incorporeals rather than corporeals. Isidore of Seville (ob. 636), who devoted the first book of his *Etymologiae* to technical grammar, offered a more subtle solution to the same problem that Cledonius faced. Among common nouns,

---

30 Consentius, *De duabus partibus orationis nomine et uerbo* (*GL* 5.338): 'Corporeal things are signified both generally and specifically: generally, such as *man, mountain*, and *sea*; specifically, such as *Cicero, Caucasus*, and *Adriatic*. There are incorporeals, such as *dutifulness, justice*, and *eloquence*; and with the exception of the names of gods, they are almost always signified generally.'

31 On Cledonius, see Kaster, *Guardians of Language*, 255–6.

32 Cledonius, *Ars grammatica* (*GL* 5.34): 'Corporeal things are those which are touched and seen, such as *person, earth*, and *sea*. There are incorporeals which are not both touched and seen, such as *sky, sun*, and *air*, and there are other incorporeals which are neither touched nor seen, such as *dutifulness, justice*, and *worthiness*.'

Isidore writes, some are called *corporalia* 'quia uel uidentur uel tanguntur, ut *caelum, terra.* Incorporalia, quia carent corpus; unde nec uideri nec tangi possunt, ut *ueritas, iustitia.*'[33] His use of *uel* rather than *et* or enclitic *-que* allows him to include among the *corporalia* a noun such as *caelum*, which refers to something that can be seen but not touched. These modifications by Cledonius and Isidore are indicative of a growing interest in bringing the traditional teaching on *corporalia* and *incorporalia* in line with the way these categories were perceived in nature: an interest that would continue to flourish among Insular grammarians of the early Middle Ages, as the discipline of grammar became more integrated with other elementary studies, and technical grammars became accordingly more encyclopedic and digressive in content.

Anglo-Saxon Reception of Latin Technical Grammars

In the previous chapter I surveyed Platonist- and Stoic-oriented Christian psychologies but could offer only scant evidence for the reception of most of the relevant texts in pre-Conquest England. In contrast, an impressive variety of late antique technical grammars was known and consulted in England during the late seventh, eighth, tenth, and eleventh centuries. The following list summarizes the evidence for Anglo-Saxon reception of technical grammars and commentaries (most of which have been discussed above) that divide nouns into those signifying *corpus* and those signifying *res*, or that divide common nouns or their external referents into *corporalia* and *incorporalia*.[34]

Audax, *De Scauri et Palladii libris excerpta* survives in one pre-Conquest MS with tenth-century Winchester provenance, and it was used by Aldhelm, Boniface, and Bede.

Cassiodorus, *Institutiones* survives in four Anglo-Saxon MSS, of which one has English provenance predating the eleventh century, plus one MS associated from the region of Anglo-Saxon missionary activity in Germany.

---

33 Isidore, *Etym.* 1.7.3 (ed. Lindsay, *Etym.*): 'because they are either seen or touched, such as *sky* and *earth*; incorporeals are so called because they lack a body and therefore can be neither seen nor touched, such as *truth* and *justice*.'

34 The contents of this list are based on the alphabetical catalogue of classical and patristic authors in Lapidge, *Library* (as well as 228–31, concerning Alcuin); and Law, 'The Study of Latin Grammar in Eighth-Century Southumbria.'

The booklist of Sæwold (ca. 1070) also mentions the *Institutiones*, and Sæwold's own MS of the text survives.[35]

Charisius, *Ars grammatica* is preserved in a MS from the milieu of the Anglo-Saxon missionaries in Germany; it was known to Boniface, Bede, Alcuin, and Abbo.

Cledonius, *Ars grammatica* is quoted by Bede; this may be the work identified as 'Glossa super Donatum' in the inventory of books belonging to the tenth-century grammarian Æthelstan.

Consentius, *Ars de nomine et uerbo* survives in a MS associated with the area of Anglo-Saxon missionary activity; it was used by Tatwine and Bede.

Diomedes, *Ars grammatica* survives in a MS from the region of Anglo-Saxon missionary activity in Germany; it was used by Boniface and Bede.

Donatus, *Ars maior* survives in two extant Anglo-Saxon MSS, one dated s. x med. and the other s. x/xi. It is mentioned in the booklist of the grammarian Æthelstan and quoted by Theodore and Hadrian, Aldhelm, Tatwine, Boniface, Bede, Alcuin, Abbo, and Byrhtferth.

Donatus, *Ars minor* is included in the booklist of the tenth-century grammarian Æthelstan; it was used by Aldhelm, Tatwine, and Boniface.

Isidore, *Etymologiae* survives in over two dozen MSS used in Anglo-Saxon England or in the region of the Anglo-Saxon missions in Germany: for additional details, see chapter 4 above. Book 1 of the *Etymologiae* deals with grammar; quotations and echoes of this book appear in the works of Aldhelm, Tatwine, Boniface, Bede, Abbo, and Byrhtferth.

Julian of Toledo, *Ars grammatica* survives in one MS associated with the region of the Anglo-Saxon missions in Germany; it is quoted by Bede.

Pompeius, *Commentarius in artem Donati* survives in one extant Anglo-Saxon MS of the early eighth century. This may be the work referred to as 'Glossa super Donatum' in the booklist of the grammarian Æthelstan. Quotations and echoes of Pompeius appear in the works of Aldhelm, Tatwine, Bede, and Alcuin.

Priscian, *Institutiones grammaticae* is attested by seven extant Anglo-Saxon MSS, of which two predate the eleventh century, plus one MS from the region of the Anglo-Saxon missions in Germany. This work is mentioned in a late eleventh-century booklist, possibly from Worcester, and it was used by Aldhelm, Bede, possibly Alcuin, Lantfred, Abbo, and Byrhtferth.

Probus, *Instituta artium* was known to Bede and possibly to Alcuin.

---

35 At *Institutiones* 2.1.2, Cassiodorus quotes the definitions of the parts of speech from Donatus's *Ars maior*. On Sæwold's MS, see Lapidge, *Library*, 137–8.

Sergius, *Explanationes in artem Donati* (= *GL* 4.486–565) survives in one extant Anglo-Saxon MS of the early eighth century. This may be the text referred to as 'Glossa super Donatum' in the booklist of Æthelstan the grammarian; it is quoted by Bede.

Sergius (Pseudo-Cassiodorus), *Commentarium de oratione et de octo partibus orationis artis secundae Donati*[36] is quoted by Boniface.

Servius, *Comm. in Donati artem maiorem* and *Comm. in Donati artem minorem* are quoted by Bede.

This survey of the evidence demonstrates that the late antique Latin technical grammars were plentiful in the classrooms of pre-Conquest England. The pattern of dissemination shows the same ninth-century decline that characterized the dissemination of Augustine's works, but in the periods when these grammars were available, they were not restricted to the richest libraries; they reached Tatwine at Breedon-on-the-Hill, and Boniface at Nursling or some unidentified centre in southwest England. Compared with the meager witnesses for theological and philosophical psychologies presented in chapter 4, this abundant evidence for the technical grammars makes it clear that anyone who learned his Latin from an Anglo-Saxon master, in England or on the continent, was much more likely to learn about incorporeality from a grammatical perspective than from a philosophical or theological one. The evidence presented thus far has not even taken into account the proliferation of elementary grammars written by Insular authors, many of which not only preserved but embellished the definition of corporeality that they inherited from the late antique technical grammars.

The Insular Latin Grammars

The most sweeping innovations made by the early Insular grammarians were motivated by the needs of students whose native language was Germanic or Celtic rather than Latin or proto-Romance: specifically, the new genre of the 'elementary grammar' focused more on formal, morphological classification and less on semantics, adding extensive lists of examples

---

36 This grammar is to be disambiguated from aforementioned grammars circulating under the name 'Sergius.' This text does not appear in *GL* but was printed at PL 70.1219–40 and has now been re-edited by C. Stock as the work of Sergius (Ps.-Cassiodorus), *Commentarium de oratione et de octo partibus orationis artis secundae Donati*. For *corpus* and *res*, see 43, and for *corporalia* and *incorporalia*, see 47.

to illustrate the declension of nouns and adjectives and the conjugation of verbs.[37] Concurrent with these developments was a trend in which the content of the grammars was growing more eclectic and encyclopedic, replete with digressions that had little bearing on the discipline of grammar itself. Vivien Law has observed that some features of these 'exegetical grammars' parallel the eclectic tendencies of Insular authors' literal commentaries on scripture and works such as the *Irish Reference Bible*;[38] I would add that encyclopedism in the grammars was likely also encouraged by a significant change in the structure of elementary education. Donatus and his contemporaries had written their technical grammars for students who studied grammar and literature in relative isolation from other disciplines, preparatory to advancing to another master's school for training in rhetoric, and then a career in public service.[39] With the disintegration of the educational system of the Roman Empire, the discipline of grammar became less isolated from other studies. This change was partly pragmatic, in that the Romans' separate schools for grammar, rhetoric, and law were replaced by self-contained monastic or cathedral or palace schools, but it was also a matter of educational philosophy, as prominent Christian scholars, including Augustine, Cassiodorus, and Bede, reconceived the study of grammar and literature as ancillary to the interpretation of the Bible.[40] In such an environment it was hardly appropriate to teach students engaged in the study of Donatus a grammatical definition of corporeality that would later be unfit for use in their study of scripture; it was more efficient to account for Christian concerns when the question of corporeality first arose with the study of nouns. And since the literal mode of scriptural exegesis drew upon knowledge from all relevant disciplines, including the natural sciences and philosophy, it was useful for even elementary students to possess an

---

37 Law, *GG*, 54–69; Law, *ILG*, 53–6.

38 Law, *ILG*, 81–5.

39 On educational institutions and disciplinary distinctions in the late antique West, see Kaster, *Guardians of Language*, 15–50; and Law, *The History of Linguistics in Europe*, 58–65. See also Vessey's introduction to Cassiodorus, *Institutions*, trans. Halporn, 24–38; and Marrou, *History of Education*, 314–39, on the transition from the Roman system to more integrated Christian schools. For the role of grammatical instruction within the framework of Anglo-Saxon education, see Gneuss, 'The Study of Language in Anglo-Saxon England.'

40 Among the *loci classici* on the implementation of the techniques of the *trivium* in scriptural interpretation are Augustine, *De doctrina christiana* 2.9–16; Cassiodorus, *Institutiones* 1.15; and Bede, *De schematibus et tropis* (= Book 2 of *De arte metrica*). On the pertinence of this educational theory for the development of medieval grammars, see Holtz, 'Les innovations théoriques,' 134; Law, 'The Study of Grammar,' 99–103; and Munzi, 'Testi grammaticali e *renovatio studiorum* carolingia,' 360–5.

understanding of corporeality and incorporeality that would remain viable when they encountered these other discourses in their study of scripture.

Not every elementary grammar bears signs of this encyclopedic impulse or, more specifically, of any interest in refining the meaning of corporeality. The grammar written by Boniface (Wynfrith), probably before 716 when he undertook his missionary work among the Frisians, is deliberately old-fashioned. In the dedicatory letter that prefaces his *Ars grammatica*, Boniface even promises that his own work will not depart from the authority of classical sources, except insofar as he has had to choose among conflicting authorities and add some supporting explanations.[41] Not surprisingly, his discussion of the first two classes of common nouns is a pastiche of the least speculative things that Charisius and Isidore say on the subject: 'Primae ergo speciei sunt corporalia, quae uideri tangique possunt, ut *terra, homo, mare*. Secundae incorporalia, quae carent corpore et nec uideri nec tangi possunt, ut *ueritas, iustitia, pietas*.'[42] He prefers Isidore's sensory criteria over Charisius's assertion that incorporeals can be perceived by the *intellectus*, and he prefers Charisius's *uideri tangique* to Isidore's more flexible formulation 'uel uidentur uel tanguntur, ut *caelum, terra*.'[43]

Among seventh- and eighth-century Insular grammars, Boniface's old-fashioned *Ars* represents the exception rather than the rule. As Vivien Law has demonstrated, Boniface had access to much of the same source material available to Aldhelm, who also worked in the south of England, but Tatwine, who presumably wrote his grammar at Breedon-on-the-Hill in Mercia before becoming archbishop of Canterbury (731–4), shares the bulk of his source material with the *Expossitio latinitatis* and other apparently Irish elementary grammars.[44] I have no new claims to advance with respect to the dating, localization, and transmission of these possibly Irish grammars, but in the present chapter, regardless of their geographical origins, they serve to flesh out the conceptual innovations characteristic of the grammatical tradition within which Tatwine's *Ars* was composed.

---

41 Boniface, *Ars grammatica*, preface, lines 64–6 (ed. Gebauer and Löfstedt, CCSL 133B, 9). Although Boniface's grammar is backward-looking with respect to its self-conscious deference to *auctoritates*, it is innovative in its inclusion of postclassical Latin vocabulary: see Law, *GG*, 169–99 (esp. 194, on Boniface's definition of the noun).

42 Boniface, *Ars grammatica*, lines 28–31 (ed. Gebauer and Löfstedt, CCSL 133B, 16): 'Corporeals belong therefore to the first class [of appellative noun], which can be seen and touched, such as *earth, person*, and *sea*. Incorporeals belong to the second class, which lack a body and can be neither seen nor touched, such as *truth, justice*, and *kindness*.'

43 Cf. Charisius, *Ars grammatica*, 193–4; and Isidore, *Etym.* 1.7.3–4, both quoted above.

44 Law, 'The Study of Latin Grammar in Eighth-Century Southumbria,' 66–7.

Insular Innovations

The author of the *Ars Ambrosiana*, who was possibly an Irish *peregrinus* of the seventh or eighth century,[45] embraced opportunities to refine the material he inherited from the Donatus tradition, even paying meticulous attention to the meaning of conjunctions in his source texts. Although it is usually said that a body is anything that is touched *and* seen (*tangitur et uidetur*), the author asserts that 'Etsi utrumque simul non continuerit, per alterum corpus nominatur,'[46] thereby taking a firm stand on a problem that had caused confusion for Cledonius and Isidore. The author also scrutinizes the relationship between *corpus* and *res* in the formulation *corpus aut rem significans*. He quotes the opinion of the grammarian 'Sergius' that the conjunction *aut* has a disjunctive meaning: '*Aut* etiam si naturam habeat disiungendi, tamen coniungit sermones, ut si dicas "ego aut tu": iunctum est uerbis, licet disiunctum est sensu.' On this basis, he concludes that 'cum corpus significet, non res significare uidetur, et cum res pronuntiat, non tunc corpora significare.'[47] As they pertain to external referents rather than nouns, on the other hand, *corpus* and *res* are not mutually exclusive: the plural noun *res* can mean 'things' generally, including corporeal things. It was not entirely necessary for Donatus to mention both *corpus* and *res* in his definition of the noun, the author concludes: 'Item Donatum dicunt diuidisse creaturas in duas partes; item potuit tantum dicere "rem significans," sed notior est partis substantia, cum sit diuisa.'[48]

---

45   Lapidge and Sharpe count the *Ars Ambrosiana* among the works of Celtic scholars on the continent (*BCLL* no. 750); Law favours an origin 'in the Mediterranean world in the sixth or seventh century,' and finds little about the methods or sources of this text to suggest that an Irishman wrote it, on the continent or otherwise (*ILG*, 93–7).

46   *Ars Ambrosiana*, lines 27–8 (ed. Löfstedt, CCSL 133C, 6): 'Even if a thing is not perceptible to both [*scil.* touch and sight] at the same time, it is called a body by virtue of either one of the two.'

47   *Ars Ambrosiana*, lines 39–43 (ed. Löfstedt, CCSL 133C, 7): 'The word *aut*, although it has a disjunctive nature, nevertheless joins words, as when you say "I or you": the phrase joins the words together although it is disjunctive in meaning ... When a noun signifies a body, it appears not to signify a thing, and when it signals things, then it does not signify bodies.'

48   *Ars Ambrosiana* lines 31–4 (ed. Löfstedt, CCSL 133C, 7): 'They also say that Donatus divided created beings into two groups; he could have said simply "signifying a thing," but the substance of each group is more readily recognized when it is divided.' Löfstedt has erroneously emended the sentence that immediately precedes this passage: in his edition it reads 'sed non omne corpus res esse potest,' and in the *apparatus criticus* he indicates that he has emended MS *omnis* to *omne*. Unusual word order notwithstanding,

To an extent that is unusual among his predecessors, the author of the *Ars Ambrosiana* is also a stickler about the distinction between signifier and signified: the noun *nomen*, he explains, refers to something incorporeal, i.e., the noun as it is conceived in the mind, unless the noun is written down.[49] Although conscious of the distinction between the noun and its external referent, the author does not restrain the impulse to explore questions pertaining to the substance of external referents where appropriate. For example, although Donatus maintains that only a *corpus* can be named *proprie communiterue*, both Consentius's grammar and the Christian understanding of spiritual beings demanded that the question be reconsidered; therefore the author of the *Ars Ambrosiana* writes, 'Aliter: et res utrumque continet, licet raro, ut sunt deorum et angelorum nomina.' To bridge the gap between grammatical and philosophical concepts of *corporalia*, he also adds a brief digression: 'Quattuor genera sunt corporalia principalia: aqua, terra, aer, ignis. Quinque res Plato numerauit.'[50] The diverse remarks concerning *corpus* and *res* in the *Ars Ambrosiana* thus illustrate multiple influences that shaped the evolution of the Insular grammarians' treatments of this topic. Even while they were eager to keep their illustrative examples of *corporalia* and *incorporalia* up-to-date with the concerns of a Christian audience in a more self-contained educational environment, for the most part they wanted to introduce subtle innovations that largely preserved the organizational structures inherited from their source texts. Sometimes, as the *Ars Ambrosiana* exemplifies, an overly subtle scrutiny of the details of earlier grammarians' teachings could obscure the main grammatical points.

In this respect, the *Ars Ambrosiana* is one of several grammars that bear out a comment made by Virgilius Maro Grammaticus[51] in connection

---

this sentence clearly should mean that not all *res* are bodies, and this is what the MS reading means; the emended version contradicts the passage that follows, in which it is said that all bodies can be called *res*. Cf. *Quae sunt quae* 14, quoted below.

49 *Ars Ambrosiana*, lines 8–11 (ed. Löfstedt, CCSL 133C, 6): '*Nomen* autem indicat rem incorporalem, ut superius diximus, nisi scripturam significat, et secundum naturam et traductionem uerbi a se orientis actum mentis indicat.'

50 *Ars Ambrosiana*, lines 53–5 and 63–4 (ed. Löfstedt, CCSL 133C, 7–8): 'Another opinion is that the category of *res* also contains both common and proper nouns, although rarely, such as the names of gods and angels ... There are four principal classes of bodily material: water, earth, air, fire; Plato counted five such things.'

51 With caution Law concludes that Virgilius Maro Grammaticus was probably Irish or Spanish and active in the mid-seventh century (*GG*, 224 and 240 n. 1; cf. *BCLL* nos. 295–7).

with the traditional teaching on nouns: 'De re autem et corpore multi hessitant.'[52] Such 'doubts,' presumably arising from perceived insufficiencies in the authoritative texts, were confronted by the Insular grammarians with varying degrees of success. Malsachanus, likely an Irishman of the eighth century,[53] integrates angels into his treatment of nouns fairly smoothly, qualifying the usual teaching that a *res* is always signified by a common noun: 'cum re semper appellatiua, ut *pietas* (extra pauca nomina angelorum, quae propria sunt, ut *Michahel* et cetera).'[54] The *Ars Bernensis*, an eighth-century work whose author was likely Irish or Anglo-Saxon,[55] cites Isidore by name as the source of his teaching on common nouns before making significant Christian additions to Isidore's list of incorporeals: 'Incorporalia quare dicuntur? Quia carent corpore, ut *iustitia, dignitas, angelus, anima.*'[56]

Thus far, the grammarians who have included *deus* or *angelus* in their consideration of the referents of nouns have done little to distinguish these animate incorporeals from the time-honoured examples of inanimate incorporeals such as *pietas, iustitia, dignitas*. The Insular grammar known by its incipit as *Aggressus*, which is possibly the work of an Irish *peregrinus* in France during the seventh or eighth century,[57] cleverly formulates an efficient way to differentiate between abstract nouns and nouns that signify incorporeal living beings, within the scope of grammatical discourse. Recognizing that the twofold division into *corporalia* and *incorporalia* that was prevalent in the Donatus tradition could not readily accommodate such a distinction, the author of *Aggressus* instead followed the precedents set by Probus's *Instituta artium* and the *Ars maior* attributed to Asper, both of which include *animalia* and *inanimalia* among the classes into which

---

52 Virgilius Maro Grammaticus, *Epitomae*, ch. 5 (ed. Polara, *Virgilio Marone grammatico: Epitomi ed Epistole*, 44): 'Many people are in doubt concerning *corpus* and *res*.'

53 BCLL no. 306; Law, 'Malsachanus Reconsidered: A Fresh Look at a Hiberno-Latin Grammarian.'

54 Malsachanus, *Congregatio Salchani filii de uerbo* (ed. Löfstedt, *Der hibernolateinische Grammatiker Malsachanus*, 173.21–2): 'a thing [res] always has a common name, such as *dutifulness* (with the exception of a few names of angels, which are proper, such as *Michael* and so forth).'

55 BCLL no. 1237 indicates that this work is a possible Irish composition; Law (*ILG*, 74–5) finds an Anglo-Saxon origin, either in England or in a missionary centre on the continent, more likely, but cf. Löfstedt, *Der hibernolateinische Grammatiker Malsachanus*, 20–4.

56 *Ars Bernensis* (*GL* 8.67.13–14): 'Why are incorporeals so called? Because they lack a body, such as *justice, worthiness, angel*, and *soul*.'

57 BCLL no. 751; Law, *ILG*, 92–3; Munzi, *Multiplex latinitas*, 72.

they divide nouns.[58] *Aggressus* uses a fourfold division that accounts for both substance and animation: 'Omnia nomina aut sunt animalia, ut *homo*, *pecus*, aut sunt inanimalia, ut *arbor, lapis*, aut sunt incorporalia, ut *pietas*, *iustitia*, aut sunt locales et ante oculos humanos incorporalia, ut *anima* et *angelus*.'[59] Particularly noteworthy is the careful characterization of the animate incorporeals: first, they are 'localized' or 'circumscribed,' an attribute associated with souls and angels chiefly within the context of Stoicizing Christian discourse. Because souls and angels are not completely free from spatial constraints – that is, because they exist within a circumscribed space – they must be less incorporeal than God, who is the only truly incorporeal entity.[60] Second, the phrase 'incorporeal before human eyes' also suggests a limited sort of incorporeality: souls and angels are incorporeal *enough* to be invisible and therefore to appear incorporeal to human vision, although they are not incorporeal to the same extent as *pietas* and *iustitia* (and presumably *deus*, though the latter is not mentioned in *Aggressus*). The effect of the *Aggressus*-author's characterization of incorporeality is qualitatively different from that of Cledonius but has a similar effect, in that it challenges the idea, typical of Platonist thought, that corporeality and incorporeality are two sides of a coin, and it favours the Stoicizing Christian understanding of incorporeality and corporeality as relative rather than absolute attributes, as if they represented opposite ends of a spectrum. That Latin grammarians during this period continued to take seriously the authority of Stoicizing Christian views on incorporeality is corroborated by an unedited treatise *De uoce* copied into the late-eighth-century grammatical compilation in Berlin, Staatsbibliothek Preussischer Kulturbesitz, Diez. B Sant. 66. Pondering whether *uox* is corporeal or incorporeal, the author paraphrases the opinions of Pompeius and 'Sergius' before adding, 'Alii dicunt incorporalis est secundum grammaticos. Tractatores autem omnes res

---

58 Probus, *Instituta artium*, divides nouns into *animalia, inanimalia,* and *accidentia,* that is, adjectives (*GL* 4.51). Asper divides nouns into *animalia, inanimalia,* and *incorporalia,* but all his examples of *incorporalia* are inanimate, such as *perfidia, clementia, sapientia, prudentia* (*GL* 5.549). Munzi (*Multiplex latinitas*, 92) maintains that Asper was a direct source for the author of *Aggressus.*

59 *Aggressus*, ch. 10 (ed. Munzi, *Multiplex latinitas*, 77): 'All nouns are either animate, such as *person* and *beast*, or they are inanimate, such as *tree* and *stone*, or they are incorporeals, such as *dutifulness* and *justice*, or they are localized, and before human eyes they are incorporeal, such as *soul* and *angel*.' Munzi emends to *corporalia* where the MSS read *localis* or *locales*: I have retained the reading *locales* which, apart from its grammatical gender, is wholly sensible in context.

60 On this strand of patristic discourse, see chapter 4 above.

corporales esse absque sola trinitate.'[61] This brief statement is sufficient to identify the grammarian's sources, the *tractatores* or exegetes, as subscribers to a Stoicizing rather than a Platonizing concept of corporeality.

This concept of relative incorporeality was developed further by two other Insular grammarians, Tatwine and the author of the *Expossitio latinitatis* (also known as the *Anonymus ad Cuimnanum*), but before I discuss these two in detail, it is worthwhile to pause over a few idiosyncracies of a grammar related to these two, known by its incipit as *Quae sunt quae*, which is likely an Irish production of the late seventh or early eighth century.[62] In some ways, it shares the interests of the other Insular grammars; for example, it includes an improved version of the sensory criteria for corporeality: 'quid interest inter corpus et rem? Omne corpus potest res esse, ut dicitur *caelum, terra, mare*; quae uidentur aut audiuntur aut tanguntur aut gustantur corporalia sunt, sed non omnis res corpus est, illa utique quae nec auditur nec tangitur, sicut dicitur *iustitia, pietas* et reliqua.'[63] The attention to the relationship between *corpus* and *res* is familiar from the *Ars Ambrosiana*; the longer catalogue of sensory criteria may have been prompted by nothing more than the tendency toward encyclopedism – why name just two senses when you can name them all? – or it may have arisen from classroom discussion of how objects in nature, such as *caelum* or *uox* or *odor*, problematize the usual definition of corporeals as 'quae uidentur et tanguntur.' (It is more difficult to work out what the author meant when, in introducing the eight parts of speech, he

---

61 *De uoce* (facs. ed. Bischoff, *Sammelhandschrift Diez. B Sant. 66*, 344.28–345.1): 'Some say sound is incorporeal, following the grammarians. The exegetes, however, say that all things are corporeal except the Trinity.' This unedited treatise *De uoce* appears in the MS at p. 343 line 7–p. 347 line 5. On the dating of the hands in the MS, see of Bischoff's introduction, 21–3, and on the content and sources of *De uoce*, see ibid., 31. The presence of this passage is signaled by Bischoff and Löfstedt in their edition of the *Expossitio latinitatis* (CCSL 133D, 24). Gennadius of Marseilles was very likely among the *tractatores* in question: in his *De ecclesiasticis dogmatibus* he writes, 'Nihil incorporeum et inuisibile natura credendum nisi solum Deum, id est patrem et filium et spiritum sanctum' (ed. Turner, 'The *Liber ecclesiasticorum dogmatum*,' 91); for translation and discussion, see my chapter 6 below.

62 *BCLL* no. 332; Law, *ILG*, 85–7. On MSS of *Quae sunt quae* and its affiliation with other seemingly Irish grammars, see Munzi, *Multiplex latinitas*, 9–15.

63 *Quae sunt quae* 14 (ed. Munzi, *Multiplex latinitas*, 20): 'What is the difference between a body and a thing? Every body can be a thing, such as *sky, earth*, and *sea*; things which are seen or heard or touched or tasted are corporeal. But not every thing is a body: certainly, a thing which is neither heard nor touched, such as *justice* or *dutifulness*, et cetera, is not a body.'

asks, 'Quae sunt de his octo partibus corporalia aut incorporalia? Nomen, pronomen, uerbum, aduerbium, haec IIII incorporalia sunt; participium, coniunctio, praepositio, interiectio corporalia sunt.'[64] I have seen nothing in the other Insular grammars to parallel this assertion, and frankly I cannot grasp what the author might have meant, regardless of whether he was assessing corporeality based on the signifiers themselves or on the things they signify.)

A lexical puzzle arises in *Quae sunt quae* at the discussion of common nouns, where the author does not use the term *incorporalia* at all but instead substitutes *spiritalia*. Bodily things can be signified generally or specifically, he explains, but '*communiter* ad rem coniungis, scilicet spiritalem, quae corpus esse non potest, ut dicitur *iustitia, pietas, dignitas*: quia illa semper communia, idest appellatiua, dicuntur: quia omnia spiritalia nomina his similia numquam proprium, sed semper appellatiuum habent.'[65] There is nothing inherently unusual in using *spiritalia* as a synonym for *incorporalia*, but the substitution does not seem to carry with it any special connotations, for the list of *spiritalia* does not include *anima* or *angelus* or *deus*. The two aforementioned grammars related to *Quae sunt quae*, in contrast, apply the term *spiritalia* to the category of the animate incorporeals that they (like *Aggressus*) set apart from the abstract *pietas, iustitia* and the like. The two grammars in question are the *Expossitio latinitatis* and the *Ars Tatuini*, each of which merits close scrutiny for its complex response to the difficulties attending grammatical treatments of corporeality and incorporeal beings.

Substance and Sensory Perception in the *Expossitio latinitatis*

The exegetical grammar entitled *Expossitio latinitatis* (also known as the *Anonymus ad Cuimnanum*) is most likely the work of an Irish author of the mid-seventh to mid-eighth century; its addressee Cuimnanus has an

---

64 *Quae sunt quae* 11 (ed. Munzi, *Multiplex Latinitas*, 19): 'Among these eight parts of speech, which are corporeals and which are incorporeals? Noun, pronoun, verb, adverb: these four are incorporeals; participle, conjunction, preposition, and interjection are corporeal.'

65 *Quae sunt quae* 14 (ed. Munzi, *Multiplex Latinitas*, 20; the editorial punctuation has been changed): 'You associate the word *generally* [as in Donatus's formulation "signifies specifically or generally"] with a thing, particularly a spiritual thing, which cannot be a body, such as *justice, dutifulness*, or *worthiness*, for these are always spoken as common nouns – that is, appellatives – because all spiritual nouns like these never have a proper name but only a common noun.'

Irish name.[66] Of all the early Insular grammars, the *Expossitio latinitatis* preserves by far the most ambitious and encyclopedic teaching on corporeality. Under the rubrics *De nomine* and *De qualitate* the author interweaves grammatical theory (e.g., that a noun must have case, be corporeal or incorporeal, and be proper or common) with the related digressions typical of the Insular grammars: every *corpus* can also be a *res*, but not vice versa; a corporeal thing is seen and touched, and incorporeals can be neither seen nor touched.[67] The author is particularly sensitive to the lack of consensus concerning some of the *De nomine* material, and he declares that he is 'eager to reply to the naysayers and quibblers' concerning the accuracy of Donatus's teaching that a *res* cannot be named with a proper noun.[68] He grants that Donatus's teaching is mostly true, but that exceptions must be made, as per the example of Consentius (whom he does not cite by name) and Christian doctrine concerning angels:

> Et haec [*scil.* incorporalia], exceptis deorum nominibus, fere semper commoniter significantur; gentiles enim deos, propriis quos uocant, spiritales esse opinantur, ut Saturnus et Iouis et Vlcanus et reliqua. Cum Christianis autem Michael Gabrihel Vrihel Raphel et reliqua angelorum nomina, qui quamuis proprie in caelo non uocantur, nos tamen per officia eorum nobis cognita propriis hiis nominibus eos censemus in terra.[69]

This author's use of the term *spiritales* is markedly different from that of *Quae sunt quae*, for it is applied to animate beings alone, setting them apart from the inanimate incorporeals *iustitia*, *pietas*, *eloquentia* that the author has named just before this passage.

---

66 *BCLL* no. 331. On the identity of the 'Anonymus,' see Bischoff's introduction to the edition of the text (CCSL 133D, xx–xxiii); Law indicates that the text was written 'in an Irish milieu, if not in Ireland itself' and dates the text between the mid-seventh and mid-eighth centuries (*ILG*, 87–90).

67 *Expossitio latinitatis* 3.4–22 and 4.91–4 (ed. Bischoff and Löfstedt, CCSL 133D, 23 and 30).

68 *Expossitio latinitatis* 3.76–85 (ed. Bischoff and Löfstedt, CCSL 133D, 25).

69 *Expossitio latinitatis* 3.85–91 (ed. Bischoff and Löfstedt, CCSL 133D, 25): 'And these incorporeals, except for the names of gods, are almost always signified generally; the pagans, however, consider the gods, whom they call by proper names, to be spiritual beings, such as Saturn and Jupiter and Vulcan and so forth. Among the Christians there are the names Michael, Gabriel, Uriel, Raphael, and the rest of the names of the angels, and although they are not called by proper names in heaven, we on earth nevertheless characterize them by means of proper names according to their actions, which are manifest to us.'

The most innovative digressions in the *Expossitio latinitatis* are those that stray furthest outside the disciplinary boundaries of grammar itself, again attesting to this author's compulsively eclectic tendencies. Still under the rubric *De nomine*, he enumerates the four 'classes of bodies' (*genera corporum*), which are moist, dry, cold, and hot, and he proceeds to discuss how in different combinations these classes of bodies constitute the elemental substances of earth, water, air, and fire and determine the properties of each. He subdivides bodies into the heavenly and the earthly: the heavenly bodies include sun, moon, stars, 'clouds with their bones, i.e., the wind,' and birds, of which the natural philosophers (*phisici*) enumerate 153 kinds, while earthly bodies are further subdivided into the 153 kinds of land animals and 153 kinds of fish.[70] Eventually the author offers some supplementary information on incorporeals as well:

> De corpore dicto rerum sciamus gradus uel defferentias, quae plures corporibus sunt, quippe dum res corporale et incorporale in se continet. Auctores autem ferunt rerum defferentias esse sex, hoc est non uiuentia ut saxa, uiuentia ut arbores, mortalia ut pecora rationis experta, mortalia rationabilia ut homines, inmortalia rationabilia ut angeli; sextus gradus, id est Deus, nam et ipse in rebus dici potest, ut alibi dicitur: Periet omnis res, quae est sub caelo, praeter Trinitatem.[71]

In this passage the author of the *Expossitio latinitatis* restructures the fundamental relationship between corporeals and incorporeals in order to accommodate living beings that were understood to be incorporeal (or, within a Stoicizing framework, relatively less corporeal). His rendering of this new structure is certainly more elegant than the clumsy four-part division that appears in rather garbled form in *Aggressus*, but it is also less complete, as there is no room in this six-level hierarchy for the inanimate incorporeals *pietas*, *iustitia*, and so forth. The most remarkable feature of

---

70 *Expossitio latinitatis*, 3.23–42 (ed. Bischoff and Löfstedt, CCSL 133D, 23–4).

71 *Expossitio latinitatis*, 3.43–50 (ed. Bischoff and Löfstedt, CCSL 133D, 24): 'Concerning the aforementioned word *body*: we ought to be aware of the ranks and grades of the numerous things that pertain to bodies, especially when a thing contains both the corporeal and the incorporeal within itself. Our sources maintain that there are six grades of things: that is, non-living things such as stones, living things such as trees, mortal things such as beasts lacking in reason, mortal rational things such as human beings, immortal rational things such as angels, and a sixth grade, namely God, for even he can be considered among "things," as it says elsewhere: "Everything that is under heaven will pass away, except for the Trinity."'

this passage is the way in which the author makes plain something that the grammars of Cledonius and Isidore only hinted at: setting Platonism aside, the everyday experience of the natural world suggests that corporeality and incorporeality are not two sides of a coin but opposite ends of a spectrum, and that something can be more corporeal or more incorporeal without being fully in either category (as in the case of Cledonius's *caelum, sol, aer*). Although several of the Insular elementary grammars discussed thus far have juxtaposed *corpus* and *res* or *corporalia* and *incorporalia* in a less rigidly dichotomous relationship (e.g., 'omne corpus res potest esse') than was characteristic of the fourth- and fifth-century grammars, the *Expossitio latinitatis* is the first text to claim outright that entities in the natural world contain different proportions of *corporale* and *incorporale* within them, ranging between the wholly corporeal *saxa* to the wholly incorporeal *Deus*. The only extant Insular grammar that matches the *Expossitio latinitatis* in its clear and straightforward restructuring of the relationship between corporeality and incorporeality is the *Ars* of the early eighth-century Anglo-Saxon bishop Tatwine.

A Spectrum Model of Corporeality in the *Ars Tatuini*

Tatwine begins his discussion of nouns with the definition that is characteristic of the Donatus tradition: a noun signifies *corpus aut rem*. But when Tatwine explicates this basic definition, he abandons the rigid conception of *corporalia* and *incorporalia* as two sides of the same coin and replaces it with a continuum, in which bodies and incorporeal things lie at the extremes and moderately corporeal things, which are only partly accessible to the senses, occupy the intermediate positions.

> Item omne quod nomine significatur corpus est aut corporale, uel incorporale: corpus est quicquid tangi et uideri potest, ut *terra*; corporale quod tangi et non uideri, ut *uentus*, uel uideri et non tangi, ut *caelum*; incorporale uero quod nec tangi nec uideri ualet, ut *sapientia*.[72]

Tatwine conforms to the structure of his source texts where he is able to, and so he downplays his radical restructuring of the relationship between

---

72 *Ars Tatuini* 1.4.25–9 (ed. De Marco, CCSL 133, 5): 'Everything that is signified by a noun is either a body or a bodily thing or an incorporeal thing. A body is whatever can be touched and seen, such as *earth*. A bodily thing is that which can be touched and not seen, such as *wind*, or seen and not touched, such as *sky*. But an incorporeal thing is that which can be neither seen nor touched, such as *wisdom*.'

corporeal and incorporeal when he shifts his focus from the external referents (*omne quod nomine significatur*) back to the nouns themselves. With
respect to general and specific signification, the nouns that name *corpora*
are no different from the nouns that name *corporalia*, so Tatwine reverts to
a binary opposition, with *corpora* and *corporalia* on one side and *incorpo-*
ralia on the other: 'Quicquid autem corporale est uel corpus proprie siue
communiter significatur ... incorporale uero, ut *pietas, iustitia, eloquentia* –
et hoc exceptis deorum nominibus – fere semper communiter significatur.'[73]
As long as Tatwine continues to focus on signifiers rather than what is signified, he structures his remarks around this binary; he reassures the reader,
for instance, that when they run across any 'signifier of corporeality or
incorporeality' (corporalitatis significantiam uel incorporalitatis), proper
or common, inflected according to case, then it must be a noun.[74] He manages to reintroduce the spectrum model when he addresses the classification of common nouns, although he collapses two categories (this time
called *corpus* and *corporalitas*) into one, lest an additional category force
him to add one to the traditional number of twenty-seven items in the list
of types of common nouns: 'Sunt autem alia [*scil.* appellatiua] uel corpus
uel corporalitatem significantia, ut *terra, humus, ensis, caelum, uentus.*
Alia incorporalitatem, ut *pietas, iustitia, dignitas, doctrina*: haec enim officia spiritus sunt, non corporis.'[75]

This last remark sheds light on the rationale behind Tatwine's restructuring of the relationship between corporeals and incorporeals. Sensory
criteria alone are not sufficient to capture the important difference between *uentus* and *pietas*; the incorporeals that are roughly equivalent to
the modern classification of abstract nouns are not only imperceptible to
the senses but they occupy a different realm, namely that of the *spiritus*
rather than that of the natural world at large. Tatwine is also sensitive
to the distinction between these *officia spiritus* and the *spiritus* 'spiritual
creatures' themselves, and accordingly he proposes a subdivision of the
incorporalia to account for this distinction: 'Corpus quidem est quicquid
tangi aut uideri potest, incorporale uero quod nec tangi nec uideri ualet,

---

73 *Ars Tatuini* 1.4.29–36 (ed. De Marco, CCSL 133, 5–6): 'Whatever is a bodily thing or a
    body is signified specifically or generally ... but an incorporeal thing, such as *dutiful-*
    ness, justice, or *eloquence* – here setting aside the names of gods – is almost always signi-
    fied generally.'
74 *Ars Tatuini* 1.5.37–40 (ed. De Marco, CCSL 133, 6).
75 *Ars Tatuini* 1.13.91–6 (ed. De Marco, CCSL 133, 7): 'There are some common nouns
    that signify either a body or corporeality, such as *earth, soil, sword, sky,* and *wind*; there
    are others that signify incorporeality, such as *dutifulness, justice, worthiness, teaching*:
    for these are the activities of a spiritual being, not of a body.'

sed spiritale per se ipsum naturaliter est ut Deus et omnis caelestis creatura animarumque substantia et quicquid ab his in officio agitur spiritaliter.'[76] He has set aside the intermediate class of *corporalia* for the moment; here it is the *incorporalia*, which are wholly inaccessible to the senses, that need to be subdivided. Interestingly, Tatwine does not separate them into living and non-living; rather, he distinguishes the ordinary incorporeals (including accidents) from the *spiritalia*, which 'naturally exist in and of themselves.'[77]

For Tatwine, therefore, it is untrue that 'a noun is never found such that it is neither corporeal nor incorporeal,' as Pompeius firmly asserted. For Tatwine, if something is somewhat perceptible, then it is somewhat bodily, but not fully a body. His common-sensical continuum model of corporeality is better able than the dichotomist model to accommodate problematic objects observed in nature, such as *aer*, which is incorporeal according to Cledonius but corporeal according to the *Ars Ambrosiana*; Tatwine's model also permits a distinction between *caelum* and *terra*, both of which meet Isidore's criteria for corporeality, even though they are not equally perceptible. Despite its practical utility, very few grammars retained or developed the spectrum model of incorporeality after the late eighth century, and I have found only one Anglo-Saxon author who applied such a model to a problem in theological or philosophical discourse: this was Candidus Wizo, whose letter concerning Christ's bodily vision will be discussed below in chapter 6. Instead, subsequent developments in Carolingian and eventually in Anglo-Saxon education demanded that grammars harmonize with an understanding of essence and epistemology more firmly rooted in the Platonist tradition, and hence that they return

---

76 *Ars Tatuini* 1.5.40–4 (ed. De Marco, CCSL 133, 6): 'A body is indeed whatever can be touched or seen, and an incorporeal thing is that which can be neither touched nor seen, but a spiritual being exists naturally in its own right, such as God and every celestial creature and the substance of souls and whatever is effected spiritually by these things in their capacity.'

77 The way Tatwine makes this distinction shows that, despite his opinion that souls and angels are incorporeal, he is not working within a fully Platonic philosophical framework, within which the incorporeal Forms of *pietas, doctrina*, and so forth would 'naturally exist in and of themselves' just as much as souls and angels do. Instead, Tatwine's conception of *pietas* and *doctrina* is aligned with that of the author of the *Expossitio latinitatis*, who in his discussion of incorporeals asserts that *pietas, iustitia, dignitas* are dependent on the corporeal beings that possess these qualities: see 4.94–5 (ed. Bischoff and Löfstedt, CCSL 133D, 30): 'Haec tamen a corporalibus oriri dicuntur, ut *pio, iusto, digno*' (These incorporeal things are said to originate in corporeal things, such as *dutiful man, just man*, and *worthy man*).

to the conception of corporeality and incorporeality as opposite sides of the same coin. Because the advances made in Carolingian grammar exerted little influence upon Anglo-Saxon thought prior to the later tenth century, at this juncture it is necessary only to say a few words about how and why the Insular grammarians' adventurous exploration of the meaning of corporeality was eclipsed by the Carolingians' more rigid approach.

Philosophical Influences on Carolingian and Later Anglo-Saxon Grammars

Insular authors continued to generate grammar textbooks of various genres during the ninth century, but they did so within continental milieux and with no discernible influence on their contemporaries in Anglo-Saxon England. Moreover, by the mid-ninth century, grammarians in these Carolingian circles were producing more parsing grammars and fewer of the elementary and exegetical grammars that had dominated during the previous two centuries, and the more advanced grammar textbooks generated by the Carolingians began to absorb new methods and new content from the discipline of dialectic as well as from Priscian.[78]

Although Priscian's *Institutiones grammaticae* had not been wholly absent from early Insular libraries, it was rare, and before the late eighth century Priscian was known chiefly through his shorter *Institutio de nomine et uerbo*.[79] Alcuin of York is credited with the revival of Priscian's *Institutiones grammaticae* on the continent in the late eighth century, and its influence was soon discernible in numerous grammars generated in Carolingian circles;[80] among the areas of discourse particularly transformed by the turn toward Priscian was the discussion of *corporalia* and *incorporalia*. Like the definition of the noun that was repeated by Donatus and his later fourth-century contemporaries, the definition put forth by Priscian in the late fifth or early sixth century had its roots in Stoic dialectic, and in fact its shared origins are reflected in a shared structure.[81] In the *Institutiones*,

---

78 Law, 'The Study of Grammar,' 92–9; Gibson, 'Milestones in the Study of Priscian, circa 800–circa 1200,' 17–28.
79 Law, 'The Study of Grammar,' 90–1; Lapidge, *Library*, 326–7.
80 Law, 'The Study of Grammar,' 95–6.
81 On Priscian's career as *grammaticus*, see Kaster, *Guardians of Language*, 346–8; on Priscian's definition of the noun, and the importance of the noun's signification of quality rather than substance, see Luhtala, *Grammar and Philosophy in Late Antiquity*, 84–95.

under the rubric *De nomine*, Priscian teaches, 'Nomen est pars orationis, quae unicuique subiectorum corporum seu rerum communem uel propriam qualitatem distribuit ... Et communem quidem corporum qualitatem demonstrat, ut *homo*, propriam uero, ut *Virgilius*, rerum autem communem, ut *disciplina, ars*, proprium, ut *arithmetica Nichomachi, grammatica Aristarchi*.'[82] Priscian's formulation of the definition of *nomen* did not by any means eclipse the definition used in the Donatus tradition, and in fact many of the ninth-century grammars employ both definitions side by side. Yet Priscian's definition served as a corrective to some of the careless approaches to the distinction between the noun and its external referent that had arisen in some of the Donatus commentaries and Insular grammars: he distinguishes the noun from its referent more sharply, and creates more conceptual distance between them, by enunciating that the noun's function is to 'attribute quality' to an entity that is either corporeal or incorporeal. Moreover, although many of the Carolingian grammars that draw on Priscian retain sensory criteria for assessing corporeality, Priscian's own discussion of *corpus* and *res* does not foreground such criteria and consequently does not encourage digressions about *anima* and *caelum* that have more to do with natural philosophy than with the discipline of grammar. The whole of Priscian's *Institutiones*, in fact, is more attentive to the rhetorical and philosophical implications of grammar, and more precise in its terminology, than the grammars of the Donatus tradition tended to be, and as such, the study of Priscian demanded that readers cultivate a greater degree of philosophical precision in their approach to grammar as well.

In addition to the influence of Priscian, other pressures compelled the Carolingians to bring greater linguistic and philosophical precision to their grammatical texts. Both ideally and in practice, the Carolingian study of grammar served as a stepping-stone to the rest of the liberal arts and ultimately to the pursuits of scriptural exegesis, theology, and philosophy. As an ideal, this attitude was several centuries old, and it had been put

---

82 Priscian, *Institutiones grammaticae* 2.22 (*GL* 2.56–7): 'A noun is a part of speech which attributes a general or specific quality to each one of the bodies or things subjected to it ... In fact, a noun communicates the general quality of bodies, such as *man*, or specific quality, such as *Virgilius*, or the general quality of (non-bodily) things, such as *discipline* and *art*, or the specific quality of things, such as *Nichomachean arithmetic* or *the grammar of Aristarchus*.' Priscian reiterates these four combinations of quality and substance shortly thereafter (*GL* 2.59), illustrating them with the nouns *homo, Terentius, uirtus*, and *Pudicitia* (i.e., the personification of the virtue of Modesty).

into practice by scholars of earlier centuries, particularly by Irish biblical exegetes,[83] but the ideal was re-energized by Charlemagne's educational reforms of the late eighth century,[84] and the subsequent decades produced copious textual evidence of the profound impact that fundamental grammatical concepts had on philosophical and theological debates, on topics that varied from etymology and translation theory to predestination and the existence of *nihil*.[85] It was not only the need to prepare future theologians and philosophers that influenced the way Carolingian grammarians handled the problem of corporeality, but a more specific need to prepare these students for a particular sort of theological and philosophical discourse, whose content was indebted to the Platonizing Christian tradition and whose method was indebted to Aristotelian dialectic, mediated by Boethius and by Themistius's *De decem categoriis*.[86] The Platonist understanding of incorporeality – specifically, of the existence and perception of Forms and of other incorporeals – was indispensable to this mode of discourse. A slightly relativizing concept of incorporeality, of the sort proposed by Stoicizing Christian thinkers, might have had limited applicability within the framework of Carolingian theological disputation, but it is hard to see how the full spectrum model of corporeality could be made compatible with a mode of disputation that regularly invoked the stark binary opposition between the incorporeal and the corporeal, with all of their respective ontological and epistemological implications. If the Carolingian grammarians took seriously their duty to prepare future Carolingian theologians, then they were obliged to instil in their youngest students the Platonist understanding of corporeality and incorporeality as two sides of the same coin, never blending and never overlapping.

Though it is useful to recognize the dominant forces that shaped Carolingian treatments of *corporalia* and *incorporalia*, it is not the case that from the late eighth century every Carolingian grammarian adopted a wholly Platonist view of substance or, under the influence of Priscian, resisted the temptation to digress about the substance of the things named by nouns.

---

83 See, for instance, Poli, 'La *beatitudine* fra esegesi e grammatica nell'Irlanda altomedioevale.'
84 Holtz ('Les innovations théoriques,' 134–5) discusses the implications of the *Admonitio generalis* of 789 for Carolingian grammatical instruction and writing.
85 See Contreni, 'Carolingian Biblical Studies'; Colish, 'Carolingian Debates over *Nihil* and *Tenebrae*'; Evans, 'The Grammar of Predestination in the Ninth Century'; Holtz, 'L'enseignement de la grammaire au temps de Charles le Chauve'; Kavanagh, 'The Philosophical Importance of Grammar for Eriugena.'
86 Marenbon, *From the Circle of Alcuin*, 12–29; see also chapter 4 above.

In fact, Erchanbert, a continental grammarian active between the 820s and 840s,[87] adapts Tatwine's spectrum model of corporeality:

Diffinitio corporis substantialiter hoc modo fit: corpus est quicquid tangi uel uideri potest. Sed hoc tribus intellegitur modis: est enim corpus quod tam uideri et tangi potest, ut *terra*; est aliud quid non uidetur et tangi potest, ut *uentus*; quodlibet autem uisui patet sed a mortalibus tangi minime ualet, ut *caelum*.[88]

These types of *corpora* are then contrasted with *res*, which can never be apprehended by bodily eyes ('corporalibus oculis nequaquam cerni potest').[89] It is noteworthy that Erchanbert esteemed Tatwine's treatment of substance and sensory perception enough to borrow from it when composing his own Donatus commentary; however, in accord with the Carolingian preference for a Platonizing theory of substance, Erchanbert has imposed a new taxonomic structure on the material he has borrowed from Tatwine. Instead of Tatwine's arrangement of *corpus, corporalis,* and *incorporalis* across a continuum, Erchanbert has simply divided *corpus* into three groups and opposed them all to *res.* Reading further in Erchanbert's treatment of nouns, we learn that he has been influenced by Priscian's *Institutiones,* for he adduces *arithmetica Nicomachi* and *grammatica Aristarchi* as examples of proper nouns that signify *res.* Yet, lest we conclude that the influences of Platonism and Priscian led to uniformity of thought among the Carolingian grammarians, Erchânbert's concluding remark hints at some dissent over the incorporeality of angels, perhaps a reference to ongoing conflicts between Platonizing and Stoicizing views:

---

87 Clausen dates Erchanbert's grammar later than that of pseudo-Clemens (written in the 820s) and before that of Hrabanus Maurus (written 842 x 856): see his edition of Erchanbert's *Tractatus super Donatum,* viii–xix. On the identity of Erchanbert, who is no longer thought to be the bishop of Freising by that name, see ibid., iv–vii; and Law, 'Erchanbert and the Interpolator: A Christian *Ars minor* at Freising (Clm 6414),' 238 n. 3.

88 Erchanbert, *Tractatus super Donatum* (ed. Clausen, 'Erchanberti Frisingensis Tractatus super Donatum,' 7): 'The definition of a body, in accord with its substance, is rendered in this way: a body is whatever can be touched or seen. But this is understood in three ways: for a body is that which can be both seen and touched, such as *earth*; a body is alternatively that which is not seen and can be touched, such as *wind*; or whatever is revealed to the sense of sight but cannot be touched by mortals, such as *heaven*.'

89 Erchanbert, *Tractatus super Donatum* (ed. Clausen, 'Erchanberti Frisingensis Tractatus super Donatum,' 8).

'Alii dicunt rem esse propriam angelorum siue deorum nomina; sed illud non adeo firmum.'[90]

Louis Holtz has argued that faithfulness to their *auctoritates* stifled the creativity of the Carolingian grammarians, whose capacity for innovation has in turn been defended by Vivien Law, on the grounds that they produced far more diverse texts than did their seventh- and eighth-century predecessors.[91] With respect to Carolingian grammatical treatments of corporeality, both of these assessments are accurate. These texts abandon the Insular grammarians' speculative and digressive approach and promote the Platonist concept of incorporeality, so there are few doctrinal idiosyncracies among the different grammarians' treatments of this topic. However, they travel different paths to the same destination. Smaragdus is preoccupied with the all-encompassing nature of the assertion that every named thing is corporeal or incorporeal, and he even accompanies his treatment of *corpus* and *res* with some elegiac couplets on that subject.[92] Murethach, like some of his Insular predecessors, explicates Donatus's treatment of nouns by paying meticulous attention to his diction and occasionally criticizing Donatus for failing to distinguish sufficiently between nouns and their referents.[93] With the help of terminology borrowed from dialectic, Sedulius Scottus enumerates five substances and accidents that qualify as *res*.[94] Remigius of Auxerre quarrels with the philosophers over the corporeality of *lux, calor,* and *uox* in one commentary, and in another he provides 'careful analysis of how *risus* and *uisus* could be said to be the names of invisible things.'[95]

To say more about these intriguing texts would, unfortunately, lead us too far away from the topic of Anglo-Saxon thought, as many of these

---

90 Erchanbert, *Tractatus super Donatum* (ed. Clausen, 'Erchanberti Frisingensis Tractatus super Donatum,' 8): 'Some people say that the names of angels or gods are proper nouns signifying incorporeals, but that is not entirely agreed upon.'

91 Holtz, 'Les innovations théoriques,' 137 and 142–3; cf. Law, 'The Study of Grammar,' 88.

92 Smaragdus, *Liber in partibus Donati* 1.7, 2 Praef., and 2.4–6 (ed. Löfstedt, Holtz, and Kibre, CCCM 68, at 10, 12, 14–15).

93 Murethach, *In Donati artem maiorem* 2, lines 3–10 (ed. Holtz, CCCM 40, 53), lines 9–21 (ibid., 56), and lines 38–42 (ibid., 61).

94 Sedulius Scottus, *In Donati artem minorem* (ed. Löfstedt, CCCM 40C, 8.28–35).

95 Remigius pursues the problem of light, heat, and sound in an encyclopedic digression under the rubric *De uoce* in his *In artem maiorem Donati commentum* (GL 8.219–20). (GL provides only a partial edition; for further bibliography see Law, 'The Study of Grammar,' 109.) The discussion of *risus* and *uisus* occurs in a yet unedited passage of Remigius's commentary on Priscian's *Institutio de nomine*; I quote Law's description of the passage in question ('The Study of Grammar,' 106 and n. 47).

Carolingian texts did not reach England, and those that did arrived with the Benedictine reform movement of the later tenth century, accompanying a revival of Priscian studies. Instead, it remains to discuss two groups of texts that served as companions to the grammars in early medieval classrooms: the Latin *enigmata* and riddle-dialogues. Not only did the *enigmata* often circulate in manuscripts with the grammars, but they also share the grammarians' preoccupation with problems pertaining to corporeality and sensory perception, and as such they can help us bridge the gap between abstract learning and practical application: the riddles show that the way grammarians presented corporeality and incorporeality had a demonstrable influence on the way grammarians and students perceived the substance of the things around them.

Playful and Practical Applications of the Grammarians' Theories of Corporeality in the Anglo-Latin *enigmata*

Through the combined efforts of several Anglo-Saxon scholars of the late seventh and early eighth centuries, Latin riddles became a fixture of elementary education in England. This development originated with the *Epistola ad Acircium*, a composite work written by Aldhelm of Malmesbury for King Aldfrith of Northumbria between 685 and 705. One section of the *Epistola*, entitled *De metris*, teaches the reader about the structure of the dactylic hexameter, and another section, called *De pedum regulis*, provides descriptions and illustrations of different types of quantitative metrical feet.[96] Between *De metris* and *De pedum regulis*, Aldhelm inserted 100 original verse *enigmata* to illustrate the principles of his metrical treatises; in setting the number of *enigmata* at 100 Aldhelm was imitating the precedent set by a group of 100 *enigmata*, each consisting of three hexameters, attributed to the otherwise unknown fourth- or fifth-century poet Symposius.[97]

Within a few years, Aldhelm's *enigmata* were inspiring imitation by other authors of grammatical and metrical treatises. Boniface, an eighth-century missionary to Germany and author of the exceedingly conservative *Ars grammatica* discussed above, may also have authored a brief metrical treatise and certainly composed twenty verse *enigmata*, ten on

---

96 On the *De metris* and *De pedum regulis*, see Neil Wright's appendix on Aldhelm's prose writings on metrics, in Aldhelm, *The Poetic Works*, trans. Lapidge and Rosier, 183–90.

97 See Lapidge and Rosier's commentary in their translation of Aldhelm, *The Poetic Works*, 61–3.

the virtues and ten on the vices.[98] Tatwine, author of the innovative *Ars Tatuini* discussed above, composed a series of forty *enigmata* on diverse topics. The two manuscripts that preserve Tatwine's riddles also contain a series of sixty *enigmata* whose author called himself Eusebius: this is thought to be the same Hwætberht, abbot of Monkwearmouth-Jarrow from 716 until around the middle of the eighth century, to whom Bede 'gave the name "Eusebius" because of his love and concern for holiness.'[99] The sixty *enigmata* of Eusebius are thought to have been produced as a complement to the forty of Tatwine, such that the two groups together form a corpus of 100 riddles, after the models of Symposius and Aldhelm; in fact, Eusebius's riddles immediately follow those of Tatwine in their two extant manuscript witnesses, both of which also contain the riddles of Symposius and Aldhelm.[100]

The intimate connection between the *enigmata* and the culture of the elementary classroom is manifest in the transmission history of the *enigmata* as well as their content. Several manuscripts copied or used in tenth- and eleventh-century England preserve one or more series of riddles alongside theoretical treatises on metre or among other verse texts used in the early stages of literary study.[101] As for the early Anglo-Saxon period, it is probable that the *enigmata* were already circulating with grammars and metrical treatises in the early eighth century and were thus transmitted to the continent in elementary classbooks brought by the Anglo-Saxon missionaries, because continental manuscript evidence and library inventories

---

98   Ibid., 67 and 245–6 n. 30. The *Ars metrica* (or *Caesurae uersuum*) attributed to Boniface is edited by Löfstedt, CCSL 133B, 109–13; on its authorship, see ibid., 105.

99   Bede renders this praise of Hwætberht in his *In Samuhelem prophetam allegorica expositio* (CPL 1346); for the few known details of his career, see Lapidge, 'Hwætberht,' in the *Blackwell Encyclopaedia of Anglo-Saxon England*, 245–6.

100 See Lapidge and Rosier's commentary in their translation of Aldhelm, *The Poetic Works*, 66–7.

101 In the massive mid-eleventh-century compendium of school texts in Cambridge, UL, Gg. 5. 35, the riddles of Eusebius, Tatwine, Boniface, Symposius, and Aldhelm, plus another nineteen anonymous riddles, appear alongside the *Versus de alphabeto*, the *Disticha Catonis*, Prosper of Aquitaine's *Epigrammata*, and several Latin biblical epics with glosses (Gneuss, *Handlist* no. 12; see further Rigg and Wieland, 'A Canterbury Classbook of the Mid-Eleventh Century'). See also London, BL, Royal 12. C. xxiii (Ker, *Catalogue* no. 263; Gneuss, *Handlist* no. 478); BL, Royal 15. A. xvi (Gneuss, *Handlist* no. 489); and Oxford, Bodleian Library, Rawlinson C. 697 (Gneuss, *Handlist* no. 661). Glorie's *conspectus codicum* (CCSL 133, 152–62) is useful in forming a general understanding of how the different riddle collections, Anglo-Latin and otherwise, were transmitted together.

document the frequent inclusion of Anglo-Latin riddles in codices containing technical grammars and metrical treatises.[102] Moreover, references to the culture of the classroom and to the trappings of literacy pervade the *enigmata* of Aldhelm, Tatwine, and Eusebius, which include riddles about parchment, a quill pen, a lectern, the letter *X*, an ink-horn, a book-wallet, the alphabet, writing-tablets, and a book-cupboard.[103] Eusebius's riddle about wax focuses on writing-tablets and mentions candles only as an afterthought.[104] Tatwine composed several riddles that nobody but students, current and former, could appreciate: one is about the four types of scriptural exegesis (*De historia et sensu et morali et allegoria*),[105] and in another riddle, the 'four sisters' (*bis binae ... sorores*) who speak in the first person are the four prepositions that can take an object in either the accusative or the ablative case (*in, sub, super,* and *subter*). Only a very sharp student would have solved the latter riddle on the basis of the grammatical puns by which the 'four sisters' describe themselves:

Emerita gemina sortis sub lege tenemur:
Nam tollenti nos stabiles seruire necesse est,
Causanti contra cursus comitamur eundo.[106]

---

102 Aldhelm's *De metris* and *Enigmata* were copied together in a late-eighth-century book 'written most likely in a German centre with Anglo-Saxon traditions,' which now survives only in fragmentary form, in several pages in St Gall, Stiftsbibliothek 1394: Lapidge (*Library*, 158, item 25) quotes Lowe's opinion (*Codices latini antiquiores* 7.982) on the date and origin of the MS. Several early German library inventories in Becker, *Catalogi bibliothecarum antiqui*, attest to the transmission of riddles alongside grammars and metrical treatises. A St Gall library inventory of the ninth century mentions one volume (item 22.391) that holds Aldhelm's *De metris, Enigmata,* and *De pedum regulis,* and another (22.393) that preserves Aldhelm's *Enigmata* with Bede's *De arte metrica* and the riddles of Symposius. A Reichenau inventory with a *terminus ante quem* of 842 mentions one volume (ibid., item 10.2) that contains, among other things, 'libri grammaticae artis Donati, et de metrica arte Bedae presbyteri, et libellus de centum metris [*scil.* Servius, *Centimetrum*]. Et liber de aenigmatibus Symphosii.' Additionally, Becker's items 37.417 and 38.73 describe a book that may survive as Vatican City, BAV, Pal. lat. 1753, containing the *Lorsch Riddles* (on which see below).
103 Parchment: Tatwine 5, Eusebius 32. Quill pen: Aldhelm 59, Tatwine 6, Eusebius 35, *Lorsch Riddles* 9. Lectern: Tatwine 10. The letter *X*, ink-horn, book-wallet: Eusebius 14, 30, 33. Alphabet, writing-tablets, and book-cupboard: Aldhelm 30, 32, and 89. Ink: *Lorsch Riddles* 12.
104 Eusebius, *Enigma* 31 (ed. Glorie, CCSL 133, 241).
105 Tatwine, *Enigma* 3 (ed. Glorie, CCSL 133, 170).
106 Tatwine, *Enigma* 16.1–3 (ed. Glorie, CCSL 133, 183): 'We are bound by a double law, old and venerable, that governs our allotted duties: for when we stand still, we must be

Tatwine uses the participle *tollens* (from *tollo, tollere, sustuli, sublatum*) to refer to the case 'that takes away,' rather than the verb *aufero, auferre, abstuli, ablatus* from which the adjective *ablatiuus* is derived; he uses the participle *causans*, 'that which accuses,' to refer to the *casus accusatiuus*. Yet beneath Tatwine's word-play is the elementary grammatical principle that these four prepositions take objects in the ablative when they signify a stationary position but in the accusative when they signify the direction of motion – a teaching that Tatwine treats under the rubric *De praepositione* of his grammatical treatise.[107]

I stress the intimate connection between the Anglo-Latin *enigmata* and the elementary classroom because the *enigmata* also betray their authors' intense interest in the ideas of corporeality and incorporeality, and I would argue that this interest arises directly from the influence of the Latin grammars on their perceptions of the world around them, both natural and man-made. In their riddles, Tatwine and Eusebius playfully invoke the relationship between corporeality and sensory perceptibility to create the paradoxes upon which the 'enigmatic' character of the poems depends. It is significant, moreover, that this fascination with the substance of things is most pronounced in the riddles of Tatwine, a highly innovative contributor to Insular grammatical discourse, and in the riddles of Eusebius, who was clearly familiar with Tatwine's writings. In contrast, Aldhelm, who wrote on metrics but not on grammar, and Boniface, whose grammar is highly conservative and devotes no special attention to *corpus* and *res* or *corporalia* and *incorporalia*, both wrote riddles that are correspondingly uninterested in the application of these categories to the real world. The Anglo-Latin riddles corroborate my theory that the foregrounding of corporeality and incorporeality in the very earliest stages of elementary education did exercise a significant influence on conceptions of real-world substances, and they also show that for those students who used the *enigmata* while studying metre and literature, their cultivation of a non-Augustinian notion of incorporeality (and hence of the human soul) was

---

subject to the one who takes away, but while making our travels we accompany the one who accuses.' In line 3 Glorie emends *causanti* (the reading of both MSS) to *causantis*, which improves neither the metre nor the syntax and disrupts the parallel structure between this and the preceding line.

107 *Ars Tatuini* 7.4 (ed. De Marco, CCSL 133, 86): 'Praepositiones utriusque casus, accusatiui scilicet et ablatiui, hae quattuor commones sunt: *in sub super subter*' (These four are the prepositions construed with both cases, namely of the accusative and the ablative: *in, under, above, beneath*).

264 Anglo-Saxon Psychologies

likely to be extended past the time when they graduated from the study of basic grammar.

Substance and Sensory Perception in Tatwine's Riddles

In his first riddle, *De philosophia*, Tatwine crafts a paradox by elaborating on the well-known perceptible attributes of *Philosophia* personified, and then undercutting that part of the characterization by asserting the incorporeality of philosophy as a discipline. The speaker of the riddle is a winged being who can penetrate every corner of heaven, hell, and earth (lines 1–2), and her merits outshine those things that most delight the senses of sight, hearing, and taste:

> Sum Salomone sagacior et uelocior euro,
> Clarior et Phoebi radiis, pretiosior auro,
> Suauior omnigena certe modulaminis arte,
> Dulcior et fauo gustantum in faucibus aeso.[108]

Yet this being of remarkable mobility and beauty is also incorporeal, which she reveals without using the word *incorporalis*: 'Nulla manus poterit nec me contingere uisus.'[109] Here the speaker echoes Tatwine's own grammatical definition of the incorporeal ('incorporale uero quod nec tangi nec uideri ualet')[110] while also cleverly contradicting what she has just said about herself in the previous four lines.

This definition of the incorporeal is not Tatwine's alone but is common to many grammars of the Donatus tradition. Nonetheless, Tatwine's more idiosyncratic understanding of the relationship between the corporeal and the incorporeal has left its mark on the last of his forty *enigmata*, whose structure is similar to that of *De philosophia*. In the first four lines of the poem, the speaker reveals not only that he can be perceived by human eyes

---

108 Tatwine, *Enigma* 1.4–7 (ed. Glorie, CCSL 133, 168): 'I am wiser than Solomon and swifter than the wind, brighter too than the rays of the sun, more precious than gold, more delightful indeed than all kinds of music, and sweeter than honey tasted in the mouths of those who savour it.' By cleverly characterizing herself with only comparative adjectives in these four lines (and a present active participle in line 9), the speaker is able to keep hidden her feminine grammatical gender and the feminine natural gender of her personification.

109 Tatwine, *Enigma* 1.8 (ed. Glorie, CCSL 133, 168): 'No hand nor gaze will be able to grasp me.'

110 *Ars Tatuini* 1.5 (quoted above).

but that he can somehow be seen in two places at once, both indoors and stretching throughout the sky:

> Summa poli spatians dum lustro cacumina laetus,
> Dulcibus allecti dapibus sub culmine curuo
> Intus ludentem sub eodem temporis ortu
> Cernere me tremulo possunt in culmine caeli. [111]

The speaker, though he can be seen, cannot be touched: in the concluding line, he says, 'Corporis absens plausu quid sum pandite sophi!'[112] In characterizing himself as visible but 'free from contact with the body,' the speaker is paraphrasing Tatwine's definition of the *corporale*, that which is neither fully incorporeal nor fully a body: 'corporale quod tangi et non uideri, ut *uentus*, uel uideri et non tangi, ut *caelum*.'[113] The solution to the riddle turns out to be a sunbeam. Although *radius solis* is not on Tatwine's own list of partly corporeal things, Cledonius includes 'sun' among the problematic, partly perceptible incorporeals: 'incorporalia sunt quae non tanguntur et uidentur, ut *caelum, sol, aer*.'[114]

Grades of Being and Corporeality in Eusebius's Riddles

Eusebius knew Tatwine's *enigmata*, but this is no guarantee that he also knew Tatwine's grammar, for there is no evidence that Tatwine's writings circulated together. Nonetheless, the contents of Eusebius's *enigmata* suggest that his own understanding of substance and sensory perception had been shaped by the more innovative strain of Insular grammatical discourse, not that of Boniface but rather that of Tatwine, the *Expossitio latinitatis*, and

---

111 Tatwine, *Enigma* 40.1–4 (ed. Glorie, CCSL 133, 207; editorial punctuation has been changed): 'When I stretch out happily and cross the highest summits of the sky, people who are lured beneath the bowed roof by tasty banquets can perceive me playing indoors, and at the same point in time, in the shimmering height of heaven.' Where Glorie prints *allectis*, the MSS read *allecti* and *at lectis* respectively; I have followed Ebert, who prints *adlecti* ('Die Räthselpoesie der Angelsachsen,' 42).

112 Tatwine, *Enigma* 40.5 (ed. Glorie, CCSL 133, 207): 'O wise men, explain what I am, who stay far away from contact with the body!'

113 *Ars Tatuini* 1.4 (quoted above).

114 Cledonius, *Ars grammatica* (quoted above). The solution-title for Tatwine's riddle is given in the MSS as *De radiis solis* in the plural, but the speaker of the riddle is singular, and throughout his other *enigmata* Tatwine is careful to use plural forms where the solution to the riddle is plural.

Quae sunt quae.[115] Seven of the first ten of Eusebius's *enigmata* describe entities that the Insular grammarians regularly name as paradigmatic examples of the classifications of nouns based on substance: *Deus, angelus, homo* (this riddle emphasizes the incorporeality of the human *anima*), *caelum, terra, uentus et ignis,* and *sol.* In three of these riddles, Eusebius focuses not on the nature of the substance but on a specific feature of the cosmos; in other words, *caelum, terra,* and *sol* are not sky, soil, and sunbeams but Heaven, Earth, and the Sun.[116] In the remaining four, however, Eusebius follows Tatwine's example and uses the concepts of incorporeality and partial corporeality as the foundation for each *enigma,* often paraphrasing the grammarians' teachings on substance and sensory perception.

Eusebius's riddle *De uento et igne* is the one most obviously inspired by the grammars. Speaking together, wind and fire explain that each of them has a distinct behaviour, and that one originates in the sky and the other 'in the depths.' They also say, 'Vnus contingi patitur nec forte uideri; / Sed prope aspicitur pulcher nec tangitur alter.'[117] Given the very brief array of semi-corporeals typically listed by the grammarians, a reader might be able to deduce the solution *uentus* without difficulty. *Ignis* is not classified as a semi-corporeal in any grammars or other riddles known to me, but *caelum* and *sol,* the two typical representatives of things that are seen but not touched, are eliminated from consideration because one of the two solutions has to 'abide in the depths.'[118]

In his riddles *De Deo* (1), *De angelo* (2), and *De homine* (4), Eusebius describes three different incorporeal entities. Several Insular grammars, including the *Ars Tatuini,* call attention to the category of animate incorporeals, including gods or God, angels, and the human soul (*anima*), but only the

---

115 See Law, 'The Study of Latin Grammar in Eighth-Century Southumbria,' esp. 66–71, on the distinct groups of texts used by Boniface and Tatwine respectively.

116 Eusebius, *Enigmata* 5 (*De caelo*), 6 (*De terra*), and 10 (*De sole*) (ed. Glorie, CCSL 133, 215–16 and 220).

117 Eusebius, *Enigma* 8.1–2 (ed. Glorie, CCSL 133, 218): 'One of us submits to being touched but, as it happens, not to being seen; the other appears beautiful up close but is not touched.' Wind and fire are paired again in the pseudo-Bedan *Collectanea,* §§80–1, concerning the three victories of wind (whose invisibility is again foregrounded) and the three victories of fire (ed. Lapidge et al., *Collectanea Pseudo-Bedae,* 130).

118 It is intriguing that the authors of grammars and riddles regularly claimed that things such as *sol, radius solis,* and *ignis* could be seen but not touched, even though the heat emanating from them can be felt by the body. Possibly it was understood that the sunbeam or the fire itself was not tangible even though its heat was perceptible; why the same distinction was not also made between the wind and its chill is unclear.

Expossitio latinitatis proposes a spectrum of beings ranging from the most corporeal to the most incorporeal, with God, then angels, and then human beings (rather than souls) occupying the more incorporeal end of the spectrum.[119] Eusebius's riddles parallel this spectrum in the *Expossitio latinitatis* in meaningful ways that go beyond the simple collocation of *Deus, angelus,* and *homo.* First of all, Eusebius characterizes God not as one of several animate incorporeals but as the most incorporeal of all beings, because God alone is uncircumscribed and non-localized. The paradox of Eusebius's first *enigma,* in fact, is founded upon the juxtaposition of God's non-locality with spatial representations of God's sublimity and his abode among the humble.

> Cum sim infra cunctos, sublimior omnibus adsto,
> Nullus adestque locus in quo circumdatus essem;
> Alta domus mea, cum sit sedes semper in imis.[120]

If Eusebius had been working within a strictly Platonizing understanding of incorporeality, he could have ascribed to all of the incorporeals the same qualities of indivisibility and non-spatial distribution, regardless of the fact that souls and angels are circumscribed. Instead, in a manner attuned to the spectrum model of the *Expossitio latinitatis* as well as the Stoicizing Christian strain of discourse on substance, Eusebius reserves non-locality for God alone, and he finds other ways of communicating the incorporeality of angels and human souls, which, though comparatively incorporeal, cannot share in God's complete incorporeality. In his second riddle, Eusebius's depiction of the angel is again indebted to the grammarians, and not only because the angel's incorporeality is associated with his invisibility. The angel identifies himself as a messenger whose labours keep him in constant motion, although his 'footsteps' are imperceptible to human sight:

> Nuntius emissus discurro more ministri;
> Non labor ac tedium, nulla molestia cursum
> Tardat, et intrantis uestigia nulla uidentur.[121]

---

119 *Expossitio latinitatis* 3.43–50 (ed. Bischoff and Löfstedt, CCSL 133D, 24).
120 Eusebius, *Enigma* 1.1–3 (ed. Glorie, CCSL 133, 211): 'Although I am beneath all people, I stand elevated above everything, and there is no space in which I could be surrounded; my house is high, but my seat is always among the lowest.'
121 Eusebius, *Enigma* 2.1–3 (ed. Glorie, CCSL 133, 212): 'Sent out as a messenger, I run about in the manner of a servant. No work, boredom, or annoyance slows my journey, and no traces of me are seen when I enter.'

Isidore's *Etymologiae* underlies Eusebius's invocation of the etymological link between *angelus* (Greek *angelos*, 'messenger') and *nuntius*, as well as his characterization of the angel as a creature in constant motion.[122] Eusebius's juxtaposition of the angel's unceasing labours with his invisibility also has an Isidorian parallel,[123] but the confluence of these ideas is equally reminiscent of the *Expossitio latinitatis*, which explains that angels themselves are incorporeal and therefore invisible, though humans assign to them proper names 'on the basis of their labours, which are manifest to us' (per officia eorum nobis cognita).[124] The third-most incorporeal being on the spectrum is the human being. It is important to clarify that in the *Expossitio latinitatis* third position on the spectrum is assigned not only because of the soul's lesser incorporeality; rather, the whole human being is placed in that position because he is composed of both *anima* and flesh. Similarly, Eusebius's fourth riddle treats the mixed substance of the human being rather than the soul alone:

> Haec mea materiae substantia bina creata est.
> Sed grauis una uidetur, quae tamen ipsa peribit –
> Cuius et ipse fugax defectum gessit helidrus – ;
> Tenuior est alia, et que semper fine carebit.[125]

The paradox here relies on the claim that of the two substances that constitute the speaker, the one that 'seems weighty' is impermanent and corruptible, while the 'thinner' or 'more subtle' substance will endure. Although the mixed substance of the whole human is what both Eusebius and the

---

122 Isidore, *Etym.* 7.5.1, on *angeli* and *nuntii*; at 7.5.3 Isidore explains that angels do not actually have wings, but painters portray angels with wings 'in order to depict rapid movement in all their undertakings' (ut celerem eorum in cuncta discursum significent).
123 Isidore, *Etym.* 7.5.2.
124 *Expossitio latinitatis* 3.85–91 (ed. Bischoff and Löfstedt, CCSL 133D, 25).
125 Eusebius, *Enigma* 4 (ed. Glorie, CCSL 133, 214): 'This, my substance, was created twofold with respect to its material. One material appears weighty, but nevertheless it will itself perish; the serpent, itself fleeting, brought about its weakness. The other is more delicate, and this one will always be free from death.' Where I retain MS *helidrus* in line 3, Glorie has emended to *chelidrus*, though adding initial c- in emulation of classical spelling disrupts the metre. Glorie's emended version of line 4 is not metrically viable, so I have followed the much simpler emendation proposed by Ebert, 'Die Räthselpoesie der Angelsachsen,' 43. The twofold nature of man is a common enough topic in early Christian and medieval literature that no single source need be posited, although Isidore, *Etym.* 11.1.4–6 is likely among Eusebius's proximate inspirations.

Expossitio latinitatis focus on, it is worth noting that Eusebius's diction in this riddle further reinforces the impression that he understood incorporeality to be relative, not absolute. Both soul and flesh are called *materia*, whereas a strictly Platonic opposition of the corporeal and the incorporeal would classify the flesh as *materia* and the soul as *forma*; moreover, the substance of the soul is not said to be incorporeal but only less corporeal or 'more subtle' than the substance of the flesh.

Substance, Soul, and Mind in Latin and OE Riddle-Dialogues

Notably, though they devote a great deal of attention to the soul (*anima*), the Insular grammarians say nothing about the mind (*mens, animus*): not a single one of the grammatical texts cited thus far discusses the mind's substance, its disposition within the body, or its relationship to the soul. As the grammars demonstrate, opinions on substance and epistemology that were inculcated in the early medieval classroom were by no means uniformly Platonizing. It is not surprising, therefore, that cardiocentric psychology is well represented in the Anglo-Latin verse riddles as well as in another genre associated with the elementary classroom, namely the prose riddle-dialogues. In the absence of a rigidly Platonizing approach to psychology, there is little in the eclectic and Stoicizing notions of substance to challenge or conflict with cardiocentrism.

The riddle-dialogues do not present themselves as doctrinally cohesive works, so it is difficult to offer any systematic evaluation of their contents, other than to observe certain thematic preoccupations. For instance, there is noticeable overlap between the grammars and the riddle-dialogues concerning things that resist simple categorization as corporeals and incorporeals, such as wind. In the pseudo-Bedan *Collectanea* the wind's ubiquity and immense powers of destruction are paradoxically juxtaposed with its inaccessibility to the senses: 'Dic mihi quae est illa res quae coelum totamque terram repleuit, siluas et surculos confringit, omniaque fundamenta concutit: sed nec oculis uideri, aut manibus tangi potest?'[126] In another Latin riddle-dialogue (printed by Suchier as Text K) the question is posed, 'Ventus

---

126 Pseudo-Bede, *Collectanea*, §79 (ed. Lapidge et al., *Collectanea Pseudo-Bedae*, 130): 'Tell me, what is that thing which fills the sky and the whole earth, destroys forests and seedlings, and smashes all foundations, but cannot be seen with the eyes or touched with the hands?' (trans. ibid., 131). See also §81 (ibid., 130–1), on the three victories of the wind, among which the first is 'inflat et non uidetur' (it blows and is not seen).

quit est?' and the response reads, 'Creatura inuisibilis ... et in alio loco uenti anime sanctorum sunt.'[127] In an untitled riddle-dialogue in a ninth-century German manuscript, the two opening questions are both clearly inspired by the grammarians' method of evaluating substance, although the answer to the first of the two is surprising: 'Quis est quod tangitur et non uidetur? Anima hominis. Quid est quod uidetur et non tangitur? Caelum.'[128] It is not unexpected that a text of this period might attribute to the human soul an incomplete sort of incorporeality, but I know of no other text that actually claims that the soul is tangible, which is tantamount to classifying it among the semi-corporeals such as *radius solis* and *aer*. Like the soul, the mind is invisible, but whether because of its substance or its hidden residence within the body is left unsaid: in the *Disputatio Adriani Augusti et Epicteti philosophi*, Adrian asks, 'Quid est quod homo non potest uidere in mundo?' and Epictetus replies, 'Alterius animum.'[129]

Another preoccupation of the riddle-dialogues is the bodily seat of the mind and of the soul, although their special attention to this topic did not produce any definitive opinions. Three of the dialogues in the *Altercatio Hadriani*-group printed by Daly and Suchier favour cardiocentrism: the interlocutor asks 'Cor quid est?' and the reply is 'Origo cogitationum et finis';[130] the interlocutor asks 'Quid est oculus?' and the reply is 'Nunctius cordis.'[131] In contrast, in the *Disputatio Adriani* the question is posed, 'Vbi

---

127 Text K, §25 (ed. Daly and Suchier, *Altercatio Hadriani Augusti et Epicteti philosophi*, 119): 'What is wind? An invisible creature ... and according to another text, winds are the souls of saints.' Cf. Ps 103:3. Text K is printed alongside the *Altercatio Hadriani*, *Disputatio Adriani*, and *Disputatio Pippini*, and another riddle-dialogue designated as Text G, and all are related to varying degrees: on the relationship among the texts, and on the ninth-century continental MSS of Texts K and G see ibid., 70–84, 115–18, and 125.

128 *Interrogationes* 1–2 (ed. Wilmanns, 'Ein Fragebüchlein aus dem neunten Jahrhundert,' 167): 'What is it that is touched and not seen? The human soul. What is it that is seen and not touched? The sky.' The text is preserved in a composite manuscript, Munich, BSB, Clm 19417, which Wilmanns identifies as a ninth-century codex with a Tegernsee provenance.

129 *Disputatio Adriani Augusti et Epicteti philosophi*, §7 (ed. Daly and Suchier, *Altercatio Hadriani*, 113): '*Adrian*: What is it that a person cannot see in this world? *Epictetus*: The mind of another person.' A nearly identical passage appears at §15 of the related text *Altercatio Hadriani et Epicteti* (ibid., 104).

130 Text G, §2 (ed. Daly and Suchier, *Altercatio Hadriani*, 126): '*Question*: What is the heart? *Answer*: The source and object of thoughts.' See also Text K, §37 (ibid., 120).

131 Text M, §51 (ed. Daly and Suchier, *Altercatio Hadriani*, 132): 'What is the eye? The messenger of the heart.' Text M is a very late witness to this riddle tradition, surviving in Munich, BSB, Clm 4424, dated 1532.

est memoria?' to which the reply is 'In cerebro';[132] and the pseudo-Bedan *Collectanea* includes this exchange: 'Vbi est memoria? In sensu. Vbi est sensus? In cerebro. Cui non datur sensus, non datur et cerebrum.'[133] Alcuin, too, leans toward cephalocentrism in his *Disputatio Pippini cum Albino*: when Pippin asks 'Quid est cerebrum?' Albinus replies 'Seruator memoriae'; and subsequently, when Pippin asks what the heart is, Albinus does not attribute to it any mental faculties but says only that it is the 'receptaculum uitae.'[134] These questions and answers do not necessarily contradict one another; it depends on whether their authors and readers understood all of the mental faculties and the life-force to be united in a single *anima* or not. Additionally, some of the riddle-dialogues suggest that their authors were resigned to being unable to make a definitive pronouncement on the location of the soul, since several texts include a version of this exchange, which I quote from the pseudo-Bedan *Collectanea*: 'Dic mihi ubi sit anima hominis, quando dormiunt homines? In tribus locis: aut in corde, aut in sanguine, aut in cerebro.'[135]

The Latin riddle-dialogues cited above were not all known to the Anglo-Saxons. Alcuin was familiar with the *Altercatio Hadriani*, and the aforementioned sections of the pseudo-Bedan *Collectanea* were likely compiled by an Insular author.[136] As for the rest, we know only that a selection of texts related to the riddle-dialogues quoted above was known to the Anglo-Saxons, specifically to the authors of the OE prose riddle-dialogues *Adrian and Ritheus* and *Solomon and Saturn*.[137] In fact, it is thanks to the influence of the Latin riddle-dialogues that their OE counterparts provide

132 *Disputatio Adriani Augusti et Epicteti philosophi*, §15 (as numbered in MS A) (ed. Daly and Suchier, *Altercatio Hadriani*, 113): '*Adrian*: Where is memory? *Epictetus*: In the brain.'
133 Pseudo-Bede, *Collectanea*, §§ 112–14 (ed. Lapidge et al., *Collectanea Pseudo-Bedae*, 134): 'Where is the memory? In the perception. Where is the perception? In the brain. Whoever is not given perception is also not given a brain' (trans. ibid., 135).
134 Alcuin, *Disputatio Pippini cum Albino*, §§23 and 35 (ed. Daly and Suchier, *Altercatio Hadriani*, 138–9): '*Pippin*: What is the brain? *Albinus*: The preserver of memory ...' *Pippin*: What is the heart? *Albinus*: The container of life.'
135 Pseudo-Bede, *Collectanea*, §2 (ed. Lapidge et al., *Collectanea Pseudo-Bedae*, 122): 'Tell me, where is the soul of man when men are asleep? In three places: either in the heart or in the blood or in the brain' (trans. ibid., 123). Similar passages occur at Text K, §64 and Text G, §20 (ed. Daly and Suchier, *Altercatio Hadriani*, 121 and 127).
136 Daly and Suchier, *Altercatio Hadriani*, 75–6 and 79–80; Lapidge, 'The Origin of the *Collectanea*,' 3–8; BCLL no. 1257 (among works of possible Celtic origins).
137 Cross and Hill, *The* Prose Solomon and Saturn *and* Adrian and Ritheus, examine the complicated relationships among the OE and Latin dialogues (7–13) and provide sources and analogues for the OE passages wherever possible.

272   Anglo-Saxon Psychologies

something extremely rare in the whole corpus of Anglo-Saxon literature: attestations of the idea that the mind might reside in the head.

The prose *Solomon and Saturn* includes a translation of the Latin passage that proposes three possible locations for the soul: 'Saga me hwar rested þas mannes sawul þone se lychaman slepð. Ic þe secge, on þrim stowum heo byð; on þam bragene, oððe on þere heortan, oððe on þam blode.'[138] Of course, whether the OE author and his audience thought that the brain was involved in mental activity depends on whether they regarded the *sawol* as a unitary soul or not. The OE dialogue *Adrian and Ritheus* localizes the *mod* rather than the *sawol* in the head, but in the context of a saying whose meaning is not wholly clear to me or to the most recent editors of the text: 'Saga me hwær byð mannes mod. Ic þe secge, on þam heafde and gæð ut þurh þone muð.'[139] This seems to mean that the contents of a man's mind are put on display in the form of speech, an interpretation that is lent credence by analogues in the vernacular proverb tradition, such as the twelfth of the *Durham Proverbs*: 'Eall on muðe þæt on mode.'[140] These hints of cephalocentric psychology certainly represent exceptions to the rule. Across the corpora of OE and Anglo-Latin literature, there are signs of familiarity with the structural tripartition of the brain and its role in sensory processing, but there are no other intimations that the head housed the transcendent *sawol* or all of the mental and emotional faculties that constituted the *mod*.[141]

Cardiocentrism and the Hydraulic Model in the Anglo-Latin *enigmata*

As mentioned above, *animus* and *mens* were excluded from Insular discussions of *incorporalia* in the grammars and from the playful treatment of incorporeality and partial corporeality in the Anglo-Latin riddles. The simplest explanation is that at least some of the Insular grammarians and enigmatists, though moderately well educated, still thought of the mind as part of the body, specifically as residing in or identical to the heart, rather

---

138 Prose *Solomon and Saturn*, §41 (ed. Cross and Hill, *The* Prose Solomon and Saturn, 31): 'Tell me where a person's soul remains when the body sleeps. I tell you, it will be in three places: in the brain, or in the heart, or in the blood.'
139 *Adrian and Ritheus* §23 (ed. Cross and Hill, *The* Prose Solomon and Saturn, 38): 'Tell me where a person's mind is. I tell you, it is in the head and it goes out through the mouth.' See also Cross and Hill's comments (ibid., 147).
140 *Durham Proverbs* 12 (ed. Arngart, 'The Durham Proverbs,' 292): 'All that is in the mind is in the mouth.'
141 Lockett, 'Anglo-Saxon Knowledge of the Functions of the Brain.'

than as part of the incorporeal soul. I would like to adduce just a few examples of cardiocentrism and hydraulic-model narratives in the Anglo-
Latin riddles prefatory to a closer examination of the second *Lorsch
Riddle*, which provides striking evidence for a community of moderately
learned readers with a shared understanding of the activities, the corporeality, and the mortality of the mind-in-the-heart.

There is little to separate the Anglo-Saxon enigmatists' depictions of
the mind-in-the-heart from those of OE poetry. Boniface's riddles on
the virtues and vices, for instance, correlate psychological distress with
cardiocentric heat. The personification of Anger (*Iracundia*) describes
herself as 'burning,' and the psychological damage that she inflicts targets
the victim's abdomen and heart: 'Ignea sum feruens, turbo precordia bel-
lis, / Rixarum iactans iugiter per corda uenenum.'[142] The personification
of Drunkenness (*Ebrietas*) also insinuates immoderate desires (*luxuria*)
into the midsection of the body, bearing 'dark firebrands' which mark as
damned the souls that she victimizes:

Dulcem semper amat me sic luxoria matrem.
Illius in gremio iugiter nutrimina porto,
Crudeles animas urens cum torribus atris,
Edita stelligeri ut non scandant culmina caeli.[143]

Tatwine's riddle *De caritate* makes more sophisticated use of the hydraulic
model, building a paradox upon the correlation of cardiocentric heat with
both intense love and intense suffering:

Haut tristis gemino sub nexu uincula gesto.
Vincta resoluo ligata iterumque soluta ligabo.
Est mirum dictu: ardent quod mea uiscera flammis,
Nemo tamen sentit fera uinctus dampna cremandi;
Sed mulcent ea plus uinctum quam dulcia mella.[144]

---

142 Boniface, *Enigma de uitiis* 2, lines 1–2 (ed. Glorie, CCSL 133, 313): 'I am fiery and
  burning; I disturb the chest with strife, spreading the poison of contention perpetually
  throughout the heart.'
143 Boniface, *Enigma de uitiis* 6, lines 9–12 (ed. Glorie, CCSL 133, 331): 'So dissipation
  always adores me, its sweet mother; I bring fodder for dissipation continually into the
  belly, burning cruel souls with dark firebrands, so that they might not ascend the lofty
  heights of starry heaven.'
144 Tatwine, *Enigma* 14 (ed. Glorie, CCSL 133, 181): 'I carry my chains under a double
  restraint but without sadness: I loosen tight bonds and again I bind those that are

274 Anglo-Saxon Psychologies

Precisely as in the OE narratives discussed in chapter 2, the experience of intense suffering entails both cardiocentric heat and constriction, while the joyful experience of intense love entails only the cardiocentric heat associated with various forms of passion. The paradox of love is that love itself is a burning passion (line 3), but the one who is 'bound' by the love of another feels only pleasure from its burning; one who is unloved, on the other hand, is also said to be 'bound,' but he is bound by the cardiocentric burning and constriction brought on by suffering in the absence of love. Adding to the paradox is the speaker's claim that it both frees and binds. Love can free the sufferer from cardiocentric constriction (*uincta resoluo ligata*), but love can also bind what is now loosed (*soluta ligabo*): in context, the speaker may be referring to the capacity of love to bind together two people who were formerly alone, or equally to the notion that unrequited love can induce sorrow and sensations of cardiocentric constriction in one whose breast was formerly free from suffering. If a complex *enigma* such as this was to be understood by Tatwine's readers, they must have shared an understanding of the relationship between emotional states and cardiocentric symptoms that is characteristic of the hydraulic model.

Two Anglo-Latin riddles have as their solution the mind-in-the-heart. The first of these is by Eusebius; one manuscript copy bears the solution-title *De corde*, and *De animo* is written in the margin of the other copy. Eusebius does not explore the mechanisms of cardiocentric psychology but invokes the biblical topos of the mind-in-the-heart as a secluded dwelling for Christ.

Vnus inest homo, qui tantum in me clausa uidebit,
Quique suis me non oculis conspexerat umquam.
Non sum magna domus, cum peruenit accola magnus,
Nulla est ianua, cum tamen omnes me simul implent.[145]

---

loosened. It is marvellous to say that my insides blaze with flames; nevertheless, no one who is restrained feels the savage injuries of burning, but they delight the one who is restrained more than sweet honey.'

145 Eusebius, *Enigma* 25 (ed. Glorie, CCSL 133, 235): 'One person dwells within me, who alone will see the secrets hidden in me, and who never looked at me with his own eyes. I am not a great dwelling, although the inhabitant who arrives is great: there is no door, although everyone fills me all at once.' Where Glorie prints *Quisque*, I prefer the reading of MS L, which is *Quique*, and I have changed the editorial punctuation accordingly. Glorie's *apparatus fontium* indicates that line 3 is a reminiscence of Is. 54:15, which prophesies the coming of Christ: 'Ecce, accola ueniet qui non erat mecum;

This riddle reminds us of Eusebius's fondness for using sensory perception as the basis for the paradoxes in his riddles – Christ has seen all that the heart contains although he has never seen the heart itself – but note that the invisibility of the mind-in-the-heart can be truly paradoxical only if the mind is *not* incorporeal, as its invisibility leads the reader to suppose. Eusebius's riddle suggests that his audience shared an understanding of cardiocentric psychology as a biblical topos. It does not necessarily corroborate the claim that they also understood cardiocentrism to be a physiological reality, but such corroboration can be found in the second of the two Anglo-Latin mind-in-the-heart *enigmata*, namely the second *Lorsch Riddle*.

The Mind-in-the-Heart in the Second *Lorsch Riddle*

In some ways, the *enigmata* represent a gray area between literary fiction and discourse that aims to be accurate. Certainly there is great scope for figurative language in a riddle, but if a riddle is to be solvable, then it ought to communicate some of its subject's characteristics plainly enough to be identifiable. The solution of the second riddle in the series known as the *Lorsch Riddles* (*Aenigmata Laureshamensia*) has been disputed, but undoubtedly it is *cor*, the heart; it portrays the heart as a bodily organ responsible for mental activity, and it does so not as part of a narrative of individual psychological events, but in the form of a precise and descriptive, if nonetheless enigmatic, discourse of how the human mind operates and is constituted.

Vatican City, BAV, Pal. lat. 1753 exemplifies the habit, noted above, of including riddles among compilations used in the instruction of grammar and metrics. Its contents include grammars by Marius Victorinus and Sergius, the *Cento Probae*, the *De orthographia* of Quintus Papirius, Aldhelm's *De metris* and *De pedum regulis* including his *Enigmata*, the *enigmata* of Symposius, and the treatise *Caesurae uersuum* attributed to Boniface.[146] Near the end of the codex is a series of twelve Latin *enigmata*, known as the *Lorsch Riddles* because they survive only in this manuscript, which was

---

aduena quondam tuus adiungetur tibi' (Behold, an inhabitant shall come, who was not with me, he that was a stranger to thee before, shall be joined to thee).

146 Reifferscheid, *Bibliotheca patrum latinorum Italica*, 1.307–10; and Dümmler, 'Lorscher Rätsel,' 261–2. As several scholars have observed, the contents of Pal. lat. 1753 bear a remarkable resemblance to a compendium of grammatical and metrical materials listed in the Lorsch library inventories of the tenth century: see Dümmler, 'Lorscher Rätsel,' 261; and Becker, *Catalogi bibliothecarum antiqui*, items 37.417 and 38.73.

compiled in the monastic scriptorium at Lorsch around the turn of the ninth century, in a milieu strongly influenced by the Anglo-Saxon missionaries of the eighth century.[147] Between the fourth and fifth riddles, the series is interrupted by a brief excerpt from Isidore's *Etymologiae* and a 32-line verse epitaph for Dombercht, an Anglo-Saxon priest who was a student of Boniface and later a teacher at Lorsch.[148] Moreover, several of the *Lorsch Riddles* are copied in a format that is highly unusual for Latin hexameters, with no line breaks separating individual verses; among Latin verse manuscripts of the eighth and ninth centuries, the nearest parallels are found in manuscripts of English origin or provenance.[149] Based on these Anglo-Saxon connections, as well as on parallels of style and content identified by Patrizia Lendinara, the riddles are believed to be the work of multiple Anglo-Saxon authors, probably composed and compiled in England.[150]

In the manuscript, none of the twelve *Lorsch Riddles* has a solution-title. The solution of the second riddle, in particular, has long been debated. When Dümmler first edited the *Lorsch Riddles* in 1879, he proposed that the solution to the second riddle was 'die menschliche Seele,' but he acknowledged that this solution was difficult to reconcile with the riddle's concluding lines.[151] The following year Paris persuasively argued that the riddle was about 'le coeur (et non l'âme),' based on the biblical allusion in the first line of the poem; Dümmler, convinced by Paris's argument, provided the solution-title '[De corde]' and included the relevant biblical verse (Sg 5:2) in his *apparatus fontium* when he re-edited the *Lorsch Riddles* for MGH two years later.[152] It is unclear to me why twentieth-century scholars have reverted to Dümmler's earlier solution: Minst proposes 'die menschliche Seele,' Glorie's edition supplies the solution-title '*De anima*,'

147 Bischoff, *Die Abtei Lorsch im Spiegel ihrer Handschriften*, points out that Anglo-Saxon minuscule exercised a formative influence over the development of a distinctive Lorsch script style around the turn of the ninth century (31–2 and 35); plate 7 shows fol. 81v where an Anglo-Saxon hand has corrected the text of Aldhelm's *De metris* in minuscule script. Vivien Law hypothesizes that the lost MS consulted by this Anglo-Saxon corrector was Boniface's own copy of the *De metris*, brought to the continent from southern England (Law, *GG*, 95–6 and 117 n. 31).

148 Dombercht's epitaph is edited by Dümmler, MGH PLAC 1.19–20.

149 On the early Anglo-Saxon habit of copying Latin verse without line breaks, see O'Brien O'Keeffe, *Visible Song*, 26. I am grateful to the staff of the Vatican Films Library at St Louis University for the opportunity to view the film of Pal. lat. 1753.

150 Lendinara, 'Gli *Aenigmata Laureshamensia*'; see also Dümmler, 'Lorscher Rätsel,' 262; and Ebert, 'Zu den Lorscher Rätseln,' 200.

151 Dümmler, 'Lorscher Rätsel,' 262.

152 Paris, review of *ZdA* 22, 139; *Aenigmata anglica* 2 (ed. Dümmler, MGH PLAC 1.21).

Bieler claims that the solution is 'anima,' and Lendinara argues that the entity portrayed in the riddle is the mens uel animus as Alcuin conceived of it in his treatise De ratione animae.[153] The second Lorsch Riddle and Alcuin's treatise on the soul undeniably share distinctive diction and imagery, but the entity that describes itself in this riddle possesses characteristics that are antithetical to the nature of the immortal anima, as discussed below. De corde is the most accurate solution proposed to date, although I propose that the best answer to this riddle can only be named in OE and not in Latin: it is the breostsefa, the mind-in-the-heart.

For ease of reference, I give here the full Latin text of the second Lorsch Riddle along with my translation, followed by more specific commentary. The text follows Dümmler's second edition[154] except where noted otherwise.

Dum domus ipsa mea dormit, uigilare suesco,
Atque sub angusto tenear cum carcere semper,
Liber ad aetheream transcendo frequentius aulam,
[4] Alta supernorum scrutans secreta polorum.

When my house is itself asleep, I am accustomed to be awake, and although I may be ever kept under a narrow prison, I often freely climb through the heavenly court, examining the heights of heaven and the mysteries of the skies.

Omnia quin potius perlustro creata sub orbe,
Rura peragro salumque peto, tunc litora linquens
Finibus inmensum fundum rimabor abyssi.

But indeed, I traverse all of creation under the sun, I pass through fields and seek the open sea; then, leaving the shores, I will swim the immense depth of the ocean to its limits.

[8] Horriferae[155] minime pertranseo claustra gehennae,
Ignea perpetue[156] subeo sed tartara Ditis.

I never penetrate the prisons of horrifying Gehenna, but I pass under eternally fiery Tartarus, ruled by Dis.

---

153   Minst, 'Die Lorscher Rätsel,' 104; Glorie, Collectiones aenigmatum, CCSL 133, 348; Bieler, 'Some Remarks on the Aenigmata Laureshamensia,' 12; Lendinara, 'Gli Aenigmata Laureshamensia,' 75.
154   Aenigmata anglica 2 (ed. Dümmler, MGH PLAC 1.21).
155   I emend to horriferae, which is metrically preferable to MS horrifera; either is syntactically viable.
156   I follow Bieler's construal of MS perpetuae as the adverb perpetue, although Bieler does not change the spelling of the word when he prints his emended version of these lines: see 'Some Remarks on the Aenigmata Laureshamensia,' 12–13.

Haec modico peragro speleo, si[157] claudar in aruis,
Mortifero concussa ruant ni ergastula casu.

If I am enclosed in my tiny cave during this earthly life, I pass through these places, unless my prison-house should collapse, struck by the occasion of death.

[12] Sin uero propria dire de sede repellor,
Mortis in occasu extimplo fio pulpa putrescens:
Sic sunt fata mea diuersa a patre creata.

But if I am fearfully propelled from my proper seat, on the occasion of death I promptly become rotting flesh: thus are my different fates ordained by the Father.

The first line of the poem reveals the speaker's identity by echoing Song of Songs 5:2, 'Ego dormio et cor meum uigilat' (I sleep, and my heart watcheth). This echo prompted Paris to favour 'heart' rather than 'soul' as the riddle's solution. I suspect that the reason why several scholars have rejected Paris's astute suggestion is that the poem goes on to characterize the heart in a fashion that is irreconcilable with Platonist and cephalocentric psychologies, both of which the modern reader likely expects to find here.

Lines 2–4 establish the central paradox of this riddle: the speaker is spatially confined yet capable of travelling through the heavens. As he elaborates in lines 5–7, his itinerary also takes him over land and through the sea, to every corner of the universe. Here the speaker closely resembles the *anima* or *animus* of Alcuin's *De ratione animae*, as Lendinara has observed, and he also resembles the *hyge* or *modsefa* that flies forth from the *hreþerloca* in *The Seafarer*.[158] What the speaker says in lines 8–9, however, points toward the *breostsefa* and away from the unitary *anima*. The two lines appear to be direct contradictions of one another: the speaker never goes to Gehenna (i.e., hell), but he does go to Tartarus (which also means hell). If the speaker is the mind-in-the-heart, it is easy to resolve this paradox, for the mind-in-the-heart travels to hell figuratively by thinking about hell, but because the mind-in-the-heart is a part of the transient body rather than the immortal soul, it will not actually travel to hell when soul and body part at death.

In lines 10–11, the speaker refines the first paradox: he retains the capacity for vast travels only as long as he is confined within his narrow cave. Should

---

157 I do not accept Bieler's emendation of MS *si* to *sic* (ibid., 13).
158 Lendinara, 'Gli *Aenigmata Laureshamensia*,' 74–6; *Sea* 58–9.

his prison-house disintegrate – should the body perish and decay – he loses the ability to escape from it by thinking about distant places. And when death takes away the speaker's ability to travel, he becomes nothing more than putrescent flesh, as he reveals in line 13: this line provides the strongest evidence that the speaker of the riddle cannot be the incorporeal, immortal *anima* that Alcuin describes in the *De ratione animae*.[159] The speaker of the second *Lorsch Riddle* must be the heart, not as the present-day reader conceives of it, but as the organ responsible for thought, which the OE poets called *breostsefa*, and which, when the *sawol* and the *feorh* departed from the body, ceased to think and began to decay with the rest of the flesh.

The second *Lorsch Riddle* therefore complements the many representations of cardiocentric psychology in OE narrative, because it offers a rare example of Anglo-Latin descriptive discourse focused on the nature of the mind-in-the-heart, and it emanates from a moderately learned environment. The riddle is transmitted with elementary school-texts, and its author was clearly familiar with the Latin *enigmata* of Aldhelm; it also displays verbal parallels with Lactantius's *De opificio Dei*, Vergil's *Aeneid*, Caelius Sedulius's *Carmen paschale*, and Bede's *Vita metrica sancti Cuthberti*, though some of these parallels may have been mediated by other works.[160] In other words, this detailed, if deliberately enigmatic, depiction of the mind-in-the-heart was produced by someone who had attained a moderate amount of Latin learning; thus it refutes the presupposition that the concept of the mind-in-the-heart persisted only among the naive and the illiterate, and it also demonstrates that those who received an education in Latin literature did not necessarily espouse an Augustinian psychology.

Conclusions

The impressionable elementary students who read (and perhaps wrote) the *Lorsch Riddles*, or studied Tatwine's *enigmata*, or internalized the late antique and Insular grammarians' opinions on *corporalia* and *incorporalia* would have, from an early point in their education, developed their view of the visible and invisible worlds under the influence of an eclectic and sometimes Stoicizing Christian perspective on substance. Consequently, because the grammarians did not advance a technically precise Platonizing teaching

---

159 On Alcuin's conception of the incorporeal, unitary soul, see chapter 6 below.
160 Parallels with Aldhelm are cited in Dümmler's *apparatus fontium*, MGH PLAC 1.21; other verbal parallels may result from direct knowledge or from knowledge of quotations in grammars, metrical treatises, and other riddles.

on substance or on the unitary soul, there was little in the elementary phase of Anglo-Saxon education to contradict the popular concept of the *breost-sefa*, the mind-in-the-heart, whose corporeality and mortality are clearly depicted in the second *Lorsch Riddle*. When we ask, therefore, whether literate Anglo-Saxon authors and copyists of OE verse would necessarily have regarded cardiocentric psychology and the hydraulic model as metaphors, the answer is an emphatic *no*. The Latin grammars and riddles demonstrate that cardiocentrism and the corporeality of the mind were wholly compatible with the grammarians' teachings on substance. As for the few gifted Anglo-Saxon students who advanced to higher levels of education (such as Bede), those who undertook such education in the most auspicious times and places (such as eighth-century Wearmouth-Jarrow) did have access to a greater selection of works by Augustine and by other authors who employed a firmly Platonizing view of incorporeality and the unitary soul. But as the case of Alcuin's student Candidus Wizo will illustrate in chapter 6, it is a mistake to presuppose that access to the works of Augustine automatically led learned Anglo-Saxons to espouse Augustine's views and to reject the Stoicizing teachings on substance that they were first exposed to during grammar school.

6 Anglo-Saxon Psychology among the Carolingians: Alcuin, Candidus Wizo, and the Problem of Augustinian Pseudepigrapha

The short treatise *De animae ratione liber ad Eulaliam uirginem* by Alcuin of York (ca. 735–804) stands at the head of the intellectual genealogy that Godden has called the 'classical tradition' in Anglo-Saxon psychology.[1] *De ratione animae* (hereafter *DRA*) takes the form of a letter to 'Eulalia,' which was Alcuin's byname for Gundrada, the sister of Adalhard, abbot of Corbie. If Gundrada is also the addressee of Alcuin's *epistola* 204, she possessed enough learning to appreciate Alcuin's use of logic in his arguments against Adoptianism.[2] *DRA* covers a wide range of teachings pertaining to the soul, but those which most influenced the course of Anglo-Saxon psychology have to do with the unitary nature of the *anima*, its incorporeality, and its interactions with the body.

Alcuin resided at York until he was well into middle age, yet most of his extant writings were penned on the continent, during or after his employment at Charlemagne's court, so they cannot be considered typical of

---

1 Godden, 'Anglo-Saxons on the Mind,' 271–4. Quotations of *De ratione animae* are drawn from PL 101.639–50; much of my information about Alcuin's sources comes from Curry's unpublished PhD dissertation: 'Alcuin, *De ratione animae*: A Text with Introduction, Critical Apparatus, and Translation.' Paul Szarmach is preparing a new edition of *DRA* for CCCM, which he discusses in 'A Preface, Mainly Textual, to Alcuin's *De ratione animae*.'

2 Alcuin's *ep.* 241 (ed. Dümmler, MGH Epist. 4.386–7) clearly identifies Gundrada as 'Eulalia.' Into his *ep.* 204 to an unnamed noblewoman, Alcuin incorporated a dialectical question-and-answer text to assist her in refuting any Adoptianists she might encounter, because, as Alcuin writes, 'noui prudentiam uestram optime in dialecticis subtilitatibus eruditam esse' (I know you to be a prudent woman who has been supremely well educated in the nuances of dialectic) (ibid., 338). On *ep.* 204 see Close, 'L'itinéraire de Candide Wizo,' 21–2.

philosophical discourse in England during his lifetime. This is certainly true of *DRA*, which belongs to the last few years of his distinguished career, ca. 801–4, when he was in semi-retirement as abbot of St Martin's at Tours.[3] Alcuin attained a remarkably advanced education at home in York, thanks to the tutelage and the abundant library of his dedicated teacher Ælberht, who would later become archbishop of York (767–78). Both Ælberht and his library are memorialized in Alcuin's poem on the history of York; this poem, along with his personal florilegium known as *De laude Dei*, which he compiled while still resident in England, attests to the richness of the library resources upon which he built his impressive education before moving to the continent.[4] In 781, Alcuin was returning from Rome bearing the pallium for the newly consecrated archbishop of York, when he stopped at Parma and there met Charlemagne, who asked Alcuin to join his circle of court scholars. He subsequently served Charlemagne as an adviser on political and theological policies, as a liturgical reformer and editor of texts, and as an educator and educational reformer, from the early or mid-780s until at least 796.[5] Based on the evidence of the York poem and *De laude Dei*, however, some of the writings that most influenced Alcuin's opinions about the soul were not available to him until he was in the employ of Charlemagne.[6]

Alcuin's intellectual portrait was long painted in very broad and even exaggerated strokes. Recent scholarship assesses his influence and his philosophical initiative in a manner that is less inflated and more faithful to the

---

3 Szarmach, 'A Preface, Mainly Textual, to Alcuin's *De ratione animae*,' 397.
4 Alcuin's *Versus de patribus, regibus, et sanctis Euboricensis ecclesiae* is edited by Dümmler (MGH PLAC 1.169–206); on the contents of the York library, see Godman's edition, translation, and commentary (*Alcuin: The Bishops, Kings, and Saints of York*, lx–lxxv); as well as Bullough, *Alcuin: Achievement and Reputation*, 252–86; and Lapidge, *Library*, 40–2 and 229–31. *De laude Dei* has not yet appeared in print. For a summary of its contents see Constantinescu, 'Alcuin et les *Libelli precum* de l'époque carolingienne'; and on progress toward a new edition, see Ganz, 'Le *De Laude Dei* d'Alcuin.'
5 Bullough, *Alcuin: Achievement and Reputation*, argues that Alcuin was attached to Charlemagne's court from 786–90 and 793–6 only. This hypothesis remains controversial; the more traditional chronology of his career has Alcuin attached to the court from 781/2 to 796 and perhaps periodically after his acquisition of the abbacy of St Martin's in 796 (see Godman's remarks in his translation of Alcuin's *Versus de patribus*, xxxiii–lx).
6 Marenbon remarks that 'although some of Alcuin's brightest followers were also Englishmen, there is no reason to suppose that the interests and methods of the continental school were merely those of York transplanted.' At York he probably developed his mastery of Latin and read Vergil and the Christian Latin poets as well as Aldhelm and Bede, but 'his interest in more abstract speculations,' facilitated by classical logic, 'developed only after he had moved to the Continent' (*Early Medieval Philosophy*, 46).

textual evidence,[7] and at the same time demonstrates that his theological works are more sophisticated and rhetorically complex than earlier generations of scholars have given him credit for.[8] These trends suggest useful approaches to *DRA* beyond an analysis of its psychological content. In this chapter I first analyse Alcuin's opinions on the unitary nature and the incorporeality of the soul and discern reasons why he considered the soul's incorporeality to be more than an esoteric question of natural philosophy. For the remainder of the chapter, I explore the possibility that Alcuin's highly selective treatment of his sources conceals an anxiety about the persistence of psychological materialism of a Stoicizing variety. Despite Alcuin's confident portrayal of a serene, Neoplatonizing intellectual landscape, we need look no further than the writings of Alcuin's own pupil Candidus Wizo to find evidence that Stoicizing Christian psychological materialism remained viable into the ninth century, at least in part because Stoicizing opinions on the substance of the soul commonly circulated under the name of Augustine.

The Hallmarks of 'The Classical Tradition' in Alcuin's *De ratione animae*

Early medieval homilies and didactic materials rarely focused on the characterization of the soul as an entity in the natural world. Too esoteric to be wholly germane to the daily pursuit of Christian virtue, this topic was more the domain of philosophers than of preachers and teachers. Alcuin did not subscribe to this view. In *DRA*, he teaches Gundrada that she can only love God as well as she knows God, and the best way for her to know God is to understand the nature of the soul, since God created the soul in his own image and likeness.[9] Alcuin's rationale follows the example of

---

7 Alcuin was once credited with single-handedly initiating the use of classical logic in addressing theological controversies; Marenbon and Bullough have demonstrated, however, that court scholars were already using logic to support their opposition to Greek image-veneration prior to Alcuin's involvement in the *Libri Carolini*. It is nonetheless reasonable to credit Alcuin with the revival of interest in Boethius's *De consolatione philosophiae*, which had not been read since the mid-sixth century. See Marenbon, 'Alcuin, the Council of Frankfort and the Beginnings of Medieval Philosophy'; and Bullough, *Alcuin: Achievement and Reputation*, 403–4.

8 E.g., Marenbon, *From the Circle of Alcuin to the School of Auxerre*, 30–66; and Cavadini, 'The Sources and Theology of Alcuin's *De fide sanctae et individuae Trinitatis*.'

9 Alcuin, *DRA* 1–2 (PL 101.639): 'Quantum enim quisque Deum agnoscit, in tantum diligit, qui minus agnoscit, minus diligit ... Et haec sola anima nobilis est, si illum amat a quo est quod est; qui illam talem creauit, ut in se sui ipsius imaginem et similitudinem haberet impressam' (One loves God only as much as one knows him; he who knows God less, loves him less ... And this soul is noble only if it loves him [*scil.* God] from

Augustine's *De Trinitate*, in that he teaches Gundrada to know the Trinity through the coexistence of memory, will, and understanding in the indivisible soul, but Alcuin also extends this principle to other characteristics of the soul, resulting in a work that directs natural philosophy toward the service of theology, to an extent not undertaken in Christian psychology since Cassiodorus's *De anima* in the mid-sixth century.

Three Models of the Unitary anima

Thanks to later quotations by Alfred and Ælfric, some of the best-known passages of *DRA* are the three schemata that delineate the activities of the unitary *anima*: one is adapted from Cassian's twenty-fourth *Collatio*, one from Augustine's *De Trinitate*, and one from Isidore's *Differentiae* and *Etymologiae*. It is tempting to try to harmonize the three schemata, or to evaluate them as though they were commensurable statements of doctrine. However, the three schemata serve distinct and largely non-complementary purposes within Alcuin's treatise, and none of the three is intended as a precise definition of the unitary *anima*.

Alcuin adduces the first tripartite schema in support of his characterization of the *anima* as governor of the living body. The soul governs the body, Alcuin explains, 'as if from the seat of royal power' (quasi de sede regalis culminis), relying on the mind to execute the tasks of oversight and moral deliberation: 'haec omnia rationabili mentis intuitu oportet eam discernere, ne quid indecens fiat in officio suae carnis alicubi.'[10] To underscore the rational nature of the *anima* as well as its domination of the body, Alcuin invokes an ancient Platonic tripartition: 'Triplex est enim animae, ut philosophi uolunt, natura: est in ea quaedam pars concupiscibilis, alia rationalis, tertia irascibilis.'[11] With the phrase *ut philosophi uolunt*, Alcuin distances himself from this schema, which originated in pagan philosophy

---

whom the soul is what it is, who created the soul such that it might have impressed upon it his very own image and likeness).

10 Alcuin, *DRA* 2 (PL 101.639): 'It is incumbent upon the soul to decide all these things by means of the rational consideration of the mind, lest anything improper happen with respect to the conduct of any part of the body.'

11 Alcuin, *DRA* 3 (PL 101.639): 'The nature of the soul, as the philosophers would have it, is threefold. Within it there is one part that is appetitive, another that is rational, and a third that is passionate.' Cf. Cassian, *Collationes* 24.14, and Isidore, *Diff.* 2.28. (Those who consult Curry's *apparatus fontium* should note that the section numbers that Curry cites from the PL edition of the *Differentiae uerborum* do not match those in Andrés Sanz's new edition for CCSL.)

(even though Alcuin actually found it in the works of Cassian and Isidore), but the distance is only slight, because the philosophers' tripartition usefully reinforces what Alcuin has already said regarding the rational soul's responsibility for preventing the body from 'indecent' actions:

> Duas enim habent harum partes nobiscum bestiae et animalia communes, id est, concupiscentiam, et iram. Homo solus inter mortales ratione uiget, consilio ualet, intellegentia antecellit. Sed his duobus, id est, concupiscentiae et irae, ratio, quae mentis propria est, imperare debet.[12]

Alcuin goes on to explain how the four cardinal virtues of the soul can be deployed against *concupiscentia* and *ira* as well as more specific vices. The theme of domination – of soul over body, of the rational soul over the appetitive and the passionate, of virtue over vice – continues through the end of the fourth chapter of *DRA*.

The fifth chapter prolongs Alcuin's discussion of the pre-eminence of the rational soul, but the emphasis shifts from its domination of the body to its pre-eminent merit. It is within this context that Alcuin reintroduces the Augustinian teaching that one can know God through his knowledge of the rational soul, where God's image and likeness reside.

> Est quoque anima imagine et similitudine sui Conditoris in principali sui parte, quae mens dicitur, excellenter nobilitata ... quanquam scilicet magna sit natura anima humana, tamen uitiari potest, quia summa non est: tamen quia summae naturae imago est, id est, diuinae, magna est natura, et nobilis.[13]

The soul is analogous to God not only by virtue of its power and its merit but also because three faculties coexist within it: one who can grasp this trait of the soul can thereby learn something of the mystery of the Trinity. Again borrowing from Augustine, Alcuin writes,

---

12 Alcuin, *DRA* 3 (PL 101.639–40): 'Beasts and animals have two of these parts in common with us: namely appetite and passion. Among mortal beings, man alone is esteemed for his reason, has the capacity for deliberation, and is marked out by virtue of his intelligence. But reason, which is peculiar to the mind, must dominate the other two, namely appetite and passion.' Cf. Augustine, *De diuersis quaestionibus* 83, and Isidore, *Diff.* 2.28.

13 Alcuin, *DRA* 5 (PL 101.641): 'The soul is wonderfully ennobled by the image and likeness of its Creator, in its foremost part, which is called the mind ... Though in its human nature the soul is obviously great, it can still be corrupted, because its nature is not the greatest of all; yet because it is the image of the greatest nature – namely, the divine nature – the nature of the soul is great and noble.' Cf. Augustine, *De Trinitate* 14.4.

Habet igitur anima in sua natura, ut diximus, imaginem sanctae Trinitatis in eo quod intellegentiam, uóluntatem, et memoriam habet. Una est enim anima, quae mens dicitur, una uita, et una substantia, quae haec tria habet in se: sed haec tria non sunt tres uitae, sed una uita; nec tres mentes, sed una mens: consequenter utique, nec tres substantiae sunt, sed una substantia.[14]

Alcuin does not try to reconcile the Augustinian triad with the philosophical tripartition adduced earlier, but the juxtaposition of the two schemata raises questions. Of course the image of the Trinity is borne by the *anima rationalis* alone, but what is the relationship among the rational, appetitive, and passionate souls in humans? Are they all of one substance? Are the *anima concupiscibilis* and the *anima irascibilis* mortal or immortal in humans, and if they are mortal, are they bodily entities? Alcuin does not pursue these questions in *DRA*, probably because he never intended for these two tripartite schemata to be reconciled. The first is a definition of the *anima* according to natural philosophy but without specifically Christian content, and the second is a heuristic device that is useful in teaching someone about the Trinity, but it is incomplete as a definition of the rational soul.

The third psychological schema presented in *DRA* is similarly irreconcilable with the first two. In chapter 11, Alcuin adapts from Isidore a catalogue of names applied to the unitary soul in its various capacities.

Atque secundum officium operis sui uariis nuncupatur nominibus: anima est, dum uiuificat; dum contemplatur, spiritus est; dum sentit, sensus est; dum sapit, animus est; dum intelligit, mens est; dum discernit, ratio est; dum consentit, uoluntas est; dum recordatur, memoria est. Non tamen haec ita diuidentur in substantia, sicut in nominibus; quia haec omnia, una est anima.[15]

---

14 Alcuin, *DRA* 6 (PL 101.641): 'So the soul has in its nature, as I mentioned, the image of the holy Trinity, because the soul has understanding, will, and memory. For there is a single soul that is called the mind, a single life, and a single substance which has these three things within it. But these three are not three lives but a single life; not three minds but a single mind; it follows that truly there are not three substances but a single substance.' Cf. Augustine, *De Trinitate* 10.11.

15 *DRA* 11 (PL 101.644): 'The soul is called by various names according to the purpose in which it is engaged: it is *anima* when it animates; when it contemplates it is *spiritus*; when it feels it is *sensus*; when it knows it is *animus*; when it understands it is *mens*; when it makes a judgment it is *ratio*; when it consents it is *uoluntas*; when it remembers it is *memoria*. Nevertheless, these things are not divided in substance as they are in name, because the one soul is all these things.' Alcuin here combines features of Isidore's names for the soul at *Diff.* 2.27 with the similar passage at *Etym.* 11.1.12–13.

Like the philosophers' tripartition of the *anima*, the Isidorian catalogue associates the term *anima* with the animating principle; additionally, it resolves a discrepancy between the two tripartite schemata by asserting that the animating principle is of one substance with the rational faculties of the human soul. On the other hand, the Isidorian catalogue is taxonomically incompatible with the trinitarian tripartition, since the catalogue does not subsume the faculties of *memoria* and *uoluntas* under the umbrella of *mens* or *anima rationalis* but rather places the more specific faculties on equal footing with *animus, mens,* and even *ratio*. A reader who encountered the Isidorian catalogue within the context of the *Differentiae* would have recognized that this list is meant to distinguish among names commonly applied to the unitary *anima*; it is not an authoritative definition of the soul, and one can easily find, within Isidore's own works, philosophical and theological assertions about the meaning of *anima, mens,* and *ratio* that are incompatible with this catalogue of names. When Alcuin transplants the Isidorian catalogue into a context where it is surrounded by philosophical and theological treatments of the faculties of the soul, it is easy to forget that it is, first and foremost, a catalogue of names.

Why Must the Soul Be Incorporeal?

In the tenth chapter of *DRA*, just before the Isidorian catalogue, Alcuin crafts a thorough and precise definition of the *anima*. Due to its complexity, it lacks the pithy and memorable character of the three schemata adduced so far, but it gains elegance and rhythm from the way Alcuin has grouped together complementary traits.

> Hoc modo anima definiri potest iuxta suae proprietatem naturae: anima[16] est spiritus intellectualis, rationalis; semper in motu, semper uiuens; bonae malaeque uoluntatis capax, secundum benignitatem Creatoris libero arbitrio nobilitatus; sua uoluntate uitiatus, Dei gratia liberatus in quibus Deus ipse uoluit; ad regendum carnis motus creatus; inuisibilis, incorporalis; sine pondere, sine colore; circumscriptus, in singulis suae carnis membris totus; in quo est imago Conditoris spiritaliter primitiua creatione impressa.[17]

---

16 The PL text reads *anima seu animus*, but cf. Curry's *apparatus criticus* ('Alcuin: De ratione animae,' 54).

17 *DRA* 10 (PL 101.643–4; I have altered the editorial punctuation): 'The soul can be defined thus according to the particular character of its nature: the soul is a spirit, possessing *intellectus* [*scil.* the faculty that apprehends incorporeals] and reason; always in

This definition begins with characteristics that the Platonic tradition ascribed to the soul before the Christian era: intellect and reason, ceaseless motion, and immortality. Alcuin then carefully adds Christian tenets that insulate him from any heterodoxy: the soul, being free to choose good or evil, is responsible for its own corruption and is utterly dependent on God for its salvation. The latter part of the definition includes traits that pertain to the soul as an entity within the natural world per se and also relative to the body. Among these traits, the soul's incorporeality deserves closer scrutiny, because of its profound implications for the soul's capacity to interact with incorporeals (especially God and the immortal Forms) and corporeals (especially the human body).

It is one thing to assert that the soul is 'incorporeal' insofar as it is distinct from the human body, and it is quite another thing to espouse the Platonic notion that the soul is utterly incorporeal, or that it is not a body of any kind. Platonic incorporeals differ significantly from the incorporeals of classical Stoicism, which were thought to participate in a diminished form of existence, and from the *incorporalia* of the grammatical tradition, which were defined on the basis of their imperceptibility to one or more of the five senses (see chapter 5 above). A Platonic incorporeal is necessarily imperceptible to all the senses, and it does not occupy space. Accordingly, Alcuin writes that the soul is 'invisible, incorporeal, without weight, without colour,' although for a reader who already shared Alcuin's Platonic understanding of incorporeals, the mention of invisibility, weightlessness, and colourlessness was redundant. Alcuin also carefully specifies that the soul is circumscribed but nonetheless whole in every part of the body. In other words, the soul is neither diffused throughout the universe as God is or as a world-soul would be, nor is it distributed throughout a space in such a way that it can be divided.

If incorporeality makes the soul imperceptible to the senses, it is even more important that incorporeality allows the soul to apprehend other

---

motion and always living; capable of good and evil desire, and ennobled by free will thanks to the kindness of its Creator; corrupted by its own will but freed by the grace of God (to the extent that God himself has willed); created to govern the movements of the flesh; invisible and incorporeal; without weight and without colour; circumscribed, but whole in every part of the fleshly body. Upon it the image of the Creator was impressed spiritually at the very first Creation.' Curry identifies Isidore's *Diff.* 2.25 and 2.28 as the source for Alcuin's information on the substance of the soul; I would add that the lines pertaining to free will, corruption, and salvation paraphrase *Diff.* 2.30, and the comment about non-spatial disposition likely depends on Augustine, *De Trinitate* 6.8, or Claudianus Mamertus, *De statu animae* 1.17.

things that are imperceptible to the senses. The idea that like perceives like goes back to the Greek Presocratics, and in its medieval Latin iterations, it did not have to carry strictly Platonic connotations.[18] Yet principally from Augustine's early dialogues and *De Trinitate*, Alcuin and other Carolingian thinkers inherited many rational demonstrations of theological doctrines, worked out according to a method of argumentation that combined Neoplatonist metaphysics with Aristotelian logic.[19] Within this mode of discourse, it was exceedingly useful to have recourse to the concept of true incorporeality, and to be able to attribute true incorporeality to the unitary, rational *anima*, with all of the ontological and epistemological implications that it entails. For instance, the demonstrations of the soul's immortality that Augustine advances throughout the *Soliloquia* depend implicitly upon the Platonic theory of Forms and explicitly upon the Aristotelian distinction between accidents and inseparable properties. More precisely, Augustine's demonstrations depend not merely on the Platonic assertion that an incorporeal substance is immortal, but upon the epistemological implications of incorporeality: since Forms such as truth and purity are incorporeal and immortal, their incorporeal residence in the *anima* must be immortal as well; otherwise they would have no 'place' in which to exist.[20]

Given that a strict, Platonic concept of incorporeality did not underlie the term *incorporalia* as it was used in pre-Carolingian grammars, and given that those Latin Fathers with a Stoicizing bent attributed true incorporeality to God but not to angels and souls, it is worth asking why Alcuin took the trouble to crystallize the esoteric notion of the incorporeal soul into a prominent point of orthodox doctrine. After all, a looser concept of incorporeality could sustain most practical teachings about virtue, self-restraint, and the afterlife.[21] In very general terms, this crystallization likely

---

18 For instance, one need not understand Platonic incorporeals to grasp Isidore's meaning when he writes at *Diff.* 2.24 (ed. Andrés Sanz, CCSL 111A, 56): 'Inter *intelligibilia* et *sensibilia* taliter ueteres discreuerunt: intelligibilia esse quae in mente animoque percipiuntur; sensibilia autem, quae uisu tactuque corporeo sentiuntur' (The ancients distinguished between intelligible things and things perceptible to the senses in this way: intelligible things are those that are perceived by the *mens* and the *animus*, while things perceptible to the senses are those that are apprehended by bodily sight and touch).

19 Marenbon, *From the Circle of Alcuin*, 4–8 and 12–29.

20 On Augustine's *Soliloquia* see chapter 4 above.

21 For instance, an effective homily that privileges the needs of the soul above those of the body need only convince the audience that the soul is distinct from, and will outlive, the fleshly human body; a strict Platonic concept of incorporeality does not advance this argument appreciably for the audience of homiletic or catechetical material.

owed something to Alcuin's very public role as one of Charlemagne's defenders of orthodoxy, and also to Alcuin's unprecedented exaltation of the
authority of Augustine above all other authorities except the Bible: either
or both of these tendencies could understandably have inclined Alcuin to
insist upon uniformity of thought in an arena where conflicting opinions
had coexisted peacefully. Even more urgent than either of these motivations, I suspect, was the fact that true incorporeality, as an attribute of the
soul, was immensely useful within the framework of Aristotelian logic.
Reliance on a looser concept of incorporeality could scarcely sustain the
sort of rational demonstrations of theological truths that the Carolingians
admired and emulated in the works of Augustine as well as Claudianus
Mamertus and Boethius, among others. So in order for Alcuin to promote
successfully the revival of dialectic in theology, he also needed to promote
a metaphysics that attached the soul's incorporeality to all the ontological
and epistemological implications that it carried in the Platonic tradition.

Body and Soul in De ratione animae

Although the truly incorporeal *anima* facilitated the rational demonstration
of many theological doctrines, it created difficulties in discussions of the
relationship between body and soul. An incorporeal *anima* is necessarily
non-spatial, so how can it 'travel' in thought, or 'recede' away from the
sense organs? An incorporeal *anima* can only apprehend other incorporeal
entities, so how can it receive the data garnered by sensory perception, and
how can it exert the force of its governance on the fleshly body? Alcuin cannot resolve such questions in *DRA*, but neither had Augustine, his chief
authority, proposed a wholly satisfactory Neoplatonist account of soul-
body interactions for Alcuin to incorporate into his own writings.

Consider, for instance, Alcuin's discussion of memory at *DRA* 7–8 and
in the poem 'Qui mare, qui terram,' which Alcuin appended to his letter
to Gundrada. First, drawing on Augustine's *De Trinitate*, Alcuin writes
of the 'marvellous speed' and 'ineffable swiftness' with which the mind
'hastens back' to places it has seen before: 'Et dum nomen audierit uel
rememorat Romae, statim recurrit animus illius ad memoriam, ubi con-
ditam habet formam illius, et ibi recognoscit eam[22] ubi recondidit illam.'[23]

---

22 The PL text reads *eam ad memoriam*, but cf. Curry's *apparatus criticus* ('Alcuin: *De
    ratione animae*,' 49).
23 Alcuin, *DRA* 7 (PL 101.642): 'And when one hears or remembers the name of Rome,
    suddenly the mind hastens back to his memory of it, where it keeps the mental picture

Not long after, Alcuin quotes at length Lactantius's *De opificio Dei* on the 'great mobility and speed' with which the mind surveys everything throughout creation:

> Nec etiam aliquis potest satis admirari, quod sensus ille uiuus atque coelestis, qui mens uel animus nuncupatur, tantae mobilitatis est, ut ne tum quidem, cum sopitus est, conquiescat: tantae celeritatis, ut uno temporis puncto coelum collustret, et si uelit, maria peruolet, terras et urbes peragret: omnia denique, quae libuerit, quamuis longe lateque submota sint, in conspectu sibi ipse cogitando constituat.[24]

If interpreted too materialistically, the language that Alcuin borrows from both Augustine and Lactantius threatens to undercut his definition of the soul as incorporeal, circumscribed, and non-spatially distributed. To preclude misunderstandings, Alcuin adds a disclaimer, clarifying that the mind does not travel spatially outside the body when engaged in memory or imagination.[25]

The purpose of introducing the 'flight of the mind' topos, as used by both Lactantius and Alcuin, is to establish an analogy between the soul and God: if the mind is capable of surveying all of creation even though it cannot leave the walls of the body, God's power to survey all of creation must be infinitely greater, since bodily boundaries cannot hem him in. Since Lactantius conceived of both the soul and God as *pneuma*, a material substance with spatial extent,[26] he attributed spatial motion and diffusion

---

(*formam*) of Rome stored, and there, where it stores that mental picture, it recognizes Rome.' Cf. Augustine, *De Trinitate* 8.5–6.

24 Alcuin, *DRA* 8 (PL 101.642–3): 'Nor can anyone sufficiently marvel at the fact that the living and heavenly faculty of perception, which is called *mens* or *animus*, possesses such great mobility that, even when it is asleep, it does not lie still. It has such great speed that it surveys the heavens in an instant of time, and if it should wish to do so, it may soar over the seas and the land and travel through the cities; by thinking it may place within its sights all things that it might want, however far and wide they may be removed from it.' Cf. Lactantius, *De opificio Dei* 16.9.

25 Alcuin, *DRA* 7 (PL 101.642): 'non quod anima exeat de sede sua ad cognoscendum aliquid, sed in seipsa manet, et in seipsa illam formam recognoscit, quam pridem mira uelocitate formauit' (Not that the soul departs from its proper seat in order to get acquainted with anything, but it remains within itself and recognizes within itself that form which it earlier formed with marvellous speed). Cf. Augustine, *De Genesi ad litteram* 12.16.

26 Lactantius calls the mind an 'incorporeal thing' (*res incorporalis*) at *De opificio Dei* 16.11, but he does not use this term as a Neoplatonist would: this becomes evident when he applies the term *incorporalis* to the breath (*spiritus*). As Lactantius explains, the

to both the soul and God. Accordingly, in his *De opificio Dei* Lactantius unfolds the analogy between the soul and God in these words:

> Et miratur aliquis si diuina mens dei **per** uniuersas mundi partes **intenta discurrit** et omnia regit, omnia **moderatur**, ubique praesens, ubique **diffusa**, cum tanta sit uis ac potestas mentis humanae intra mortale corpus inclusae, ut ne saeptis quidem grauis huius ac pigri corporis, cum quo inligata est, coerceri ullo modo possit?[27]

The spatial motion and diffusion that Lactantius associates with the divine *pneuma* do not harmonize with Alcuin's understanding of incorporeals; thus where Alcuin paraphrases Lactantius's analogy, he excises the words that I have placed in bold type, which connote spatiality. Moreover, to reinforce the idea that God's non-spatial distribution may be understood by analogy to that of the soul, Alcuin replaces Lactantius's phrase *ubique diffusa* 'poured out everywhere' with *ubique tota* 'everywhere whole,' echoing the language he uses in his aforementioned definition of the human soul.[28]

The poem 'Qui mare, qui terram,' which Alcuin attached at the end of his letter to Gundrada, recapitulates the teaching that one may better know God by learning about the soul, especially about its capacity to perceive things not present to the senses. The poem formally illustrates that the soul is the *imago Dei* by introducing the soul in line 11 with an echo of the description of God in line 1:

---

breath consists of a material substance so thin (*tenuis*) that it cannot force open a space through which it might leave the body; this is why the larynx is formed in such a way as to remain wide open at all times (*De opificio Dei* 11.7; ed. Perrin, SC 213, 170–2).

27 Lactantius, *De opificio Dei* 16.10 (ed. Perrin, SC 213, 196): 'And is it surprising to anyone that the divine mind of God, stretched out through every part of the cosmos, travels throughout all things, governs all things, and establishes a boundary around all things, being present everywhere and poured out everywhere, since the strength and power of the human mind, although enclosed within a mortal body, is so great that it cannot be hemmed in, even by the walls of this ponderous and sluggish body that traps it inside?'

28 Alcuin, *DRA* 8 (PL 101.643). The first clause in Alcuin's reworking of the analogy reads, 'Et miratur aliquis, si diuina mens Dei, uniuersas mundi partes simul, et semper praesentes habeat, quae omnia regit ubique praesens, ubique tota?' (Is it surprising to anyone that the divine mind of God, which governs all things and is everywhere present and everywhere whole, grasps all parts of the cosmos, which are present all at once and at all times?)

Qui mare, qui terram, coelum qui condidit altum   [1]
   Qui regit imperio cuncta creata suo;
Iusserat hic hominem rebus dominare sub astris.
... Quae mare, quae terras, coelum quae peruolat altum,   [11]
   Quamuis sit carnis carcere clausa suae:
Corporis utque oculus, uisus ad sidera tendit,
   Uno stet quamuis carnis in arce loco.[29]

As in the prose, Alcuin guards against the misconception that the soul can travel through space, carefully reiterating that the soul stays 'in one place.' And although it is not the stuff of great poetry, he subsequently clarifies that the soul occupies that place indivisibly and non-spatially: 'Spiritus est anima, in membris iam totus ubique.'[30]

It is curious that Alcuin finds so many ways and opportunities to articulate the non-spatial motion and non-spatial distribution of the soul, which is of course a corollary of its incorporeality, while using the word *incorporalis* only once in *DRA*. Alcuin was probably well aware that the word *incorporalis* meant different things to different readers, and so to argue strenuously that the soul was *incorporalis* did not necessarily convey all of the corollaries of true incorporeality as Neoplatonists conceived of it. Moreover, as will be explored more fully in the latter part of the chapter, if Alcuin faced any opposition to his Neoplatonizing teaching on the incorporeal soul, it likely came from the Stoicizing Christian tradition, whose proponents argued that the soul's circumscription in the body implied a spatial (*localis*) nature, which in turned implied some degree of corporeality. Alcuin's peculiarly determined emphasis on the soul's circumscription *and* non-spatial distribution suggests that if he envisioned any hypothetical opposition to his argument, it was of a Stoicizing nature: but all this will become clearer when we turn to the writings of Alcuin's pupil Candidus.

First, however, it remains to consider a problem in Christian psychology that was exacerbated by the Neoplatonists' insistence that the soul was truly incorporeal: by what mechanism can an incorporeal soul interact

---

29 Alcuin, 'Qui mare, qui terram,' lines 1–3 and 11–14 (PL 101.647): 'He who created the deep sea, the earth, the lofty heaven, who rules all created things by his own power: he commanded man to rule over all things beneath the stars ... [The soul,] which flies throughout the deep sea, the earth, and the lofty heavens, like an eye directs the gaze of the body toward heaven, although it is enclosed by the prison of its own flesh, and though it remains in one place, in its stronghold.'
30 Alcuin, 'Qui mare, qui terram,' line 33 (PL 101.648): 'The soul is a spirit, presently whole everywhere and in every part of the body.'

with bodies? Even Lactantius, whose concept of incorporeality was relative rather than absolute, found this problem challenging: he declares that the mind itself can neither witness nor understand how an incorporeal thing might be joined with a body.[31] The Neoplatonizing psychology of Augustine, moreover, does not satisfactorily resolve the problem of soul-body interactions. Augustine's most detailed and confident examinations of this problem actually invoke Stoic concepts such as *krasis* (mixture), *tonos* (spatial extension or tensional force), and *pneuma* (spiritual material) in order to articulate a mechanism of soul-body interaction, even though he always maintains firmly that the soul is incorporeal.[32] What Alcuin's *DRA* borrows from Augustine's *De Genesi ad litteram* is a rather vague account of how light and air mediate between soul and body and allow the former to govern the latter:

> Sicut enim Deus omnem creaturam, sic anima omnem corpoream creaturam naturae dignitate praecellit. Quae etiam per lucem et aerem, quae sunt excellentiora mundi corpora, corpus administrat suum. Omnium rerum species lux animae annuntiat, quas ipsa in se acceptas specificat, specificatasque recondit.[33]

This explanation raises more questions than it answers. Alcuin's readership may not all have agreed on whether light and air were corporeals or incorporeals,[34] and at any rate there remains the question of how the incorporeal soul interacts with corporeal air and light, or how incorporeal air and light interact with the flesh. Alcuin only compounds the difficulty when he discusses *exstasis*, that is, the withdrawal of the soul from the senses. In these lines Alcuin relies heavily on Augustine:

---

31 Lactantius, *De opificio Dei* 16.11 (ed. Perrin, SC 213, 196): 'animus se ipsum non uidet aut qualis aut ubi sit nec si uideat, tamen perspicere possit quo pacto rei corporali res incorporalis adiuncta sit' (The mind does not see itself or what sort of thing it is or where it is, nor, if it should see these things, would it be able to comprehend under what conditions an incorporeal thing should be joined to a corporeal thing).

32 O'Daly, *Augustine's Philosophy of Mind*, 40–5 and 80–2.

33 Alcuin, *DRA* 12 (PL 101.645): 'For just as God surpasses every creature, so does the soul, by the worthiness of its nature, surpass every corporeal creature. The soul also governs its body by means of light and air, which are the more rarefied types of earthly bodies. Light communicates to the soul the appearances of all things, and the soul receives those appearances into itself and classifies them, and it stores them as they have been classified.' Cf. Augustine, *De Genesi ad litteram* 7.19.

34 Light and air are among the entities that the grammarians sometimes placed at intermediate positions along the spectrum between bodies and true incorporeals, depending upon the sensory criteria used: see chapter 5 above.

Si enim uel Deum, uel seipsam, uel spiritale aliquid considerare gestit, auertit se a sensibus carnis, ne fiant ei impedimento, spiritalia rimanti. Saepe etiam in tantum affectata erit qualibet cogitatione, ut, quamuis apertos habeat oculos, quae praesto sunt, non uideat; nec sonantem uocem intelligat, nec tangentem corpus sentiat. Regit enim corpus per quinque sensus, quae horum nihil est. Dum de ea cogitamus, nihil corporeum cogitare debemus.[35]

Alcuin reminds the reader that the soul itself is not one of the five senses, as if this fact were enough to explain how the soul can detach itself from the recognition of sensory stimuli; however, the question of how the soul was connected to those stimuli in the first place has not yet been answered. Lactantius proposes (but does not wholeheartedly endorse) a phenomenological, materialist explanation for *exstasis*, namely that the mind sequesters itself from the sense organs in the head by withdrawing spatially to the chest cavity,[36] but Augustine and Alcuin were compelled to reject this explanation if they were to maintain the incorporeality and nonspatiality of the soul.

Alcuin Smoothes the Wrinkles in the Intellectual Landscape

For the sections of *DRA* discussed thus far, Alcuin's chief sources of information included Lactantius's *De opificio Dei*, Augustine's *De Trinitate* and *De Genesi ad litteram*, and Isidore's *Differentiae*. Given that Lactantius's work bears the marks of Stoicizing materialism, it is not surprising that when faced with a choice between Lactantius and Augustine, Alcuin prefers Augustine's Neoplatonizing opinions. In the aforementioned problem of *exstasis*, Alcuin even prefers Augustine's perplexity over the materialist explanations proffered by Lactantius. Yet Alcuin's adherence to, and exaltation of, Augustine's authority goes beyond a simple preference for the Neoplatonic over the Stoic. The way Alcuin handles his sources in *DRA* gives the impression that all of his teachings represent

---

35 Alcuin, *DRA* 12 (PL 101.644–5): 'For if the soul yearns to ponder either God or itself or any spiritual thing, it turns itself away from the senses of the flesh, lest they become an impediment to it when it examines spiritual things. Often it will even be affected by some sort of deep thought to such a degree that, although the eyes remain open, the soul does not see things which are at hand, nor does it understand a voice that is speaking, nor does it feel when someone is touching the body. For it rules the body through its five senses, but it is not one of them. So when we think about the soul, we must not conceive of it as a corporeal entity.' Cf. Augustine, *De Genesi ad litteram*, 12.12.
36 Lactantius, *De opificio Dei*, 16.5–8 (ed. Perrin, SC 213, 194.)

points of consensus throughout the ranks of Christian thinkers. He never names the authors whom he quotes and paraphrases in *DRA*, and this reticence prevents any of those quotations from being interpreted as the opinion of just one thinker.[37]

Alcuin's highly selective use of his source texts brings about an illusion of historical and contemporary unanimity within Christian discourse on psychology. Where his source texts mention points of disagreement within the philosophical and Christian traditions, either to condemn them or merely to record them, Alcuin refuses to acknowledge such disagreement, even in cases where heterodoxy was not at issue. For instance, Alcuin quotes Lactantius's *De opificio Dei* 16 extensively, but he says nothing of the varying opinions on the seat of the soul that Lactantius records in that chapter. Alcuin relies heavily on the second book of Isidore's *Differentiae*, particularly on chapters 25–30, but he does not acknowledge Isidore's report, at *Diff.* 2.27, of a philosophical opinion that the soul and the mind were separate entities. Isidore shows contempt for the folly of those who believe the soul to be corporeal, at *Diff.* 2.26 and *Etym.* 11.1.7–8 (both passages adjacent to the catalogue of names for the soul that Alcuin consulted), but Alcuin refuses to repeat this information, even to condemn it. One might suppose that Alcuin regarded Lactantius and Isidore as encyclopedic rather than theological authorities, in which case their doxographic tendencies might not have been compatible with Alcuin's didactic objectives. Yet Augustine, too, discussed controversies pertinent to the nature of the soul. Book 7 of *De Genesi ad litteram*, in particular, tells the history of disputes over the origin of the soul, its substance, and its relationship with the faculty of thought and with the body; Book 12 of the same work weighs conflicting opinions about the phenomena of dreams and mystical visions. Alcuin consulted both of these books but, in *DRA*, he refused to consider variant opinions on any of these matters.

Alcuin's most active effort to whitewash over pertinent controversies appears near the end of *DRA*, where he enumerates several doctrines, about which (he claims) all orthodox Christian authors agree:

> In hoc enim omnes consentiunt catholici scriptores, quod anima a Deo sit condita; nec partem eam esse Dei naturae, quia si ex Dei esset natura assumpta, peccare non posset. Nec eam corpus esse palpabile uel uisibile: nec mori

---

37 Alcuin names his authorities only at *DRA* 13 (PL 101.645), where he mentions Jerome and Augustine's unfruitful epistolary exchange concerning the origin of the soul and lists some works of Augustine on the soul that he has been unable to find.

eam posse, ita ut non sit; nec a reatu primae praeuaricationis liberari posse, nisi per gratiam et mysterium mediatoris Dei.[38]

Several of these opinions attained the status of orthodoxies precisely *because* of disputes within the early Church, although Alcuin would have Gundrada think otherwise.[39] The third opinion on the list – that the soul is not a body, palpable or visible – is cleverly articulated and even misleading, perhaps intentionally so. It is entirely fair to say that not even the most Stoicizing of early Christian thinkers posited that the soul was perceptible to the bodily senses of sight and touch. And it is absolutely true that in the tradition of the elementary grammarians, a body is defined as that which is apprehended by touch and sight. What Alcuin conveniently neglects to mention is that numerous credible Christian authors, such as Lactantius, Hilary, Cassian, and Gennadius, did indeed teach that the soul was a bodily or material substance, but one so subtle that it could not be touched or seen: this opinion even appears in works that Alcuin has quoted earlier in *DRA*.[40] Alcuin's carefully worded claim that no orthodox author ever supposed the soul to be a 'tangible or visible body' effectively sweeps under the rug the entire problem of Stoicizing psychological materialism. It is striking that in order to do so, he must invoke a definition of *corpus* that meets only the standards of elementary grammar rather than those of Neoplatonizing Christian thought.

Many present-day scholars regard Stoicizing psychological materialism as already passé by the onset of the early Middle Ages, thanks to the Neoplatonist influence of Augustine, Claudianus Mamertus, and eventually Boethius, among others. Alcuin's handling of his sources suggests that this is exactly what he wanted Gundrada to think: that the Augustinian material that he imparted to her had no viable intellectual opposition. It is conceivable that Alcuin crafted *DRA* as a straightforward psychological primer rather than as a polemic, or alternatively, that he was anxious to overturn a materialist folk psychology of the sort that persisted in England; however,

---

38 Alcuin, *DRA* 13 (PL 101.645): 'All Catholic writers agree about this: that the soul was created by God; that the soul is not a part of the nature of God, because if it had taken on the nature of God it would not have been able to sin; that the soul is not a body, tangible or visible; that the soul is unable to die in such a way that it no longer exists; and that it cannot be freed from the guilt of original sin except through the grace and the mystery of God our mediator.'
39 The second tenet listed here opposes the Origenist heresy; the last one opposes Semipelagianism.
40 Namely Cassian's *Collationes* and Lactantius's *De opificio Dei.*

since *DRA* was addressed to a learned noblewoman, probably one with some knowledge of dialectic, it is more likely that he wanted to root out a competing *philosophical* psychology. Several classes of evidence reinforce the impression that Stoicizing psychological materialism remained a significant challenge to Neoplatonizing psychology in Alcuin's day and even within his own circle.

The Persistence of Stoicizing Materialism

In earlier chapters I have written in more detail about classical Stoic and Stoicizing Christian ontology and psychology, so my reprise of these topics here will be brief. Stoic and Platonist ontologies should, in principle, be irreconcilable. For the Stoics, incorporeality is characteristic of things at the bottom of the ontological hierarchy, which do not even truly exist but can only subsist; everything that truly exists is corporeal. In the Platonist tradition (broadly speaking), incorporeality is characteristic of things at the very top of the ontological hierarchy; they are the only things that truly exist, because corporeal things are corruptible and therefore cannot exist as fully as the immutable incorporeals. In early Christian discourse, a number of Western theologians espoused a blend of these two positions: God alone is incorporeal, while all creatures, including angels and human souls, are corporeal to some extent. In hindsight, and under the influence of Alcuin's claim of unanimity within Christian psychological discourse, it is easy to dismiss Stoic materialism as a relic of late antiquity that had lost the battle with Augustine and with Neoplatonism long before the Carolingian period; however, it is a useful corrective to consider that we derive our holistic understanding of Augustine's thought from generations of scholars who have weeded out many pseudepigraphal writings from the corpus of Augustine's authentic works.

One of the works that circulated widely under Augustine's name in the eighth and ninth centuries was Gennadius of Marseilles' *De ecclesiasticis dogmatibus*, a brief treatise that articulates a series of orthodox positions and contrasts each with its heterodox alternatives.[41] Gennadius consistently condemns strains of Christian thought that posit too slim a difference between the substance of God and that of his creatures, and in this vein he insists that God alone is incorporeal, while souls and angels are corporeal:

---

41 See chapter 4 above.

XI. Nihil incorporeum et inuisibile natura credendum nisi solum Deum, id est patrem et filium et spiritum sanctum; qui ideo incorporeus creditur quia ubique est et omnia inplet adque constringit, ideo inuisibilis omnibus creaturis quia incorporeus est.
XII. Creatura omnis corporea: angeli et omnes caelestes uirtutes corpore, licet non carne, subsistunt. Ex eo autem corporeas esse credimus intellectuales naturas, quod localitate circumscribuntur, sicut et anima humana quae carne clauditur, et demones qui per substantiam angelicae naturae sunt.[42]

Because this sort of Stoicizing materialism contradicts Platonist-Christian teachings on the soul and is incompatible with dialectical arguments about the soul, in hindsight we assume that Platonist-Christian psychology had completely eclipsed Stoicizing Christian psychology by Alcuin's day. If that were so, it would be hard to account for the vast numbers of manuscript copies of *De eccl. dogm.* that were generated during the early medieval period.[43] I will have more to say below about the early medieval manuscript witnesses of *De eccl. dogm.*, but first I would like to explore the surprising use of Gennadius's materialist psychology by two of Alcuin's own pupils: Candidus Wizo (ob. post 804), an Anglo-Saxon and a long-time companion of Alcuin, and Hrabanus Maurus, who as a young man studied the liberal arts with Alcuin at Tours and later became archbishop of Mainz (848–56).

Hrabanus Maurus, Candidus, and Gennadius

Hrabanus's invocation of Gennadius requires only a brief mention. In his encyclopedic *De uniuerso*, composed in the mid-840s, Hrabanus reproduces the entirety of the first recension of *De eccl. dogm.*, including paragraph 54 ('Propter nouellos legislatores'), without comment.[44] He does not actively engage with any of Gennadius's opinions, and it is likely that

---

42 Gennadius, *De eccl. dogm.* 11–12 (ed. Turner, 'The *Liber ecclesiasticorum dogmatum*,' 91–2): '11. We must believe that nothing is by nature incorporeal and invisible except God alone, that is, the Father and Son and Holy Spirit. We believe God to be incorporeal because he exists everywhere and he infuses and contains all things; we believe him to be invisible to all creatures because he is incorporeal. 12. Every creature is corporeal; angels and all the heavenly powers subsist as a body, but not as flesh. For this reason we believe that intellectual creatures are corporeal: because they are circumscribed in space, and so also is the soul which is enclosed in flesh, and demons which, by virtue of their essence, are angelic natures.'
43 Turner, 'The *Liber Ecclesiasticorum Dogmatum*,' 80–8.
44 On the significance of *De eccl. dogm.* par. 54, see chapter 4 above.

the inclusion of *De eccl. dogm.* in an encyclopedic context – specifically in Book 4 which treats heresies, rather than in Book 1 which treats the persons of the Trinity – signals Hrabanus's interest in collecting Gennadius's extensive list of heresies, rather than his tacit endorsement of every paragraph.[45] It is nonetheless noteworthy that as late as the 840s a scholar such as Hrabanus saw no reason to comment on, or to excise, the Stoicizing material when he incorporated Gennadius's work into his own.

Candidus Wizo's use of *De eccl. dogm.* deserves closer scrutiny, because he was one of Alcuin's closest associates, yet he did not shrink from arguing in favour of the corporeality of the soul, an argument that he based chiefly on material from paragraphs 11 and 12 of Gennadius's treatise. Candidus had been a pupil of Alcuin's when the latter was master of the cathedral school at York. After he joined Alcuin on the continent in the 790s, he often conveyed Alcuin's letters to and from correspondents, and he travelled at least twice to Rome, once with Arn of Salzburg.[46] Among Candidus Wizo's extant works is a letter to an unnamed correspondent, who has asked him to explain whether Christ had been able to see God while he was living as a human being on earth, and whether God can be seen by means of the eyes of the body.[47]

---

45   Hrabanus, *De uniuerso* 4.10 (PL 111.96–104).
46   On Candidus's biography, see Jones, 'The Sermons Attributed to Candidus Wizo,' 260–1; and Marenbon, *From the Circle of Alcuin*, 38–40 and 58–9. The attribution of the *Epistola 'Num Christus'* to Candidus Wizo is now secure (Marenbon, *From the Circle of Alcuin*, 39–40), but doubts have arisen concerning the attribution of the Neoplatonizing *Dicta Candidi* to Candidus Wizo (Dolbeau, 'Le *Liber XXI sententiarum*,' 162–5; the *Dicta*, with the other 'Munich Passages,' are edited by Marenbon, *From the Circle of Alcuin*, 152–66).
47   Candidus Wizo, *Epistola 'Num Christus corporeis oculis Deum uidere potuerit'* (ed. Dümmler, MGH Epist. 4.558): 'Est autem quaestio, de qua pulsatum te a quodam dicis: quod Christus dominus noster, in quantum homo fuit, cum hic mortalis inter mortales uiueret, Deum uidere non potuisset? … interrogare dicitur, uidelicet, si corporeis eius oculis Pater uideretur?' (This is the question which you say somebody has pressed you with: was Christ our Lord, insofar as he was a human being, not able to see God while he was living here as a mortal among mortals? … [Your correspondent] is said to have posed the question: namely, would the Father have been seen with Christ's corporeal eyes?) The gist of Candidus's reply is that Christ could not have seen God the Father with corporeal eyes. For God, there is nothing separating will and ability (*uelle* and *posse*). Since Christ could have seen the Father with his spiritual eyes any time he wished, he had no need or desire to use the inferior sight of his corporeal eyes to see the Father. Therefore, because he did not will it, he was not able. Candidus delivers this reply early in the letter (MGH Epist. 4.558.24–560.12) and then devotes the remainder of the letter to unrelated topics.

The few scholars who have paid attention to the *Epistola 'Num Christus'* have neglected one of its most interesting features: Candidus builds his argument upon the Stoicizing Christian notion that God alone is truly incorporeal. He writes:

> Deus sicut summus spiritus est, sic et summe incorporalis est. Hoc autem ideo dico, quia et angeli et animae et quicunque spiritus creati sunt, licet incorporales et dicantur et sint, eius tamen incorporalitatis et, ut ita dicam, spiritalitatis conparatione corporales quodammodo sunt. Licet namque alias forte inlocales, uel animae uel angeli dici possint, in conparatione tamen summae illius diuinitatis locales sunt, quia etsi non altero, ipso tamen mundo, qui utique locus est, continentur. Deus autem non mundo nec creatura aliqua continetur, quia ab ipso continentur omnia creata, ut sint et maneant.[48]

Candidus is obviously aware of two competing opinions on the corporeality of angels and human souls, one Stoicizing and one Neoplatonizing. His rejection of the latter is respectful, but he favours the former. Candidus asserts that angels and souls *are* corporeal and *are* localized, while conceding that one might *call* angels and souls incorporeal and non-localized as a means of facilitating discourse: they 'are called, and are, incorporeal,' and they 'can perhaps be called non-localized in some respects.' It sounds as though Candidus aimed to justify his adherence to a Stoicizing Christian ontology within a milieu that pressured him to adopt a Neoplatonizing perspective instead.[49]

---

48 Candidus Wizo, *Ep. 'Num Christus'* (ed. Dümmler, MGH Epist. 4.558): 'Just as God is the highest spirit, so also is he incorporeal to the highest degree. I say this because the angels and souls and whatever kind of spirits have been created, although they too are called incorporeal and are incorporeal, are nonetheless corporeal in a certain way, in comparison with God's incorporeality and, I would say, his spiritual nature. And so, although souls and angels can perhaps be called non-localized in some respects, they are still localized in comparison with that highest divinity: because even if they are not contained by another thing, they are still contained by the world itself, which is certainly a place. But God is contained neither by the world nor by any creature, because all creatures are contained by him, so that they may exist and endure.' I am grateful to Drew Jones for bringing to my attention the *Ep. 'Num Christus'* and the parallels in Junillus's *Instituta* discussed below.

49 To clarify, Candidus would not have labelled either of these strains of thought according to their classical philosophical roots, but he likely thought of both as patristic opinions: one favoured by the likes of Hilary and Cassian, and the other by Claudianus Mamertus and Boethius. Where Augustine, as Candidus knew him, would have fit into this dichotomy is a matter I will discuss further below.

But from what sources did Candidus learn his Stoicizing ontology, and why would he have considered them persuasive and authoritative enough to bolster his rebuttal of the Neoplatonizing position? He could have had several Stoicizing Christian sources at his disposal; I have not identified any verbatim quotations. Cassian's seventh *Collatio* was perhaps available to him, since Alcuin quotes it in *DRA*, but Cassian's discussion of the soul's corporeality is not immediately relevant to Candidus's purposes, since the former occurs in the context of an argument that demons do not have access to the thoughts of the soul, and furthermore, Cassian says nothing about God's visibility.[50] Faustus's *Epistola* 3 (*Quaeris a me*) parallels the content and context of Candidus's letter much more closely. Not only does Faustus link God's incorporeality with non-locality and invisibility,[51] as Candidus does, but he also provides a precedent for defying Neoplatonizing authorities and for the use of 'the corporeal' as a relative category rather than an absolute one. Faustus writes, 'Nam sicut in quodam sancti Hieronymi tractatu legimus: "globos," inquit, "siderum corporatos esse spiritus arbitrantur," et item: "si angeli," inquit, "caelestia etiam corpora ad conparationem dei inmunda esse dicuntur, quid putas homo aestimandus est?"'[52] Although Candidus may have consulted Faustus's letter as one of multiple sources for his Stoicizing opinions, I hesitate to conclude that Candidus's chief *authority* was Faustus. His *Epistola* 3 was probably available to Candidus's circle, but its reputation must have been rather dim, since it had been the direct target of Claudianus Mamertus's anti-Stoicizing polemic in *De statu animae*, a text known and frequently used within Alcuin's circle.[53] Both Cassian and Faustus, moreover, were authors whom Christian thinkers ought to avoid, according to the pseudo-Gelasian *De libris recipiendis et non recipiendis*, which members of Charlemagne's circle trusted to help them distinguish orthodox writings from heterodox ones.[54]

---

50 Cassian, *Collationes* 7.13, discussed in chapter 4 above.
51 See chapter 4 above for this section of Faustus's letter.
52 Faustus, *Ep.* 3 (*Quaeris a me*) (ed. Engelbrecht, CSEL 21, 173–4): 'For in a certain treatise of St Jerome we read: "They consider the spheres of the heavens to be embodied spirits," and likewise, "If the angels are said to be celestial bodies, unclean in comparison with God, what do you think man ought to be considered?"' Faustus is quoting Jerome's *Comm. in Iob* 25.
53 Claudianus Mamertus's *De statu animae* often circulated with part of Faustus's *Ep.* 3 attached as a preface; see Engelbrecht's discussion in his editions of Claudianus (CSEL 11, viiii–x and 1) and Faustus (CSEL 21, xlviii).
54 Von Dobschutz, *Das Decretum Gelasianum*, 13, lines 322 and 324; the inclusion of Faustus and Cassian on this list is due to their Semipelagian tendencies rather than to their

However, the language and Stoicizing content of Candidus's argument have very close parallels in two works that were held in high regard in Carolingian circles: Gennadius's *De ecclesiasticis dogmatibus* and the *Instituta regularia diuinae legis* of Junillus Africanus. The *Instituta*, composed during the period 542–ca. 549 when Junillus held the office of *Quaestor sacri palatii* under the emperor Justinian, is a Latin treatise on the methods of historical biblical exegesis characteristic of the Antiochene school, composed in the form of a question-and-answer catechesis.[55] Junillus's objective was not to propound dogmas per se but to teach the reader how to engage with the language of the Bible; hence Cassiodorus, in his *Institutiones*, recommends reading Junillus's *Instituta* alongside other works that introduce the reader to exegetical methods, such as Augustine's *De doctrina christiana*.[56] In the second book of the *Instituta*, under the heading 'Quot modos et differentias in operatione creaturarum scriptura posuerit,'[57] Junillus asserts that creatures created out of something else are corporeal (*corporea sunt*), while creatures created *ex nihilo* are incorporeal (*incorporea*). Immediately he qualifies this assertion: 'Haec uero incorporea accipienda sunt, non sicut deus incorporeus dicitur; eius enim conparatione nihil incorporeum est, sicut nec inmortale nec inuisibile. Alius enim modus est, quo haec uerba soli diuinitati conueniunt, alius, quo de creaturis loquitur sicut animabus uel angelis.'[58] Junillus treats incorporeality as a relative category, but he emphasizes the differential application of language, rather than the actual substance of the beings to which the language is applied. In this respect the *Instituta* appears to be a very plausible source of inspiration to Candidus, who claims that souls and angels can be *called* incorporeal, even if comparison with God shows them not to be incorporeal or spiritual in the highest degree. Moreover, because Junillus

---

Stoicizing ontology. On the use of the pseudo-Gelasian *Decretum* by the court scholars who produced the *Libri Carolini*, see W. Otten, 'The Texture of Tradition,' 18–21.

55 Maas, *Exegesis and Empire*, 1–2.

56 Ibid., 32–4; see Cassiodorus, *Institutiones* 1.10.1.

57 Junillus, *Instituta regularia diuinae legis* 2.2 (ed. Maas, *Exegesis and Empire*, 168): 'How many senses and differences in the working of created beings has Scripture set forth?' (trans. ibid., 169).

58 Junillus, *Instituta regularia diuinae legis* 2.2 (ed. Maas, *Exegesis and Empire*, 178): 'But these things must not be considered incorporeal in the same way that God is said to be incorporeal, for in comparison with him nothing is incorporeal, just as nothing is immortal nor invisible. For there is one sense in which these words are suitably applied to the deity alone, and another sense in which it is said of creatures such as souls and angels' (my translation).

makes invisibility a corollary of incorporeality, it is not difficult to see why Candidus might have turned to Junillus while searching for authoritative textual precedents concerning God's invisibility. Junillus's work was certainly circulating in Carolingian milieux at the turn of the ninth century when Candidus wrote his *Epistola 'Num Christus'*; Laistner lists fourteen extant MSS of the *Instituta* dating to the eighth and ninth centuries, most of which he assigns to French and German centres.[59]

I do not believe, however, that Junillus can have been Candidus's only authority for his statement on the relative corporeality of souls. Ultimately Candidus justifies his relativizing view of incorporeality on the basis of the substance of things – specifically, whether things are spatial and circumscribed or not – rather than on the basis of language alone, as Junillus does. For this line of argument Candidus likely relied upon the authority of Gennadius's *De ecclesiasticis dogmatibus*. In the passages of *De eccl. dogm.* examined above, Gennadius (like Junillus) professes that invisibility is a corollary of incorporeality, so again, it is not difficult to see how Candidus might have selected Gennadius as one of his authorities on the invisibility of God. Yet unlike Junillus, Gennadius also names non-locality and non-circumscription as corollaries of God's total incorporeality, and Candidus follows his lead, arguing that the word *inlocalis*, when applied to creatures that are obviously localized and circumscribed, cannot have the same meaning as when it is applied to God, who alone is not contained, even by the cosmos. Where Candidus broaches the topic of locality and circumscription, he leaves behind the linguistic questions pertinent to Junillus's treatise on exegesis and enters the arena where Platonist-Christian and Stoicizing opinions on substance competed with one another through the works of Faustus, Gennadius, Claudianus Mamertus, and the like.

Another reason why I suspect that Gennadius's treatise exerted the strongest influence on the opening of Candidus's *Epistola 'Num Christus'* is that the *De eccl. dogm.* circulated more widely and was held in even higher regard than Junillus's *Instituta*. Unlike his fellow Stoicizers Cassian and Faustus, Gennadius does not appear on the list of heterodox authors in *De libris recipiendis et non recipiendis*, and moreover, a catechetical manual emanating from the circle of Arn of Salzburg (with whom Candidus was closely affiliated) lists Gennadius among the *doctores* of the Church, alongside the likes of Hilary, Jerome, Ambrose, and Augustine. This same manual proceeds to quote numerous paragraphs of *De eccl. dogm.* and to

---

59 Laistner, 'Antiochene Exegesis in Western Europe during the Middle Ages,' 24–6.

recommend that they be imparted to catechumens. Among the passages quoted in the manual, paragraph 54, in which Gennadius rebukes the *nouellos legislatores* and confirms that the soul is corporeal, is reproduced in full under the rubric *De immortalitate animae*.[60] Finally, the most intriguing clue to understanding how and why Candidus used *De eccl. dogm.* lies in the circumstances of its manuscript transmission, which in turn bear significant implications for the relationship between Stoicizing and Neoplatonizing thought in Carolingian circles.

Transmission and Misattribution of *De ecclesiasticis dogmatibus*

By supplementing the list of manuscripts in Turner's century-old study of *De eccl. dogm.* with the data available through *HÜWA*,[61] I count a remarkable total of sixty-seven copies of Gennadius's *De eccl. dogm.* that were generated between ca. 600 and ca. 1000.[62] Turner's catalogue of manuscript witnesses of *De eccl. dogm.* is sorted into four groups, according to the attribution that each manuscript gives to Gennadius's treatise. Among those that belong to the period ca. 700–ca. 1000, only seven attribute the text to Gennadius,[63] while another eight bear a title identifying *De eccl. dogm.* as a set of canons promulgated by the first Nicene Council of 325.[64] In twenty-three further copies, *De eccl. dogm.* is anonymous and without attribution to any specific ecclesiastical meeting; nearly all of the manuscripts in this group are collections of canons.[65] Finally, eighteen manuscripts from this

---

60 This catechetical manual, entitled *Ordo de catecizandis rudibus uel quid sint singula quae geruntur in sacramento baptismatis*, is edited by Bouhot, 'Alcuin et le *De cate-chizandis rudibus* de saint Augustin' 205–30; the quotation of *De eccl. dogm.* par. 54 appears at 209. Only the oldest (and most corrupt) of the three known manuscripts of the *Ordo* includes the list of *doctores*: Munich, BSB, Clm 6325, produced at Freising in the first third of the ninth century (ibid., 195–7).

61 Primmer (series ed.), *Die handschriftliche Überlieferung der Werke des heiligen Augustinus* (*HÜWA*), publishes the fruits of an ongoing project to catalogue all known manuscripts of the works of Augustine as well as Augustinian pseudepigrapha, with two volumes (*Werkverzeichnis* and *Verzeichnis nach Bibliotheken*) devoted to the manuscript holdings of each individual country or region.

62 As of this writing, *HÜWA* volumes for France, the United States, Russia, and Hungary have yet to appear, so this total will climb when those volumes are available, although some manuscripts held in these countries are already listed by Turner.

63 Turner, 'The *Liber ecclesiasticorum dogmatum*,' 83.

64 Turner, 'The *Liber ecclesiasticorum dogmatum*,' 81–2; the titles in this group read 'Incipit doctrina dogma ecclesiastica secundum Nicenum concilium' or some variation thereon.

65 Ibid., 85–7.

period attribute Gennadius's work to Augustine of Hippo, either by attaching Augustine's name to the top of *De eccl. dogm.* itself, or by including the text in a series of works that bear an attribution to Augustine at the head of the series.[66]

According to Turner, attributions to Augustine first arose in the late eighth century, in manuscripts of canons that preserve the second recension of *De eccl. dogm.* He hypothesizes that in the earliest cases, Augustine's name was added when *De eccl. dogm.* was copied from an exemplar that transmitted it anonymously.[67] Yet Turner also highlights two manuscripts in which ninth-century scribes apparently 'corrected' the attribution, from Gennadius *to* Augustine. Apparently, once the attribution to Augustine had been added to anonymous copies of *De eccl. dogm.*, 'the influence of the name now chosen was so powerful that it began, even as early as the ninth century, to suppress the rival and doubtless earlier ascription to Gennadius.'[68]

The transmission history of *De eccl. dogm.* problematizes certain generalizations commonly applied to the Carolingian intellectual milieu. First of all, the survival of a boldly Stoicizing[69] text in several dozen manuscripts from the period ca. 700 to ca. 1000 challenges the claims, made implicitly by Alcuin and explicitly by modern scholars, that Stoicizing ontology and psychology held no sway in Christian discourse as late as the ninth

---

66 Ibid., 83–5.

67 Ibid., 83–5; the second recension lacks par. 53 and 54 (the latter being the 'nouellos legislatores' passage).

68 Ibid., 85. In Verona, Biblioteca Capitolare, LX (58), dating to the early eighth century, a later hand has added the words *Beatissimi Augustini episcopi* over the original attribution to Gennadius; in the ninth-century MS Paris, BNF, lat. 2796, an attribution to Gennadius appears with the treatise itself, but it is attributed to Augustine in the table of contents. With such an abundance of manuscript copies and competing attributions, it is not surprising that a library might accumulate multiple copies with contradictory attributions. The scribe of a Bobbio MS of ca. 900 (Milan, Biblioteca Ambrosiana, G. 58 sup.) confronted such a situation by retaining all three attributions: 'Incipit liber beati Augustini, siue ut alii uolunt Gennadii presbyteri Massiliensis, uel certe diffinitio dogmatum aecclesiasticorum Niceni concilii in regulis LVI ad aedificationem catholicae fidei' (ibid., 82).

69 Among the manuscripts listed by Turner, just over half include par. 54, and all but one include par. 11 and 12. Note, too, that unlike Cassian's *Collationes*, which buries a few Stoicizing paragraphs in a work long enough to occupy over 700 pages in the modern CSEL edition, Gennadius's work is very short, just over ten pages in Turner's edition. When three out of fifty-four paragraphs favour psychological materialism, it lends a Stoicizing flavour to the entire work.

century. In fact, if early medieval readers trusted the titles and attributions in their manuscripts, most readers of De eccl. dogm. believed that they were reading a collection of canons, that is, an express proclamation by the Church that the statements contained therein had been deemed orthodox. When the famous name of the first Nicene Council was attached to De eccl. dogm. in a collection of canons, it lent an even greater weight of authority to Gennadius's words. Perhaps most authoritative of all, for a Carolingian reader, were the numerous copies of De eccl. dogm. that bore an attribution to Augustine. Based on the relative frequency of each different attribution in surviving manuscripts, Candidus was more likely to have encountered De eccl. dogm. as a collection of canons or as a work of Augustine than under Gennadius's own name. If he did indeed read that work under the guise of the canons of the Nicene Council or a work of Augustine, it is no wonder that he considered it authoritative enough to support his rejection of the Neoplatonizing opinion that the soul was incorporeal. The irony is that Alcuin probably imparted to Candidus his view that Augustine's writings were among the most reliable indices of orthodoxy, and that Candidus may well have thought he was borrowing from a work of Augustine when he built his argument about the invisibility of God upon paragraphs 11 and 12 of De ecclesiasticis dogmatibus.

Beyond Alcuin and Candidus

The significance of the misattributions of De eccl. dogm. stretches far beyond Candidus Wizo. Carolingian writings abound in implicit and explicit elevations of Augustine's authority above the other Fathers; their deference to Augustine's teachings is so pervasive that modern scholars do not hesitate to explain intellectual decisions – those of compilers, redactors, authors, and participants in theological debates – as a consequence of Carolingian perceptions of Augustine's authority. Yet for the Carolingians, the 'authoritative works of Augustine' consisted of a smaller selection of genuine works than modern readers have access to, mixed with a significant corpus of pseudepigrapha. A work promoting Semipelagianism and a Stoicizing ontology, as did Gennadius's De eccl. dogm., must have muddled the Carolingians' understanding of Augustine's thought when it circulated under Augustine's name. Conversely, it is startling to find that anyone who was at all acquainted with Augustine's thought would have attributed De eccl. dogm. to Augustine in the first place. The fact that numerous ninth-century scribes did precisely this serves as a stark reminder that, although the Carolingians held up Augustine as an arbiter of orthodoxy, an educated Carolingian may not have had a clear and holistic view of what 'Augustinian thought' might be, even on as plain a question as whether the soul was incorporeal.

The two Anglo-Saxon figures of Alcuin and Candidus Wizo, master and pupil, therefore exemplify two sides of the Carolingians' relationship with Augustine. Alcuin was so enthusiastic a proponent of Augustine's authority that in a didactic work such as *DRA* he would efface all traces of pertinent controversy and present Augustine's views as though they represented points of wholehearted consensus in patristic and Carolingian discourse. In contrast, Candidus Wizo brought to light, perhaps unintentionally, one of the very points of contention from which Alcuin shielded Gundrada when composing *DRA*. Clearly Candidus felt justified in mounting a challenge to the Neoplatonizing position on the soul's incorporeality. It is not easy to determine whether Candidus garnered the confidence to do so from his own mistaken apprehension of *De eccl. dogm.* as a canonical or Augustinian text, or whether he was one of a sizable minority, among the literati of York or of Alcuin's continental circle, who still considered the Stoicizing ontology to be a viable alternative to the Neoplatonizing one, no matter whose name was attached to it.

Over the few decades following Alcuin's death, Carolingian scholars composed several treatises on the nature of the soul. One of these, by Ratramnus of Corbie, argued expressly against the existence of a world-soul.[70] Four others responded to a circular letter disseminated around 850 by Charles the Bald (840–77), in which the king solicited scholarly opinions on the nature of the soul, especially on whether the soul was corporeal, circumscribed, and spatial (*localis*). Replies were generated by Ratramnus, by Alcuin's former pupil Hrabanus Maurus, by Hrabanus's former pupil Gottschalk of Orbais (ca. 804–ca. 869), and by Hincmar, archbishop of Rheims (845–82).[71] All four authors argue in favour of an incorporeal and non-spatial soul, so it is tempting to suppose that such

---

70 Around 863, Odo, bishop of Beauvais, commissioned from Ratramnus a refutation of the Irish monk Macharius and a pupil of his, who maintained that there was one world-soul rather than many individual souls. Ratramnus's work is edited by Lambot, *Liber de anima ad Odonem Bellovacensem*; see also Bouhot, *Ratramne de Corbie*, 57–60.

71 Ratramnus, *De anima* (ed. Wilmart, 'L'opuscule inédit de Ratramne sur la nature de l'âme,' 210–23); Hrabanus, *De anima* (PL 110.1109–20); Gottschalk, *Quaestiones de anima* (ed. Lambot, *Oeuvres théologiques et grammaticales de Godescalc d'Orbais*, 283–94); and Hincmar, *De diuersa et multiplici animae ratione* (PL 125.929–52), though the attribution to Hincmar is now in doubt (Matter, 'The Soul of the Dog-Man,' 50). On Carolingian psychological discourse in the mid-ninth century, see Wilmart, 'L'opuscule inédit';

a position no longer faced significant challenges by the mid-ninth century. On the other hand, the fact that Charles the Bald took the trouble to solicit these scholars' opinions hints that some uncertainty or confusion about the matter persisted. A few passages from Ratramnus's *De anima* shed light on the source of that confusion.

Ratramnus begins by restating the specific questions at hand. Addressing Charles, he writes, 'Duo, quantum memini, proposuistis ecclesiasticorum uobis auctoritate soluenda, sitne anima circumscripta siue localis. Non facilis sane quaestio, et quantum perscrutanda doctis, tantum minus intelligentibus abscondenda, quoniam panis, qui prouectioribus uitam ministrat, lacte nutriendos necat.'[72] Ratramnus's attitude is, in one way, strikingly like Alcuin's: he thinks that unsophisticated minds should be shielded from the intricate difficulties attending an investigation of the *ratio animae*. Yet at the same time, Ratramnus does not hide from Charles that such difficulties exist. The king's questions are 'not easy,' and they demand close scrutiny by learned men. If this is not empty flattery on Ratramnus's part, it suggests that the question of the soul's substance and dimensions had not been definitively settled.

Ratramnus proceeds to explain to Charles that the soul is not *circumscripta* in the sense that such a word applies to a corporeal entity, which is limited by its finite extension in space, but it is *circumscripta* in the sense that an individual soul is distinct from other creatures and is not coextensive with them. As for its dimensions, the soul is not spatial (*localis*) in any sense of the word: it is neither extended in space nor divisible into parts.[73] Recall that a few decades earlier, Alcuin called the soul a *spiritus circumscriptus* without explaining precisely what he meant by *circumscriptus*, while Candidus Wizo argued that because the soul is circumscribed it must be *localis* and *corporalis*, at least compared with the wholly uncircumscribed nature of God. Ratramnus's *De anima* implicitly responds to the disagreement between Alcuin and Candidus by clarifying that the soul is said to

---

Bouhot, *Ratramne de Corbie*, 41–51; and Tolomio, *L'Anima dell'uomo*, which includes translations of all four of these treatises into Italian, with commentary.

72 Ratramnus, *De anima*, lines 1–8 (ed. Wilmart, 'L'opuscule inédit,' 210): 'As far as I recall, you set forth two things to be solved for you by the authority of the churchmen: whether the soul is circumscribed, and whether it is spatial. Of course, this question is not easy, and as much as these things must be closely examined by learned men, so must they be concealed from those who are less able to understand, since the bread which provides life to those who are more advanced does harm to those who need to be nourished on milk.'

73 Ratramnus, *De anima*, lines 21–40 (ed. Wilmart, 'L'opuscule inédit,' 210–11).

be circumscribed with respect to its individual identity, not with respect to spatial extension. In this light Candidus's reasoning, that the circumscribed soul must also be spatial and therefore corporeal, does not follow.

While Ratramnus favours the Neoplatonizing notion of the non-spatial and incorporeal soul, he is willing (unlike Alcuin) to acknowledge that wise men have disagreed and continue to disagree on this matter. In the course of his comments on Ambrose's treatment of the 'flight of the mind' topos in the *Hexameron*, Ratramnus expresses admiration for the way in which Ambrose has corrected others' errors concerning the substance of the soul. Among Ambrose's contemporaries, Ratramnus reports, 'Nonnulli denique putarunt animae magnitudinem mole corporis metiendam.'[74] He concludes his *De anima* with a parallel statement in the present tense, indicating that such errors persist in his own day: 'Sunt autem nonnulli, forte non contemnendae scientiae uiri, qui et corporalem et localem docuerunt eam [*scil.* animam] fore.'[75] Again, it is possible that Ratramnus simply wished to avoid offending his royal addressee by attributing errors about the soul to 'men of not insignificant knowledge,' but if we can take his words at face value, the challenge posed to Neoplatonizing psychology in Ratramnus's own day was not a common-sense Germanic psychological materialism but rather the learned, Stoicizing brand of materialism.[76] This impression is affirmed by passages in the treatises on the soul by Hrabanus and Hincmar, in which, like Alcuin, they first establish the soul's non-spatial nature, and thence its incorporeality, directly refuting the Stoicizing argument that the soul's circumscription implies spatial distribution and thence corporeality.[77]

---

74 Ratramnus, *De anima*, lines 473–4 (ed. Wilmart, 'L'opuscule inédit,' 221): 'Quite a few men believed that the size of the soul could be measured in the same way as the mass of a body.'
75 Ratramnus, *De anima*, lines 557–8 (ed. Wilmart, 'L'opuscule inédit,' 223): 'There are plenty of people, however – even men of not insignificant knowledge – who have taught that the soul is both corporeal and spatial.'
76 Cristiani, 'L'Espace de l'âme,' has observed certain continuities of thought between the fifth-century and ninth-century controversies over the nature of the soul, especially concerning the importance of space and place. See also Verbeke, *The Presence of Stoicism in Medieval Thought*, 35–8; and cf. Spanneut, *Permanence du Stoïcisme*, who suggests that ninth-century Carolingian materialism was not solely a perpetuation of Stoicizing doctrines of late antique Latin Christianity but gained new momentum from the materialist statements made by Paulus Alvarus of Cordoba, who Spanneut hypothesizes may have been influenced by the psychological materialism of Ibn Ḥazm of Cordoba, the so-called 'Tertullian of Islam' (181).
77 Hrabanus, for instance, demonstrates that the soul cannot have shape (*forma*) in space: see *De anima* 3 (PL 110.1113). The diction of (?Pseudo-)Hincmar's *De diuersa et multiplici*

As I proceed in the next chapter to consider King Alfred's engagement with philosophical psychology in works by Augustine, Boethius, and Alcuin, it should be kept in mind that the refutation of Stoicizing psychological materialism was not an end in itself. The mode of argumentation that the Carolingians encountered in Augustine's early dialogues and emulated in their own writings could ill accommodate a relatively or comparatively incorporeal soul; it was far more efficient to advance arguments about the soul if one had recourse to all of the ontological and epistemological corollaries that the Platonic tradition attached to incorporeality. Consider this brief example, which demonstrates that place (*locus*) is incorporeal because it exists in the mind:

> Si aliud est corpus et aliud est locus, sequitur ut locus non sit corpus. Aer autem istius corporalis atque uisibilis mundi quarta pars est; locus igitur non est ... Si rationalis anima incorporea est (unde nullus sapiens dubitat) necessario quicquid in ea intellegitur incorporeum esse manifestum est. Et locus in anima intellegitur, sicut prius dictum est. Incorporalis igitur est.[78]

Such an argument relies on the diametrical opposition of corporeals and incorporeals: if something is demonstrated not to be corporeal, then it must be incorporeal, and vice versa. This mode of discourse cannot operate on the premise that a given entity can be more or less incorporeal. If that were the case, then once having demonstrated that a given entity is not wholly corporeal, one would be left to determine whether it is subtly

---

ratione animae 1.4 (PL 125.937–8) strongly suggests that he knew and opposed the Stoicizing material in Gennadius's *De eccl. dogm.*: 'Quartum locum tenet percontatio, utrum omnis creatura corporea sit, et solus Deus incorporeus. Iam quidem in superioribus satis superque, ut putabamus, ostensum est, nec Deum esse corporeum, neque angelicam dignitatem, sed nec humanarum substantiam animarum' (In fourth position on the list is your inquiry as to whether every creature is corporeal and God alone incorporeal. Now it has already been shown in the foregoing pages, and well enough, as I see it, that God is not corporeal, nor is the rank of angels, nor is the substance of human souls).

78 These passages appear as paragraphs 11 and 16 in a florilegium compiled from Eriugena's *Periphyseon*, surviving in Paris, BNF, lat. 13953, copied in the early tenth century (excerpts ed. Marenbon, *From the Circle of Alcuin*, 171): 'If a body is one thing and a place is another, it follows that a place is not a body. Air, however, is the fourth part of the corporeal and visible world, so it is not a place ... If the rational soul is incorporeal (as no wise man doubts) whatever is understood to exist in the soul is necessarily shown to be incorporeal. And place is understood to exist in the soul, as was mentioned earlier. Therefore place is incorporeal.'

corporeal or wholly incorporeal, and to apply the epistemological corollaries of incorporeality on a sliding scale as well, if such were even possible.

The foregoing passage states that no wise man could doubt the incorporeality of the soul, but as this chapter has made clear, this assertion describes the Carolingian intellectual landscape of the later ninth century more accurately than the reality of Alcuin's day. Back in England, the Platonic understanding of incorporeality was slow to catch on, and a much looser understanding of incorporeality was still applied to the soul in the late ninth century, when King Alfred and his circle of scholars generated Old English translations of several important Latin books. The next chapter analyses the very strange result of Alfred's attempt to render Augustine's *Soliloquia* into Old English *without* invoking the notion of strict incorporeality – an omission that precludes him from successfully replicating most of Augustine's philosophical reasoning.

7 The Alfredian *Soliloquies*: One Man's Conversion to the Doctrine of the Unitary *sawol*

Ac þa ðe firwetgeorne weorþað and onginnað þonne leornian, gif him God abrit of þam mode þæt dysig þæt hit ær mid oferwrigen was, þonne ne wundriað hi no fela þæs þe hi nu wundriað.[1]

This chapter brings us to the first clear and self-conscious confrontation between the vernacular and classical traditions in Anglo-Saxon psychology, a confrontation that unfolds in the pages of the *OE Boethius* and *Soliloquies*, which most scholars attribute to King Alfred the Great (871–899).[2] If we can judge from the epigraph above, which is unparalleled in Boethius's Latin, the translator of the *OE Boethius* valued intellectual curiosity and cultivated an open-mindedness to philosophical alternatives to old, familiar beliefs. Such an outlook is easily attributable to Alfred, who accumulated a lifetime's worth of experience with the vernacular concepts of *sawol* and *mod* before he first encountered patristic discourse on the nature of the soul, in such works as Boethius's *De consolatione philosophiae*,

---

1 Alfred, *OE Boethius*, B-text ch. 39, lines 75–8 (ed. Godden and Irvine, 1.360): 'But as for those who become curious and then begin to learn: if God draws back from their mind the foolish error in which it was formerly cloaked, they will not then consider very strange the things that they currently consider strange.'

2 At the end of this chapter I explore some alternatives to Alfredian authorship; in the meantime, my arguments about the *Boethius* and *Soliloquies* presuppose, but are not wholly dependent upon, the currently prevalent view that the historical Alfred wrote or supervised the writing of the *Pastoral Care*, the *OE Boethius*, the *Soliloquies*, and a prose translation of the first fifty Psalms; and that he bore some resemblance to the man whom we are acquainted with through the prologues attributed to him and through Asser's *De rebus gestis Ælfredi*.

Augustine of Hippo's *Soliloquia*, and Alcuin's *De ratione animae*. This particular educational profile, which is considered rather extraordinary for a ninth-century lay Anglo-Saxon, makes it likely that Alfred gleaned from his study of these discourses an awareness that the rational, immortal *anima* of the Platonist-Christian tradition was incompatible with his life-long understanding of the two entities *sawol* and *mod*.

Malcolm Godden has rightly foregrounded the Alfredian *Boethius* as a crucial witness to the classical tradition in Anglo-Saxon psychology. Rather than focusing solely on the *Boethius* as a finished product, however, I would like to consider how Alfred might have reacted to, and sought to resolve, discrepancies between his deeply ingrained understanding of the *sawol-mod* relationship and the new Platonist-Christian psychology he encountered as he studied Boethius's *Consolatio*. Crucial to our understanding of Alfred's response to the *Consolatio* is his engagement with Augustine's *Soliloquia*. As I propose below, Alfred's circle studied the Latin *Soliloquia* because it addressed questions that would have troubled Anglo-Saxon readers of Boethius's *Consolatio*: Does the mind participate in the afterlife of the soul? Is the soul engaged in mental activity while it resides in the body? In the afterlife, do we retain individual consciousness or are we subsumed into the world-soul, to spend eternity deprived of the pleasure and stimulation of our own minds? Having used the Latin *Soliloquia* to further his understanding of the unitary *anima* in the Latin *Consolatio*, Alfred completed OE translations of both texts, supplementing the psychology of the OE *Boethius* with new information gleaned from his study of the *Soliloquia*.

In the pages that follow, my discussion of the OE *Boethius* serves only as a brief prologue to a closer examination of the Alfredian *Soliloquies*. This is partly because the *Soliloquies*, unlike the *Boethius*, is underrepresented in studies of Anglo-Saxon psychology;[3] but it is also because the present moment is not a propitious one for advancing new interpretations of the

---

3 On psychology in the *Soliloquies*, see esp. M. Wilcox, 'Alfred's Epistemological Metaphors,' 201–10; as well as a brief mention in Godden, 'Anglo-Saxons on the Mind,' 275, and Low, 'The Anglo-Saxon Mind,' 163–6. The psychology of the OE *Boethius* is treated by (among others) Szarmach, 'Alfred, Alcuin, and the Soul'; K. Otten, *König Alfreds Boethius*, 165–80; Low, 'The Anglo-Saxon Mind,' 161–3; Mize, 'The Representation of the Mind as an Enclosure in Old English Poetry,' 61–3 and 71; Šileikytė, 'In Search of the Inner Mind'; Godden, 'Anglo-Saxons on the Mind,' 274–7; and M. Wilcox, 'Alfred's Epistemological Metaphors,' 194–201.

OE Boethius. As I write, the first true critical edition of the prose and verse *Boethius*, edited by Malcolm Godden and Susan Irvine, has just been published under the auspices of the Alfredian Boethius Project.[4] Additionally, only a small portion of the corpus of ninth- and tenth-century commentaries on the Latin *Consolatio* has been printed; editions and studies of these are currently being generated by the successor to the Alfredian Boethius Project.[5] Rather than advance a necessarily inchoate study of the *Boethius* without having all of the pertinent materials at my disposal, I have focused the present chapter on the much maligned and generally ignored *Soliloquies* instead – although I anticipate that the publication of the commentaries on the Latin *Consolatio* will significantly advance our understanding of the OE *Soliloquies* too.

The Alfredian Reception of Boethius's *De consolatione philosophiae*

The rationale behind Alfred's study of the Latin *Consolatio* was likely a simple one. On the continent, the Carolingians had revived the study of this text nearly a century earlier, and such study was, by the end of the ninth century, generating abundant commentary. Alfred's continental helpers, such as Grimbald of Saint-Bertin and John the Old Saxon, probably regarded the *Consolatio* as indispensable to an intermediate or advanced course of study, so when Alfred desired to study Christian literature, the *Consolatio* was an obvious choice, once the king had learned

---

4 Sedgefield (ed.), *King Alfred's Old English Version of Boethius*, has now been superseded by Godden and Irvine (eds), *The Old English Boethius*, which appeared in 2009. Though this edition appeared too recently for me to take into account their hundreds of pages of commentary, I have used their OE text (cited below simply as Godden and Irvine), following the B-text for the prose and the C-text for the metres. On earlier editions, see Szarmach, 'Editions of Alfred: The Wages of Un-influence,' 137–40; see also Kiernan, 'Alfred the Great's Burnt *Boethius*,' on the technologically enhanced study of London, British Library, Cotton Otho A. vi, the only manuscript witness (other than Junius's transcript) to the prosimetrical form of the OE *Boethius*, which was seriously damaged in the Cotton library fire of 1731.

5 The Boethius in Medieval Europe Project posts its objectives and progress at http://www.english.ox.ac.uk/boethius/; see also Godden, 'The Alfredian Boethius Project,' 31–2. Several partial editions of individual commentaries were published in the twentieth century; for further bibliography, and discussion of the commentaries and their MSS, see Bolton, 'The Study of the Consolation of Philosophy in Anglo-Saxon England'; Wittig, 'The "Remigian" Glosses on Boethius's *Consolatio Philosophiae* in Context,' 196; and Szarmach, 'Alfred, Alcuin, and the Soul.'

sufficient Latin.[6] As little as we know about the elementary instruction in Latin that Alfred finally received as an adult, we can be confident that Alfred, unlike boys and young men educated on the continent in the ninth century, was not thoroughly trained in the mode of argumentation characteristic of Carolingian theologians: Alfred's translations show no signs that he could reproduce logical demonstrations that depended upon Platonic metaphysics and Aristotelian logic. Without formal instruction in these areas, Alfred would have brought to his reading of Boethius no clear understanding of the Platonic concept of incorporeality, nor of its epistemological, ontological, and psychological implications. Consequently, some of the philosophical fundamentals that underpin Boethius's *Consolatio* would, at first, have been obscure to Alfred: the difference between perception of corporeals and intellection of Forms, for instance; the true incorporeality of the *anima* (according to Platonic criteria rather than those of the grammarians); the presence of Forms in the *anima* that preexists the body; the permanence of those Forms in the intellect in such a way that, with effort, the living human can 'recollect' them. I do not mean to suggest that Alfred *never* acquired an understanding of such concepts; on the contrary, his translations show that he accepted and assimilated some of them. But what we see of his *OE Boethius* is the final product of a period of study, with the assistance of his helpers and the commentary tradition, rather than a record of his first, relatively uninformed reaction to a philosophically challenging Latin text.

Additionally, Alfred brought to his reading of the Latin *Consolatio* the presuppositions characteristic of vernacular psychological narratives, including that the *mod* died with the body, and that the impersonal *sawol* alone would experience the afterlife. It would have been easy enough for an Anglo-Saxon to learn that the *anima* is something like the *sawol* because it represents the individual in the afterlife, and that the *animus* and *mens* are something like the *mod* because they are responsible for thought. It is another matter entirely to transcend this simplistic approximation and then to grasp that the *animus/mens* is the rational and noblest part of the human *anima*; or that the *animus/mens* must be incorporeal because

---

6 Bately, 'Those Books That Are Most Necessary for All Men to Know,' 49 and 68 nn. 23–8; Beaumont, 'The Latin Tradition of the *De consolatione philosophiae*,' 279–81; Courcelle, *La Consolation de Philosophie dans la tradition littéraire*, 241–99 (but see also Marenbon, *Boethius*, 173–4 with notes; and Wittig, 'The "Remigian" Glosses,' 169–71, regarding parts of Courcelle's argument that require modification, particularly on Asser's and Alfred's putative use of commentaries).

it possesses the capacity to apprehend the incorporeal Forms; or that because the *animus/mens* is incorporeal, it is therefore an unchanging and
immortal repository of those Forms.[7] For the majority of Anglo-Saxons,
the *mod* was none of these things, as I have argued above. For this reason,
much of what Boethius wrote about the *mens* and *animus* would have
conflicted with what Alfred knew of the *mod*, and I suspect that this conflict played a significant role in shaping the king's engagement with the
Latin text.

Alfred's method of translating the words *anima, animus,* and *mens* in
the *Consolatio* is, in brief, surprisingly inconsistent. Or perhaps it would
be more accurate to say that Alfred employed three different translation
strategies as context demanded, and unless we can discern his rationale,
his method will *appear* inconsistent. The first of the three strategies is the
most passive: where Boethius uses the term *anima* to refer to the unitary
soul in the afterlife, or the terms *animus* and *mens* to refer to the unitary
soul engaging in thought during life, Alfred translates *anima* as *sawol,* and
animus/mens as *mod,* superficially retaining the meaning of both the Latin
and the OE terms. For example, in the Latin *Consolatio philosophiae,* Circe
changes Odysseus's crew into wild animals, but only with respect to their
bodies: she cannot touch their *mens* or their *cor,* the locus of their true self
and human identity.[8] Since it is normal for the word *mod* to represent the
locus of thought and personality, Alfred uses *mod* throughout the corresponding OE passage, to the exclusion of all other psychological terms.[9]

---

7 The approximation of *anima* to *sawol* and *animus/mens* to *mod* exemplifies what D.H.
Green calls 'loan-meanings,' in which 'a word in the recipient language acquired a wider
(Christian) semantic range under the influence of a word in the giving language,' as in the
Christianization of Latin *dominus* under the influence of Greek *kyrios,* or of Old High
German *sêla* (cognate with OE *sawol*) under the influence of Latin *anima.* Among methods of importing loan-words, loan-meanings involve 'the least degree of artificiality,
producing a term which was readily understood and making the transition to Christianity largely painless. However, this success was achieved at the cost of deleting the essential difference between paganism and Christianity, so that the initial gain concealed the
fact of a deferred payment' (*Language and History in the Early Germanic World,* 284–5).
8 Boethius, *Cons.* 4 m. 3 and 4 pr. 4 (ed. Bieler, CCSL 94, 72–3).
9 Alfred, *OE Boethius,* B-text ch. 38, lines 38–49 (ed. Godden and Irvine, 1.351). In the
following pages, except where noted otherwise, the sourcing of passages in the *OE Boethius* follows Discenza, 'The Sources of [the OE Translation of] Boethius, *The Consolation of Philosophy*'; translations are my own but have been made in consultation with
Green's translation of the Latin *Cons.* and Godden and Irvine's translation of the *OE
Boethius.*

The second of Alfred's three translation strategies demanded a greater sensitivity to context on the part of the translator. Where Boethius uses the words *mens* and *animus* in a discussion of the unitary soul's activities before or after its residence in the body, Alfred renders these words as *sawol*, in accord with the vernacular tradition, within which only the *sawol* outlasts the body and the *mod* is mortal. For example, in the Latin text, Philosophia knows that her interlocutor already believes that human minds (*mentes hominum*) are immortal; she says to him, 'tu idem es cui persuasum atque insitum permultis demonstrationibus scio mentes hominum nullo modo esse mortales.'[10] Within the vernacular tradition, however, there is no reason to presuppose that the *mod* is immortal, because immortality is proper to the *sawol* alone. Accordingly, in the corresponding lines of the OE dialogue, Wisdom (as Alfred has renamed Philosophia's vernacular counterpart) speaks about the *sawol* instead: 'Ic wene nu þæt ic hæfde ær genog sweotole gereht be manegum tacnum þætte monna sawula sint undeaþlice and ece.'[11] In another instance, where Philosophia introduces the familiar topos of God as the physician of souls, she asks, 'Quid uero aliud animorum salus uidetur esse quam probitas, quid aegritudo quam uitia? Quis autem alius uel seruator bonorum uel malorum depulsor quam rector ac medicator mentium deus?'[12] The 'health' offered by the divine physician is not short-term mental health but the eternal salvation of the soul; accordingly, Alfred uses *sawol* rather than *mod* when he translates: 'Hwæt is sawla hælo bute ryhtwisnes? Oððe hwæt hiora untrymnes bute unþeawas? Hwa is þonne betera læce þære sawle þonne se þe hi gesceop, þæt is God? He arað þa godan and witnað ða yflan; he wat hwæs ælc wyrðe bið.'[13]

---

10 Boethius, *Cons.* 2 pr. 4, lines 80–2 (ed. Bieler, CCSL 94, 25): 'You likewise are a man whom I know to have been persuaded by, and to have internalized, numerous proofs that the minds of humans are in no way mortal.'

11 Alfred, *OE Boethius*, B-text ch. 11, lines 82–4 (ed. Godden and Irvine, 1.263): 'I suppose now that I have already explained clearly enough, by means of many examples, that the souls of humans are immortal and eternal.'

12 Boethius, *Cons.* 4 pr. 6, lines 104–7 (ed. Bieler, CCSL 94, 81): 'Indeed, what do you think the health of the mind is, if not uprightness? And what is illness of the mind, if not the vices? And who is it that protects good men and frustrates the evil, if not God, the governor and healer of minds?'

13 Alfred, *OE Boethius*, B-text ch. 39, lines 238–41 (ed. Godden and Irvine, 1.365): 'What is the health of souls, if not uprightness? Or what is the illness of souls, if not vices? Who, then, is a better physician for the soul than he who fashioned it, that is, God? He cares for the good and chastises the evil; he knows what each soul is worthy of.'

In at least one instance, Alfred very meticulously employs this particular translation strategy in such a way that the unitary soul of Boethius's text is essentially split into the functionally discrete entities *sawol* and *mod*. In the Latin text of 3 m. 11, Philosophia expounds the Platonic theory of anamnesis or recollection.[14] It seems as though truth must be learned from scratch, she explains, but in fact truth always resides in the *animus*, even if we are unaware of it: 'Quisquis profunda mente uestigat uerum / ... animumque doceat quicquid extra molitur / suis retrusum possidere thesauris.'[15] At issue in these lines is the forgetfulness of the mind during its residence in the living body, so Alfred renders *mens* and *animus* as *mod*: 'Swa hwa swa wille dioplice spirigan mid inneweardan mode æfter ryhte ... gesecge þonne his agnum mode þæt hit mæg findan oninnan him selfum ealle þa god þe hit ute secð.'[16] As the *metrum* continues, Philosophia continues to speak of recollection in the living *mens*, but she also alludes to another facet of the theory of recollection, namely, that the truth latent in the *mens* was acquired before it inhabited the body, when it existed on the plane of the incorporeal Forms.

Non omne namque mente depulit lumen
obliuiosam corpus inuehens molem;
haeret profecto semen introrsum ueri
quod excitatur uentilante doctrina.[17]

---

14 In brief, the theory of recollection posits that the incorporeal *anima* existed before the formation of its body, and during its pre-existence it absorbed knowledge of the incorporeal Forms. The truth of the Forms abides within the soul while it inhabits the body, but the flesh hinders the soul's apprehension or recollection of this truth.

15 Boethius, *Cons.* 3 m. 11, lines 1 and 5–6 (ed. Bieler, CCSL 94, 59): 'Whoever hunts down what is true in the depths of his mind ... must also teach his mind that, tucked away among its stores of treasure, it possesses everything that it labours to find outside itself.'

16 Alfred, *OE Boethius*, B-text ch. 35, lines 2–8 (ed. Godden and Irvine, 1.330): 'Whoever wishes earnestly to follow after what is true, employing his inner mind ... should then tell his own mind that it can find within itself every good thing that it seeks outside itself.'

17 Boethius, *Cons.* 3 m. 11, lines 9–12 (ed. Bieler, CCSL 94, 59): 'Now, the body, though it lays on its forgetful bulk, has not driven out every bit of light from the mind; actually, a seed of what is true abides within, which is brought to life when the breath of teaching blows upon it.' Godden points out that in this passage 'Boethius's seed of truth in the heart becomes Alfred's seed of truth dwelling in the soul when the soul and body are joined' ('Anglo-Saxons on the Mind,' 275), but in fact Alfred's treatment of mind and soul throughout this *metrum* is more complicated than he indicates.

For Boethius, *mens* is a suitable name for the mind that pre-exists the body as well as that which inhabits the body, but the Anglo-Saxon reader would not have expected the word *mod* to be applied to an entity that has life outside the body. Alfred's translation, though ponderous, judiciously uses *mod* to name the locus of forgetfulness during life and *sawol* to name that entity which acquired the 'seed of reason' during its pre-existence:

> Forðam nan hefignes þæs lichoman ne nan unðeaw ne mæg eallunga ation of his mode þa rihtwisnesse, swa þæt he hire hwæthwegu nabbe on his mode, þeah sio swærnes ðæs lichoman and þa unþeawas oft abisegien þæt mod mid ofergiotulnesse, and mid þam gedwolmiste hit fortio þæt hit ne mæge swa beorhte scinan swa hit wolde. And þeah bið simle corn þære soðfæstnesse sædes on þære sawle wunigende, þa hwile þe sio sawl and se lichoma gegaderode bioð. Þæt corn sceal bion aweht mid ascunga and mid lare gif hit growan sceal.[18]

Finally, in the closing lines of the Latin *metrum*, Philosophia reiterates that the living human being recollects truths rather than learns them anew: 'Quodsi Platonis Musa personat uerum, / quod quisque discit immemor recordatur.'[19] Although these lines mention neither mind nor soul, Alfred's translation uses the word *mod* to signal that Wisdom is once again talking about thought processes that occur during life:

> Forþam hit is swiðe ryht spell þæt Plato se uðwita sæde. He cwæð swa hwa swa ungemyndig sie rihtwisnesse, gecerre hine to his gemynde. Þonne fint he þær þa ryhtwisnesse gehydde mid þæs lichoman hefignesse and mid his modes gedrefednesse and bisgunga.[20]

---

18 Alfred, *OE Boethius*, B-text ch. 35, lines 11–20 (ed. Godden and Irvine, 1.330): 'Therefore neither any heaviness of the body nor any vice can entirely take away reason from a person's mind, to the extent that he would have none of it [*scil.* reason] in his mind; nevertheless, the sluggishness of the body and the vices often distract the mind with forgetfulness, and with the mist of error they obscure it so that it cannot shine as brightly as it would like. And yet there will always be a grain of a seed of truth dwelling in the soul, as long as the soul and the body are united. That grain must be awakened by inquiry and instruction, if it is to grow.' For *rihtwisnes* meaning *reason*, see BT s.v. *rihtwisness* II.
19 Boethius, *Cons.* 3 m. 11, lines 15–16 (ed. Bieler, CCSL 94, 60): 'So if the Muse of Plato proclaims the truth, that which a person learns he actually recollects, though he be unaware.'
20 Alfred, *OE Boethius*, B-text ch. 35, lines 26–8 (ed. Godden and Irvine, 1.330): 'Therefore it is a very true message that Plato the philosopher spoke. He said: Whoever is not

By virtue of careful attention to his psychological vocabulary, Alfred supplies much information that is only implicit in the Latin *metrum*,[21] and moreover, by employing the words *mod* and *sawol* in accordance with the vernacular tradition, he makes the meaning of the text more accessible to his vernacular audience.

There are places in the text, however, where the translator would have seriously undermined the substance of Boethius's teaching if he had insisted on maintaining the vernacular division of labour between *mod* and *sawol*: this is especially true where Boethius underscores the unitary nature of the soul. In such instances, Alfred adopts a third distinct translation strategy. Contrary to the conventions of the vernacular tradition, he uses the word *sawol* to represent the rational, unitary soul, regardless of whether the Latin text calls it *anima, animus,* or *mens*, and Alfred even adds material from other Latin texts to elucidate his characterization of the unitary soul, since Boethius's Latin text never explains outright that the *animus/mens* is part of the *anima*. This strategy is most clearly discernible in Alfred's rendition of 3 m. 9. In the first dozen lines of the Latin *metrum*, Philosophia addresses God in his capacity as the source of order in the cosmos. Next, continuing her address, Philosophia says, 'Tu triplicis mediam naturae cuncta mouentem / conectens animam per consona membra resoluis.'[22] In these notoriously opaque lines, Boethius almost certainly intended to invoke the Neoplatonic conception of the world-soul, though some early medieval commentators explicated these lines as a depiction of God sending out threefold human souls to animate individual bodies.[23]

---

conscious of his faculty of reason, let him turn back to his memory: there he will find reason, hidden by the heaviness of the body and by the confusion and preoccupations of his mind.'

21 Notably, however, Alfred's rendition of 3 m. 11 conspicuously neglects to mention the incorporeality of the *anima* and of the Forms, which is a necessary component of the theory of recollection in its full-fledged form.

22 Boethius, *Cons.* 3 m. 9, lines 13–14 (ed. Bieler, CCSL 94, 52). Reading these lines as a reference to the human soul, I translate: 'In your capacity to unify, you send out the soul, threefold in nature, throughout all the harmonious limbs; acting as your intermediary, the soul sets all things in motion.' Cf. R. Green's translation, which takes the *anima* to be the world-soul: 'You release the world-soul throughout the harmonious parts of the universe as your surrogate, threefold in its operations, to give motion to all things' (*The Consolation of Philosophy*, 60).

23 For a brief overview of the relationship between *Cons.* 3 m. 9 and Plato's *Timaeus*, see Marenbon, *Boethius*, 151–3; on early medieval commentary on 3 m. 9, see Huygens, 'Mittelalterliche Kommentare zum *O qui perpetua*'; and Beaumont, 'The Latin Tradition of the *De consolatione philosophiae*,' 282–95.

Alfred, following the commentators, elaborates at length on these two lines of the Latin *metrum*, synthesizing from several sources an explanation of what it means for the *sawol* to be threefold.

Þu eac þa ðriefealdan sawla on geðwærum limum styrest, swa þæt ðære sawle þy læsse ne bið on ðam læstan fingre ðe on eallum þam lichoman. For þi ic cwæð þæt sio sawul wære þreofeald forþam þe uðwitan secgað þæt hio hæbbe þrio gecynd. An ðara gecynda is þæt heo bið wilnigende, oðer þæt hio bið irsiende, þridde þæt hio bið gesceadwis. Twa þara gecyndu habbað netenu swa same swa men; oðer þara is willnung, oðer is irsung. Ac se mon ana hæfð gesceadwisnesse, nalles nan oðru gesceaft; forði he hæfð oferþungen ealle þa eorðlican gesceafta mid geðeahte and mid andgite. Forþam seo gesceadwisnes sceal wealdan ægðer ge þære wilnunga ge þæs yrres, forþam hio is synderlic cræft þære saule.[24]

First, prompted by Boethius's image of the soul's diffusion among the *consona membra*, Alfred asserts that the *sawol* is whole in every part of the body, a counterintuitive notion at odds with the emphatic cardiocentrism of the vernacular tradition. Alfred possibly borrowed this characterization from a 'Remigian' commentary on the *Consolatio*, but he also could have found similar information in Alcuin's *De ratione animae*.[25] Next, Alfred

---

24 Alfred, *OE Boethius*, B-text ch. 33, lines 215–25 (ed. Godden and Irvine, 1.317): 'You also govern the threefold souls in the obedient limbs [*scil.* of the body], so that there is no less of that soul in the smallest finger than in the entire body. For this reason I said that the soul was threefold: because philosophers say that it has three natures. One of those natures is that it is appetitive, the second that it is irascible, the third that it is rational. Beasts, like humans, have two of these natures: one of the two is appetite, the other is irascibility. But the human alone, and no other creature, possesses reason, so he has surpassed all earthly creatures by means of deliberation and understanding. Therefore reason must dominate both appetite and passion, because it is the special virtue of the soul.'

25 For instance, the 'Remigian' commentary in Cambridge, UL, Kk. 3. 21 includes in its glosses of lines 13–14 the phrase 'nec minus in digito quam in toto corpore' (no smaller in a finger than in the whole body) (fol. 49v), but Alcuin writes simply that the soul is 'in singulis suae carnis membris totus' (whole in every part of its flesh): see *DRA* 10 (PL 101.644). The 'Remigian' gloss may derive ultimately from Augustine's *Contra epistolam Manichaei quam uocant Fundamenti*, 16 (ed. Zycha, CSEL 25, 213.28–214.3). Parallels in Claudianus Mamertus's *De statu animae* (e.g. 1.17 and 3.2; ed. Engelbrecht, CSEL 11, at 63 and 155) match the diction of the gloss less precisely but are more plausible than Augustine's *Contra ep. Manichaei* as a direct source, given that Claudianus Mamertus is named as an authority shortly thereafter on the same folio (49v) of the Kk. 3. 21 commentary. For a much fuller consideration of Alfred's possible reliance on commentaries and Alcuin in his rendition of 3 m. 9, see Szarmach, 'Alfred, Alcuin, and the Soul.'

further complicates the notion of *sawol* by ascribing to it three faculties that are typically proper to the *mod*, namely reason, passion, and appetite; here Alfred borrows directly from Alcuin's *De ratione animae*.[26] Finally, Alfred intimates that the individual will belongs to the *sawol*, insofar as the subordination of passion and appetite to reason is 'the special virtue of the *sawol*.' Here too Alfred follows *De ratione animae*, but Alcuin actually says that reason is 'a particular characteristic of the mind' (*mentis propria*),[27] so it would appear that in attributing reason to the soul, Alfred was carefully controlling his diction to ensure that his version of 3 m. 9 communicated a consistent teaching on the unitary nature of the soul.

Alfred must have been eager to disseminate his new learning about the unitary soul, because even in passages where it is not wholly germane to the content of his source text, he adds information about the unitary soul from other Latin works. In Boethius's *Consolatio*, Philosophia criticizes those vain individuals who prize ostentatious clothes above the innate dignity that they derive from being 'in mind, similar to God' (Deo mente consimiles).[28] In translating this passage, Alfred was less interested in the problem of vanity than in elaborating on the phrase *Deo mente consimiles*, as is suggested by Wisdom's brief digression in the corresponding passage of the OE text:

> Hwæt, ge þonne þeah hwæthwega godcundlices on eowerre saule habbað, þæt is andgit and gemynd and se gesceadwislica willa þæt hine þara twega lyste. Se þe þonne þas ðreo hæfð, þonne hæfð he his sceoppendes onlicnesse, swa forð swa swa ænegu gesceaft furemest mæg hiere sceppendes onlicnesse habban.[29]

The triad of memory, will, and understanding originates in Augustine's *De Trinitate*, but Alfred likely borrowed it directly from Alcuin's *De ratione animae*.[30] Though Alfred's digression turns the focus away from Philosophia's main point, it also generates an additional opportunity for him to teach his

---

26 Alcuin, *DRA* 3 (PL 101.639–40).
27 Alcuin, *DRA* 3 (PL 101.640); Godden, 'Anglo-Saxons on the Mind,' 274–5.
28 Boethius, *Cons.* 2 pr. 5, lines 66–9 (ed. Bieler, CCSL 94, 28).
29 Alfred, OE *Boethius*, B-text ch. 14, lines 76–80 (ed. Godden and Irvine, 1.269): 'Listen: you still possess something godlike in your soul: that is, understanding and memory, as well as the rational will, which takes pleasure in the other two [*scil.* understanding and memory]. So he who possesses these three therefore has the likeness of his creator to the greatest degree that any creature can have the likeness of its creator.'
30 Alcuin, *DRA* 5 and 6 (PL 101.641).

audience that the *sawol* possesses a triad of mental faculties. A similar digression appears in Alfred's translation of 3 pr. 10, where Philosophia inquires whether the relationship between true happiness and other desirable things is like the relationship among the many parts of one body.[31] This question prompts a considerable digression in the corresponding chapter of the OE text, concerning 'the spiritual and bodily virtues' (good ge gastlicu ge lichomlicu). Bodily virtues, such as strength, are not the same thing as the body itself, Wisdom maintains; likewise, 'Þonne is ðære sawle god wærscipe and gemetgung and geþild and ryhtwisnes and wisdom and manege swelce cræftas, and swa þeah bið oðer sio sawl, oðer bið hire cræftas.'[32] This digression does nothing to clarify the point that Philosophia makes in the Latin text, but it does allow Alfred to impart two lessons gleaned from his study of Augustine's *Soliloquia*: first, that the moral virtues belong to the unitary *sawol*, and second, that abstract qualities are not identical to the persons or things in which those qualities reside.[33]

Elsewhere it has been suggested, on the basis of passages discussed thus far, that during the period when he was producing the *OE Boethius*, Alfred already thought of *sawol* and *mod* as indistinguishable, and therefore that he used these OE terms interchangeably to render *anima*, *animus*, and *mens*.[34] On that interpretation of the evidence, Alfred had already fully assimilated the concept of the unitary soul before undertaking his translation, and he used the OE terms *mod* and *sawol* indiscriminately and with scant regard for how his audience – not a highly educated audience, if they were reading Boethius in OE rather than in Latin – might be confused by a *mod* that participates in the afterlife and a *sawol* that possesses a full complement of mental faculties. Moreover, this interpretation cannot account for the many passages in which Alfred chooses between *mod* and *sawol* on

31 Boethius, *Cons.* 3 pr. 10, lines 80–101 (ed. Bieler, CCSL 94, 54–5).
32 Alfred, *OE Boethius*, B-text ch. 34, lines 132–4 (ed. Godden and Irvine, 1.322): 'Prudence, then, and moderation and patience and uprightness and wisdom and many such good things are the virtues of the soul; yet the soul is one thing and its virtues are another.'
33 That the spiritual virtues belong to the *eagan modes* is first intimated in the OE *Soliloquies* at Carnicelli 62.4–10, and the relationship of the *eagan modes* to the *sawol* is developed slowly. On the difference between a person's virtues and the person himself, see Augustine, *Soliloquia* 1.15.27 (ed. Hörmann, 41.1–17); and Alfred, *Soliloquies* (ed. Carnicelli, 81.12–29).
34 Godden, 'Anglo-Saxons on the Mind,' 275, refers to three of the four passages that I have considered here and proposes that Alfred 'frequently substitutes *sawl* for Boethius' *mens* or *cor* in reference to the inner self, and seems to treat mind (*mod*) and soul (*sawl*) as very closely related concepts.'

the basis of their distinct functions according to the vernacular tradition, rather than on the basis of a simplistic substitution of *sawol* for *anima* and of *mod* for *animus/mens*.

I favour an alternative interpretation of the evidence, namely that the *OE Boethius* is a record of Alfred's evolving responses to the *Consolatio* during a period of time when he was learning and gradually assimilating the concept of the unitary soul, which came to replace his long-held concept of the *sawol* and *mod* as wholly discrete entities. Though scholars have long maintained that Alfred wrote the *Soliloquies* after writing the *Boethius*, the very same scholars have acknowledged that the Latin *Soliloquia* as well as the OE *Soliloquies* exerted a discernible influence upon the content and diction of the *Boethius*,[35] which suggests that at least some revision of the *Boethius* occurred after a period of serious engagement with the Latin *Soliloquia*. This mutual influence, as well as Alfred's application of multiple and conflicting translation strategies to the psychological terminology of the Latin *Consolatio*, are congruent with the sequence of events that I envision. While studying the *Consolatio*, and perhaps even beginning to work out a translation, Alfred realized how great a difference separated Boethius's unitary *anima* from his own understanding of *sawol* and *mod*; he sought clearer explanations of the unitary *anima* in the commentaries on the *Consolatio*, Alcuin's *De ratione animae*, and especially Augustine's *Soliloquia*; and then he transferred his new understanding of the unitary *anima* into OE as he completed the *Boethius*.

Viewed in this light, Alfred's translation strategies are not aimlessly inconsistent; rather, they conform to two identifiable, if contrary, objectives, perhaps belonging to two distinct phases of his translation project, corresponding to the periods before and after his study of Augustine's Latin *Soliloquia*. If this is the case, then the OE *Boethius* passages adduced above are enormously useful in unravelling one of the longstanding puzzles of Alfredian studies: of all the Latin texts available, why would Alfred have selected the *Soliloquia* for inclusion in his translation program?

---

35 Frantzen, *King Alfred*, 82–5; Hubbard, 'The Relation of the "Blooms of King Alfred" to the Anglo-Saxon Translation of Boethius'; Carnicelli, 29–40. The influence of the Latin *Soliloquia* on the content of the OE *Boethius* may be more extensive than is suggested by the few direct borrowings identified to date: Discenza, 'The Sources of [the OE Translation of] Boethius, *The Consolation of Philosophy*,' identifies borrowings from the *Soliloquia* in B-text ch. 21, lines 4–5 (ed. Godden and Irvine, 1.285) and ch. 35, lines 154–5 (ibid., 1.334) as well as two loci for which the *Soliloquia* are one of multiple possible sources (ch. 23 lines 13–14 and ch. 27 lines 6–8; ibid., 1.289 and 1.297), to which we may add the *Soliloquies*-inspired digression on the bodily and spiritual virtues that I discussed above.

Contextualizing the *Soliloquies* within the Alfredian Canon

Among the Alfredian translations, the adaptation of Augustine's *Soliloquia* most staunchly resists efforts to deduce why it was selected for translation. Alfred's circle clearly appreciated the dialogue format, since they also selected Gregory's *Dialogi* and Boethius's *Consolation of Philosophy*;[36] they may also have been swayed by the prestige and authority attached to the name of Augustine.[37] Or, as Richard Gameson points out, 'it is possible that the choice of texts by Augustine was very limited' in Alfred's milieu; moreover, 'in comparison with Augustine's numerous greater works,' the *Soliloquia* is 'very short.'[38] The practical considerations of form, prestige, availability, and brevity seem inconsequential, however, when balanced against the challenges that Augustine's sophisticated philosophical discourse presented to the ninth- or early tenth-century Anglo-Saxon reader. Accordingly, it has become commonplace in studies of the *Soliloquies* to remark that its presence among the Alfredian translations is inexplicable. '[I]t remains almost impossible to understand how [Alfred] became attracted to the *Soliloquia*,' writes Milton McC. Gatch, since this dialogue must have been 'one of the least congenial of Augustine's works to the reader of the age of Alfred.'[39] Malcolm Godden observes that because Alfred characteristically privileged faith and patristic authority over rational proof, it is 'bewildering that Alfred should have taken up such a work as the *Soliloquia* in the first place.'[40] The transmission history of the OE *Soliloquies* reveals little about how later generations used the text: only one (nearly) complete copy survives,[41] and one brief fragment is preserved as a prayer in a miscellany.[42]

---

36 Godden, 'The Player King: Identification and Self-Representation in King Alfred's Writings,' 137.

37 Gatch, 'King Alfred's Version of Augustine's *Soliloquia*: Some Suggestions on Its Rationale and Unity,' 20.

38 Gameson, 'Alfred the Great and the Destruction and Production of Christian Books,' 204; see also Frantzen, 'The Form and Function of the Preface in the Poetry and Prose of Alfred's Reign,' 136.

39 Gatch, 'King Alfred's Version of Augustine's *Soliloquia*,' 20.

40 Godden, 'Text and Eschatology in Book III of the Old English *Soliloquies*,' 189.

41 London, BL, Cotton Vitellius A. xv, fols 4–93, copied in the mid-twelfth century (Ker, *Catalogue*, no. 215). Although the origin of this manuscript is wholly distinct from that of the *Beowulf*-manuscript, with which it is bound, a facsimile of fols 4–93 is included in Kiernan et al. (eds), *Electronic Beowulf 2.0*.

42 London, BL, Cotton Tiberius A. iii, copied in the mid-eleventh century (Ker, *Catalogue*, no. 186; Gneuss, *Handlist*, no. 363); see also Szarmach, 'Alfred's *Soliloquies* in London, BL, Cotton Tiberius A. iii.'

A number of scholars have understood the preface to the *Pastoral Care* to represent Alfred's plan for a 'six-book basic library in English that was to be used in his educational reform,'[43] but if this is accurate, one can scarcely defend the appropriateness of the *Soliloquies* as a representative work of theology or philosophy within such a library.[44] 'It seems preposterous,' Allen Frantzen comments, 'that of all the theological books he might have translated, Alfred would have chosen the *Soliloquies* ... and that he would have allowed a marginally competent companion [*scil.* Wærferth] to struggle with Gregory's *Dialogues* (which, unlike the *Soliloquies*, really is a useful text).'[45]

I agree with Frantzen that Alfred's circle probably did not translate Augustine's *Soliloquia* in order to fill a basic requirement within a putative condensed library in the vernacular, but I disagree with the suggestion that Augustine's *Soliloquia* and the process of translating it into OE were not 'useful' to Alfred's circle. If present-day readers are under the impression that the OE *Soliloquies* was not useful, it is only because present-day scholars have stubbornly looked in the wrong places for evidence of the *Soliloquies*' purpose. It is understandable (if perhaps theoretically misguided) that scholars are more keenly interested in the parts of the Alfredian translations that we consider to be 'original' Alfredian material, because the thoughts and interests of the translator(s) seem to be more vividly communicated to us by way of their purposeful additions and alterations to the text than by the parts that are faithfully translated.[46] It is wholly illogical, however, to suppose that the clues that can reveal why Alfred's circle deemed a text worthy of translation in the first place are to be found in the additions and alterations. The decision to translate a text into OE is based on the merits of the *Latin* text, whether these merits are known first-hand through study of the text or by reputation. Scholarship on the OE *Soliloquies* has largely neglected to investigate why Alfred's circle might have studied the Latin *Soliloquia*, which they must have

---

43 Payne, *King Alfred and Boethius*, 3.
44 'Augustine's *Soliloquia* would not be anybody's obvious choice' for an endeavour of this sort, Szarmach observes, 'even when bolstered by Epistola 147 *De uidendo Deo* – and especially from a later perspective that values *Confessions* or *De ciuitate Dei* or even *De trinitate*' ('Alfred's *Soliloquies* in London, BL, Cotton Tiberius A. iii,' 160).
45 Frantzen, 'The Form and Function of the Preface,' 136.
46 For further critiques of the scholarly tendency to detach and privilege the 'original' material from the Alfredian translations, see Frantzen, 'The Form and Function of the Preface,' 121–5; and Davis, 'The Performance of Translation Theory in King Alfred's National Literary Program,' esp. 149.

undertaken to do before deciding it was worthy of translation. In order to elucidate the impetus behind the creation of an OE *Soliloquies*, therefore, we must begin by determining what the Alfredian audience found worthwhile in the study of Augustine's Latin *Soliloquia*.[47]

Alfredian Reception of Book 1 of the Latin Soliloquia

In chapter 4 above, I surveyed the objectives and methods of Augustine's Latin *Soliloquia*. To be sure, some of the biographical and philosophical anxieties that motivated the historical Augustine to compose the *Soliloquia* would have been obscure to an Alfredian audience. Having no knowledge of Cicero's *Hortensius*, and probably lacking direct knowledge of the *Confessiones* or of *De Trinitate* in which Augustine reflects on his early engagement with the problem of scepticism,[48] the Alfredian audience could not have had more than a superficial grasp of the intellectual and spiritual conflicts that Augustine addressed through the *Soliloquia*, nor could they have sympathized fully with Augustine's urgent desire to repudiate Academic scepticism, which had long since ceased to pose a viable threat to Platonist-Christian teachings. However, the central question which the interlocutor 'Augustine' poses repeatedly during the *Soliloquia* was highly relevant to the intellectual and doctrinal concerns of learned Anglo-Saxons such as Alfred. Pervading and shaping the Latin dialogue is 'Augustine's' fear that even if the soul is immortal – which he does not take for granted – its afterlife might be devoid of individual mental activity, without which his existence will be dreary and futile. This fear is first articulated near the end of the first day of Ratio's conversation with 'Augustine':

---

47 In the discussion that follows, the name Augustine refers to the historical Augustine of Hippo, while 'Augustine' in inverted commas refers to the interlocutor portrayed in the Latin *Soliloquia*, and the name Agustinus refers to the interlocutor portrayed in the OE *Soliloquies*. Concerning the respective strengths and weaknesses of Carnicelli's and Endter's editions of the OE *Soliloquies*, see Szarmach, 'Editions of Alfred: The Wages of Un-influence,' 140–2. Translations of both Augustine's *Soliloquia* and the OE *Soliloquies* are my own, but I have consulted Watson's commentary in his translation of Augustine, *Soliloquies and Immortality of the Soul*; and Hargrove, *King Alfred's Old English Version of St. Augustine's Soliloquies Turned into Modern English*.

48 The *Hortensius* was not known in Anglo-Saxon England, and I know of no manuscript or source-study evidence to suggest that Alfred's circle had access to the *Confessiones* or *De Trinitate*.

R[*atio*]. Quid? si docereris tam te relicto isto corpore quam in ipso consti-
tutum posse ad sapientiam peruenire, curares, utrum hic an in alia uita eo
quod diligis frueris?

A[*ugustinus*]. Si nihil me peius excepturum intellegerem, quod retroageret ab
eo, quo progressus sum, non curarem.

R. Nunc ergo propterea mori times, ne aliquo peiore malo inuoluaris, quo
tibi auferatur diuina cognitio.

A. Non solum ne auferatur timeo, si quid forte percepi, sed etiam ne inter-
cludatur mihi aditus eorum quibus percipiendis inhio, quamuis quod iam
teneo, mecum mansurum sit.[49]

Because 'Augustine' is unsure of the immortality of the soul, he worries
that death will end his soul's search for wisdom or even deprive him of
wisdom that he has worked hard to attain. Over the course of Book 2,
Ratio convinces 'Augustine' that his soul is immortal, but at the end of
Book 2, he voices a related concern, which Ratio would have addressed in
Book 3 if Augustine had ever completed the *Soliloquia*:

R. ... Non enim credo te parum formidare, ne mors humana, etiamsi non
interficiat animam, rerum tamen omnium et ipsius, si qua comperta fuerit,
ueritatis obliuionem inferat.

A. Non potest satis dici, quantum hoc malum metuendum sit. Qualis enim
erit illa aeterna uita uel quae mors non ei praeponenda est, si sic uiuit anima,
ut uidemus eam uiuere in puero mox nato? ut de illa uita nihil dicam, quae in
utero agitur; non enim puto esse nullam.[50]

---

49 Augustine, *Soliloquia* 1.12.20 (ed. Hörmann, CSEL 89, 32.2–12): '*R*. What if you could
be convinced that you would be able to attain wisdom whether you had left behind this
body or you were still ensconced within it? Would you care whether it was in this life
or in another that you enjoyed that which you value? *A*. It would not matter to me, as
long as I understood that I would not later encounter anything worse, which might
drive me back from the level [*scil.* of wisdom] to which I had advanced. *R*. Currently,
then, you fear death because you might be subjected to some worse evil, which would
rob you of your knowledge of the divine. *A*. Not only do I fear that my knowledge
might be taken away – if I have, by chance, absorbed any – but I also fear that the access
to those things which I yearn to grasp might be closed to me, even if that which I already grasp were to remain with me.'

50 Augustine, *Soliloquia* 2.20.36 (ed. Hörmann, CSEL 89, 97.15–98.5): '*R*. I believe that
you are sorely afraid that the death that befalls human beings, even if it does not extinguish the soul, will nonetheless lead to the forgetting of everything, even of truth itself,
if one has discovered any truth. *A*. I can scarcely put into words how fearsome that
misfortune would be: for if the soul lives as we see it live in a newborn child (not to

For 'Augustine,' it is not enough that the soul merely survive the death of the body; he is still terrified by the prospect of a perpetually static, mindless, and non-individuated existence.

Now, when 'Augustine' asks repeatedly to know the fate of the mind after death, he already takes for granted that the *animus* or *mens* is a faculty or property of the *anima*; what he needs to be persuaded of is the immortality of the whole unitary *anima*. A reader such as Alfred, on the other hand, would have taken for granted the immortality of the *anima*, so from his perspective, Ratio's proof that the *anima* and the *animus* both pursue wisdom in the afterlife served to demonstrate the unity of these two entities: the *animus* participates in the afterlife of the *anima*, and the *anima* encompasses the mental faculties of the *animus*. This proof of the unitary nature of the soul, I argue, was the primary reason why Alfred and his associates consulted and studied Augustine's *Soliloquia*. Other related aspects of the *Soliloquia* would have enhanced its appeal for the Alfredian audience. For instance, Ratio offers 'Augustine' something more than a sterile dialectical proof of the immortality of the soul and mind together; she reveals the moral and spiritual benefits of believing that one's individual mental faculties remain intact after death.[51] Additionally, over the course of the dialogue, the unity of mind and soul is continually reinforced, as Ratio and 'Augustine' model the Platonizing Christian usage of the terms *anima*, *animus*, and *mens* to represent a single rational and immortal entity, and as Ratio founds her demonstration of the soul's immortality upon the soul's possession of *intellectus* or *animus*, where *ueritas* can reside eternally.

Given that the vernacular conceptions of the unpsychologized, immortal *sawol* and the mortal, corporeal *mod* complicated the Anglo-Saxon assimilation of Platonist-Christian psychology, the Latin *Soliloquia* offered to its Anglo-Saxon readers a valuable solution to this impediment, in the form of a decisive argument in favour of the unitary soul. Alfred himself appears to have absorbed the doctrine of the unitary soul from the *Soliloquia* and then applied his new understanding to certain passages of the *Boethius*. Thus the ultimate conclusion of the argument of the *Soliloquia* found favour with Alfred's circle, but the same may not be true of its philosophical method. On the second day of conversation in Book 1, Ratio rapidly works out a logical proof that true things do not exist unless

---

mention the sort of life that goes on *in utero*, for I believe that it too exists), what sort of life would it be, and what death would not be preferable to that life?'
51 Augustine, *Soliloquia* 1.6.13–7.14 (ed. Hörmann, CSEL 89, 21.10–23.5).

they are immortal.[52] Her reasoning relies implicitly and unquestioningly on Platonic ontology and epistemology, and because Augustine took for granted that these were familiar to his target audience, he did not explicate their fundamentals within the *Soliloquia*. As others have pointed out, Alfred's lack of prior knowledge of this method of argumentation must have made comprehending the Latin *Soliloquia* a formidable challenge.

The Alfredian Reader and Book 2 of the Soliloquia

The early chapters of Book 2 offered the Alfredian reader further information on the unitary character of the immortal *anima*. To begin, the way in which Ratio reframes 'Augustine's' inquiry is particularly well suited to Anglo-Saxon interests: '[E]sse uis, uiuere, et intellegere; sed esse ut uiuas, uiuere ut intellegas,' Ratio recapitulates. '... Sed utrum ista semper futura sint an nihil horum futurum sit an maneat aliquid semper et aliquid intercidat an minui et augeri haec possint, cum omnia mansura sint, nosse uis.'[53] In Ratio's restatement of the question, rather than presuming that all faculties of the unitary *anima* will be equally affected by the death of the body, 'Augustine' wants to know whether existence and life (which are proper to the *sawol*) will necessarily be coupled with understanding (which is proper to the *mod*) after death. The Alfredian reader may have been surprised to discover, while studying the section of Book 2 that addresses the continuation of life and understanding after death, that 'Augustine' identifies the *anima* as the locus of understanding and of the self. He readily assents when Ratio asks, 'Quid? intellectus uidetur tibi ad animam pertinere?'[54] and shortly thereafter, 'Augustine' accepts that his *anima*, rather than his bodily senses, are the essence of his individual self:

> R. Non igitur est in rebus falsitas, sed in sensu; non autem fallitur, qui falsis non adsentitur. Conficitur ut aliud simus nos, aliud sensus, siquidem, cum ipse fallitur, possumus nos non falli.

---

52 Augustine, *Soliloquia* 1.14.26–15.29 (ed. Hörmann, CSEL 89, 39.3–43.13; see chapter 4 above).

53 Augustine, *Soliloquia* 2.1.1 (ed. Hörmann, CSEL 89, 47.7–13): 'R. You want to exist, to live, and to understand, but you want to exist in order to live, and to live in order to understand ... But you desire to know whether these [*scil.* existence, life, and understanding] will exist forever; or whether none of them will continue to exist; or whether one might endure always while another perishes; or whether, if all of them are going to endure, they can be diminished or increased.'

54 Augustine, *Soliloquia* 2.3.3 (ed. Hörmann, CSEL 89, 49.4): 'Then does it seem to you that the intellect belongs to the soul?'

A. Nihil habeo quod contradicam.

R. Sed numquid, cum anima fallitur, audes te dicere non esse falsum?

A. Quo pacto istud audeo?[55]

By this point, early in Book 2 of the *Soliloquia*, it could not have escaped a reader steeped in the vernacular tradition of psychology that Ratio and 'Augustine' ascribe to the *anima* a wide range of mental faculties and characteristics that most Anglo-Saxons associated with the *mod* rather than the *sawol*.

It is more difficult to gauge how an Alfredian reader might have responded to Ratio's introduction of Aristotle's Categories and her return to the Platonic theory of Forms. Alfred's circle probably gained a superficial acquaintance with the Categories through Isidore's *Etymologiae*,[56] and it is possible that they were able to study the Categories in more depth by way of the pseudo-Augustinian *De decem categoriis* or Porphyry's *Isagoge* in Boethius's Latin translation.[57] Even if Alfred's circle had not studied dialectic, Augustine's use of the Categories was not necessarily beyond their grasp, because Ratio and 'Augustine' define 'accident' and 'inseparable property' and use examples to illustrate the distinction between them.[58] Where Ratio relies on the theory of Forms, on the other hand, her argument

---

55 Augustine, *Soliloquia* 2.3.3 (ed. Hörmann, CSEL 89, 50.14–21): 'R. Therefore falsity is not in things but in sensory perception; one who does not assent to that which is false is not deceived. One concludes that we ourselves are one thing, and our sensory perception is something else, because we ourselves are capable of avoiding deception when our sensory perception is deceived. A. I have no reason to contradict you. R. But would you dare to say that, when the soul has been deceived, *you* have not been deceived? A. How could I be so bold as to say that?'

56 Isidore, *Etym.* 2.26, 'De categoriis Aristotelis,' is a very brief treatment of the Categories synthesized from several sources. On the *Etym.* and other vehicles of transmission of the *Categories* in the early Middle Ages, see Minio-Paluello, 'The Text of the *Categoriae*: The Latin Tradition,' esp. 31–5; and Minio-Paluello, 'Dalle *Categoriae decem* pseudo-Agostiniane (Temistiane) al testo vulgato Aristotelico Boeziano.'

57 *De decem categoriis* is a Latin paraphrase and abridgement of Aristotle's *Categories*, penned by Themistius in the fourth century but commonly attributed to Augustine from the late eighth century until the early modern period. Among the MSS of this work listed by Lapidge (*Library*, 334), three were potentially available in England around the turn of the tenth century; the most intriguing is Bern, Burgerbibliothek, C. 219 + Leiden, Bibliotheek der Rijksuniversiteit, Voss. lat. Q. 2, fol. 60, copied in the late ninth century in either Wales or southwest England (Gneuss, *Handlist*, no. 795), which preserves Themistius alongside a fragment of Boethius's translation of Porphyry's *Isagoge*, an introductory commentary on Aristotle's *Categories*.

58 Augustine, *Soliloquia* 2.12.22 (ed. Hörmann, CSEL 89, 75.4–76.7; see chapter 4 above).

may have been less accessible to the Alfredian reader. Like Boethius's Latin *Consolatio*, Augustine's *Soliloquia* leaves unsaid what his audience would already have known concerning the epistemological and ontological implications of incorporeality, and there was no single condensed primer on the Forms available to Alfred's circle, as there was on the Categories.[59] At times in the *Soliloquia* even the interlocutor 'Augustine' is temporarily stumped by Ratio's profoundly Realist assertions, such as the notion that if a body actually achieved its ideal Form, it would not be a body anymore but an *animus*.[60] It is difficult to see how this aspect of Ratio's reasoning could have made sense to Alfred if his background in Platonist thought was as sparse as it appears. I hesitate to use the OE *Soliloquies* as an index of what an Alfredian reader failed to grasp in the Latin *Soliloquia*, because the translator may have omitted material that he himself understood but deemed too sophisticated for his intended audience. However, as will be detailed below, Alfred radically overhauled the content of the OE *Soliloquies* so that its arguments might proceed without recourse to the theory of Forms, even though it would have been much simpler to add to the OE *Soliloquies* a brief introduction to the Platonist meaning and implications of incorporeality. It is difficult to avoid the conclusion that Alfredian students of the Latin *Soliloquia* did not grasp the ontological and epistemological implications of the soul's incorporeality well enough to understand how they operated in Augustine's philosophical discourse.

Despite all this, the Latin *Soliloquia* could undoubtedly have proven very useful to an Anglo-Saxon reader if he was willing to accept the content of Augustine's argument on the basis of authority even though the logic of the argument eluded him. If Alfred was such a reader, then the *Soliloquia* filled in gaps in his understanding of the unitary *anima* – gaps brought to light by his study of Boethius's *Consolatio* – and presented the concept of the unitary *anima* not merely as right doctrine but also as a comfort and a source of hope for one who formerly believed that his *mod*, his individual consciousness and his true self, would die with the

---

59 See Gersh, 'The Medieval Legacy from Ancient Platonism'; and Marenbon, 'Platonism – A Doxographic Approach,' on early medieval knowledge of Platonic philosophy. Perhaps the closest thing to a substantial précis of the theory of Forms that might have been consulted by the Anglo-Saxons is Augustine's mostly favourable discussion of Plato's natural philosophy, in Book 8 of *De ciuitate Dei*, but there is scant evidence for direct knowledge of this work during the interval between Bede's day and Ælfric's (see chapter 4 above).

60 Augustine, *Soliloquia* 2.18.32 (ed. Hörmann, CSEL 89, 91.1–8).

body. Study of the Latin *Soliloquia* could, in fact, have offered all this to any Anglo-Saxon readers who were intellectually curious or spiritually anxious to resolve the conflict between their everyday concept of the mind and that which they absorbed through their first encounters with patristic theology. But how many such readers of patristic theology were there outside Alfred's immediate circle? Although I will argue below that Alfred's intellectual profile was not as extraordinary as is commonly assumed, it is unquestionably true that middle-aged laypersons did not typically take up the study of patristic theological and philosophical treatises, and therefore never confronted the conflict between the two psychologies. For an audience who persisted in blissful ignorance of the difference between the vernacular and philosophical definitions of the soul, an OE translation of the *Soliloquia* was an efficient means for Alfred to disseminate the lessons that he had learned through his study of Platonist-Christian psychology in the *Soliloquia* as well as in Alcuin's *De ratione animae* and Boethius's *Consolatio*.

The Philosophical and Rhetorical Achievement of the OE *Soliloquies*

Both Gatch and Godden convincingly attribute many omissions and additions in the *Soliloquies* to Alfred's preference for arguments based on dogma and patristic authority rather than on philosophical proof.[61] Yet Gatch and Godden profess not to understand why Alfred considered it useful to study or to translate Augustine's *Soliloquia* in the first place, so there is much scope to sharpen our understanding of the OE *Soliloquies* in light of my foregoing arguments: namely that Alfred studied the *Soliloquia* in order to learn about the unitary soul; that he succeeded in applying his new learning on the unitary soul to his translation of Boethius's *Consolatio*; and that as a translator he was either unable or unwilling to engage with any of Augustine's lines of reasoning that demanded prior knowledge of Platonist metaphysics or Aristotelian dialectic. Realizing that the utility of the *Soliloquies* project lay in its demonstration of the unitary nature of the soul permits a much more focused assessment of the philosophical and rhetorical character of the *Soliloquies* than has been undertaken to date.

Among the Alfredian additions, omissions, and alterations that directly affect what the *Soliloquies* communicates about the unitary soul, I discern three salient patterns, each of which dominates a different section of the OE dialogue. First, a series of subtle adjustments to the diction in the early part

---

61 Gatch, 'King Alfred's Version of Augustine's *Soliloquia*'; Godden, 'Text and Eschatology.'

of Book 1 contributes to a radical change in the characterization of the interlocutor Agustinus: whereas his Latin counterpart 'Augustine' was a sceptic who needed to be persuaded that the unitary *anima* was immortal, Alfred turns Agustinus into an adherent of vernacular psychology, who needs to be persuaded that the *mod* forms part of the immortal *sawol*. Second, from the middle of Book 1 through most of Book 2, Alfred minimizes the role of Platonic metaphysics, especially the concept of incorporeality with all of its epistemological implications, which is indispensable to the logical demonstrations of the Latin *Soliloquia*. Third, the concluding section of Book 2 and all of Book 3 consist of material (including the theory of recollection and the story of Dives and Lazarus) that Alfred has added in order to bolster the message that the *mod* will participate in the afterlife and is therefore part of the *sawol*. All three of these manoeuvers shape the dialogue into a form far better suited for an Anglo-Saxon audience than a verbatim translation of Augustine's *Soliloquia* would have been. In Figure 1 below, these three changes appear in the top row, as items I, II, and III.

Among these three large-scale reworkings of the dialogue, Alfred's decision to minimize the role of Platonic metaphysics and Aristotelian dialectic is the most disruptive and the most significant. As I argued earlier, the dialectical proofs of the immortality of the soul that Ratio unfolds in the Latin *Soliloquia* are utterly reliant on the premise that the soul is truly incorporeal and on all of the epistemological implications that attach to that premise. In order for Alfred to bring the OE *Soliloquies* to roughly the same conclusion that Ratio and 'Augustine' reach in the Latin dialogue, he had to find alternative forms of argumentation that would attain those conclusions without recourse to the concept of incorporeality. Alfred's decision to minimize the role of Platonic metaphysics in the middle section of the *Soliloquies* therefore triggers a complicated cascade of further changes to the content as well as the rhetoric of the dialogue, which are schematized in the lower three rows on Figure 1; the arrows indicate that a number of the smaller changes implemented by Alfred were necessitated, directly or indirectly, by Alfred's decision to remove all forms of argumentation that demand knowledge of Platonic metaphysics.

The Transformation of the *Soliloquies* into a Conversion Story (Fig. 1, item I)

At the outset of the Latin *Soliloquia*, 'Augustine' is motivated by a reasoned curiosity. He initiates a conversation with Ratio because he 'desired to know' (*scire cupiebam*); he mulls over 'many and varied' (*multa ac uaria*) matters, of which he lists three: himself, his good, and what evil should be

Figure 1
Changes and additions to the content and rhetoric of the OE *Soliloquies*

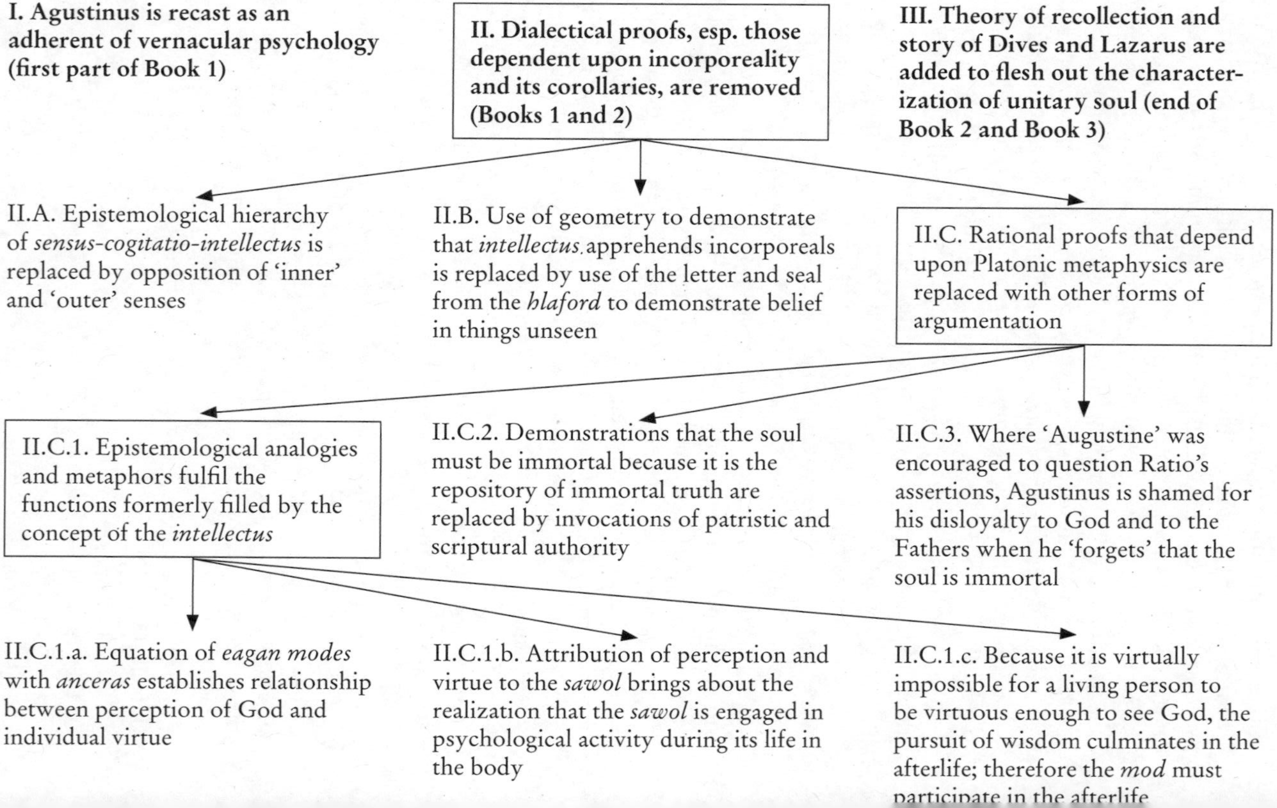

I. Agustinus is recast as an adherent of vernacular psychology (first part of Book 1)

II. Dialectical proofs, esp. those dependent upon incorporeality and its corollaries, are removed (Books 1 and 2)

III. Theory of recollection and story of Dives and Lazarus added to flesh out the characterization of unitary soul (end of Book 2 and Book 3)

II.A. Epistemological hierarchy of *sensus-cogitatio-intellectus* is replaced by opposition of 'inner' and 'outer' senses

II.B. Use of geometry to demonstrate that *intellectus* apprehends incorporeals is replaced by use of the letter and seal from the *blaford* to demonstrate belief in things unseen

II.C. Rational proofs that depend upon Platonic metaphysics are replaced with other forms of argumentation

II.C.1. Epistemological analogies and metaphors fulfil the functions formerly filled by the concept of the *intellectus*

II.C.2. Demonstrations that the soul must be immortal because it is the repository of immortal truth are replaced by invocations of patristic and scriptural authority

II.C.3. Where 'Augustine' was encouraged to question Ratio's assertions, Agustinus is shamed for his disloyalty to God and to the Fathers when he 'forgets' that the soul is immortal

II.C.1.a. Equation of *eagan modes* with *anceras* establishes relationship between perception of God and individual virtue

II.C.1.b. Attribution of perception and virtue to the *sawol* brings about the realization that the *sawol* is engaged in psychological activity during its life in the body

II.C.1.c. Because it is virtually impossible for a living person to be virtuous enough to see God, the pursuit of wisdom culminates in the afterlife; therefore the *mod* must participate in the afterlife

avoided.[62] In contrast, from the opening lines of his translation, Alfred imbues the words of the interlocutor Agustinus with an urgency unparalleled in the Latin. Agustinus's mind is plagued by doubts (*modis ... tweounga*; *þæt mod ... tweonode*), and he yearns to understand something that has been beyond his grasp ('*þæs þe hit [scil.* mod] ær for sweotol ongytan ne meahte'). The matters that have stirred up doubt and confusion are not only *mislicu* 'varied' but also *selcuð*, literally 'little-known,' perhaps 'novel' or 'esoteric.' Most important, Agustinus expands the list of questions that he hopes to answer, and prominent among the additions is that he desires to know whether the mind *and* the soul are mortal or immortal ('hwæþer hys mod and hys sawel deadlic were and gewitendlice, þe heo were alibbendu and ecu').[63] Within a few sentences, Alfred has transformed an exercise in dialectic into a dramatic conversion story. He foreshadows that what was doubtful, obscure, and alienating for Agustinus will become credible, clear, and familiar; and that prominent among these 'novel' or 'esoteric' lessons, he will learn whether both mind *and* soul are immortal.

The reason why Agustinus needs to learn something 'novel' about the mind and the soul is that, unlike the sceptic 'Augustine' in the Latin dialogue, who accepts the soul's unitary nature but doubts its immortality, Agustinus is an adherent of vernacular psychology. He believes that the *sawol* is immortal but excluded from mental activity, while the *mod*, the locus of mental activity and personality, cannot participate in the afterlife. Alfred must have devoted painstaking attention to Agustinus's diction early in Book 1 in order to effect this transformation. For example, during the lengthy prayer near the beginning of the dialogue, Agustinus uses the word *sawol* to signify the entity that survives while the body decays and that receives recompense in the afterlife for an individual's deeds,[64] and he

---

62 I quote both Augustine, *Retractationes* 1.4.1 (ed. Mutzenbacher, CCSL 57, 13–14) and *Soliloquia* 1.1.1 (ed. Hörmann, CSEL 89, 3.2–7). This sentence of the *Retractationes* appears at the head of many manuscript copies of the Latin *Soliloquia*, and it must have appeared there in Alfred's exemplar, because the OE *Soliloquies* begins with a paraphrase of this sentence (see Godden, 'The Sources of [the OE Translation of] Augustine, *Soliloquies*'). Editors and translators of the OE *Soliloquies* typically treat the paraphrase of *Retractationes* 1.4.1 as part of the new preface composed by Alfred, though this is unwarranted by the *mise-en-page* of this material in the manuscript: see Kiernan et al., *Electronic Beowulf* 2.0, fols 2r–v.

63 Alfred, *Soliloquies* (ed. Carnicelli, 48.13–49.3).

64 In the OE *Soliloquies* at Carnicelli 52.21–4, Agustinus condemns the 'error' (*dwolan*) of those who believe that 'manna sawla næbben nan edlean æfter þisse worulde heora gearnunge' (the souls of men will have no reward after this world); the corresponding

localizes a mental or spiritual state in the *mod*, where the corresponding Latin mentions neither the mind nor the soul.[65] Another complex series of changes illustrates how attentively Alfred conformed Agustinus's diction to the usage of the vernacular tradition. In the Latin version of the opening prayer, 'Augustine' addresses God 'per quem melius nostrum deteriori subiectum non est.'[66] In rendering this line, Alfred interprets the 'better' part of us to be the mind and the 'worse' part to be the body: 'þu þe us lærdesd þæt we underþieddan urne lycuman ure mode.'[67] Alfred's interpretation was probably suggested to him by a passage that appears later in the Latin dialogue, in which 'Augustine' quotes an opinion attributed to Cornelius Celsus, a physician of the early first century AD: '"duabus," inquit, "partibus compositi sumus, ex animo scilicet et corpore, quarum prior melior, deterius corpus est."'[68] It is intriguing that after Alfred applies Celsus's interpretation of 'better' and 'worse' to the foregoing passage, he rejects it when he comes to translate the quotation of Celsus in its proper context, choosing *sawol* rather than *mod* to render the term *animus*: '"Of twam ðingum we sint þæt we sint, þæt ys, of saule and of lichaman; seo sawel is gastlic and se lichaman, eordlic."'[69] The principle

---

passage in the Latin makes no mention of the afterlife of the soul (Augustine, *Soliloquia* 1.1.3; ed. Hörmann, CSEL 89, 7.9–11). At Carnicelli 53.26–7, Agustinus declares, 'þeah se lichaman er were gemolsnod, þeah wæs seo sawl simle lybbende siððam heo ærest gesceapen wes' (although the body will have already decayed, nonetheless the soul has always been alive ever since it was first fashioned); this statement has no parallel in the Latin (cf. Augustine, *Soliloquia* 1.1.4; ed. Hörmann, CSEL 89, 8.9–9.7).

65 At *Soliloquia* 1.1.2 (ed. Hörmann, CSEL 89, 5.1), 'Augustine' addresses God 'qui nisi mundos uerum scire noluisti' (who was unwilling that anybody except the pure know what is true); cf. the corresponding passage in the OE *Soliloquies* (ed. Carnicelli, 50.25–6), in which Agustinus specifies that God reveals himself to those who are pure *on mode*: 'þu þe nelt þe eallunga geeowian openlice nanum oðrum buton þam, þam geclænsode beoð on heora mode' (you who were unwilling to openly reveal yourself fully to anyone other than those who were cleansed in their mind).

66 Augustine, *Soliloquia* 1.1.3 (ed. Hörmann, CSEL 89, 6.16–17): 'through whom the better part of us has not been subjugated to the worse.'

67 Alfred, *Soliloquies* (ed. Carnicelli, 52.10–11): 'you who taught us that we subjugate our body to our mind.'

68 Augustine, *Soliloquia* 1.12.21 (ed. Hörmann, CSEL 89, 33.7–9): 'we are composed of two parts, namely of body and mind; between these two, the first is the better and the body is the worse.'

69 Alfred, *Soliloquies* (ed. Carnicelli, 75.12–13): 'Out of two things we are what we are: that is, of soul and body; the soul is spiritual and the body is earthly.'

guiding the translator's decisions is the division of labour between *sawol* and *mod* in the vernacular tradition: it is the *mod* that governs the body but the transcendent *sawol* that complements the transient body to make up a whole human being.

The vernacularization of Agustinus's conception of the soul continues as he begins his conversation with Gesceadwisnes in earnest. Recall that early in the Latin dialogue, Ratio elicits from 'Augustine' a distinction between the souls of beasts and those of humans: he does not love all ensouled beings (*animalia*) but only humans, because they possess rational souls (*rationales animas habent*); moreover, he loves humans more in proportion to how well they use their rational souls ('quanto magis bene utuntur anima rationali').[70] Agustinus cannot use the word *sawol* in this way to distinguish among beasts, humans, and more beloved humans, because the vernacular tradition does not attribute reason to the human *sawol* any more than to the *sawol* of beasts, nor does it characterize human beings as 'users' of the *sawol* during their bodily life. Accordingly, Agustinus denies loving everything that has a soul ('ælc þing þe sawle hæfð'); rather, he loves humans because they possess reason in the mind ('habbað gesceadwisnesse on here mode'), and he loves his friends in proportion to how well they use their reason and how virtuous their will is: 'ælcne þara [*scil.* freonda] ðe ic ma lufige þonne oðerne, ic hine lufige swa mycele ma þonne ðone oðerne swa ic ongyte þæt he betran willan hæfð þonne se oðer, and his gesceadwisnesse nyttran wille to donne.'[71]

The nuanced changes to Agustinus's diction up to this point firmly establish that he recognizes a sharp division of labour between *sawol* and *mod*, as is typical of the vernacular tradition. As Gesceadwisnes begins to lay the groundwork that will prepare Agustinus for his conversion to belief in the unitary soul, Alfred begins to refashion Gesceadwisnes's arguments so that they might proceed without recourse to the Platonic notion of incorporeality. Alfred immediately faces a difficult puzzle: if he dispenses with the concept of *intellectus*, the faculty by which humans perceive incorporeals, how can he talk about the vision of God?

---

70 Augustine, *Soliloquia* 1.2.7 (ed. Hörmann, CSEL 89, 12.16–23).

71 Alfred, *Soliloquies* (ed. Carnicelli, 57.18–58.4): 'if I love any one of my friends more than another, I love him more than another to the same degree that I perceive him to possess a better will, and to put his reason to a more useful purpose, than the other does.'

How Can Agustinus See God without *intellectus*?
(Fig. 1, items II.A and II.B)

In the Latin *Soliloquia*, in preparation for her teaching on the vision of God, Ratio leads 'Augustine' to articulate a hierarchy of types of perception. At its base is *sensus* or sensory perception, which is exceeded by *cogitatio*, or abstract thought built upon information gleaned by sensory perception. Superior to both of these is *intellectus*, the faculty of the incorporeal *anima* that apprehends incorporeal entities, including God and the immortal truths of the Forms, although the power of the *intellectus* is blunted while it is attached to a fleshly body.[72] Rather than add to Gesceadwisnes's teachings some introduction to the concept of incorporeality, Alfred dispenses with *intellectus* altogether, and instead of a tripartite epistemological hierarchy, he establishes a binary opposition between sensory or 'outer perception,' which he calls *uttor gewit* and *uttor andgiet*, and 'inner thought,' which he calls *innor gewit* and *ingeþanc*.

Agustinus is appropriately suspicious of 'outer perception.' He earnestly agrees when Gesceadwisnes proposes,

> me þincð nu þæt þu ne truwie ðam uttram gewitte, naðer ne þam eagum, ne þam earum, ne ðam stence, ne ðam swece, ne ðam hrinunge, ðað þu ðurh ðara ænig swa sweotole ongytan mæge þæt þæt þu woldest, buton þu hyt on þinum ingeþance ongytæ þurh ðin gesceadwisnesse.[73]

But 'inner thought,' although it is directed toward the apprehension of a different class of entities, is no more immune to deception than is 'outer perception.' Gesceadwisnes inquires whether Agustinus knows his *cniht* Alypius 'þe mid ðam utram gewitum, þe mið þam inran.' Agustinus replies, 'ic hine can nu swa ic hine of ðam uttram gewitum cunnan mæge. Ac ic wilnode þæt ic cuðe hys ingeþanc of minum ingeþance. Ðonne wiste ic hwilce treowða he hæfde wið me.'[74] Agustinus's concluding comment,

---

72 On Alfred's reception of Augustine's epistemological hierarchy, see M. Wilcox, 'Alfred's Epistemological Metaphors,' 203–9 and 217.

73 Alfred, *Soliloquies* (ed. Carnicelli, 59.5–8): 'It seems to me now that you do not trust the outer understanding – neither the eyes nor the ears nor odour nor taste nor touch – or that through any of them you could understand so clearly that which you wish to understand, unless you grasp it in your inner thought by means of your reason.'

74 Alfred, *Soliloquies* (ed. Carnicelli, 59.10–14): Gesceadwisnes asks Agustinus whether he knows his servant Alypius 'by means of the outer senses or by means of the inner understanding?' Agustinus replies, 'I currently know him as well as I can know him by

which has no parallel in the Latin, confirms that the category of 'inner thought' is not the equivalent of *cogitatio* and *intellectus* joined together; it is the equivalent of *cogitatio* alone, which is vulnerable to deception, because it depends upon information gathered by the senses. If Alypius wished to conceal the disloyalty of his *ingeþanc* from Agustinus's *ingeþanc*, he could easily do so by means of words and actions apprehended by Agustinus's *uttor gewit*. For this reason, *ingeþanc* generates belief or disbelief, rather than certain knowledge.

In the absence of *intellectus*, wherein lies the capacity to generate certain knowledge by apprehending incorporeal truths, belief and disbelief play a disproportionately large role in Alfred's version of the dialogue. In the Latin text, as part of their discussion of epistemology, Ratio and 'Augustine' ponder the relationship between the shapes that are perceptible in nature and the Forms of shapes that the *intellectus* apprehends in the study of geometry, leading 'Augustine' to an important conclusion: he is absolutely certain that his *intellectus* can apprehend these incorporeal, ideal shapes, even though the sceptical Academics would argue otherwise.[75] Not surprisingly, in his translation Alfred curtails the discussion of geometry before the problem of Forms arises.[76] However, in doing so, Alfred sacrifices an indispensable phase of Agustinus's conversion: it is crucial that he, like 'Augustine,' come to realize that he can reliably know things that are not perceived by the senses. So Alfred crafts an analogy that will bring Agustinus to this realization by another path. Gesceadwisnes asks Agustinus whether he can reliably know, on the basis of a letter accompanied by a seal, the intention and will of his temporal lord:

geþenc nu gyf ðines hlafordes ærendgewrit and hys insegel to ðe cymð, hwæðer þu mæge cweðan þæt ðu hine be ðam ongytan ne mægæ, ne hys willan þær-on gecnawan ne mæge. gyf þu ðonne cwyst þæt þu hys willan ðer-on

---

means of my outer senses. But I wanted to know his inner thought by means of my inner thought. Then I would know what sort of loyalty he held toward me.'
75 Augustine, *Soliloquia* 1.4.9 (ed. Hörmann, CSEL 89, 15.12–16.18).
76 Gesceadwisnes asks a few questions that pertain to geography and astronomy rather than geometry; then the conversation leaps ahead, and she asks Agustinus whether he fears the censure of the Academics (Alfred, *Soliloquies*; ed. Carnicelli, 60.11–61.5). Note that the analogy of the lord's letter and seal is inserted not where the discussion of geometry has been excised but at a slightly later position in the dialogue (ibid., 62.22–63.19), in response to Agustinus's hesitation to accept the recommendation that he give up even more worldly pleasures.

gecnawan magæ, cweð þonne hweðer þe rihtra þince þe þu hys willan folgie,
þe þu folgie þam welam þe he ðe er forgeaf to-eacan hys freondscype.[77]

Agustinus dutifully replies that it is better to follow his lord's will, as he
knows it from the letter, and thereby to continue in loyal friendship.[78]
Note, however, that Agustinus has arrived at a conclusion significantly
different from that of his Latin counterpart. His consideration of geometry led 'Augustine' to assert that one can possess certain *knowledge* of
truths that are utterly imperceptible to the senses. The analogy constructed
by Gesceadwisnes, on the other hand, illustrates that objects perceptible
to the senses – in this case, written words and a seal – can provide a firm
basis for *belief* in something that is not currently present to the senses.

What may seem like a philosophical shortcoming is, in the context of
Alfred's translation, an enormous rhetorical advantage, because belief, as
Gesceadwisnes and Agustinus conceive of it, is not just a form of perception but a virtue and a sign of loyalty. As we saw earlier, Agustinus is
inclined to doubt whether Alypius's outward signs of loyalty really match
what lies hidden in his *ingeþanc*, but in that case, doubt is not a mark of
disloyalty, because Alypius is a social subordinate, a servant (*cniht*). Faced
with a visible and tangible sign of the will of his lord, his social superior,
Agustinus is inclined to believe rather than to doubt, and Gesceadwisnes
praises him for this display of loyalty. Unlike the *intellectus* of 'Augustine,' which by its incorporeal nature is theoretically capable of perceiving
truth in the Forms, Agustinus's *ingeþanc* cannot overcome its own fal-
libility in this lifetime. Yet as long as Agustinus is a loyal subject, he will
not dare to think that outward signs from the Lord – in the form of the
Bible and the writings of the Fathers, which Agustinus reads or hears with
his *uttor gewit* and ponders in his *ingeþanc* – could ever be less than fully
trustworthy.

---

77 Alfred, *Soliloquies* (ed. Carnicelli, 62.22–7): 'Now consider this: if a message from your
    lord and his seal were sent to you, would you be able to say that you were unable to
    understand him by means of those things, and would you be unable to know his will
    thereby? If you then say that you are able to know his will thereby, tell me whether you
    think it is more correct for you to follow his will, or that you follow the wealth that he
    has already given to you in addition to his friendship?'
78 Alfred, *Soliloquies* (ed. Carnicelli, 62.28–33).

Epistemological Analogies and Metaphors (Fig. 1, items II.C.1 and II.C.1.a)

Having no recourse to the concept of *intellectus*, Gesceadwisnes advances her teachings by relying on two different links between perception and virtue. The aforementioned link between belief and loyalty is the simpler of the two, and its role in the dialogue is more rhetorical than doctrinal: later in the dialogue, it will give Gesceadwisnes incredible rhetorical leverage, because she can shame Agustinus for hesitating to believe those Christian teachings of which he cannot have certain knowledge in the present life. In the meantime, Gesceadwisnes addresses the issue of how, and how much, an individual can know of God during the present life. To this end, she uses elaborate analogies and metaphors to show Agustinus how the cultivation of virtue leads to a clearer vision of God. Once Agustinus has grasped this point, he will finally be fully prepared to learn about the unitary nature of the soul.[79]

It is actually Agustinus who first introduces ship metaphors into their consideration of epistemology. He likens his bodily eyes to a ship and his *ingeþanc* to dry ground. If one has to cross deep waters, it is better to have the ship of sensory perception than nothing at all, but if one can walk on the sturdy ground of the *ingeþanc*, the ship of sensory knowledge can be left at the shore. Continuing to rely on sensory knowledge when one could have recourse to *ingeþanc* is no more efficient than dragging a ship along on dry ground.[80] Agustinus's images of the eyes and the ship are immediately taken up by Gesceadwisnes, but she changes their figurative significance and builds upon them the two metaphors that will pervade the rest of the dialogue: the *eagan modes* 'eyes of the mind' and *scip modes* 'ship of the mind.' She encourages Agustinus to fix his contemplation on God 'with the eyes of the mind,' and then she likens these eyes to the rope that attaches a ship to its anchor, and also to the anchor itself, which is fixed in solid ground and keeps the ship safe in turbulent seas.[81] '[H]wæt is þæt ðæt þu hehst modes eagan?' Agustinus asks – an understandable

79 On Alfred's elaboration of these metaphors in the *Soliloquies*, above and beyond the presence of such figures in his source text, see M. Wilcox, 'Alfred's Epistemological Metaphors,' 204–9, 213–15.
80 Alfred, *Soliloquies* (ed. Carnicelli, 61.13–22); here the OE closely follows the Latin (Augustine, *Soliloquia* 1.4.9; ed. Hörmann, CSEL 89, 16.5–11).
81 Alfred, *Soliloquies* (ed. Carnicelli, 61.23–62.3).

question, in the face of these mixed metaphors.[82] The eyes of the mind, explains Gesceadwisnes, are reason and the many other virtues that anchor the mind to God: 'myd þisum ancrum þu scealt gefastnian ðone streng on gode, þæt ðæt scyp healdan sceal þines modes.'[83] Therefore Agustinus can keep his mind firmly anchored to God if he cultivates virtues by renouncing worldly pleasures. Yet Agustinus despairs. He does not believe absolutely that he will be able to see God clearly, and this doubt makes it very burdensome to cultivate virtue.[84] To put Agustinus's doubt in a different light, here Gesceadwisnes introduces the aforementioned analogy of the lord's letter and seal, and she points out that if Agustinus is disposed to be loyal to his temporal lord, he should be even more loyal to his eternal Lord, which should in turn make it easier to cultivate virtue.

At this particular moment, the topic of conversation seems to have wandered irretrievably far from the central problem of whether the *mod* will participate in the eternal life of the *sawol*, but in fact Agustinus is only one step from completing his spiritual and intellectual preparation for the 'novel' teachings that Gesceadwisnes has in store for him. He understands the connection between virtue and the vision of God, but he does not understand that both of these persist after the death of the body. Here the analogy of the lord's sealed letter provides Gesceadwisnes the opportunity to turn the conversation toward the topic of eternity. When Gesceadwisnes asks whether God and the 'anchors' or virtues are eternal or transient, Agustinus is confident that God is eternal, but he can offer no reply as to the virtues.[85] This is significant, because the virtues belong to the *mod*, so his ignorance confirms that he is still unaware that the *mod* can share in the eternal life of the *sawol*.[86] Gesceadwisnes next asks Agustinus whether he still desires to see God clearly, and although he affirms this wholeheartedly, he senses that it will be nearly impossible to achieve. His presently dim knowledge of God makes it difficult to be virtuous,

---

82 Alfred, *Soliloquies* (ed. Carnicelli, 62.4): 'What is this that you call the eyes of the mind?' M. Wilcox, 'Alfred's Epistemological Metaphors,' makes sense of the mixing of ocular and nautical imagery by correlating them in tables: see esp. 217, Table 4.
83 Alfred, *Soliloquies* (ed. Carnicelli, 62.9–10): 'with these anchors you must fasten that rope onto God, so that the ship can protect your mind.'
84 Alfred, *Soliloquies* (ed. Carnicelli, 62.19–21).
85 Alfred, *Soliloquies* (ed. Carnicelli, 63.1–10).
86 That the virtues are proper to the mind is true not only from Agustinus's perspective, which up to this point has conformed to the vernacular tradition in Anglo-Saxon psychology, but also from Gesceadwisnes's perspective, for she has just taught Agustinus that the virtues are the 'eyes of the mind.'

and unless he is virtuous, he will never be able to see God.[87] Agustinus is stumped and frustrated, yet Gesceadwisnes praises him: he understands the problem and has been humbled by it.[88] He is now prepared, intellectually and spiritually, for Gesceadwisnes to teach him that the *mod* and the immortal *sawol* are one.

Gesceadwisnes Introduces the Unitary *sawol* (Fig. 1, item II.C.1.b)

Thus far, Gesceadwisnes has avoided any suggestion that the *sawol* and the *mod* might be the same entity. To bring this about has required diligent attention from Alfred, since the interlocutors of the Latin *Soliloquia* freely use both *anima* and *animus* to refer to the rational soul. But as soon as Gesceadwisnes determines that Agustinus is prepared to grasp the unitary nature of the soul, she begins to articulate an intimate relationship between *sawol* and *mod*, although she communicates this information more obliquely and imagistically than, say, Alcuin does in *De ratione animae*. First she reveals that the mind is the eye of the soul, and that reason (that is, Gesceadwisnes herself) is to the mind what sight is to the eyes.[89] Next she adds that the soul, too, has sight, in the form of its capacities for reason and scrutiny, although some souls cannot exercise these capacities to their fullest because the eyes of the soul are unhealthy.[90] Finally, Gesceadwisnes ties together all the disparate images she has employed so far, re-establishing that the eyes of the mind are virtues, and that the cultivation of virtue makes it possible to see God: 'Ac se ðe god geseon wille, he scel habban his modes eagan hale: þæt is, ðæt he hebbe festne geleafan and rihte tohopan

---

87 The reciprocal relationship between faith and virtue, already touched on above, is reiterated at Carnicelli 63.25–64.3, after Gesceadwisnes has introduced the analogy of the sealed letter from a temporal lord.

88 Alfred, *Soliloquies* (ed. Carnicelli, 64.4–12).

89 Alfred, *Soliloquies* (ed. Carnicelli, 65.1 and 65.6–8): 'wite þæt erest gewiss, þæt ðæt mod byð þære sawle æge ... Ac þu scealt witan ðæt ic þe þe nu wið sprece, ic eom gesceadwisnes, and ic eom ælcum manniscum mode on þam stale þe seo hawung byð þam eagum' (First, know with certainty that the mind is the eye of the soul ... But you must know that I, who am speaking with you now, am Reason, and I am in the mind of every man, playing the role that the faculty of looking plays in the eyes).

90 Alfred, *Soliloquies* (ed. Carnicelli, 67.1–3): 'þare saule hawung is gescadwisnes and smeaung. Ac manige sawle hawiað mid ðam and þeah ne geseoð þæt þæt hi wilniað, forðamþe hi næbbað ful hale eagan' (the sight of the soul is reason and scrutiny. But many souls look with reason and scrutiny and nevertheless they do not see what they desire, because they do not have really healthy eyes).

and fulle lufe.'[91] This is good news for Agustinus, who longs to see God clearly. However, as Gesceadwisnes continues, her message becomes rather less encouraging.

> Ac þeah seo saule si fulfremed and fulclæne þa hwile þe heo on þam licuman byt, heo ne mæg god geseon swa swa heo wilnað for þæs licuman hefenesse and gedrefednesse, buton mid miclum geswince þurh geleafan and tohopan and þurh lufe. ðæt sint þa þreo anceras þe þæt scyp ðes modes healdað on gemang ðam brogan þara yða. þæt mod þeah hæfð micle frofre on ðam þe hit gelyfð and geare wot þæt þa ungelimp and þa ungesælþa þisse wurlde ne beoð æce.[92]

It seems that what Gesceadwisnes promised Agustinus earlier – that the cultivation of virtue could bring him to a clearer vision of God – was a best-case scenario. Impeded by the body, even an excellent soul can scarcely attain the vision of God during the present life, so the anchors of faith, hope, and love typically can do no more than keep the ship of the mind from drifting irretrievably away from God.

The foregoing passage concludes with Gesceadwisnes's first intimation that the *mod* will share in the afterlife of the *sawol*, and that the belief in the afterlife of the mind should be a great source of comfort. What she is really trying to tell Agustinus, very gently, is that all but the most extraordinarily virtuous people must suffer the death of the body before attaining a clear vision of God. But this meaning is lost on Agustinus, who impatiently reminds Gesceadwisnes that she earlier promised to teach him how he could 'see God with my mind's eyes every bit as clearly as I can presently see the sun with my bodily eyes.'[93] Gesceadwisnes explains again, more deliberately and pointedly this time: a man might look at the sun with his bodily eyes, and although the sun shines on him, yet he cannot see it as it really is. Likewise, he might desire to know God the eternal and almighty Sun, and

---

91 Alfred, *Soliloquies* (ed. Carnicelli, 67.3–5): 'But he who wishes to see God must keep his eyes healthy: that is, he should hold a firm faith and right hope and complete love.'

92 Alfred, *Soliloquies* (ed. Carnicelli, 67.20–68.6): 'But even if the soul were wholly perfected and wholly purified while in the body, it cannot see God as it desires because of the heaviness and turmoil of the body, except through strenuous effort, by means of faith and hope and love. These are the three anchors that steady the ship of the mind amid the terror of the waves. The mind nevertheless has much comfort in the thought that it believes and knows with confidence that the misfortune and unhappiness of this world will not be eternal.'

93 Alfred, *Soliloquies* (ed. Carnicelli, 69.14–15).

God's light will shine on him who looks at him. But only a 'very foolish person' (swiðe dysi man) would be sad because he cannot look closely at the sun with his bodily eyes, and it is equally foolish to insist upon seeing God clearly during the present life.[94]

Now, Gesceadwisnes's teaching is not wholly in harmony with Augustine's anti-Academic agenda in the Latin *Soliloquia*, because Augustine intended for his dialogue to demonstrate that faith and hope and love could facilitate the intellection of incorporeal truths, even during life in the body.[95] Gesceadwisnes does not foreclose this possibility entirely; later on she will explain that a few saints have been able to attain the vision of God during their lifetimes by vigorously rejecting everything of the present world. But compared with Ratio, Gesceadwisnes is noticeably more pessimistic about her interlocutor's prospects, to the point where she maintains that it is 'foolish' to expect to see God before death. On the other hand, Gesceadwisnes's epistemological pessimism goes hand-in-hand with her optimism about the mind's immortality, because it has been promised to Agustinus that he will be able to see God, and if he cannot do so during this life, then it must be the case that his mind will accompany the *sawol* to the afterlife, where he can look upon God and see him as he really is.

Why Does Agustinus Not Confess That He Fears the Death of the Mind?

If my account of Alfred's motivations is correct – if Alfred produced the *Soliloquies* in order to teach other Anglo-Saxons that the *mod* would enjoy the afterlife along with the *sawol* – then we would certainly expect him to include in his translation that part of the conversation, near the end of the first day, in which 'Augustine' explains that his fear of death is actually a fear that death will end the life of the mind.[96] Some explanation is needed, therefore, for the fact that the OE *Soliloquies*, as it has come down to us, includes nothing that corresponds to the majority of *Soliloquia* 1.12.20, although it does include a fairly faithful translation of the lines just before and just after the passage in question. Alfred's deliberate omission of this passage would cast considerable doubt on my interpretation of Alfred's rationale; however, as Karl Jost first demonstrated and as Carnicelli has

---

94 Alfred, *Soliloquies* (ed. Carnicelli, 69.26–70.5).
95 See O'Daly, *Augustine's Philosphy of Mind*, 162–71 on Augustine's critique of scepticism, and 211–16 on the extent to which the soul in the body can perceive God.
96 Augustine, *Soliloquia* 1.12.20 (discussed above).

corroborated, the OE dialogue originally included a rendering of all of *Soliloquia* 1.12.20, but this section had been lost by the time our sole manuscript of the *Soliloquies* was copied. Jost noticed the presence of a brief and nonsensical exchange between Gesceadwisnes and Agustinus,[97] which apparently joins together the first part of a question spoken by Ratio early in 1.12.20 with the first two words of 1.12.21.[98] We can be confident that this material was lost rather than intentionally omitted by the translator because there are three subsequent references to the missing material, and two of these references are Alfred's own additions, unparalleled in the Latin.[99] Therefore, although it is frustrating that we can no longer read precisely how Alfred handled this crucial passage of the Latin *Soliloquia*, its absence does not threaten the hypothesis that the afterlife of the mind was the driving concern behind the study of the Latin *Soliloquia* and the production of the OE *Soliloquies*.

Alfred Replaces Dialectic with Dogma (Fig. 1, item II.C.2)

At this point in the Latin *Soliloquia*, the soul's immortality has been asserted but not proven. To establish a definitive proof, Ratio turns to dialectic to bolster her assertions. Likewise, at this point in the OE dialogue, the unitary nature of the *sawol* has been asserted but not proven. Gesceadwisnes turns to Christian dogma rather than dialectic to strengthen her assertions. It has been suggested that Alfred made such a change because he expected that an Anglo-Saxon audience, with no experience of dialectic, would find the authority of Church teachings greater than that of reasoned demonstrations.[100] This was doubtless part of Alfred's motivation, but it is also the case that once Alfred decided to excise the concept

---

97 Alfred, *Soliloquies* (ed. Carnicelli, 74.26–75.1; I have omitted the editor's reconstructed text): 'Ða cwæð heo: ac hu ðonne gyf hi ðe myrrað and lettað þæs lichoman mettrimnysse. Ða cwæð ic: þæt is soð.' As the text stands in the MS, these lines mean 'Then she said: But how then if they lead you astray and hinder the frailty of the body. Then I said: That is true.'

98 Ratio's question reads 'Quid, si te ab inquirendo etiam impediat eorum praesentia,' and *Soliloquia* 1.12.21 begins with the words 'Dolor corporis.'

99 See Carnicelli, 74–5. The clearest visual representation of the fault in the OE text appears in Endter (ed.), *König Alfreds des Grossen Bearbeitung der Soliloquien*, 41.20–9, where the relevant Latin passage ('Quid? si docereris … mecum mansurum putem') forms part of a larger section that Endter prints in small type, indicating that it has no corresponding OE passage in the extant version of the *Soliloquies*.

100 Gatch, 'King Alfred's Version of Augustine's *Soliloquia*,' 30–4.

of incorporeality from his rendering of the *Soliloquies*, he foreclosed the possibility of reproducing the dialectical demonstrations advanced by Ratio in the Latin dialogue.

The opening of the second day's conversation plainly illustrates the challenge facing Alfred. Gesceadwisnes can replicate Ratio's reasoning for as long as she can avoid invoking the Platonist concept of incorporeality; accordingly, Gesceadwisnes's argument can follow Ratio's through the point where she establishes that the true is not the same as truth, and that truth survives when a truthful man passes away.[101] Then she asks Agustinus some questions about the location and substance of truth and other abstract entities:

> ic wolde witan hwæder þu wene þæt se wisdom þonne gelænde, oððe seo clennes, oððe seo soðfæstnes, ðonne se man gewite; oððe hwanon heo ær cumen, oððe hwær hy sien, gyf hi sien, oððe hwæðer hi lichamlice sien þe gastlice. Forðam þes nis nan tweo, þæt ælc þincg þara ys hwærhwugu is.[102]

Gesceadwisnes is suddenly in deeper philosophical waters than she can stay afloat in without recourse to the concept of Forms or of incorporeality, or a subtler understanding of the difference between place and space. In the corresponding lines of the Latin *Soliloquia*, the question of where truth exists is a prologue to Ratio's demonstration that there must exist immortal, incorporeal things in which truth can abide. If Gesceadwisnes were to pursue this line of reasoning, she would first have to provide a philosophically sound answer to the question of 'whether truth is bodily or spiritual' (which, incidentally, is a given rather than a question in the Latin dialogue).

Gesceadwisnes extracts herself from this morass by changing the subject without seeming to do so. She does not know the location or the substance of truth, but she knows that God is truth, so she says, 'þæt þu soðfestnes hætst, þæt ys god; he wæs a, and a byd, undeadlic and æce.'[103] And she cannot use dialectic to prove that the *mod* is part of the immortal

---

101　Alfred, *Soliloquies* (ed. Carnicelli, 81.12–26).

102　Alfred, *Soliloquies* (ed. Carnicelli, 81.26–30): 'I would like to know where you suppose wisdom goes, or chasteness, or truth, when the man departs; or where it first came from, or where they exist if they exist, or whether they are bodily or spiritual. Because there is no doubt of this: that everything that exists is somewhere.'

103　Alfred, *Soliloquies* (ed. Carnicelli, 82.12–13): 'that which you call truth is God: he always existed, and always will exist, immortal and eternal.'

sawol, but she can invoke the basic tenets of Church teaching to render a different sort of proof:

> Se god hæfð ealle creftas on hym gesunde and ful medeme. se hæft gesceapena twa æca gesceafta, þæt sint, engelas and manna sauwela, þam he sealde sumne dæl ecra gyfa, swilcra swilce nu wisdom is, and rihtwisnes, and oðre manega þe us lang ðincð to rimanne: engelum he gef be heora andefne, and manna saulum he gyfð, ælcre be hyre andefne, swilca gyfa. Ða swilcan gifa hi ne þurfon næfre forlætan, forðam heo beoð æca.[104]

There is no need to look to esoteric theological authorities for this information. The assertion that God created angels and souls to be immortal is fundamental and ubiquitous; it can be found in homilies, catechetical texts, commentaries on the *Consolatio*, and even in Insular grammars. For Agustinus to doubt such an elementary teaching would be ridiculous. As Agustinus will learn in Book 2, the 'gifts' that abide eternally in the *sawol* are wisdom and virtues – that is, gifts that are proper to the *mod* – and so it follows that the *mod* must share in the eternity of the *sawol*. As Book 1 ends, Agustinus goes away to ponder what Gesceadwisnes has taught him, and he promises to report back to her if he has any doubts.[105]

Agustinus 'Forgets' That the *sawol* Is Immortal (Fig. 1, items II.C.2 and II.C.3)

When Agustinus reconvenes with Gesceadwisnes in Book 2, he has clearly been mulling things over. He has narrowed the focus of his enquiry, and he is now chiefly interested in the state of his knowledge (*gewit*) in the afterlife. Unfortunately, he has also 'forgotten' that he is immortal, even though throughout Book 1 he took his immortality for granted. Agustinus demands of Gesceadwisnes:

---

104 Alfred, *Soliloquies* (ed. Carnicelli, 82.13–19): 'God possesses all the virtues in himself, complete and entirely perfect. He has fashioned two eternal creations, which are angels and the souls of men, to whom he gives a certain portion of each gift: now, among these are gifts such as wisdom, and righteousness, and many others that I think would take too long to enumerate. He provides such gifts for the angels according to their nature, and he provides such gifts for the souls of men, each according to its nature. Gifts of this sort need never be surrendered, because they are eternal.'
105 Alfred, *Soliloquies* (ed. Carnicelli, 82.22–6).

sege þeah hwet ic þe æfter acsode, hwæðer ic a lybbende were; and siððan ic wolde witan hwæðer ic, æfter þæs lychoman gedale and þære sawle, a mare wisse þonne ic nu wot æalles þæs þe ic nu lange wilnode to witanne; forðam ic ne mæg nanwiht ongytan bætre on men þonne he wite, and nanwith wyrse ðonne he nyte.[106]

Gesceadwisnes affirms her understanding of Agustinus's demands by restating the questions: Agustinus knows that he currently exists, lives, and possesses some knowledge, but he wants to know 'hweðer þa ðreo þing æalle æce weron ðe neron; oððe hweðer heora enig æce weræ; oððe, gyf heo æallu æce wæren, hweðer heora enig æfter ðisse weorlde on ðam æcan lyfe awðer dide, wexse oððe wanede.'[107] Both Gesceadwisnes and Agustinus depart from the Latin in a small but significant way. Whereas 'Augustine' was concerned with his capacity to understand (*intellegere*) after death, Agustinus is preoccupied with the fate and changeability of his personal store of knowledge (*gewit*) after death: this preoccupation will drive all of the conversation in Book 3.[108] For the moment, however, Gesceadwisnes is chiefly concerned to address Agustinus's newfound doubts about his own immortality. She scolds him – gently, for now – and recapitulates the argument for the immortality of the *sawol*, based on Christian dogmas, that she presented at the end of Book 1.[109]

How could Agustinus 'forget' that the soul is immortal? His sudden and unexplained doubt is out of keeping with Agustinus's tenacious adherence to vernacular psychology in Book 1, and furthermore, it violates

---

106 Alfred, *Soliloquies* (ed. Carnicelli, 84.16–20): 'But tell me what I asked you about more recently: whether I would be alive always. And then I would like to know whether, after the separation of this body and the soul, I will ever know more than I now know of everything that I have now long desired to know: for I can imagine nothing better in a man than that he have knowledge, and nothing worse than that he have no knowledge.' Agustinus's gnomic remark about knowledge is more forceful than that of his Latin counterpart, who merely says that if knowledge brings misery, then nobody can ever be happy (Augustine, *Soliloquia* 2.1.1; ed. Hörmann, CSEL 89, 47.1–4).
107 Alfred, *Soliloquies* (ed. Carnicelli, 85.12–14): 'whether the three things are all eternal or not; or whether any one of them were eternal; or if they were all eternal, whether any of them did one or the other, grow larger or grow smaller, after this world in that eternal life.'
108 Knowledge and dynamic change are emphasized again in Gesceadwisnes's second restatement of Agustinus's question at Carnicelli 86.2–3: 'hweðer ðu æfter þæs lichaman gedale and þære sawle mare wisse þonne ðu nu wast, þe læsse' (whether you will know more, after the separation of this body and the soul, than you now know, or less).
109 Alfred, *Soliloquies* (ed. Carnicelli, 85.16–19).

any pretence of realistic literary characterization when a Christian such as Agustinus forgets his own immortality in the interim between Books 1 and 2. Although unsatisfying as a literary device, Agustinus's preposterous forgetfulness serves as a stepping-stone to the two most important arguments of Book 2: first, that it is a shameful sign of disloyalty for a Christian to doubt the basic tenets of the faith; and second, that 'forgetfulness' can be remedied by the *mod*'s recollection of truths it learned before entering the body, which in turn proves that the *mod* participates in the *sawol*'s life outside the body. These two arguments represent necessary departures from the method of reasoning used throughout Book 2 of the Latin dialogue, which depends upon the theory of Forms as well as Aristotle's Categories. The trajectory of the OE dialogue will not converge again with that of the Latin source until the very end of Book 2.

Forgetfulness, Disloyalty, and Recollection (Fig. 1, items II.C.1.c and III)

Even before Gesceadwisnes proceeds to address her interlocutor's doubts at greater length, Agustinus enumerates a long list of fundamental Christian doctrines that he does *not* doubt. He believes that God is eternal; that he is unity and trinity; that he is without beginning and without end. He believes that the complexity and order of the visible universe (*gesewena gesceafta*) testify to God's sovereignty over all of it, and that earthly kings rule only by God's permission.[110] Some of these statements are found in the ancient creeds, and others are acclamations of God's ultimate authority, but most of them are irrelevant to the nature of the soul. Only after expressly affirming all of these beliefs does Agustinus sheepishly admit, 'Ac ic tweoge gyt be heora [*scil.* sawla] ecnesse, hweðer hi a lybbende sien.'[111] Agustinus's list of affirmations strikes the reader as an anticipation of, and a defence against, suspicions of heterodoxy or disloyalty that might be aroused when he admits his doubts about the soul's immortality.

Agustinus's defensive posture is soon justified. At first, Gesceadwisnes responds mildly to Agustinus's doubts, pointing out that 'holy books' contain so many authoritative claims of the soul's immortality that it would be tedious to enumerate them all.[112] In reply, Agustinus claims that

---

110 Alfred, *Soliloquies* (ed. Carnicelli, 86.5–15).
111 Alfred, *Soliloquies* (ed. Carnicelli, 86.17–18): 'But I still have doubt concerning the eternity of souls and whether they will be alive always.'
112 Alfred, *Soliloquies* (ed. Carnicelli, 86.19–21).

he is familiar with the teachings of the holy books, but (like the lord's seal and letter that were discussed in Book 1) these holy books sustain belief rather than certain knowledge, and he would prefer the latter.[113] Just as Gesceadwisnes earlier taught Agustinus that a clear vision of God in the present life is virtually impossible, here she claims that certain knowledge of the soul's immortality is, likewise, unattainable to most people during life on earth.

> ic wundrige hwi ðu swa swiðe georne and swa gewislice þæt to witanne, þætte nefre nan man of ðisse carcerne þises andweardan lyfes swa gewislice witan ne myhte swa swa ðu wilnast, þeah ðe manige gearnodon þæt hi hyt on þis andweardan life sweotolor ongeaton þonne oððre mænege hyt gelyfden be þisra and be unleasra manna sægena ... and þeah þa halgan fæderas þe ær us weron swiðe georne wisson be ðam þe ðu ær acsodest, þæt is, be undeadlicnesse manna sawla. þæt wæs swiðe sweotol on þam þæt hi nanwiht ne tweode, ðonne hy swiðost forsawen þis andwearde lyf.[114]

Although Gesceadwisnes chides Agustinus for his presumptuous desire for certain knowledge, Gesceadwisnes herself is in a difficult position, rhetorically and doctrinally. If it is true that the 'holy books' contain authoritative testimony of the soul's immortality, she must grant that the

---

113 Alfred, *Soliloquies* (ed. Carnicelli, 86.22–3): 'Ac me lyste hyt nu bet to witanne þonne to gelyfanne' (But now it would please me better to know than to believe).

114 Alfred, *Soliloquies* (ed. Carnicelli, 86.24–87.10): 'I am amazed that you yearn so greatly and so certainly to know that which no person has ever, from within the prison of this present life, been able to know as certainly as you desire, although many have laboured to understand it more clearly in this present life than many others have believed it based on the proclamations of these and reliable men ... and nonetheless the holy Fathers who lived before us knew very well about that which you earlier asked, that is, about the immortality of the souls of human beings. That was very clear to them, so that they had no doubt at all, when they most strenuously despised this present life.' It makes a great difference in the meaning of this passage whether the verb *gearnodon* is a form of *ge-earnian*, 'to merit, win,' as Carnicelli construes it, or a form of *geornian* 'to yearn for,' which appears earlier in the same sentence. If Carnicelli is correct, then Gesceadwisnes is claiming that many men have merited certain knowledge of the soul's immortality. This interpretation might harmonize with Augustine of Hippo's anti-sceptical agenda, but it contradicts what Gesceadwisnes says here and reiterates later: that only the holiest of men, who utterly despise earthly life, have been able to attain certain knowledge of the immortality of the soul; the rest of us only 'yearn' after such knowledge. Thus I construe *gearnodon* as a form of *geornian* 'to yearn for.'

Fathers (either the authors of the New Testament or the Fathers of the Church), by their self-denial, have attained certain knowledge of this truth. However, it is also crucial to Gesceadwisnes's argument for the immortality of the *mod* that certain knowledge of truths and of God be deferred until after death for ordinary people. This is one of the peculiarities of the OE *Soliloquies*, in fact: to demonstrate the immortality of the *mod*, Gesceadwisnes must, to some extent, reject the anti-sceptical agenda that Augustine advances in the Latin *Soliloquia*.

Rather than address these subtleties, Gesceadwisnes continues to criticize Agustinus, with ever inflating rhetoric. '[Þ]urh swylcra manna gesewenan sculon gelyfan ða þe hyt swa sweotolo ongytan ne magon swa swa hi meahton,' Gesceadwisnes repeats, before adding reproachfully, 'and þeah be þære undeadlicnesse þere sawle, gyf ðu hys get geðafa ne eart, ic gedo þæt ðu hyt ongyst, and ic gedo æac þæt ðe sceamað þæt ðu hyt swa late ongeate.'[115] To emphasize that Agustinus's doubt is not a purely intellectual shortcoming, Gesceadwisnes reprises an argument she deployed in Book 1, likening faithful belief in the immortality of the soul to the unbroken loyalty that a man owes to his temporal lord in the present life.[116] She concludes this phase of her argument by impugning Agustinus's loyalty to God himself: 'hwi tweost ðu þonne ymbe Cristes, godes sunu, and ymbe hera þegena sæcgena, þe hy selfe to sprecon? ... Hwy ne myhte þu ðonne þam æallum gelyfan, and cwæde ær þæt þu were heora mann?'[117] This overwrought appeal to the ideal of loyal servitude represents the culmination of the many changes to the content and rhetoric of the *Soliloquies* that were necessitated back in Book 1 when Alfred decided not to pursue arguments that depended on Platonic metaphysics: this decision in turn removed the *intellectus* from consideration and placed belief, rather than certain knowledge through intellection, at the pinnacle of the epistemological hierarchy.

---

115 Alfred, *Soliloquies* (ed. Carnicelli, 87.12–16): 'Those who are incapable of understanding it as well as the Fathers could understand it ought to believe it based on the teachings of such men [*scil.* the Fathers]. But as for the immortality of the soul: if you still do not assent to that, I will make you understand it, and I will also make you ashamed that you came to understand it so slowly.'

116 On the Alfredian addition concerning Theodosius and Honorius, see Gatch, 'King Alfred's Version of Augustine's *Soliloquia*,' 34–5.

117 Alfred, *Soliloquies* (ed. Carnicelli, 89.13–18): 'Why then do you have doubts concerning the sayings of Christ, the Son of God, and the sayings of his servants, which they themselves speak about? ... How could you not believe in them all, and have stated earlier that you were their servant?'

Gesceadwisnes's chastisement has the desired effect: Agustinus is ashamed to have doubted and grateful to have been corrected. The only excuse he can muster is that his doubt was not wilful but rather the result of forgetfulness. '[Æ]all þis ic wiste þeah ær, ac ic hyt forgeat, swa ic ondrede æac þæt ic ðis do,' he explains. 'Ic wat æac þæt ic hyt hæfde swa clene forgieten þæt ic hyt næfre eft ne ofmunde, þær ðu me þy sweotoloran bysena ne sede, ægðer ge be minum hlaforde ge be manegum bispellum.'[118] Gesceadwisnes does not browbeat Agustinus further but instead offers to teach him something that can remedy his forgetfulness about the immortality of the *sawol* and also persuade him that the *mod* participates in the *sawol*'s life outside the body. Remarkably, given Alfred's avoidance of Platonic metaphysics up to this point, Gesceadwisnes's solution to 'forgetfulness' is the Platonic theory of anamnesis or recollection, which is nowhere invoked by Augustine in the Latin *Soliloquia*.

To be precise, what Gesceadwisnes teaches is a watered-down version of anamnesis, which makes no mention of incorporeality or the Forms and consequently sounds more like part of a creation myth than Neoplatonist doctrine. To overcome his 'wretched forgetfulness' Agustinus must ask his mind ('Acsa ðin agen mod') how it retains knowledge of the present and thirsts for knowledge of the distant past and of the future.[119] If the mind is rational (*gesceadwis*), Gesceadwisnes predicts, it will tell Agustinus that 'hit forði wilnige þæt to witanne þæt ær us wæs, forði hit simle wære syððan god þone forman man gesceape hafde.'[120] Notably, Gesceadwisnes's exposition of the theory of recollection never mentions the *sawol* but focuses entirely on the *mod*,[121] whose life outside the body was the focus of Agustinus's original inquiry, before he 'forgot' the immortality of the *sawol*.

Alfred's decision to invoke the theory of anamnesis, which does not appear at all in Augustine's Latin dialogue, was very likely made in direct response to the one outstanding philosophical flaw that vitiates Ratio's arguments in Book 2 of the *Soliloquia*. Recall that Ratio attempts to

---

118 Alfred, *Soliloquies* (ed. Carnicelli, 89.25–8): 'All this I nevertheless knew before, but I forgot it, as I fear also that I will forget this. I know also that I had so entirely forgotten it that I would never again have remembered it, if you had not explained it to me by means of clearer examples, both about my lord and about the many parables.'

119 Alfred, *Soliloquies* (ed. Carnicelli, 90.13 and 19).

120 Alfred, *Soliloquies* (ed. Carnicelli, 90.24–91.1): 'it therefore desires to know what existed before us, because it has always existed since God created the first human.'

121 Alfred, *Soliloquies* (ed. Carnicelli, 90.19–91.8). In these 14 lines of text the neuter pronoun *hit*, referring back to the *mod*, appears twenty-two times.

demonstrate that the mind must be immortal because truth, such as the truth contained in the discipline of dialectic, is an inseparable property of the mind. 'Augustine' objects, not once but twice, on the grounds that this cannot be maintained of uneducated minds, which are surely as immortal as those minds that have learned dialectic, yet Ratio declines to address this issue in the two books of the dialogue that were completed.[122] The theory of recollection neatly counters 'Augustine's' objection, because if the soul or mind was able to apprehend truth in the Forms from the time when all souls were created, but its apprehension of that truth is merely impeded by the body, then it follows that the minds of the uneducated still possess those truths, though they remain latent until they are recollected.

The Conclusion of Book 2: The *mod* Is More Than Reason and Virtue

When Gesceadwisnes finishes explaining that the *mod* pre-existed the body, Agustinus summarizes all he has learned so far. He concedes that every human soul is eternal and immortal, and moreover, that the *mod* exercises its reason, virtues, and knowledge as it participates in the *sawol*'s life outside the body: 'eall þæt min mod and min gescadwisnesse goodra crefta gegadrad, [þæt mot] þæt mod þa simle habban. and ic gehere æac þæt min gewit is æce.'[123] It would appear that all of Agustinus's doubts and anxieties have been resolved, so why does Alfred add an entire third book to the *Soliloquies*? As Agustinus reminds Gesceadwisnes in the closing lines of Book 2, she has yet to answer the specific question that he articulated at the beginning of the book:

> Ac me lyste gyt witan be ðam gewitte þæt ic ær acsode: hweðer hyt æfter þæs lichaman gedale and þare sawle weoxe þe wanede, þe hyt swa on stæle stode, þe hyt swa dyde swa hyt ær dæð on þisse weorulde – oðre hwile weoxe, oðre hwile wanode. Ic wat nu þæt þæt lyf a byð and þæt gewit. Ac ic ondrede þæt hyt beo on þære weorulde swa hyt her byt on cildum. Ne wene ic na þæt þæt

---

122   Augustine, *Soliloquia* 2.19.33 (ed. Hörmann, CSEL 89, 93.7–12), discussed above in chapter 4.

123   Alfred, *Soliloquies* (ed. Carnicelli, 91.22–3): 'my mind will then always be able to possess all the good virtues that my mind and my reason have accumulated, and I hear also that my knowledge is eternal.' In this quotation I follow Endter (*König Alfreds des Grossen Bearbeitung der Soliloquien*, 64.25), who adds *þæt mot* before the MS reading *þæt mod*; Carnicelli only emends MS *mod* to *mot*.

lyf þær beo butan gewitte, þe ma þe hyt hær byð on cildum; þonne byð þær
forlytlu wynsumnes æt þam lyfe.[124]

Like 'Augustine' of the Latin dialogue, Agustinus anticipates no pleasure
in an afterlife where his mind will not be fully actualized and fully individualized. The Latin *Soliloquia*, remaining unfinished, does not address this
problem, but Alfred adds a third book to the OE *Soliloquies* for precisely
this purpose. Godden considers Book 3 to be 'arguably the most ambitious writing Alfred ever undertook, both in its attempt to complete an
argument that Augustine had abandoned unfinished, and in its determined
pursuit of eschatological ideas that were remarkably more expansive than
the orthodox formulations.'[125] If Alfred was willing to stretch the boundaries of what his patristic authorities taught about existence in the afterlife,
it was in the service of showing that the *mod* would retain all of its faculties: not just the noble but static capacity for reason and virtue, but also an
awareness of individuality, the capacity for change, personal memories,
and emotions.

The Rich Life of the Individual *mod* in the Afterworld (Fig. 1, item III)

At first, in the closing lines of Book 2, Gesceadwisnes declines to answer
Agustinus's question about the changeability of his *gewit*. Instead, in a jar-
ring disruption of the fiction that the interlocutor Agustinus is based on
the historical Augustine of Hippo, Gesceadwisnes instructs Agustinus to
read Augustine of Hippo's *Epistola* 147, better known as *De uidendo Deo*.
As Book 3 opens, Agustinus again asks whether his *gewit* will be changeable in the afterlife; he has not studied *De uidendo Deo* after all, he says,

---

124 Alfred, *Soliloquies* (ed. Carnicelli, 91.24–92.2): 'But it would still please me to know
what I earlier asked about knowledge: whether it would increase or diminish after the
separation of the body and the soul, or whether it would thus remain in one condition,
or whether it would thus do as it did before in this world – that is, that it sometimes
increases and sometimes decreases. Now I know that life and knowledge will always
exist. But I fear that it will be in that world [i.e., in the afterlife] just as here it is in children. I do not hope that that life in that world will be deprived of knowledge, more
than it is here in children; in that case, there is very little that is appealing about that
life.' Cf. Augustine, *Soliloquia* 2.20.36 (discussed above).
125 Godden, 'Text and Eschatology,' 205.

because it is inconvenient for him to read the whole thing.[126] Gesceadwisnes does not relent until Agustinus manages to formulate a more specific question: 'Ac ic wolde þæt þu me [secgan hweðer þa fordgefarenan heora freonda helpan] meahte oððe mosten on þas wurlde, oððe hweðer hy enige geminde hefde þara freonda þe hi beæftan heom lefdon on þisse weorulde.'[127]

Gesceadwisnes bases her reply[128] on the gospel story of Dives and Lazarus (Lk 16:19–31). After death, the stingy rich man Dives is consigned to hell, while the beggar Lazarus is comforted in the bosom of Abraham. Dives and Lazarus can see one another, but Abraham will not allow Lazarus to approach Dives with water to quench his thirst, nor to pay an admonitory visit to family members whom Dives would like to have warned about the reality of hell. This story, with its accompanying tradition of patristic exegesis, provides Gesceadwisnes with much of the evidence that supports her portrayal of a more dynamic and individualized mental life in the afterworld.[129] The wretched Dives can remember his friends and family on earth, indicating that people retain their personal stores of memories when they die.[130] The blessed retain their memories of both good and bad deeds committed during life, and they rejoice in their righteousness.[131] Nor is this privilege reserved to the blessed: in fact, just as Dives and Lazarus

---

126 Alfred, *Soliloquies* (ed. Carnicelli, 92.3–20). On Alfred's borrowings from *De uidendo Deo* later in Book 3, see Gatch, 'King Alfred's Version of Augustine's *Soliloquia*,' 35–6.

127 Alfred, *Soliloquies* (ed. Carnicelli, 92.21–2 and 95.2–3): 'But I would like for you to tell me whether the departed can or may give aid to their friends in this world, or whether they have any memory of the friends whom they left behind them in this world.' In my discussion of Book 3 I follow Godden's reordering of its fragments ('Text and Eschatology,' 181–5), and the OE text that I supply here in square brackets follows Godden's MnE reconstruction (ibid., 205).

128 This reply is not introduced by the usual 'Ða heo cwæð,' but rather by a garbled line that Carnicelli (95.4) reasonably emends to 'Ða answarede he an his agnum ingeþancum and cwæð' (Then he answered in his own inner thoughts and spoke). Since the opening lines of the *Soliloquies* explain that Agustinus wrote these two books about 'his agnum ingeþance' and about 'hu hys gesceadwisnes answarode hys mode þonne þæt mod ymbe hwæt tweonode' (Carnicelli 48.13–16), the speaker here is certainly Gesceadwisnes; cf. Godden's weighing of other possibilities ('Text and Eschatology,' 185).

129 Godden, 'Text and Eschatology,' discusses patristic parallels and possible sources – chiefly Gregory's *Dialogi* and *Homiliae in euangelia* and Julian of Toledo's *Prognosticon* – for Gesceadwisnes's unusual assertions about knowledge in the afterlife and their relationship to patristic teachings on the subject (190–202).

130 Alfred, *Soliloquies* (ed. Carnicelli, 95.4–9 and 95.25–6).

131 Alfred, *Soliloquies* (ed. Carnicelli, 96.19–23).

regard one another from opposite sides of the abyss, so the damned and the blessed can see one another in the afterworld. This sight reminds each person of the earthly deeds that sent him there, while it also makes the damned feel more wretched in comparison with the blessed whom they can see, and it makes the blessed feel more honoured in comparison with the damned.[132] Gesceadwisnes's exegesis of the gospel account portrays a very rich mental life in the afterworld, including personal memories, a clear awareness of one's separation from other individuals, and the capacity for emotional reactions to one's own memories and condition.

But most enticing to Agustinus, who is preoccupied with his *gewit*, is Gesceadwisnes's next promise: when the mind is no longer weighed down by the body, we will know (*witon*) everything we desire to know and become wiser than anyone has ever been on earth, and this knowledge will be augmented yet again on Judgment Day.[133] This universal gift will not render every *mod* equal in wisdom and knowledge, but rather, each individual will be granted new wisdom in proportion to the amount of wisdom he accumulated during life:

> nis þæs æac na to wenanne þæt ealle men hæbben gelicne wisdom on heofenum[.] Ac ælc hefð be þam andefnum þe he ær æfter æarnað; swa ær he hær swiðor swincð and swiðor giornð wisdomes and rihtwisnesse, swa he hys þær mare hæft, and æac maren are and maren wuldor.[134]

The learned Agustinus can therefore take comfort in the thought that his own hard-earned wisdom will be retained and augmented at death, but he will not lose the intellectual advantage that he has over other, less learned persons.

Gesceadwisnes has finally accounted for all the features of the *mod* that Agustinus dearly hopes to retain after death, and she has assuaged his fear that he might regress to a state of childlike knowledge and self-awareness. Now that Agustinus knows that the *mod* and the *sawol* are one, and that his *mod* is fully actualized when it participates in the immortal existence

---

132 Alfred, *Soliloquies* (ed. Carnicelli, 93.24–94.2).
133 Alfred, *Soliloquies* (ed. Carnicelli, 92.22–93.2 and 93.14–20).
134 Alfred, *Soliloquies* (ed. Carnicelli, 94.9–13): 'Likewise, it is not to be expected that all men will have the same wisdom in heaven. But each possesses according to his own capacity whatever he formerly earned; just as earlier he worked hard here and eagerly yearned for wisdom and reason, so will he have more of it there, and also more honour and more glory.'

of the *sawol*, he has a great deal to look forward to after death. Book 3 thus fulfils the objectives that Alfred initiated in his radical transformations of Books 1 and 2: in a mode of discourse accessible and persuasive to an Anglo-Saxon audience, the *Soliloquies* teaches that the concept of the unitary *sawol* is not only doctrinally correct but also a source of hope and a compelling motivation to cultivate virtue and wisdom.

This last conclusion is pointedly reinforced by Gesceadwisnes in the closing lines of the dialogue. Because people who are exceptionally wise on earth retain their exceptional wisdom in heaven, she observes, 'me þincð swiðe dysig man and swiðe unlæde, þe nele hys andgyt æcan þa hwile þe he on þisse weorulde byð, and simle wiscan and willnian þæt he mote cuman to ðam æcan lyfe þær us nanwiht ne byð dygles.'[135] If the *Soliloquies* did in fact emanate from Alfred's circle, these lines may represent an attempt to defend Alfred's strenuous efforts to spread literacy, even to the point of threatening to remove from their posts those secular officials who refused to learn to read.[136] But as long as the question of Alfred's authorship remains unresolved, our interpretations of 'Alfredian' texts ought not to be pinned too firmly on the premise of Alfred's own authorship or even his supervision. To conclude this chapter, I would like to consider the question of authorship: not whether Alfred himself penned the *Soliloquies*, but whether it is plausible that somebody else did, and if so, what the implications might be for the intellectual landscape of Anglo-Saxon England in the decades around the year 900.

If Alfred Did Not Write the *Soliloquies*, Who Did?

There is no shortage of reasonable arguments favouring Alfred's authorship of the OE *Soliloquies*, or at least his close involvement in its production.[137] Some have implicitly accepted Wuelcker's opinion that history has

---

135   Alfred, *Soliloquies* (ed. Carnicelli, 97.14–16). Godden translates: 'I think anyone is foolish and idle if he will not increase his understanding while he is in the world, and always desire and seek that he may come to the eternal life where nothing will be hidden from us' ('Text and Eschatology,' 204).

136   Asser, *De rebus gestis Ælfredi*, ch. 106 (ed. Stevenson, *Asser's Life of King Alfred*, 92–4). Asser reports that the men whose posts were threatened were *perterriti* 'thoroughly terrified' and *correcti* 'chastened,' but I suspect that they were also understandably resentful and sought to convince the king that they could render satisfactory verdicts without learning to read.

137   See esp. Whitelock, 'The Prose of Alfred's Reign,' 71–3; Frantzen, *King Alfred*, 68–9; and M. Wilcox, 'Alfred's Epistemological Metaphors,' 201–10.

given us no evidence of any Anglo-Saxon layperson other than Alfred who was suitably equipped to produce the OE *Soliloquies*, and many have called attention to changes in the characterization of the interlocutor Agustinus that seem to reflect the interests and needs of a temporally powerful layman, if not necessarily a king.[138] In the Latin *Soliloquia*, for instance, Ratio advises 'Augustine' to write in solitude, but in the OE *Soliloquies*, Gesceadwisnes advises Agustinus to secure a group of companions to help him write, perhaps communicating a sympathetic attitude toward Alfred's need for helpers in his translation endeavours.[139] In the Latin dialogue, 'Augustine' has renounced wealth and material comforts in excess of what he needs to maintain his health and *usus liberalis*, the practice of generosity; he denies a desire for any worldly honours at all; and he opines that any sort of physical contact with a woman, even procreative sex, 'casts down the masculine mind from its stronghold' (ex arce deiciat animum uirilem).[140] In the OE version, Agustinus adopts a more relaxed attitude toward worldly pursuits. He disavows any selfish interest in luxuries but insists on the importance of providing them for the men who depend on him; he circumspectly rejects only those temporal honours that are 'immoderate' or 'intemperate and unlawful'; and he allows that the need to procreate is an acceptable reason to marry, although it is less than ideal for priests to do so.[141]

While Alfred's authorship provides the simplest explanation for these features of the OE *Soliloquies*, it is not the only plausible explanation, and in the few years since his essay on 'Text and Eschatology' appeared, Godden has published a more sceptical opinion of Alfred's involvement in any OE translation program. Additions and changes to the *Soliloquies* that seem to reflect a powerful layman's own interests and anxieties, Godden maintains, 'no more imply the king's own authorship than do similar references to royal concerns in the works written on Charlemagne's behalf

138 Wuelcker, 'Ueber die angelsaechsische Bearbeitung der Soliloquien Augustins,' 105; see also Carnicelli, 38–9; Waterhouse, 'Tone in Alfred's Version of Augustine's *Solilo-quies*,' 71–8. Godden's nuanced reading leads him to conclude that these and other changes reflect more the position of a courtier than of the king himself ('The Player King,' 146–50).

139 Augustine, *Soliloquia*, 1.1.1 (ed. Hörmann, CSEL 89, 3.12–14); Alfred, *Soliloquies* (ed. Carnicelli, 49.20–1). On Alfred's helpers, see Asser, *De rebus gestis Ælfredi*, chs 77–9 (ed. Stevenson, *Asser's Life of King Alfred*, 62–6); and Alfred's Preface to the *Pastoral Care* (ed. Sweet, *Pastoral Care*, 7.17–25).

140 Augustine, *Soliloquia* 1.10.17 (ed. Hörmann, CSEL 89, 26.11–28.12).

141 Alfred, *Soliloquies* (ed. Carnicelli, 72.11–73.25).

or in Æthelred's laws.'[142] Yet Wuelcker's observation remains a viable objection to arguments against Alfred's authorship: 'What we are missing is a plausible alternative author, or authors,' Godden concedes.[143] It remains highly probable that the author(s) of the *OE Boethius* also produced the *Soliloquies*, but there is no firm evidence that these works emanated from Alfred's circle, and Godden raises the possibility that both works were produced as late as the mid-tenth century.[144] I remain reasonably satisfied that Alfred himself authored or at least closely supervised the production of the *OE Boethius* and *Soliloquies*. Nonetheless, it is worth considering how my intepretation of the dialogue would be affected should a definitive argument eventually be advanced for the removal of the *Soliloquies* from the Alfredian canon.

The starting point for my arguments about the Anglo-Saxon use of the Latin *Soliloquia* as well as the production of the OE *Soliloquies* has been the premise that most Anglo-Saxons recognized a sharp division of labour between *sawol* and *mod*, and that most Anglo-Saxons would never encounter any cause to question their conception of *sawol* and *mod*, unless they read about the unitary nature and the incorporeality of the soul in the context of philosophical or theological discourse. Alfred's intellectual profile makes him a particularly convincing candidate to have authored the OE *Soliloquies*, because (as I have reasoned) he first took up the study of theology and philosophy late in life and therefore would have had a more firmly ingrained vernacular conceptualization of *sawol* and *mod* than would a person who learned about the unitary soul at a young age. Alfred would therefore have been likely to recognize and to wish to resolve the conflicts he observed between the two psychologies.

---

142 Godden, 'Did King Alfred Write Anything?' 11; cf. Godden, 'The Player King,' esp. 142–9.

143 Godden, 'Did King Alfred Write Anything?' 17. He explains that all of the putative Alfredian translations were evidently produced by native speakers of English, so their primary author could not have been Grimbald of Saint-Bertin, John the Old Saxon, or Asser of St David's in Wales; Wærferth's style is too peculiar and his grasp of Latin too shaky; Plegmund and the 'learned priests' Æthelstan and Werwulf were all Mercians, while the texts all show chiefly West Saxon features.

144 Godden, 'Did King Alfred Write Anything?' 16 and 18; see also ibid., 17, on the common authorship of these two texts. The *terminus ante quem* for the *Boethius*, and (if common authorship is accepted) therefore for the *Soliloquies* as well, is set just before or around the mid-tenth century by the earliest manuscript witness to the *Boethius* (ibid., 16 and 22–3 n. 72).

As neatly as this explanation conforms to what we think we know about the historical Alfred, it is not necessary to accept Alfredian authorship in order to accept my rationale for the study of the *Soliloquia* and the production of the *Soliloquies*, because, contrary to the prevailing perception, Alfred's educational profile was not unique among learned Anglo-Saxons of the ninth and early tenth centuries, with respect to the very late age at which he first engaged in the serious study of theology. Several classes of evidence indicate that in Alfred's day, even Latin-literate Anglo-Saxons rarely undertook serious study of the sophisticated theological treatises of the Fathers – an endeavour which must be distinguished from the reading of patristic homilies and hagiographies – and that those who did progress to such an advanced level were nearing or in middle age by that stage of their education.

Patristic Theology and the Anglo-Saxon Curriculum

Most of the works of Ambrose, Augustine, and Jerome that were available in early eighth-century Wearmouth-Jarrow virtually disappeared from the Anglo-Saxon intellectual landscape until the eleventh century, at which time libraries accumulated more thorough collections of patristic works, most often by importing or copying continental manuscripts.[145] During the interim, the works of these theologians were much less familiar to the Anglo-Saxons than were the homilies of Caesarius of Arles (ob. 542), which offered no sustained discourse on the *ratio animae*, and the works of Gregory and Isidore, whose approaches to the soul were partly Platonizing and partly common-sensical. Even a sophisticated philosophical work such as Boethius's *De consolatione philosophiae*, when available, could not really serve as an introduction to Platonizing psychology, because Boethius wrote for an audience whom he assumed already to be familiar with the metaphysical background of his arguments.

The works of the Fathers, moreover, were not a vital part of the Anglo-Saxon school curriculum. According to Michael Lapidge, an oblate who began his education at a monastery around age seven would first memorize the psalms and hymns of the Divine Office; next he would learn Latin grammar and elementary metrics, after which 'he proceeded to those Latin texts which constituted the medieval curriculum, a course lasting some

---

145 See chapter 4 above and epilogue.

ten years.'[146] This curriculum was by no means standardized, but extant manuscripts, glossaries, and booklists suggest that it commonly included the *Disticha Catonis*, Prosper of Aquitaine's *Epigrammata*, Prudentius's *Psychomachia*, and four lengthy Latin poems based on scriptural narratives, by Juvencus, Caelius Sedulius, Arator, and Alcimus Avitus. More advanced students sometimes studied Vergil's *Aeneid* and Lucan's *Pharsalia*, and beginning in the tenth century, Persius's *Satires* and Boethius's *De consolatione philosophiae* were perhaps added to the list.[147] With the occasional exception of the *Consolatio*, this curriculum included no texts that posed a significant challenge to the vernacular concepts of *sawol* and *mod*.

When a student had completed a literary curriculum of this nature he studied the quadrivium, or alternatively, 'if he became a monk, spent the remainder of his life reading Scripture and the patristic authorities ... [M]editation on the writings of Ambrose, Augustine, Jerome, and Gregory,' or at least such as were available, 'would have been the lifelong occupation of a monk.'[148] According to the timetable outlined by Lapidge, even a young boy, embarking on a ten-year literary curriculum after mastering Latin grammar and metrics, could scarcely have graduated to the study of patristic texts before reaching his early twenties. Nor can we assume that a student in Alfred's day typically began his career at age seven: early Anglo-Saxon monasteries did not systematically promote oblature in the way that reformed Benedictine communities would do during the later tenth and eleventh centuries, so many students' careers must have begun much later and stretched further into adulthood.[149]

Texts emanating from Alfred's milieu offer some specific corroboration of these generalizations. Æthelweard, Alfred's youngest child, learned both English and Latin from a young age; Asser says he was engaged in *liberalibus artibus* and *ludis literariae disciplinae*.[150] The precise significance of

---

146 Lapidge, 'Anglo-Latin Literature,' 2–3.
147 Ibid., 3–4. Though Prosper's *Epigrammata* is based on excerpts from the works of Augustine, it emphasizes moral teachings and explication of basic credal statements, with no attention to Augustine's psychology, ontology, or natural philosophy.
148 Ibid., 4.
149 On the rise and fall of oblature among English Benedictine communities, see P.A. Quinn, *Better than the Sons of Kings*, esp. 195–202. Where oblature was practised, it was regarded as a moral and spiritual advantage more than an intellectual one; see Jones, 'Ælfric and the Limits of the "Benedictine Reform,"' esp. 80).
150 Asser, *De rebus gestis Ælfredi*, ch. 75, lines 11–21 (ed. Stevenson, *Asser's Life of King Alfred*, 58; see also Keynes and Lapidge (trans.), *Alfred the Great: Asser's* Life of King Alfred, 90 and 257).

Asser's words is elusive, and the phrase *liberales artes* does not necessarily refer to the trivium (grammar, rhetoric, and dialectic), but it is highly unlikely that such a phrase would signify philosophy and theology, to which the liberal arts served as *ancillae*, and the word *ludi* 'games' that Asser applies to Æthelweard's literary studies suggests anything but the gravitas of patristic discourse. Outside the ambit of the royal family, the textual evidence tells of ideal rather than realized education. Alfred's Preface to the *Pastoral Care* states that one objective of his translation program is to engage all the *geoguþ* of the free classes in learning to read English, and only those who were to be promoted 'to a superior position,' either in secular or in ecclesiastical employment, would graduate to the study of Latin after they could read in English.[151] Notably, the word *geoguþ* (rather than *cildru*) suggests that Alfred did not envision seven-year-old boys as his ideal elementary students, but young men, anywhere between their teens and their thirties.[152] These and other glimpses of real and ideal educational practice in works associated with Alfred's milieu show plainly that children were not the only ones to learn to read, and that those who did read did not pick up Augustine or Boethius until they had passed many other educational milestones.

The Educational Profile of the Monk-Priest

The most familiar categories of literate Anglo-Saxons cannot be very fruitfully compared with Alfred, in terms of their educational profiles. Those who began as seven-year-old *oblati* brought a significantly narrower range of secular experience to their advanced studies than Alfred did; the *conuersi*

---

151 Alfred, Preface to the *Pastoral Care* (ed. Sweet, *Pastoral Care*, 7.10–15). The phrase *to hieran hade* is usually thought to refer to the priestly order, but Godden argues persuasively that it could equally have referred to the monastic habit or even to prestigious secular offices: see 'King Alfred's Preface and the Teaching of Latin in Anglo-Saxon England.'

152 The word *geoguþ* is more flexible than its Latin counterparts (e.g., *adolescens,* young man, between ages fifteen and thirty; *iuuenis,* young man, between the ages of twenty and forty), but a search of Healey et al., *The Dictionary of Old English Corpus on the World Wide Web,* indicates that where *geoguþ* appears in glosses and translations, it is most likely to render either *iuuenis* or *iuuentus* 'the period between ages twenty and forty,' while *puer* 'boy,' up to age seventeen, is most likely to be rendered by OE *cild* or *cnapa*. The *DOE* notes that *geoguþ* was often used to distinguish the period of youth from that of childhood as well as from that of maturity: see s.v. *geoguþ*, A.1; specialized uses recorded in the *DOE* signify young persons who were old enough to have taken up a livelihood (e.g., young monks and nuns, untried warriors).

who entered monastic life after years or decades in a secular career share Alfred's timetable, but the majority of *conuersi* were unlikely to progress past the memorization of psalms and liturgical texts.[153] Though Alfred's policies encouraged adult laypersons to acquire vernacular literacy for secular purposes, it is improbable that many lay adults attained an advanced level of Latin literacy or read works of theology, except possibly in the form of the Alfredian translations.

There is one class of scholars whose educational careers likely paralleled that of King Alfred: those men who were first ordained as priests and subsequently entered monastic life. Historians of education and of monasticism have focused most of their attention on the *oblati* and the *conuersi*, but significant numbers of men also entered the monastery by way of the priesthood, and therefore must have deferred their advanced monastic studies until they were nearing middle age, since the canonical age for ordination to the priesthood was thirty. I am unaware of any studies or statistics that might indicate what proportion of monks followed this path to the monastery in England.[154] Asser, at least, did not call attention to anything out of the ordinary in his account of King Alfred's foundation of a new monastery at Athelney. Since the king was unable to find enough Englishmen to constitute as large a monastic community as he desired to have there, he imported continental priests and deacons, who became monks straightaway, while a select group of their children were educated in the monastery as oblates.[155]

For more specific information about the career path of the monk-priest, we can consult the *uitae* of two Anglo-Saxon men who managed to acquire very advanced educations as monks, even though they deferred this stage of their careers until after they were ordained as priests. The first of these is Dunstan, archbishop of Canterbury (960–88), whose *uita* was written between 995 and 1005 by a cleric who identified himself only by his initial 'B.,' who knew Dunstan personally for some years prior to the

---

153 On the monastic careers of *conuersi*, see Foot, *Monastic Life in Anglo-Saxon England, c. 600–900*, 146–52.

154 A more general picture of the career path of the monk-priest on the continent may be found in Nussbaum, *Kloster, Priestermönch und Privatmesse*; and Häussling, *Mönchskonvent und Eucharistiefeier*.

155 Asser, *De rebus gestis Ælfredi*, ch. 92–4 (ed. Stevenson, *Asser's Life of King Alfred*, 79–81; see also Keynes and Lapidge (trans.), *Alfred the Great: Asser's Life of King Alfred*, 102–3).

latter's elevation to the archbishopric.[156] The second is Æthelwold, bishop of Winchester (963–84): his hagiographer Wulfstan of Winchester (also known as Wulfstan Cantor) had been Æthelwold's pupil at Winchester, and the editors of his *Vita sancti Æthelwoldi*, written around 996, have suggested that this text is based largely on biographical information that Æthelwold recounted to Wulfstan first-hand during his lifetime.[157] Naturally we cannot interpret every detail of a saint's *uita*, especially of his childhood years, as unfiltered historical fact. As Sarah Foot has observed, 'Early medieval hagiographers frequently stressed the precociously young age at which their subject's notable piety became manifest, for to choose religion in childhood was a recognized mark of holiness and an indication of future sanctity.'[158] Given that both Dunstan and Æthelwold were revered for their learning as well as for their ecclesiastical leadership, it would not be surprising to find that Dunstan's and Æthelwold's hagiographers exaggerated the amount of learning that each attained in boyhood. Yet unexpectedly, the *uitae* of both men portray them as as late bloomers, arriving at their monastic vocation and their advanced learning when they were in their thirties or older.

Both B. and Wulfstan are vague about the content of their subjects' boyhood studies, and both portray their subjects as good students, but not miraculously precocious. Dunstan's parents dedicated him to the 'holy pursuit of letters' (sacris … litterarum otiis), and he sailed quickly through his elementary studies.[159] Æthelwold too was given over to the 'holy pursuit of letters' (sacris litterarum studiis).[160] These phrases do little to tell us what the boys studied, but Wulfstan's description of Æthelwold's disposition as a student offers some clues:

qui aliis uiam salutis erat ostensurus ipse cum Maria secus pedes Domini humiliter sederet et uerbum ex ore illius salubriter audiret. Erat enim agilis

156 Lapidge, 'B. and the *Vita S. Dunstani*,' 279–83; Lapidge also hypothesizes that B. 'was a sort of Latin secretary to Dunstan sometime during the years of Dunstan's abbacy at Glastonbury' (289).
157 See Lapidge and Winterbottom's introduction to Wulfstan, *Life of St Æthelwold*, c–ci.
158 Foot, *Monastic Life in Anglo-Saxon England*, 140.
159 *Sancti Dunstani uita auctore B.*, ch. 4 and 5 (ed. Stubbs, *Memorials of Saint Dunstan*, 7 and 10–11).
160 Wulfstan of Winchester, *Vita Sancti Æthelwoldi*, ch. 6 (ed. Lapidge and Winterbottom, *Life of St Æthelwold*, 8).

natura atque acutus ingenio, ita ut quicquid maiorum traditione didicerat non
segniter obliuioni traderet sed tenaci potius memoriae commendaret.[161]

Wulfstan compares the boy Æthelwold to the contemplative archetype of
Mary, emphasizing his attentive listening and his skill in memorization.[162]
If Wulfstan's comments have any basis in biographical fact, they intimate
that at this stage of boyhood Æthelwold was engaged in passive, non-
literate learning, such as memorizing the psalms and catechetical dialogues
or colloquies, rather than reading and writing Latin.

Wulfstan's next reference to learning occurs when Æthelwold is an *ado-*
lescens, spending a significant period of time attached to King Athelstan's
court: 'ibique indiuiduo comitatu multum temporis agens in palatio plura
a sapientibus regis utilia ac proficua sibi didicit.'[163] Lapidge and Winterbottom take this to mean 'that Æthelwold pursued a secular career at
court until he was ordained by Bishop Ælfheah.'[164] The learning that occupied him in his teens and twenties, therefore, was not book-learning but
practical secular skills, which may or may not have demanded literacy. If
the canonical age for ordination to the priesthood was observed in early
tenth-century England, then this secular work kept Æthelwold busy until
he was at least thirty.[165] Dunstan's career followed a similar trajectory:

---

161 Wulfstan of Winchester, *Vita Sancti Æthelwoldi,* ch. 6 (ed. Lapidge and Winterbottom,
     Life of St Æthelwold, 9–11): 'one who was destined to show others the "way of salva-
     tion" was himself with Mary able to sit humbly at the feet of the Lord [cf. Lk 10:39],
     listening to the words of salvation from his lips. He was naturally quick and sharp of
     mind, so that he did not lazily consign to oblivion what he learnt from the elders'
     teaching, but rather stored it in a retentive memory' (trans. ibid., 10).

162 For the significance of Mary as a symbol of the contemplative life in the works of
     Gregory the Great and within the discourse of the tenth-century English Benedicti-
     nism, see Clayton, 'Hermits and the Contemplative Life in Anglo-Saxon England,'
     150–1 and 158–62. The classic study of the figures of the contemplative Mary and the
     active Martha in medieval spirituality is Constable, 'The Interpretation of Mary and
     Martha'; see esp. 26–35 on Anglo-Saxon and Carolingian praise for the contemplative
     life of Mary.

163 Wulfstan of Winchester, *Vita Sancti Æthelwoldi,* ch. 7 (ed. Lapidge and Winterbottom,
     Life of St Æthelwold, 10): 'He spent a long period there in the royal *burh* as the king's
     inseparable companion, learning much from the king's *witan* that was useful and prof-
     itable to him' (trans. ibid., 11). On Æthelwold's surprisingly extensive entanglements
     in secular business, see Yorke, 'Æthelwold and the Politics of the Tenth Century.'

164 See Lapidge and Winterbottom's commentary on Wulfstan, *Life of St Æthelwold,* 11 n. 7.

165 Lapidge and Winterbottom consider the canonical age for priesthood to be a reliable
     enough criterion to support their claim that Æthelwold could have been born no later
     than c. 909 if his ordination took place (as Wulfstan maintains) during the reign of

B. reports that Dunstan entered minor orders at Glastonbury, and Wulfstan's *Life of Æthelwold* records that Æthelwold's kinsman Ælfheah, bishop of Winchester (934–51), ordained Dunstan and Æthelwold to the priesthood at the same time, probably between 934 and 939.[166]

It must be stressed that very little education was an absolute prerequisite to ordination to the priesthood at any time during the Anglo-Saxon period. Scholars and ecclesiastical administrators had been complaining about priestly illiteracy and ignorance since Bede's day. Alfred complains of the same in his preface to the *Pastoral Care*, and Ælfric (perhaps echoing Alfred) claims that even in the earlier tenth century, 'nan englisc preost ne cuðe dihtan oððe asmeagan anne pistol on leden, oðþæt Dunstan arcebisceop and Aðelwold biscop eft þa lare on munuclifum arærdon.'[167] The *mæssepreost* who was the first tutor to Ælfric of Eynsham, and was therefore a younger contemporary of Dunstan and Æthelwold, had little command of Latin: 'he cuðe be dæle Lyden understandan,' as Ælfric recalls.[168] Even in the early eleventh century, Byrhtferth would mock the priests to

---

Athelstan (924–39): see their comments in Wulfstan, *Life of St Æthelwold*, xlii and 11 n. 11. If Dunstan, like Æthelwold, was ordained by 939 it is implausible that he could have been born as late as 924, so it is commonly assumed that B. was mistaken when he wrote that Dunstan was born (*oritur*) during the reign of Athelstan (ibid., 14 n. 4). Brooks, who suggests that canonical ages were not strictly observed during the tenth century, defends the plausibility of B.'s dating, on the grounds that if Dunstan were born as late as 924 he could still have become a monk during Athelstan's reign and have received the abbacy of Glastonbury during Eadmund's reign (939–46), as B. maintains ('The Career of St Dunstan,' 3–5). Brooks does not take into consideration the passage (quoted above) in Wulfstan's *Vita Sancti Æthelwoldi* that suggests, but does not say definitively, that Dunstan and Æthelwold were both ordained priests before Athelstan's death, that is, by 939. Dunstan could conceivably have become a monk by age fifteen, but he was surely not ordained a priest by that age, so there is little reason to defend B.'s dating of Dunstan's birth.

166 On Dunstan's entry into minor orders, see B., *Sancti Dunstani uita auctore B.*, ch. 5 (ed. Stubbs, *Memorials of Saint Dunstan*, 10); on his priestly ordination, see Wulfstan, *Vita Sancti Æthelwoldi*, ch. 8 (ed. Lapidge and Winterbottom, *Life of St Æthelwold*, 12), and Lapidge and Winterbottom's comments on the date of this event (ibid., xlii).

167 Ælfric, *Grammar*, Preface (ed. Zupitza, *Ælfrics Grammatik und Glossar*, 3): 'no English priest was capable of composing or fully comprehending a letter in Latin, before Archbishop Dunstan and Bishop Æthelwold re-established learning in the monasteries.' The parallel with Alfred is noted by J. Wilcox in his edition of *Ælfric's Prefaces*, 153.

168 Ælfric, *Old English Preface to the Translation of Genesis*, lines 12–13 (ed. J. Wilcox, *Ælfric's Prefaces*, 116): 'he could partly understand Latin.' On the implications of Ælfric's statement, see Jones, '*Meatim sed et rustica*: Ælfric of Eynsham as a Medieval Latin Author,' 53–4; and Jones, 'Ælfric and the Limits of "Benedictine Reform,"' 96–107.

whom he taught the computus, because their knowledge was so rudiment-
ary compared to that of the *oblati*.[169] We have no cause to suppose that
either Dunstan or Æthelwold was so deficient in Latin that he would have
been delinquent in his priestly duties, but on the other hand, their hagiographers give us no cause to think that either of them had, by the time
of their ordination, attained more advanced learning than their priestly
duties required.

After his ordination, Æthelwold next spent some time attached to the
retinue of Bishop Ælfheah, at the recommendation of the king (presumably Athelstan), in order to continue his education.[170] We know very little
about Ælfheah; there survive no writings of his, nor any attestation that
he was highly learned, so it is unlikely that he was able to advance Æthelwold's education appreciably.[171] Thereafter, Dunstan's and Æthelwold's
careers followed the same trajectory once again. Though ordained a priest,
Dunstan could still have chosen to marry, but Bishop Ælfheah persuaded
him to become a monk instead,[172] and only after he had committed himself
to the monastic life, according to B., did Dunstan pursue more advanced
learning. As a Glastonbury monk, Dunstan read widely and diligently in
'sacred and divine volumes' (*sacrorum et diuinorum uoluminum*) and took
advantage of the library belonging to the 'wandering Irishmen' (*Hiber-
nensium peregrini*) who resided at Glastonbury: 'Horum etiam libros

169   On the low level of learning required of priests across the Anglo-Saxon period, and on
Alfred's assessment of priestly Latinity in the Preface to the *Pastoral Care*, see esp.
Godden, 'King Alfred's Preface and the Teaching of Latin in Anglo-Saxon England,'
598–9. Byrhtferth's *Enchiridion* is punctuated by frequent mockery of the dull priests
to whom he taught computus in OE: see *Enchiridion* 1.1.172–5, 1.2.323–5, and 1.3.1–4,
among many others (ed. Baker and Lapidge, *Byrhtferth's Enchiridion*, 18–19, 42–3,
and 46–7).

170   Wulfstan of Winchester, *Vita Sancti Æthelwoldi*, ch. 9 (ed. Lapidge and Winterbottom,
Life of St Æthelwold, 14): 'Aput quem [*scil.* Ælfeagum] praecipiente rege quo melius
imbueretur aliquandiu commoratus est' (With [Ælfheah] he stayed for some time at
the king's wish to improve his education) (trans. ibid., 15).

171   On the connections, professional and familial, that linked Bishop Ælfheah with
Æthelwold and Dunstan, see Yorke, 'Æthelwold and the Politics of the Tenth Century,' 66–8 and 73–4; and Brooks, 'The Career of St Dunstan,' 5–7.

172   It is not clear how much time elapsed between Dunstan's ordination and his entry into
the monastic life: see B., *Sancti Dunstani uita*, ch. 5 (ed. Stubbs, *Memorials of Saint
Dunstan*, 10–11). Brooks writes that Dunstan spent 'the years of his puberty' engaged
in advanced study ('The Career of St Dunstan,' 5), but B.'s *uita* leaves little doubt that
Dunstan's advanced studies occurred while he was a monk in Glastonbury, *after* he
had been ordained as a priest, probably at age 30 or later.

rectae fidei tramitem phylosophantes, diligenter excoluit, aliorumque
prudentum, quos ab intimo cordis aspectu patrum sanctorum assertione
solidatos esse persensit, solubili semper scrutamine indagauit.'[173] This is
the first time in B.'s *uita* that he portrays Dunstan engaging with the sort
of books that might have exposed him to discourses on the nature of the
soul, whether in the Irishmen's 'philosophizing books' or in those books
that bore the 'authority of the holy Fathers.'

Æthelwold was next to come to Glastonbury, where he undertook a
program of study under Dunstan's tutelage; after studying with Dunstan
for a time, he too became a monk. Remarkably, according to his hagiographer, Æthelwold began his studies at Glastonbury at the very lowest
level of the literary curriculum:

> Cuius [*scil.* Dunstani] magisterio multum proficiens, tandem monastici ordi-
> nis habitum ab ipso suscepit, humili deuotione eius regimini deditus. Didicit
> namque inibi liberalem grammaticae artis peritiam atque mellifluam metricae
> rationis dulcedinem, et more apis prudentissimae, quae solet boni odoris
> arbores circumuolando requirere et iocundi saporis holeribus incumbere,
> diuinorum carpebat flores uoluminum. Catholicos quoque et nominatos stu-
> diose legebat auctores, insuper uigiliis et orationibus perseueranter insistens,
> et abstinentia semet ipsum edomans, et fratres ad ardua semper exhortans.[174]

Lapidge and Winterbottom accept at face value Wulfstan's narrative of
Æthelwold's formal education: nearly all of his study of Latin literature
and patristic theology was deferred until he was at Glastonbury.[175] If

---

173 B., *Sancti Dunstani uita*, ch. 5 (ed. Stubbs, *Memorials of Saint Dunstan*, 11): 'Dunstan
assiduously pored over the Irishmen's books, which proffered wisdom concerning the
path of orthodox faith, and with unclouded powers of discrimination he continually
sought out the books of other wise men, which he knew with certainty, by means of the
deepest insight of his heart, to be supported by the corroboration of the holy Fathers.'

174 Wulfstan of Winchester, *Vita Sancti Æthelwoldi*, ch. 9 (ed. Lapidge and Winterbottom,
Life of St Æthelwold, 14): 'He profited greatly by Dunstan's teaching, and eventually
received the habit of the monastic order from him, devoting himself humbly to his
rule. At Glastonbury he learned skill in the liberal art of grammar and the honey-
sweet system of metrics; like a provident bee that habitually flits around looking for
scented trees and settling on greenery of pleasant taste, he laid toll on the flowers of
religious books. He was eager to read the best-known Christian writers, and was in
addition constant in vigils and prayer, taming himself by fasting and never ceasing to
exhort his fellow monks to strive for the heights' (trans. ibid., 15).

175 See Lapidge and Winterbottom's introduction to Wulfstan, *Life of St Æthelwold*,
lxxxvi.

Wulfstan's narrative is accurate, his statement that Æthelwold had to study grammar and metrics with Dunstan is a strong indication that before 939 his Latin literacy was not sufficiently advanced to allow him to read sophisticated literary Latin on his own. If his ordination occurred when he was no younger than thirty, Æthelwold would have attained his mid-thirties if not his forties during his course of study of grammar, metrics, and 'religious books,' which, if he was following the typical curriculum, probably means Christian Latin poetry.[176] Only after completing the literary curriculum was Æthelwold appropriately 'eager to read the best-known Christian writers,' who, based on their mention at the end of the sequence of educational stages, may have been the Fathers, although it is also possible that for a late tenth-century audience, the 'best-known Christian writers' were not the Fathers but the Christian Latin poets. There is no reason to doubt that as a monk Æthelwold eventually read such works of Boethius, Augustine, Ambrose, and Jerome as were available; but on the other hand, the authors whose influence Lapidge has detected in Æthelwold's known Latin writings are not the aforementioned Fathers but Venantius Fortunatus, Juvencus, and Aldhelm, as well as St Benedict and Bede.[177]

I do not wish to argue that Dunstan or Æthelwold actually wrote the OE *Soliloquies*, but rather that their *uitae* demonstrate that an educational career like Alfred's was not unique in southern England during the late ninth and

---

176 From my interpretation of Wulfstan's account, it follows that Æthelwold was, at first, one of the students rather than one of the leaders in the 'hypothetical Aldhelm seminar' that was ongoing at Glastonbury in the 940s and 950s according to Mechthild Gretsch, *The Intellectual Foundations of the English Benedictine Reform* (382). This is not to say that Æthelwold did not attain, between his arrival in 939 and his departure for Abingdon in 955, the very high level of literary expertise that Gretsch attributes to him, and that could have made him an influential participant in the creation of the glosses on the Royal Psalter and on Aldhelm's prose *De uirginitate* preserved in Brussels, Bibliothèque Royale, MS 1650, which Gretsch identifies as emanating from Glastonbury in the 940s. My point is simply that Æthelwold did not bring this expertise to Glastonbury with him; that he had already reached middle age when he participated in the 'Aldhelm seminar'; and that even when he was a fine Latinist engaged in the glossing of Aldhelm, he was still preoccupied with a stage in the literary curriculum that did not include any Latin theological discourse other than Boethius's *Consolatio*.

177 On the writers emulated by Æthelwold, see Lapidge, 'Æthelwold as Scholar and Teacher,' 197. Lapidge indicates that Æthelwold was certainly familiar with Bede's *Historia ecclesiastica*; there is no evidence that he knew Bede's exegetical and scientific writings.

early tenth centuries.[178] Their intellectual approach to the patristic discourses they read through the eyes of worldly experience would doubtless have been significantly different from that of their oblate brethren, particularly with respect to the irreconcilable differences between vernacular and classical opinions on the relationship between soul and mind. Recognizing the educational similarities among Alfred, Dunstan, and Æthelwold, as well as the class of monk-priests as a whole, makes it more plausible that someone other than Alfred could have been responsible for the idiosyncratic treatment of the psychological content of the *OE Boethius* and the *Soliloquies*, and it also suggests a broader target audience for these texts, since other men of moderate and advanced learning likely shared Alfred's struggle to understand the unitary nature of the *sawol*.

---

178 For markedly different reasons, Godden has recently suggested that Dunstan and his teachers at Glastonbury are plausible alternative authors of the *OE Boethius* and *Soliloquies*: see 'The Alfredian Project and Its Aftermath,' 118.

8 Ælfric's Battle against Materialism

None of the evidence considered up to this point suggests that a Platonizing philosophical psychology was capable of supplanting any facet of vernacular psychology at any stratum of Anglo-Saxon society beyond those who progressed to an advanced stage of the literary curriculum and studied Boethius's *De consolatione philosophiae* with the aid of commentaries. At middling and lower levels of education, the eclectic, often Stoicizing theories of substance and the strongly cardiocentric psychology of the Insular grammars and riddles posed no serious challenge to the vernacular tradition. Alcuin's *De ratione animae* taught that the soul was both incorporeal and unitary, but he wrote this text on the continent in the form of a Latin epistle, and it did not reach a broad audience in pre-Conquest England; the *OE Boethius* and *Soliloquies* provided the first vernacular discourse on the unitary soul but did not assimilate the concept of incorporeality in the strictest Platonizing sense.[1]

Only at the very end of the tenth century would Ælfric of Eynsham (ca. 950–ca. 1010) pioneer a vernacular discourse that had the potential to bring the concept of the strictly incorporeal, unitary soul to a broad audience. The key textual witness to this discourse is Ælfric's Nativity homily (*Lives of Saints* 1; Belfour homily 9), which adapts into OE a large portion of Alcuin's *De ratione animae*. The decision to use Alcuin's Platonizing philosophical psychology as the vehicle for his teachings on the unitary soul made Ælfric's job significantly more difficult than it had to be. In contrast to Alfred, who promulgated the doctrine of the unitary soul but

---

1 On the dissemination of the Latin Boethius commentaries, Alcuin's *DRA*, and the *OE Boethius* and *Soliloquies*, see chapter 4 above.

without the supporting framework of Platonist ontology and epistemology, Ælfric endeavoured to teach his audience about the strict incorporeality of the soul and its epistemological implications. The first half of the present chapter examines the nature and the extent of materialism among the Anglo-Saxons of the tenth and eleventh centuries, especially as attested in homiletic and hagiographic materials outside the Ælfrician corpus; following this, I evaluate Ælfric's efforts to inculcate in his contemporaries a less materialist understanding of the mind, of the soul, and of the transformation wrought during the eucharist.

What Does 'Materialism' Entail?

Historians have devoted significantly more attention to the popular materialist mentality that was current in ninth-century Francia than to the materialism that Ælfric battled in England around the year 1000. To define more precisely the meaning of 'materialism' as it existed in Ælfric's milieu, therefore, it is helpful to begin with an overview of some recent insights into Carolingian materialism and the Carolingian anti-materialist eucharistic treatises that Ælfric would later rely upon, one by Pascasius Radbertus and the other by Ratramnus of Corbie.

Frequent reception of the eucharist was not a central component of the devotional practices of Christian laypersons in eighth- and ninth-century Francia. Some scholars have attributed this circumstance not to custom alone but to a popular preference for manifestations of God's presence that were vividly materialized and perceptible to the senses.[2] The laity recognized such manifestations to reside in the relics of the saints, which attracted enthusiastic popular devotion, but they were apathetic about a devotional practice such as the eucharist, which occurred during the course of a Sunday rite that apparently did little to encourage lay participation. In comparison with the countless narratives of miracles effected through the relics of saints, this period gave rise to relatively few reports of miracles related to the eucharist, suggesting that the laity did not view the body and blood of Christ as a locus of contact with God's real presence and of access to divine power and favour.[3]

---

2 Cristiani, 'La controversia eucaristica nella cultura del secolo IX,' 218–19; Chélini, 'La pratique dominicale des laïcs dans l'église franque sous le règne de Pépin,' 168–9.
3 Cristiani, 'La controversia eucaristica,' 216–19 and n. 205; Chélini, 'La pratique dominicale des laïcs,' 168–9.

The Frankish laity's indifference to and incomprehension of the eucharist was treated as a pastoral problem, but when similar attitudes surfaced within a prominent monastic community, the response was as much doctrinal as pastoral. Early in the 830s Warino, abbot of Corvey, grew anxious about what he perceived to be barbaric ignorance among his monks, many of whom were Saxons recently converted to Christianity: like many of their contemporaries, the monks thought that the presence of Christ in the eucharist was merely symbolic or figural, but not real, because it was not perceptible to the senses. Warino sought to cultivate in his monks a greater reverence for the eucharist, surpassing their enthusiasm for the more palpable forms of devotional practice, and to this end, he commissioned from Pascasius Radbertus a treatise entitled *De corpore et sanguine Domini* during the period 831–3.[4] In his explication of the eucharist, Pascasius appeals to the Corvey monks' preference for devotions that engage the senses, and he emphasizes the reality and immediate accessibility of Christ's presence in the bread and wine of the eucharist. In his opening chapter Pascasius writes,

> Et ideo nullus moueatur de hoc corpore Christi et sanguine, quod in misterio uera sit caro et uerus sit sanguis, dum sic ille uoluit qui creauit: *Omnia* enim *quaecumque uoluit Dominus fecit in caelo et in terra*. Et quia uoluit licet figura panis et uini haec sic esse, omnino nihil aliud quam caro Christi et sanguis post consecrationem credenda sunt.[5]

Pascasius clearly aims to persuade an audience who denies the reality of Christ's presence in the sacrament because all they can see and taste in the eucharist is bread and wine. In his efforts to cater to such an audience, later in his treatise Pascasius resorts to vivid, corporealizing images that could easily have been misconstrued as assertions that Christ's presence was physically real and perceptible to the senses. This is especially true of the series of eucharistic miracle stories that Pascasius compiles in chapter 14, in which people who doubt the reality of Christ's presence in the eucharist

---

4 Chazelle, *The Crucified God in the Carolingian Era*, 210–11; Cristiani, 'La controversia eucaristica,' 215.

5 Pascasius, *De corpore et sanguine Domini* 1.44–9 (ed. Paulus, CCCM 16, 14–15): 'And therefore let no one have doubts concerning this body and blood of Christ, that they are true flesh and true blood, since he who made it willed it to be so: for *whatsoever the Lord hath pleased he hath done, in heaven and in earth* [Ps 134:6]. And since he willed it to be so, although its appearance be that of bread and wine, you must not on any account believe other than that they are the flesh and blood of Christ after the consecration.' See also ch. 2.9–14 and 3.1–18 (ibid., 20 and 23–4).

change their minds after experiencing gruesome visions of a living child bloodily sacrificed on the altar as the priest breaks the bread, or of a bloody finger on the paten.[6] Even though he introduces these miracle stories under the somewhat misleading chapter title 'Quod haec saepe uisibili specie apparuerint' ('That the body and blood often appear in visible form'), it was not Pascasius's intent to teach that the transformation of the bread and wine into the body and blood of Christ was a material change; elsewhere in *De corpore et sanguine Domini*, and in other writings as well, he clearly asserts that Christ is *not* sensibly perceptible in the eucharist except in extraordinary, miraculous manifestations.[7]

Pascasius's rhetoric makes clear that he understood one particular error to be current among his audience: they denied the reality of the transformation of the eucharist because they could not see it. Yet it is also argued that precisely the opposite error was thriving in ninth-century Francia. Celia Chazelle writes that Pascasius 'uphold[s] the doctrine of the eucharist that most closely approaches popular tendencies in the ninth century to think that the consecrated elements contain or become flesh and blood in a physical sense,' and that contemporary scholarly opposition to Pascasius's treatise was but one manifestation of a broader anxiety about the increasingly sensual nature of Christian devotion.[8] And indeed, when Pascasius's chief opponent, Ratramnus of Corbie, penned a treatise also called *De corpore et sanguine Domini* in the 840s or 850s, he had in mind an audience whose error lay in their expectation that the consecration of the bread and wine would render Christ's physical presence in the elements perceptible to the senses of sight and taste.[9] '[Q]uidam fidelium,'

---

6 Pascasius, *De corpore et sanguine Domini* 14 (ed. Paulus, CCCM 16, 85–92).

7 One of the passages cited above (*De corpore et sanguine Domini* 3.1–18) as suggestive of the perceptible presence of Christ in the eucharist is meant to express that sacraments make visible something that is invisible. Less vulnerable to misreading is the chapter immediately preceding the eucharistic miracle stories (*De corpore et sanguine Domini* 13.3–5; ed. Paulus, CCCM 16, 83), where Pascasius teaches, 'Quod uero colorem aut saporem carnis minime praebet, uirtus tamen fidei et intelligentiae quae nihil de Christo dubitat, totum illud spiritaliter sapit et degustat' (The power of faith and understanding, which has no hesitation where Christ is concerned, spiritually tastes and savours all of that which does not at all exhibit the colour or the flavour of flesh). See Cristiani, 'La controversia eucaristica,' 215–16; and Chazelle, 'Figure, Character, and the Glorified Body in the Carolingian Eucharistic Controversy,' 6–7.

8 Chazelle, *The Crucified God in the Carolingian Era*, 216 and 219.

9 For the purposes of the present discussion I am chiefly interested in the popular mentalities to which Pascasius and Ratramnus were responding, rather than the controversy that unfolded among the scholarly elites of mid-ninth-century Francia: on the specific issues

writes Ratramnus, 'corporis sanguinisque Christi misterium quod in ecclesia cotidie celebratur dicant, quod nulla sub figura, nulla sub obuelatione fiat, sed ipsius ueritatis nuda manifestatione peragatur.'[10] Speaking to these misguided faithful, Ratramnus exhorts them to taste, smell, and examine the consecrated wine: it will still exhibit the flavour, odour, and colour of wine. Only if they examine it 'more inwardly' (interius) will they find the blood of Christ manifested to 'the minds of believers.' The body and blood of Christ indeed exist in the bread and wine, but they 'exist figurally' (figurate ... existit).[11] Ratramnus's goal is to convince an audience who is already willing to accept the reality of Christ's presence in the eucharist that this presence is accessible only through faith and intellection, not through sensory perception.

What, then, was the nature of popular belief about the eucharist, if the error targeted by Pascasius appears to have been the diametrical opposite of that targeted by Ratramnus? To characterize the mentality that underlay the ninth-century Frankish misapprehensions of the eucharist, scholars often invoke the term 'materialism,' though this term is very elastic and prone to oversimplification, which in turn obscures its potential effects on popular mentalities. In the case of the Carolingians, I maintain that the two major errors concerning the presence of Christ in the eucharist share a single origin: a materialist mentality that is most accurately characterized as a common-sense supposition that reality is constituted by material entities, or by that which is perceived by the senses. Some scholars have oversimplified this popular materialism by asserting that it is manifested only as a habit of corporealizing that which is incorporeal. Brian Stock, for instance, claims that prior to the rise of formal exegesis of the sacraments, there was no 'existing basis for allegory and interpretation' of the eucharist, and therefore, 'For the unlettered ... the concrete representation

---

at stake in this controversy and the intellectual context from which it emanated, see esp. Chazelle, *The Crucified God in the Carolingian Era*, 211–15, for her revised dating of Ratramnus's treatise; 215–25 on the eucharistic theology of Pascasius and Hincmar; and 225–38 on that of Ratramnus and other opponents of the Pascasian teaching. See also Matter, 'The Soul of the Dog-Man'; Bouhot, *Ratramne de Corbie*, 77–88; and Chazelle, 'Figure, Character, and the Glorified Body.'

10 Ratramnus, *De corpore et sanguine Domini* 2 (ed. van den Brink, *De corpore*, 43): 'Certain of the faithful are saying that the sacrament of the body and blood of Christ, which is celebrated daily in church, is effected not in any figural sense nor under any veil of secrecy, but is wrought as an uncloaked display of the truth itself.'

11 Ratramnus, *De corpore et sanguine Domini* 10 (ed. van den Brink, *De corpore*, 45).

of the eucharist and its associated rituals were the norm.'[12] But this is only a partial account of the effects of materialism, and it effectively denies that a population in which materialism thrives has any capacity for symbolic and allegorical thought – a position that is surely untenable. If materialism is the identification of reality with what is physical and accessible to the senses, then it is likely to shape popular mentalities in two distinct ways. People who are convinced that a given entity is real will expect it to be accessible to the senses, and people who observe that a given entity is inaccessible to the senses will deny that it is fully real, although this does not, I contend, preclude the possibility of symbolic or allegorical reality. The first materializing error is the one Ratramnus sought to rectify, and the second is the one that Pascasius sought to rectify, but both errors emanate from a materialism that does not acknowledge the existence of incorporeal, imperceptible realities.

The fact that Ælfric saw fit to rework parts of Pascasius's and Ratramnus's eucharistic theology into the form of an OE homily implies that Ælfric believed certain misperceptions of the eucharist to be current among his audience, and that those misperceptions were sufficiently similar to those that had been current in ninth-century Francia that Ælfric could remedy them by means of the same arguments that his Carolingian predecessors had formulated. Several of Ælfric's remarks, apparently based on personal experience, confirm this implication: he knew of individuals who simply could not grasp that the transformation that occurred during the eucharist could be simultaneously real and imperceptible.[13] Carolingian popular materialism therefore provides a useful comparandum as we proceed to consider the nature and extent of Anglo-Saxon materialism in the tenth and eleventh centuries. Marta Cristiani has proposed that the Corvey monks' materialist misconceptions about the eucharist were the product of their peculiar background, insofar as they were 'recent converts, still tied to their pagan mentality,'[14] but I see no reason to tie materialism to paganism. It is characteristic of common sense, not of paganism, to believe that reality is constituted by what is perceptible to the senses. Chazelle's observation about the extent of materialism in Francia is equally valid for the Anglo-Saxons: as long as the modicum of education afforded to ordinary clergy and religious did not inculcate in them the concept that something could be at

---

12 Stock, *The Implications of Literacy*, 265.
13 Ælfric, Easter Day homily (*CH II* 15), lines 86–90 (discussed below).
14 Cristiani, 'La controversia eucaristica,' 215: 'persone di recente conversione, ancora legate alla mentalità pagana.'

once real and also immaterial and imperceptible, materialism would persist, with its corollary errors concerning the eucharist, even among populations of dedicated Christians.[15] This means that the target audience of Ælfric's preaching was not a particularly backward or superficially Christianized segment of the population, but rather it encompassed all laypersons, clergy, and professed religious who had not been taught to conceive of a category of incorporeal, imperceptible realities.

Moreover, because Ælfric relied upon Platonizing philosophical treatises as the foundations of his anti-materialist preaching, his battle was necessarily waged on multiple conceptual fronts. He taught that the imperceptible transformation effected in the eucharist was real rather than symbolic; at the same time, he maintained that the real entity known as the *sawol* was imperceptible to the senses, and that the *mod* derived its power to perceive the incorporeal by virtue of its being part of the incorporeal *sawol* rather than part of the body. On each of these issues, Ælfric laboured in opposition to the teachings that prevailed in homiletic and hagiographical texts of his day, which routinely depicted the eucharist according to a materializing mentality, anthropomorphized the soul, and portrayed the soul as an impersonal and ineffectual victim or beneficiary of the actions executed by the mind-body complex. In the following pages I examine each of these trends in the anonymous homiletic and hagiographic literature of tenth- and early eleventh-century England in order to flesh out our understanding of Anglo-Saxon materialism. In non-Ælfrician texts these three materializing tendencies are scarcely, if at all, interrelated, but within the Ælfrician corpus they are inseparable, by virtue of the tightly interwoven relationship among ontology, epistemology, and psychology in the Platonizing philosophical discourse that Ælfric borrowed from his Carolingian sources.

Materializing Tendencies in OE Representations of the Eucharist

Exegesis of the eucharist is rare in OE homilies; preachers more often had recourse to narratives of the Last Supper or to exhortations to be shriven before receiving the eucharist. But where interpretation of the sacrament does occur, it usually underscores the typological significance of the eucharist and neglects the reality of the transformation of the elements or of Christ's presence, and thereby it reinforces the materialist inclination to

---

15 Chazelle, 'Figure, Character, and the Glorified Body,' 7.

equate the imperceptible with the symbolic and the unreal. A few examples – there are scarcely more than a few in extant OE homilies – will suffice to illustrate this pattern. Tristram homily 4 explains that a person may experience three forms of 'spiritual birth' (accennednyss gastlicu): baptism, confession, and reception of the eucharist. The homilist adds a few words about the significance of this third spiritual birth: 'He [*scil.* se drihten] geanlicode his lichaman heofonlican hlafe . and he onlihte his blod wine on lifes calice . and us þa onsende hider on þisne middaneard to earnan . and to wedde eces lifes.'[16] According to the words of this homilist, Christ instituted a ritual 'likening' of the eucharistic meal to his sacrifice of flesh and blood; there is no suggestion that the linguistic and conceptual act of 'likening' effects a substantial, sacramental change. Other homilies reinforce the focus on the symbolism of the eucharist by virtue of typological links between the eucharistic meal and other biblical events. Vercelli homily 5, for instance, likens Christ's birth in the manger to his presence in the sacrament:

> We gehyrdon þæt ure hælend wæs on binne aseted þa he wæs acenned. Þæt wæs sio stow þær man nytenum hira andlifan sealde. Sio binne getacnode Godes wiofod, þær bið þam halgum nytenum, þæt is þam geleaffulum mannum, bið seald þæt gastlice gereord Cristes lichoman, ðe he us to wedde forlet þætte we sien dælnimende Godes rices.[17]

In a third example, in Assmann homily 13, the typological significance of the eucharist serves to warn listeners of the consequences of receiving the sacrament in a state of spiritual impurity. Jesus tells John that he will be betrayed by whoever first takes the bread he has dipped in the salt-cellar. As Judas takes and eats the salted bread, he also ingests a devil, who drives him out of his senses. 'Ac uton nu geþæncan, men,' the homilist urges his listeners, 'be ðære bysene, þe se hælend þam Scariothiscan Iudan þone hlaf

---

16 Tristram homily 4, lines 162–5 (ed. Tristram, 'Vier altenglische Predigten aus der heterodoxen Tradition,' 179): 'He [*scil.* the Lord] likened his body to the bread of heaven and he likened his blood to wine in the cup of life, and he delivered them to us here on this earth as a reward and as a pledge of eternal life.'
17 Vercelli homily 5, lines 139–44 (ed. Scragg, *Vercelli Homilies*, 118): 'We have heard that our Saviour was laid in a manger when he was born: a manger was the place where people gave food to their livestock. The manger symbolized the altar of God, where there will be given to the holy beasts, that is, to the faithful people, that spiritual feast of the body of Christ, who left it for us as a covenant, so that we might be partakers of the kingdom of God.'

sealde, þæt us is on ðam mycel wærlicnys getacnad and æteowed on ðære onfangennysse ures drihtnes lichaman, þæt is þonne þæs halgan husles.' The figural significance of the narrative is meant to guide listeners to purify themselves before receiving the bread of the eucharist and thereby avoid a similar fate: 'Uton forðan tilian, þæt we syn clæne and unwæmme þam to onfonne, swa swa þa oðre apostolas wæron, næs na swa swa Iudas wæs.'[18] Each of these three homilies uses words such as *geanlicod* or *getacnod* to communicate the similarity between the eucharist and an event in the life of the historical Christ. To underscore the symbolic or typological significance of the eucharist is entirely within the bounds of orthodoxy, but each of these homilies stops short of communicating the idea that both Pascasius and Ratramnus promoted: the presence of Christ in the eucharist, though imperceptible, is wholly real. It bears mention that the anonymous homilies adduced above do not represent an unusually naive strain of thought. Ælfric's younger contemporary, the prolific homilist Wulfstan, archbishop of York (1002–23), explains in his *Institutes of Polity* how the duties of each of the seven ecclesiastical grades figurally re-enact important moments in Christ's life. The priest and the altar, for example, respectively symbolize (*getacnað*) Christ and his cross; 'and seo oflete getacnaþ Cristes lichaman, and win and wæter on ðam calice geswutelað þa halignessa, þe of Cristes sidan ut fleowan, þæt wæs blod and wæter.'[19] Again, there is nothing doctrinally objectionable in Wulfstan's explanation, but like other OE homilists he foregrounds the figural and neglects to comment on the relationship between the figural and the real.

---

18 Assmann homily 13, lines 262–7 (ed. Assmann, 163): 'Let us now ponder, people, this exemplum in which the Saviour gave the bread to Judas Iscariot; ponder the fact that in that exemplum a great warning is betokened and made manifest to us in the reception of our Lord's body, that is, the holy eucharist ... Therefore let us endeavour to be pure and spotless to receive that bread, as the other apostles were, not at all as Judas was.'
19 Wulfstan II of York, *Institutes of Polity* 24.36 (ed. Jost, *Die 'Institutes of Polity,'* 236): 'and the sacrifice [*scil.* the communion bread; *oflete* is derived from Latin *oblata*] symbolizes the body of Christ, and the wine and the water in the chalice are visible signs of the sacred things that flowed out from Christ's side, namely blood and water.' The language of symbolism is Wulfstan's own; his source text, the Latin *Ordinals of Christ*, illustrates how the duties performed by each of the seven grades of ecclesiastics typologically re-enacts an event in the life of Christ, but the *Ordinals* do not include language suggesting that the eucharist itself is chiefly or solely a symbolic act. On the *Ordinals of Christ* in the early medieval West, see Reynolds, *The Ordinals of Christ*, esp. 28–83; and on Anglo-Saxon treatments of this material, see ibid., 84–90.

The Corporealized Soul in Anglo-Saxon Preaching and Hagiography

The effects of materialism on Anglo-Saxon perceptions of the soul were less complicated than its effects on their understanding of the eucharist, probably because there was little or no doubt that the soul was fully real, and consequently, materialism was likely to lead in just one direction: toward the belief that the soul was a material and perceptible entity, even if a very subtle and elusive one. Discourse on the *ratio animae* is, like exegesis of the eucharist, extremely rare in Anglo-Saxon homilies outside the Ælfrician corpus. As Joyce Hill has observed, 'Complex theological issues (such as the opening of John's Gospel, the nature of the Trinity, or the meaning of the eucharist), which Ælfric readily tackles in the course of his exegesis, are rarely discussed' in the anonymous homilies.[20] Narratives of the soul's activities in the afterlife, however, are prominent in OE and Latin homilies and hagiography, and these narratives conform to and reinforce a materialist understanding of the soul by underscoring its bodily shape, spatial dimensions, and material substance. What is more, the rhetorical impact of numerous homilies actually depends upon the vivid corporealization of the soul, which strengthens the reality of the terrible punishments awaiting the souls of sinners in the afterworld.

First of all, homiletic portrayals of hell capitalize on the audience's fear of bodily pains.[21] According to one OE homily, the seven eternal torments that await the souls of the damned are hunger, thirst, cold, the heat of fire, the biting of serpents, a rotten stench, and haze and smoke;[22] in another OE homily, hell is characterized by fire and cold, black smoke and boiling pitch, and the wails of souls in torment.[23] A Latin homily preached in twelfth-century Winchester warns listeners to remember that souls in hell will endure serpents and 'burning pains amid the ceaseless fire.'[24]

---

20 J. Hill, 'Reform and Resistance: Preaching Styles in Late Anglo-Saxon England,' 21.

21 On the parallels among the eschatological homilies cited here, see Wright, 'The Old English "Macarius" Homily, Vercelli Homily IV, and Ephrem Latinus, *De paenitentia*'; and Tristram, 'Stock Descriptions of Heaven and Hell in Old English Prose and Poetry.'

22 Homily 'Nu bidde we eow for Godes lufon,' lines 2–6 (ed. Wenisch, '*Nu bidde we eow for Godes lufon*: A Hitherto Unpublished Old English Homiletic Text in CCCC 162,' 50); see also Robinson, 'The Devil's Account of the Next World: An Anecdote from Old English Homiletic Literature,' 366, lines 21–6.

23 Napier homily 29 (ed. Napier, 138.25–139.4).

24 Christmas Sermon in Bodley 451, fols 95r–6v, par. 5 (ed. Hall, 'Preaching at Winchester in the Early Twelfth Century,' 215).

And one particularly sadistic OE homily forebodes that hell will contain unquenchable fire and 'egesfulle wyrmas, þa þe wundiað and slitað þa synnfullan sawle.' In the end times, the homilist continues, St Peter will lock the gates of hell and throw the key over his shoulder into hell: then 'Hlud bið se cnyll ofer ealle eorðan, þonne seo cæg fealleð innan helle,' he concludes menacingly.[25]

Now, it is entirely within the bounds of patristic orthodoxy to conceive of hell as a corporeal space replete with corporeal torments; in the *Dialogi*, Gregory the Great maintains that the fires in hell are corporeal.[26] But in the *Dialogi* there also arises this question: how can an incorporeal soul be tormented by a corporeal fire? Gregory must admit that the corporeal fire cannot actually burn the incorporeal soul; rather, the incorporeal soul is psychologically tormented by seeing itself burned.

> Teneri autem per ignem spiritum dicimus, ut in tormento ignis sit uidendo atque sentiendo. Ignem namque eo ipso patitur quo uidet, et quia concremari se aspicit crematur. Sicque fit ut res corporea incorpoream exurat, dum ex igne uisibili ardor ac dolor inuisibilis trahitur, ut per ignem corporeum mens incorporea etiam incorporea flamma crucietur.[27]

Doctrinal accuracy is maintained at the expense of eschatological rhetoric: hellfire *sounds* considerably less menacing when the most it can do is to make the incorporeal soul feel *as though* it were being burned. Though the *Dialogi* was among the very best-known Latin works in Anglo-Saxon England,[28] I have yet to encounter a single OE homiletic or hagiographical work that follows Gregory's lead and asserts that the torments of hell are only psychological, or in other words, that they are real and efficacious yet also incorporeal. The reason, I think, is simple. Even if a homilist himself

---

25 Assmann homily 14, lines 129–39 (ed. Assmann, 168–9): 'terrible serpents which will wound and tear at the sinful souls ... Loud will be the crash resounding over the whole earth when the key falls into hell.'

26 Gregory, *Dialogi* 4.30.4–5 (ed. de Vogüé, SC 265, 102).

27 Gregory, *Dialogi* 4.30.2 (ed. de Vogüé, SC 265, 100): 'We say that the soul is enveloped by the fire in such a way that it is tormented by the fire, by seeing and feeling it. For the soul suffers from the fire to the same extent that it sees the fire, and because the soul observes itself being burned up, it is burned up. And thus it happens that a bodily thing burns an incorporeal thing, when the invisible heat and pain are taken over from the visible fire, so that, by means of the corporeal fire, the incorporeal mind is tormented by a flame that is likewise incorporeal.'

28 See chapter 4 above.

accepted that the incorporeal could also be real and efficacious, he likely recognized that the threat of bodily suffering could deter sin far more effectively than a subtle explanation of how the damned soul would suffer psychological torment while observing an illusion of its own burning by hellfire that could not actually burn it.

Rhetorical impact, it appears, motivated Anglo-Saxon homilists not only to reject Gregory's example but also to adopt vividly corporealized and anthropomorphized portrayals of the soul, which enhance the reality and intensity of the punishments that damned souls would have to endure in hell. The corporealized soul typically possesses spatial extension and a visible, palpable physical substance. The OE 'Macarius' homily forebodes that in hell there will be 'þa earman sawla ahangene ofer þa hatestan ligeas, and þær þonne beoð forðriccede, and gebundene, and ofdune aworpene on þa sweartestan stowe.'[29] In Vercelli homily 4, the soul shares the body's involuntary physiological responses to terror at the Last Judgment. The resurrected body 'sweats a very disgusting sweat' and changes colours: 'Hwilum he bið swiðe laðlicum men gelic, þonne wannað he Ᵹ doxað; oðre hwile he bið blæc Ᵹ æhiwe; hwilum he bið collsweart.' The soul is still distinct from its resurrected body, but outwardly it responds to this awful scene 'just the same as the body': 'Ᵹ gelice sio sawl hiwað on yfel bleoh swa same swa se lichoma, Ᵹ bið gyt wyrsan hiwes. Ᵹ standaþ butu swiðe forhte Ᵹ bifigende onbidað domes.'[30] A number of OE homilies take this corporealization of the soul a step further and attribute to it bodily limbs, each of which is subject to a particularly cruel torment in hell. The depiction of hell in Napier homily 29 endows the souls of the damned with all the organs of the bodily senses:

hwylon þær eagan ungemetum wepað for þæs ofnes bryne, hwylon eac þa teð for mycclum cyle manna þær gnyrrað ... ne hi mid heora nosum ne magon naht elles gestincan, buton unstenca ormætnessa. ðær beoð þa wanjendan

---

29 OE 'Macarius' homily, lines 152–5 (ed. Sauer, *Theodulfi capitula*, 416): 'wretched souls suspended over the hottest flames, and then they will be crushed and bound and hurled down into the darkest place.'

30 Vercelli homily 4, lines 289–94 (ed. Scragg, *Vercelli Homilies*, 101–2): 'Sometimes the body is like a very foul man, when it grows black and darkens; sometimes it is pale and without colour; sometimes it is black as coal. And likewise the soul transforms into an evil colour in the same manner as the body, and it is of still worse a colour. And both [soul and body] stand very frightened, and trembling, they await judgment.'

weleras afylde ligspiwelum bryne on þam hellican fyre, and hi wælgrimme wyrmas slitað, and heora ban gnagað byrnendum toðum.[31]

A variation on this theme in Fadda homily 1 includes among hell's torments 'eagona wop ond toþa gristbitung ond welera ðurst ... heortan fyrhtu ... ond þrotena drygnesse.'[32] Other analogous homilies attribute to the souls in hell all the various limbs by which they can be strung up, or the various parts high and low on the body, up to which they can be submerged in burning pitch, as in Tristram homily 3:

> sume þær hangiað be þam fotum . þæs þe us halige gewritu onwrigen habbað . and sume þær hangiað be þam handum . and sume þær hangiað be þam sweorum . and sum þær beoð besenced oð ða cneow on þam hatan pice . and on ðam fyre . and sum þær bið besenced oð ðæne nafelan . and sum þær bið besenced oð ðone muð . and sume þær hangiað be heora feaxe . on þam þuruhhatan fyre.[33]

Elsewhere, a certain Theban anchorite hears a similar account of hell when he converses with a devil, who tells him first-hand that in hell they suspend *people* – he does not even use the word *sawol* – upside-down from a tree over a cliff, 'þæt him sige þæt blod on ælcere healfe ut þurh þane muþ and þurh þa nosþyrle.'[34] Other homilies that make use of this form of anthropomorphization include Blickling 4 and Blickling 16, both of which

---

31 Napier homily 29 (ed. Napier, 138.27–9 and 139.6–11): 'In that place, sometimes the eyes weep excessively on account of the heat of the inferno, and sometimes teeth are clenched because of the great chill inflicted upon the people ... With their noses they can smell nothing other than an excess of foul odour; moaning lips are defiled by the belching flames in the heat of the hellish fire, and fierce serpents tear them apart and chew on their bones with burning teeth.'

32 Fadda homily 1, lines 213–16 (ed. Luiselli Fadda, *Nuove omelie anglosassoni*, 23): 'weeping of the eyes, gnashing of the teeth, thirst of the lips ... trembling of the heart ... and dryness of the throat.'

33 Tristram homily 3, lines 156–63 (ed. Tristram, 'Vier altenglische Predigten,' 168): 'Some people there hang by their feet – the holy books have explained to us about these people. Others there hang by their hands, and others there hang by their necks, and some people there are submerged up to the knees in the hot pitch and in the fire, and others are submerged up to the navel, and some there are submerged up to the mouth, and others there hang by their hair in the fire, which is hot through and through.'

34 *The Devil's Account of the Next World*, lines 10–11 (ed. Robinson, 'The Devil's Account of the Next World,' 365): 'so that the blood falls out of him through his mouth and through his nostrils, on both sides.'

draw from the rich stock of images in the apocryphal *Visio Pauli*.[35] According to Blickling 4, during his vision of the afterworld, St Paul witnessed a priest hurled by an iron hook into a river of pitch, and an old man chained and plunged into the fire up to his knees.[36] Blickling 16 concludes with St Paul's vision of souls tormented in the afterworld: 'he geseah þæt on ðæm clife hangodan on ðæm isigean bearwum manige swearte saula be heora handum gebundne.' These black souls are found hanging all along the twelve-mile interval separating the cliff from the water beneath, '7 ðonne ða twigo forburston þonne gewitan þa saula niðer þa þe on ðæm twigum hangodan, 7 him onfengon ða nicras.'[37]

Though the apocryphal *Visio Pauli*, which inspired these images of anthropomorphic souls, was not universally regarded as a trustworthy text,[38] other depictions of corporealized and anthropomorphic souls had wholly respectable reputations among the Anglo-Saxons. Fursey's and Dryhthelm's visions of corporealized souls and vivid bodily torments in the afterlife were deemed worthy of inclusion in Bede's *Historia ecclesiastica* (3.19 and 5.12), and it was the missionary Boniface who first recorded the vision of the Monk of Much Wenlock; all three of these visions were subsequently translated into OE at least once.[39] After his visionary experience, the Monk of Much Wenlock reports that the damned souls in hell appear in the guise of black birds (*on sweartra fugela onlicnissum*), who wail and gnash their teeth and weep in human voices as they are plunged repeatedly into fiery pits. Across a river of fiery pitch there lies a tree, which the blessed souls can use as a bridge to escape this awful place, but when the souls of the damned try to cross the tree, 'sume hig befiollan in

---

35 On the wide influence, direct and indirect, of the *Visio Pauli* in Anglo-Saxon England, see Healey, *The Old English Vision of St. Paul*, 41–57, where there is discussion of many of the narratives adduced in this section and below. On the relationship between the landscapes of hell in the Latin *Visio Pauli* and in Blickling 16, and the depiction of Grendel's mere in *Beowulf*, see Wright, *The Irish Tradition in Old English Literature*, 116–36.

36 Blickling homily 4 (ed. Morris, *Blickling Homilies*, 43).

37 Blickling homily 16 (ed. Morris, *Blickling Homilies*, 209): 'And on that cliff he saw many black souls hanging in the icy woods, bound by their hands ... and when the branches snapped, then the souls that were hanging on the branches went downward, and the water-monsters took hold of them.'

38 Healey, *The Old English Vision of St. Paul*, 41.

39 See chapter 1 above on soul-travel in the *OE Bede* and in the OE version of Boniface's letter to Eadburga.

fotes deopnesse; sume mid ealne lichaman; sume oð ða cneowu; sume oð ðone middel; sume oð ða helan.'[40]

The account of the Monk of Much Wenlock corporealizes the soul to such an extent that it claims that some of these damned souls are mired in the river of pitch 'with the whole body,' but the manuscript setting of the OE version of Boniface's letter places it alongside texts that take significantly different approaches to the substance of the soul. It survives only in London, BL, Cotton Otho C. i, vol. 2, which Ker dates to the early and middle eleventh century. In this codex, the OE letter is preceded by Wærferth's OE translation of Gregory's *Dialogi*, which asserts, at least in a few discursive contexts, that the soul is incorporeal, though this discourse is far outweighed by narratives of anthropomorphic and visible souls.[41] Also in this manuscript is an Ælfrician text, now only partly legible, entitled *De creatore et creatura*, which incorporates a long section of Ælfric's Nativity homily and over 200 lines of his *Hexameron*, including remarks on the invisibility and ineffability of the soul; on the incorporeality of the angels, who are called 'bodiless, living in the spirit' (lichamlease lybbende on gaste); and on the presence of the soul in humans alone and not in beasts.[42] The preservation of these three texts together – one firmly Platonizing, one eclectic, and one firmly within the vernacular tradition – exemplifies Thomas N. Hall's observation that, in matters of psychology and eschatology, what seem like gross inconsistencies to the modern audience did not necessarily trouble the typical Anglo-Saxon compiler or scribe: 'The frequency with which these themes are explored in Old English literature might lead one to expect that at some point the Anglo-Saxons arrived at a reasonably secure set of ideas that add up to a coherent body of eschatological doctrine, but in reality the situation turns out to be far from secure or coherent.'[43]

---

40 *Wynfrith's Letter*, lines 127–9 (ed. Sisam, 'An Old English Translation of a Letter from Wynfrith to Eadburga,' 219): 'Some of them fall in to the depth of a foot; others, with the whole body; others, up to the knees; others, up to the waist; others, up to the neck; others, up to the heels.' This passage is a close rendering of Boniface's Latin original, which Sisam prints alongside the OE text.

41 Ker, *Catalogue*, no. 182; Sisam, 'An Old English Translation of a Letter from Wynfrith to Eadburga,' 201–4; on this MS see also Godden, 'Wærferth and King Alfred: The Fate of the Old English *Dialogues*.'

42 This text is unedited. Ker, *Catalogue*, no. 182, provides the line numbers of the passages in *LS* 1 and the *Hexameron* that are replicated in *De creatore et creatura*. The aforementioned references to the soul and to incorporeality correspond to lines 88–90, 105, 373–5 of Ælfric's *Hexameron* (ed. Crawford, *Exameron anglice*, 40, 42, and 61). On *De creatore et creatura*, see Kleist, 'Ælfric's Corpus: A Conspectus,' 126.

43 Hall, 'The Psychedelic Transmogrification of the Soul in Vercelli Homily IV,' 309.

For each of the foregoing homiletic or hagiographical narratives about corporealized and anthropomorphized souls, we might ask whether the audience 'knew better' or whether they took the corporealized soul at face value. Whatever the homilist himself may have known of Platonizing doctrines of the soul's incorporeality, he had little to gain from passing it on to his listeners within the context of a menacing eschatological homily. The hortatory force of such a homily depends upon the listeners' belief in the reality of hell and its torments, as illustrated by the warning delivered near the opening of the OE 'Macarius' homily: 'Geeadmedað eow her, þæt ge ne syn þær geniðrade, and þæt ge ne syn sende on þa ytemestan þistro and on þæt unadwescedlice fyr. Eala, men þa leofestan, hwa is æfre swa heardre heortan, þæt he ne mæge wepan þa toweardan witu and him þa ondrædan?'[44] There is no textual evidence, nor any other good reason to suspect, that Anglo-Saxon preachers (other than Ælfric) took pains to ensure that their listeners understood that the souls of the damned were not as corporealized as they appear in the homilies. Commenting on the parallel behaviours of soul and body in Vercelli homily 4, Hall observes that 'we as latter-day readers are likely to come to this homily with the false expectation that the body and soul are somehow fundamentally different. But this is not at all the case in Vercelli IV, which presents the body and soul virtually as mirror images of one another.'[45]

At the same time, it should not be overlooked that Anglo-Saxon preachers frequently delineated a sharp boundary between the human soul and the flesh – which is not the same as claiming that the soul is wholly lacking in physical substance – and that this too fulfilled a specific rhetorical purpose. Since the soul is immortal and the body is destined to rot in the grave, the needs of the soul ought to be valued and pursued above those of the body. Says the homilist of Blickling 5: 'myccle swiðor we sceolan þencan be þæm gastlicum þingum þonne be þæm lichomlicum. Se lichoma on þisse worlde þingum gewiteþ, swa þonne seo saul mid gastlicum þingum on ecnesse leofaþ.'[46] In a similar vein, the homilist of Blickling 8 encourages his audience to worry less about food and clothing, because 'gelimpeð

---

44 OE 'Macarius' homily, lines 17–22 (ed. Sauer, *Theodulfi capitula*, 411): 'Humble your-selves here, so that you will not be humiliated there, and so that you will not be sent into the outermost darkness and the unquenchable fire. Alas, dearest people, who is so hard-hearted that he cannot weep and fear for himself in the face of impending punishments?'
45 Hall, 'The Psychedelic Transmogrification of the Soul,' 314.
46 Blickling homily 5 (ed. Morris, *Blickling Homilies*, 57): 'We should think about spiritual matters much more than about bodily ones. The body takes care of our affairs in this world, as later on the soul will live amid spiritual things for eternity.'

þæt eft æfter feawum dagum oþþe feawum gearum, þæt se ilca lichoma byð on byrgenne from wyrmum freten ⁊ forglendred. Forþon us is myccle mare nedþearf þæt we winnon ymbe ure saule þearfe, seo biþ geondweard on heofnum beforan Gode ⁊ his englum.'[47] Once more, in Bazire and Cross homily 6, the homilist declares, 'we ne sceolon on þysum dagum ymbe ures lichaman glenga þencan ac hu we magon ure sawle mid godum weorcum gefrætwian.'[48] Note, however, that in all such cases, the impact of this sort of preaching does not depend in any way on the soul's being wholly immaterial: to set his listeners' priorities right, the homilist need only underscore that the soul is distinct from the flesh and therefore cannot retain any bodily goods or achievements when the flesh dies.

The Mind-Body Complex in Anglo-Saxon Preaching

Though we might label it a form of materialism, the localization of the mental faculties in the body rather than in the soul is conceptually unrelated to the materializing tendencies considered thus far, whose shared origin is the premise that reality is constituted by what is perceptible to the senses. Cardiocentrism and the notion of a mind-body complex originate elsewhere, in the subjective perception of cardiocentric sensations accompanying intense mental events. All the same, as background to Ælfric's anti-materialist writings, we need to consider what his contemporaries were preaching about the mind-body complex. This is because Ælfric's approach to inculcating an understanding of the reality of incorporeals was rooted in the Platonizing discourse of the Carolingians and was therefore inextricable from certain epistemological premises, including the ascription of the faculties of thought and intellection to the unitary, incorporeal soul.

As in the *Soul and Body* poems and *Riddle* 43 of the Exeter Book, in the homiletic corpus the notion of the mind-body complex is most clearly manifest in the portrayal of an impersonal, impotent soul who is utterly at the mercy of the body's decisions and actions. Above I quoted the homilist of Blickling 5, who maintains that it is the body that bears responsibility

---

47 Blickling homily 8 (ed. Morris, *Blickling Homilies*, 99): 'It will happen, after a few days or a few years, that the very flesh in the tomb will be eaten up and swallowed by worms. Therefore it is much more urgent for us to strive for the needs of our soul, which will be present before God and his angels in heaven.'

48 Bazire and Cross homily 6, lines 23–5 (ed. Bazire and Cross, *Eleven Old English Rogationtide Homilies*, 83): 'In these days we must contemplate not the splendour of the body but how we can ornament our soul with good works.'

for earthly affairs ('Se lichoma on þisse worlde þingum gewiteþ'), while the soul is not called upon to do anything until it reaches the afterlife. He then proceeds to remind his listeners that the soul 'eft onfehþ hire lichoman on þæm ytmestan dæge, ꜿ mid þæm sceal beon riht agyldende for ealles þæs lichoman dædum.'[49] The remarks of the Vercelli 4 homilist bear a similar implication, though he focuses instead on the mental side of the mind-body complex: 'Þy us sealde dryhten þæt andgyt þe he wolde þæt we ongeaton ·his willan ꜿ ure sawle hælo.'[50] Both homilists intimate that the responsibility for an individual's actions and welfare lies somewhere other than in the soul itself: it is the body that performs outward deeds, and the mind or understanding that deliberates about what is best for the soul. Even if these brief statements cannot be granted the status of authoritative doctrine, they undeniably betray a radically different way of thinking about the body-soul relationship than that which Alcuin proposes in *De ratione animae*, in which the soul dominates the actions of the body, governing 'as if from the seat of royal power.'[51]

Much of the OE homiletic material that establishes a similar characterization of the mind-body complex is found in narratives of the soul's address to the body after death.[52] Vercelli homily 4 exemplifies the passivity of the soul and the willfulness of the body. The damned soul, speaking first to the body, says, 'Æghwylce dæge þu geworhtest þine byrðenne scylda ꜿ næfre nane ne gebetest ... Eall þin yfel þe ðu a worhtest, a hie þe wel licodon. ꜿ þæt wæs þin gamen, hu ðu mæst unrihtest geworhtest, ꜿ hit is nu min hæft.'[53] Next the damned soul complains to Death about the body it once inhabited: 'On anum dæge he geworhte oft þusend scylda, ꜿ to nænigre

---

49 Blickling homily 5 (ed. Morris, *Blickling Homilies*, 57): '[The soul] will take up its body again on the last day, and with it the soul must atone fully for all the deeds of the body.'

50 Vercelli homily 4, lines 77–9 (ed. Scragg, *Vercelli Homilies*, 93): 'The Lord granted us understanding because he desired that we understand his will and the salvation of our soul.'

51 Alcuin, *DRA* 2 (PL 101.639). Hall makes a similar observation, contrasting *DRA* with Vercelli homily 4 ('The Psychedelic Transmogrification of the Soul,' 314).

52 I am less concerned with the literary conventions by which the soul is personified and the corpse is made to speak; the crucial thing to observe is that all participants in these scenes, including souls both blessed and damned, angels and demons, and even God, attribute virtually all responsibility for an individual's actions to the body, in ways that reinforce the idea that the mind is not at all part of the soul.

53 Vercelli homily 4, lines 213–14 and 218–20 (ed. Scragg, *Vercelli Homilies*, 98–9): 'Every day you performed your regimen of sins and never did you make amends for them in any way ... All the evils that you have continually wrought, these have always pleased you well. And it was amusing to you to behave in the most abominable manner, and now it will be my enslavement.'

hreowe gehweorfan nolde ... Oft eodon fram his huse wydwan Ᵹ steopcild, þær hie næfdon are ne frofre æt him, Ᵹ he symlede æt his beodgereordum, þæt ic wæs oft swiðe neah ofðylmed Ᵹ asmorod.'⁵⁴ The damned soul is not claiming that it achieved virtue while the body behaved sinfully; the soul's moral rectitude is irrelevant, since it has no influence over the body.

Variations on this theme are to be found in numerous OE homilies. Assmann homily 14 and Fadda homily 8 include addresses of the soul to the body in which the damned soul is willing to shoulder a tiny portion of the blame – if only the soul had loved heaven and remembered the torments that were stored up in hell! But throughout these accounts of the soul's address it is never suggested that the soul could govern or even counsel the body efficaciously. The body wrought 'evil deeds' and set out to deceive men; the body is even responsible for faithlessness, for the soul demands of it, 'Hwi noldest ðu gelyfan þinum scrifte? Ac seldan þu gemundest þine sawle.'⁵⁵ When the damned soul of Fadda homily 8 turns a critical eye upon itself, it nonetheless continues to implicate the body, saying, 'Wa me, forðæm ic þa awirgedan þinc mid ðe lufode! ... Wa me, forðæm þe ic geþafode ealle ða yfel þe þu dydest! Forþon ic nu for ðinum gewyrhtum eom cwylmed, and for þinum yfelum dædum ic eom on helle wite bescofen.'⁵⁶ In an unusual adaptation of the soul's address motif, the homilist of Napier 29 even urges his listeners, right then and there, to address their own bodies ('nu we magon sylfe þus to urum lichaman sprecan'), and to demand to know 'hwæt dest þu, la flæsc, oððe hwæt drihst þu nu? hwæt miht þu on þa tid þearfe wepan? ... hwi ne forhttast þu ðe fyrene egesan and þe sylfum ondrætst swiðlice witu, þa drihten geo deoflum geworhte, awyrgedum gastum?'⁵⁷

---

54 Vercelli homily 4, lines 236–7 and 244–7 (ed. Scragg, *Vercelli Homilies*, 99–100): 'Every day the body sinned a thousand times, and he was unwilling to be converted to any repentance ... Often widows and orphans went away from his house without receiving any pity or comfort from him, and he had a great time at his feasts, so that I was often very nearly choked and smothered.'

55 Assmann homily 14, lines 90–1 (ed. Assmann, 167): 'Why were you unwilling to believe your confessor? Instead you rarely gave a second thought to your soul.'

56 Fadda homily 8, lines 25–31 (ed. Luiselli Fadda, *Nuove omelie anglosassoni*, 165–7; editorial punctuation has been altered): 'Woe is me, because along with you I loved shameful things! ... Woe is me, because I tolerated all the evil things that you did! Therefore I am now tormented because of what you have wrought, and because of your evil deeds I am hurled into the torment of hell.'

57 Napier homily 29 (ed. Napier, 138, lines 17–23): 'What are you doing, O flesh? What are you up to now? What might give you cause to weep at that time [*scil.* the end times]? ... Why do you not fear the terrible fire and shrink from the mighty punishments which the Lord inflicts upon you devils, wretched spirits?'

One of the more protracted eschatological narratives, including the soul's address to the body, appears in the OE 'Macarius' homily. Here too, only a tiny fraction of the individual's culpability is placed upon the soul, while the soul heaps all of the individual's failings upon the 'vilest and most evil body' (fulestan and wyrrestan lichoman). 'Wa þe, þu earma lichoma!' begins the soul. 'Ðu þe wære nimende fremdra manna speda, and þu þe æfre wære ofer eorðan welena strynende, and þu þe gefrætwodest þe mid deorwurðe hrægle; and þu þe wære reod, and ic me wæs blac; þu wære glæd, and ic me wæs unrot; þu hloge, and ic weop.'[58] A pack of demons gathers around the corpse to escort the soul to hell, and when the terrified soul refuses to come out, the demons drive it out by attacking each guilty member of the body.

Se lichoma ongan þa swiðe swætan and mislic hiw bredan. Ðæt deofol ongan þa cleopian and cwæð: 'Stingað hyne mid sare on his eagan; forþan eal, swa hwæt swa he mid his eagan geseah unrihtes, ealles he his gyrnde. Stingað hyne mid sare on his muð; forþon eal, swa hwæt swa hyne lyste etan oððe drincan oððe sprecan, eall he hit aræfnde. Stingað hyne mid sare on his heortan; forþon þe on hyre ne wunode arfæstnis ne mildheortnes ne Godes lufu.'[59]

As the masculine pronoun *hyne* indicates, the demon clearly orders his companions to attack the body (*lichoma*, masc.) in order to drive out the soul (*sawol*, fem.). The demon's ascription of vices and sins to each part of the body that they attack represents a very concrete manifestation of the Anglo-Saxon habit of ascribing responsibility and agency to the mind-body complex instead of the soul.[60]

---

58 OE 'Macarius' homily, lines 91–6 (ed. Sauer, *Theodulfi capitula*, 414): 'Woe to you, you wretched body! You were accustomed to seize for yourself the sustenance of those who needed protection; you ceaselessly amassed wealth for yourself while you were on earth, and you adorned yourself with expensive clothing; and you were ruddy while I was pale, you were joyful while I was unhappy; you laughed, and I wept.'

59 OE 'Macarius' homily, lines 99–107 (ed. Sauer, *Theodulfi capitula*, 414): 'Then the body began to sweat profusely and to be transformed into different colours. Then the devil began to shout, saying, "Pierce him with a wound to the eyes, because he desires every improper thing that he has seen with his eyes. Pierce him with a wound to the mouth, because whatever he wished to eat or drink or say, so he did. Pierce him with a wound to the heart, because therein dwelled no virtue nor mercy nor love of God."'

60 Interestingly, the corresponding passage in the Latin 'Macarius' homily (or at least in the version printed by Batiouchkof) employs only one gendered pronoun, and it is feminine: 'Apprehendite eam et pungite oculos illius, quia quicquid uidit siue iustum siue iniustum omnia concupiuit,' begins the demon (Batiouchkof, 'Le débat de l'âme et du corps,' 577). In context, the antecedent of the feminine pronoun *eam* is almost certainly

If further evidence is needed that the impotence of the soul is its natural condition rather than just a personal weakness of those who end up
damned, consider that the souls of the blessed likewise admit that they
were ineffectual during earthly life, and that good works and self-restraint
must be credited to the body. In Vercelli 4, the blessed soul speaks to the
angels about its body, saying, 'He swanc for me, ⁊ ic gefeah on him ... He
swencte hine mid fæstenne, ⁊ ic gamenode in oferfyllo ... Uncra synna he
sworette ⁊ uncra scylda, ⁊ ic glædlice in wynsumnesse wæs ferende.'⁶¹ Next
the blessed soul says to its body, 'Æghwæt godes þe wæs yðe to donne
on Godes naman, þæt ðu woldest þæt ic wære in wuldre æfter uncrum
gedale,'⁶² and finally, it says to God that its former body 'hæfde hiht in
þe. He wæs strang ⁊ staðolfæst ⁊ fæstrad on þinum bebodum. On godum
worcum he wæs arod. Næs he æfstig ne eaðbilge ne hatheort, ne oferfyllo ne lufude he. Næs he gytsere ne strudere ne ofermod ne niðig ne
leasfyrhð, ne deofulcræftas ne lufode he.'⁶³ The blessed soul of Assmann
homily 14 likewise commends its body, saying, 'Wel þe, forþam þe þu
godes cyrican eadmodlice gelome sohtest and þine ælmessan eadmodlice
sealdest and þinum gebedum georne lufedest and þinne scrift oft gesohtest
and godes willan þu eac worhtest.'⁶⁴ The blessed soul of the Lenten homily

---

anima, since the feminine noun *caro* 'flesh' has not occurred for several lines prior to
the passage quoted here; therefore these lines present a strikingly different rationale for
the anthropomorphization of the soul and, incidentally, an unusual degree of psychologization of the soul during life, in contrast to the Anglo-Saxon vernacular tradition.
One wonders whether the author of the OE 'Macarius' homily had an exemplar that
read *Apprehendite eum* rather than *eam*, or whether he deliberately changed the target
of the devils' attack from the soul to the body because the Latin version psychologized
the soul to such an extent that it clashed with his vernacular audience's expectations.

61 Vercelli homily 4, lines 127–32 (ed. Scragg, *Vercelli Homilies*, 95): 'The body toiled for
me and I rejoiced in him ... He tormented himself with fasting, and I made merry with
gluttony ... He groaned under the weight of our sins and our guilt, while in pleasure I
was travelling joyfully.'

62 Vercelli homily 4, lines 135–6 (ed. Scragg, *Vercelli Homilies*, 95): 'You were willing to
do any kind of good deed in God's name because you desired that I live in glory after
our parting.'

63 Vercelli homily 4, lines 137–41 (ed. Scragg, *Vercelli Homilies*, 96): '[he] had hope in you;
he was strong and resolute and constant in your commandments. He was quick to do
good works. He was never envious or easily angered or hot-hearted, nor did he love
gluttony. He was not a miser nor a robber, not rash nor malicious nor false, nor did he
love witchcraft.'

64 Assmann homily 14, lines 94-7 (ed. Assmann, 167): 'Good for you! For you visited God's
church respectfully and frequently, and you gave alms humbly, and you cherished your
prayers and visited your confessor often, and you also carried out God's will.'

in Oxford, Bodleian Library, Junius 85 and 86 employs a memorable image to illustrate its understanding of the body's role in the individual's moral and spiritual striving: 'Ðu wære þæt scearpuste scyrsex,' says the soul to the body, 'forþon ðu cuðest synna þe fram aceorfan.'[65] This image epitomizes the relationship between the soul and the mind-body complex that pervades OE homilies: in the face of any challenges posed by earthly life, it falls to the body to be keen and hard and to protect the soul, which otherwise would be unarmed.

Clearly the vernacular homiletic and hagiographical materials generated anonymously during the tenth and eleventh centuries did little to promote the concept of incorporeality in its strict philosophical sense, nor to encourage audiences to think of the soul as an incorporeal entity encompassing the rational mind. Ignoring the standards set by his contemporaries, Ælfric aimed to bring to ordinary audiences in the vernacular something of the Platonist-Christian understanding of incorporeality. His primary motivation may have been to rescue his listeners from the spiritual danger of receiving the eucharist while misapprehending its incorporeal nature, a problem addressed most pointedly in his Easter Day homily (*CH II* 15); his teachings there are complemented by further lessons on incorporeality and its epistemological implications in his Nativity homily (*LS* 1). Prefatory to a consideration of these two homilies, it is useful to examine how Ælfric's concern to minimize materialist errors manifested itself in subtle ways and with reference to a variety of topics, across the corpus of his OE homilies.

Anti-Materialist Tactics throughout the Ælfrician Corpus

Ælfric's impulse to correct excessive materialism often manifested itself in accordance with broader habits of mind that shaped his methods as a homilist and as a translator, such as his mistrust of the preaching of his contemporaries and contempt for popular New Testament apocrypha. Ælfric prefaces his first series of *Catholic Homilies* with a complaint that in his day there are too few people 'who are willing to teach well and to instruct well.' The target of his complaint becomes clearer when he explains that his homilies are meant to elevate the quality of the religious instruction available in the vernacular: he has composed the *Catholic Homilies*, he says, 'for ðan ðe ic geseah Ᵹ gehyrde mycel gedwyld on manegum engliscum bocum.

---

65 Fadda homily 8, lines 60–1 (ed. Luiselli Fadda, *Nuove omelie anglosassone*, 169): 'You were the keenest razor, because you were able to shear away sins from yourself.'

ðe ungelærede menn ðurh heora bilewitnysse to micclum wisdome tealdon.'[66] Ælfric's mistrust extended to texts that his contemporaries considered doctrinally acceptable. Among those that he denounces by name are the apocryphal *Visio Pauli*, which had inspired numerous homiletic depictions of vividly corporealized souls in the afterworld, and the apocryphal *transitus Mariae* accounts, which narrate the bodily assumption of the Virgin Mary into heaven.[67] Ælfric was also wary of the *Vitas Patrum*, and in his preface to the *Lives of Saints* he mentions that he has avoided translating narratives from the *Vitas Patrum* 'in quo multa subtilia habentur quae non conueniunt aperiri laicis.'[68] Where he did draw on the *Vitas Patrum* in his other writings, Ælfric took care to efface hints of psychological materialism present in his source text. One narrative in the *Vitas Patrum* reports that a certain monk desired 'uidere animam peccatoris et iusti, quomodo abstrahitur a corpore,' that is, to witness first-hand the blessed soul's reception by angels and the damned soul's being dragged out of the body by demons – an event of which he must have heard tell in homilies and hagiographies. Rather than encourage the notion that one could actually see the soul, Ælfric relates that this monk simply wished to observe the conduct of a damned man and a blessed man as they die: he prays to God 'þæt he moste geseon hu se synnfulla mann his sawle ageafe, ꞇ hu se rihtwise gewite of life.'[69] God then bestows upon the monk a miraculous vision of these events, in which he can see demons and angels performing their expected roles in great detail, but in contrast to typical anonymous narratives of the same ilk, in Ælfric's account the monk sees nothing of the shape or substance of the souls, and there is no hint of their corporealization or anthropomorphization.

Ælfric's anti-materializing impulse also harmonizes with a tendency that Malcolm Godden has identified especially in the *Lives of Saints*: on those

---

66 Ælfric, *CH I*, Preface, lines 110 and 50–2 (ed. Clemoes, *CH I*, 176 and 174): 'because I have seen and heard great error in many English books, which uneducated men in their simplicity receive as great wisdom.'

67 On Ælfric's unusually suspicious attitude toward New Testament apocrypha and the teachings of his contemporaries, see J. Hill, 'Reform and Resistance,' 24–34; Godden, 'Ælfric's Saints' Lives and the Problem of Miracles,' 86–92; Healey, *The Old English Vision of St. Paul*, 41.

68 Ælfric, Preface to *LS*, lines 12–13 (ed. Skeat, *LS* 1.2): 'in which are contained many elusive matters which should not be made available to laypersons.'

69 *Vitas Patrum* 6.3.13 (printed in the *apparatus* of Pope's edition, *Suppl.* 775; also at PL 73.1011): 'to see the soul of a sinner and the soul of a just man, how each was drawn out of the body.' Ælfric, *Suppl.* 27.19–21 (ed. Pope, *Suppl.*, 776): 'that he be able to see how the sinful man gives up his soul, and how the righteous man departs from life.'

occasions when he is compelled to acknowledge that miracles make incorporeal realities manifest to the senses, Ælfric emphasizes that such manifestations are extraordinary and in no way represent the natural state of that which is spiritual.[70] Godden supplies many different pieces of evidence to demonstrate that in the *Lives of Saints* Ælfric habitually maintains the boundary between the incorporeal and the manifest in this manner; to those examples we may add Ælfric's account of Fursey in *CH II* 20. There would have been little point in retelling the visions of Dryhthelm and Fursey without retaining the anthropomorphism of the souls that these men witnessed during their miraculous visions of the afterworld, which were of course sanctioned by their inclusion in Bede's *Ecclesiastical History*.[71] All the same, near the end of the account of Fursey's vision, when the burn inflicted upon Fursey's incorporeal soul during his vision is thereafter made visible on his body for the rest of his life, Ælfric makes sure his audience knows that something outside the natural order has occurred: 'wæs ðeah þæt bærnet þe he gelæhte æt ðam unrihtwisum were. on his sculdre. and on ansyne æfre gesewen; Micel wunder þæt hit wearð gesyne on ðam lichaman. þæt þæt seo sawul ana underfeng.'[72] Given his habitual insistence on the miraculous and unnatural character of such manifestations, it is noteworthy that he does not apply this tactic when he retells eucharistic miracles, as I discuss below.

Assmann Homily 4: A Reconfiguration of the Mind-Body Relationship

Even though the corporealization of the mind as an organ in the chest cavity is a categorically different phenomenon from the sort of materialism that refuses to acknowledge the reality of incorporeals, it was essential that Ælfric address the nature of the soul from an epistemological angle as well as an ontological one, because his teachings on incorporeals were rooted in

---

70 Godden, 'Ælfric's Saints' Lives and the Problem of Miracles.'
71 Bede, *Historia ecclesiastica* 5.12 and 3.19; these visions appear in Ælfric, *CH II* 20 and 21. Ælfric ranks Bede among the most authoritative of his sources for the *Catholic Homilies* (see Preface to *CH I*, lines 14–17; ed. Clemoes, *CH I*, 173); his immediate source for most of his account of Fursey (*CH II* 20) was actually not Bede but an anonymous Latin *uita Fursei* similar to BHL 3210, printed by Bolland et al. in *Acta Sanctorum* Jan. 2.36–41 (see Godden, *CH Comm.*, 529–30).
72 Ælfric, *CH II*, 20.248–51 (ed. Godden, *CH II*, 197): 'That burn, which he had received from the wicked man, was still seen there on his shoulder and his face ever after. It was a great miracle that that which the soul alone had undergone became visible on the body.' Emphasis on the miraculous nature of the manifestation has antecedents in both the anonymous *uita Fursei* and Bede's version; this is perhaps one of the reasons why Ælfric found the story suitable to recount.

Platonism. In his Nativity homily, discussed below, Ælfric advances the concept of the unitary soul by asserting repeatedly that all of the mental faculties that the vernacular tradition typically assigned to the mind-body complex are actually proper to the *sawol*. But in his second homily for the feast of a confessor (Assmann homily 4) – which was apparently composed with a non-monastic audience in mind, and may in practice have reached a very large audience[73] – Ælfric adopts a more subtle approach and encourages his audience to conceive of an oppositional relationship between mind and body rather than a close-knit partnership.

This is not a homily whose central focus is the mind. Ælfric preaches on the pericope Mt 24:42, 'Vigilate ergo quia nescitis qua hora Dominus uester uenturus sit,'[74] and on the similar text at Lk 12:35–41. Nearly half of Ælfric's homily follows Bede's discussion of these verses in his commentary on Luke as well as Haymo of Auxerre's reworking of the Bedan material in a homily *De confessoribus*.[75] Bede's commentary focuses on the meaning of *uigilia* 'wakefulness.' He correlates childhood, the prime of life, and old age with the three *uigiliae* 'watches,' or opportunities to emend and atone for one's errors and be saved.[76] Going beyond the precedents supplied by Bede and Haymo, Ælfric also distinguishes between awakenings of the body and awakenings of the mind. To illustrate wakefulness of the body Ælfric describes the monastic practice of rising in the middle of the night for the Night Office, and he affirms that bodily wakefulness is virtuous *if* it leads to virtuous deeds.[77] Even better, however, is

---

73 Ælfric describes the office of *uhtsang* or Night Office as the time when 'we' monks wake up and pray 'for *you*' (Assmann homily 4, lines 37–40; ed. Assmann, 51): 'we waciað on cyrcan / æt urum uhtsange, þonne oðre men slapaþ, / and we tobrecað urne slæp and gebiddað for eow / and heriað urne drihten mid halgum lofsangum' (We are awake in the church at our Night Office when other men sleep, and we interrupt our sleep and pray for you). According to Clayton, 'If Æthelwold II of Winchester [probably 1006–12] preached this text on the feast of a major saint, such as one of the Winchester confessor-saints, then it could well have reached a large audience of influential people' ('Of Mice and Men: Ælfric's Second Homily for the Feast of a Confessor,' 18). Clayton also narrows the likely date of composition of Assmann 4 to the years 1006–7: see ibid., 1–2 and 19–20.

74 'Watch ye therefore, because ye know not what hour your Lord will come.'

75 See Clayton, 'Of Mice and Men,' on the relationship between the two biblical texts and on Ælfric's use of Bede and Haymo.

76 Lines 48–50 of the homily depend on Bede's *In Marci euangelium expositio* 4.358–65; the chief source for most of the material in lines 67–167 of the homily is Bede's *In Lucae euangelium expositio* 4.1039–66 and 4.1106–25: see Clayton, 'The Sources of Assmann 4 (Homily for the Common of a Confessor).'

77 Ælfric, Assmann homily 4, lines 35–46 (ed. Assmann, 51).

wakefulness of mind: 'þæs modes wæcce is micele betere, / þæt se man hogie, hu he gehealdan beo / wið ðone swicolan deofol, þe hine beswican wyle / mid mislicum leahtrum and manfullum dædum.'[78] One who cultivates wakefulness of mind will be 'pure with respect to what he eats' and 'firm of faith.'[79] It is this same mental wakefulness, Ælfric continues, that the evangelist Luke had in mind when he wrote that the Lord will bless those servants whom he finds ready to do his bidding even during the second or third watch: he who is not vigilant during the first watch, during childhood, must by all means 'rouse his mind from earthly errors' (his mod awrecce of middaneardlicum gedwyldum) during the prime of life.[80]

There is nothing unusual in Ælfric's use of the word *mod* to describe the entity that is capable of will and deliberation and virtue, but Ælfric's teaching is set apart from the vernacular tradition by virtue of the oppositional relationship that he establishes between mind and body. Even the most thoroughly Christianized OE literature of the vernacular tradition tends not to map its assessment of lesser and greater virtue onto body and *mod* respectively, but rather onto the mind-body complex and the *sawol*; it is the job of the mind-body complex to set its own needs to the side and to privilege those of the immortal *sawol*. Ælfric's homily encourages his audience to reconfigure the relationship between body and *mod* so that it more closely resembles the oppositional relationship between body and *sawol*. The purpose of this reconfiguration is not merely to make the doctrinal point that the *mod* is part of the *sawol*; in fact, he leaves the *sawol* out of this part of the homily altogether, even though both Bede and Haymo use the words *anima, animus, mens,* and *spiritus* interchangeably in the corresponding passages of their Latin texts. The point, I think, is to place the potent and efficacious *mod* in the role of the body's governor, a role that the vernacular tradition usually fills with the impotent and inefficacious *sawol*.

Ælfric confirms this reconfiguration as he proceeds to explicate Lk 12:39: 'Hoc autem scitote quia si sciret pater familias qua hora fur ueniret, uigilaret utique et non sineret perfodiri domum suam.'[81] In Bede's commentary, the *paterfamilias* is likened to the *spiritus*, and when he is asleep,

78 Ælfric, Assmann homily 4, lines 47–50 (ed. Assmann, 51–2): 'wakefulness of mind is much better: that is, that one consider how he may be preserved from the deceitful devil, who wishes to seduce him with all sorts of vices and evil deeds.'
79 Ælfric, Assmann homily 4, lines 52 and 56 (ed. Assmann, 52).
80 Ælfric, Assmann homily 4, lines 57–75 (ed. Assmann, 52–3); cf. Lk 12:36–40.
81 'But this know ye, that if the householder did know at what hour the thief would come, he would surely watch, and would not suffer his house to be broken into.'

the thief Death breaks into the house of the body and snatches the *spiritus* away to hell.[82] Ælfric, however, continues to develop the relationship between the *mod* and the body: as he explicates this passage, the head of the household 'is our own mind' (is ure agen mod), and the thief Death steals the body rather than the soul.[83] If the hour of the thief's arrival were known to the *paterfamilias*, he would be able to defend his household, 'forðam ðe þæt mod wolde micclum hogian, / þæt hit awoce and geworhte dædbote / his swærran synna.'[84] Ælfric's allegoresis of the gospel text is not quite as smooth as Bede's or Haymo's, but by keeping the *sawol* and the *gast* entirely out of this discussion, he achieves a clear reconfiguration of the mind-body relationship in which the mind, the *paterfamilias*, is the dominant figure with the potential to rouse itself to a virtuous state of wakefulness, while the body has no agency whatsoever. Ælfric's meticulous attention to his psychological terminology, furthermore, led him to omit from his own diction the cardiocentric imagery that he found in his Latin sources for this section of the homily. Within the passages that Ælfric borrows from the commentaries on Luke and Mark, Bede uses the phrases *cum angusto cordi* and *ianuas cordium nostrorum*, but OE equivalents of these expressions are absent from the corresponding passages of Ælfric's homily, as though he reckoned that the mind-in-the-heart had no place in a discourse that otherwise sets mind and body in a firmly oppositional relationship.[85]

The Eucharistic Transformation Made Manifest in Ælfric's Life of St Basil

There is no doubt that Ælfric was more ambitious than his contemporaries with respect to his intention to bring sophisticated theological teachings to a broader audience, but he was not idealistic to the point of being

---

82 Bede, *In Lucae euangelium expositio* 4.1056–60 (ed. Hurst, CCSL 120, 257); see also Clayton, 'Of Mice and Men,' 9–10.

83 Ælfric, Assmann homily 4, lines 95–8 (ed. Assmann, 54): the thief is 'se gemænelica deaþ, ðe þæs mannes lichaman / mid his digelan tocyme to deaðe gebringð' (that death that is common to all, that with its stealthy encroachment carries the body away to death).

84 Ælfric, Assmann homily 4, lines 101–3 (ed. Assmann, 54): 'because the mind would have staunchly strived to keep itself awake and to atone for its weighty sins.'

85 *cum angusto cordi*: Bede, *In Lucae euangelium expositio* 4.1108–9 (ed. Hurst, CCSL 120, 258–9); cf. lines 129–32 of Ælfric's homily. *ianuas cordium nostrorum*: Bede, *In Marci euangelium expositio* 4.358–9 (ed. Hurst, CCSL 120, 604); cf. lines 48–50 of the homily. Ælfric does not always reject the cardiocentric imagery of his source texts, as Ælfrician passages cited above in chapter 2 demonstrate. I have not undertaken any systematic study of the treatment of cardiocentrism across Ælfric's writings, though my initial impression is that he was much more likely to retain the cardiocentric imagery of his sources in narrative contexts than in discourses that aspire to theological precision.

impractical. As we shall see, Ælfric seems to have decided that the best way to combat all of the errors rooted in popular materialism was to convince his audience of the existence of incorporeal realities. Yet at the same time, he occasionally had recourse to less sophisticated, 'quick-fix' tactics, such as miracle stories that graphically illustrate the real presence of Christ in the eucharist, which were useful correctives for those in his audience who denied the reality of the eucharistic transformation because it was imperceptible to the senses. Consider his account of St Basil (LS 3), which Ælfric adapted directly from an anonymous Latin *uita*.[86] The fifth chapter tells of a Jew who attends Mass out of curiosity. When the Jew sees the celebrant Basil break the eucharistic bread, 'þa þuhte þam Iudeiscan swylce he todælde an cyld. Eode swaþeah mid oðrum mannum earhlice to husle and him wearð geseald an snæd flæsces, and he seap of ðæm calice eac swylce blod.'[87] He takes a portion of the eucharist home to show his wife, and the next day he asks Basil to baptize him and his entire household. Ælfric's translation of this episode is faithful to the content of the Latin *uita*, and – contrary to his usual treatment of miraculous manifestations of the incorporeal – Ælfric does not go out of his way to make sure his audience realizes that this manifestation is miraculous and therefore not representative of what one typically sees on the paten and in the chalice. Some readers have argued that graphic eucharistic miracles such as this were at odds with Ælfric's overarching aims, but I suspect that such arguments are rooted in an oversimplified understanding of the nature of Anglo-Saxon popular materialism. If told with caution, eucharistic miracles served to proclaim that the bread and wine were truly transformed into Christ's body and blood during the eucharist, and so they served that portion of the materialist audience who denied the reality of the sacrament because of its inaccessibility to the senses. The miracle story in the *Life of St Basil* therefore had a specific didactic purpose, which Ælfric would have undermined if he had (as was his habit) emphasized the unnaturalness of the manifestation. For precisely the same didactic purpose Ælfric makes two eucharistic miracle-stories the centrepiece of his Easter Day homily, which

---

86 A new edition and translation of the OE *Life* are found in Corona (ed.), *Ælfric's Life of Saint Basil the Great*; she identifies BHL 1023 as Ælfric's direct source and prints the Latin text (ibid., 14–28 and 223–47).

87 Ælfric, *Life of St Basil* (LS 3), lines 158-61 (ed. Corona, *Ælfric's Life of Saint Basil the Great*, 160): 'Then it appeared to the Jew as if Basil was splitting apart a child. Still, he went fearfully with the other people to receive the eucharist, and a morsel of flesh was given to him, and he likewise sipped blood from the chalice.' Cf. BHL 1023, ch. 5, lines 4–8 (ibid., 229).

is entirely devoted to persuading his listeners that spiritual and imperceptible entities can also be real, and that the presence of Christ in the eucharist is one such incorporeal reality.

Ælfric's Easter Day Homily on the Eucharist

Ælfric's intended audience for both series of *Catholic Homilies* included ordinary, uneducated laypersons, many of whom received the eucharist only
rarely.[88] Like certain of his Carolingian and Anglo-Saxon forebears, Ælfric
thought laypersons should receive the eucharist more often, and his homily
De doctrina apostolica (Suppl. 19) includes exhortations to that effect. 'Is eac
to witenne þæt Cristene men sceoldon gan to husle oftor þonne hi doð, swa
swa man deð þær ðær man þone Cristendom wel hylt,' Ælfric states; he goes
on to list sixteen occasions during the liturgical year when the eucharist was
available to 'pious persons,' though he grants that it is acceptable for a layperson to receive the eucharist a mere three times a year.[89] Lay reception of
the eucharist was also a source of anxiety for Ælfric, because laypersons were
prone to misunderstand the sacrament. In the homily *De doctrina apostolica*,
Ælfric indicates that one who receives the eucharist must be free from both
sin and doctrinal error.[90] In the same spirit, he introduces his Easter Day
homily (*CH II* 15) by explaining that he will clarify the meaning of the
eucharist for those about to receive the sacrament on this important feast day,
'þy læs ðe ænig twynung eow derian mage. be ðam liflicum gereorde.'[91]

From what sort of error was Ælfric so concerned to rescue his lay audience? The answer becomes clear over the course of the Easter Day homily, but it is expressed more concisely in his mid-Lent Sunday homily
(*CH II* 12): 'On ðam halgan husle we ðicgað cristes lichaman. se hlaf is
soðlice his lichama gastlice. ðeah ðe se ungelæreda þæs gelyfan ne cunne.'[92]

---

88 On the frequency of lay reception of the eucharist in the early medieval West, see Ché-
    lini, 'La pratique dominicale des laïcs'; and Browe, *De frequenti communione in ecclesia
    occidentali.*
89 Ælfric, *Suppl.* 19, lines 119–30 (ed. Pope, *Suppl.*, 628): 'You should know, moreover,
    that Christian persons ought to go to eucharist more often than they do, just as people
    do in the places where they hold firmly to Christian customs.'
90 Ælfric, *Suppl.* 19, lines 126–7 (ed. Pope, *Suppl.*, 628).
91 Ælfric, Easter Day homily (*CH II* 15), lines 6–7 (ed. Godden, *CH II*, 150): 'lest any
    uncertainty about that life-giving food be able to harm you.'
92 Ælfric, *CH II* 12, lines 212–14 (ed. Godden, *CH II*, 116): 'In the holy eucharist we eat
    the body of Christ: the bread is truly his body in a spiritual sense, although an un-
    learned person is unable to believe it.'

The difficulty for this unlearned person is that *soðlice* and *gastlice* are mutually exclusive: he is not inclined to acknowledge the existence of spiritual or imperceptible realities.[93] Accordingly, when Ælfric devotes an entire homily to the explication of the eucharist – an exceedingly rare topic for an early medieval homily in either Latin or OE – he treats the unlearned audience's materialist error as a failure to grasp the ways in which something can be true or real in Christian discourse; they persist in conceiving of the spiritual and the real as mutually exclusive categories.

The structure of the Easter Day homily reveals Ælfric's strategy for teaching his audience how to bridge the gap between the spiritual and the real. The homily is 337 lines long in the modern edition. In roughly eighty lines at the beginning and roughly eighty lines at the end of the homily, Ælfric delivers the sort of typological characterization of the eucharist that his audience might have heard from other OE preachers: he begins by showing how the Passover narrative 'spiritually prefigures' (hæfde getacnunge æfter gastlicum andgite) Christ's historical passion and the sacrifice of the eucharist,[94] and he closes with a discussion of the manifold historical and typological significance of the lamb in both the Old and New Testaments.[95] At the midpoint of the homily he recounts two eucharistic miracles in which the presence of Christ is made visibly manifest, in the form of human flesh and blood, to celebrants and recipients of the sacrament.[96] Finally, in roughly seventy lines immediately preceding and roughly eighty lines immediately following the eucharistic miracles, Ælfric teaches his audience that truth and reality inhere in the imperceptible and spiritual, and that they are not mutually exclusive categories; here his teaching

---

93 To clarify: the reader ought *not* to assume that the terms 'spiritual' and 'invisible' imply strict incorporeality or a total lack of physical substance in most early medieval literature. Only in a minority of cases – and I believe we can include Ælfric in this small group – is it safe to assume that an author used the term *spiritualis* or *gastlic* to represent the incorporeal realities of Platonizing Christian thought.

94 Ælfric, Easter Day homily (*CH II* 15), lines 8–85 (ed. Godden, *CH II*, 150–2). The quotation occurs at lines 38–9 (ibid., 151); a more literal rendering might say that the Passover narrative 'has the figural meaning, according to the spiritual understanding,' of Christ's passion.

95 Ælfric, Easter Day homily (*CH II* 15), lines 255–337 (ed. Godden, *CH II*, 157–60). Most of Ælfric's teaching in this section follows Gregory, *Homiliae in Euangelia* 22; for this and subsequent identifications of Ælfric's Latin source texts I follow Godden, *CH Comm*, 489–500.

96 Ælfric, Easter Day homily (*CH II* 15), lines 159–73 (ed. Godden, *CH II*, 154–5).

relies heavily on Ratramnus's *De corpore et sanguine Domini*.[97] The overall structure is an envelope pattern, in which two very different conceptualizations of the eucharist – the first emphasizing its typological meaning and the second emphasizing the reality and accessibility of Christ's presence – are reconciled, as Ælfric teaches his audience that there exists an imperceptible, spiritual, incorporeal reality, and that Christ's presence in the eucharist can therefore be simultaneously invisible, figural, and real.

For our present purposes, little needs to be said about the typological interpretations of the eucharist that begin and end the Easter Day homily. As for the eucharistic miracles placed at the midpoint of the homily, their message is the same as that which occurs during the *Life of St Basil* cited above. In the first of the two stories, two monks pray for 'some manifestation concerning the holy eucharist' (sume swutelunge be ðam halgan husle), which God grants while they are concelebrating a Mass: they see a child lying on the altar, and when the priest breaks the bread, they see an angel cutting apart the child with a dagger, his flesh going onto the paten and his blood into the chalice.[98] In the second story, Gregory the Great beseeches God to bestow upon a certain 'doubting woman' a marvellous vision that will affirm for her the mystery of Christ's presence in the eucharist. When Gregory next celebrates Mass, this woman receives the eucharist from him, and both of them see a bloody finger lying on the paten. The woman's doubt vanishes at once.[99] Neither the typological interpretations nor the miracles are particularly remarkable on their own, but for several centuries, readers have found it incongruous that Ælfric juxtaposed these graphic miracle-stories with the typological material and with arguments borrowed from Ratramnus, since their respective purposes appear to be diametrically opposed.[100] Ælfric's

---

97 Ælfric, Easter Day homily (*CH II* 15), lines 86–158 (ed. Godden, *CH II*, 152–4) and 174–254 (ibid., 155–7).

98 Ælfric, Easter Day homily (*CH II* 15), lines 159–67 (ed. Godden, *CH II*, 154–5). Cf. Pascasius, *De corpore et sanguine Domini* 14.71–119 (ed. Paulus, CCCM 16, 88–9). It is possible that Ælfric drew these eucharistic miracles not directly from the *De corpore* but from Pascasius's collection of eucharistic miracle-stories, known as the *Exaggeratio plurimorum auctorum de corpore et sanguine Domini*, formerly attributed to Heriger of Lobbes. See Godden, *CH Comm.* 488 and 494–5; and van den Brink's commentary in Ratramnus, *De corpore et sanguine Domini*, 3, 6–7, and 29–32.

99 Ælfric, Easter Day homily (*CH II* 15), lines 167–73 (ed. Godden, *CH II*, 155). Cf. Pascasius, *De corpore et sanguine Domini* 14.44–70 (ed. Paulus, CCCM 16, 87–8); but see the previous note.

100 See, e.g., Leinbaugh, 'Ælfric's *Sermo de Sacrificio in Die Pascae*: Anglican Polemic in the Sixteenth and Seventeenth Centuries,' esp. 54–5; Grundy, 'Ælfric's *Sermo de sacrificio in die pascae*: Figura and Veritas,' 266; and N. Thompson, 'Anglo-Saxon Orthodoxy,' 46–7.

rationale is not particularly obscure, however, if we keep in mind that popular materialism led to more than one type of error among his audience. He needed to convince some people that things they believed were real were also incorporeal, and he needed to convince other people that things they knew to be imperceptible were also real. Typology served the first group; eucharistic miracles served the second group. Arguments borrowed from Ratramnus served both. And since Ælfric makes clear that the stories borrowed from Pascasius depict miracles rather than the everyday perceptibility of Christ's presence in the sacrament, there is no inherent conflict between these miracles and the material borrowed from Ratramnus.

The Reality of Incorporeals and the Incorporeality of Spiritual Realities

In the centuries following the Carolingian eucharistic controversy, unsubtle readers would polarize the debate between Pascasius and Ratramnus, attributing to the former a belief in Christ's physical presence, and to Ratramnus (and hence to Ælfric), belief in Christ's *merely* symbolic presence.[101] Though this view exaggerates the extent of their disagreement, it is true that Ratramnus devotes much attention to the fact that the transformation of the eucharistic elements is not perceptible in the appearance or the taste of the bread and wine, because it is a spiritual presence and a mystery. For Ælfric, it must not have been easy to adapt material from Ratramnus's *De corpore et sanguine Domini* into a vernacular homily accessible to a lay audience, because (unlike the first edition of Pascasius's eucharistic treatise), Ratramnus's teachings unfold within the framework of Carolingian grammatical theory and dialectic; they were formulated for an educated audience, whom he could reasonably expect to have acquired some familiarity with the concept of incorporeal realities.[102] Some parts of Ratramnus's treatise would have been scarcely comprehensible to readers who did not already concede the existence of incorporeal realities. According to a few of Ælfric's own remarks in the Easter Day homily, the target audience of the *Catholic Homilies* included people who were troubled by the assertion

101 For a thoughtful reconsideration of early modern reception of the Easter Day homily, see Bjorklund, 'Parker's Purposes for his Manuscripts: Matthew Parker in the Context of his Early Career and Sixteenth-Century Church Reform.'

102 In his commentary on Ratramnus's *De corpore*, chapters 1–4, 15, and 102, van den Brink adduces evidence that Ratramnus composed this work at the behest of Charles the Bald (*De corpore et sanguine Domini*, 27); see also Bouhot, *Ratramne de Corbie*, 83–5; and on the modes of theological discourse associated with the Carolingian court in the mid-ninth century, see Matter, 'The Soul of the Dog-Man'; and Chazelle, *The Crucified God in the Carolingian Era*, 233–5.

that something could be both real and incorporeal. For these people, the physical impossibility of changing bread and wine into body and blood stood in the way of their belief in the sacraments.

Prefatory to the argument he borrows from Ratramnus, Ælfric tells his audience, 'Nu smeadon gehwilce men oft. and gyt gelome smeagað. hu se hlaf þe bið of corne gegearcod and ðurh fyres hætan abacen. mage beon awend to cristes lichaman. oððe þæt win ðe bið of manegum berium awrungen. weorðe awend þurh ænigre bletsunge to drihtnes blode.'[103] Ælfric's explanation of this mystery is not about the transformation of the elements themselves but about how Christians are supposed to understand the transformation. Some things are said of Christ figurally or 'by means of figural language' (þurh getacnunge), and some things are said historically or 'by means of something certain' (ðurh gewissum þinge), that is, a concrete and perceptible reality. Christ was born of Mary historically and crucified historically, but Christ is called 'bread' figurally, just as he is called 'lamb' or 'lion' figurally, but not historically, and not 'according to his true nature' (æfter soðum gecynde).[104]

As soon as Ælfric invokes the idea of figural language, he risks leading his audience to conclude that Christ's presence in the eucharist is not real. Keenly anticipating this risk, Ælfric poses a rhetorical question: 'Hwi is ðonne þæt halige husel gecweden cristes lichama. oþþe his blod. gif hit nis soðlice þæt þæt hit gehaten is?'[105] His wording of this question implies that his audience had trouble believing that something was 'real' or 'true' if it was neither perceptible to the senses nor identical to something that had historically been perceptible to the senses. Ælfric answers his own question thus:

Soðlice se hlaf and þæt win ðe beoð ðurh sacerda mæssan gehalgode. oðer ðing hi æteowiað menniscum andgitum wiðutan. and oðer ðing hi clypiað wiðinnan geleaffullum modum; Wiðutan hi beoð gesewene hlaf and win.

103 Ælfric, Easter Day homily (CH II 15), lines 86–90 (ed. Godden, CH II, 152): 'Some men have frequently sought to find out, and still continually seek to find out, how the bread, which is prepared from grain and baked by the heat of the fire, can be transformed into the body of Christ, or how that wine, which is pressed from many grapes, may become transformed by any blessing into the blood of the Lord.'

104 Ælfric, Easter Day homily (CH II 15), lines 90–9 (ed. Godden, CH II, 152–3).

105 Ælfric, Easter Day homily (CH II 15), lines 100–1 (ed. Godden, CH II, 153): 'Then why is that holy eucharist said to be the body of Christ, or his blood, unless it truly *is* that which it is called?'

ægðer ge on hiwe. ge on swæcce. ac hi beoð soðlice æfter ðære halgunge cristes lichama. and his blod þurh gastlicere gerynu.[106]

With Ratramnus's help, Ælfric teaches a simplified lesson about the epistemological and ontological implications of incorporeality. With their eyes they can see the appearance of the bread and wine, but with another faculty, the 'faithful mind,' they can perceive the hidden, spiritual part of the eucharist that is imperceptible to the bodily senses. This teaching superficially resembles the epistemological binary of *uttor gewit* and *innor andgiet* that Alfred established in the first book of the OE *Soliloquies*, although in fact a philosophically significant distinction separates Alfred's and Ælfric's respective schemata. Recall that Alfred's *innor andgiet* is roughly the equivalent of Augustine's *cogitatio*, that is, the faculty of abstract thought founded upon sensory data. Except in extraordinarily holy individuals, Alfred's *innor andgiet* can *believe* in incorporeal truths but cannot apprehend them or gain first-hand knowledge of them during earthly life, and consequently Alfred's epistemological hierarchy includes no real counterpart to Augustine's *intellectus*.[107] For Ælfric, faith still plays a role in the apprehension of incorporeals, since he specifies that the hidden spiritual reality of the eucharist is available to the *geleafful mod*; however, faith is not a substitute for first-hand knowledge. The *mod* can actually perceive spiritual realities that are imperceptible to the senses. And although Ælfric does not pursue this point in the present context, the reason why the *mod* can do so is because it is part of the incorporeal soul rather than a fleshly organ in the chest cavity.

It is doubtful that many Anglo-Saxon readers or auditors of this homily were equipped to understand the full implications of Ælfric's insistence that the transformation of the eucharistic elements was a spiritual or incorporeal reality that could be apprehended by means of an incorporeal faculty. But Ælfric found clever ways to make the concept of incorporeal realities more familiar. He points out that when a child is baptized, he is cleansed of sins on the inside, imperceptibly but truly, though his outward

---

106 Ælfric, Easter Day homily (*CH II* 15), lines 101–7 (ed. Godden, *CH II*, 153): 'Truly the bread and the wine, which are consecrated by the Masses of the priests, reveal one thing outwardly to human understanding, and they communicate another thing inwardly to believing minds. Outwardly they are seen to be bread and wine, both in appearance and in taste, but after the consecration they are truly the body of Christ and his blood, through the spiritual mystery.'

107 See chapter 7 above.

appearance does not change; and when the priest's blessing is said over the water in the baptismal font, the water is invisibly transformed into holy water, with the spiritual power to wash away sins, even though to sensory perception it looks like ordinary corruptible matter.[108] This is an astute approach to the problem, partly because even the uneducated in Ælfric's audience may well have had a simplified understanding of the purpose of baptism and would have witnessed first-hand that the sacrament works no visible change upon the child, nor does the blessing upon the water. The reality of an invisible action or power may, moreover, have been easier for his audience to grasp than the reality of an invisible presence. In fact, for the minority of readers and auditors who already accepted that the soul was an incorporeal reality, the comparison of eucharist to baptism would be particularly effective, because it would be easy to grasp that changes wrought upon the incorporeal soul were themselves incorporeal.

Ælfric next illustrates the nature of the real presence in three different ways, and at the conclusion of each he returns to the same refrain: Christ's presence in the eucharist is not bodily (*lichamlic*) but spiritual (*gastlic*). First, Ælfric distinguishes the outwardly visible, corruptible nature of the bread and wine from the invisible, salvific power of the eucharist, which is perceptible only by means of faith. Second, he points out the physical impossibility of the identity of the historical body and the eucharistic body of Christ, since one was made of flesh and bone, but the other is perceptibly made of grain.[109] Third, he explains that the body of Christ is eternally immutable while the bread of the eucharist is chewed, swallowed, and digested.[110] Ælfric directs these assertions at listeners who think that the real is also necessarily perceptible and concrete, so at each stage, in order to lead his audience to a better understanding of the eucharist, Ælfric offers a vivid illustration of the meaning of incorporeality. In fact, while he is on the subject of the physical disintegration of the eucharistic bread, Ælfric points out that even though the bread is broken into pieces and shared among many people, the incorporeal presence of Christ within is neither divided nor diminished by the breaking of the bread, because that which

---

108 Ælfric, Easter Day homily (*CH II* 15), lines 107–16 (ed. Godden, *CH II*, 153).
109 Ælfric, Easter Day homily (*CH II* 15), lines 119–36 (ed. Godden, *CH II*, 153–4); Godden identifies several selections from Ratramnus's *De corpore* that Ælfric has reworked in this section (*CH Comm.*, 492–3).
110 Ælfric, Easter Day homily (*CH II* 15), lines 143–8 (ed. Godden, *CH II*, 154); cf. Ratramnus, *De corpore et sanguine Domini*, 76–7 (ed. van den Brink, *De corpore*, 61–2).

is incorporeal is not spatially distributed: 'Manega underfoð þone halgan lichaman. and he bið swa ðeah on ælcum dæle eall æfter gastlicere gerynu; Þeah sumum men gesceote læsse dæl. ne bið swa ðeah na mare miht on ðam maran dæle þonne on ðam læssan.'[111] As in the earlier comparison between eucharist and baptism, this line of reasoning is more likely to be appreciated by someone who already has an understanding of the implications of incorporeality, especially as those implications have been applied to the soul. In fact, Ælfric did not find this reference to the eucharist's indivisible and non-spatial nature in any of the Latin sources that have been identified for the Easter Day homily; his inspiration for this passage may well have been a discourse on the soul, such as that of Claudianus Mamertus or a commentary on Boethius's *Consolatio*, where the indivisible and non-spatial nature of the soul is characterized in similar terms: there is no less of it in the littlest finger than in the whole body.[112]

At the close of this segment of the Easter Day homily, just before the eucharistic miracles, Ælfric sternly reminds his audience that if they still cannot comprehend *how* Christ is spiritually present in the eucharist, they are obligated to have faith *that* he is spiritually present, and not to ask ceaseless questions about it: 'Soðlice hit is swa swa we ær cwædon cristes lichama and his blod. na lichamlice. ac gastlice; Ne sceole ge smeagan hu hit gedon sy. ac healdan on eowerum geleafan þæt hit swa gedon sy.'[113] It is reasonable for Ælfric to encourage his audience to believe before they fully understand; after all, he has just reminded them that the eucharist is a 'spiritual mystery.' Yet at the same time, he is determined to bring his audience closer to understanding the mystery of the eucharist by convincing them of the reality of incorporeals.

Accordingly, after presenting the Pascasian eucharistic miracles summarized above, Ælfric turns again to Ratramnus for further demonstrations that the invisible can be real and substantial. At the Last Supper, Ælfric observes, Christ 'awende ðurh ungesewenlicere mihte þone hlaf

---

111 Ælfric, Easter Day homily (*CH II* 15), lines 148–51 (ed. Godden, *CH II*, 154): 'Many people receive the holy body, and nonetheless it is whole in every portion, according to the spiritual mystery. Although one may get a smaller piece, there is still no more power in the bigger piece than in the smaller one.'
112 See chapters 6 and 7 above.
113 Ælfric, Easter Day homily (*CH II* 15), lines 156–8 (ed. Godden, *CH II*, 154): 'As we said earlier, it is truly called the body and blood of Christ, not in a bodily sense, but in a spiritual sense. You should not seek to know how it happens, but you should maintain in your faith that it does so happen.'

to his agenum lichaman. and þæt win to his blode.'[114] It is worth noting that, in contrast to Tristram homily 4, discussed earlier, in which Christ 'likened' the elements of the Passover meal to his body and blood, Ælfric maintains that Christ actually effected a transformation of (*awende*) the bread and wine. Ælfric additionally uses the Last Supper episode to correct the error of those who expect to see and taste flesh and blood in the eucharist: Christ must have transformed the Passover bread and wine into his body and blood spiritually (*gastlice*) rather than bodily (*licham-lice*) because at the time of the Last Supper, his actual, historical flesh and blood had not yet become a sacrifice on the Cross.[115] As Ælfric goes on to borrow more typological commentary from Ratramnus, he establishes a model that the faithful can follow if they wish to approach the sacrament in the correct frame of mind and reap its benefits. Christ's sacrifice of his body and blood is prefigured in the account of the Israelites' wandering in the desert, when God provides manna to eat and when Moses miraculously brings forth water from a rock. Those who ate the physical manna and drank the physical water nonetheless died a physical death. But Moses and Aaron and others did not die the eternal death of the spirit, Ælfric explains, because they perceived the spiritual realities that were hidden in the food they consumed: 'Hi gesawon þæt se heofonlica mete wæs gesewenlic. and brosniendlic. ac hi understodon gastlice be ðam gesewenlican ðinge. and hit gastlice ðigdon.'[116] This is the example that Ælfric's listeners are to follow when they receive the eucharist after hearing this Easter homily: observe that the bread and wine retain the outward form of bread and wine, but know that the incorporeal reality of Christ's presence is hidden within.

Though Ælfric addresses two different types of materializing error in his Easter Day homily on the eucharist, his objectives in the Nativity homily on the soul are, in one respect, simpler. There is no evidence that serious doubts about the reality of the soul plagued the Anglo-Saxons, and so the effects of materialism led in just one direction, toward the assumption that

---

114 Ælfric, Easter Day homily (*CH II* 15), lines 193–5 (ed. Godden, *CH II*, 156): 'transformed the bread and wine into his own body and blood by means of an invisible power.' Here Ælfric follows Ratramnus's argument (*De corpore et sanguine Domini* 27–8; ed. van den Brink, *De corpore*, 50) against the Pascasian teaching that the eucharist transforms the bread and wine into Christ's historical body (see Godden, *CH Comm.*, 496).
115 Ælfric, Easter Day homily (*CH II* 15), lines 190–3 (ed. Godden, *CH II*, 155–6).
116 Ælfric, Easter Day homily (*CH II* 15), lines 206–8 (ed. Godden, *CH II*, 156): 'They saw that the heavenly food was visible and corruptible, but they had a spiritual understanding of that visible thing, and they ate it spiritually.' Cf. Ratramnus, *De corpore et sanguine domini* 78 (ed. van den Brink, *De corpore*, 62); see Godden, *CH Comm.*, 496.

the soul was corporeal and perceptible. At the same time, Ælfric's objectives were complicated by the need to combine a lesson on the soul's incorporeality with a lesson on its unitary nature. Ælfric achieves this primarily
by adapting the firmly Platonist-Christian doctrines that he found in Alcuin's *De ratione animae*. Remarkably, Ælfric shapes his adaptation of this
relatively sophisticated philosophical discourse on the soul in such a way
that it pointedly refutes the doctrinal errors of the anonymous vernacular homilies and also complements the Easter Day homily by fleshing out
what it means for something to be real and incorporeal at the same time.

Ælfric's Nativity Homily on the Incorporeal, Unitary *sawol*

In the first piece in his *Lives of Saints* series, Ælfric's discourse on the soul
is not set forth as a purely natural-philosophical exposition. As is fitting
for a Christmas homily, he begins with a discussion of the Incarnation and
from there proceeds to the coeternity of Christ with the Father and the
nature of the Trinity. After eighty-three prose lines in the modern edition,
Ælfric turns to the nature of the *sawol*; taking his cue from Alcuin's *De
ratione animae*, he justifies his subject matter by asserting that knowledge
of the nature of the soul is a stepping-stone to understanding the nature of
the Trinity.[117] From that point onward, Ælfric's discourse on the soul is
heavily indebted to Alcuin's *De ratione animae*.[118] For both of these authors the soul's incorporeality was conceptually intertwined with its unitary
nature and its powers of perception, although for the sake of clarity I have
treated Ælfric's approaches to each of these topics separately.

The Earliest Vernacular Discourse on the True Incorporeality of the sawol

Ælfric's audience already knew the soul was real, but many of them were
not aware that it was incorporeal and utterly imperceptible to the senses.
To convince them of this demanded that Ælfric contradict much of what
they would have heard from other vernacular preachers. He addresses the

---

117 Ælfric, Nativity homily (*LS* 1), lines 79–83 and 112–16 (ed. Skeat, *LS* 1.14–16). For
specific correspondences between Ælfric's text and Alcuin's, see Godden, 'The Sources
of *Lives* [*of Saints*] 1 (Nativity of Christ)'; most of the relevant passages of *DRA* are
quoted or discussed above in chapter 6.
118 In the present discussion I quote the version of the Nativity homily that is preserved
as *LS* 1; on the other OE version (Belfour homily 9) and their proximate and ultimate
Latin sources, see below.

412 Anglo-Saxon Psychologies

topic of the soul's substance and appearance from several angles. To begin, although we conventionally speak of the size (*mycelnyss*) or growth of the soul, these qualities are meant in a non-spatial sense, in which greater size signifies an accumulation of virtues: 'Gescead wexð on cildrum na seo sa-·wul . and seo sawul þihþ on mægenum . and ne bið namare þonne heo æt fruman wæs ac bið betere ne heo ne underfæhð lichomlice mycelnysse.'[119] Drawing on Alcuin's fundamental and formal definition of the *anima*, Ælfric asserts that 'Seo sawul is gesceadwis gast . æfre cucu ... Heo is ungesæwenlic . and unlichomlic . butan hæfe and butan bleo.'[120] Though Ælfric is here translating almost verbatim from Alcuin's *De ratione animae*, his description of the incorporeal soul sounds like a pointed refutation of the portrayals of the corporealized soul in the anonymous vernacular homilies. In Blickling 16, the souls of the wicked men hang from the rimy trees until the limbs give way beneath them and they plunge down the cliff: these souls clearly have *hæf*. And in Vercelli 4 and its analogues, souls are endowed with a *bleo* that reflects their merits or failings.[121] Ælfric's teaching therefore directly challenges the homiletic tradition of the anthropomorphized and corporealized soul by rejecting any notion that the soul has weight or colour. Near the end of the Nativity homily, Ælfric departs briefly from his source text in order to reiterate this crucial point: 'nan lichamlic gesceaft ne mæg beon hyre [*scil.* sawle] wiðmeten . We cwæden ær þæt heo wære butan bleo . forþan ðe heo nis na lichamlic . On lichaman bið bleoh . and seo sawul bið swa gewlitegod . swa heo on worulde geearnode.'[122] Given the rhetorical value of the promise of rewards and punishments in the afterlife, it was wise for Ælfric to affirm

---

119 Ælfric, Nativity homily (*LS* 1), lines 110–12 (ed. Skeat, *LS* 1.16): 'In children it is the faculty of reason, not the soul, that increases; and the soul grows in virtues and yet is no larger than it originally was, although it is better; nor does it take on size in a bodily sense.' Notably, this passage does not depend on Alcuin's *DRA*; the corresponding lines of the Latin homily in Boulogne-sur-Mer 63, which is the proximate source of *LS* 1, appears to be synthesized from similar statements in Augustine, *De quantitate animae* 16.28, and Cassiodorus, *De anima* 7.57–8, suggesting that if he was indeed the author of the Latin homily, Ælfric searched outside Alcuin's *DRA* for further affirmations of the soul's incorporeality. See Godden, 'Anglo-Saxons on the Mind,' 282.
120 Ælfric, Nativity homily (*LS* 1), lines 171 and 176–7 (ed. Skeat, *LS* 1.20): 'The soul is a rational spirit, always living ... It is invisible and incorporeal, without weight and without colour.'
121 On Blickling 16 and Vercelli 4, see above.
122 Ælfric, Nativity homily (*LS* 1), lines 207–10 (ed. Skeat, *LS* 1.22): 'No bodily creature can be likened to the soul. We stated earlier that the soul was without colour, because it is not corporeal. In a body there is colour, and the soul will be adorned just as it merited in the world.'

that the soul will be 'adorned' after death as the vernacular homilies suggest, but he makes it clear that such adornment does not take the form of colour or any other property of bodies.

A few subtle adjustments that Ælfric made to the information he received from Alcuin may reveal a bit more about how he perceived his audience's conception of the *sawol*. Where Alcuin writes that the soul is 'circumscribed and whole in every member of its body,' the attribute of circumscription distinguishes the individual soul from the Neoplatonic world-soul and from the *pneuma* of the Stoic tradition; the soul's wholeness in every part of the body results from its indivisibility and its non-spatial distribution, which are important corollaries of its incorporeality, but difficult to comprehend. It would not be fair to say that Ælfric 'dumbs down' the content of his source text for the sake of his audience, but he does choose his battles carefully. To characterize the soul as 'circumscribed' in an absolute sense was not a meaningful philosophical distinction for Ælfric's audience; he instead writes that the soul is 'mid þam lichaman befangen . and on eallum limum wunigende.'[123] When Ælfric asserts that the soul resides in all the limbs but not that it is *whole* in all the limbs, he sets aside the difficult concept of non-spatial distribution. This is a somewhat surprising decision, given that here Ælfric had an opportunity to elaborate on non-spatial distribution as a corollary of incorporeality, and thereby to reinforce the parallel point that he makes in the Easter Day homily: namely that the presence of Christ is incorporeal and therefore non-spatial, which is why the salvific power of the eucharist remains whole in every piece of bread that is broken and distributed. On the other hand, the simpler statement that the soul resides in all the limbs directly challenged the cardiocentric localization of the soul that was typical of the vernacular tradition. Later in the homily, Ælfric even confirms that cardiocentrism was current among his audience and that he regards cardiocentrism as erroneous. 'Nis seo orþung þe we ut blawaþ . and in ateoð oþþe ure sawul ac is seo lyft þe ealle lichamlice þing on lybbað . butan fixum anum þe on flodum lybbað,' he observes, in a remark that has no parallel in Alcuin's *De ratione animae*.[124] The perception of the soul as identical to the air that enters and leaves the lungs is likely the same popular perception that underlay the frequent narrative depictions of the soul leaving the breast at death.

---

123 Alcuin, *DRA* 10 (PL 101.644); Ælfric, Nativity homily (*LS* 1), line 177 (ed. Skeat, *LS* 1.20): 'enclosed by the body and residing in all the limbs.'
124 Ælfric, Nativity homily, lines 214–16 (ed. Skeat, *LS*, 1.22): 'Nor is our breath, which we blow out and draw in, our soul; but [our breath] is the air in which all bodily things live, except only the fish who live in water.'

Ælfric's discussion of the substance of the soul marks a milestone in early medieval psychology, because he was the first to supply a detailed discourse in the vernacular on the soul's incorporeality and its implications, and thereby the first to mount a challenge to the prevailing corporealization of the *sawol* in the anonymous OE homilies.[125] Because Ælfric's audience was not inclined to doubt the reality of the soul, if they grasped his teachings in this homily they would be well on their way to accepting that something could be simultaneously incorporeal and real, and therefore much closer to sharing in the understanding of the eucharist that Ælfric promoted. But Ælfric's depiction of the soul, and of incorporeals in general, would be incomplete without examining the unitary nature of the soul – that is, its union with the mind – because the soul's incorporeality had an important epistemological dimension. That dimension would have been very new to the typical Anglo-Saxon audience as well, given the vernacular tradition's functional and substantial distinction between *sawol* and *mod*.

Ælfric's Discursive Assertion of the Unitary Nature of the sawol

The first OE discourses on the unitary nature of the soul were already a century old by Ælfric's day: these of course were the Alfredian translations of the *Boethius* and the *Soliloquies*. The *OE Boethius* was even consulted by Ælfric as he sought material for his Nativity homily to supplement what he borrowed from Alcuin,[126] although Ælfric rejected the pre-existence of souls and the theory of recollection,[127] which play

---

125 The earliest applications of the word *unlichamlic* 'incorporeal' to the *sawol* actually belong to Wærferth's translation of Gregory's *Dialogues*. As discussed in chapter 4 above, there is good reason to suspect that even the Latin source text did not convey to readers the full array of Platonist corollaries of incorporeality; given Alfred's own struggles with this aspect of Boethius's and Augustine's thought, I cannot imagine that his colleague Wærferth brought to his translation of the *Dialogues* the same philosophical understanding of the word *unlichamlic* that underlies Ælfric's use of the term.

126 Godden, 'The Sources of *Lives* [*of Saints*] 1.' Godden maintains that the *OE Boethius* was a direct source for Ælfric's Nativity Homily ('Anglo-Saxons on the Mind,' 296–8), and Godden and Irvine indicate that Ælfric drew directly upon the *OE Boethius* in other writings as well (1.207–8 and 1.545–7); Leinbaugh, however, maintains that Ælfric may not have known the *OE Boethius* directly ('Ælfric's *Lives of Saints* 1 and the Boulogne Sermon,' 195–204).

127 See chapter 7 above on recollection and the pre-existence of souls in the *OE Boethius* and *Soliloquies*. Cf. *CH II* 14, lines 55–7 (ed. Godden, *CH II*, 139), where Ælfric comments on Christ's statement that the traitorous Judas would have been better off if he had never been born: 'Nis þæt na to understandenne ænigum gesceadwisum swilce

such an important role in both the *Boethius* and the *Soliloquies*. Most of Ælfric's borrowings from the *Boethius* have to do with the position of the human soul in the hierarchy of creatures,[128] rather than with characteristics of the soul per se, but when Ælfric first attributes mental faculties to the soul, he is apparently informed by both Alcuin's *De ratione animae* and the adaptation of the Alcuinian text that appears in the *Boethius*. 'Uþwytan sæcgað,' begins Ælfric, 'þæt þære sawle gecynd is ðryfeald . An dæl is on hire gewylnigendlic . oðer yrsiegendlic . þrydde gesceadwislic. Twægen þissera dæla habbað deor and nytenu mid us . þæt is gewylnunge and yrre. Se man ana hæfð gescead . and ræd . and andgit.'[129] Though this is territory that Alfred has already covered in OE, Ælfric's treatment is nonetheless a landmark in the history of Anglo-Saxon thought, because he presents this material in a work that could potentially reach a significant and diverse audience, for whom the attribution of appetite, passion, and reason to the *sawol* was a striking departure from their everyday idiom.

The same can be said for Ælfric's next statements about the *sawol*. He explains the purpose of each of these three faculties of the soul, concluding with the assertion that 'Gescead is ðære sawle forgifen to gewyssienne and to styrenne hire agen lif . and ealle hire dæda.'[130] Like Alcuin, he then proposes a second tripartition of the soul, into the faculties of 'gemynd . and andgit . and wyllan' (memory and will and understanding), wherein resides its likeness to the Trinity.[131] In the vernacular homiletic tradition, the soul plainly does not govern its own life and deeds; it is at the mercy of the mind-body complex, which has the autonomy to deliberate and to act as it pleases, unmoved by the inefficacious wishes of the *sawol*. Ælfric

---

he awar wære. ær ðan ðe he geboren wære,' clarifies Ælfric, 'Ac hit is anfealdlice gecweden. þæt him betere wære. þæt he næfre nære. ðonne he yfele wære' (This should not be taken to mean in any way that he existed somewhere before he was born, but it is generally agreed that it would be better that he never existed than that he existed evilly). Godden, 'Anglo-Saxons on the Mind,' adduces further evidence of Ælfric's opposition to the theory of anamnesis (284–5).

128 E.g., Ælfric, Nativity homily (*LS* 1), lines 25–32 and 41–59 (ed. Skeat, *LS* 1.12–14).

129 Ælfric, Nativity homily (*LS* 1), lines 96–100 (ed. Skeat, *LS* 1.16): 'Philosophers maintain that the nature of the soul is threefold. One part of it is appetitive, the second passionate, and the third rational. Wild animals and cattle, along with us, have two of these parts, namely appetite and passion. Humankind alone possesses reason and speech and understanding.' It is Godden's opinion that here Ælfric's language is influenced by both Alcuin and Alfred: see 'The Sources of *Lives* [*of Saints*] 1.'

130 Ælfric, Nativity homily (*LS* 1), lines 107–8 (ed. Skeat, *LS* 1.16): 'Reason is bestowed upon the soul so that it might guide and control its own life and all its deeds.'

131 Ælfric, Nativity homily (*LS* 1), lines 112–14 (ed. Skeat, *LS* 1.16).

leaves no room for misunderstanding but makes clear that the *sawol* that animates the body is one and the same as these three mental faculties: 'An sawul is . and an lif . and an edwist . þe þas ðreo þing hæfð on hire . and þas ðreo þing na synd na ðreo lif ac an . ne þreo ædwiste ac an.'[132] Toward the end of the homily Ælfric makes an even stronger statement, ascribing to the unitary *sawol* not merely agency but even dominance over the body: 'Seo sawul is þæs lichoman hlæfdige . and heo gewissað þa fif andgitu þæs lichaman . swa swa of cynesætle.'[133] Unlike the *sawol* of *Riddle* 43 in the Exeter Book, who was *hlaford* 'lord' over the body in name more than in practice, the unitary *sawol* of Ælfric's homily is actually capable of deliberation, will, and governance of the body.

Ælfric's psychology again directly contradicts the vernacular tradition when he adapts Alcuin's treatment of the flight of the mind. *Sawol* is the name Ælfric gives to the entity that is said figuratively to travel to the people and places conjured up by memory and imagination: 'Uton nu behealden þa wundorlican swyftnysse þære sawle . heo hæfð swa mycele swyftnysse þæt heo on anre tide gif heo swa wyle . besceawað heofonan and ofer sæ flyhð . land . and burga geondfærð . and ealle þas þing mid geþohte on hire sihðe gesæt.'[134] The *sawol* is also the entity responsible for dreaming: 'And swa styrigende is seo sawul . þæt heo furðon on slæpe ne gestylþ.'[135] In this account the *mod* is nothing more than the faculty

---

132 Ælfric, Nativity homily (*LS* 1), lines 114–16 (ed. Skeat, *LS* 1.16): 'It is one soul and one life and one substance that possesses these three things within itself, and these three things are not three lives but one, not three substances but one.'

133 Ælfric, Nativity homily (*LS* 1), lines 195–6 (ed. Skeat, *LS* 1.22): 'The soul is the mistress of the body and she instructs the five senses of the body as if from a royal throne.'

134 Ælfric, Nativity homily (*LS* 1), lines 122–6 (ed. Skeat, *LS* 1.18): 'Let us now consider the marvellous swiftness of the soul. It possesses such great swiftness that, if it so desires, in a single moment it can contemplate heaven and fly over the sea, travel throughout lands and towns, and by means of thought form all those things that it has seen.'

135 Ælfric, Nativity homily (*LS* 1), lines 131–2 (ed. Skeat, *LS* 1.18): 'And the soul is so mobile that even in sleep it does not stand still.' Here Ælfric is probably talking about ordinary dreams, but a subsequent passage (lines 178–80; ed. Skeat, *LS* 1.20) may allude to visionary experiences: he states that the soul 'ne mæg be hyre agenre mihte of þam lichoman gewytan . ne æft ongean cyrran . butan se wylle þe hi geworhte . and on þonne lichaman asænde' (cannot depart from the body under its own power nor return to it again, unless he who created the soul and sent it into the body desires that to happen). In the *OE Boethius*, Alfred likewise denies that the soul's travel from the body occurs according to its own will and power, though he says so in the context of discussing

that the *sawol* uses to conjure images of things both remembered and imagined.[136] By imputing all these activities to the *sawol*, Ælfric challenges the vernacular poetic tradition, in which memory and imagination are the purview of the *mod* (or *hyge* or *sefa*), and the *sawol* leaves the body only to visit the afterworld, either at death or during a mystical vision.

This brings us to the frequently discussed passage in which Ælfric renders in OE the list of names given to the unitary soul to account for all the different roles it plays within the body. The list drives home Ælfric's teaching that the *sawol* is a unitary soul, incorporating the *mod*, rather than the impersonal and flaccid creature that the OE poets and anonymous homilists envisioned inhabiting the body.

Heo is on bocum manegum naman gecyged . be hyre weorces þenungum . Hyre nama is anima þæt is sawul and seo nama gelympð to hire life . And spiritus gast . belimpð to hire ymbwlatunge . Heo is sensus . þæt is andgit . oððe felnyss . þonne heo gefret . Heo is animus . þæt is mod . þonne heo wat . Heo is mens . Þæt is mod þonne heo understent . Heo is memoria . þæt is gemynd . þonne heo gemanð . Heo is ratio . þæt is gescead . þonne heo toscæt . Heo is uoluntas . þæt is wylla . þonne heo hwæt wyle . Ac swa þeah ealla þas naman syndon sawul.[137]

Some studies of Anglo-Saxon psychology have understood this passage to represent the way most or all Anglo-Saxons conceived of the relationship between *mod* and *sawol*,[138] but as I hope I have made clear, this passage marks the culmination of an extraordinary vernacular discourse in which

---

dreams rather than visionary experiences: see the *OE Boethius*, B-text ch. 34, lines 307–9 (ed. Godden and Irvine 1.328); and Godden, 'Anglo-Saxons on the Mind,' 277.

136 Ælfric, Nativity homily (*LS* 1), lines 129–30 (ed. Skeat, *LS* 1.18): 'Eal swa be gehwylcum oðrum þingum þe heo ær cuðe . oððe ne cuðe . heo mæg on hire mode gescyppan' (All such things as the soul earlier knew of, or did not know of, the soul can conjure in its mind).

137 Ælfric, Nativity homily (*LS* 1), lines 180–8 (ed. Skeat, *LS* 1.20–2): 'In books, the soul is called by many names, according to the services of its labour. Its name is *anima*, that is soul, and this name pertains to its life. And *spiritus*, spirit, pertains to its contemplation. It is *sensus*, that is perception or feeling, when it perceives. It is *animus*, that is mind, when it knows. It is *mens*, that is mind, when it understands. It is *memoria*, that is memory, when it remembers. It is *ratio*, that is reason, when it discerns. It is *uoluntas*, that is will, when it desires something. But nevertheless, the name of all these things is soul.' Cf. Alcuin, *DRA* 11 (PL 101. 644; see chapter 6 above).

138 Notably Phillips, 'Heart, Mind, and Soul in Old English,' 16–17.

Ælfric makes repeated assertions about the *sawol* that starkly disagree with the vernacular tradition. As I have argued, the psychology of the vernacular tradition is not an artificial and formulaic idiom used by a handful of barely Christianized OE poets to describe the mind in an elevated literary register. The vernacular psychological idiom inhabited every type of poetry, prose narratives, and especially homilies, both Latin and OE, and it was entirely compatible with the cardiocentric understanding of the mind and the eclectic attitudes toward corporeality that were cultivated, without polemic, in the schoolrooms of England down to the tenth century and later. In short, what Ælfric achieves in his Nativity homily is a remarkable novelty. He was only the second Anglo-Saxon to generate vernacular discourse on the unitary nature of the *sawol*, and he was the first author working in England to assimilate the Platonizing concept of the incorporeal unitary soul, to recognize the interdependence of the ontological and the epistemological ramifications of the soul's incorporeality, and to render such a discourse in a form that had the potential to be disseminated to a broad audience. Now it remains to examine the potential and the actual dissemination of Ælfric's anti-materialist writings and to consider their impact on the Anglo-Saxon intellectual landscape, broadly conceived.

The Dissemination and Influence of Ælfric's Anti-Materializing Homilies

How much did Ælfric's teachings instigate widespread change in the way unlearned and moderately learned Anglo-Saxons conceived of incorporeal realities, especially the unitary soul? Did his homilies exert enough influence to begin to dissolve the common-sense connection between mind and heart, and thereby to undermine the status of cardiocentrism and the hydraulic model as tenets of folk psychology? To answer this question we need to take into account Ælfric's intended audiences, the manuscript evidence that attests to the nature of his actual audiences, and evidence for widespread change in the eleventh century.

Ælfric composed both series of *Catholic Homilies* during the period 987 x 995, while he was at Cerne.[139] His own prefaces to the *Catholic Homilies* make clear that unlearned layfolk were an important part of Ælfric's target

---

139 Godden, *CH Comm*, xxxi–xxxvi; J. Wilcox, 'Ælfric in Dorset and the Landscape of Pastoral Care,' 52.

audience, although whether and how these homilies might actually have reached a lay audience is still in question.[140] Most of the surviving *Catholic Homilies* manuscripts are high-status productions in which the text is not pointed for oral delivery, which strongly suggests that they were used in non-liturgical situations, either for private devotional reading or on occasions when religious texts might be read aloud for groups of ordinary laypersons or of professed religious.[141] At the same time, the *Catholic Homilies* were copied in enormous quantity: Jonathan Wilcox cites the figure of 34 extant copies of *CH I*, 'with a further 50 postulated from the textual evidence,' a volume of textual reproduction that according to Wilcox 'demonstrates the official, institutionally-adopted status of these homilies.'[142] Admittedly Wilcox's opinions about the exposure of non-monastic audiences to Ælfric's homilies represent the more optimistic end of the spectrum, far from the circumspection of Godden's and Clayton's conservative estimates.[143] I hesitate to embrace Wilcox's proposition that in Ælfric's day, in 'virtually every church, minster, and monastery throughout England, people of both sexes and all classes, in some places including among them communities of priests or monks and nuns,' were hearing a consistent program of preaching every Sunday and feast day.'[144] Nonetheless, copious manuscript evidence supports Wilcox's conclusion that the wide dissemination of the *Catholic Homilies* 'represents something quite revolutionary – the beginning of a form of mass communication that must have played a significant part in defining a sense of English identity at the turn of the millennium.'[145]

Dissemination of the *Lives of Saints* in general, and of the Nativity homily in particular, was considerably more restricted.[146] Between 992 and 1002, Ælfric composed the series of short hagiographies and homilies known as his *Lives of Saints* at the behest of two wealthy laymen, Ealdorman Æthelweard and his son Æthelmær,[147] and the first piece in this series is Ælfric's

---

140 Godden, *CH Comm.*, xxi–xxix; Clayton, 'Homiliaries and Preaching,' 176–86.
141 J. Wilcox, 'Ælfric in Dorset,' 61; for further discussion of 'pseudo-liturgical' occasions, see ibid., 55; and J. Wilcox, 'The Audience of Ælfric's *Lives of Saints*,' 258–9.
142 J. Wilcox, 'Ælfric in Dorset,' 61.
143 See n. 140 above.
144 J. Wilcox, 'Ælfric in Dorset,' 62.
145 Ibid., 62.
146 J. Hill, 'The Dissemination of Ælfric's *Lives of Saints*: A Preliminary Survey,' 243–52. Note that the last manuscript in Hill's Group B should be Bodley 343 (containing Belfour 9), not 340 (ibid., 244; cf. Ker, *Catalogue*, no. 310, item 77).
147 Clemoes, 'The Chronology of Ælfric's Works,' 56.

OE Nativity homily, which in this form survives in just one manuscript.[148] During the years 1002–5 Ælfric produced an OE revision of this homily, now known as Belfour homily 9, which survives only in a twelfth-century homiliary, Oxford, Bodleian Library, Bodley 343.[149] Also extant is the Latin epitome of Alcuin's *De ratione animae*, in the early eleventh-century MS Boulogne-sur-Mer, Bibliothèque Municipale 63, but scholars have not reached consensus regarding the date and authorship of this Latin piece, nor about its precise relationship with *LS* 1 and Belfour 9.[150]

As a group, the *Lives of Saints* were intended for private reading rather than liturgical preaching, but the Nativity homily is one of several pieces in *LS* that takes the form of a liturgical homily: Ælfric opens with a reference to the Gospel that would have been preached earlier during the Christmas Mass, and he refers to Christmas Day as 'this day.'[151] Belfour homily 9, moreover, was reworked by Ælfric into a more rhythmic and alliterative style, perhaps suggesting that he intended to make the homily more suitable for oral delivery. The new material that Ælfric added to Belfour 9 'in several instances … acts as a reminder of the occasion for which the homily was intended,'[152] and thereby links the homily more closely to the context of the liturgy of Christmas Day, a feast on which the laity certainly were expected to attend Mass. Wilcox has proposed no fewer than twelve specific scenarios in which the *Lives of Saints* were likely to have been read, publicly and privately, by lay and clerical and mixed audiences,[153] and though his vision may have been a reality for other pieces in the *Lives of Saints* series, it is not likely to have been realized in the case of the Nativity homily. The slim number of surviving manuscripts and

---

148 London, BL, Cotton Julius E. vii (s. xi in.); see Ker, *Catalogue*, no. 162, item 4.

149 Belfour homily 9 (ed. and trans. Belfour, *Twelfth-Century Homilies in MS. Bodley 343*, 78–97); see Clemoes, 'The Chronology of Ælfric's Works,' 56.

150 Godden attributes the Latin homily to Ælfric ('Anglo-Saxons on the Mind,' 296–8), while Leinbaugh argues against Ælfric's authorship ('Ælfric's *Lives of Saints* I and the Boulogne Sermon,' 197–9); on the relationship between Ælfric and the Latin homily see also Gatch, 'MS Boulogne-sur-Mer 63 and Ælfric's First Series of Catholic Homilies.' An edition of the Latin homily in Boulogne-sur-Mer 63 appears in Leinbaugh's unpublished 1980 PhD dissertation, 'The Liturgical Homilies in Ælfric's *Lives of Saints*.'

151 Ælfric, Nativity homily (*LS* 1), lines 1–5 (ed. Skeat, *LS*, 1.10); see Clayton, 'Homiliaries and Preaching,' 186; and Clemoes, 'The Chronology of Ælfric's Works,' 37–8.

152 Leinbaugh, 'Ælfric's *Lives of Saints* I and the Boulogne Sermon,' 194; see, for instance, the added material near the opening of Belfour 9 (ed. Belfour, *Twelfth-Century Homilies in MS. Bodley 343*, 84, lines 19–20).

153 J. Wilcox, 'The Audience of Ælfric's *Lives of Saints*,' 258–9.

also the nature of those manuscripts leaves it uncertain that the Nativity homily ever reached a significant audience of any kind.[154] In sum, both *LS* 1 and Belfour 9 appear to be liturgical homilies, but their surviving manuscript copies do not provide firm evidence of their actual use in the liturgy. It is appropriate therefore to be circumspect about the relationship between Ælfric's intended audience and the actual dissemination of his Nativity homily on the soul.

The Status of Cardiocentrism and the Hydraulic Model in the Age of Ælfric

Without any clear idea of how widely and how often lay audiences were exposed to Ælfric's teachings on the reality of incorporeals, we must look to texts of the eleventh century for signs of Ælfrician influence on popular materialism and folk psychology: this is the task I have undertaken in the epilogue that follows this chapter. Regardless of the actual degree to which the Anglo-Saxons assimilated Ælfric's teachings about incorporeality and the unitary soul, it is crucial to recognize that his homilies mark the very *earliest* efforts to transmit such ideas to a wide audience, and therefore this is the very earliest point in the history of Anglo-Saxon thought when any sustained and authoritative challenge threatened to uproot embodied concepts such as the cardiocentric localization of the soul, the mind-body complex, and the hydraulic model of mental activity. These features of the folk psychology that we have called the vernacular tradition, therefore, persisted among most Anglo-Saxons at least until Ælfric's day, and probably for a considerable length of time after that.

Because Ælfric's discourse on the eucharist is best known for its later appropriation by Protestant partisans in the early modern disputes over the nature of the eucharist, the pioneering significance of Ælfric's thought per se has been rather obscured and, as Paul Szarmach has pointed out, distorted by those who would impose the scholastic concept of transubstantiation upon

---

154 As for Belfour 9, Susan Irvine has observed that Oxford, Bodleian Library, Bodley 343, bearing none of the markings typically found in homiliaries used in preaching, was most likely intended for private devotional reading by monastics, or perhaps as 'a reading book for secular clergy which could be assimilated and adapted for use in preaching.' She further theorizes that the section of Bodley 343 in which Belfour 9 appears may have been culled from an earlier collection of homilies *quando uolueris*, since Belfour 9 is not known to have circulated with any of the other six pieces (three Ælfrician and three anonymous) in this section of the manuscript (*Old English Homilies from MS Bodley 343*, lii–liii and xlvii–l).

the 'bodily' transformation of the eucharist that Ælfric denies. Szarmach corrects those who would misconstrue Ælfric's word *lichamlice* as a reference to the real presence of Christ's body in the eucharistic bread: 'Ælfric is really talking about typological understanding, not transubstantiation.'[155] I agree, and I would add that Ælfric actually creates an oppositional relationship between that which is bodily (*lichamlice*) present and that which is truly present. On this point, Szarmach is more circumspect: 'The implication is that one might draw out of [Ælfric's] concept of *gastlice* the Christian-Platonic notion that only the spiritual is really real, but this gloss has yet to be established in Ælfrician vocabulary.'[156] Szarmach is prudent to withhold judgment on this matter on the basis of evidence within the Easter Day homily alone. Yet when we contextualize the Easter Day homily amid Ælfric's other discourses on the eucharist and on the soul, the most sensible way to account for his consistent anti-materializing stance is to conclude that Ælfric did indeed harbour a Platonist-Christian understanding of incorporeals as participants in a reality superior to that of visible bodies.

155 Szarmach, 'Ælfric as Exegete: Approaches and Examples in the Study of the *Sermones Catholici*,' 244.
156 Ibid., 244.

Epilogue: Challenges to Cardiocentrism and the Hydraulic Model during the Long Eleventh Century (ca. 990–ca. 1110)

According to the model of emergent metaphoricity that I proposed in chapter 3, a concept rooted in an embodied reality is reinforced by subjective experience and by idioms congruent with that experience; such a concept will function non-metaphorically in language and in thought until such time as a highly authoritative or inherently persuasive rival theory mounts a sustained challenge to the perception that the embodied reality and objective reality are one and the same. I have identified specific textual communities within Anglo-Saxon England that confronted challenges to cardiocentric psychology and the hydraulic model of the mind, most notably those challenges posed by Platonist-Christian discourse on the unitary and incorporeal soul. Before the end of the ninth century, assimilation of this rival psychology was restricted to the exceptionally learned, such as Bede and Alcuin. Persons of little or moderate education learned Donatus's grammatical concept of incorporeality rather than that of the Platonists, and they digested much more of the eclectic psychology of Gregory's *Dialogi* and Isidore's encyclopedic works than the philosophical psychology of Augustine or Claudianus Mamertus. Beginning in the late ninth or early tenth century, the integration of Boethius's *De consolatione philosophiae* into the literary curriculum and the availability of commentaries on this text increased the likelihood that an individual who attained an advanced, but not exceptional, education might also arrive at a more thoroughly Platonist understanding of the unitary soul and its incorporeality. But as the anonymous homilies suggest, among the functionally literate and the illiterate, vernacular psychology continued to thrive, including cardiocentrism, the hydraulic model, and the division of labour between *sawol* and *mod*.

Ælfric's homilies therefore represent the first evidence of a potential challenge to vernacular psychology at the lowest educational strata. Of course Ælfric's homilies did not single-handedly revolutionize Anglo-Saxon folk psychology; the point is rather that we have no evidence that vernacular psychology was seriously challenged at any but the highest educational strata prior to the dissemination of Ælfric's homilies during the period ca. 990–ca. 1010. By this time, most of our extant OE poetry, rich in cardiocentric and hydraulic-model idioms, had already been committed to parchment: in the Exeter Book (s. x^2), the Vercelli Book (s. x^2), Junius 11 (ca. 960 x 990), the Nowell Codex (s. x/xi), and the metres of the OE Boethius (s. x med.).[1] The poems in these codices – not to mention other verse such as Solomon and Saturn and the poems of the Anglo-Saxon Chronicle, and a substantial body of historical and hagiographical prose in OE – date to an era when only a tiny minority of literate Anglo-Saxons had any exposure to the sort of teachings on substance and on the soul that posed a serious challenge to vernacular psychology.

Present-day readers have typically approached the idiom of vernacular psychology with the initial assumption that it was used and understood metaphorically, but since this assumption is based more on our own deeply ingrained mind-body dualism and an overestimation of the availability of Platonist-Christian discourse in pre-Conquest England, I urge readers to adopt a different approach. Most authors and audiences of extant OE literature used and understood cardiocentric psychology and the hydraulic model literally rather than metaphorically, and therefore the burden of proof ought to rest upon the reader who wishes to demonstrate that a specific author or work employs hydraulic-model idioms metaphorically – a demonstration that could be effected by showing that the author or work in question emanated from a milieu that had already assimilated learned forms of discourse that conflicted with and supplanted the embodied concepts associated with the vernacular tradition in Anglo-Saxon psychology.

Two brief examples will illustrate how such a demonstration might work (and how the two halves of this book fit together). As a very simple example, consider The Seafarer: is the idea of the mind-in-the-breast used metaphorically in this poem? Clemoes has argued that The Seafarer

---

1 For the Exeter Book, Vercelli Book, Nowell Codex, and metres of the OE Boethius (London, BL, Cotton Otho A.vi) I follow Ker's dating (Catalogue, nos 116, 394, 216, and 167). I have elsewhere argued for an earlier and narrower window of time, ca. 960 x 990, for the inception of the Junius 11 manuscript and the copying of its first four texts (Genesis A, Genesis B, Exodus, Daniel): see Lockett, 'An Integrated Re-examination of Oxford, Bodleian Library, MS Junius 11.'

draws its material on the flight of the mind directly from Alcuin's *De ratione animae*, while Diekstra points out that the relevant passage in Alcuin is quoted nearly verbatim from Lactantius's *De opificio Dei*; it is difficult to tell which served as the *Seafarer*-poet's proximate source.[2] If Clemoes's argument could be bolstered by the identification of further source texts that transmit Platonist-Christian discourse on the nature of the unitary, incorporeal soul, then one could build a solid case that *The Seafarer* emerged from a textual community that understood the *sawol* and the *mod* in much the same way that Alfred, or perhaps even Ælfric, did: in which case the idea of the *breostsefa* must be an archaism, an ornament, or even a conceptual metaphor, but not a literal expression of folk psychology, from the perspective of the author and his nearest audience. However, if no further psychological discourses can be securely identified as sources for *The Seafarer*, the Stoicizing text by Lactantius is the more likely inspiration for the flight-of-the-mind material, since the vernacular psychology evidenced throughout *The Seafarer* is sharply at odds with the unitary, incorporeal *anima* of Alcuin's *DRA*. It would follow that *The Seafarer* invokes the concept of the *breostsefa* most likely as a literal representation of one aspect of the vernacular tradition in psychology, and that the poem was generated by a milieu that had access to Lactantius's Stoicizing opinions, including the cardiocentric localization of the mind and the corporeality of the soul. As this example shows, when evaluating the psychological content of OE literature, it is important to keep in mind that the identification of a Latin source text for an OE work does *not* imply that the work emerged from a milieu whose Latin textual resources approached substance, soul, and mind from an exclusively Platonist-Christian perspective.

A second example, worthy of further investigation, is that of the metrical *Solomon and Saturn*. Daniel Anlezark has recently advanced a compelling argument that links the corpus of *Solomon and Saturn* materials to Dunstan's circle at Glastonbury in the 940s and 950s, based on similarities of technical vocabulary, style, and subject matter between *Solomon and Saturn* and certain texts thought to have been studied and copied at Glastonbury.[3] None of the similarities noted by Anlezark has to do with the *ratio animae*, but the intellectual community at Glastonbury was demonstrably

---

2 See chapter 4 above, as well as chapter 5 for a similar ambiguity in the source study of the second *Lorsch Riddle*.
3 Anlezark, *The Old English Dialogues of Solomon and Saturn*, 49–57.

engaged in the study of Boethius's *Consolatio*[4] and therefore may well have absorbed the Platonist-Christian doctrine of the unitary soul. An understanding of *sawol* as pragmatically synonymous with *sefa* and *mod* may even underlie a passage in the metrical *Solomon and Saturn*, where God is called 'seofan snytro and saule hunig / and modes meolc.'[5] If further study reinforces the impression that the Glastonbury community of the mid-tenth century was studying Platonist-Christian discourse on the soul while also composing OE verse, then any poems composed there would have to be counted among the earliest witnesses to the metaphorization of the mind-in-the-heart, of the hydraulic model (which is invoked at *MSol* 59b–62), and of any features of vernacular psychology that conflict with the unitary, incorporeal soul of Platonist-Christian discourse.

I have chosen Ælfric's homilies as the endpoint of the present study for two reasons. I do not suppose that Ælfric's homilies actually exercised an immediate and far-reaching influence on Anglo-Saxon folk psychology, but only that his homilies represent the first texts that had the *potential* to do so, even if their practical effects were rather limited. The fact that this change was initiated after most OE poetry was already preserved in written form is sufficient to address the central question that launched this study, concerning the relationship between what the Anglo-Saxons wrote about the mind and what they believed about the mind; consequently, to extend this study through the end of the Anglo-Saxon period would not appreciably advance our understanding of the psychological idiom of most of the texts in the OE poetic corpus.

The second reason to conclude with Ælfric is that his career coincided with the onset of several significant and rapid changes in the Anglo-Saxon intellectual landscape. A study of the changes in Anglo-Saxon psychological narrative and discourse throughout the century or so following Ælfric's death would have to account for a massive influx of new theological, philosophical, and medical texts; the assimilation of dialectic into the psychological discourse of authors such as Lanfranc and Anselm, whose illustrious careers were spent partly in England; changes in the elementary educational curriculum; and changes in the liturgy and in the administrative structure of the Church, which altered the organization of pastoral care and increased the lay population's exposure to catechesis and

---

4 See Godden's discussion, with bibliography, of the Glastonbury hands that glossed and annotated the copy of the *Consolatio* in Vatican City, BAV, Vat. lat. 3363 ('Alfred, Asser, and Boethius,' 335–7).
5 *MSol* 66–7a: 'wisdom of the mind and honey of the soul and milk of the mind.'

preaching. By the early twelfth century the dynamics of psychological discourse itself and of its dissemination were markedly different from those that existed in Ælfric's day. I close this study, therefore, with brief illustrations of the ways in which these changes expanded the range of textual communities that confronted Platonist-Christian psychological discourse and other challenges to the vernacular psychological tradition.

The Importation and Copying of Patristic Theological Texts

During the past two or three decades, as literary scholars have moved away from the pan-allegorical interpretation of all OE literature through an Augustinian lens, historians have shown that the eleventh- and twelfth-century availability of many Augustinian and other patristic texts in England was a new development. From the point of view of the continental scholars who arrived in the later tenth century to assist in the work of reforming English Benedictine monasticism, and even more from the perspective of continental ecclesiastics who occupied many English abbacies and episcopacies after the Conquest, Anglo-Saxon libraries seemed 'eccentric,' as Rodney Thomson has observed, because of the 'noticeable absence of central patristic works, in particular the major works of Augustine, Jerome and Ambrose (there is of course some Gregory).' Carolingian biblical commentaries were scarce, while books belonging to the elementary educational curriculum, particularly grammars, were proportionally overrepresented in Anglo-Saxon libraries.[6] From the late tenth century up to the first half of the twelfth, the acquisition and copying of new patristic texts increased markedly. At first, around the year 1000, the trend is noticeable but limited in scope. By the later eleventh century, several centres – mostly cathedrals – were engaged in a program of systematic acquisition and copying of patristic texts with which to augment their libraries, and by the middle of the twelfth century, most major libraries had a fairly large and standardized collection of patristic writings.[7] Based on the large proportion

---

6 Thomson, 'The Norman Conquest and English Libraries,' 29. See also Webber, 'The Patristic Content of English Book Collections in the Eleventh Century,' 192. Webber additionally points out that in the tenth century, many continental libraries were no better stocked with patristic materials than were Anglo-Saxon libraries; the surge in the transmission of patristic literature in post-Conquest England was part of a larger movement across western Europe to acquire the staples of patristic teaching (ibid., 197).
7 Thomson, 'The Norman Conquest and English Libraries,' 33–8; Webber, 'The Patristic Content of English Book Collections,' 197, 203.

of manuscripts of patristic literature used in late Anglo-Saxon England that were either imported from the continent or copied from continental exemplars, it appears that such works had been unavailable in England when demand for them arose in the late tenth and eleventh centuries, and that many of the patristic works known to Aldhelm, Bede, and Alcuin had been lost during the ninth century.[8] That such books were neglected, lost, and destroyed during the ninth century is corroborated not only by Alfred's late ninth-century lament about the state of learning in England but also by several studies demonstrating that manuscript and charter evidence support Alfred's gloomy assessment.[9]

The upsurge in the importation and copying of patristic texts expanded the range and quality of psychological discourse available to scholars in England. Chapter 4 above included a list of the major patristic discussions of the soul, with summaries of the evidence for their presence and use in England. Among those that I classified as Platonist-Christian in orientation, many that became available in eleventh-century manuscripts were either wholly unattested in England in previous centuries, or else were attested only by eighth-century evidence. Among the texts that were copied or acquired anew between the late tenth and late twelfth centuries are numerous works by Augustine in which discourse on the nature of the soul features prominently: there survive from this period two manuscripts of the *Confessiones*, two of *De ciuitate Dei*, three of *De Genesi ad litteram*, two of *De Trinitate*, one of *Epistola* 147 (*De uidendo Deo*), one of the *Soliloquia*, three of *De anima et eius origine*, one of *De quantitate animae*, and two of *De uera religione*. This period also saw the copying or acquisition of one extant copy of Cassiodorus's *De anima*, two extant copies of Alcuin's *De ratione animae*, and four extant copies of Ambrose's *Hexameron*.[10] Over the course of the eleventh century, Salisbury Cathedral Library became a veritable repository of psychological doctrines: the

8 Rella, 'Continental Manuscripts Acquired for English Centers,' 107; Webber, 'The Patristic Content of English Book Collections,' 194–5; Hall, 'Biblical and Patristic Learning,' 334–6.

9 Alfred, Preface to the *Pastoral Care* (ed. Sweet, *Pastoral Care*, 3–7). Gneuss, 'King Alfred and the History of Anglo-Saxon Libraries,' argues that the Vikings were not entirely to blame for the decline in English learning; evidence suggests that available books were sorely neglected already prior to the climax of the Vikings' violence against English centres of learning in the mid-to-late ninth century. See also Gameson, 'Alfred the Great and the Production and Destruction of Christian Books,' who makes the interesting argument that the ninth-century losses suffered by Anglo-Saxon libraries, though devastating, were the norm rather than the exception among book-owning cultures of antiquity and the Middle Ages.

10 Lapidge, *Library*; Gneuss, *Handlist*; see also chapter 4 above.

books held or produced there by the year 1100 included Augustine's *Confessiones, De quantitate animae, De uera religione, De Genesi ad litteram, De anima et eius origine,* and *Soliloquia;* Gregory's *Dialogi,* Gennadius's *De ecclesiasticis dogmatibus,* Alcuin's *De ratione animae,* and by the early twelfth century, even Calcidius's commentary on Plato's *Timaeus.*[11] Salisbury's holdings were unusually rich in patristic psychologies, even for the eleventh century, but it is fair to say that most centres of English learning that were thriving during the eleventh century acquired some texts that gave their communities of users better access to Platonist-Christian concepts of the soul and of incorporeality.

Theological Discourse in Post-Conquest England

Scholars trained on the continent who took up ecclesiastical posts in England during the post-Conquest period brought not only their patristic source texts but also their own theological writings, many of which demonstrate the same facility with Platonist-Christian ontology and Aristotelian dialectic that characterized Carolingian conversations about the soul. The last two men to hold the archbishopric of Canterbury during the eleventh century, Lanfranc of Bec (1070–89) and his student and successor Anselm of Bec (1093–1109) were both continental scholars, trained in cathedral schools. Among Lanfranc's writings are a set of notes concerning Latin translations of Plato's *Timaeus* and a treatise *De corpore et sanguine Domini* refuting the eucharistic theology of Berengar of Tours;[12] Anselm's *Proslogion* and *Cur Deus homo,* among others, represent the earliest phase of scholastic theology. Admittedly Lanfranc and Anselm are representative

---

11 Gneuss, *Handlist,* nos 581, 697, 715, 717, 720, 728, 749.5, 752; on the copy of Calcidius, see Webber, *Scribes and Scholars at Salisbury Cathedral,* 85. This is not an exhaustive list. One continental manuscript with an eleventh-century Salisbury provenance suggests that it was compiled by somebody with a particular interest in Platonist-Christian discourse on the soul: Oxford, Bodleian Library, Bodley 516 contains Augustine's *De uidendo Deo,* Cassiodorus's *De anima,* and part of Augustine's *De quantitate animae* all in one volume (Gneuss, *Handlist,* no. 581; Rella, 'Continental Manuscripts Acquired for English Centers,' 114). Webber describes the codex as 'a ninth-century miscellany of patristic and penitential texts, copied in northern Italy: It was in Brittany or Wales by the tenth century, and in England by the eleventh' (*Scribes and Scholars at Salisbury Cathedral,* 79). Another Salisbury holding suggests a more eclectic attitude toward the nature of the soul: Salisbury, Cathedral Library 165, fols 122–78, contains Alcuin's *De ratione animae* back-to-back with Gennadius's *De ecclesiasticis dogmatibus* (Gneuss, *Handlist,* no. 749.5; copied at Salisbury in the late eleventh century).

12 See Gibson, *Lanfranc of Bec,* esp. 12–15 on Lanfranc's early education on the continent, and 39–50 on the role of grammar and dialectic in his scholarship.

of the most sophisticated theological influences on English thought rather than of the typical theological output of English writers of the eleventh century. Such a topic is impossible to survey in a short space, but I would like to adduce one example of an author, now little known to literary historians, whose education was fairly mediocre for his day but who nonetheless assimilated Platonist-Christian psychology to an extent that would have made him an outstanding figure on the intellectual landscape just a century earlier.

Patrick of Dublin's De tribus habitaculis animae

Several poems and a prose treatise *De tribus habitaculis animae* are attributed to a certain Patrick, bishop of Dublin (1074–84), a native of Ireland who became a Benedictine monk and was educated at Worcester, under the tutelage of St Wulfstan, who was prior of the Benedictine monastery and later bishop of Worcester (1062–95). Patrick sent a copy of his prose treatise to his old friends at Worcester, accompanied by at least one of the poems attributed to him (*Perge, carina*).[13] The prose treatise was already circulating in England before the end of the eleventh century and became quite popular in English Cistercian circles during the twelfth century; the poems were less widely disseminated, and the earliest surviving manuscript of *Constet quantus honos*, a poem of considerable interest in the present discussion, dates to the later twelfth century.[14] Patrick was learned but not extraordinarily so, and the diction and style of his works are accessible rather than ostentatiously erudite.

One of Patrick's poems begins 'Constet quantus honos humane conditionis / Scire uolens, huius serie uideat rationis': these lines foreshadow that the remainder of the poem takes up the theme that human nature

---

13 Gwynn reconstructs Patrick's career and demonstrates his authorship of the prose treatise and four poems (*The Writings of Bishop Patrick*, 8–13). He estimates that none of Patrick's extant Latin poems was composed before he undertook his schooling at Worcester; the poem *Perge, carina*, which serves as the *envoi* to the *Liber de tribus habitaculis animae*, indicates that the prose treatise and that poem were written in Ireland after Patrick had departed from Worcester. On the intellectual life and manuscript culture at Worcester during Patrick's time, see Gameson, 'St Wulfstan, the Library of Worcester and the Spirituality of the Medieval Book.'

14 Gwynn, *The Writings of Bishop Patrick*, 21–8; MSS of Patrick's works are catalogued at 28–53. Gwynn notes that Mario Esposito generated a list of several dozen MSS containing *De tribus habitaculis animae*; in contrast, Gwynn knew of only two copies of the poem *Constet quantus honos* (ibid., 13–14 and 27).

is noble because humans were made in the image of God.[15] The opening section paraphrases parts of the Creation story in Genesis and underscores that humans alone have reason and free will, because humans are the only creatures that God made deliberately and attentively, rather than by simply saying 'Fiant' (lines 3–20). As Patrick explores the many ways in which the image of God is reflected in human nature, he begins with the idea that both God and the human soul are non-spatially distributed and therefore indivisible, being whole in every part of the space with which they are associated.

Rex immortalis non dicitur esse localis.	25
Perfectus quippe deus est et totus ubique,	
Viuificando mouens et cunta mouendo gubernans.	
In cuntis totus manet et per singula totus,	
Non in maiori maior quam parte minori:	
Omnia sed totum capiunt et singula totum.	30
Spiritus humanus sic a factore creatus	
Est indiuisus mortali corpore missus,	
Viuificando mouens et membra mouendo gubernans.	
In cunctis eque uiget et per singula queque.	
Est in maiori pariter membroque minori	35
Integer et totus, perlustrans intima solus.[16]	

15 Patrick, *Constet quantus honos*, lines 1–2 (ed. Gwynn, *The Writings of Bishop Patrick*, 72): 'He who wishes to know how high the honour stands of man's nature, let him see it from the sequence of my reasoning' (trans. ibid., 73). This poem exhibits some striking resemblances to (but no verbatim quotations of) Alcuin's poem 'Qui mare, qui terram,' which also explores several aspects of the correspondence between the nature of God and the *ratio animae* (see chapter 6 above). Both poems consider the problem of the non-spatial distribution of incorporeals (an awkward discourse to adapt to quantitative Latin verse), and both authors employ the stylistic device of re-using a memorable verse describing God a few lines later in describing the soul, formally illustrating the notion that the *imago Dei* is impressed upon the soul. In Alcuin's case, he uses the line 'Qui mare, qui terram, coelum qui condidit altum' to refer to God, and a few lines later, he introduces the section on the soul with the line 'Quae mare, quae terras, coelum quae peruolat altum' (lines 1 and 11); Patrick writes that God is 'Viuificando mouens et cunta mouendo gubernans' and the soul is 'Viuificando mouens et membra mouendo gubernans' (lines 27 and 33; ed. Gwynn, *The Writings of Bishop Patrick*, 72).

16 Patrick, *Constet quantus honos*, lines 25–36 (ed. Gwynn, *The Writings of Bishop Patrick*, 72–4): 'The immortal King, we are taught, is not confined to space. For God is perfect and whole everywhere, giving life and movement to all, and ruling all by movement. In all things He abides, whole in all and whole in each: not greater in a greater part, not

Less than a century before, Ælfric was struggling to make his audience, laity and religious alike, understand the concept of strict incorporeality as it applied to the eucharist and to the human soul; by the mid-to-late eleventh century, the same idea was so elementary to an Irishman educated at Worcester that he could communicate it in leonine hexameters.

Patrick next explains how God's trinitarian nature is manifest in the unitary soul, which he calls both *mens* and *spiritus*. Like God, who is immutable, the soul will not die but will always exist, live, and know; like the triune God, the one mind is three distinct faculties, namely memory, will, and understanding.[17] The remainder of the poem, which runs to 107 lines altogether, is occupied with exhortations to make the *imago Dei* outwardly manifest, not by words alone, but by 'good character and actions.' A closer examination of Patrick's diction might reveal whether he adapted all his material directly from Augustine's *De Trinitate* or whether he also bolstered his psychological discourse with the *Soliloquia* or Claudianus Mamertus's *De statu animae*; for our purposes, it is significant enough that Patrick had access to one or more of these texts, read them, internalized them, and produced a literary rendering of several points of thoroughly Augustinian psychology, including the non-spatial distribution of the soul, which is one of the most counterintuitive corollaries of the notion of strict incorporeality.

Patrick's prose treatise *Liber de tribus habitaculis animae* likewise includes discourse on the notion of incorporeality, as both an ontological and an epistemological condition, but here it is blended in an unexpected fashion with traditional homiletic and apocryphal images of the corporeal torments of hell. The treatise begins with a description of the three dwellings of the soul: heaven, where everything is incomprehensibly wonderful; hell, where everything is incomprehensibly horrible; and earth, where the good and the bad mingle, and whence all souls are supplied to the other two dwellings. The pit of hell is haunted by the shades of tangible terrors such as 'doloris, fetoris, adustionis, sitis, famis, ignis inextinguibilis.'[18]

---

less in less, but all parts hold Him wholly and each wholly. Man's spirit, thus made by its Creator, is sent, undivided, to be in mortal body: giving life and movement, and ruling the limbs in movement. It lives equal in all, and in each separate limb: it is equally present in the greater and lesser limbs, whole and entire, penetrating alone the innermost parts' (trans. ibid., 73–5).

17 Patrick, *Constet quantus honos*, lines 39–71 (ed. Gwynn, *The Writings of Bishop Patrick*, 74–6).

18 Patrick, *Liber de tribus habitaculis animae*, lines 32–3 (ed. Gwynn, *The Writings of Bishop Patrick*, 108; editorial punctuation has been altered): 'pain, stench, burning, thirst, hunger, inextinguishable fire.'

As the Gospel of Matthew warns, there will be wailing and gnashing of teeth; Patrick further anthropomorphizes the souls of the damned as he explains, 'Fletus nanque et liquefactio oculorum ex calore nascitur: stridor uero dentium de frigore nascitur.'[19] Patrick does not follow the example of the *Dialogi*, in which Gregory modifies the traditionally corporeal-ized vision of hell by explaining that the suffering of the damned is purely psychological.[20] Yet in contrast to the anonymous OE homilies exam-ined in chapter 8 above, Patrick demands that his audience engage with a philosophically subtler understanding of the afterlife of the soul, during which its incorporeality is the basis for its capacity to see God face to face: 'uisibilibus delectari et corporalibus nichil est comparandum delectationi et gaudio quod nascitur ex inuisibilibus et incorporeis et ex societate an-gelorum et iustorum omnium et ex certa scientia et cognitione ipsius diuine nature et ex Dei ipsius uisione facie ad faciem.'[21] If the reader harbours any suspicion that Patrick might have taken literally the anthropomorphism of spiritual beings, that suspicion is effaced when Patrick characterizes God's 'body parts' as functionally interchangeable because they are incorporeal: 'cuius [*scil.* Dei] oculus flammiuomi profundum penetrat inferni: cuius auris tacitam cordis uocem audit, id est cogitationem: cuius oculus non minus audit quam uidet, cuius auris non minus uidet quam audit, quia non corpus sunt sed summa sapientia et certa cognitio.'[22] Patrick speaks of God in Boethian terms, as experiencing the entirety of creation in an eternal and simultaneous present;[23] additionally, to the souls of the blessed, Patrick attributes three epistemological faculties – *uisio corporalis, uisio*

---

19 Patrick, *Liber de tribus habitaculis animae*, lines 49–50 (ed. Gwynn, *The Writings of Bishop Patrick*, 108–110): 'Then weeping and watering of the eyes are caused by the heat, but the gnashing of teeth is caused by the cold.'
20 Gregory, *Dialogi* 4.30.2 (discussed in chapter 8 above).
21 Patrick, *Liber de tribus habitaculis animae*, lines 133–7 (ed. Gwynn, *The Writings of Bish-op Patrick*, 116): 'To be delighted by visible and corporeal things is nothing in comparison with the delight and joy which are born of invisible and incorporeal things, and from the company of angels and all the just, and from certain knowledge and understanding of the divine nature and from the experience of seeing God himself, face to face.'
22 Patrick, *Liber de tribus habitaculis animae*, lines 146–9 (ed. Gwynn, *The Writings of Bishop Patrick*, 116): 'God's eye penetrates into the abyss of hell that spews forth flames; God's ear hears the silent voice of the heart, that is, the understanding; God's eye no less hears than sees, and his ear no less sees than hears, because they are not a body but the highest wisdom and certain understanding.'
23 Patrick, *Liber de tribus habitaculis animae*, lines 183–4 and 216–19 (ed. Gwynn, *The Writings of Bishop Patrick*, 120 and 122).

spiritalis, and *uisio intellectualis* – paralleling Augustine's tripartite epistemological hierarchy of *sensus, cogitatio,* and *intellectus*.[24]

The fact that Patrick's works are little studied – that Patrick does not stand out as a major figure on the eleventh-century English intellectual landscape – is a testimony to the rapid advance of Platonist-Christian doctrines on the soul and on substance among men of moderate learning and unpretentious literary output. In terms of Patrick's achievement of an assimilation of Platonist-Christian thought into literary Latin, perhaps the most comparable writings to emerge from the previous three centuries of Anglo-Saxon literary history are the *De ratione animae*, which Alcuin wrote in Francia after years of access to some of the best collections of patristic literature available, and a certain *Carmen de libero arbitrio*, likely the work of Lantfred, a Frankish scholar whose knowledge of patristic and classical literature far outweighed that which was available to his colleagues during his stay in Winchester in the 970s (or, if not Lantfred, some other foreign scholar attached to Æthelwold's school in the later tenth century).[25] In other words, no English-educated scholar working with Insular library resources had produced anything quite like Patrick's *Constet quantus honos* and *De tribus habitaculis animae* since perhaps the time of Bede.

The Rise of Dialectic and Priscian's Grammar in English Elementary Education

Patrick's education might be called modest but it cannot be considered elementary. Yet the changes that make Patrick's work seem unremarkable for the product of a mid-eleventh-century English school were anchored in an increase in dialectic and a proportional decrease in Donatus-based study of grammar at the elementary stage of the curriculum. Manuscript evidence indicates that the turn toward dialectic was already occurring in the early tenth century, when copies of Themistius's *De decem categoriis*, Boethius's works on logic (which included translations, from the Greek, of Aristotle's

---

24   Patrick, *Liber de tribus habitaculis animae*, lines 249–55 (ed. Gwynn, *The Writings of Bishop Patrick*, 124).

25   The *Carmen de libero arbitrio* is edited and translated by Lapidge, 'Three Latin Poems from Æthelwold's School at Winchester,' 266–77; on the Boethian content and non-English authorship of the *Carmen de libero arbitrio*, see ibid., 242–7. Kleist reprints Lapidge's edition and translation and examines the theology of free will and grace in the *Carmen de libero arbitrio*: see *Striving with Grace: Views of Free Will in Anglo-Saxon England*, 121–44 and 272–81.

Categories and Porphyry's *Isagoge* as well as commentaries and manuals), and Alcuin's *De dialectica* were being produced and acquired in England. For example, Cambridge, CCC, 206, which was copied in England in the early tenth century, juxtaposes multiple works on dialectic, including Themistius, Boethius's translation of and second commentary on the *Isagoge*, and Alcuin's *De dialectica*, as well as Boethius's *Opuscula sacra*, which model the use of dialectic in theological argumentation.[26]

As discussed in chapter 5, the majority of late antique and Insular grammarians define the incorporeal as 'that which can be neither seen nor touched,' or some variation upon this sensory-based definition. The student who learned this definition of incorporeality, if he went on to study dialectic, had to discard the grammatical definition and replace it with a complex concept of incorporeality that was attached to qualities of immortality, immutability, and the capacity to perceive or to be perceived by other incorporeals. Consequently, where dialectic entered the early medieval curriculum, it was more expedient for students not to be misled by a Donatus-type definition of incorporeality in the first place. In his weighty *Institutiones grammaticae* Priscian treats both signifiers and things signified in a manner that is more philosophically precise and more compatible with a student's preparation for the study of dialectic than the grammars of the Donatus tradition. Among the Carolingians, the popularity of Priscian's *Institutiones* grew markedly in the century after the revival of dialectic and of the works of Boethius (both logical and theological), and eventually Priscian's unwieldy text was abridged and supplied with commentaries to make it more suitable for classroom use.[27] Roughly the same thing happened in Anglo-Saxon England. The copying of works of logic was on the rise in the early tenth century; at the end of the century, Ælfric used the *Excerptiones de Prisciano* as the basis for an OE grammar for students who were only beginning to learn Latin; and there survive four Anglo-Saxon copies of Priscian's *Institutiones* that are dated 's. xi?' or 's. xi/xii.' In comparison, the latest surviving Anglo-Saxon copy of either of Donatus's grammars is a Canterbury copy of the *Ars maior* dated 's. x/xi.'[28]

---

26 Gneuss, *Handlist*, no. 67; on Boethius's works on dialectic, see Marenbon, *Boethius*, 17–65.

27 Holtz, 'Les nouvelles tendances de la pédagogie grammaticale au Xᵉ siècle,' 167–71.

28 Lapidge, *Library*, 326 and 300. On the parallel prominence of Priscian in continental education in the mid-eleventh century, and the impact of Priscian's language theory on theological argumentation, see Gibson, *Lanfranc of Bec*, esp. 46–8; and Gibson, 'Milestones in the Study of Priscian, circa 800–circa 1200,' 28–33.

Priscian's *Institutiones* and related grammars (i.e., the *Excerptiones* and Ælfric's *Grammar*) did not fix the problem of the oversimplification of incorporeality; they merely circumvented it. The compiler of the *Excerptiones de Prisciano* used Priscian's other works as well as Donatus's *Ars maior* to supplement what he gleaned from the *Institutiones*, and he reorganized the Priscianic material into an arrangement that users of Donatus would already have been familiar with.[29] The compiler of the *Excerptiones* defines the noun as a part of speech 'that attributes common or proper quality to each of the bodies or things subject to it,' and he asserts that both common and proper quality can be attributed to *incorporalia* as well as to *corporalia*. Although the compiler substitutes the Christian incorporeals *angelus* and *Michael* for Priscian's *uirtus* and *Pudicitia*,[30] he remains true to Priscian's example by paying no special attention to the substances of the things to which nouns refer. The nouns *God* and *reason* and *mind* are singled out not as incorporeals but only because they belong to another semantic class, that of 'absolute' nouns: 'que per se intelliguntur et non egent alterius conexione nominis, ut *deus, ratio, mens*.'[31]

Ælfric's chief source for his vernacular *Grammar* was the *Excerptiones*, but because he intended his *Grammar* to be used by beginners, he omitted the most complex material retained in the Latin *Excerptiones*, to the extent that 'the level of the doctrine rarely rises above that of the *Ars maior*,' and he added a greater selection of conjugational and declensional paradigms.[32] Like the compiler of the Latin *Excerptiones*, Ælfric refused to indulge in digressions about the substance of the referents of nouns.[33] His definition

---

29 As Vivien Law has characterized the *Excerptiones*, 'The compiler's aim was to discover what Priscian had to say about the subjects included in Donatus's *Ars maior*' (Law, *GG*, 204). Porter argues cautiously in favour of Ælfric's authorship of the *Excerptiones* (*Excerptiones de Prisciano*, 23–30), but Law points out that a French manuscript of the *Excerptiones*, roughly contemporary with the two early eleventh-century Anglo-Saxon copies but textually antecedent to them, makes a continental origin more probable (Law, *GG*, 203–4).

30 *Excerptiones de Prisciano* 2.1 and 2.7 (ed. Porter, *Excerptiones de Prisciano*, 60 and 62); cf. Priscian, *Institutiones grammaticae*, 2.22 and 2.26 (*GL* 2.56.28–57.1 and 2.59.10–13).

31 *Excerptiones de Prisciano* 2.21 (ed. Porter, *Excerptiones de Prisciano*, 66): 'These nouns are understood on their own and do not need to be further specified by a second name, such as *God, reason, mind*.' Cf. Priscian, *Institutiones grammaticae*, 2.31 (*GL* 2.62.5–6), where *deus* and *ratio* are named but not *mens*.

32 Law, *GG*, 207–8.

33 For instance, Ælfric retains Priscian's definition of *uox* (*Institutiones* 1.1; *GL* 2.5.1–4) but does not suggest that this definition was ever philosophically controversial, and he neither reproduces nor contradicts Priscian's characterization of sound as a body with

of the noun conspicuously omits the distinction between *corpus* and *res* that had been a permanent fixture in both the Donatus tradition and in Priscian: 'Nomen is nama, mid ðam we nemnað ealle ðing ægðer ge synderlice ge gemænelice. Synderlice be agenum naman: *Eadgarus, Aðelwoldus*; gemænelice: *rex* cyning, *episcopus* bisceop.'[34] Where Ælfric introduces the different classes of noun, he defies countless precedents and removes *corporalia* and *incorporalia* from the head of the list, beginning instead with *primitiua* or simplex nouns. The fifth class on Ælfric's list is '*incorporalia*, þæt is, unlichamlice, swa swa is *angelus* engel, *Michael, Gabriel, Raphael,*' but *corporalia* are not distinguished as a class unto themselves.[35] Like the compiler of the Latin *Excerptiones*, Ælfric pays special attention to the nouns '*deus* god, *ratio* gescead, *mens* mod' only because they belong to the class of absolute nouns; no mention is made of the substance of their referents.[36]

In fact, at the loci where the grammarians of the Donatus tradition indulge their curiosity about the meaning of incorporeality, Ælfric says so little about substance that a student would likely learn more about incorporeals from altogether unrelated loci in the *Grammar*, such as appearances of the term *unlichamlice* in morphological contexts. Third-declension nouns in –*or*, explains Ælfric, include agentive masculine nouns such as *doctor* and *salinator*, as well as '*incorporalia*, þæt synd unlichamlice: *hic furor* ðeos hatheortnyss, *horror* oga, *labor* geswinc, *sudor* swat, *pallor* blacung, *pudor* sceamu, *decor* wlite, *calor* hæte, *feruor* wylm, *rubor* readnys oððe sceamu, *algor* cyle.'[37] It is wholly counterintuitive to consider physical attributes such as sweat and heat and redness to be incorporeal, but here Ælfric is laying the groundwork for his students to understand one of the most prominent concerns in the Porphyrian and Boethian

---

threefold extension in space. See Ælfric, *Grammar* (ed. Zupitza, *Aelfrics Grammatik und Glossar*, 4): 'Stemn is geslagen lyft gefredendlic on hlyste, swa micel swa on ðære heorcnunge is' (Sound is air that has been struck, perceptible to the sense of hearing, to the extent that someone is listening).

34 Ælfric, *Grammar* (ed. Zupitza, *Aelfrics Grammatik und Glossar*, 8): 'A *nomen* is the name with which we name all things, either specifically or generally: specifically, by an individual's name, such as *Edgar, Æthelwold*; generally, such as *rex* "king," or *episcopus* "bishop."'

35 Ælfric, *Grammar* (ed. Zupitza, *Aelfrics Grammatik und Glossar*, 11–12): 'incorporeals, that is, non-bodily things, such as *angelus* "angel," *Michael, Gabriel*, and *Raphael*.'

36 Ælfric, *Grammar* (ed. Zupitza, *Aelfrics Grammatik und Glossar*, 14).

37 Ælfric, *Grammar* (ed. Zupitza, *Aelfrics Grammatik und Glossar*, 47). The nouns listed mean *anger, horror, toil, sweat, paleness, modesty, beauty, heat, seething, redness* or *shame*, and *coldness*.

writings on dialectic and on universals: sweat (or perhaps 'sweatiness'), heat, and redness are incorporeals because they are not bodies that exist on their own but rather accidental qualities that inhere in bodies. Ælfric does not supply any further explanation of the incorporeality of accidents; that topic is proper to dialectic, not morphology. Nor does he teach an oversimplified, sensory-oriented concept of incorporeality that would ill serve those students who would later proceed to the study of dialectic. The general neglect of substance per se in eleventh-century Priscianic treatments of nouns may have left elementary grammar students without any firm understanding of the practical meaning of incorporeality, but when those same students advanced to the *De decem categoriis* or Alcuin's *De dialectica*, it was surely better for them to harbour no preconceptions about substance than to have a philosophically inadequate conception of incorporeality.

Stasis in the Homiletic Corpus

For evidence of what the general populace was learning about the nature of the soul in the eleventh century, we may turn again to the homiletic corpus. Although the homilies of Ælfric represent a major turning-point in the history of Anglo-Saxon thought about psychology and ontology, the homilies copied and composed in the century that followed Ælfric's career did not adopt his anti-materialist zeal. I have not performed an exhaustive study of psychological discourse, eschatological narratives, and soul-body dialogues in eleventh- and twelfth-century homilies, but the texts that I have examined demonstrate that (aside from the proliferation of Ælfric's *Catholic Homilies*) any new developments in homiletics, whether in the form of new Anglo-Saxon compositions or of newly available Latin texts, offered very little that might challenge the vernacular tradition of cardiocentrism and the division of labour between *sawol* and *mod*.

In a very broad sense, the increased availability of patristic texts in the eleventh century likely led some homilists and preachers to promote a more Platonizing psychology than their predecessors, possibly in ways that are not prominent in the textual record. We have no way to know, for instance, how often a preacher who had access to a manuscript like Bodley 516 might have rejected apocrypha and soul-body dialogues as sources for his own homilies because he no longer considered the anthropomorphic soul to be sufficiently orthodox.[38] But I have found little specific textual

---

38 On Bodley 516, see n. 11 above.

evidence that Platonist-Christian thought exercised any greater influence over Anglo-Saxon preaching during the eleventh century than it had pre- viously. Gregory the Great's *Homiliae in Hiezechihelem* deserve special mention, because homily 2.5 in this series incorporates a brief discussion of the non-spatial distribution of the soul within the body and the rela- tionship between that indivisibility and the soul's powers of perception.[39] This series of homilies seems not to have circulated as a group in pre- Conquest England, and while some of the *Homiliae in Hiezechihelem* ap- peared earlier in augmented versions of the homiliary of Paul the Deacon, homily 2.5 was not among them. In the eleventh century, however, Greg- ory's *Homiliae in Hiezechihelem* came to be very popular: eight surviving Anglo-Saxon manuscripts of the series belong to the period between the mid-eleventh and early twelfth centuries.[40]

At the same time, the materialism that Ælfric had battled in the preach- ing of his contemporaries persisted in the homilies that were copied during the eleventh and twelfth centuries. Quite a few of the anonymous hom- ilies adduced above in chapter 8, which depict anthropomorphic souls in the afterworld and cast the *sawol* as an ineffectual and impersonal entity while it resides in the body, are preserved in eleventh- and twelfth-century copies; in fact, some of the most fascinating compilations of vernacular psychological material postdate Ælfric. In the previous chapter I briefly mentioned the early- and mid-eleventh-century compilation London, BL, Cotton Otho C. i, vol. 2, which juxtaposes Ælfric's *De creatore et crea- tura* with Wærferth's translation of Gregory's *Dialogues*, the OE transla- tion of Boniface's account of the Monk of Much Wenlock, and a homily incorporating the 'Evil tongues' motif associated with the *Visio Pauli* tradition.[41] The OE *Visio Pauli* itself appears in another mid-eleventh cen- tury compilation, Oxford, Bodleian Library, Junius 85 and 86, alongside a soul's-address homily (Fadda homily 8) and a homily that threatens the souls of the damned with vividly corporeal punishments (Fadda homily 1).[42] Ælfric's anti-materialist writings offered a corrective to the vernacular tradition, but throughout the eleventh century Ælfric's homilies still had to compete for the lay audience's attention with homilies that reinforced aspects of vernacular psychology.

---

39 Gregory, *Homiliae in Hiezechihelem* 2.5.9–10 (ed. Morel, SC 360, 242–6).
40 Hall, 'The Early English Manuscripts of Gregory the Great's *Homilies on the Gospel and Homilies on Ezechiel*,' 130–5; see also Lapidge, *Library*, 305.
41 Ker, *Catalogue*, no. 182.
42 Ker, *Catalogue*, no. 336.

Cephalocentrism and the Influx of Medical Texts

Aside from homilies, another segment of the textual record that may be pertinent to the status of folk psychology among the general population is the medical literature of Anglo-Saxon England. Though the relationship between written medical texts and the practice of medicine is fairly obscure across the early medieval West,[43] it is reasonable to suppose that medical doctrines might occasionally be transmitted orally by practising physicians, and that such doctrines might be received very favourably by patients if they were associated with efficacious medical practices. Some of the Latin medical texts that became available during the eleventh century are the foremost sources of cephalocentric psychology attested in Anglo-Saxon England. These texts therefore deserve attention for their potentially compelling challenge to the cardiocentrism of the vernacular tradition.

If we base our assessment on surviving manuscripts alone, the corpus of medical literature that was demonstrably in circulation during the ninth and tenth centuries was small and was dominated by OE texts.[44] The most significant of these are Bald's *Leechbook*, probably compiled in the circle of Alfred during the late ninth century and preserved in a manuscript of the mid-tenth century;[45] *Leechbook III*, also preserved in a manuscript of the mid-tenth century;[46] the OE *Herbarium*, translated from the Latin in the mid-to-late tenth century;[47] and *Lacnunga*, compiled in the late tenth or early eleventh century.[48] Audrey Meaney has demonstrated that several further manuscript witnesses to OE materials in these texts are either datable to the period before Alfred or show linguistic signs of predating Alfred.[49] In addition to these OE texts, there circulated in pre-1000 England at least one recension of the

---

43 On the relationship between text and practice in Anglo-Saxon medicine, see Meaney, 'The Practice of Medicine in England about the Year 1000'; and for a broader view of the problem, see Riddle, 'Theory and Practice in Medieval Medicine.'

44 For an overview of the medical literature available in ninth- and tenth-century England, see Banham, 'A Millennium in Medicine?' 230–2; and Hollis, 'Scientific and Medical Writings.' Hollis also surveys evidence for knowledge of classical medicine in England during the seventh and eighth centuries (ibid., 194–6).

45 *Bald's Leechbook* is edited by Cockayne, *Leechdoms, Wortcunning and Starcraft*, 2.2–298; on this text, its dating, and its sources, see esp. Meaney, 'Variant Versions of Old English Medical Remedies'; and M.L. Cameron, 'Bald's *Leechbook*: Its Sources and their Use in its Compilation.'

46 *Leechbook III* is edited by Cockayne, *Leechdoms, Wortcunning and Starcraft*, 2.300–60.

47 The *OE Herbarium* is edited, with facing-page Latin text, by de Vriend, *The Old English Herbarium and Medicina de Quadrupedibus*.

48 The *Lacnunga* is now edited by Pettit, *Anglo-Saxon Remedies, Charms, and Prayers*.

49 Meaney, 'Variant Versions of Old English Medical Remedies.'

Latin *Herbarium*,[50] as well as the fourth book of Isidore's *Etymologiae*, entitled *De medicina*, which treats the history of medicine, humoral theory, diseases, and medical remedies and equipment.[51] Neither individually nor as a group do these medical texts articulate any coherent theory of the mind-body relationship, although they all exhibit some degree of mind-body holism, in that they address (what we would consider to be) mental disturbances by prescribing special diets and ingested medicines that target the organic origins of such disturbances. A few passages in these texts identify the brain as the organic origin of illnesses with a mental component, particularly in the case of epilepsy; yet other organs, including the heart and the belly, are also implicated in mental disorders and changes in temperament, so on the whole these texts promote no *special* relationship between the brain and the mind.[52]

To some extent, the eclectic nature of the medical texts surviving from pre-1000 England is a consequence of the accumulation of doctrines from diverse medical traditons: some of the recipes and remedies are apparently derived from native traditions in practical medicine, while Latin medical texts and Latin translations of Greek medical texts have been identified as the ultimate sources of a significant portion of this material as well.[53] Except for the *Herbarium*, there survives no manuscript evidence for the circulation of these Latin and Greek works in England before ca. 1000, so it is unclear whether the compilers of OE medical texts had direct access to their source texts in unabridged form, or whether they had recourse only to florilegia and digests. Banham maintains that the eleventh century saw the *first* arrival of many complete Latin medical texts that hitherto had been known indirectly or in excerpts; Cameron, in contrast, argues that many if not most of the identifiable Latin sources of the OE medical literature were directly available to the compilers.[54]

Most of the Latin and Greek sources identified by Cameron and others belong to the Galenic tradition, which localizes the mind in the brain. James McIlwain has demonstrated that unequivocally cephalocentric psychological doctrines are present in most of the Latin works identified as sources of the OE medical texts:

---

50 Banham, 'A Millennium in Medicine?' 232–3.
51 On the dissemination of Isidore's *Etym.* in Anglo-Saxon England, see chapter 4 above.
52 For further discussion, see Lockett, 'Anglo-Saxon Knowledge of the Functions of the Brain.'
53 See esp. M.L. Cameron, *Anglo-Saxon Medicine*, 65–99.
54 Banham, 'A Millennium in Medicine?' 232–7; cf. M.L. Cameron, 'Bald's *Leechbook*: Its Sources and Their Use in its Compilation,' who assumes that a Latin source was known directly if it is translated verbatim by the compiler of an OE medical text (154–5).

For example, the *Practica Alexandri* or *Latin Alexander* refers to the head as the place 'where exists the chief comprehension of all senses' (*ubi princeps omnium sensuum est intellectus*) and identifies the *cerebrum* as 'where the soul dwells' (*ubi anima habitat*). The *Liber tertius* also speaks of the *cerebrum* 'in which the soul primarily lives' (*in quo principaliter anima habitat*).'[55]

McIlwain then takes Cameron's approach to the source-study evidence one step further. Although none of these Galenic texts survives in any pre-1000 Anglo-Saxon manuscript, he theorizes that a considerable body of Latin medical texts – integral texts, not excerpts or florilegia – must have been present in England from at least the late ninth century, when *Bald's Leechbook* was compiled, and perhaps even from the time of Bede; consequently, because of the overwhelmingly cephalocentric orientation of the psychological doctrines in these texts, the Anglo-Saxons must have been familiar with and favourably disposed toward cephalocentric theories of mind.[56]

This is not the only way to interpret the source-study evidence, however. McIlwain does not account for the fact that not a single one of the aforementioned passages that unequivocally localize the mind in the brain is quoted or paraphrased in any extant OE medical compilation. This suggests to me that *if* these Latin source texts actually were in circulation in pre-1000 England, then the compilers of the OE medical texts avoided and rejected passages localizing the mind in the brain, even as they approved and borrowed other content from the same texts. As for the putative pre-1000 circulation of Galenic source texts in Latin, in other scholarship on the state of Anglo-Saxon medical knowledge it has been observed that the presence of a few recipes or bits of lore from a particular Latin or Greek medical text cannot serve as definitive evidence that the compiler of an OE medical text had the whole of that Latin or Greek source at his disposal.[57]

Though I disagree with McIlwain's interpretation of the evidence for pre-1000 England, the great value of his essay is that he demonstrates

---

55 McIlwain, 'Brain and Mind in Anglo-Saxon Medicine,' 105; he also adduces evidence of cephalocentrism in Vindicianus's *Epitome altera*, in Marcellus's *De medicamentis liber*, the *Liber Esculapii*, and the *Passionarius Galeni*, all of which represent ultimate sources of material found in the OE medical literature (ibid., 105–8).
56 McIlwain, 'Brain and Mind in Anglo-Saxon Medicine.' The 'key assumption' underlying his interpretation of the source-study evidence, he writes, is 'that ideas articulated in identified sources, especially ideas found in more than one text, formed part of the collective, medical knowledge base of the Anglo-Saxons' (105).
57 P. Thompson, 'The Disease That We Call Cancer,' 4.

the prevalence of cephalocentrism in the medical texts that flowed into England during the eleventh century, and thereby he makes clear the potential for this material to pose a serious challenge to the cardiocentrism of Anglo-Saxon folk psychology once it began to circulate in England. Debby Banham has identified a number of Galenic writings that arrived in England, as integral texts rather than as excerpts, around the year 1000 or later: the *Passionarius Galeni* attributed to Gariopontus, the pseudo-Galenic *Liber tertius*, the *Liber Esculapii*, Galen's *Ad Glauconem de methodo medendi*, the *Liber Aurelii*, the *Practica Petrocelli*, and pseudo-Soranus's *In artem medendi isagoge*.[58] The simplest explanation for this influx of new medical learning in Latin, Banham hypothesizes, is that such books were required by Norman medical practitioners, whose arrival in England likely began during the reign of Edward the Confessor, and who would have been poorly served by the mostly vernacular medical compilations already available there.[59] I cannot begin to speculate how much time might have elapsed between the arrival of these texts and their assimilation by practising physicians, but I am confident that when this occurred, their localization of the mind in the brain served as a counterintuitive yet very persuasive theory to rival the concept of the mind-in-the-heart.

I suspect, moreover, that in those textual communities where cephalocentrism was accepted, its effects impinged not solely upon the community's perception of the mind's localization. Because the brain has no nerve endings that respond instantly to intense emotions, the adoption of a cephalocentric psychology is, effectively, the uncoupling of one's concept of the mind from the embodied experience of its activity, which is felt in the abdomino-thoracic cavity. Therefore, although any localization of the soul within a portion of the fleshly body is technically at odds with a strict Platonist understanding of the soul's incorporeality and non-spatial disposition, it is easier to reconcile a loosely incorporealist understanding of the unitary soul with a cephalocentric conception of the mind than with the embodied concept of the mind-in-the-heart.

Even this brief introduction to the fundamental changes to the content and size of Anglo-Saxon libraries during the long eleventh century brings to light a series of potential challenges to the cardiocentrism, the hydraulic model, and the division of labour between *mod* and *sawol* that characterized

---

58 Banham, 'A Millennium in Medicine?' 233.
59 Ibid., 237–9.

the vernacular tradition in Anglo-Saxon psychology. Further study of these changes to the English intellectual landscape through, say, the end of Anselm's archiepiscopacy in 1109 would be able to identify more precisely when and at which educational strata vernacular psychology was supplanted by Platonist-Christian doctrines on the soul and by cephalocentric medical doctrines. The content of libraries, the dominant mode of theological argumentation, the philosophical orientation of the school curriculum, the structure of Church administration and pastoral care, and the principles of practical medicine all underwent rapid and profound transformations during the long eleventh century. Nonetheless, the method by which I have evaluated the evolving relationship between embodied realities and counterintuitive rival theories in pre-1000 England, by assessing the degree of conflict between embodied and counterintuitive concepts at each intellectual stratum of Anglo-Saxon culture, is equally valid for the long eleventh century, and permits a more nuanced understanding of the gradual metaphorization of the idioms of vernacular psychology, which was brought about at different rates and by different means in various textual communities.

Bibliography

Primary Sources

Abbo of Fleury. *The Commentary on the Calculus of Victorius of Aquitaine.* Edited by A.M. Peden. Auctores Britannici Medii Aevi 15. Oxford: Oxford University Press, 2003.

Ælfric of Eynsham. *Admonitio ad filium spiritualem.* Edited and translated by Henry W. Norman. In *The Anglo-Saxon Version of the Hexameron of St. Basil ... and the Anglo-Saxon Remains of St. Basil's* Admonitio ad filium spiritualem, 31–57. 2nd ed. London, 1849.

– *Ælfric's Catholic Homilies: The First Series.* Edited by Peter Clemoes. EETS s.s. 17. Oxford: Oxford University Press, 1997.

– *Ælfric's Catholic Homilies: The Second Series.* Edited by Malcolm Godden. EETS s.s. 5. London: Oxford University Press, 1979.

– *Ælfric's De temporibus anni.* Edited by Heinrich Henel. EETS o.s. 213. London: Oxford University Press, 1942.

– *Ælfrics Grammatik und Glossar: Text und Varianten.* Edited by Julius Zupitza. Berlin, 1880. Reprinted with introduction by Helmut Gneuss. Hildesheim: Weidmann, 2003.

– *Ælfric's Lives of Saints.* Edited by Walter W. Skeat. EETS o.s. 76, 82, 94, and 114. London: Trübner, 1881–1900.

– *Ælfric's Prefaces.* Edited by Jonathan Wilcox. Durham: Durham Medieval Texts, 1994.

– *Exameron anglice, or The Old English Hexameron.* Edited by S.J. Crawford. BaP 10. Hamburg: H. Grand, 1921. Repr. Darmstadt: Wissenschaftliche Buchgesellschaft, 1968.

– *Die Hirtenbriefe Ælfrics in altenglischer und lateinischer Fassung.* Edited by Bernhard Fehr. BaP 9. Hamburg: H. Grand, 1914. Reprinted with introduction by Peter Clemoes. Darmstadt: Wissenschaftliche Buchgesellschaft, 1966.

- *Homilies of Ælfric: A Supplementary Collection.* Edited by John C. Pope. EETS o.s. 259–60. London: Oxford University Press, 1967–8.
- *Life of Saint Basil.* Edited by Gabriella Corona. In *Ælfric's Life of Saint Basil the Great: Background and Context.* Anglo-Saxon Texts 5. Cambridge: D.S. Brewer, 2006.

Æthelwold of Winchester. 'An Account of King Edgar's Establishment of Monasteries.' In *Councils and Synods with Other Documents Relating to the English Church I: A.D. 871–1204; Part I: 871–1066*, edited by Dorothy Whitelock, M. Brett, and C.N.L. Brooke, 142–54. Oxford: Clarendon Press, 1981.
- *Die angelsächsischen Prosabearbeitungen der Benediktinerregel*, edited by Arnold Schröer. BaP 2. Kassel: 1885–8. Reprinted with additions by Helmut Gneuss. Darmstadt: Wissenschaftliche Buchgesellschaft, 1964.

Alcuin of York. *De animae ratione liber ad Eulaliam·uirginem* [*De ratione animae*]. PL 101.639–50.
- *De ratione animae.* Edited and translated by J.J.M. Curry. In 'Alcuin, *De ratione animae*: A Text with Introduction, Critical Apparatus, and Translation.' PhD diss., Cornell University, 1966.
- *Epistolae.* Edited by Ernst Dümmler. MGH Epist. 4.18–481. Berlin, 1895.
- *Versus de patribus, regibus, et sanctis Euboricensis ecclesiae.* Edited by Ernst Dümmler. MGH PLAC 1.169–206. Berlin, 1881.
- *Versus de patribus, regibus, et sanctis Euboricensis ecclesiae.* Edited and translated by Peter Godman. In *Alcuin: The Bishops, Kings, and Saints of York.* Oxford: Clarendon Press, 1982.

Aldhelm of Malmesbury. *Aenigmata Aldhelmi.* Edited by Fr. Glorie. In *Collectiones aenigmatum merouingicae aetatis*, 367–540.
- *The Poetic Works.* Translated by Michael Lapidge and James Rosier. With an appendix by Neil Wright. Cambridge: D.S. Brewer, 1985.

Alfred the Great. *King Alfred's Old English Prose Translation of the First Fifty Psalms.* Edited by Patrick P. O'Neill. Cambridge, MA: The Medieval Academy of America, 2001.
- *King Alfred's Old English Version of Boethius, De consolatione philosophiae.* Edited by Walter John Sedgefield. Oxford, 1899. Repr. Darmstadt: Wissenschaftliche Buchgesellschaft, 1968.
- *King Alfred's Old English Version of St. Augustine's Soliloquies Turned into Modern English.* Translated by Henry Lee Hargrove. New York: Henry Holt, 1904.
- *King Alfred's Version of St. Augustine's Soliloquies.* Edited by Thomas A. Carnicelli. Cambridge, MA: Harvard University Press, 1969.
- *King Alfred's West-Saxon Version of Gregory's Pastoral Care.* Edited and translated by Henry Sweet. 2 vols. EETS o.s. 45, 50. London, 1871.

– *König Alfreds des Grossen Bearbeitung der Soliloquien des Augustinus*. Edited by Wilhelm Endter. BaP 11. Hamburg: H. Grand, 1922. Repr. Darmstadt: Wissenschaftliche Buchgesellschaft, 1964.

[?Alfred the Great.] *The Old English Boethius: An Edition of the Old English Versions of Boethius's* De Consolatione Philosophiae. Edited and translated by Malcolm Godden and Susan Irvine with Mark Griffith and Rohini Jayatilaka. 2 vols. Oxford: Oxford University Press, 2009.

Anlezark, Daniel, ed. and trans. *The Old English Dialogues of Solomon and Saturn*. Anglo-Saxon Texts 7. Cambridge: D.S. Brewer, 2009.

Aristotle. *Aristotle's Problems*. Edited and translated by W.S. Hett. 2nd ed. 2 vols. Loeb Classical Library, 316–17. Cambridge, MA: Harvard University Press, 1961.

– *Ars rhetorica*. Edited by Adolphus Roemer. Leipzig: Teubner, 1914.

– *De anima (On the Soul)*. Translated by Hugh Lawson-Tancred. London: Penguin, 1986.

– *Problèmes*. Edited and translated by Pierre Louis. 3 vols. Paris: Les Belles Lettres, 1991–4.

Arngart, Olof, ed. 'The Durham Proverbs.' *Speculum* 56 (1981): 288–300.

Asper. *Ars maior*. *GL* 5.547–54.

Asser. *Asser's Life of King Alfred, together with the Annals of Saint Neots*. Edited by William Henry Stevenson. With an introduction by Dorothy Whitelock. Oxford: Clarendon Press, 1959.

– *Life of King Alfred*. Translated by Simon Keynes and Michael Lapidge. In *Alfred the Great: Asser's Life of King Alfred and Other Contemporary Sources*, 66–110. New York: Penguin, 1983.

Assmann, Bruno, ed. *Angelsächsische Homilien und Heiligenleben*. BaP 3. Kassel, 1889. Reprinted with an introduction by Peter Clemoes. Darmstadt: Wissenschaftliche Buchgesellschaft, 1964.

Audax. *De Scauri et Palladii libris excerpta*. *GL* 7.320–61.

Augustine of Hippo. *Confessionum libri XIII*. Edited by Lucas Verheijen. CCSL 27. Turnhout: Brepols, 1981.

– *Contra epistolam Manichaei quam uocant Fundamenti*. Edited by J. Zycha. CSEL 25/1, 191–248. Vienna, 1891.

– *De civitate Dei*. Edited by Bernard Dombart and Alphonse Kalb. CCSL 47–8. Turnhout: Brepols, 1955.

– *De Genesi ad litteram libri duodecim*. Edited by J. Zycha. CSEL 28/1, 1–435. Vienna, 1894.

– *De Trinitate libri XV*. Edited by W.J. Mountain with Fr. Glorie. CCSL 50–50A. Turnhout: Brepols, 1968.

– *Retractationum libri II*. Edited by Almut Mutzenbecher. CCSL 57. Turnhout: Brepols, 1984.

– *Soliloquies and Immortality of the Soul*. Translated by Gerard Watson. Facing-page Latin text edited by Wolfgang Hörmann. Warminster: Aris and Phillips, 1990.

– *Soliloquiorum libri duo; De inmortalitate animae; De quantitate animae*. Edited by Wolfgang Hörmann. CSEL 89. Vienna: Hoelder-Pichler-Tempsky, 1986.

– *The Trinity*. Translated by Edmund Hill. Brooklyn: New City Press, 1991.

B. *Sancti Dunstani uita auctore B*. Edited by William Stubbs. In *Memorials of Saint Dunstan, Archbishop of Canterbury*, 3–52. Rolls Series 63. London, 1874. Repr. Millwood, NY: Kraus Reprint, 1965.

Bately, Janet, ed. *The Old English Orosius*. EETS s.s. 6. London: Oxford University Press, 1980.

Batiouchkof, Th. 'Le débat de l'âme et du corps.' *Romania* 20 (1891): 1–55 and 513–78.

Bazire, Joyce, and James E. Cross, eds. *Eleven Old English Rogationtide Homilies*. London: King's College London Medieval Studies, 1989.

Becker, Gustavus, ed. *Catalogi bibliothecarum antiqui I: Catalogi saeculo XIII uetustiores*. Bonn, 1885.

Bede. *Bede's Ecclesiastical History of the English People*. Edited and translated by Bertram Colgrave and R.A.B. Mynors. Oxford: Clarendon Press, 1969.

– *In Lucae euangelium expositio*. Edited by David Hurst. CCSL 120, 1–425. Turnhout: Brepols, 1960.

– *In Marci euangelium expositio*. Edited by David Hurst. CCSL 120, 431–648. Turnhout: Brepols, 1960.

Pseudo-Bede. *Collectanea*. Edited and translated by Michael Lapidge et al. In *Collectanea Pseudo-Bedae*, edited by Martha Bayless and Michael Lapidge, 122–286. Scriptores Latini Hiberniae 14. Dublin: Dublin Institute for Advanced Studies, 1998.

Behaghel, Otto, ed. *Heliand und Genesis*. Revised by Burkhard Taeger. 9th ed. Tübingen: Max Niemeyer Verlag, 1984.

Belfour, A.O., ed. and trans. *Twelfth-Century Homilies in MS. Bodley 343*. EETS o.s. 137. London: K. Paul, Trench, Trübner, and Company, 1909.

Bergin, Osborn, ed. and trans. *Irish Bardic Poetry: Texts and Translations, Together with an Introductory Lecture*. Compiled by David Greene and Fergus Kelly. Foreword by D.A. Binchy. Dublin: Dublin Institute for Advanced Studies, 1970.

Bischoff, Bernhard, facs. ed. *Sammelhandschrift Diez. B Sant. 66: Grammatici latini et catalogus librorum. Vollständige Faksimile-Ausgabe*. Graz: Akademische Druck- und Verlagsanstalt, 1973.

Bischoff, Bernhard, and Bengt Löfstedt, eds. *Anonymus ad Cuimnanum: Expossitio latinitatis*. CCSL 133D. Turnhout: Brepols, 1992.

Boethius. *Philosophiae consolatio*. Edited by Ludwig Bieler. CCSL 94. Turnhout: Brepols, 1957.

– *The Consolation of Philosophy*. Translated by Richard Green. New York: Macmillan, 1962.

Bolland, J., et al., eds. *Acta sanctorum*. Antwerp and Brussels, 1643–.

Boniface (Wynfrith). *Aenigmata Bonifatii*. Edited by Fr. Glorie. In *Collectiones aenigmatum merouingicae aetatis*, 278–343.

– *Ars grammatica; accedit Ars metrica*. Edited by George John Gebauer and Bengt Löfstedt. CCSL 133B. Turnhout: Brepols, 1980.

Bradley, S.A.J., trans. *Anglo-Saxon Poetry*. London: Dent, 1982.

Breatnach, Liam, ed. and trans. '*The Caldron of Poesy*.' *Ériu* 32 (1981): 45–93.

Brooks, Kenneth R., ed. *Andreas and the Fates of the Apostles*. Oxford: Clarendon Press, 1961. Repr. 1998.

Browe, Peter, ed. *De frequenti communione in ecclesia occidentali … Documenta varia*. Rome: Pontificia Università Gregoriana, 1932.

Byrhtferth of Ramsey. *Byrhtferth's Enchiridion*. Edited and translated by Peter S. Baker and Michael Lapidge. EETS s.s. 15. Oxford: Oxford University Press, 1995.

Calder, Daniel G., and Michael J.B. Allen, trans. *Sources and Analogues of Old English Poetry: The Major Latin Texts in Translation*. Cambridge: D.S. Brewer, 1976.

Candidus Wizo. *Epistola 'Num Christus corporeis oculis Deum uidere potuerit.'* Edited by Ernst Dümmler. MGH Epist. 4.557–61. Berlin, 1895.

Cassian, John. *Collationes*. Edited by Michael Petschenig. Revised by Gottfried Kreuz. 2nd ed. CSEL 13. Vienna: Verlag der Österreichischen Akademie der Wissenschaften, 2004.

– *The Conferences*. Translated by Boniface Ramsey. Ancient Christian Writers 57. New York: Newman Press, 1997.

Cassiodorus. *De anima*. Edited by James W. Halporn. CCSL 96, 534–75. Turnhout: Brepols, 1973.

– *'Institutions of Divine and Secular Learning' and 'On the Soul.'* Translated by James W. Halporn. Introduction by Mark Vessey. Translated Texts for Historians 42. Liverpool: Liverpool University Press, 2004.

Cathey, James E., ed. and comm. *Hêliand: Text and Commentary*. Morgantown: West Virginia University Press, 2002.

Chardonnens, László Sándor, ed. *Anglo-Saxon Prognostics, 900–1100: Study and Texts*. Brill's Texts and Sources in Intellectual History 3. Leiden: Brill, 2007.

Charisius, Flavius Sosipater. *Charisii Artis grammaticae libri V*. Edited by Karl Barwick. Revised by F. Kühnert. 2nd ed. Leipzig: Teubner, 1964.

Chickering, Howell D., Jr, ed. and trans. *Beowulf: A Dual-Language Edition*. 2nd ed. New York: Anchor Books, 2006.

Claudianus Mamertus. *De statu animae libri tres.* Edited by Augustus G. Engel-brecht. CSEL 11. Vienna, 1885.

Cledonius. *Ars grammatica. GL* 5.9–79.

Cockayne, Oswald, ed. and trans. *Leechdoms, Wortcunning, and Starcraft of Early England.* 3 vols. Rolls Series 35. London, 1864–6. Repr. Millwood, NY: Kraus Reprint, 1965.

Consentius. *De duabus partibus orationis nomine et uerbo. GL* 5.338–85.

Cross, James E., and Thomas D. Hill, eds. *The Prose* Solomon and Saturn *and* Adrian and Ritheus. Toronto: University of Toronto Press, 1982.

Cynewulf. *Cynewulf's 'Elene.'* Edited by P.O.E. Gradon. Rev. ed. Exeter: University of Exeter Press, 1977.

Daly, Lloyd William, and Walther Suchier, eds. *Altercatio Hadriani Augusti et Epicteti philosophi.* Urbana: University of Illinois Press, 1939.

De Nonno, Mario, ed. *La Grammatica dell'*Anonymus Bobiensis *(GL I.533–565 Keil).* Rome: Edizioni di Storia e Letteratura, 1982.

de Vriend, Hubert Jan, ed. *The Old English Herbarium and Medicina de Quadrupedibus.* EETS o.s. 286. London: Oxford University Press, 1984.

Diels, Hermann, ed. *Die Fragmente der Vorsokratiker.* Revised by W. Kranz. 6th ed. Berlin: Weidmann, 1952.

Diomedes. *Ars grammatica. GL* 1.299–529.

Dionysius Thrax. *Ars grammatica [Tekhnê grammatikê].* Edited by Gustavus Uhlig. Leipzig, 1883.

Doane, A.N., ed. *Genesis A: A New Edition.* Madison: University of Wisconsin Press, 1978.

Donatus, Aelius. *Ars maior.* Edited by Louis Holtz. In *Donat et la tradition de l'enseignement grammatical: Étude sur l'*Ars Donati *et sa diffusion (IVᵉ–IXᵉ siècle) et édition critique,* 603–74. Paris: CNRS, 1981.

– *Ars minor.* Edited by Louis Holtz. In *Donat et la tradition de l'enseignement grammatical: Étude sur l'*Ars Donati *et sa diffusion (IVᵉ–IXᵉ siècle) et édition critique,* 585–602. Paris: CNRS, 1981.

Dositheus. *Ars grammatica. GL* 7.376–436.

Dronke, Ursula, ed. and trans. *The Poetic Edda, Volume I: Heroic Poems.* Oxford: Clarendon Press, 1969.

Dümmler, Ernst, ed. *Aenigmata anglica [Lorsch Riddles].* MGH PLAC 1.20–3. Berlin, 1881.

– ed. *Epitaphium Domberchti.* MGH PLAC 1.19–20. Berlin, 1881.

– ed. 'Lorscher Rätsel.' *Zeitschrift für deutsches Altertum und deutsche Literatur* 22 (1878): 258–63.

Ebert, Adolf, ed. 'Die Räthselpoesie der Angelsachsen, insbesondere die Aenigmata des Tatwine und Eusebius.' *Berichte über die Verhandlungen der königlich sächsischen Gesellschaft der Wissenschaften zu Leipzig, Philologisch-historische Classe* 29 (1877): 20–56.

Empedocles. *The Poem of Empedocles.* Edited and translated by Brad Inwood. Rev. ed. Phoenix Presocratics 3. Toronto: University of Toronto Press, 2001.

Erchanbert. 'Erchanberti Frisingensis Tractatus super Donatum.' Edited by Wendell Vernon Clausen. PhD diss., University of Chicago, 1948.

Eusebius (Hwætberht). *Aenigmata Eusebii.* Edited by Fr. Glorie. In *Collectiones aenigmatum merouingicae aetatis,* 211–71.

Faustus of Riez. *Epistola* 3 *(Quaeris a me).* Edited by Augustus G. Engelbrecht. CSEL 21, 168–81. Vienna, 1891.

Gennadius of Marseilles. *De ecclesiasticis dogmatibus.* Edited by C.H. Turner. In 'The *Liber ecclesiasticorum dogmatum* attributed to Gennadius.' *Journal of Theological Studies* 7 (1906): 78–99.

Glorie, Fr., ed. *Collectiones aenigmatum merouingicae aetatis.* CCSL 133, 167–540. Turnhout: Brepols, 1968.

Gonser, Paul, ed. *Das angelsächsische Prosa-Leben des heiligen Guthlac.* Anglistische Forschungen 27. Heidelberg: Carl Winter's Universitätsbuchhandlung, 1909.

Gottschalk of Orbais. *Quaestiones de anima.* Edited by D.C. Lambot. In *Oeuvres théologiques et grammaticales de Godescalc d'Orbais,* 283–94. Louvain: Spicilegium Sacrum Lovaniense, 1945.

Gregory the Great. *Dialogues.* Edited and translated by Adalbert de Vogüé. SC 251, 260, 265. Paris: Les Éditions du Cerf, 1978–80.

– *Homélies sur Ézéchiel.* Edited and translated by Charles Morel. SC 327 and 360. Paris: Les Éditions du Cerf, 1986–90.

Halsall, Maureen, ed. *The Old English* Rune Poem: *A Critical Edition.* Toronto: University of Toronto Press, 1981.

Harsley, Fred, ed. *Eadwine's Canterbury Psalter.* EETS o.s. 92. London, 1889. Repr. Millwood, NY: Kraus Reprint, 1973.

Healey, Antonette diPaolo, ed. *The Old English Vision of St. Paul.* Speculum Anniversary Monographs 2. Cambridge, MA: The Mediaeval Academy of America, 1978.

Hesiod. *Theogony.* Edited by M.L. West. Oxford: Clarendon Press, 1966.

– *Theogony; Works and Days.* Translated by M.L. West. Oxford: Oxford University Press, 1988.

– *Works and Days.* Edited by M.L. West. Oxford: Oxford University Press, 1978.

Hilary of Poitiers. *Sur Matthieu.* Edited and translated by Jean Doignon. SC 254 and 258. Paris: Les Éditions du Cerf, 1978–9.

(?Pseudo-)Hincmar of Reims. *De diuersa et multiplici animae ratione.* PL 125.929–48.

The Holy Bible: Douay Rheims Version. Baltimore, 1899. Repr. Rockford, IL: TAN Books, 2000.

Homer. *Iliad.* Edited by David B. Monro and Thomas W. Allen. In *Homeri opera,* vols 1–2. 3rd ed. Oxford: Clarendon Press, 1920. Repr. 1978.

– *The Iliad of Homer.* Translated by Richmond Lattimore. Chicago: University of Chicago Press, 1951.

Hrabanus Maurus. *De anima.* PL 110.1109–20.

– *De uniuerso.* PL 111.9–614.

Irvine, Susan, ed. *Old English Homilies from MS Bodley 343.* EETS o.s. 302. Oxford: Oxford University Press, 1993.

Isidore of Seville. *Etymologiarum sive Originum libri XX.* Edited by W.M. Lindsay. 2 vols. Oxford: Clarendon Press, 1911.

– *The Etymologies of Isidore of Seville.* Translated by Stephen A. Barney, W.J. Lewis, J.A. Beach, and Oliver Berghof with Muriel Hall. Cambridge: Cambridge University Press, 2006.

– *Liber differentiarum [II].* Edited by María Adelaida Andrés Sanz. CCSL 111A. Turnhout: Brepols, 2006.

– *Sententiae.* Edited by Pierre Cazier. CCSL 111. Turnhout: Brepols, 1998.

– *Synonymorum de lamentatione animae peccatricis libri duo.* PL 83.827–68.

Julian of Toledo. *Ars Iuliani Toletani Episcopi: Una gramática latina de la España visigoda.* Edited by Maria A.H. Maestre Yenes. Toledo: Publicaciones del Instituto Provincial, 1973.

Junillus Africanus. *Instituta regularia diuinae legis.* Translated by Michael Maas. In *Exegesis and Empire in the Early Byzantine Mediterranean: Junillus Africanus and the Instituta Regularia Divinae Legis.* With a contribution by Edward G. Mathews, Jr. With the Latin text established by Heinrich Kihn. Tübingen: Mohr Siebeck, 2003.

Keil, Heinrich, ed. *Grammatici Latini.* 7 vols. Leipzig, 1857–80. With supplemental vol. 8, *Anecdota helvetica,* edited by Hermann Hagen. Leipzig, 1870. All vols reprinted Hildesheim: Georg Olms, 1961.

Kelly, S.E., ed. *The Electronic Sawyer: An Online Version of the Revised Edition of Sawyer's* Anglo-Saxon Charters, *Section One [S 1–1602].* Adapted for the WWW by S.M. Miller. http://www.trin.cam.ac.uk/chartwww/eSawyer.99/eSawyer2.html.

Kiernan, Kevin, et al., eds. *Electronic Beowulf 2.0.* CD-ROM. London: British Library, 2004.

Klaeber, Frederick. *Klaeber's Beowulf and the Fight at Finnsburg.* Edited by R.D. Fulk, Robert E. Bjork, and John D. Niles. Introduction by Helen Damico. 4th ed. Toronto: University of Toronto Press, 2008.

Krapp, George Phillip, and Elliott Van Kirk Dobbie, eds. The Anglo-Saxon Poetic Records. 6 vols. New York: Columbia University Press, 1931–42.

Lactantius. *L'Ouvrage du Dieu créateur* [*De opificio Dei*]. Edited by Michel Perrin. 2 vols. SC 213 and 214. Paris: Les Éditions du Cerf, 1974.

Langefeld, Brigitte, ed. *The Old English Version of the Enlarged Rule of Chrodegang: Edited together with the Latin Text and an English Translation.* Frankfurt am Main: Peter Lang, 2003.

Löfstedt, Bengt, ed. *Ars Ambrosiana: Commentum anonymum in Donati Partes maiores.* CCSL 133C. Turnhout: Brepols, 1982.

Long, A.A., and D.N. Sedley, eds and trans. *The Hellenistic Philosophers.* 2 vols. Cambridge: Cambridge University Press, 1987.

Luiselli Fadda, A.M., ed. *Nuove omelie anglosassone della rinascenza benedettina.* Florence: Felice Le Monnier, 1977.

Macrae-Gibson, O.D., ed. *The Old English Riming Poem.* Cambridge: D.S. Brewer, 1983.

Magennis, Hugh, ed. *The Anonymous Old English Legend of the Seven Sleepers.* Durham: Durham Medieval Texts, 1994.

Magnusson, Magnus, and Hermann Pálsson, trans. *Njal's Saga.* London: Penguin, 1960.

Malsachanus. *Congregatio Salchani filii de uerbo.* Edited by Bengt Löfstedt. In *Der hibernolateinische Grammatiker Malsachanus,* 169–260. Uppsala: Uppsala University Press, 1965.

Mariotti, Scevola, ed. 'Il *fragmentum Bobiense de nomine (Gramm. lat.* VII 540–44 Keil).' In *Il Libro e il testo,* edited by Cesare Questa and Renato Raffaelli, 39–68. Urbino: Università degli Studi di Urbino, 1984.

Metzger, Bruce M., and Roland E. Murphy, eds. *The New Oxford Annotated Bible.* New York: Oxford University Press, 1994.

Migne, J.-P., ed. *Patrologia Latina.* 221 vols. Paris, 1844–64.

Milfull, Inge B., ed. *The Hymns of the Anglo-Saxon Church.* CSASE 17. Cambridge: Cambridge University Press, 1996.

Miller, Thomas, ed. and trans. *The Old English Version of Bede's Ecclesiastical History of the English People.* EETS o.s. 95, 96, 110, 111. London, 1890–8.

Moffat, Douglas, ed. and trans. *The Old English Soul and Body.* Wolfeboro, NH: D.S. Brewer, 1990.

Morris, Richard, ed. and trans. *The Blickling Homilies.* EETS o.s. 58, 63, 73. London, 1874–80. Reprinted as one volume. London: Oxford University Press, 1967.

Muir, Bernard J., ed. *A Digital Facsimile of Oxford, Bodleian Library, MS. Junius 11.* Software by Nick Kennedy. CD-ROM. Oxford: Bodleian Library, 2004.

Munzi, Luigi, ed. and comm. *Multiplex latinitas: Testi grammaticali latini dell'Alto Medioevo.* AION Quaderni 9. Naples: Istituto universitario orientale, 2004.

Murethach. *In Donati artem maiorem.* Edited by Louis Holtz. CCCM 40. Turnhout: Brepols, 1977.

Murphy, G. Ronald, trans. *The Heliand: The Saxon Gospel.* New York: Oxford University Press, 1992.

Napier, Arthur, ed. *Wulfstan: Sammlung der ihm zugeschriebenen Homilien nebst Untersuchungen über ihre Echtheit.* Berlin, 1883. Reprinted with additions by Klaus Ostheeren. Dublin: Weidmann, 1967.

Oess, Guido, ed. *Der altenglische Arundel-Psalter: Eine Interlinearversion in der Handschrift Arundel 60 des Britischen Museum.* Anglistische Forschungen 30. Heidelberg: Carl Winter's Universitätsbuchhandlung, 1910. Repr. Amsterdam: Swets and Zeitlinger, 1968.

O'Rahilly, Cecile, ed. *Táin Bó Cúailnge, Recension I.* Dublin: Dublin Institute for Advanced Studies, 1976.

– ed. *Táin Bó Cúalnge from the Book of Leinster.* Irish Texts Society 49. Dublin: Dublin Institute for Advanced Studies, 1967.

Orchard, Andy. *Pride and Prodigies: Studies in the Monsters of the* Beowulf-*Manuscript.* Cambridge: D.S. Brewer, 1995. Repr. Toronto: University of Toronto Press, 2003.

Pascasius Radbertus. *De corpore et sanguine Domini.* Edited by Beda Paulus. CCCM 16. Turnhout: Brepols, 1969.

Patrick, Bishop of Dublin. *The Writings of Bishop Patrick, 1074–1084.* Edited and translated by Aubrey Gwynn. Scriptores Latini Hiberniae 1. Dublin: Dublin Institute for Advanced Studies, 1955.

Pettit, Edward, ed. *Anglo-Saxon Remedies, Charms, and Prayers from British Library MS Harley 585: The Lacnunga.* 2 vols. Lewiston: Edwin Mellen Press, 2001.

Phocas [Foca]. *De nomine et verbo.* Edited by F. Casaceli. Naples: Libreria Scientifica Editrice, 1974.

Plato. *Timaeus.* Translated by Benjamin Jowett. In *The Collected Dialogues of Plato, Including the Letters,* edited by Edith Hamilton and Huntington Cairns, 1151–1211. New York: Pantheon Books, 1966.

– *Timaeus.* Edited and translated by Albert Rivaud. In *Oeuvres complètes, tome X: Timée – Critias,* 125–228. Paris: Les Belles Lettres, 1925. Repr. 1985.

Pompeius. *Commentum artis Donati. GL* 5.95–312.

Porter, David W., ed. and trans. *Excerptiones de Prisciano: The Source for Ælfric's Latin-Old English Grammar.* Anglo-Saxon Texts 4. Cambridge: D.S. Brewer, 2002.

Priscian. *Institutiones grammaticae. GL* 2.1–3.377.

Probus. *Instituta artium. GL* 4.47–192.

Ratramnus of Corbie. *De anima.* Edited by André Wilmart. In 'L'opuscule inédit de Ratramne sur la nature de l'âme.' *RB* 43 (1931): 207–23.

– *De corpore et sanguine Domini: Texte original et notice bibliographique.* Edited by J.N. Bakhuizen van den Brink. Rev. ed. Amsterdam: North-Holland Publishing House, 1974.

– *Liber de anima ad Odonem Bellovacensem.* Edited by D.C. Lambot. Namur: Éditions Godenne, 1951.

Remigius of Auxerre. *In artem maiorem Donati commentum.* GL 8.219–66 (partial edition).

Rhodes, E.W., ed. *Defensor's* Liber scintillarum *with an Interlinear Anglo-Saxon Version.* EETS o.s. 93. London, 1889.

Rosier, James L., ed. '*Instructions for Christians*: A Poem in Old English.' *Anglia* 82 (1964): 4–22.

Sauer, Hans, ed. *Theodulfi capitula in England.* Munich: Wilhelm Fink Verlag, 1978.

Scragg, Donald G., ed. *The Vercelli Homilies and Related Texts.* EETS o.s. 300. Oxford: Oxford University Press, 1992.

Sedulius Scottus. *In Donati artem minorem.* Edited by Bengt Löfstedt. CCCM 40C, 2–54. Turnhout: Brepols, 1977.

Sergius. *Explanationes in artem Donati.* GL 4.486–565.

'Sergius.' *Primae explanationes Sergii de prioribus Donati grammatici.* GL 8.143–58.

Sergius (Ps.-Cassiodorus). *Commentarium de oratione et de octo partibus orationis artis secundae Donati.* Edited by Christian Stock. Munich: K.G. Saur, 2005.

Servius. *Comm. in Donati artem maiorem.* GL 4.421–48.

– *Comm. in Donati artem minorem.* GL 4.405–420.

Sisam, Kenneth. 'An Old English Translation of a Letter from Wynfrith to Eadburga (A.D. 716–17) in Cotton MS. Otho C 1.' In *Studies in the History of Old English Literature*, 199–224. Oxford: Clarendon Press, 1953. Repr. 1998.

Skeat, Walter W., ed. *The Holy Gospels in Anglo-Saxon, Northumbrian, and Old Mercian Versions.* Cambridge, 1871–87. Repr. Darmstadt: Wissenschaftliche Buchgesellschaft, 1970.

Smaragdus. *Liber in partibus Donati.* Edited by B. Löfstedt, L. Holtz, and A. Kibre. CCCM 68. Turnhout: Brepols, 1986.

Snorri Sturluson. *The Prose Edda: Norse Mythology.* Translated by Jesse L. Byock. London: Penguin, 2003.

Sveinsson, Einar Ólafur, ed. *Brennu-Njáls Saga.* Íslenzk Fornrit 12. Reykjavik: Hið íslenzka fornritafélag, 1954.

Tatwine. *Aenigmata Tatuini.* Edited by Fr. Glorie. In *Collectiones aenigmatum merouingicae aetatis*, 167–208.

– *Ars Tatuini.* Edited by Maria de Marco. CCSL 133, 1–141. Turnhout: Brepols, 1968.

Tertullian. *De anima.* Edited by J.H. Waszink. CCSL 2, 779–869. Turnhout: Brepols, 1954.

Thurneysen, Rudolf, ed. *Scéla mucce Meic Dathó*. Dublin: Dublin Institute for Advanced Studies, 1935. Repr. 1951.

Tolomio, Ilario, trans. *L'Anima dell'uomo: Trattati sull'anima dal V al IX secolo*. Milan: Rusconi, 1979.

Treharne, Elaine M., ed. *The Old English Life of St Nicholas with the Old English Life of St Giles*. Leeds: Leeds Studies in English, 1997.

Tristram, Hildegard L.C., ed. 'Vier altenglische Predigten aus der heterodoxen Tradition, mit Kommentar, Übersetzung und Glossar sowie drei weiteren Texten im Anhang.' PhD diss., Albert-Ludwigs-Universität (Freiburg im Bresgau), 1970.

Virgilius Maro Grammaticus. *Epitomi ed Epistole*. Edited by Giovanni Polara. Naples: Liguori Editore, 1979.

Von Dobschütz, Ernst, ed. *Das Decretum Gelasianum de libris recipiendis et non recipiendis*. Texte und Untersuchungen 38. Leipzig: J.C. Hinrichs, 1912.

Wærferth of Worcester. *Bischof Wærferths von Worcester Übersetzung der Dialoge Gregors des Grossen*. Edited by Hans Hecht. BaP 5. Leipzig and Hamburg: Wigand, 1900–7. Repr. Darmstadt: Wissenschaftliche Buchgesellschaft, 1965.

Warner, Rubie D.-N., ed. *Early English Homilies from the Twelfth Century MS. Vesp. D. XIV*. EETS o.s. 152. London: Kegan Paul, Trench, Trübner, and Co., 1917. Repr. Millwood, NY: Kraus Reprint, 1981.

Weber, Robert, ed. *Le Psautier romain et les autres anciens psautiers latins*. Vatican City: Libreria Vaticana, 1953.

Weber, Robert, Bonifatius Fischer, et al., eds. *Biblia Sacra iuxta vulgatam versionem*. 4th ed. Stuttgart: Deutsche Bibelgesellschaft, 1994.

Wenisch, Franz. '*Nu bidde we eow for Godes lufon*: A Hitherto Unpublished Old English Homiletic Text in CCCC 162.' In *Words, Texts, and Manuscripts: Studies in Anglo-Saxon Culture Presented to Helmut Gneuss on the Occasion of His Sixty-Fifth Birthday*, edited by Michael Korhammer with Karl Reichl and Hans Sauer, 43–52. Cambridge: D.S. Brewer, 1992.

Williamson, Craig, ed. and trans. *The Old English Riddles of the Exeter Book*. Chapel Hill: University of North Carolina Press, 1977.

Wilmanns, W. 'Ein Fragebüchlein aus dem neunten Jahrhundert.' *Zeitschrift für deutsches Altertum und deutsche Literatur* 15 (1872): 166–80.

Wouters, Alfons, ed. *The Grammatical Papyri from Graeco-Roman Egypt: Contributions to the Study of the 'Ars Grammatica' in Antiquity*. Verhandelingen van de Koninklijke Akademie voor Wetenschappen, Letteren en Schone Kunsten van België, Klasse der Letteren 41, no. 92. Brussels: Paleis der Academiën, 1979.

Wulfstan II of York. *Die 'Institutes of Polity, Civil and Ecclesiastical': Ein Werk Erzbischof Wulfstans von York*. Edited by Karl Jost. Bern: Francke Verlag, 1959.

Wulfstan of Winchester. *Life of St Æthelwold*. Edited and translated by Michael Lapidge and Michael Winterbottom. Oxford Medieval Texts. Oxford: Clarendon Press, 1991.

Yerkes, David, ed. *The Old English Life of Machutus*. Toronto: University of Toronto Press, 1984.

Secondary Sources

Alcamesi, Filippa. 'The *Sibylline Acrostic* in Anglo-Saxon Manuscripts: The Augustinian Translation and the Other Versions.' In *Foundations of Learning: The Transfer of Encyclopaedic Knowledge in the Early Middle Ages*, edited by Rolf H. Bremmer, Jr, and Kees Dekker, 147–73. Mediaevalia Groningana n.s. 9. Leuven: Peeters, 2007.

Alexander, P.J., S.G.S. Prabhu, E.S. Krishnamoorthy, and P.C. Halkatti. 'Mental Disorders in Patients with Noncardiac Chest Pain.' *Acta Psychiatrica Scandinavica* 89 (1994): 291–3.

Anderson, Earl R. *Folk-Taxonomies in Early English*. Madison, NJ: Fairleigh Dickinson University Press, 2003.

Annas, Julia. *Hellenistic Philosophy of Mind*. Berkeley: University of California Press, 1992.

Augustyn, Prisca. *The Semiotics of Fate, Death, and the Soul in Germanic Culture: The Christianization of Old Saxon*. Berkeley Insights in Linguistics and Semiotics 50. New York: Peter Lang, 2002.

Averill, James R. 'Autonomic Response Patterns during Sadness and Mirth.' *Psychophysiology* 5 (1969): 399–414.

Bains, Jatinder. 'Race, Culture and Psychiatry: A History of Transcultural Psychiatry.' *History of Psychiatry* 16 (2005): 139–54.

Banham, Debby. 'A Millennium in Medicine? New Medical Texts and Ideas in England in the Eleventh Century.' In *Anglo-Saxons: Studies Presented to Cyril Roy Hart*, edited by Simon Keynes and Alfred P. Smyth, 230–42. Dublin: Four Courts Press, 2006.

Bankert, Dabney Anderson, Jessica Wegmann, and Charles D. Wright. *Ambrose in Anglo-Saxon England with Pseudo-Ambrose and Ambrosiaster*. Old English *Newsletter* Subsidia 25. Kalamazoo: The Medieval Institute, Western Michigan University, 1997.

Bately, Janet. 'Those Books That Are Most Necessary for All Men to Know: The Classics and Late Ninth-Century England, A Reappraisal.' In *The Classics in the Middle Ages*, edited by Aldo S. Bernardo and Saul Levin, 45–78. Medieval and Renaissance Texts and Studies 69. Binghamton, NY: Center for Medieval and Renaissance Studies, 1990.

Beaumont, Jacqueline. 'The Latin Tradition of the *De Consolatione Philosophiae*.' In *Boethius: His Life, Thought and Influence*, edited by Margaret Gibson, 278–305. Oxford: Blackwell, 1981.

Becker, Gertraud. *Geist und Seele im Altsächsischen und im Althochdeutschen: Der Sinnbereich des Seelischen und die Wörter* gêst-geist *und* seola-sêla *in den Denkmälern bis zum 11. Jahrhundert*. Heidelberg: C. Winter, 1964.

Bibliotheca hagiographica latina. 2 vols. Brussels: Socii Bollandiani, 1899–1901. With *Supplementum* by Henryk Fros. Brussels: Sociéte des Bollandistes, 1986.

Bieler, Ludwig. 'Some Remarks on the *Aenigmata Laureshamensia*.' *Romanobarbarica* 2 (1977): 11–15.

Bischoff, Bernhard. *Die Abtei Lorsch im Spiegel ihrer Handschriften*. 2nd ed. Lorsch: Verlag Laurissa, 1989.

Bjorklund, Nancy Basler. 'Parker's Purposes for His Manuscripts: Matthew Parker in the Context of His Early Career and Sixteenth-Century Church Reform.' In *Old English Literature in Its Manuscript Context*, edited by Joyce Tally Lionarons, 217–41. Morgantown: West Virginia University Press, 2004.

Blank, David, and Catherine Atherton. 'The Stoic Contribution to Traditional Grammar.' In *The Cambridge Companion to the Stoics*, edited by Brad Inwood, 310–27. Cambridge: Cambridge University Press, 2003.

Bolton, Diane K. 'The Study of the *Consolation of Philosophy* in Anglo-Saxon England.' *Archives d'histoire doctrinale et littéraire du Moyen Âge* 44 (1977): 33–78.

Bosworth, Joseph. *An Anglo-Saxon Dictionary*. Edited and revised by T. Northcote Toller. Oxford, 1898. Repr. Oxford: Oxford University Press, 1991. With *Supplement* by T. Northcote Toller, revised by Alistair Campbell. Oxford: Oxford University Press, 1921. Repr. 1992.

Bouhot, Jean-Paul. 'Alcuin et le *De catechizandis rudibus* de saint Augustin.' *Recherches Augustiniennes* 15 (1980): 176–240.

– *Ratramne de Corbie: Histoire littéraire et controverses doctrinales*. Paris: Études Augustiniennes, 1976.

Bremmer, Jan N. *The Early Greek Concept of the Soul*. Princeton, NJ: Princeton University Press, 1983.

Britt-Krause, Inga. 'Sinking Heart: A Punjabi Communication of Distress.' *Social Science and Medicine* 29 (1989): 563–75.

Brittain, Charles. 'No Place for a Platonist Soul in Fifth-Century Gaul? The Case of Mamertus Claudianus.' In *Society and Culture in Late Antique Gaul: Revisiting the Sources*, edited by Ralph W. Mathisen and Danuta Shanzer, 239–62. Aldershot: Ashgate, 2001.

Brooks, Nicholas. 'The Career of St Dunstan.' In *St Dunstan: His Life, Times and Cult*, edited by Nigel Ramsay, Margaret Sparks, and Tim Tatton-Brown, 1–23. Woodbridge: Boydell Press, 1992.

Brown, Harriet. 'The *Other* Brain Also Deals with Many Woes.' *The New York Times*, 23 August 2005. http://www.nytimes.com/2005/08/23/health/23gut/html.

Brunschwig, Jacques. 'Stoic Metaphysics.' In *The Cambridge Companion to the Stoics*, edited by Brad Inwood, 206–32. Cambridge: Cambridge University Press, 2003.

Bullough, Donald A. *Alcuin: Achievement and Reputation*. Education and Society in the Middle Ages and Renaissance 16. Leiden: Brill, 2004.

Cacioppo, John T., Gary G. Berntson, Jeff T. Larsen, Kirsten M. Poehlmann, and Tiffany A. Ito. 'The Psychophysiology of Emotion.' In *Handbook of Emotions*, edited by Michael Lewis and Jeannette M. Haviland-Jones, 173–91. 2nd edition. New York: Guilford Press, 2000.

Cameron, M.L. *Anglo-Saxon Medicine*. CSASE 7. Cambridge: Cambridge University Press, 1993.

– 'Bald's *Leechbook*: Its Sources and Their Use in Its Compilation.' *ASE* 12 (1983): 153–82.

Carey, John. '*Fir Bolg*: A Native Etymology Reconsidered.' *Cambridge Medieval Celtic Studies* 16 (1988): 77–83.

Cavadini, John. 'The Sources and Theology of Alcuin's *De fide sanctae et individuae Trinitatis*.' *Augustinian Studies* 12 (1981): 11–18.

Chazelle, Celia. *The Crucified God in the Carolingian Era: Theology and Art of Christ's Passion*. Cambridge: Cambridge University Press, 2001.

– 'Figure, Character, and the Glorified Body in the Carolingian Eucharistic Controversy.' *Traditio* 47 (1992): 1–36.

Chélini, J. 'La pratique dominicale des laïcs dans l'église franque sous le règne de Pépin.' *Revue d'histoire de l'Église de France* 42 (1956): 161–74.

Clayton, Mary. 'Blood and the Soul in Ælfric.' *NQ* 54 (2007): 365–7.

– 'An Edition of Ælfric's *Letter to Brother Edward*.' In *Early Medieval English Texts and Interpretations: Studies Presented to Donald G. Scragg*, edited by Elaine Treharne and Susan Rosser, 263–83. Medieval and Renaissance Texts and Studies 252. Tempe: ACMRS, 2002.

– 'Hermits and the Contemplative Life in Anglo-Saxon England.' In *Holy Men and Holy Women: Old English Prose Saints' Lives and Their Contexts*, edited by Paul E. Szarmach, 147–75. Albany: State University of New York Press, 1996.

– 'Homiliaries and Preaching in Anglo-Saxon England.' *Peritia* 4 (1985): 207–42. Reprinted with corrections in *Old English Prose: Basic Readings*, edited by Paul E. Szarmach with the assistance of Deborah A. Oosterhouse, 151–98. New York: Garland, 2000.

– 'Of Mice and Men: Ælfric's Second Homily for the Feast of a Confessor.' *Leeds Studies in English* n.s. 24 (1993): 1–26.

– 'The Sources of Assmann 4 (Homily for the Common of a Confessor) (Cameron B.1.5.11).' In *Fontes Anglo-Saxonici*. 1991.
Clemoes, Peter. 'The Chronology of Ælfric's Works.' In *The Anglo-Saxons: Studies in Some Aspects of Their History and Culture*, edited by Peter Clemoes. London: Bowes and Bowes, 1959. Reprinted with addenda in *Old English Prose: Basic Readings*, edited by Paul E. Szarmach with the assistance of Deborah A. Oosterhouse, 29–72. New York: Garland, 2000.
– '*Mens absentia cogitans* in *The Seafarer* and *The Wanderer*.' In *Medieval Literature and Civilization: Studies in Memory of G.N. Garmonsway*, edited by D.A. Pearsall and R.A. Waldron, 62–77. London: Athlone, 1969.
Close, Florence. 'L'Itinéraire de Candide Wizo: Un élément de datation des oeuvres anti-adoptianistes d'Alcuin?' *Revue d'histoire de la spiritualité* 103 (2008): 5–26.
Colish, Marcia L. 'Carolingian Debates over *Nihil* and *Tenebrae*: A Study in Theological Method.' *Speculum* 59 (1984): 757–95.
– *The Stoic Tradition from Antiquity to the Early Middle Ages*. 2 vols. Leiden: E.J. Brill, 1985.
Collins, Terence. 'The Physiology of Tears in the Old Testament.' *Catholic Biblical Quarterly* 33 (1971): 18–38 and 185–97.
Constable, Giles. 'The Interpretation of Mary and Martha.' In *Three Studies in Medieval Religious and Social Thought*, 3–141. Cambridge: Cambridge University Press, 1995.
Constantinescu, Radu. 'Alcuin et les *Libelli precum* de l'époque carolingienne.' *Revue d'Histoire de la Spiritualité* 50 (1974): 17–56.
Contreni, John J. 'Carolingian Biblical Studies.' In *Carolingian Essays*, edited by Uta-Renate Blumenthal, 71–98. Washington, DC: The Catholic University of America Press, 1983.
Courcelle, Pierre. *La Consolation de Philosophie dans la tradition littéraire: Antécédants et postérité de Boèce*. Paris: Études Augustiniennes, 1967.
Cristiani, Marta. 'La controversia eucaristica nella cultura del secolo IX.' *Studi medievali* 3rd ser. 9 (1968): 167–233.
– 'L'Espace de l'âme: La controverse sur la corporéité des esprits, le *De statu animae* de Claudien Mamert et le *Periphyseon*.' In *Eriugena: Studien zu seinen Quellen*, edited by Werner Beierwaltes, 149–63. Heidelberg: Carl Winter Universitätsverlag, 1980.
Cross, F.L., and E.A. Livingstone, eds. *The Oxford Dictionary of the Christian Church*. 3rd ed. Oxford: Oxford University Press, 1997.
Cross, James E. 'Aspects of Microcosm and Macrocosm in Old English Literature.' In *Studies in Old English Literature in Honor of Arthur G. Brodeur*, edited by Stanley B. Greenfield, 1–22. Eugene: University of Oregon Books, 1963.

- 'Ubi Sunt Passages in Old English: Sources and Relationships.' Vetenskaps-
  Societetens i Lund, Arsbok (1956): 23–44.
Davis, Kathleen. 'The Performance of Translation Theory in King Alfred's
  National Literary Program.' In Manuscript, Narrative, Lexicon: Essays on
  Literary and Cultural Transmission in Honor of Whitney F. Bolton, edited by
  Robert Boenig and Kathleen Davis, 149–70. Lewisburg, PA: Bucknell Univer-
  sity Press, 2000.
Dean, Cornelia. 2005. 'Scientific Savvy? In U.S., Not Much.' New York Times,
  30 August 2005. http://www.nytimes.com/2005/08/30/science/30profile.html.
DeGregorio, Scott. 'Cassiodorus.' In Sources of Anglo-Saxon Literary Culture.
  Volume 4, C, edited by Thomas N. Hall. Kalamazoo: Medieval Institute Publi-
  cations, Western Michigan University, forthcoming.
Deignan, Alice. 'Metaphorical Expressions and Culture: An Indirect Link.'
  Metaphor and Symbol 18 (2003): 255–71.
Dekker, Kees. 'King Alfred's Translation of Gregory's Dialogi: Tales for the Un-
  learned?' In Rome and the North: The Early Reception of Gregory the Great in
  Germanic Europe, edited by Rolf H. Bremmer, Jr, Kees Dekker, and David F.
  Johnson, 27–50. Paris: Peeters, 2001.
Dekkers, Eligius, and Aemilius Gaar. Clavis patrum latinorum. 3rd ed. Steen-
  brugge: Brepols, 1995.
De Leemans, Pieter, and Michèle Goyens, eds. Aristotle's Problemata in Different
  Times and Tongues. Leuven: Leuven University Press, 2006.
Diekstra, F.N.M. 'The Seafarer 58–66a: The Flight of the Exiled Soul to Its
  Fatherland.' Neophilologus 55 (1971): 433–46.
Discenza, Nicole Guenther. 'The Sources of [the OE Translation of] Boethius, The
  Consolation of Philosophy (Cameron B.9.3).' In Fontes Anglo-Saxonici. 2001.
Di Sciacca, Claudia. Finding the Right Words: Isidore's Synonyma in Anglo-
  Saxon England. Toronto: University of Toronto Press, 2008.
- 'Isidorian Scholarship at the School of Theodore and Hadrian: The Case of the
  Synonyma.' Quaestio 3 (2002): 76–106.
Dolbeau, François. 'Le Liber XXI Sententiarum (CPL 373): Édition d'un texte
  de travail.' Recherches Augustiniennes 30 (1997): 113–65.
Dutton, Paul Edward. 'Medieval Approaches to Calcidius.' In Plato's Timaeus as
  a Cultural Icon, edited by Gretchen J. Reydams-Schils, 183–205. Notre Dame,
  IN: University of Notre Dame Press, 2003.
Ebert, Adolf. 'Zu den Lorscher Rätseln.' Zeitschrift für deutsches Altertum und
  deutsche Literatur 23 (1879): 200–2.
Eggers, Hans. 'Altgermanische Seelenvorstellungen im Lichte des Heliand.'
  In Der Heliand, edited by Jürgen Eichhoff and Irmengard Rauch, 270–304.
  Darmstadt: Wissenschaftliche Buchgesellschaft, 1973.

Ekman, Paul, Robert W. Levenson, and Wallace V. Friesen. 'Autonomic Nervous System Activity Distinguishes among Emotions.' *Science* n.s. 221 (1983): 1208–10.

Enright, Michael J. 'Fires of Knowledge: A Theory of Warband Education in Medieval Ireland and Homeric Greece.' In *Ireland and Europe in the Early Middle Ages: Texts and Transmission*, edited by Próinséas Ní Chatháin and Michael Richter, 342–67. Dublin: Four Courts Press, 2002.

Evans, G.R. 'The Grammar of Predestination in the Ninth Century.' *Journal of Theological Studies* n.s. 33 (1982): 134–45.

Fabrega, Horacio, Jr. 'Somatization in Cultural and Historical Perspective.' In *Current Concepts of Somatization: Research and Clinical Perspectives*, edited by Laurence J. Kirmayer and James M. Robbins, 181–99. Washington, DC: American Psychiatric Press, 1991.

Fauconnier, Gilles, and Mark Turner. *The Way We Think: Conceptual Blending and the Mind's Hidden Complexities*. New York: Basic Books, 2002.

Flowers, Stephen E. 'Toward an Archaic Germanic Psychology.' *Journal of Indo-European Studies* 11 (1983): 117–38.

Fludernik, Monika, Donald C. Freeman, and Margaret H. Freeman. 'Metaphor and Beyond: An Introduction.' *Poetics Today* 20 (1999): 383–96.

Fontes Anglo-Saxonici Project, ed. *Fontes Anglo-Saxonici: World Wide Web Register.* http://fontes.english.ox.ac.uk/.

Foot, Sarah. *Monastic Life in Anglo-Saxon England, c. 600–900.* Cambridge: Cambridge University Press, 2006.

Fortin, Ernest L. *Christianisme et culture philosophique au Ve siècle: La querelle de l'âme humaine en Occident.* Paris: Études Augustiniennes, 1959.

Frank, Roberta. 'Poetic Words in Late Old English Prose.' In *From Anglo-Saxon to Early Middle English: Studies Presented to E.G. Stanley*, edited by Malcolm Godden, Douglas Gray, and Terry Hoad, 87–107. Oxford: Clarendon Press, 1994.

Frantzen, Allen J. 'The Body in *Soul and Body I*.' *The Chaucer Review* 17 (1982): 76–88.

– 'The Form and Function of the Preface in the Poetry and Prose of Alfred's Reign.' In *Alfred the Great: Papers from the Eleventh-Centenary Conferences*, edited by Timothy Reuter, 121–36. Aldershot: Ashgate, 2003.

– *King Alfred*. Boston: Twayne Publishers, 1986.

Frede, Michael. 'The Stoic Notion of a *lekton*.' In *Language*, edited by Stephen Everson, 109–28. Companions to Ancient Thought 3. Cambridge: Cambridge University Press, 1994.

Fulk, R.D. *A History of Old English Meter.* Philadelphia: University of Pennsylvania Press, 1992.

Gameson, Richard. 'Alfred the Great and the Destruction and Production of Christian Books.' *Scriptorium* 49 (1995): 180–210.

– 'St Wulfstan, the Library of Worcester and the Spirituality of the Medieval Book.' In *St Wulfstan and His World*, edited by Julia S. Barrow and N.P. Brooks, 59–104. Aldershot: Ashgate, 2005.

Ganz, David. 'Le *De laude Dei* d'Alcuin.' In *Alcuin, de York à Tours: Écriture, pouvoir et réseaux dans l'Europe du haut Moyen Âge*, edited by Philippe Depreux and Bruno Judic, 387–91. (= *Annales de Bretagne et des Pays de l'Ouest* 111.) Rennes: Presses Universitaires de Rennes, 2004.

Gatch, Milton McCormick. 'King Alfred's Version of Augustine's *Soliloquia*: Some Suggestions on Its Rationale and Unity.' In *Studies in Earlier Old English Prose*, edited by Paul E. Szarmach, 17–45. Albany: State University of New York Press, 1986.

– 'MS Boulogne-sur-Mer 63 and Ælfric's First Series of Catholic Homilies.' *JEGP* 65 (1966): 482–90.

Geeraerts, Dirk, and Stefan Grondelaers. 'Looking Back at Anger: Cultural Traditions and Metaphorical Patterns.' In Taylor and MacLaury, *Language and the Cognitive Construal of the World*, 153–79.

Gersh, Stephen E. 'The Medieval Legacy from Ancient Platonism.' In *The Platonic Tradition in the Middle Ages: A Doxographic Approach*, edited by Stephen Gersh and Maarten J.F.M. Hoenen with Pieter Th. van Wingerden, 3–30. Berlin: Walter de Gruyter, 2002.

Gevaert, Caroline. 'Anger in Old and Middle English: A "Hot" Topic?' *Belgian Essays on Language and Literature* (2001): 89–101.

– 'The ANGER IS HEAT Question: Detecting Cultural Influence on the Conceptualization of Anger through Diachronic Corpus Analysis.' In *Perspectives on Variation: Sociolinguistic, Historical, Comparative*, edited by Nicole Delbecque, Johan van der Auwera, and Dirk Geeraerts, 195–208. Berlin: Mouton de Gruyter, 2005.

– 'The Evolution of the Lexical and Conceptual Field of ANGER in Old and Middle English.' *A Changing World of Words: Studies in English Historical Lexicography, Lexicology, and Semantics*, edited by Javier E. Díaz Vera, 275–99. New York: Rodopi, 2002.

Gibson, Margaret. *Lanfranc of Bec.* Oxford: Clarendon Press, 1978.

– 'Milestones in the Study of Priscian, circa 800–circa 1200.' *Viator* 23 (1992): 17–33.

Gneuss, Helmut. 'Addenda and Corrigenda to the *Handlist of Anglo-Saxon Manuscripts*.' *Anglo-Saxon England* 32 (2003): 293–305.

– *Handlist of Anglo-Saxon Manuscripts: A List of Manuscripts and Manuscript Fragments Written or Owned in England up to 1100.* Tempe: ACMRS, 2001.

– 'King Alfred and the History of Anglo-Saxon Libraries.' In *Modes of Interpretation in Old English Literature: Essays in Honour of Stanley B. Greenfield*, edited by Phyllis Rugg Brown, Georgia Ronan Crampton, and Fred C. Robinson, 29–49. Toronto: University of Toronto Press, 1986.

– 'The Study of Language in Anglo-Saxon England.' *Bulletin of the John Ry-lands Library* 72 (1990): 3–32.

Godden, Malcolm R. *Ælfric's Catholic Homilies: Introduction, Commentaries, and Glossary.* EETS s.s. 18. Oxford: Oxford University Press, 2000.

– 'Ælfric's Saints' Lives and the Problem of Miracles.' *Leeds Studies in English* n.s. 16 (1985): 83–100.

– 'Alfred, Asser, and Boethius.' In *Latin Learning and English Lore*, edited by O'Brien O'Keeffe and Orchard, 1.326–48.

– 'The Alfredian Boethius Project.' *Old English Newsletter* 37 (2003): 26–34.

– 'The Alfredian Project and Its Aftermath: Rethinking the Literary History of the Ninth and Tenth Centuries.' *Proceedings of the British Academy* 162 (2009): 93–122.

– 'Anglo-Saxons on the Mind.' In *Learning and Literature in Anglo-Saxon England: Studies Presented to Peter Clemoes on the Occasion of his Sixty-Fifth Birthday*, edited by Michael Lapidge and Helmut Gneuss, 271–98. Cambridge: Cambridge University Press, 1985.

– 'Did King Alfred Write Anything?' *Medium Ævum* 76 (2007): 1–23.

– 'King Alfred's Preface and the Teaching of Latin in Anglo-Saxon England.' *English Historical Review* 117 (2002): 596–604.

– 'The Player King: Identification and Self-Representation in King Alfred's Writings.' In *Alfred the Great: Papers from the Eleventh-Centenary Conferences*, edited by Timothy Reuter, 137–50. Aldershot: Ashgate, 2003.

– 'The Psyche and the Self: Some Issues in *Beowulf*.' In *Studies in Middle English Language and Literature*, edited by J.L. Chamosa and T. Guzmán, 49–67. León: Universidad de León, 1997.

– 'The Sources of *Lives [of Saints]* 1 (Nativity of Christ) (Cameron B.1.3.2).' In *Fontes Anglo-Saxonici.* 2002.

– 'The Sources of [the OE Translation of] Augustine, *Soliloquies* (Cameron B.9.4).' In *Fontes Anglo-Saxonici.* 2001.

– 'Text and Eschatology in Book III of the Old English *Soliloquies*.' *Anglia* 121 (2003): 177–209.

– 'Wærferth and King Alfred: The Fate of the Old English *Dialogues*.' In *Alfred the Wise: Studies in Honour of Janet Bately*, edited by Jane Roberts and Janet L. Nelson, 35–51. Woodbridge: D.S. Brewer, 1997.

Good, Byron J. 'The Heart of What's the Matter: The Semantics of Illness in Iran.' *Culture, Medicine and Psychiatry* 1 (1977): 25–58.

Green, D.H. *Language and History in the Early Germanic World.* Cambridge: Cambridge University Press, 1998.

Gretsch, Mechthild. *The Intellectual Foundations of the English Benedictine Reform.* CSASE 25. Cambridge: Cambridge University Press, 1999.

Griffith, M. 'The Sources of *The Phoenix* (Cameron A.3.4).' In *Fontes Anglo-Saxonici*. 2001.

Grondeux, Anne. '*Corpus dicitur quidquid videtur et tangitur*: Origines et enjeux d'une définition.' *Voces* 14 (2003): 35–76.

– '*Res* Meaning a Thing Thought: The Influence of the *Ars Donati*.' *Vivarium* 45 (2007): 189–202.

Grundy, Lynne. 'Ælfric's *Sermo de sacrificio in die pascae*: Figura and Veritas.' *NQ* 235 (1990): 265–9.

Gwara, Scott. '*Forht* and *fægen* in *The Wanderer* and Related Literary Contexts of Anglo-Saxon Warrior Wisdom.' *Mediaeval Studies* 69 (2007): 255–98.

Hadot, Pierre. 'Sur divers sens du mot *pragma* dans la tradition philosophique grecque.' In *Concepts et Catégories dans la pensée antique*, edited by Pierre Aubenque, 309–19. Paris: J. Vrin, 1980.

Hall, Thomas N. 'Biblical and Patristic Learning.' In *A Companion to Anglo-Saxon Literature*, edited by Phillip Pulsiano and Elaine Treharne, 327–44. Oxford: Blackwell, 2001.

– 'The Early English Manuscripts of Gregory the Great's *Homilies on the Gospel* and *Homilies on Ezechiel*: A Preliminary Survey.' In *Rome and the North: The Early Reception of Gregory the Great in Germanic Europe*, edited by Rolf H. Bremmer, Jr, Kees Dekker, and David F. Johnson, 115–36. Paris: Peeters, 2001.

– 'Preaching at Winchester in the Early Twelfth Century.' *JEGP* 104 (2005): 189–218.

– 'The Psychedelic Transmogrification of the Soul in Vercelli Homily IV.' In *Time and Eternity: The Medieval Discourse*, edited by Gerhard Jaritz and Gerson Moreno-Riano, 309–22. Turnhout: Brepols, 2003.

Hankinson, R.J. 'Greek Medical Models of Mind.' In *Psychology*, edited by Stephen Everson, 194–217. Companions to Ancient Thought 2. Cambridge: Cambridge University Press, 1991.

Harbus, Antonina. '*Exeter Book Riddle 39* Reconsidered.' *Studia Neophilologica* 70 (1998): 139–48.

– *The Life of the Mind in Old English Poetry*. Costerus n.s. 143. Amsterdam: Rodopi, 2002.

Häussling, Angelus Albert. *Mönchskonvent und Eucharistiefeier. Eine Studie über die Messe in der abendländischen Klosterliturgie des frühen Mittelalters und zur Geschichte der Messhäufigkeit*. Münster Westfalen: Aschendorff, 1973.

Healey, Antonette diPaolo, Dorothy Haines, Joan Holland, David McDougall, and Ian McDougall, with Pauline Thompson and Nancy Speirs. *The Dictionary of Old English: A to G Online*. Web interface by Peter Mielke and Xin Xiang. Toronto: Dictionary of Old English Project, 2007.

Healey, Antonette diPaolo, John Price Wilkin, and Xin Xiang. *The Dictionary of Old English Corpus on the World Wide Web*. Toronto: Dictionary of Old English Project, 2009.

Henry, P.L. 'Furor Heroicus.' *Zeitschrift für celtische Philologie* 39 (1982): 235–42.

Hill, Joyce. 'Confronting *Germania Latina*: Changing Responses to Old English Biblical Verse.' In *Latin Culture and Medieval Germanic Europe*, edited by Richard North and Tette Hofstra, 71–88. Mediaevalia Groningana 11. Groningen: Egbert Forsten, 1992. Reprinted in *The Poems of MS Junius 11*, edited by R.M. Liuzza, 1–19. New York: Routledge, 2002.

– 'The Dissemination of Ælfric's *Lives of Saints*: A Preliminary Survey.' In *Holy Men and Holy Women: Old English Prose Saints' Lives and Their Contexts*, edited by Paul E. Szarmach, 235–59. Albany: State University of New York Press, 1996.

– 'Reform and Resistance: Preaching Styles in Late Anglo-Saxon England.' In *De l'homélie au sermon: Histoire de la prédication médiévale*, edited by Jacqueline Hamesse and Xavier Hermand, 15–46. Louvain-la-Neuve: Université Catholique de Louvain Publications de l'Institut d'Études Médiévales, 1993.

Hill, Thomas D. ' "Hwyrftum scriþað": *Beowulf*, line 163.' *Mediaeval Studies* 32 (1970): 379–81.

Hinton, Devon, and Susan Hinton. 'Panic Disorder, Somatization, and the New Cross-Cultural Psychiatry: The Seven Bodies of a Medical Anthropology of Panic.' *Culture, Medicine and Psychiatry* 26 (2002): 155–78.

Hogan, Patrick Colm. *Cognitive Science, Literature, and the Arts: A Guide for Humanists*. New York: Routledge, 2003.

Hollan, Douglas. 'Emotion Work and the Value of Emotional Equanimity among the Toraja.' *Ethnology* 31 (1992): 45–56.

Hollis, Stephanie. 'Scientific and Medical Writings.' In *A Companion to Anglo-Saxon Literature*, edited by Phillip Pulsiano and Elaine Treharne, 188–208. Oxford: Blackwell, 2001.

Holthausen, Ferdinand. *Altenglisches etymologisches Wörterbuch*. 3rd ed. Heidelberg: Carl Winter Universitätsverlag, 1974.

Holtz, Louis. 'L'enseignement de la grammaire au temps de Charles le Chauve.' In *Giovanni Scoto nel suo tempo: L'organizzazione del sapere in età carolingia*, 153–69. Spoleto: Centro italiano di studi sull'alto medioevo, 1989.

– 'Les innovations théoriques de la grammaire carolingienne: peu de chose. Pourquoi?' In *L'Héritage des grammairiens latins de l'antiquité aux lumières*, edited by Irène Rosier, 133–45. Louvain: Peeters, 1988.

– 'Les nouvelles tendances de la pédagogie grammaticale au Xe siècle.' *Mittellateinisches Jahrbuch* 24/25 (1989/90): 163–73.

- 'La typologie des manuscrits grammaticaux latins.' *Revue d'histoire des textes* 8 (1978): 247–69.

Hubbard, Frank G. 'The Relation of the "Blooms of King Alfred" to the Anglo-Saxon Translation of Boethius.' *Modern Language Notes* 9 (1894): 161–71.

Hultin, Neil. 'The External Soul in *The Seafarer* and *The Wanderer*.' *Folklore* 88 (1977): 39–45.

Hupka, Ralph B., Zbigniew Zaleski, Jürgen Otto, Lucy Reidl, and Nadia V. Tarabrina. 'Anger, Envy, Fear, and Jealousy as Felt in the Body: A Five-Nation Study.' *Cross-Cultural Research* 30 (1996): 243–64.

Huygens, Robert B.C. 'Mittelalterliche Kommentare zum *O qui perpetua*.' *Sacris erudiri* 6 (1954): 373–427.

Jager, Eric. 'Speech and the Chest in Old English Poetry: Orality or Pectorality?' *Speculum* 65 (1990): 845–59.

- 'The Word in the "Breost": Interiority and the Fall in *Genesis B*.' *Neophilologus* 75 (1991): 279–90.

Johnson, David F. 'Who Read Gregory's *Dialogues* in Old English?' In *The Power of Words: Anglo-Saxon Studies Presented to Donald G. Scragg on His Seventieth Birthday*, edited by Hugh Magennis and Jonathan Wilcox, 171–204. Morgantown: West Virginia University Press, 2006.

Johnson, Mark. *The Meaning of the Body: Aesthetics of Human Understanding*. Chicago: University of Chicago Press, 2007.

Johnson, Mark, and George Lakoff. 'Why Cognitive Linguistics Requires Embodied Realism.' *Cognitive Linguistics* 13 (2002): 245–63.

Johnson, William C., Jr. '*The Ruin* as Body-City Riddle.' *Philological Quarterly* 59 (1980): 397–411.

Jolly, Karen Louise. *Popular Religion in Late Saxon England: Elf Charms in Context*. Chapel Hill: University of North Carolina Press, 1996.

Jones, Christopher A. 'Ælfric and the Limits of "Benedictine Reform."' In *A Companion to Ælfric*, edited by Hugh Magennis and Mary Swan, 67–108. Leiden: Brill, 2009.

- '*Meatim sed et rustica*: Ælfric of Eynsham as a Medieval Latin Author.' *Journal of Medieval Latin* 8 (1998): 1–57.

- 'The Sermons Attributed to Candidus Wizo.' In *Latin Learning and English Lore*, edited by O'Brien O'Keeffe and Orchard, 1.260–83.

Kaster, Robert A. *Guardians of Language: The Grammarian and Society in Late Antiquity*. Berkeley: University of California Press, 1988.

Kavanagh, Catherine. 'The Philosophical Importance of Grammar for Eriugena.' In *History and Eschatology in John Scotus Eriugena and His Time*, edited by James McEvoy and Michael Dunne, 61–76. Leuven: Leuven University Press, 2002.

Kay, Christian J. 'Metaphors We Lived By: Pathways between Old and Modern English.' In *Essays on Anglo-Saxon and Related Themes in Memory of Lynne Grundy*, edited by Jane Roberts and Janet Nelson, 273–85. London: King's College London Centre for Late Antique and Medieval Studies, 2000.

Kelly, J.F. 'The Use of Augustine among the Anglo-Saxons.' *Studia Patristica* 28 (1993): 211–16.

Ker, N.R. *Catalogue of Manuscripts Containing Anglo-Saxon.* Oxford: Clarendon Press, 1957. Reprinted with supplement, 1990.

Kiernan, Kevin. 'Alfred the Great's Burnt *Boethius.*' In *The Iconic Page in Manuscript, Print, and Digital Culture*, edited by George Bornstein and Theresa Tinkle, 7–32. Ann Arbor: University of Michigan Press, 1998.

Kirk, G.S., J.E. Raven, and M. Schofield. *The Presocratic Philosophers: A Critical History with a Selection of Texts.* 2nd ed. Cambridge: Cambridge University Press, 1983.

Kirmayer, Laurence J. 'Cultural Variations in the Clinical Presentation of Depression and Anxiety: Implications for Diagnosis and Treatment.' *Journal of Clinical Psychiatry* 62 (suppl. 13) (2001): 22–8.

Kirmayer, Laurence J., Thi Hong Trang Dao, and André Smith. 'Somatization and Psychologization: Understanding Cultural Idioms of Distress.' In *Clinical Methods in Transcultural Psychiatry*, edited by Samuel O. Okpaku, 233–65. Washington, DC: American Psychiatric Press, 1998.

Kleinman, Arthur M. 'Depression, Somatization and the "New Cross-Cultural Psychiatry."' *Social Science and Medicine* 11 (1977): 3–10.

Kleinman, Arthur M., and Joan Kleinman. 'Somatization: The Interconnections in Chinese Society among Culture, Depressive Experiences, and the Meanings of Pain.' In *Culture and Depression: Studies in the Anthropology and Cross-Cultural Psychiatry of Affect and Disorder*, edited by Arthur Kleinman and Byron Good, 429–90. Berkeley: University of California Press, 1985.

Kleist, Aaron J. 'Ælfric's Corpus: A Conspectus.' *Florilegium* 18 (2001): 113–64.

– *Striving with Grace: Views of Free Will in Anglo-Saxon England.* Toronto: University of Toronto Press, 2008.

Klibansky, Raymond. *The Continuity of the Platonic Tradition during the Middle Ages: with a New Preface and Four Supplementary Chapters; together with Plato's Parmenides in the Middle Ages and the Renaissance.* Millwood, NY: Kraus International Publications, 1982.

Kövecses, Zoltán. 'Anger: Its Language, Conceptualization, and Physiology in the Light of Cross-Cultural Evidence.' In *Language and the Cognitive Construal of the World*, edited by Taylor and MacLaury, 181–96.

– 'Embodiment, Experiential Focus, and Diachronic Change in Metaphor.' In *Selected Proceedings of the 2005 Symposium on New Approaches in English*

Historical Lexis (HEL-LEX), edited by R.W. McConchie, Olga Timofeeva, Heli Tissari, and Tanja Säily, 1–7. Somerville, MA: Cascadilla Proceedings Project, 2006.

– *Metaphor and Emotion: Language, Culture, and Body in Human Feeling.* Cambridge: Cambridge University Press, 2000.

– 'Metaphor and the Folk Understanding of Anger.' In *Everyday Concepts of Emotion: An Introduction to the Psychology, Anthropology and Linguistics of Emotion*, edited by James A. Russell, José-Miguel Fernández-Dols, Antony S.R. Manstead, and J.C. Wellenkamp, 49–71. Dordrecht: Kluwer Academic Publishing, 1995.

Kytö, Merja. 'Manual to the Diachronic Part of the Helsinki Corpus of English Texts: Coding Conventions and Lists of Source Texts,' Part 1.1. 3rd ed. Helsinki: Department of English, University of Helsinki, 1996. http://khnt.hit.uib .no/icame/manuals/HC/INDEX.HTM.

La Farge, Beatrice. *'Leben' und 'Seele' in den altgermanischen Sprachen. Studien zum Einfluß christlich-lateinischer Vorstellungen auf die Volkssprachen.* Heidelberg: C. Winter, 1991.

Laistner, M.L.W. 'Antiochene Exegesis in Western Europe during the Middle Ages.' *Harvard Theological Review* 40 (1947): 19–31.

Lakoff, George. *Women, Fire, and Dangerous Things: What Categories Reveal About the Mind.* Chicago: University of Chicago Press, 1987.

Lakoff, George, and Mark Johnson. *Metaphors We Live By.* Chicago: University of Chicago Press, 1980. Reprinted with new afterword, 2003.

– *Philosophy in the Flesh: The Embodied Mind and Its Challenge to Western Thought.* New York: Basic Books, 1999.

Lapidge, Michael. 'Æthelwold as Scholar and Teacher.' In *Bishop Æthelwold: His Career and Influence*, edited by Barbara Yorke, 89–117. Ipswich: Boydell Press, 1988. Reprinted in Lapidge, *ALL* 2, 183–211.

– 'Anglo-Latin Literature.' In Lapidge, *ALL* 1, 1–35.

– *Anglo-Latin Literature, 600–899.* London: Hambledon Press, 1996.

– *Anglo-Latin Literature, 900–1066.* London: Hambledon Press, 1993.

– *The Anglo-Saxon Library.* Oxford: Oxford University Press, 2006.

– 'B. and the *Vita S. Dunstani*.' In *St Dunstan: His Life, Times and Cult*, edited by Nigel Ramsay, Margaret Sparks, and Tim Tatton-Brown, 247–59. Woodbridge: Boydell Press, 1992. Reprinted in Lapidge, *ALL* 2, 279–91.

– 'The Comparative Approach.' In *Reading Old English Texts*, edited by Katherine O'Brien O'Keeffe, 20–38. Cambridge: Cambridge University Press, 1997.

– 'Hwætberht.' In *The Blackwell Encyclopaedia of Anglo-Saxon England*, edited by Michael Lapidge, John Blair, Simon Keynes, and Donald Scragg, 245–6. Oxford: Blackwell, 1999.

– 'An Isidorian Epitome from Early Anglo-Saxon England.' *Romanobarbarica* 10 (1988–9): 443–83. Reprinted in Lapidge, *ALL* 1, 183–223.

- 'The Origin of the *Collectanea*.' In *Collectanea Pseudo-Bedae*, edited by Martha Bayless and Michael Lapidge, 1–12. Dublin: Dublin Institute for Advanced Studies, 1998.
- 'Stoic Cosmology and the Source of the First Old English Riddle.' *Anglia* 112 (1994): 1–25.
- 'Three Latin Poems from Æthelwold's School at Winchester.' *ASE* 1 (1972): 85–137. Reprinted in *ALL* 2, 225–77.

Lapidge, Michael, and Richard Sharpe. *A Bibliography of Celtic-Latin Literature 400–1200*. With a foreword by Proinsias Mac Cana. Dublin: Royal Irish Academy, 1985.

Law, Vivien. 'Erchanbert and the Interpolator: A Christian *Ars minor* at Freising (Clm 6414).' In *History of Linguistic Thought in the Early Middle Ages*, edited by Vivien Law, 223–43. Amsterdam: John Benjamins, 1993.
- *Grammar and Grammarians in the Early Middle Ages*. London: Longman, 1997.
- *The History of Linguistics in Europe from Plato to 1600*. Cambridge: Cambridge University Press, 2003.
- *The Insular Latin Grammarians*. Woodbridge: Boydell Press, 1982.
- 'Malsachanus Reconsidered: A Fresh Look at a Hiberno-Latin Grammarian.' *Cambridge Medieval Celtic Studies* 1 (1981): 83–93.
- 'The Study of Grammar.' In *Carolingian Culture: Emulation and Innovation*, edited by Rosamond McKitterick, 88–110. Cambridge: Cambridge University Press, 1994.
- 'The Study of Latin Grammar in Eighth-Century Southumbria.' *ASE* 12 (1983): 43–71.
- *Wisdom, Authority and Grammar in the Seventh Century: Decoding Virgilius Maro Grammaticus*. Cambridge: Cambridge University Press, 1995.

Law, Vivien, and Ineke Sluiter, eds. *Dionysius Thrax and the Technê Grammatikê*. Münster: Nodus Publikationen, 1995.

Lazzari, Loredana. 'Isidore's *Etymologiae* in Anglo-Saxon Glossaries.' In *Foundations of Learning: The Transfer of Encyclopaedic Knowledge in the Early Middle Ages*, edited by Rolf H. Bremmer, Jr, and Kees Dekker, 63–93. Mediaevalia Groningana n.s. 9. Leuven: Peeters, 2007.

Leff, Julian P. 'Culture and the Differentiation of Emotional States.' *British Journal of Psychiatry* 123 (1973): 299–306.

Leinbaugh, Theodore H. 'Ælfric's *Lives of Saints 1* and the Boulogne Sermon: Editorial, Authorial, and Textual Problems.' In *The Editing of Old English: Papers from the 1990 Manchester Conference*, edited by D.G. Scragg and Paul E. Szarmach, 191–212. Woodbridge: D.S. Brewer, 1994.
- 'Ælfric's *Sermo de sacrificio in die pascae*: Anglican Polemic in the Sixteenth and Seventeenth Centuries.' In *Anglo-Saxon Scholarship: The First Three*

Centuries, edited by Carl Berkhout and Milton McCormick Gatch, 51–68. Boston: G.K. Hall, 1982.
- 'The Liturgical Homilies in *Ælfric's Lives of Saints*.' PhD diss., Harvard University, 1980.
Lendinara, Patrizia. 'Gli *Aenigmata Laureshamensia*.' *PAN: Studi dell'Istituto di Filologia Latina* 7 (1979): 73–90.
Littlemore, Jeannette. 'The Effect of Cultural Background on Metaphor Interpretation.' *Metaphor and Symbol* 18 (2003): 273–88.
Lloyd, A.C. 'Emotion and Decision in Stoic Psychology.' In *The Stoics*, edited by John M. Rist, 233–45. Berkeley: University of California Press, 1978.
- 'Grammar and Metaphysics in the Stoa.' In *Problems in Stoicism*, edited by A.A. Long, 57–84. London: Athlone, 1971.
Lockett, Leslie. 'Anglo-Saxon Knowledge of the Functions of the Brain.' Forthcoming.
- 'An Integrated Re-examination of the Dating of Oxford, Bodleian Library, MS Junius 11.' *ASE* 31 (2002): 141–73.
- 'The Role of Grendel's Arm in Feud, Law, and the Narrative Strategy of *Beowulf*.' In *Latin Learning and English Lore*, edited by O'Brien O'Keeffe and Orchard, 1.368–88.
Long, A.A. 'Language and Thought in Stoicism.' In *Problems in Stoicism*, edited by A.A. Long, 75–113. London: Athlone Press, 1971.
- 'Soul and Body in Stoicism.' *Phronesis* 27 (1982): 34–57.
- 'Stoic Psychology.' In *The Cambridge History of Hellenistic Philosophy*, edited by K. Algra, J. Barnes, J. Mansfeld, and M. Schofield, 560–84. Cambridge: Cambridge University Press, 1999.
Low, Soon Ai. 'The Anglo-Saxon Mind: Metaphor and Common Sense Psychology in Old English Literature.' PhD diss., University of Toronto, 1998.
- 'Approaches to the Old English Vocabulary for "Mind."' *Studia Neophilologica* 73 (2001): 11–22.
- 'Mental Cultivation in *Guthlac B*.' *Neophilologus* 81 (1997): 625–36.
- 'Pride, Courage, and Anger: The Polysemousness of Old English *Mod*.' In *Verbal Encounters: Anglo-Saxon and Old Norse Studies for Roberta Frank*, edited by Antonina Harbus and Russell Poole, 81–8. Toronto: University of Toronto Press, 2005.
Luhtala, Anneli. *Grammar and Philosophy in Late Antiquity*. Studies in the History of the Language Sciences 107. Amsterdam: John Benjamins, 2005.
Maalej, Zouhair. 'Figurative Language in Anger Expressions in Tunisian Arabic: An Extended View of Embodiment.' *Metaphor and Symbol* 19 (2004): 51–75.
Maas, Michael. *Exegesis and Empire in the Early Byzantine Mediterranean: Junillus Africanus and the Instituta Regularia Divinae Legis*. Tübingen: Mohr Siebeck, 2003.

Mac Cana, Proinsias. '*Laíded, gressacht* "Formalized incitement."' *Ériu* 43 (1992): 69–92.

Mac Mathúna, Liam. 'Lexical and Literary Aspects of "Heart" in Irish.' *Ériu* 53 (2003): 1–18.

Madoz, José. 'Un caso de materialismo en España en el siglo VI.' *Revista española de teología* 8 (1948): 203–30.

Marenbon, John. 'Alcuin, the Council of Frankfort, and the Beginnings of Medieval Philosophy.' In *Das Frankfurter Konzil von 794: Kultur und Theologie*, edited by Rainer Berndt, 603–15. 2 vols. Quellen und Abhandlungen zur mittelrheinischen Kirchengeschichte 80. Mainz: Selbstverlag der Gesellschaft für mittelrheinische Kirchengeschichte, 1997. Reprinted in John Marenbon, *Aristotelian Logic, Platonism, and the Context of Early Medieval Philosophy in the West*, item 4. Aldershot: Ashgate Variorum, 2000.

– *Boethius*. Oxford: Oxford University Press, 2003.

– *Early Medieval Philosophy (480–1150): An Introduction*. London: Routledge & Kegan Paul, 1983.

– *From the Circle of Alcuin to the School of Auxerre: Logic, Theology and Philosophy in the Early Middle Ages*. Cambridge Studies in Medieval Life and Thought, 3rd ser. 15. Cambridge: Cambridge University Press, 1981.

– 'Platonism – A Doxographic Approach: The Early Middle Ages.' In *The Platonic Tradition in the Middle Ages: A Doxographic Approach*, edited by Stephen Gersh and Maarten J.F.M. Hoenen, with Pieter Th. van Wingerden, 67–89. Berlin: Walter de Gruyter, 2002.

Marrou, H.I. *A History of Education in Antiquity*. Translated by George Lamb. New York: Sheed and Ward, 1956. Repr. Madison: University of Wisconsin Press, 1982.

Mathisen, Ralph. *Ecclesiastical Factionalism and Religious Controversy in Fifth-Century Gaul*. Washington, DC: The Catholic University of America Press, 1989.

Matsuki, Keiko. 'Metaphors of Anger in Japanese.' In *Language and the Cognitive Construal of the World*, edited by Taylor and MacLaury, 137–51.

Matter, E. Ann. 'The Soul of the Dog-Man: Ratramnus of Corbie between Theology and Philosophy.' *Rivista di storia della filosofia* n.s. 61 (2006): 43–53.

Matto, Michael. 'A War of Containment: The Heroic Image in *The Battle of Maldon*.' *Studia Neophilologica* 74 (2002): 60–75.

McCone, Kim. *Pagan Past and Christian Present in Early Irish Literature*. Maynooth: Department of Old Irish, National University of Ireland, Maynooth, 2000.

McGowan, Joseph P. 'Lexicon, Glosses.' In 'The Year's Work in Old English Studies 2001,' edited by Daniel Donoghue and R.M. Liuzza. *Old English Newsletter* 36 (2003): 15–36.

McIlwain, James T. 'Brain and Mind in Anglo-Saxon Medicine.' *Viator* 37 (2006): 103–12.

Meaney, Audrey L. 'The Practice of Medicine in England about the Year 1000.' In *The Year 1000: Medical Practice at the End of the First Millennium*, edited by E. Savage-Smith and Peregrine Horden, 221–37. (= *Social History of Medicine* 13.) Oxford: Oxford University Press for the Society for the Social History of Medicine, 2000.

– 'Variant Versions of Old English Medical Remedies and the Compilation of Bald's *Leechbook*.' *ASE* 13 (1984): 235–68.

Meyvaert, Paul. 'The Authentic *Dialogues* of Gregory the Great.' *Sacris erudiri* 43 (2004): 55–129.

Mikołajczuk, Agnieszka. 'The Metonymic and Metaphorical Conceptualisation of *Anger* in Polish.' In *Speaking of Emotions: Conceptualisation and Expression*, edited by Angeliki Athanasiadou and Elżbieta Tabakowska, 153–90. Berlin: Mouton de Gruyter, 1998.

Minio-Paluello, Lorenzo. 'Dalle *Categoriae decem* pseudo-Agostiniane (Temistiane) al testo vulgato Aristotelico Boeziano.' In *Opuscula: The Latin Aristotle*, 448–58. Amsterdam: Adolf M. Hakkert, 1972.

– 'The Text of the *Categoriae*: The Latin Tradition.' In *Opuscula: The Latin Aristotle*, 28–39. Amsterdam: Adolf M. Hakkert, 1972.

Minst, Karl J. 'Die Lorscher Rätsel: Ein fast vergessener Codex aus der Lorscher Bibliothek.' In *Laurissa Jubilans: Festschrift zur 1200-Jahrfeier von Lorsch*, edited by Hans Degen and Wolfgang Selzer, 101–5. Lorsch: Gemeinde Lorsch, 1964.

Mize, Britt. 'Manipulations of the Mind-as-Container Motif in *Beowulf*, *Homiletic Fragment II*, and Alfred's *Metrical Epilogue to the Pastoral Care*.' *JEGP* 107 (2008): 25–56.

– 'The Representation of the Mind as an Enclosure in Old English Poetry.' *ASE* 35 (2006): 57–90.

Morin, G. 'Le *Liber dogmatum* de Gennade de Marseille et problèmes qui s'y rattachent.' *RB* 24 (1907): 445–55.

Mumford, David B. 'Emotional Distress in the Hebrew Bible: Somatic or Psychological?' *British Journal of Psychiatry* 160 (1992): 92–7.

– 'Somatic Symptoms and Psychological Distress in the *Iliad* of Homer.' *Journal of Psychosomatic Research* 41 (1996): 139–48.

Mumford, David B., J.T. Bavington, K.S. Bhatnagar, Y. Hussain, S. Mirza, and M.M. Naraghi. 'The Bradford Somatic Inventory: A Multi-Ethnic Inventory of Somatic Symptoms Reported by Anxious and Depressed Patients in Britain and the Indo-Pakistan Subcontinent.' *British Journal of Psychiatry* 158 (1991): 379–86.

Munzi, Luigi. 'Testi grammaticali e *renovatio studiorum* carolingia.' In *Manuscripts and Tradition of Grammatical Texts from Antiquity to the Renaissance*, edited by Mario de Nonno, Paolo de Paolis, and Louis Holtz, 1.351–88. 2 vols. Cassino: Edizioni dell'Università degli Studi di Cassino, 2000.

Nicholson, Simon. 'The Expression of Emotional Distress in Old English Prose and Verse.' *Culture, Medicine and Psychiatry* 19 (1995): 327–38.

North, Richard. *Pagan Words and Christian Meanings*. Costerus n.s. 81. Amsterdam: Rodopi, 1991.

North, Robert. 'Brain and Nerve in the Biblical Outlook.' *Biblica* 74 (1993): 577–97.

Nussbaum, Otto. *Kloster, Priestermönch und Privatmesse: Ihr Verhältnis im Westen von den Anfängen bis zum hohen Mittelalter*. Bonn: Peter Hanstein Verlag, 1961.

Obeyesekere, Gananath. 'The Theory and Practice of Psychological Medicine in the Ayurvedic Tradition.' *Culture, Medicine and Psychiatry* 1 (1977): 155–81.

O'Brien O'Keeffe, Katherine. *Visible Song: Transitional Literacy in Old English Verse*. CSASE 4. Cambridge: Cambridge University Press, 1990.

O'Brien O'Keeffe, Katherine, and Andy Orchard, eds. *Latin Learning and English Lore: Studies in Anglo-Saxon Literature for Michael Lapidge*. 2 vols. Toronto: University of Toronto Press, 2005.

O'Daly, Gerard. *Augustine's Philosophy of Mind*. Berkeley: University of California Press, 1987.

Ogilvy, J.D.A. *Books Known to the English, 597–1066*. Cambridge, MA: The Mediaeval Academy of America, 1967.

Orchard, Andy. 'Artful Alliteration in Anglo-Saxon Song and Story.' *Anglia* 113 (1995): 429–63.

Orel, Vladimir. *A Handbook of Germanic Etymology*. Leiden: Brill, 2003.

Ots, Thomas. 'The Angry Liver, the Anxious Heart, and the Melancholy Spleen: The Phenomenology of Perceptions in Chinese Culture.' *Culture, Medicine and Psychiatry* 14 (1990): 21–58.

Otten, Kurt. *König Alfreds Boethius*. Tübingen: Niemeyer, 1964.

Otten, Willemien. 'The Texture of Tradition: The Role of the Church Fathers in Carolingian Theology.' In *The Reception of the Church Fathers in the West: From the Carolingians to the Maurists*, edited by Irena Backus, 1.3–50. 2 vols. Leiden: Brill, 1997.

Pang, Keum Young Chung. '*Hwabyung*: The Construction of a Korean Popular Illness among Korean Elderly Immigrant Women in the United States.' *Culture, Medicine and Psychiatry* 14 (1990): 495–512.

Paris, Gaston. Review of *Zeitschrift für deutsches Altertum und deutsche Literatur* 22 (1878). *Romania* 8 (1879): 138–9.

Parish, Steven M. 'The Sacred Mind: Newar Cultural Representations of Mental Life and the Production of Moral Consciousness.' *Ethos* 19 (1991): 313–51.

Paulsen, David L. 'Early Christian Belief in a Corporeal Deity: Origen and Augustine as Reluctant Witnesses.' *Harvard Theological Review* 83 (1990): 105–16.

Payne, F. Anne. *King Alfred and Boethius: An Analysis of the Old English Version of the* Consolation of Philosophy. Madison: University of Wisconsin Press, 1968.

Pelteret, David A.E. *Slavery in Early Mediaeval England: From the Reign of Alfred until the Twelfth Century.* Rochester, NY: Boydell Press, 1995.

Phillips, Michael Joseph. 'Heart, Mind, and Soul in Old English: A Semantic Study.' PhD diss., University of Illinois at Urbana-Champaign, 1985.

Poli, Diego. 'La *beatitudine* fra esegesi e grammatica nell'Irlanda altomedioevale.' *Giornale italiano di filologia* 36 (1984): 231–44.

Popper, Karl R. 'Comments on the Prehistoric Discovery of the Self and on the Mind-Body Problem in Ancient Greek Philosophy.' In *The World of Parmenides: Essays on the Presocratic Enlightenment,* edited by Arne F. Petersen with Jørgen Mejer, 223–50. London: Routledge, 1998.

Potter, Joyce. '*Wylm* and *weallan* in *Beowulf*: A Tidal Metaphor.' *Medieval Perspectives* 3 (1988): 191–9.

Primmer, Adolf, series ed. *Die handschriftliche Überlieferung der Werke des heiligen Augustinus.* 10 vols. Vienna: Verlag der Österreichischen Akademie der Wissenschaften, 1969–.

Quinn, Naomi. 'The Cultural Basis of Metaphor.' In *Beyond Metaphor: The Theory of Tropes in Anthropology,* edited by James W. Fernandez, 56–93. Stanford, CA: Stanford University Press, 1991.

Quinn, Patricia A. *Better than the Sons of Kings: Boys and Monks in the Early Middle Ages.* New York: Peter Lang, 1989.

Reifferscheid, August. *Bibliotheca patrum latinorum italica.* 2 vols. Vienna, 1870–1.

Rella, F.A. 'Continental Manuscripts Acquired for English Centers in the Tenth and Early Eleventh Centuries: A Preliminary Checklist.' *Anglia* 9 (1980): 107–16.

Renehan, Robert. 'On the Greek Origins of the Concepts Incorporeality and Immateriality.' *Greek, Roman and Byzantine Studies* 21 (1980): 105–38.

Reynolds, Roger E. *The Ordinals of Christ from Their Origins to the Twelfth Century.* Beiträge zur Geschichte und Quellenkunde des Mittelalters 7. Berlin: Walter de Gruyter, 1978.

Riddle, John M. 'Theory and Practice in Medieval Medicine.' *Viator* 5 (1974): 157–84.

Rigg, A.G., and Gernot R. Wieland. 'A Canterbury Classbook of the Mid-Eleventh Century: The "Cambridge Songs" Manuscript.' *ASE* 4 (1975): 113–30.

Roberts, Jane, and Christian Kay, with Lynne Grundy. *A Thesaurus of Old English in Two Volumes*. 2nd ed. Costerus n.s. 131. Amsterdam: Rodopi, 2000.

Robinson, Fred C. 'The Devil's Account of the Next World: An Anecdote from Old English Homiletic Literature.' *Neuphilologische Mitteilungen* 73 (1972): 362–71.

– 'Lexicography and Literary Criticism: A Caveat.' In *Philological Essays: Studies in Old and Middle English Language and Literature in Honour of Herbert Dean Meritt*, edited by James L. Rosier, 99–110. The Hague: Mouton, 1970.

– 'Notes and Emendations to Old English Poetic Texts.' *Neuphilologische Mitteilungen* 67 (1966): 356–64. Reprinted in *The Editing of Old English*, 116–21. Oxford: Blackwell, 1994.

Salmon, Vivian. 'The Wanderer and The Seafarer, and the Old English Conception of the Soul.' *Modern Language Review* 55 (1960): 1–10.

Sanders, Lisa. 'Heart Ache.' *The New York Times Magazine*. 18 June 2006. 27–8.

Sayers, William. 'The Smith and the Hero: Culann and Cú Chulainn.' *Mankind Quarterly* 25 (1985): 227–60.

Schaar, Claes. 'Brondhord in the Old English Rhyming Poem.' *English Studies* 43 (1962): 490–1.

Sedley, David. 'Chrysippus on Psychophysical Causality.' In *Passions and Perceptions: Studies in Hellenistic Philosophy of Mind*, edited by Jacques Brunschwig and Martha C. Nussbaum, 313–31. Cambridge: Cambridge University Press, 1993.

Sehrt, Edward Henry. *Vollständiges Wörterbuch zum Heliand und zur altsächsischen Genesis*. Göttingen: Vandenhoeck und Ruprecht, 1925. Repr. 1966.

Siegmund, P. Albert. *Die Überlieferung der griechischen christlichen Literatur in der lateinischen Kirche bis zum zwölften Jahrhundert*. Munich: Filser-Verlag, 1949.

Šileikytė, Rūta. 'In Search of the Inner Mind: Old English gescead and Other Lexemes for Human Cognition in King Alfred's Boethius.' *Kalbotyra* 54 (2004): 1–9.

Sisam, Kenneth. 'MSS. Bodley 340 and 342: Ælfric's Catholic Homilies.' In *Studies in the History of Old English Literature*, 148–98. Oxford: Clarendon Press, 1953. Repr. 1998.

Smith, Mark S. 'The Heart and Innards in Israelite Emotional Expressions: Notes from Anthropology and Psychobiology.' *Journal of Biblical Literature* 117 (1998): 427–36.

Smithers, G.V. 'The Meaning of The Seafarer and The Wanderer.' *Medium Ævum* 26 (1957): 137–53.

Sobo, E.J. 'The Jamaican Body's Role in Emotional Experience and Sense Perception: Feelings, Hearts, Minds, and Nerves.' *Culture, Medicine and Psychiatry* 20 (1996): 313–42.

Soland, Margrit. *Altenglische Ausdrücke für 'Leib' und 'Seele.'* Zürich: Juris, 1979.

Solomon, Robert C. 'Getting Angry: The Jamesian Theory of Emotion in Anthropology.' In *Culture Theory: Essays on Mind, Self, and Emotion*, edited by Richard A. Shweder and Robert A. LeVine, 238–54. Cambridge: Cambridge University Press, 1984.

Spanneut, Michel. *Permanence du Stoïcisme: De Zénon à Malraux.* Gembloux: Éditions J. Duculot, 1973.

– *Le Stoïcisme des Pères de l'Église: De Clément de Rome à Clément d'Alexandrie.* Paris: Éditions du Seuil, 1957.

Stanley, Eric G. 'Old English Poetic Diction and the Interpretation of *The Wanderer, The Seafarer*, and *The Penitent's Prayer.*' *Anglia* 73 (1956): 413–66.

Stock, Brian. *The Implications of Literacy: Written Language and Models of Interpretation in the Eleventh and Twelfth Centuries.* Princeton, NJ: Princeton University Press, 1983.

Strömbäck, Dag. 'The Concept of the Soul in Nordic Tradition.' *Arv* 31 (1975): 5–22.

Sullivan, Shirley Darcus. *Psychological and Ethical Ideas: What Early Greeks Say.* *Mnemosyne* Suppl. 144. Leiden: Brill, 1995.

Szarmach, Paul E. 'Ælfric as Exegete: Approaches and Examples in the Study of the *Sermones Catholici.*' In *Hermeneutics and Medieval Culture*, edited by Patrick Gallacher and Helen Damico, 237–47. Albany: State University of New York Press, 1989.

– 'Alfred, Alcuin, and the Soul.' In *Manuscript, Narrative, Lexicon: Essays on Literary and Cultural Transmission in Honor of Whitney F. Bolton*, edited by Robert Boenig and Kathleen Davis, 127–48. Lewisburg, PA: Bucknell University Press, 2000.

– 'Alfred's *Soliloquies* in London, BL, Cotton Tiberius A. iii (art. 9g, fols. 50v–51v).' In *Latin Learning and English Lore*, edited by O'Brien O'Keeffe and Orchard, 2.153–79.

– 'Editions of Alfred: The Wages of Un-Influence.' In *Early Medieval Texts and Interpretations: Studies Presented to Donald G. Scragg*, edited by Elaine M. Treharne and Susan Rosser, 135–49. Tempe: ACMRS, 2003.

– 'The Meaning of Alfred's *Preface* to the *Pastoral Care.*' *Mediaevalia* 6 (1980): 57–86.

– 'A Preface, Mainly Textual, to Alcuin's *De ratione animae.*' In *The Man of Many Devices, Who Wandered Full Many Ways: Festschrift in Honor of János M. Bak*, edited by Balász Nagy and Marcell Sebök, 397–408. Budapest: Central European University Press, 1999.

- 'A Return to Cotton Tiberius A. III, art. 24, and Isidore's *Synonyma*.' In *Text and Gloss: Studies in Insular Learning and Literature Presented to Joseph Donovan Pheifer*, edited by Helen Conrad-O'Briain, Anne Marie D'Arcy, and John Scattergood, 166–81. Dublin: Four Courts Press, 1999.
- 'The *Timaeus* in Old English.' In *Lexis and Texts in Early English: Studies Presented to Jane Roberts*, edited by Christian J. Kay and Louise M. Sylvester, 255–67. Costerus n.s. 133. Amsterdam: Rodopi, 2001.
Taylor, John R., and Robert E. MacLaury, eds. *Language and the Cognitive Construal of the World*. Berlin: Mouton de Gruyter, 1995.
Taylor, John R., and Thandi G. Mbense. 'Red Dogs and Rotten Mealies: How Zulus Talk About Anger.' In *Speaking of Emotions: Conceptualisation and Expression*, edited by Angeliki Athanasiadou and Elżbieta Tabakowska, 191–226. Berlin: Mouton de Gruyter, 1998.
Testard, Maurice. *Saint Augustin et Cicéron*. 2 vols. Paris: Études Augustiniennes, 1958.
Thompson, Nancy. 'Anglo-Saxon Orthodoxy.' In *Old English Literature in Its Manuscript Context*, edited by Joyce Tally Lionarons, 37–65. Morgantown: West Virginia University Press, 2004.
Thompson, Pauline. 'The Disease That We Call Cancer.' In *Health, Disease and Healing in Medieval Culture*, edited by Sheila Campbell, Bert Hall, and David Klausner, 1–11. New York: St Martin's Press, 1992.
Thomson, Rodney M. 'The Norman Conquest and English Libraries.' In *The Role of the Book in Medieval Culture*, edited by Peter Ganz, 2.27–40. 2 vols. Turnhout: Brepols, 1986.
Tieleman, Teun. *Galen and Chrysippus on the Soul: Argument and Refutation in the De placitis Books II–III*. Leiden: Brill, 1996.
Tristram, Hildegard L.C. 'Stock Descriptions of Heaven and Hell in Old English Prose and Poetry.' *Neuphilologische Mitteilungen* 79 (1978): 102–13.
Turner, C.H. 'The *Liber ecclesiasticorum dogmatum* attributed to Gennadius,' with 'The *Liber ecclesiasticorum dogmatum*: Supplenda.' *Journal of Theological Studies* 7 (1906): 78–99; and 8 (1907): 103–14.
Turville-Petre, E.O.G. *Myth and Religion of the North: The Religion of Ancient Scandinavia*. Westport, CT: Greenwood Press, 1975.
Verbeke, Gérard. *L'Évolution de la doctrine du pneuma du Stoïcisme à Saint Augustin*. Paris: Desclée De Brouwer, 1945.
- *The Presence of Stoicism in Medieval Thought*. Washington, DC: The Catholic University of America Press, 1983.
Von Staden, Heinrich. 'Body, Soul, and Nerves: Epicurus, Herophilus, Erasistratus, the Stoics, and Galen.' In *Psyche and Soma: Physicians and Metaphysicians*

on the Mind-Body Problem from Antiquity to Enlightenment, edited by John P. Wright and Paul Potter, 79–116. Oxford: Clarendon Press, 2000.

Waterhouse, Ruth. 'Tone in Alfred's Version of Augustine's *Soliloquies*.' In *Studies in Earlier English Prose*, edited by Paul E. Szarmach, 47–85. Albany: State University of New York Press, 1986.

Watters, Ethan. *Crazy Like Us: The Globalization of the American Psyche*. New York: Free Press, 2010.

Webber, Teresa. 'The Patristic Content of English Book Collections in the Eleventh Century: Towards a Continental Perspective.' In *Of the Making of Books: Medieval Manuscripts, Their Scribes and Readers: Essays Presented to M.B. Parkes*, edited by P.R. Robinson and Rivkah Zim, 191–205. Brookfield, VT: Ashgate, 1997.

– *Scribes and Scholars at Salisbury Cathedral, c. 1075–c. 1125*. Oxford: Clarendon Press, 1992.

Wehlau, Ruth. *The Riddle of Creation: Metaphor Structures in Old English Poetry*. New York: Peter Lang, 1997.

Wellenkamp, J.C. 'Everyday Conceptions of Distress: A Case Study from Toraja, Indonesia.' In *Everyday Concepts of Emotion: An Introduction to the Psychology, Anthropology and Linguistics of Emotion*, edited by James A. Russell, José-Miguel Fernández-Dols, Antony S.R. Manstead, and J.C. Wellenkamp, 267–80. Dordrecht: Kluwer Academic Publishing, 1995.

Wentersdorf, Karl P. 'The Old English *Rhyming Poem*: A Ruler's Lament.' *Studies in Philology* 82 (1985): 265–94.

Whitelock, Dorothy. 'The Prose of Alfred's Reign.' In *Continuations and Beginnings: Studies in Old English Literature*, edited by Eric Gerald Stanley, 67–103. London: Nelson, 1966.

Wierzbicka, Anna. *Emotions across Languages and Cultures: Diversity and Universals*. Cambridge: Cambridge University Press, 1999.

Wilcox, Jonathan. 'Ælfric in Dorset and the Landscape of Pastoral Care.' In *Pastoral Care in Late Anglo-Saxon England*, edited by Francesca Tinti, 52–62. Woodbridge: Boydell Press, 2005.

– 'The Audience of Ælfric's *Lives of Saints* and the Face of Cotton Caligula A. xiv, fols. 93–130.' In *Beatus Vir: Studies in Early English and Norse Manuscripts in Memory of Phillip Pulsiano*, edited by A.N. Doane and Kirsten Wolf, 228–63. Tempe: ACMRS, 2006.

Wilcox, Miranda. 'Alfred's Epistemological Metaphors: *eagan modes* and *scip modes*.' *ASE* 35 (2006): 179–217.

Wilmart, André. 'L'opuscule inédit de Ratramne sur la nature de l'âme.' *RB* 43 (1931): 207–23.

Wittig, Joseph S. 'The "Remigian" Glosses on Boethius's *Consolatio Philosophiae* in Context.' In *Source of Wisdom: Old English and Early Medieval Latin Studies in Honour of Thomas D. Hill*, edited by Charles D. Wright, Frederick M. Biggs, and Thomas N. Hall, 168–200. Toronto: University of Toronto Press, 2007.

Wright, Charles D. *The Irish Tradition in Old English Literature*. CSASE 6. Cambridge: Cambridge University Press, 1993.

– 'The Old English "Macarius" Homily, Vercelli Homily IV, and Ephrem Latinus, *De paenitentia*.' In *Via Crucis: Essays on Early Medieval Sources and Ideas in Memory of J.E. Cross*, edited by Thomas N. Hall, Thomas D. Hill, and Charles D. Wright, 210–34. Morgantown: West Virginia University Press, 2002.

Wuelcker, Richard Paul. 'Ueber die angelsaechsische Bearbeitung der Soliloquien Augustins.' *Beiträge zur Geschichte der deutschen Sprache und Literatur* 4 (1877): 101–31.

Yorke, Barbara. 'Æthelwold and the Politics of the Tenth Century.' In *Bishop Æthelwold: His Career and Influence*, edited by Barbara Yorke, 65–88. Woodbridge: Boydell Press, 1988.

Index

Some authors and works have not been listed individually but rather under generic categories such as glosses, grammars, homilies, medical texts, riddle-dialogues, riddles, and saints' lives.

218; *Hortensius*, 185, 328; lost
translation of Plato's *Timaeus*,
214–15
Claudianus Mamertus, 181; *De statu
animae*, 191–2, 196–7, 198–9, 219,
221, 223, 288n17, 301n49, 302,
322n25, 409, 423, 432
Cleanthes, 192, 193
commentaries on Boethius's *De
consolatione philosophiae*, 219–23,
315, 322, 409
conceptual metaphor theory, 7–8, 11,
110–17, 166–8, 170–2; and cognitive
science, 166; and cultural variation,
113–14; metaphorization as change
in relationship between source and
target domains, 166–72, 176. *See
also* embodied realism
container metaphor, 5. *See also*
cardiocentric psychology;
conceptual metaphor theory;
hydraulic model of mental activity
corpus. See under grammars
and grammarians, ancient
and late antique; grammars
and grammarians, medieval;
incorporeality; Stoicism, classical;
Stoicizing Christian ontology and
psychology
Cú Chulainn, 142, 145–6, 147
Cynewulf, *Christ II (Ascension)*, 19,
55, 58, 61, 64, 73; *Elene*, 21, 36,
52n133, 54n1, 55n4, 56, 58, 62, 71,
74, 76–7; *Fates of the Apostles, The*,
44, 76n78; *Juliana*, 25, 26–7, 36,
46n109, 49, 54n1

Daniel, 36–7, 55, 69
Death of Edgar, The, 9, 56, 58n15
Deor, 75

dialectic, 182, 184, 282n6, 283n7; in
Augustine, *Soliloquia*, 187–91;
in Claudianus Mamertus, *De
statu animae*, 191–2; compatible
with strict Platonist concept of
incorporeality, 289–90, 311–12;
Differentiae sermonum (in Bern,
Burgerbibliothek, Cod. 178),
206n88; influenced the study of
grammar, 255–7; in late Anglo-
Saxon education, 434–8; minimized
in Alfred's *Soliloquies*, 334–56;
simulated in Gregory, *Dialogi*,
202–3
Diogenes of Apollonia, 121n36
Diogenes Laertius, *Lives of the
Philosophers*, 230n5
'Directions to Recite the Penitential
Psalms,' 90
discourse: contrasted with
narrative, 17–19, 93, 167, 181,
200–3, 211, 275, 279, 400; its role in
metaphorization of an embodied
concept, 167–72, 178, 179–81
Disticha Catonis: Latin, 364; OE, 222
Dombercht, epitaph of, 276
Donatus. *See under* grammars and
grammarians, ancient and late antique
drunkenness, 3–4, 77–9, 95, 273
dualism, mind-body: in modern
Western (Cartesian) thought,
8–13, 111, 151, 173–7; in
Platonist-Christian thought, 9,
13–15; and global marketing of
pharmaceuticals, 176n217
Dunstan, archbishop of Canterbury:
charter S546, 227; his circle at
Glastonbury, 425–6, 370–2;
education and career, 366–72
Durham Proverbs, 89, 272

Toronto Anglo-Saxon Series

General Editor
ANDY ORCHARD

Editorial Board
ROBERTA FRANK
THOMAS N. HALL
ANTONETTE DIPAOLO HEALEY
MICHAEL LAPIDGE